THE
MUTUAL FUND DIRECTORY

THE COMPLETE
REFERENCE TO OVER
2,500 FUNDS
IDENTIFIED, DESCRIBED
AND CATEGORIZED

INVESTMENT COMPANY INSTITUTE

Probus Publishing Company
Chicago, Illinois

Library of Congress Cataloging in Publication Data Available

ISBN 1-55738-156-9

Printed in the United States of America

1   2   3   4   5   6   7   8   9   0

♦ ♦ ♦ ♦
The Mutual Fund Directory

♦ ♦ ♦ ♦
Preface

This guide has been prepared by the Investment Company Institute, which is the national association of the American investment company industry. The Institute serves as a clearinghouse to which the public, news media, and government agencies may turn for information about the mutual fund industry in the United States.

Our members include more than 2,900 open-end investment companies (mutual funds), their investment advisers, and principal underwriters. Mutual fund members have more than 30 million shareholders (individual and institutional) and account for approximately 90 percent of total industry assets.

Mutual funds have become the nation's third largest financial service—behind banks and insurance companies.

The *Guide* is made available as a public service by the members of the Institute and contains general information on mutual funds. It also lists more than 2,900 mutual funds that were members of the Institute as of November 30, 1989. Questions regarding specific information on an individual fund should be directed to the fund itself.

Investment Company Institute
1600 M Street, NW
Suite 600
Washington, DC 20036

Mutual Funds— What Are They?

A mutual fund is an investment company—a company that makes investments on behalf of individuals and institutions who share common financial goals. The fund pools the money of many people—each with a different amount to invest.

Professional money managers then use the pool of money to buy a variety of stocks, bonds, or money market instruments that, in their judgment, will help the fund's shareholders achieve their financial objectives.

Each fund has an investment objective (it's described in the fund's prospectus), which is important to both the manager and the potential investor. Investment objectives are typically described in terms of one or more main goals. These goals may include

1) stability—protecting the principal (amount invested) from loss,

2) growth—increasing the value of the principal, and

3) income—generating a constant flow of income through dividends.

The fund manager uses the investment objective as a guide when choosing investments for the fund's portfolio. Potential investors use it to determine which funds are suitable for their own needs. Mutual funds' investment objectives cover a wide range; some follow aggressive investment policies, involving greater risk, in search of higher returns; others seek current income from more conservative investments. (See pages 17-20 for definitions of 22 different investment objectives.)

When the fund earns money, it distributes the earnings to its shareholders. Money received by the fund as dividends from stocks held in its portfolio or as interest earned on its holdings of debt instruments is paid out to fund shareholders as dividends. In addition, any earnings generated from securities sold for a profit are distributed to shareholders as capital gains distributions. Dividends and capital gains produced are paid out in proportion to the number of fund shares owned. Thus, shareholders who invest a few hundred dollars get the same investment return per dollar as those who invest hundreds of thousands.

From Financial Shopper to Shareholder

Investing in a mutual fund means buying shares of the fund. An investor becomes an owner of shares in the fund just as he or she might own shares of stock in a large corporation. The difference is that a fund's only business is investing in securities, and the price of its shares is directly related to the value of the securities it holds. The collection of securities held by the fund is known as the fund's portfolio.

Mutual funds continually issue new shares for purchase by the public. A fund's share price can change from day to day, depending on the daily value of the securities held by the fund. The share price is called the net asset value (or NAV) and is calculated very simply. The total value of the fund's investments at the end of the day, after expenses, is divided by the number of shares outstanding. Money market funds are typically managed to maintain a constant share price, usually $1.00. (To learn more about buying mu-

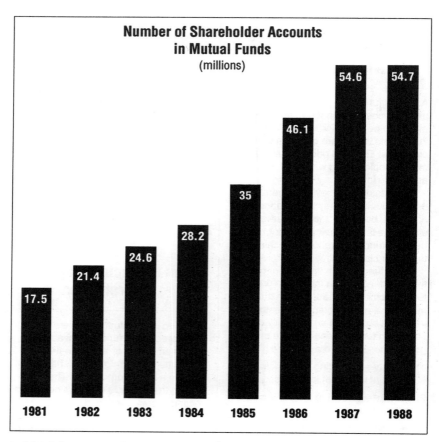

Number of Shareholder Accounts in Mutual Funds
(millions)

Year	Value
1981	17.5
1982	21.4
1983	24.6
1984	28.2
1985	35
1986	46.1
1987	54.6
1988	54.7

tual fund shares, see "Ease of Purchase" on page 4.)

◆ ◆ ◆ ◆

How Do Mutual Funds Operate?

A mutual fund is owned by its hundreds or thousands of shareholders. A board of directors elected by the shareholders is responsible for carrying out the fund's investment policies and objectives. The board is authorized to appoint officers to manage the day-to-day operation of a fund or to delegate that function to a management company.

The management company, which is often the organization that created the fund, may offer one or more mutual funds and may provide other financial products and services as well. (See pages 7-9 for a description of some of these services.) The fund's management company usually serves as the fund's investment adviser.

The investment adviser is charged with managing the fund's portfolio of securities. The adviser is usually paid for its services in the form of a fee that is based on the total value of the fund's

How to Read Newspaper Fund Tables

(1) The first column is the abbreviated fund's name. Several funds listed under a single heading indicate a family of funds.

(2) The second column is the Net Asset Value (NAV) per share as of the close of the preceding business day. In some newspapers, the NAV is identified as the sell or the bid price—the amount per share you would receive if you sold your shares (less the deferred sales charge, if any). Each mutual fund determines its net asset value every business day by dividing the market value of its total assets, less liabilities, by the number of shares outstanding. On any given day, you can determine the value of your holdings by multiplying the NAV by the number of shares you own.

(3) The third column is the offering price or, in some papers, the buy or the asked price—the price you would pay if you purchased shares. The buy price is the NAV plus any sales charges. If there are no initial sales charges, an NL for no-load appears in this column, and the buy price is the same as the NAV. To figure the sales charge percentage, divide the difference between the NAV and the offering price by the offering price. Here, for instance, the sales charge is 7.2 percent ($14.52 − $13.47 = $1.05; $1.05 ÷ $14.52 = 0.072).

(4) The fourth column shows the change, if any, in net asset value from the preceding quotation—in other words, the change over the most recent one-day trading period. This fund, for example, gained eight cents per share.

(5) A "p" following the abbreviated name of the fund denotes a fund that charges a fee from assets for marketing and distribution costs, also known as a 12b-1 plan (named after the 1980 Securities and Exchange rule that permits them).

(6) If the fund name is followed by an "r," the fund has either a contingent deferred sales charge (CDSC) or a redemption fee. A CDSC is a charge if shares are sold within a certain period; a redemption charge is a fee applied whenever shares are sold.

(7) A footnote "t" indicates a fund that habitually enters the previous day's prices, instead of the current day's.

(8) A "t" designates a fund that has both a CDSC or a redemption fee and a 12b-1 plan.

Name	NAV	Buy	Chg
Apztic:			
Aoyte	9.95	10.73	...
Bxy Xer	10.37	11.33−	.01
Dar Rippe	7.38	8.07+	.09
Income (1)	3.16	3.45−	.01
Tbq Ratl	9.97	10.47+	.01
Tbqr Dt	10.19	10.70−	.02
Xypr Ao r	10.05	10.98−	.01
Brkid:			
Blgr Drfr	15.64	16.46−	.03
Bmo Pnc	8.54	N.L.−	.06
Bto Bmd	7.27	(2)7.65	...
Cmyog:			
MIA p	11.86	12.79+	.01
MIX	11.44	12.33−	.03
MIY p	9.70	10.46−	.01
MBF p	11.58	12.49−	.04
MBI	14.77	15.92+	.20
MBR	11.99	12.93−	.03
MRI	13.47	14.52−	.04
MII	7.66	8.26+	.02
MDX	10.00	10.50	...
DMX r	9.74	10.23	(3)
GYI	6.93	7.47−	.03
JAM	10.01	10.79−	.02
JEL	10.09	10.59−	.06
MTNC	10.25	10.76−	.06
MPRS t	10.12	10.62+	.02
Jellies	20.33	N.L.+	.02
Sulter	23.81	N.L.+	.13 (4)
Drapg:			
Bākc Jau	15.45	16.52+	.06
Cryl Ba	20.68	22.12+	.05
Gryd 3	12.10	12.60−	.04
Frp Dup	9.80	10.45−	.11
Fye Fnc	12.61	N.L.	...
Hy Fnc	8.19	8.53−	.01
Hx Paple	10.96	11.42−	.06
Ierl Ely t	10.02	10.95+	.04
Ext RP	10.90	11.12−	.04
Mina SI	7.36	7.67−	.01
Msa IT	9.56	9.96+	.01
Luz Bal	9.85	9.95	...
Oceana	16.49	17.64+	.12
Rhoen	11.68	12.49−	.03
Sol Mech	8.89	9.72+	.10
Tpx Salu	12.72	13.60−	.01

Name	NAV	Buy	Chg
Urx Chl	6.67	7.39+	.03
Urbd Dvr	4.49	5.40+	.04
Etubr:			
Grvya	15.30	NL+	.04
Gsrnab p	(5)12.96	NL−	.04
Hilt ltd	10.54	NL−	.02
Holpre r	8.40	NL−	.02
Hprl Rd	13.58	NL+	.07
Nev Sra	16.65	NL+	.01
Ow Nort	13.53	NL+	.17
Sys Run	5.08	NL+	.01
Tqr Hyd	8.73	NL+	.02
Tuir IS	10.26	NL−	.03
Tysa El	5.11	NL+	.03
Veersl Yr	9.49	9.87+	.07
Fdrlk:			
Uhd Eec p	10.18	NL+	.03
Rho Ond p	10.77	NL−	.02
Iro Nico p	8.54	NL−	.06
Gpprt:			
Alllst B	24.00	NL+	.01
Cuy Nini	10.76	NL+	.03
Eqrytl r (6)	15.87	NL+	.03
Ginta Ir	12.00	NL+	.01
Gvrt Lis	10.18	NL+	.02
Heal lec	10.40	10.51−	.02
Jbd Hld	10.23	10.77−	.04
JIY Sun	14.78	15.40+	.03
Mini JN	10.93	NL+	.02
Op Sec	12.97	13.65	...
Prtn Ta	16.40	17.26+	.03
Rsil Nc	15.33	16.14−	.06
Esrch R f (7)	9.24	NL+	.11
Xill Ndix	12.13	12.77+	.22
Htpla:			
ACT trp t (8)47.99		49.22+	.06
ACT asp r	48.89	50.14+	.11
Aal AxC	14.15	14.86−	.03
Batl Pd	10.18	NL+	.03
Chrg tt	14.28	15.61−	.01
Dnrty E	11.04	12.07+	.03
Granie	12.02	13.14−	.02
Hdro le	11.53	12.60−	.01
Ilen Hc	18.82	20.57+	.12
JI Ncom	11.97	12.84−	.06
Kgh Pod p	15.46	16.58−	.01
Tbq Ratl	17.07	18.60+	.08

assets. (Management fees average around one-half of one percent.) The adviser employs professional portfolio managers who invest the fund's money by purchasing a number of stocks or bonds or money market instruments, depending on the type of fund and its investment objective.

These fund professionals decide where to invest the fund's assets. The money managers make their investment decisions based on extensive, ongoing research into the financial performance of individual companies, taking into account general economic and market trends. In addition, their decisions are backed up by extensive economic and statistical resources.

On the basis of their research, money managers decide what and when to buy, sell, or hold for the fund's portfolio, in light of the fund's specific investment objective.

The fund's portfolio managers will normally invest the fund's pool of investment dollars in 50 to 100 different securities to spread the fund's holdings over a number of investments. This diversification is an important principle in lessening the fund's overall investment risk. Such diversification is typically beyond the financial capacity of most individual investors. You can find out where a fund has invested its assets by requesting its semiannual or annual report, or the Statement of Additional Information (SAI), also known as Part B of the prospectus.

In addition to the investment adviser, the fund may also contract with a principal underwriter, a custodian, and a transfer agent. The principal underwriter arranges for the distribution of the fund's shares to the investing public. The underwriter may act as a wholesaler, selling fund shares to securities dealers, or it may retail directly to the public.

The custodian is usually a bank and its functions include safeguarding the fund's assets, making payment for the fund's portfolio of securities upon authority from the fund's adviser, and receiving payments when securities are sold.

The transfer agent performs the shareholder recordkeeping services. It will issue new shares, cancel redeemed shares, and distribute dividends and capital gains to shareholders.

◆ ◆ ◆ ◆
More About Mutual Funds

Ease of Purchase

Mutual fund shares are easy to buy. For those who prefer to make investment decisions themselves, mutual funds are as close as the telephone or the mailbox. Those who would like help in choosing a fund can draw upon a wide variety of sources.

Many funds sell their shares through representatives registered to sell securities, such as stockbrokers, financial planners, or insurance agents. These representatives can help you analyze your financial needs and objectives and recommend appropriate funds.

For these professional services, you may be charged a sales commission (usually referred to as a "load"), expressed as a percent of the total purchase price of the fund shares. Other fund organizations that maintain their own sales force to help potential investors charge a similar commission. If you write or call these funds, a sales agent will contact you.

The maximum charge for these services is 8.5 percent of the initial investment, or 9.3 percent of the net amount

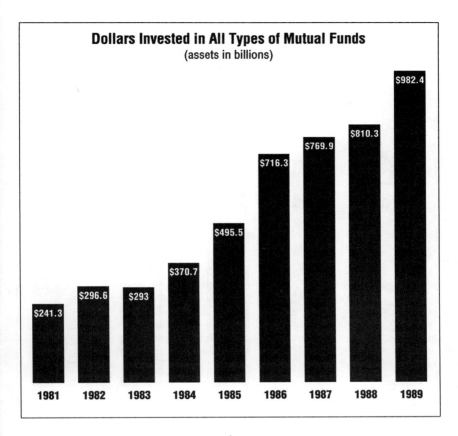

Dollars Invested in All Types of Mutual Funds
(assets in billions)

1981	$241.3
1982	$296.6
1983	$293
1984	$370.7
1985	$495.5
1986	$716.3
1987	$769.9
1988	$810.3
1989	$982.4

invested. This initial sales charge is sometimes called a "front-end" load, since it is payable when shares are first purchased. In some cases, instead of an initial sales charge or load, there is an annual fee of up to 1¼ percent of the fund's assets. This is a 12b-1 fee, which is named after a Securities and Exchange Commission rule that permits funds to charge a percentage of fund assets to pay for the costs of attracting new shareholders. Some funds that are sold through brokers or other sales professionals adopt the 12b-1 structure to compensate the seller of fund shares at the time of sale, though the investor may pay the commission over several years. Other funds may use the fee to pay for other expenses, such as advertising. Some funds charge a fee on reinvested dividends.

There also may be a charge if shares are redeemed during the first few years of ownership. This is known as a contingent deferred sales charge (CDSC), and may be expressed as a percentage of either the original purchase price or the redemption proceeds. If you remain in the fund long enough (typically one to six years), this fee will not be charged. Most CDSCs also decline over time.

The CDSC is one kind of "back-end" load i.e., a charge imposed when you withdraw money from your account; a redemption fee is another. This fee may

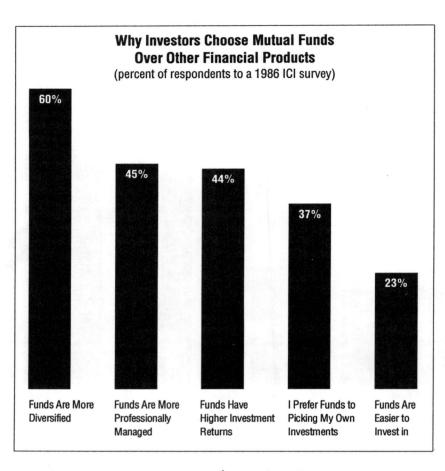

Why Investors Choose Mutual Funds Over Other Financial Products

(percent of respondents to a 1986 ICI survey)

60%	45%	44%	37%	23%
Funds Are More Diversified	Funds Are More Professionally Managed	Funds Have Higher Investment Returns	I Prefer Funds to Picking My Own Investments	Funds Are Easier to Invest in

be charged whenever shares are redeemed, and it may be either a dollar amount or a percentage of the redemption price. Information on all fees is included in the fund's prospectus.

Some funds distribute their shares directly to the public. They may advertise in magazines and newspapers and those interested can write or call for additional information. Most can be reached through toll-free telephone numbers, many of which are included in the fund listings in this directory. Some have set up their own retail offices in large metropolitan areas.

Because there are no sales agents involved, most of these direct-marketed funds, often called "no loads," charge a much lower or no sales commission. In the case of these funds, it's generally up to you to do your investment homework.

Some direct-marketed funds also charge a small 12b-1 fee against fund assets for the costs of distribution. Distribution costs for direct-marketed funds are those associated with advertising and other methods of publicizing the availability of the fund or for servicing shareholder accounts. Distribution fees

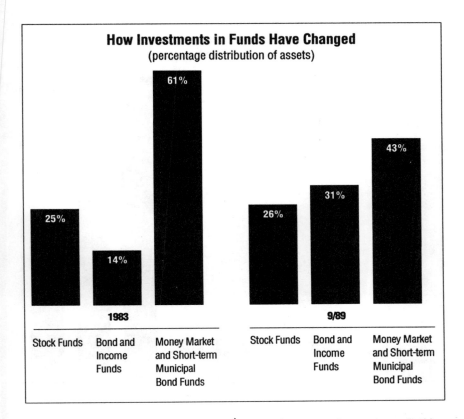

How Investments in Funds Have Changed
(percentage distribution of assets)

1983

25%	14%	61%

Stock Funds | Bond and Income Funds | Money Market and Short-term Municipal Bond Funds

9/89

26%	31%	43%

Stock Funds | Bond and Income Funds | Money Market and Short-term Municipal Bond Funds

of this type usually range between one-tenth to one-and-a-quarter percent.

Any fees charged by a fund are described in the prospectus. In addition, a fee table listing all transactional fees and all annual fund expenses can be found at the front of the prospectus. A hypothetical example accompanies the fee table showing the effect of fees on earnings over time.

Access to Your Money (Liquidity)
Mutual funds, by law, must stand ready on any day the fund is open for business to redeem (i.e., buy back) any or all of your shares at their current net asset value. Of course, the value may be up or down from the price you originally paid, depending on the market. If

you redeem your shares at a profit, this is the third way (in addition to dividends and capital gains distributions) it's possible to make money on your investment.

To redeem your shares (sell them back to the fund) all you need to do is give the fund proper notification (the procedure is explained in the prospectus) and the fund will send your check promptly. In most instances, the fund will issue a check when it receives the notification (by law it must send you the check within seven business days). You receive the price your shares are worth on the day the fund gets proper notice of redemption from you.

If you own a money market fund, you can also redeem shares by writing

7

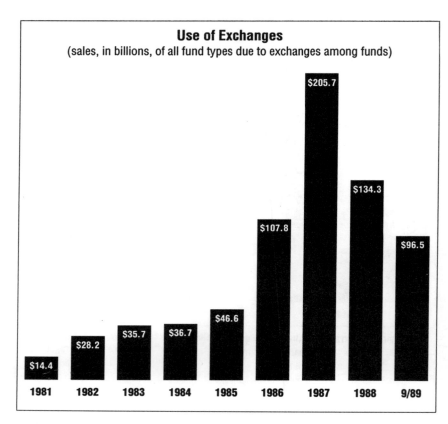

Use of Exchanges
(sales, in billions, of all fund types due to exchanges among funds)

1981	$14.4
1982	$28.2
1983	$35.7
1984	$36.7
1985	$46.6
1986	$107.8
1987	$205.7
1988	$134.3
9/89	$96.5

checks directly against your fund balance.

Exchange Privilege
As the economy or your own personal circumstances change, the types of funds you hold may no longer be the types you need.

Many mutual funds are part of a "family of funds" (a group of funds managed by the same company) and may offer an option called an exchange privilege.

How does it work? Within a family of funds, there may be several—each with a different investment objective—varying from highly conservative funds to those which are more aggressive and carry a higher degree of risk. An ex-

change privilege allows you to transfer shares from one of these funds to another.

Exchange policies vary from fund to fund. The fee for an exchange is nominal—often around $5 or less. For the specifics about a fund's exchange privilege, check the prospectus.

Detailed Recordkeeping
The fund will handle all the paperwork and recordkeeping necessary to keep track of your investment transactions. A typical statement will note such items as your most recent investment or withdrawal (as well as others within a relevant time period) and a dividend or capital gains payment to you in cash or

8

reinvested in the fund. The fund will also report to you on the federal tax status of your earnings.

Other Services

Automatic Investment
You can arrange to make regular contributions to your fund by authorizing it to withdraw a specified amount from your bank account. Some funds offer this service as a payroll deduction plan, where an amount is regularly deducted from your paycheck and invested in the fund.

Automatic Reinvestment
You can elect to have any dividends and capital gains distributions from your mutual fund investment turned back into the fund, automatically buying new shares and expanding your current holdings. (Most shareholders opt for the reinvestment privilege.)

Automatic Withdrawal
You can make arrangements with the fund to automatically send you (or anyone you designate) checks from the fund's earnings or principal. This system works well, for instance, for retirees who want to receive regular supplements to their other income or for families who want to arrange for regular monthly or quarterly payments to their children at college.

Checkwriting Privilege
Many funds offer this service for a low or no charge. This can be helpful when you have car payments or similar expenses to meet. Funds may require checks to be above a minimum dollar amount, $250 for instance, and they may limit the number of checks written

during a specific time period. Be sure to get the details from the prospectus if you are interested in this service.

Retirement Plans
Many financial experts have long viewed mutual funds as appropriate vehicles for retirement investing. They are quite commonly used in self-employed retirement plans (once referred to as Keoghs), as well as in Individual Retirement Accounts (IRAs). They are also used in many 401(k) plans (sometimes called salary-reduction plans) and other employer-sponsored pension plans.

Many funds offer prototype retirement plans and standard IRA agreements. Consult the fund's prospectus for details.

Telephone Exchange
Exchanging shares in a family of funds can be as easy as a telephone call if a fund has this feature. You need to authorize the fund in writing ahead of time if you wish to take advantage of this service. A minimum of $250 or more usually applies to this exchange. Check the prospectus for more details.

Wire Transfers
Many funds allow you to use wire transfers to purchase or redeem shares. Your bank or broker can do this. Check with the fund for specifics on this arrangement.

♦ ♦ ♦ ♦
Who Regulates Mutual Funds?

Mutual funds are highly regulated businesses that must comply with some of the toughest laws and rules in the financial services industry. All funds are regulated by the U.S. Securities and Exchange Commission (SEC).

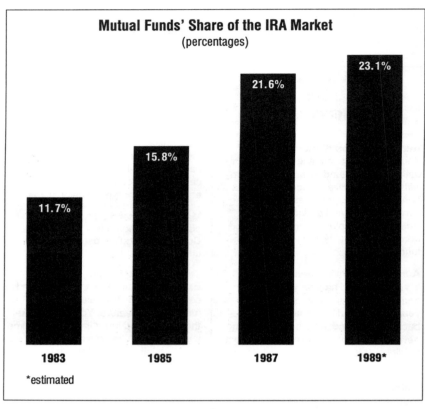

Mutual Funds' Share of the IRA Market
(percentages)

Year	Percentage
1983	11.7%
1985	15.8%
1987	21.6%
1989*	23.1%

*estimated

The SEC, with its extensive rulemaking and enforcement authority, oversees mutual fund compliance with four major federal securities statutes. Listed in chronological order, these laws cover the following areas.

The **Securities Act of 1933** requires the fund's shares to be registered with the SEC prior to their sale. In essence, the Securities Act ensures that the fund provides potential investors with a current prospectus. The prospectus makes detailed disclosures about the fund's management, its investment policies and objective, and its investment activities. This law also limits the types of advertisements that may be used by a mutual fund.

The **Securities Exchange Act of 1934** regulates the purchase and sale of all types of securities, including mutual fund shares.

The **Investment Advisers Act of 1940** is a body of law that regulates certain activities of the investment advisers to mutual funds.

The **Investment Company Act of 1940** is a highly detailed regulatory statute applying to the fund itself. This act contains numerous provisions designed to prevent self-dealing and other conflicts of interest, provide for the safekeeping of fund assets, and prohibit the payment of excessive fees and charges by the fund and its shareholders.

Fund assets must generally be held by an independent custodian, and there are strict requirements for fidelity bonding to ensure against the misappropriation of shareholder monies.

In addition to these federal statutes, almost every state has its own set of regulations governing mutual funds.

While federal and state laws cannot guarantee that a fund will be profitable, they are designed to ensure that all mutual funds are operated and managed in the interests of their shareholders. Here are some specific investor protections that every fund must follow:

• regulations concerning what may be claimed or promised about a mutual fund and its potential;

• requirements that vital information about a fund be made readily available (such as the prospectus, the Statement of Additional Information, also known as Part B of the prospectus, and annual and semiannual reports);

• requirements that a fund operate in the interest of its shareholders, rather than any special interests of its management; and

• rules in the income tax laws dictating diversification of a fund's portfolio over a wide range of investments to avoid too much concentration in a particular security.

◆ ◆ ◆ ◆
Reading a Mutual Fund Prospectus

The purpose of the fund's prospectus is to provide the reader with full and complete disclosure. The prospectus covers the following key points:

• the fund's investment objective. What financial goals is it aiming for?

• the investment methods it uses in trying to achieve these goals;

• the name and address of its investment adviser and a brief description of the adviser's experience;

• the level of investment risk the fund is willing to assume in pursuit of its investment objective. This will range from maximum to minimum risk, depending on the type of fund;

• any investments the fund will NOT make (for example, real estate or commodities);

• tax consequences of the investment for the shareholder;

• how to purchase shares of the fund, including the costs of investing;

• how to redeem shares;

• services provided, such as IRAs, automatic investment of dividends and capital gains distributions, checkwriting, withdrawal plans, and any other features. The prospectus also explains how these services work;

• a condensed financial statement (in tabular form, covering the last ten years, or the period the fund has been in existence if less than ten years), called "Per Share Income and Capital Changes." The fund's performance may be calculated from the information given in this table; and

• a tabular statement of any fees charged by the fund and their effect on earnings over time.

Here are some answers to commonly asked questions about mutual fund prospectuses.

Q. Why do mutual funds make their prospectuses so hard to read?
A. A prospectus is a legal document carrying stiff penalties for any misstatements or omissions. Thus, it must contain information that may appear overly

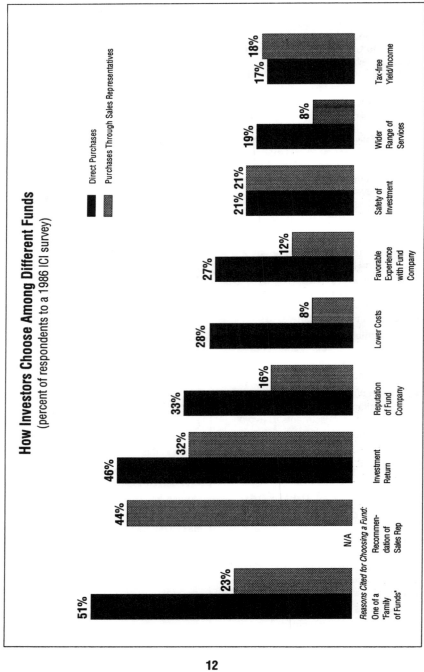

How Investors Choose Among Different Funds
(percent of respondents to a 1986 ICI survey)

■ Direct Purchases
▨ Purchases Through Sales Representatives

Reasons Cited for Choosing a Fund:

One of a "Family" of Funds: 51% / 23%

Recommendation of Sales Rep: N/A / 44%

Investment Return: 46% / 32%

Reputation of Fund Company: 33% / 16%

Lower Costs: 28% / 8%

Favorable Experience with Fund Company: 27% / 12%

Safety of Investment: 21% / 21%

Wider Range of Services: 19% / 8%

Tax-free Yield/Income: 17% / 18%

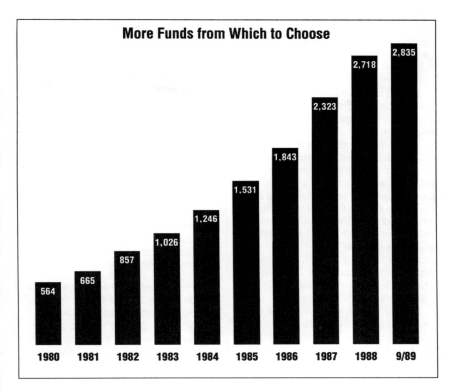

More Funds from Which to Choose

1980	1981	1982	1983	1984	1985	1986	1987	1988	9/89
564	665	857	1,026	1,246	1,531	1,843	2,323	2,718	2,835

technical to some investors. Although the U.S. Securities and Exchange Commission (SEC), the federal agency that regulates mutual funds, has simplified prospectus requirements in recent years, what remains is still relatively technical compared to, say, your daily newspaper.

Q. If it's so technical, why bother to read it?

A. First and most important, you should not make any investment until you have enough information on which to base your decision. The prospectus gives you that information. In addition, you're likely to save yourself from major headaches later on if you read the prospectus before you invest. For example:

1. You need to withdraw your money in a hurry to meet emergency medical expenses. When you try to redeem your shares by telephone, you find out you don't have the proper form on file to do this. Had you read the prospectus, you could have already filed the form.

2. You invest in one fund in a family of mutual funds and make some exchanges during the year among the different funds. You are happy with your earnings, but when each fund sends you your tax statement, you're surprised to find out you owe Uncle Sam. Had you read the prospectus, you would have known the IRS treats an exchange among different funds as a taxable transaction just as if you had

redeemed your shares for cash and then reinvested elsewhere.

3. You place an order to invest in a mutual fund with your broker. When the statement arrives confirming your order, the price is not what you expected. Had you read the prospectus, you would have known which day's price to expect.

4. You decide to invest in a money market mutual fund. You review the prospectus of a fund recommended by a friend, as well as those of two other funds whose ads you noticed. You discover that the fund recommended by your friend has a minimum checkwriting privilege of $1,000. Since one of your objectives is to use this fund for your monthly $500 car payment, you realize that your friend's fund is not for you. You look for a fund that meets your requirements.

5. Over the last year, you made a series of investments into one fund that amounted to more than $10,000. Had you read the prospectus, you could have filed a "letter of intent" to purchase, which would have entitled you to a lower sales charge on each of those investments.

Q. I'm convinced. I need to read the prospectus. But funds could still make it easier to understand. It's not just the jargon—the prospectus even looks intimidating. Why can't the funds use charts and graphs, for example—make it more like a newsletter instead of a legal document?
A. Maybe they could. But don't forget, most funds try to produce their prospectuses within a short time period that doesn't allow for a lot of artwork. And many funds must send the prospectus to hundreds of thousands of investors. Printing and postage costs tend to discourage the use of expensive paper or multicolor graphics, particularly if much of the bill must be paid from monies the fund could otherwise use for investing on behalf of its shareholders.

Q. I'm interested in several different funds. Won't it take forever to plow through all those prospectuses?
A. No. Once you get used to the language and know what to look for, you should be able to reduce the time it takes to absorb the information.

Q. How do I get a prospectus?
A. You can call or write the fund directly and ask that a prospectus be mailed to you, or you can ask your broker or financial planner for a copy. Every fund is required to provide a prospectus either prior to the sale or no later than confirmation of the sale.

Q. When comparing one prospectus to another, will I find the same type of information in the same place?
A. Certain information must appear on the cover page. Both the fee table and the per-share table must appear at the beginning of the prospectus (see page 11). Although the SEC is quite specific about what topics must be included in the rest of the prospectus, funds can present most of this information in any order they choose. This flexibility lets them organize the material in the way most appropriate for each individual fund. Prospectuses average about 10-20 pages and many include a table of contents. So even if you don't immediately see what you're looking for, it shouldn't take long to find.

Q. When I get the prospectus, what should I look for first?
A. Here are some suggestions:
1. *The Date.* Be sure you've got the most recent edition (prospectuses must be updated at least once a year). With earlier copies, you run the risk that some of the information has changed.

What Diversification Means for Stock Mutual Funds
1988
If the portfolios of 60 of the largest stock mutual funds were combined, the resulting total would be invested as indicated in the following industries:

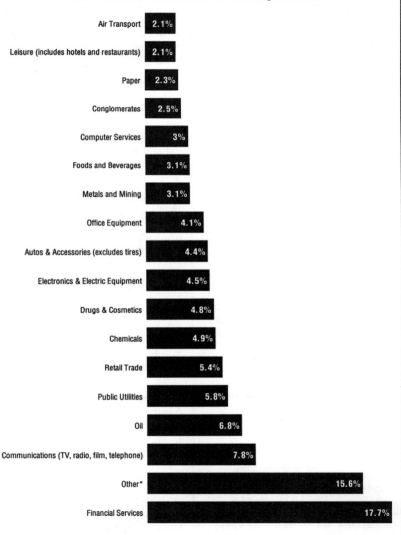

Industry	Percentage
Air Transport	2.1%
Leisure (includes hotels and restaurants)	2.1%
Paper	2.3%
Conglomerates	2.5%
Computer Services	3%
Foods and Beverages	3.1%
Metals and Mining	3.1%
Office Equipment	4.1%
Autos & Accessories (excludes tires)	4.4%
Electronics & Electric Equipment	4.5%
Drugs & Cosmetics	4.8%
Chemicals	4.9%
Retail Trade	5.4%
Public Utilities	5.8%
Oil	6.8%
Communications (TV, radio, film, telephone)	7.8%
Other*	15.6%
Financial Services	17.7%

*Each industry in this category represents less than 2% of total.

2. *The Minimum.* If the minimum dollar amount required to open an account is too high for you, read no further.

3. *The Investment Objective.* Be sure the fund's objective matches your own. For example, if you need a steady source of supplemental income, a fund whose objective is long-term capital appreciation may not be suitable for you. (See pages 17-20 for a discussion of investment objectives.)

4. *Performance.* If the numbers from the per-share table (see page 11 for description) don't please you, move on to the next prospectus. But even if they do please you, don't fill out the application just yet.

5. *Risk.* Different investors can tolerate different levels of risk. Stellar past performance won't mean much if you can't sleep nights. Review carefully what types of risk the prospectus says to expect with this fund.

6. *Services.* If any particular feature or service is essential to you, such as checkwriting, telephone exchange, automatic investing, etc., check to be sure it's there in the prospectus. (See pages 7-9 for more information on these services.)

7. *Fees.* Fees should be in line with those of similar funds operating under comparable policies and objectives. For example, if you're looking for a growth fund, you can compare the fee tables in the prospectuses of several such funds to get an idea of what to expect. Of course, fees should be only one of many considerations when selecting a mutual fund.

Q. I received a prospectus that lists several different funds on the cover page. How can one prospectus apply to more than one fund?

A. Some funds, organized as "series" funds, consist of several separate portfolios of securities, each with its own investment objective and policies. Such funds can be grouped together in one prospectus. In addition, many fund families are reducing their printing and postage costs, as well as the amount of mail in your mailbox, by publishing a "consolidated" prospectus that covers several different funds managed by the same investment adviser. Information that is the same from fund to fund, such as how to purchase shares, appears only once. Information that differs from fund to fund, such as investment objectives, will be repeated for each fund. Although there may be only one fee table, you'll see a column of figures for each fund.

Q. What if I need more information than I can find in the prospectus?
A. Ask the fund for its Statement of Additional Information (SAI), also known as Part B of the prospectus. Funds must provide this document free of charge to anyone who requests it. Among other items, the SAI includes

• a list of the securities in the fund's portfolio at the end of the fund's fiscal year,

• a list of all the directors and officers of the fund, including their occupations and compensation from the fund,

• information about anyone who owns 5 percent or more of the fund's shares, and

• the fund's audited financial statements.

While you're at it, you can also ask for the fund's latest report, which is issued at least twice a year. These reports include a description of how the fund fared during the period covered, the fund's financial statements, and a list of the securities the fund held in its portfolio at the end of the most recent accounting period.

* * * *

Mutual Fund Investment Objectives

The Investment Company Institute classifies mutual funds into 22 broad categories according to their basic investment objectives. Here is a brief description of each. The directory that follows these introductory pages groups specific funds alphabetically by investment objective. Refer to the table of contents for the beginning page numbers of each directory section.

Aggressive Growth Funds seek maximum capital gains as their investment objective. Current income is not a significant factor. Some may invest in stocks of businesses that are somewhat out of the mainstream, such as fledgling companies, new industries, companies fallen on hard times, or industries temporarily out of favor. Some may also use specialized investment techniques such as option writing or short-term trading.

Balanced Funds generally have a three-part investment objective: 1) to conserve the investors' initial principal,

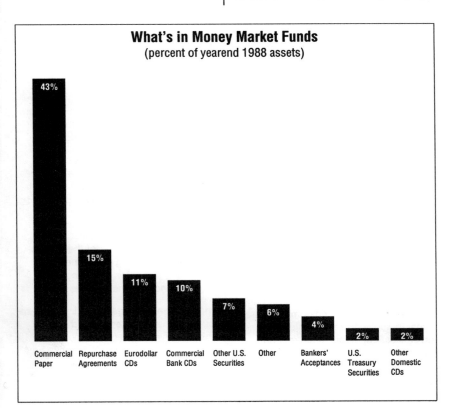

What's in Money Market Funds
(percent of yearend 1988 assets)

Commercial Paper	43%
Repurchase Agreements	15%
Eurodollar CDs	11%
Commercial Bank CDs	10%
Other U.S. Securities	7%
Other	6%
Bankers' Acceptances	4%
U.S. Treasury Securities	2%
Other Domestic CDs	2%

2) to pay current income, and 3) to promote long-term growth of both this principal and income. Balanced funds have a portfolio mix of bonds, preferred stocks, and common stocks.

Corporate Bond Funds, like income funds, seek a high level of income. They do so by buying bonds of corporations for the majority of the fund's portfolio. The rest of the portfolio may be in U.S. Treasury bonds or bonds issued by a federal agency.

Flexible Portfolio Funds may be 100 percent invested in stocks OR bonds OR money market instruments, depending on market conditions. These funds give the money managers the greatest flexibility in anticipating or responding to economic changes.

GNMA or Ginnie Mae Funds invest in mortgage securities backed by the Government National Mortgage Association (GNMA). To qualify for this category, the majority of the portfolio must always be invested in mortgage-backed securities.

Global Bond Funds invest in the debt securities of companies and countries worldwide, including the U.S.

Global Equity Funds invest in securities traded worldwide, including the U.S. Compared to direct investments, global funds offer investors an easier avenue to investing abroad. The funds' professional money managers handle the trading and recordkeeping details and deal with differences in currencies, languages, time zones, laws and regulations, and business customs and practices. In addition to another layer of diversification, global funds add another layer of risk—exchange-rate risk.

Growth Funds invest in the common stock of well-established companies.

Their primary aim is to produce an increase in the value of their investments (capital gains) rather than a flow of dividends. Investors who buy a growth fund are more interested in seeing the fund's share price rise than in receiving income from dividends.

Growth and Income Funds invest mainly in the common stock of companies that have had increasing share value but also a solid record of paying dividends. This type of fund attempts to combine long-term capital growth with a steady stream of income.

High-yield Bond Funds maintain at least two-thirds of their portfolios in lower-rated corporate bonds (Baa or lower by Moody's rating service and BBB or lower by Standard and Poor's rating service). In return for a generally higher yield, investors must bear a greater degree of risk than for higher-rated bonds.

Income-bond Funds seek a high level of current income for their shareholders by investing at all times in a mix of corporate and government bonds.

Income-equity Funds seek a high level of current income for their shareholders by investing primarily in equity securities of companies with good dividend-paying records.

Income-mixed Funds seek a high level of current income for their shareholders by investing in income-producing securities, including both equities and debt instruments.

International Funds invest in equity securities of companies located outside the U.S. Two thirds of their portfolios must be so invested at all times to be categorized here.

Individual and Institutional Dollars Compared
(yearend 1988 mutual fund assets in billions)

■ Individuals
▨ Institutions

$548.4

$261.9

All Funds

st stable securities available, reasury bills, certificates of arge banks, and commercial short-term IOUs of large rations).

:ome Funds seek a higher urn by investing primarily in aying common stocks on options are traded on na- urities exchanges. Current re- ally consists of dividends, from writing options, net gains from sales of portfolio on exercises of options or otherwise, and any profits from closing purchase transactions.

Precious Metals/Gold Funds maintain two thirds of their portfolios invested in securities associated with gold, silver, and other precious metals.

Short-term Municipal Bond Funds invest in municipal securities with relatively short maturities. These are also known as tax-exempt money market funds. For some taxpayers, portions of income from these securities may be subject to the federal alternative minimum tax.

State Municipal Bond Funds—Long-term work just like other long-term municipal bond funds (see above) except their portfolios contain the issues of only one state. A resident of that state has the advantage of receiving income free of both federal and state tax. For some taxpayers, portions of income from these securities may be subject to the federal alternative minimum tax.

State Municipal Bond Funds—Short-term work just like other short-term municipal bond funds (see above) except their portfolios contain the issues of only one state. A resident of that state has the advantage of receiving income free of both federal and state tax. For some taxpayers, portions of income from these securities may be subject to the federal alternative minimum tax.

U.S. Government Income Funds invest in a variety of government securities. These include U.S. Treasury bonds, federally guaranteed mortgage-backed securities, and other government notes.

◆ ◆ ◆ ◆
Twelve Commonly Asked Questions on Mutual Funds

Q. Are mutual funds a new type of investment?
A. No. In fact, they have roots in 18th century Britain. The first U.S. mutual fund was organized in Boston in 1924. Some mutual fund companies have been in operation for 50 years or more.

Q. How much money do you need to invest in a mutual fund?
A. Literally anywhere from a few dollars to several million! Many funds have no minimum requirements for investing. Others have established minimums in the hundreds or thousands of dollars. A few funds are open to large institutional accounts only. The vast majority of funds, however, require a minimum investment of between $250 and $1000.

Q. Do mutual funds offer a fixed rate of return?
A. No. Mutual funds invest in securities such as stocks and bonds whose yields and values fluctuate with market conditions.

But mutual funds can make money for their shareholders in three ways. One, they pay their shareholders dividends earned from the fund's investments. Two, if a security held by a fund is sold at a profit, funds pay their shareholders capital gains distributions. And three, if the value of the securities held by the fund increases, the value of each mutual fund share increases proportionally.

In none of these cases, however, can a return be guaranteed. In fact, it is against the law for a mutual fund to make a claim as to its future performance. Ads quoting returns, remember, are based on past performance and should not be interpreted as a "fixed rate" yield. Nor should past performance be taken as a predictor of future earnings.

Q. What are the risks of mutual fund investing?

A. Mutual funds are investments in financial securities with fluctuating values. The value of the stocks in a fund's portfolio, for example, will rise and fall according to general economic conditions and the fortunes of the particular companies that issue those stocks. Even the most conservative securities, such as U.S. government obligations, will fluctuate in value as interest rates change. There are resulting risks that investors should be aware of when purchasing mutual fund shares.

The more than 2,900 mutual funds available span the complete spectrum of investment risk. Some funds—the aggressive growth category, for example—attract investors who seek maximum capital appreciation through a fund that uses investment techniques that carry greater risk than other stock-type investments. Other funds, such as money market funds, emphasize low risk with the preservation of capital as a chief goal. Read the prospectus to get a feel for the risk—and possible returns—involved.

Mutual funds operate in a strict federal and state regulatory environment. (For a discussion of how shareholders are protected, see pages 9-11.)

Q. How can I evaluate a fund's long-term performance?

A. Those considering a mutual fund purchase may calculate a fund's performance by referring to the section in the prospectus headed, "Per Share Income and Capital Changes." This section will give you the figures needed to compute the annual rates of return earned by the fund each year for the past ten years (or for the life of the fund if less than ten years).

Q. What's the difference between yield and total return?

A. Yield is the income per share paid to a shareholder, from dividends and interest, over a specified period of time. Yield is expressed as a percent of the current offering price per share.

The term "total return" is a measure of the per-share change in total value from the beginning to the end of a specified period, usually a year, including distributions paid to shareholders. This measure includes income received from dividends and interest, capital gains distributions, and any unrealized capital gains or losses.

Q. How much does it cost to invest in a mutual fund?

A. A mutual fund normally contracts with its management company to provide for most of the needs of a normal business, i.e., its offices, administration, personnel, communications, equipment, etc. The management company is paid a fee for these services, which usually include managing the fund's investments.

In addition, the fund may pay directly for some of its costs, such as printing, mailing, accounting, and legal services. Typically, these two charges may average about one to one-and-a-half percent of the fund's assets annually. In such a fund, you would be paying $10-$15 a year on every $1000 invested.

Some funds' directors have adopted plans (with the approval of the fund's shareholders) that allow them to pay certain distribution costs (the costs of advertising, for example) directly from fund assets. These costs may range from one-tenth of one percent to one-and-a-quarter percent annually.

There may be other charges involved, for example, in exchanging shares. Some funds may charge a redemption fee when a shareholder redeems (cashes in) his or her shares, usually within five years of purchasing them.

All costs and charges assessed by the fund organization are given in its prospectus.

Q. Is the management fee part of the sales charge?

A. No, the management fee is paid by the fund to its investment adviser for services rendered in managing the fund's portfolio. An average fee is one-half of one percent a year of the fund's total assets. As described above, the management fee and other business expenses generally total somewhere between one and one-and-a-half percent. These expenses are paid from the fund's assets and are reflected in the price of fund shares. In contrast, most sales charges are deducted from your initial investment. See pages 4-7 for more information on sales charges.

Q. Is my money locked up for a certain period of time in a mutual fund?

A. Unlike some other types of financial accounts, mutual funds are liquid investments. That means that any shares a mutual fund investor owns may be redeemed freely, on any day the fund is open for business.

Since a mutual fund stands ready to buy back its shares at their current net asset value, you always have a buyer for your shares at current market values.

Q. How often do I get account statements from a mutual fund?

A. Mutual funds ordinarily send immediate confirmation statements when an investor purchases or redeems (sells) shares. Statements alerting sharehold-

ers to reinvested dividends are sent out periodically. At least semiannually, investors also receive statements on the status of the fund's investments. Tax statements are mailed annually.

Q. I've already purchased shares of a mutual fund. How can I tell how well my investment is doing?

A. There are two steps in judging how well your fund is faring. First, you need to know how many shares you now own. The "now" is emphasized because if you've asked the fund to plow any dividends and capital gains distributions back into the fund for you, it will do so by issuing you more shares, thereby increasing the value of your investment.

Once you know how many shares you own, look up the fund's net asset value (sometimes called the "sell" or "bid" price) in the financial section of a major metropolitan daily newspaper. (See page 3 for an example.)

Second, multiply the net asset value times the number of shares you own to figure out the value of your investment as of that date. Compare today's value against your beginning value.

You'll need to keep the confirmation statements you receive when you first purchase shares and as you make subsequent purchases in order to compare the value "then" vs. "now." You will also need these statements for tax purposes.

Q. Do investment experts recommend mutual funds for Individual Retirement Accounts?

A. Most financial experts view many mutual funds as compatible with the long-term objectives of saving for retirement. Indeed, shareholders cite this reason for investing more than any other. Many types of funds work best when allowed to ride out the ups and downs of

22

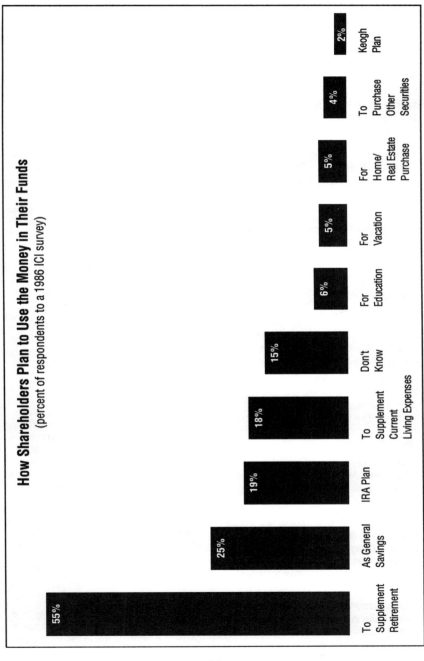

How Shareholders Plan to Use the Money in Their Funds
(percent of respondents to a 1986 ICI survey)

To Supplement Retirement — 55%

As General Savings — 25%

IRA Plan — 19%

To Supplement Current Living Expenses — 18%

Don't Know — 15%

For Education — 6%

For Vacation — 5%

For Home/Real Estate Purchase — 5%

To Purchase Other Securities — 4%

Keogh Plan — 2%

market cycles over long periods of time.

Funds can also offer the IRA owner flexibility. By using the exchange privilege within a family of funds, the investor can shift investments from one type of securities to another in response to changes in personal finances or the economic outlook or as retirement approaches.

◆ ◆ ◆ ◆
Glossary

Adviser
The organization employed by a mutual fund to give professional advice on the fund's investments and asset management practices (also called the "investment adviser").

"Asked" or "Offering" Price
The price at which a mutual fund's shares can be purchased. The asked or offering price means the current net asset value per share plus sales charge, if any.

"Bid" or "Sell" Price
The price at which a mutual fund's shares are redeemed (bought back) by the fund. The bid or redemption price usually means the current net asset value per share.

Broker/Dealer
A firm that buys and sells mutual fund shares and other securities to the public.

Capital Gains Distributions
Payments to mutual fund shareholders of profits (long-term gains) realized on the sale of the fund's portfolio securities. These amounts usually are paid once a year.

Capital Growth
An increase in market value of a mutual fund's securities, as reflected in the net asset value of fund shares. This is a specific long-term objective of many mutual funds.

Contingent Deferred Sales Charge (CDSC)
A fee imposed when shares are redeemed (bought back by the fund) during the first few years of share ownership.

Custodian
The organization (usually a bank) that keeps custody of securities and other assets of a mutual fund.

Diversification
The policy of all mutual funds to spread investments among a number of different securities to reduce the risks inherent in investing.

Dollar-cost Averaging
The practice of investing equal amounts of money at regular intervals regardless of whether securities markets are moving up or down. This procedure reduces average share costs to the investor who acquires more shares in periods of lower securities prices and fewer shares in periods of higher prices.

Exchange Privilege
An option enabling mutual fund shareholders to transfer their investment from one fund to another within the same fund family as their needs or objectives change. Typically, funds allow investors to use the exchange privilege several times a year for a low or no fee per exchange.

Income Dividends
Payments to mutual fund shareholders of dividends, interest, and/or short-term capital gains earned on the fund's portfolio securities after deducting operating expenses.

Investment Company
A corporation, trust, or partnership that invests pooled funds of shareholders in securities appropriate to the fund's ob-

jective. Among the benefits of investment companies, compared to direct investments, are professional management and diversification. Mutual funds (also known as "open-end" investment companies) are the most popular type of investment company.

Investment Objective
The goal—e.g., long-term capital growth, current income, etc.—that the investor and mutual fund pursue together.

Long-term Funds
An industry designation for funds that invest primarily in securities with remaining maturities of more than one year. Long-term funds are broadly divided into equity (stock), bond, and income funds.

Management Fee
The amount paid by a mutual fund to the investment adviser for its services. The average annual fee industrywide is about one-half of one percent of fund assets.

Mutual Fund
An investment company that pools money from shareholders and invests in a variety of securities, including stocks, bonds, and money market instruments. A mutual fund stands ready to buy back (redeem) its shares at their current net asset value; this value depends on the market value of the fund's portfolio securities at the time of redemption. Most mutual funds continuously offer new shares to investors.

Net Asset Value Per Share
The market worth of one share of a mutual fund. This figure is derived by taking a fund's total assets—securities, cash, and any accrued earnings—deducting liabilities, and dividing by the number of shares outstanding.

No-load Fund
A mutual fund selling its shares at net asset value without the addition of sales charges.

Portfolio
A collection of securities owned by an individual or an institution (such as a mutual fund). A fund's portfolio may include a combination of stocks, bonds, and money market securities.

Prospectus
The official booklet that describes a mutual fund and must be furnished to all investors. It contains information required by the U.S. Securities and Exchange Commission on such subjects as the fund's investment objectives, policies, services, and fees. A more detailed document, known as "Part B" of the prospectus or the "Statement of Additional Information," is available at no charge upon request.

Redemption Price
The amount per share (shown as the "bid" in newspaper tables) that mutual fund shareholders receive when they cash in shares. The value of the shares depends on the market value of the fund's portfolio securities at the time. This value is the same as "net asset value per share" (see above).

Reinvestment Privilege
An option available to mutual fund shareholders in which fund dividends and capital gains distributions are automatically turned back into the fund to buy new shares and thus increase holdings.

Sales Charge
An amount charged to purchase shares in many mutual funds sold by brokers or other sales agents. The maximum charge is 8.5 percent of the initial investment. The charge is added to the net asset value per share when determining the offering price (see above).

Series Funds
Funds that are organized with separate portfolios of securities, each with its own investment objective.

Short-term Funds
An industry designation for funds that invest primarily in securities with maturities of less than one year. Short-term funds include money market funds and short-term municipal bond funds.

Transfer Agent
The organization employed by a mutual fund to prepare and maintain records relating to the accounts of its shareholders. Some funds serve as their own transfer agents.

12b-1 Fee
The fee charged by some funds, named after an SEC rule. Such fees pay for distribution costs, such as advertising and dealer compensation. The fund's prospectus outlines 12b-1 fees, if applicable.

Underwriter
The organization that acts as the distributor of a mutual fund's shares to broker/dealers and investors.

Variable Annuity
An investment contract sold to an investor by an insurance company. Capital is accumulated, often through investment in a mutual fund, and converted to an income stream at a future date, perhaps retirement. Income payments vary with the value of the account.

Withdrawal Plan
A program in which shareholders receive payments from their mutual fund investments at regular intervals. Typically, these payments are drawn first from the fund's dividends and capital gains distributions, if any, and then from principal, as needed.

◆ ◆ ◆ ◆
About This Directory

On the following pages, you'll find listings for more than 2,900 mutual funds, organized by 22 broad investment objectives. For definitions of these objectives, see pages 17-20.

The information about each fund is intended to give you a head start in finding one or more that meet your investment needs. Of course, before investing, consult the fund's prospectus or an investment professional.

Information on each fund includes the following:

• Name, address, and telephone number, including toll-free numbers if available. The fund name is in bold type. Some mutual funds are organized as a series, i.e., several funds with different investment objectives are grouped under the name of a parent fund. In that case, the parent is listed in bold type and the series fund is listed separately in bold italics under the parent name. Some funds have separate "classes," or fee structures based on different criteria. These classes appear in italic beneath the fund name.

• Year the fund began.

• The fund's investment adviser. An investment adviser makes investment decisions and manages the fund's portfolio (see page 2).

• The fund's total net assets as of September 30, 1989. Net assets reflect the market worth of a fund's portfolio, cash, and any accrued earnings—minus its expenses. In cases where a fund's assets were estimated, "(e)" appears after the amount listed.

- The initial and subsequent investment amounts; how much money it takes to get started in the fund, and how much is required to make additions to your investment. The amounts listed are for regular investments only. Minimums for IRA accounts, for example, may be lower than the amounts stated.

- Fees charged by the fund. These include front-end, or initial, sales charges and back-end sales charges. Initial sales charges, i.e., those payable when shares are purchased, are indicated by an "i" in this column. Back-end charges, or charges imposed when shares are redeemed, are indicated by an "r." These could be either contingent deferred sales charges (CDSC), which are fees imposed when shares are redeemed during the first few years of share ownership, or redemption fees, which are payable whenever shares are "bought back" by the fund. A "p" is used if a fund has a 12b-1 fee. Money generated by this charge is used to pay for distribution costs such as sales or promotional expenses. If a fund has both a 12b-1 fee and either a CDSC or a redemption fee, a "t" will appear in this column. If none of these fees applies to the fund, an "n" will appear in this column.

The notation *N/A* that may appear in the assets column or fee column indicates the information was not available at the time this book was produced.

- The column headed, Where to Buy Shares, indicates the fund's primary method of distributing its shares. Many funds offer consumers multiple ways to purchase shares.

The notations in this column mean:

Fund—Call the fund directly for information. It will send a prospectus and perhaps other information, such as its most recent annual report, along with a purchase application.

Local rep—Shares are primarily sold through local sales agents for the fund including stockbrokers, financial planners, or other securities professionals in your community.

Insur—Fund shares are sold as part of a special insurance product. Consumers are able to buy into the fund only by purchasing an insurance product.

Not offering shares—This indicates that shares of the fund are not generally available for purchase at this time.

◆ ◆ ◆ ◆

Aggressive Growth Funds

Aggressive Growth

Fund	Year Began	Investment Adviser	9/30/89 Assets	Minimum Initial and Subsequent Investment	Fees*	Where to Buy Shares
ABT Investment Series, Inc. *ABT Emerging Growth Fund* 205 Royal Palm Way Palm Beach, FL 33480 407/655-7255 800/441-6580	1983	Palm Beach Capital Management, Ltd.	$21.9 Mil	$1,000/ 50	i, p	Local Rep
Aggressive Stock Trust 99 High St. Boston, MA 02110 617/338-3200 800/343-2898 800/225-1587	1982	Keystone Custodian Funds, Inc.	$16.2 Mil	Not Applicable	n	Insur
AIM Equity Funds, Inc. *AIM Constellation Fund* 11 Greenway Plaza Ste. 1919 Houston, TX 77046 713/626-1919 800/231-0803 800/392-9681 TX Only	1966	AIM Advisors, Inc.	$95.7 Mil	$1,000/ 100	i, p	Local Rep
Alger American Fund *Alger American Small Capitalization Portfolio* 75 Maiden Lane New York, NY 10038 212/806-8800 800/223-3810	1988	Fred Alger Management, Inc.	$0.1 Mil	Not Applicable	n	Insur
Alger Fund *Alger Small Capitalization Portfolio* 75 Maiden Lane New York, NY 10038 212/806-8800 800/223-3810	1986	Fred Alger Management, Inc.	$12.5 Mil	$1,000/ 100	t	Fund
American Capital Over-The-Counter Securities, Inc. 2800 Post Oak Blvd. Houston, TX 77056 713/993-0500 800/421-5666	1983	American Capital Asset Management, Inc.	$47.3 Mil	$500/ 50	i, p	Local Rep
American Capital Venture Fund, Inc. 2800 Post Oak Blvd. Houston, TX 77056 713/993-0500 800/421-5666	1969	American Capital Asset Management, Inc.	$206.8 Mil	$500/ 50	i, p	Local Rep

*Key: i=initial sales charge   r=redemption fee or contingent deferred sales charge(CDSC)
t=12b-1 fee and either CDSC or redemption fee   p=12b-1 fee   n=none of the preceding fees   N/A=not available

31

Aggressive Growth

Fund	Year Began	Investment Adviser	9/30/89 Assets	Minimum Initial and Subsequent Investment	Fees*	Where to Buy Shares
American General Equity Accumulation Fund, Inc. 2800 Post Oak Blvd. Houston, TX 77056 713/993-0500 800/421-5666	1982	American Capital Asset Management, Inc.	$74.6 Mil	Not Applicable	n	Insur
American General Series Portfolio Company *Capital Accumulation Fund* 2929 Allen Pkwy. P.O. Box 3206 Houston, TX 77253 713/526-5251	1983	Variable Annuity Life Insurance Company	$67.5 Mil	Not Applicable	r	Insur
American Investors Growth Fund, Inc. 777 W. Putnam Ave. P.O. Box 2500 Greenwich, CT 06836 203/531-5000 800/243-5353	1957	D.H. Blair Advisors, Inc.	$64.7 Mil (e)	$1,000/ 100	i	Local Rep
AMEV Fiduciary Fund, Inc. P.O. Box 64284 St. Paul, MN 55164 612/738-4000 800/872-2638	1982	AMEV Advisers, Inc.	$33.0 Mil	$500/ 50	i, p	Local Rep
Bailard, Biehl & Kaiser International Fund, Inc. 2755 Campus Dr. San Mateo, CA 94403 415/571-5800	1979	Warburg Investment Management International Limited	$68.1 Mil (e)	$1,000/ 100	n	Fund
Baron Asset Fund 450 Park Ave. New York, NY 10022 212/759-7700 800/99-BARON	1987	BAMCO, Inc.	$47.7 Mil	$10,000/ 2,000	t	Local Rep
Bull & Bear Special Equities Fund, Inc. 11 Hanover Sq. New York, NY 10005 212/785-0900 800/847-4200	1986	Bull & Bear Equity Advisers, Inc.	$3.8 Mil (e)	$1,000/ 100	p	Fund

*Key: i=initial sales charge   r=redemption fee or contingent deferred sales charge(CDSC)
t=12b-1 fee and either CDSC or redemption fee   p=12b-1 fee   n=none of the preceding fees   N/A=not available

32

Aggressive Growth

Fund	Year Began	Investment Adviser	9/30/89 Assets	Minimum Initial and Subsequent Investment	Fees*	Where to Buy Shares
CIGNA Aggressive Growth Fund One Financial Plaza Springfield, MA 01103 413/784-0100 800/56CIGNA	1983	CIGNA Investments, Inc.	$12.7 Mil	$500/ 50	i, p	Local Rep
CIGNA Annuity Fund *Aggressive Equity Fund* CIGNA Corporation Hartford, CT 06152 203/726-6000 800/562-4462	1987	CIGNA Investments, Inc.	$1.6 Mil	Not Applicable	n	Insur
Colonial/Hancock Liberty Trust *Colonial/Hancock Liberty Aggressive Growth Fund* One Financial Ctr. Boston, MA 02111 617/426-3750 800/225-2365, 800/426-3750	1987	Colonial Management Associates, Inc.	$1.0 Mil	Not Applicable	n	Insur
Colonial Value Investing Portfolios - Equity Portfolio *Aggressive Growth Fund* One Financial Ctr. Boston, MA 02111 617/426-3750 800/225-2365, 800/426-3750	1988	Colonial Management Associates, Inc.	$8.8 Mil	$500/ 100	t	Local Rep
Columbia Special Fund, Inc. 1301 SW 5th Ave. P.O. Box 1350 Portland, OR 97207 503/222-3600 800/547-1707	1985	Columbia Funds Management Company	$85.7 Mil	$2,000/ 100	n	Fund
Counsellors Emerging Growth Fund, Inc. 466 Lexington Ave. New York, NY 10017-3147 212/878-0600 800/888-6878	1988	Warburg, Pincus Counsellors, Inc.	$27.9 Mil	$25,000/ 5,000	n	Fund
Dean Witter Developing Growth Securities Trust Two World Trade Ctr. New York, NY 10048 212/392-2550 800/869-3863	1983	Dean Witter Reynolds Inc. - InterCapital Division	$89.3 Mil	$1,000/ 100	t	Local Rep

*Key: i=initial sales charge   r=redemption fee or contingent deferred sales charge(CDSC)
t=12b-1 fee and either CDSC or redemption fee   p=12b-1 fee   n=none of the preceding fees   N/A=not available

Aggressive Growth

Fund	Year Began	Investment Adviser	9/30/89 Assets	Minimum Initial and Subsequent Investment	Fees*	Where to Buy Shares
Delaware Group Trend Fund One Commerce Sq. Philadelphia, PA 19103 215/988-1200 800/523-4640	1968	Delaware Management Company, Inc.	$78.6 Mil	$25/ 25	i	Local Rep
Delaware Group Value Fund One Commerce Sq. Philadelphia, PA 19103 215/988-1200 800/523-4640	1987	Delaware Management Company, Inc.	$11.2 Mil	$1,000/ 25	i, p	Local Rep
Dreyfus Leverage Fund, Inc. 666 Old Country Rd. Garden City, NY 11530 718/895-1206 800/645-6561	1969	Dreyfus Corporation	$484.1 Mil	$2,500/ 100	i	Local Rep
Dreyfus Strategic Aggressive Investing, L.P. 666 Old Country Rd. Garden City, NY 11530 718/895-1347 800/648-9048	1987	Dreyfus Corporation	$122.4 Mil	$2,500/ 500	i, p	Fund
Dreyfus Strategic Investing 666 Old Country Rd. Garden City, NY 11530 718/895-1347 800/648-9048	1986	Dreyfus Corporation	$113.3 Mil	$2,500/ 500	i, p	Fund
Enterprise Equity Portfolios *Enterprise Aggressive Growth Portfolio* 1200 Ashwood Pkwy. Ste. 290 Atlanta, GA 30338 404/396-8118, 800/432-4320	1987	Enterprise Capital Management, Inc.	$4.3 Mil (e)	$500/ 25	t	Local Rep
Equitec Siebel Fund Group *Equitec Siebel Aggressive Growth Fund Series* 7677 Oakport St. P.O. Box 2470 Oakland, CA 94614 415/430-9900 800/869-8900	1986	Siebel Capital Management, Inc.	$34.8 Mil (e)	$1,000/ 0	t	Local Rep

*Key: i=initial sales charge   r=redemption fee or contingent deferred sales charge(CDSC)
t=12b-1 fee and either CDSC or redemption fee   p=12b-1 fee   n=none of the preceding fees   N/A=not available

Aggressive Growth

Fund	Year Began	Investment Adviser	9/30/89 Assets	Minimum Initial and Subsequent Investment	Fees*	Where to Buy Shares
Equity Portfolio: Growth 82 Devonshire St. Boston, MA 02109 617/570-7000 800/843-3001 617/570-5511 MA Only	1983	Fidelity Management & Research Company	$24.3 Mil	$500,000/ 0	n	Local Rep
Evergreen Fund 2500 Westchester Ave. Purchase, NY 10577 914/694-2020 800/235-0064	1971	Evergreen Asset Management Corporation	$791.7 Mil (e)	$2,000/ 0	n	Fund
Evergreen Limited Market Fund, Inc. 2500 Westchester Ave. Purchase, NY 10577 914/694-2020 800/235-0064	1983	Evergreen Asset Management Corporation	$36.1 Mil (e)	$25,000/ 5,000	n	Fund
Evergreen Value Timing Fund 2500 Westchester Ave. Purchase, NY 10577 914/694-2020 800/235-0064	1986	Evergreen Asset Management Corporation	$28.7 Mil (e)	$2,000/ 0	n	Fund
Explorer Fund Vanguard Financial Ctr. P.O. Box 2600 Valley Forge, PA 19482 215/648-6000 800/662-7447 800/362-0530 PA Only	1967	Wellington Management Company	$297.9 Mil	$3,000/ 100	n	Fund
Explorer II Vanguard Financial Ctr. P.O. Box 2600 Valley Forge, PA 19482 215/648-6000 800/662-7447 800/362-0530 PA Only	1985	Granahan Investment Management, Inc.	$83.9 Mil	$3,000/ 100	n	Fund
Fairfield Fund, Inc. 600 Third Ave. New York, NY 10016 203/863-5600 800/237-1718	1956	National Securities & Research Corporation	$34.4 Mil	$500/ 25	i	Local Rep

*Key: i=initial sales charge   r=redemption fee or contingent deferred sales charge(CDSC)
t=12b-1 fee and either CDSC or redemption fee   p=12b-1 fee   n=none of the preceding fees   N/A=not available

Aggressive Growth

Fund	Year Began	Investment Adviser	9/30/89 Assets	Minimum Initial and Subsequent Investment	Fees*	Where to Buy Shares
FBL Series Fund, Inc. *Aggressive Growth Common Stock Portfolio* 5400 University Ave. W. Des Moines, IA 50265 515/225-5400 800/247-4170 800/422-3175 IA Only	1987	FBL Investment Advisory Services, Inc.	$2.2 Mil	$250/ 0	t	Local Rep
Federated Growth Trust Federated Investors Twr. Pittsburgh, PA 15222-3779 412/288-1900 800/245-5000	1984	Federated Management	$151.7 Mil	$25,000/ 0	n	Local Rep
Fidelity Capital Trust *Fidelity Capital Appreciation Fund* 82 Devonshire St. Boston, MA 02109 617/570-7000 800/544-6666	1986	Fidelity Management & Research Company	$2.3 Bil	$2,500/ 250	i, r	Fund
Fidelity Financial Trust *Fidelity Freedom Fund* 82 Devonshire St. Boston, MA 02109 617/570-7000 800/544-6666	1983	Fidelity Management & Research Company	$1.5 Bil	$500/ 250	n	Fund
Fidelity Growth Company Fund 82 Devonshire St. Boston, MA 02109 617/570-7000 800/544-6666 617/523-1919 MA Only	1983	Fidelity Management & Research Company	$266.4 Mil	$1,000/ 250	i	Fund
Fidelity Magellan Fund 82 Devonshire St. Boston, MA 02109 617/570-7000 800/544-6666	1962	Fidelity Management & Research Company	$12.4 Bil	$1,000/ 250	i	Fund
Fidelity Securities Fund *Fidelity OTC Portfolio* 82 Devonshire St. Boston, MA 02109 617/570-7000 800/544-6666	1984	Fidelity Management & Research Company	$792.9 Mil	$2,500/ 250	i	Fund

*Key: i=initial sales charge   r=redemption fee or contingent deferred sales charge(CDSC)
t=12b-1 fee and either CDSC or redemption fee   p=12b-1 fee   n=none of the preceding fees   N/A=not available

Aggressive Growth

Fund	Year Began	Investment Adviser	9/30/89 Assets	Minimum Initial and Subsequent Investment	Fees*	Where to Buy Shares
Fidelity Select Portfolios *Air Transportation Portfolio* 82 Devonshire St. Boston, MA 02109 617/570-7000 800/544-6666	1985	Fidelity Management & Research Company	$9.6 Mil	$1,000/ 250	i, r	Fund
Fidelity Select Portfolios *Automation and Machinery Portfolio* 82 Devonshire St. Boston, MA 02109 617/570-7000 800/544-6666	1986	Fidelity Management & Research Company	$1.3 Mil	$1,000/ 250	i, r	Fund
Fidelity Select Portfolios *Automotive Portfolio* 82 Devonshire St. Boston, MA 02109 617/570-7000 800/544-6666	1986	Fidelity Management & Research Company	$1.1 Mil	$1,000/ 250	i, r	Fund
Fidelity Select Portfolios *Biotechnology Portfolio* 82 Devonshire St. Boston, MA 02109 617/570-7000 800/544-6666	1985	Fidelity Management & Research Company	$82.2 Mil	$1,000/ 250	i, r	Fund
Fidelity Select Portfolios *Broadcast and Media Portfolio* 82 Devonshire St. Boston, MA 02109 617/570-7000 800/544-6666	1986	Fidelity Management & Research Company	$25.0 Mil	$1,000/ 250	i, r	Fund
Fidelity Select Portfolios *Brokerage and Investment Management Portfolio* 82 Devonshire St. Boston, MA 02109 617/570-7000 800/544-6666	1985	Fidelity Management & Research Company	$4.8 Mil	$1,000/ 250	i, r	Fund
Fidelity Select Portfolios *Capital Goods Portfolio* 82 Devonshire St. Boston, MA 02109 617/570-7000 800/544-6666	1986	Fidelity Management & Research Company	$1.8 Mil	$1,000/ 250	i, r	Fund

*Key: i=initial sales charge   r=redemption fee or contingent deferred sales charge(CDSC)
t=12b-1 fee and either CDSC or redemption fee   p=12b-1 fee   n=none of the preceding fees   N/A=not available

Aggressive Growth

Fund	Year Began	Investment Adviser	9/30/89 Assets	Minimum Initial and Subsequent Investment	Fees*	Where to Buy Shares
Fidelity Select Portfolios *Chemicals Portfolio* 82 Devonshire St. Boston, MA 02109 617/570-7000 800/544-6666	1985	Fidelity Management & Research Company	$34.9 Mil	$1,000/ 250	i, r	Fund
Fidelity Select Portfolios *Computers Portfolio* 82 Devonshire St. Boston, MA 02109 617/570-7000 800/544-6666	1985	Fidelity Management & Research Company	$8.7 Mil	$1,000/ 250	i, r	Fund
Fidelity Select Portfolios *Defense and Aerospace Portfolio* 82 Devonshire St. Boston, MA 02109 617/570-7000 800/544-6666	1984	Fidelity Management & Research Company	$1.7 Mil	$1,000/ 250	i, r	Fund
Fidelity Select Portfolios *Electric Utilities Portfolio* 82 Devonshire St. Boston, MA 02109 617/570-7000 800/544-6666	1986	Fidelity Management & Research Company	$14.5 Mil	$1,000/ 250	i, r	Fund
Fidelity Select Portfolios *Electronics Portfolio* 82 Devonshire St. Boston, MA 02109 617/570-7000 800/544-6666	1985	Fidelity Management & Research Company	$5.6 Mil	$1,000/ 250	i, r	Fund
Fidelity Select Portfolios *Energy Portfolio* 82 Devonshire St. Boston, MA 02109 617/570-7000 800/544-6666	1981	Fidelity Management & Research Company	$77.9 Mil	$1,000/ 250	i, r	Fund
Fidelity Select Portfolios *Energy Service Portfolio* 82 Devonshire St. Boston, MA 02109 617/570-7000 800/544-6666	1985	Fidelity Management & Research Company	$46.6 Mil	$1,000/ 250	i, r	Fund

*Key: i=initial sales charge   r=redemption fee or contingent deferred sales charge(CDSC)
        t=12b-1 fee and either CDSC or redemption fee   p=12b-1 fee   n=none of the preceding fees   N/A=not available

38

Aggressive Growth

Fund	Year Began	Investment Adviser	9/30/89 Assets	Minimum Initial and Subsequent Investment	Fees*	Where to Buy Shares
Fidelity Select Portfolios *Financial Services Portfolio* 82 Devonshire St. Boston, MA 02109 617/570-7000 800/544-6666	1981	Fidelity Management & Research Company	$36.7 Mil	$1,000/ 250	i, r	Fund
Fidelity Select Portfolios *Food and Agriculture Portfolio* 82 Devonshire St. Boston, MA 02109 617/570-7000 800/544-6666	1985	Fidelity Management & Research Company	$19.8 Mil	$1,000/ 250	i, r	Fund
Fidelity Select Portfolios *Health Care Portfolio* 82 Devonshire St. Boston, MA 02109 617/570-7000 800/544-6666	1981	Fidelity Management & Research Company	$237.7 Mil	$1,000/ 250	i, r	Fund
Fidelity Select Portfolios *Housing Portfolio* 82 Devonshire St. Boston, MA 02109 617/570-7000 800/544-6666	1986	Fidelity Management & Research Company	$1.5 Mil	$1,000/ 250	i, r	Fund
Fidelity Select Portfolios *Industrial Materials Portfolio* 82 Devonshire St. Boston, MA 02109 617/570-7000 800/544-6666	1986	Fidelity Management & Research Company	$7.0 Mil	$1,000/ 250	i, r	Fund
Fidelity Select Portfolios *Leisure Portfolio* 82 Devonshire St. Boston, MA 02109 617/570-7000 800/544-6666	1984	Fidelity Management & Research Company	$88.5 Mil	$1,000/ 250	i, r	Fund
Fidelity Select Portfolios *Life Insurance Portfolio* 82 Devonshire St. Boston, MA 02109 617/570-7000 800/544-6666	1985	Fidelity Management & Research Company	$0.7 Mil	$1,000/ 250	i, r	Fund

*Key: i=initial sales charge   r=redemption fee or contingent deferred sales charge(CDSC)
t=12b-1 fee and either CDSC or redemption fee   p=12b-1 fee   n=none of the preceding fees   N/A=not available

Aggressive Growth

Fund	Year Began	Investment Adviser	9/30/89 Assets	Minimum Initial and Subsequent Investment	Fees*	Where to Buy Shares
Fidelity Select Portfolios *Medical Delivery Portfolio* 82 Devonshire St. Boston, MA 02109 617/570-7000 800/544-6666	1986	Fidelity Management & Research Company	$43.3 Mil	$1,000/ 250	i, r	Fund
Fidelity Select Portfolios *Paper and Forest Products Portfolio* 82 Devonshire St. Boston, MA 02109 617/570-7000 800/544-6666	1986	Fidelity Management & Research Company	$9.0 Mil	$1,000/ 250	i, r	Fund
Fidelity Select Portfolios *Property and Casualty Insurance Portfolio* 82 Devonshire St. Boston, MA 02109 617/570-7000 800/544-6666	1985	Fidelity Management & Research Company	$2.8 Mil	$1,000/ 250	i, r	Fund
Fidelity Select Portfolios *Regional Banks Portfolio* 82 Devonshire St. Boston, MA 02109 617/570-7000 800/544-6666	1986	Fidelity Management & Research Company	$21.2 Mil	$1,000/ 250	i, r	Fund
Fidelity Select Portfolios *Restaurant Industry Portfolio* 82 Devonshire St. Boston, MA 02109 617/570-7000 800/544-6666	1986	Fidelity Management & Research Company	$3.2 Mil	$1,000/ 250	i, r	Fund
Fidelity Select Portfolios *Retailing Portfolio* 82 Devonshire St. Boston, MA 02109 617/570-7000 800/544-6666	1985	Fidelity Management & Research Company	$11.2 Mil	$1,000/ 250	i, r	Fund
Fidelity Select Portfolios *Savings and Loan Portfolio* 82 Devonshire St. Boston, MA 02109 617/570-7000 800/544-6666	1985	Fidelity Management & Research Company	$21.8 Mil	$1,000/ 250	i, r	Fund

*Key: i=initial sales charge   r=redemption fee or contingent deferred sales charge(CDSC)
      t=12b-1 fee and either CDSC or redemption fee   p=12b-1 fee   n=none of the preceding fees   N/A=not available

Aggressive Growth

Fund	Year Began	Investment Adviser	9/30/89 Assets	Minimum Initial and Subsequent Investment	Fees*	Where to Buy Shares
Fidelity Select Portfolios *Software and Computer Services Portfolio* 82 Devonshire St. Boston, MA 02109 617/570-7000 800/544-6666	1985	Fidelity Management & Research Company	$9.9 Mil	$1,000/ 250	i, r	Fund
Fidelity Select Portfolios *Technology Portfolio* 82 Devonshire St. Boston, MA 02109 617/570-7000 800/544-6666	1981	Fidelity Management & Research Company	$82.8 Mil	$1,000/ 250	i, r	Fund
Fidelity Select Portfolios *Telecommunications Portfolio* 82 Devonshire St. Boston, MA 02109 617/570-7000 800/544-6666	1985	Fidelity Management & Research Company	$137.1 Mil	$1,000/ 250	i, r	Fund
Fidelity Select Portfolios *Transportation Portfolio* 82 Devonshire St. Boston, MA 02109 617/570-7000 800/544-6666	1986	Fidelity Management & Research Company	$2.9 Mil	$1,000/ 250	i, r	Fund
Fidelity Select Portfolios *Utilities Portfolio* 82 Devonshire St. Boston, MA 02109 617/570-7000 800/544-6666	1981	Fidelity Management & Research Company	$107.6 Mil	$1,000/ 250	i, r	Fund
Fidelity Special Situations Fund *Initial Class* *Plymouth Class* 82 Devonshire St. Boston, MA 02109 617/570-7000 800/522-7297	1983 1988	Fidelity Management & Research Company	$218.0 Mil	$1,000/250 $1,000/250	i i, p	LRep LRep
Fiduciary Management Associates 1345 Avenue of the Americas New York, NY 10105 212/969-1000 800/221-5672	1969	Alliance Capital Management L.P.	$187.0 Mil	$1,000/ 100	n	Fund

*Key: i=initial sales charge   r=redemption fee or contingent deferred sales charge(CDSC)
  t=12b-1 fee and either CDSC or redemption fee   p=12b-1 fee   n=none of the preceding fees   N/A=not available

Aggressive Growth

Fund	Year Began	Investment Adviser	9/30/89 Assets	Minimum Initial and Subsequent Investment	Fees*	Where to Buy Shares
First Investors Discovery Fund, Inc. 120 Wall St. New York, NY 10005 212/208-6000	1969	First Investors Management Company, Inc.	$19.7 Mil	$200/ 50	i, p	Local Rep
First Investors Fund For Growth, Inc. 120 Wall St. New York, NY 10005 212/208-6000	1965	First Investors Management Company, Inc.	$33.5 Mil	$200/ 50	i, p	Local Rep
First Investors Life Series Fund *Discovery Series* 120 Wall St. New York, NY 10005 212/208-6000	1986	First Investors Management Company, Inc.	$0.2 Mil	Not Applicable	n	Insur
Flag Investors Emerging Growth Fund, Inc. 135 E. Baltimore St. P.O. Box 515 Baltimore, MD 21203 301/727-1700 800/767-3524	1988	Flag Investors Management Corp.	$43.8 Mil (e)	$2,000/ 1,000	i, p	Local Rep
Franklin Custodian Funds, Inc. *DynaTech Series* 777 Mariners Island Blvd. San Mateo, CA 94404 415/570-3000 800/632-2180 800/632-2350	1968	Franklin Advisers, Inc.	$37.7 Mil	$100/ 25	i	Local Rep
Fund of the Southwest, Inc. 1100 Milan St., Ste. 3500 P.O. Box 3167 Houston, TX 77253-3167 713/750-8000 800/262-6631	1969	Capstone Asset Management Company	$15.4 Mil	$200/ 0	i	Local Rep
Gabelli Value Fund, Inc. Grand Central Station P.O. Box 1634 New York, NY 10163 212/490-3670 800/422-3554	1989	Gabelli Funds, Inc.	$1.1 Bil	$5,000/ 200	N/A	Local Rep

*Key: i=initial sales charge   r=redemption fee or contingent deferred sales charge(CDSC)
t=12b-1 fee and either CDSC or redemption fee   p=12b-1 fee   n=none of the preceding fees   N/A=not available

42

Aggressive Growth

Fund	Year Began	Investment Adviser	9/30/89 Assets	Minimum Initial and Subsequent Investment	Fees*	Where to Buy Shares
General Aggressive Growth Fund, Inc. 666 Old Country Rd. Garden City, NY 11530 718/895-1396 800/242-8671	1984	Dreyfus Corporation	$43.2 Mil	$2,500/ 100	p	Fund
GIT Equity Trust *GIT Equity Special Growth Portfolio* 1655 Fort Myer Dr. Arlington, VA 22209 703/528-6500 800/336-3063	1983	Bankers Finance Investment Management Corp.	$24.5 Mil	$1,000/ 0	n	Fund
Gradison Growth Trust *Opportunity Growth Fund* 580 Walnut St. Cincinnati, OH 45202-3198 513/579-5700 800/869-5999	1983	Gradison & Company, Inc.	$23.4 Mil	$1,000/ 50	p	Local Rep
Hartwell Emerging Growth Fund, Inc. c/o Furman Selz 230 Park Ave. New York, NY 10169 212/309-8400 800/624-FUND	1968	Hartwell Management Company, Inc.	$25.1 Mil	$2,000/ 100	i	Local Rep
HVA Aggressive Growth Fund, Inc. 200 Hopmeadow St. P.O. Box 2999 Hartford, CT 06104-2999 203/843-8245 800/227-1371	1984	Hartford Investment Management Company, Inc. Wellington Management Company	$56.2 Mil	Not Applicable	n	Insur
IAI Apollo Fund, Inc. 1100 Dain Twr. P.O. Box 357 Minneapolis, MN 55440 612/371-7780	1983	Investment Advisers, Inc.	$29.2 Mil	$5,000/ 1,000	n	Local Rep
IDS Discovery Fund, Inc. IDS Tower 10 Minneapolis, MN 55440 612/372-3131 800/328-8300	1981	IDS Financial Corporation	$166.7 Mil	$100/ 100	i, p	Local Rep

*Key: i=initial sales charge   r=redemption fee or contingent deferred sales charge(CDSC)
t=12b-1 fee and either CDSC or redemption fee   p=12b-1 fee   n=none of the preceding fees   N/A=not available

43

Aggressive Growth

Fund	Year Began	Investment Adviser	9/30/89 Assets	Minimum Initial and Subsequent Investment	Fees*	Where to Buy Shares
IDS Progressive Fund, Inc. IDS Tower 10 Minneapolis, MN 55440 612/372-3131 800/328-8300	1969	IDS Financial Corporation	$175.8 Mil	$100/100	i, p	Local Rep
IDS Strategy Fund, Inc. **Aggressive Equity Fund** IDS Tower 10 Minneapolis, MN 55440 612/372-3131 800/328-8300	1984	IDS Financial Corporation	$285.5 Mil	$100/100	t	Local Rep
Integrated Equity Portfolios **Aggressive Growth Portfolio** 10 Union Square East New York, NY 10003 212/353-7000 800/858-8850	1987	Integrated Resources Asset Management Corp.	$52.5 Mil	$1,000/100	i, p	Local Rep
Integrated Resources Series Trust **Aggressive Growth Portfolio** One Bridge Plaza Fort Lee, NJ 07024 201/461-0606 800/821-5100	1987	Integrated Resources Asset Management Corp.	$40.3 Mil	Not Applicable	r	Insur
Janus Venture Fund, Inc. P.O. Box 44339 Denver, CO 80201-4339 303/333-3863 800/525-3713	1985	Janus Capital Corporation	$79.7 Mil	$1,000/50	n	Fund
John Hancock Special Equities Trust 101 Huntington Ave. Boston, MA 02199-7603 617/375-1500 800/225-5291	1985	John Hancock Advisers, Inc.	$12.9 Mil	$1,000/25	i	Local Rep
J.W. Gant Fund, Inc. 2255 Glades Rd. Ste. 312-E Boca Raton, FL 33431 407/241-3846	1988	Louis Anthony Advisory Group, Inc.	$1.8 Mil	$1,000/500	i, p	Local Rep

*Key: i=initial sales charge   r=redemption fee or contingent deferred sales charge(CDSC)
t=12b-1 fee and either CDSC or redemption fee   p=12b-1 fee   n=none of the preceding fees   N/A=not available

Aggressive Growth

Fund	Year Began	Investment Adviser	9/30/89 Assets	Minimum Initial and Subsequent Investment	Fees*	Where to Buy Shares
Kaufmann Fund, Inc. 17 Battery Place Ste. 2624 New York, NY 10004 212/344-3337	1986	Edgemont Asset Management Corporation	$31.1 Mil (e)	$1,500/ 100	t	Fund
Kemper Summit Fund 120 S. LaSalle St. Chicago, IL 60603 312/781-1121 800/621-1148	1969	Kemper Financial Services, Inc.	$286.5 Mil	$1,000/ 100	i	Local Rep
Keystone America Omega Fund, Inc. 99 High St. Boston, MA 02110 617/338-3200 800/343-2898 800/225-1587	1979	Keystone Custodian Funds, Inc.	$40.2 Mil	$1,000/ 0	i, p	Local Rep
Keystone Custodian Funds, Inc. S-4 Series 99 High St. Boston, MA 02110 617/338-3200 800/343-2898 800/225-1587	1932	Keystone Custodian Funds, Inc.	$561.9 Mil	$250/ 0	t	Local Rep
Kidder, Peabody Special Growth Fund, Inc. 20 Exchange Place New York, NY 10005 212/510-5552	1984	Webster Management Corporation	$18.1 Mil	$1,500/ 500	t	Local Rep
Lazard Special Equity Fund, Inc. One Rockefeller Plaza New York, NY 10020 212/957-5343 800/854-8525	1986	Lazard Freres & Co.	$125.5 Mil	$50,000/ 2,500	n	Fund
Legg Mason Special Investment Trust, Inc. 111 S. Calvert St. P.O. Box 1476 Baltimore, MD 21203-1476 301/539-3400 800/822-5544 800/492-7777 MD Only	1985	Legg Mason Fund Adviser, Inc.	$67.7 Mil	$1,000/ 500	p	Local Rep

*Key: i=initial sales charge   r=redemption fee or contingent deferred sales charge(CDSC)
t=12b-1 fee and either CDSC or redemption fee   p=12b-1 fee   n=none of the preceding fees   N/A=not available

Aggressive Growth

Fund	Year Began	Investment Adviser	9/30/89 Assets	Minimum Initial and Subsequent Investment	Fees*	Where to Buy Shares
Lehman Capital Fund, Inc. 55 Water St. 34th Fl. New York, NY 10041 212/668-8578 800/221-5350	1976	Lehman Management Company, Inc.	$77.7 Mil	$1,000/ 100	i	Local Rep
Lexington Growth Fund, Inc. Park 80 W., Plaza Two P.O. Box 1515 Saddle Brook, NJ 07662 201/845-7300 800/526-0056	1969	Lexington Management Corporation	$30.0 Mil	$1,000/ 50	n	Fund
Lord Abbett Developing Growth Fund, Inc. The General Motors Bldg. 767 Fifth Ave. New York, NY 10153 212/848-1800 800/223-4224	1973	Lord, Abbett & Co.	$141.7 Mil	$1,000/ 0	i	Local Rep
MacKay-Shields MainStay Series Fund *MainStay Capital Appreciation Fund* 51 Madison Ave. New York, NY 10010 212/576-7000 800/522-4202	1986	MacKay-Shields Financial Corporation	$35.4 Mil	$500/ 50	t	Local Rep
Management of Managers Group of Funds *Special Equity Fund* 200 Connecticut Ave. 8th Fl. Norwalk, CT 06854 203/855-2200	1984	Evaluation Associates Investment Management Co.	$41.2 Mil	$0/ 0	n	Local Rep
ManuLife Series Fund, Inc. *Emerging Growth Equity Fund* 200 Bloor St. East N. Tower 5 Toronto, Ont., Canada M4W 1E5 416/926-6700	1984	Manufacturers Adviser Corporation	$3.3 Mil (e)	Not Applicable	n	Insur
Massachusetts Financial Emerging Growth Trust 500 Boylston St. Boston, MA 02116 617/954-5000 800/343-2829	1982	Massachusetts Financial Services Company	$229.6 Mil	$1,000/ 25	i	Local Rep

*Key: i=initial sales charge   r=redemption fee or contingent deferred sales charge(CDSC)
t=12b-1 fee and either CDSC or redemption fee   p=12b-1 fee   n=none of the preceding fees   N/A=not available

46

Aggressive Growth

Fund	Year Began	Investment Adviser	9/30/89 Assets	Minimum Initial and Subsequent Investment	Fees*	Where to Buy Shares
Massachusetts Financial Special Fund 500 Boylston St. Boston, MA 02116 617/954-5000 800/343-2829	1983	Massachusetts Financial Services Company	$139.0 Mil	$1,000/ 25	i	Local Rep
Medical Research Investment Fund, Inc. 1100 Milan St., Ste. 3500 P.O. Box 3167 Houston, TX 77253-3167 713/750-8000 800/262-6631	1985	G/A Capital Management, Inc.	$2.9 Mil	$200/ 0	i, p	Local Rep
Merrill Lynch Phoenix Fund, Inc. *Class A* *Class B* P.O. Box 9011 Princeton, NJ 08543-9011 609/282-2800 800/637-3863	1982 1988	Fund Asset Management, Inc.	$291.0 Mil $1,000/50 $1,000/50	i t	LRep LRep
MetLife-State Street Equity Trust *MetLife-State Street Capital Appreciation Fund* One Financial Ctr. 30th Fl. Boston, MA 02111 617/348-2000, 800/882-0052	1986	MetLife-State Street Investment Services, Inc.	$41.3 Mil	$250/ 25	i, p	Local Rep
MFS Lifetime Investment Program *Lifetime Emerging Growth Trust* 500 Boylston St. Boston, MA 02116 617/954-5000 800/343-2829	1986	Lifetime Advisers, Inc.	$80.3 Mil	$1,000/ 50	t	Local Rep
MidAmerica High Growth Fund, Inc. 433 Edgewood Rd., NE Cedar Rapids, IA 52499 319/398-8511 800/553-4287 800/342-4490 IA Only	1965	MidAmerica Management Corporation	$13.0 Mil	$10/ 10	i	Local Rep
MIM Mutual Funds, Inc. *Stock Appreciation Fund* 4500 Rockside Rd. Ste. 440 Independence, OH 44131-6809 216/642-3000 800/233-1240	1987	Mathematical Investing Systems, Inc.	$1.4 Mil	$250/ 50	p	Fund

*Key: i=initial sales charge   r=redemption fee or contingent deferred sales charge(CDSC)
t=12b-1 fee and either CDSC or redemption fee   p=12b-1 fee   n=none of the preceding fees   N/A=not available

Aggressive Growth

Fund	Year Began	Investment Adviser	9/30/89 Assets	Minimum Initial and Subsequent Investment	Fees*	Where to Buy Shares
NASL Series Trust *Aggressive Asset Allocation Trust* 695 Atlantic Ave. P.O. Box 9064 GMF Boston, MA 02205 617/439-6960 800/344-1029	1989	NASL Financial Services, Inc.	N/A	Not Applicable	N/A	Insur
NASL Series Trust *Conservative Asset Allocation Trust* 695 Atlantic Ave. P.O. Box 9064 GMF Boston, MA 02205 617/439-6960 800/344-1029	1989	NASL Financial Services, Inc.	N/A	Not Applicable	N/A	Insur
NASL Series Trust *Moderate Asset Allocation Trust* 695 Atlantic Ave. P.O. Box 9064 GMF Boston, MA 02205 617/439-6960 800/344-1029	1989	NASL Financial Services, Inc.	N/A	Not Applicable	N/A	Insur
Nautilus Fund, Inc. 24 Federal St. Boston, MA 02110 617/482-8260 800/225-6265	1979	Eaton Vance Management, Inc.	$13.9 Mil	$1,000/ 50	i	Local Rep
Neuwirth Fund, Inc. 140 Broadway 42nd Fl. New York, NY 10005 212/504-4000 800/225-8011 800/521-3036	1967	Wood, Struthers & Winthrop Management Corporation	$28.0 Mil (e)	$1,000/ 100	n	Fund
New England Zenith Fund *Capital Growth Series* 501 Boylston St. Boston, MA 02116 617/267-7055 800/634-8025	1983	Loomis, Sayles & Company, Inc.	$82.4 Mil	Not Applicable	n	Insur
New York Venture Fund, Inc. 124 E. Marcy St. P.O. Box 1688 Santa Fe, NM 87504-1688 505/983-4335 800/545-2098	1969	Venture Advisers, L.P.	$318.8 Mil	$1,000/ 25	i, p	Local Rep

*Key: i=initial sales charge   r=redemption fee or contingent deferred sales charge(CDSC)
t=12b-1 fee and either CDSC or redemption fee   p=12b-1 fee   n=none of the preceding fees   N/A=not available

Aggressive Growth

Fund	Year Began	Investment Adviser	9/30/89 Assets	Minimum Initial and Subsequent Investment	Fees*	Where to Buy Shares
Oberweis Emerging Growth Fund *Emerging Growth Portfolio* 30 N. LaSalle St. Ste. 4000 Chicago, IL 60602 312/444-2100	1987	Hamilton Investment Inc.	$14.9 Mil (e)	$5,000/ 1,000	i, t	Local Rep
OLDE Custodian Fund *OLDE Special Ventures Equity Series* 751 Griswold Detroit, MI 48226 313/961-6666	1988	OLDE Asset Management, Inc.	$0.7 Mil	$1,000/ 500	i	Local Rep
Olympic Trust *Small Cap Fund* 800 W. 6th St. Ste. 540 Los Angeles, CA 90017-2708 213/623-7833 800/346-7301	1985	Hotchkis & Wiley	$8.9 Mil	$25,000/ 0	n	Fund
Oppenheimer Directors Fund Two World Trade Ctr. New York, NY 10048-0669 212/323-0200 800/525-7048	1979	Oppenheimer Management Corporation	$145.5 Mil	$1,000/ 25	i	Local Rep
Oppenheimer Global Bio-Tech Fund Two World Trade Ctr. New York, NY 10048-0669 212/323-0200 800/525-7048	1988	Oppenheimer Management Corporation	$3.9 Mil	$10,000/ 25	i, p	Local Rep
Oppenheimer OTC Fund Two World Trade Ctr. New York, NY 10048-0669 212/323-0200 800/525-7048	1986	Oppenheimer Management Corporation	$53.7 Mil	$1,000/ 25	i, p	Local Rep
Oppenheimer Regency Fund Two World Trade Ctr. New York, NY 10048-0669 212/323-0200 800/525-7048	1983	Oppenheimer Management Corporation	$121.6 Mil	$1,000/ 25	i	Local Rep

*Key: i=initial sales charge   r=redemption fee or contingent deferred sales charge(CDSC)
t=12b-1 fee and either CDSC or redemption fee   p=12b-1 fee   n=none of the preceding fees   N/A=not available

49

Aggressive Growth

Fund	Year Began	Investment Adviser	9/30/89 Assets	Minimum Initial and Subsequent Investment	Fees*	Where to Buy Shares
Oppenheimer Target Fund Two World Trade Ctr. New York, NY 10048-0669 212/323-0200 800/525-7048	1980	Oppenheimer Management Corporation	$71.3 Mil	$1,000/ 25	i	Local Rep
Oppenheimer Time Fund Two World Trade Ctr. New York, NY 10048-0669 212/323-0200 800/525-7048	1971	Oppenheimer Management Corporation	$340.7 Mil	$1,000/ 25	i	Local Rep
Oppenheimer Variable Account Funds *Oppenheimer Capital Appreciation Fund* 3410 S. Galena St. Denver, CO 80231 303/671-3200 800/525-7048	1983	Oppenheimer Management Corporation	$27.9 Mil	Not Applicable	n	Insur
Pacific Horizon Funds, Inc. *Aggressive Growth Portfolio* 156 W. 56th St. Ste. 1902 New York, NY 10019 212/492-1600 800/367-6075	1984	Security Pacific National Bank	$101.6 Mil	$1,000/ 100	i, p	Local Rep
Pasadena Investment Trust *Pasadena Growth Fund (The)* 600 N. Rosemead Blvd. Pasadena, CA 91107-2101 818/351-4276 800/882-2855	1986	Roger Engemann Management Co., Inc.	$26.9 Mil (e)	$1,000/ 100	n	Fund
PBHG Growth Fund, Inc. 1100 Milan St., Ste. 3500 P.O. Box 3167 Houston, TX 77253-3167 713/750-8000 800/262-6631	1985	Pilgrim Baxter Greig & Associates	$21.5 Mil	$200/ 0	i	Local Rep
Perritt Capital Growth Fund, Inc. 680 N. Lake Shore Dr. Twr Resi Dr., Ste. 2038 Chicago, IL 60611-4402 312/649-6940 800/338-1579	1988	Perritt Investments, Inc.	$5.7 Mil	$1,000/ 250	n	Fund

*Key: i=initial sales charge   r=redemption fee or contingent deferred sales charge(CDSC)
t=12b-1 fee and either CDSC or redemption fee   p=12b-1 fee   n=none of the preceding fees   N/A=not available

Aggressive Growth

Fund	Year Began	Investment Adviser	9/30/89 Assets	Minimum Initial and Subsequent Investment	Fees*	Where to Buy Shares
Phoenix Series Fund *Phoenix Stock Fund Series* 101 Munson St. Greenfield, MA 01301 203/253-1000 800/243-1574	1981	Phoenix Investment Counsel, Inc.	$132.9 Mil	$500/ 25	i	Local Rep
Princor Aggressive Growth Fund, Inc. 711 High St. Des Moines, IA 50309 515/247-5711 800/247-4123 800/622-5344 IA Only	1987	Principal Management, Inc.	$9.1 Mil	$300/ 50	i, p	Local Rep
Professional Portfolios Trust *Aggressive Growth Fund* 429 N. Pennsylvania St. Indianapolis, IN 46204-1897 317/634-3300 800/862-7283	1988	Unified Management Corporation	$0.2 Mil	$200/ 25	p	Local Rep
Prudential-Bache Growth Opportunity Fund, Inc. One Seaport Plaza New York, NY 10292 212/214-1215 800/225-1852	1980	Prudential Mutual Fund Management	$161.0 Mil	$1,000/ 100	t	Local Rep
Prudent Speculator Fund *Prudent Speculator Leveraged Fund (The)* 4023 W. 6th St. Los Angeles, CA 90020 800/444-4778	1987	Prudent Speculator Group	N/A	$5,000/ 500	p	Fund
Putnam Capital Manager Trust *PCM Voyager Fund* One Post Office Sq. Boston, MA 02109 617/292-1000 800/225-2465	1988	Putnam Management Company, Inc.	$30.1 Mil	Not Applicable	r	Insur
Putnam Health Sciences Trust One Post Office Sq. Boston, MA 02109 617/292-1000 800/225-2465	1982	Putnam Management Company, Inc.	$273.7 Mil	$500/ 50	i	Local Rep

*Key: i=initial sales charge   r=redemption fee or contingent deferred sales charge(CDSC)
t=12b-1 fee and either CDSC or redemption fee   p=12b-1 fee   n=none of the preceding fees   N/A=not available

51

Aggressive Growth

Fund	Year Began	Investment Adviser	9/30/89 Assets	Minimum Initial and Subsequent Investment	Fees*	Where to Buy Shares
Putnam Information Sciences Trust One Post Office Sq. Boston, MA 02109 617/292-1000 800/225-2465	1983	Putnam Management Company, Inc.	$103.5 Mil	$500/ 50	i	Local Rep
Putnam OTC Emerging Growth Fund One Post Office Sq. Boston, MA 02109 617/292-1000 800/225-2465	1982	Putnam Management Company, Inc.	$192.4 Mil	$500/ 50	i, p	Local Rep
Putnam Vista Basic Value Fund One Post Office Sq. Boston, MA 02109 617/292-1000 800/225-2465	1968	Putnam Management Company, Inc.	$245.8 Mil	$500/ 50	i	Local Rep
Putnam Voyager Fund One Post Office Sq. Boston, MA 02109 617/292-1000 800/225-2465	1969	Putnam Management Company, Inc.	$730.9 Mil	$500/ 50	i	Local Rep
Quantum Fund, Inc. 605 Madison Ave. Covington, KY 41011 606/491-4271	1984	Madison Avenue Advisors Inc.	$0.2 Mil	$1,000/ 250	i, r	Local Rep
Quasar Associates, Inc. 1345 Avenue of the Americas New York, NY 10105 212/969-1000 800/221-5672	1968	Alliance Capital Management L.P.	$263.1 Mil	$1,000/ 100	i, p	Local Rep
RCS Emerging Growth Fund One Embarcadero Ctr. Ste. 3100 San Francisco, CA 94111 415/781-9700 800/288-7726	1987	Avon Capital Management Corporation	$7.7 Mil	$25,000/ 5,000	t	Local Rep

*Key: i=initial sales charge   r=redemption fee or contingent deferred sales charge(CDSC)
t=12b-1 fee and either CDSC or redemption fee   p=12b-1 fee   n=none of the preceding fees   N/A=not available

Aggressive Growth

Fund	Year Began	Investment Adviser	9/30/89 Assets	Minimum Initial and Subsequent Investment	Fees*	Where to Buy Shares
Retirement Planning Funds of America, Inc. *Equity Fund* 124 E. Marcy St. P.O. Box 1688 Santa Fe, NM 87504-1688 505/983-4335 800/545-2098	1976	Venture Advisers, L.P.	$21.6 Mil	$1,000/ 25	t	Local Rep
Royce Fund *Value Series* 1414 Avenue of the Americas New York, NY 10019 212/355-7311 800/221-4268	1982	Quest Advisory Corp.	N/A	$2,000/ 50	t	Local Rep
Schield Portfolios Series *Aggressive Growth Portfolio* 390 Union Blvd. Ste. 410 Denver, CO 80228 303/985-9999 800/826-8154 800/233-4971 CO Only	1986	Schield Management Company	$2.5 Mil	$1,000/ 100	i, p	Local Rep
Scudder Development Fund 175 Federal St. Boston, MA 02110 617/439-4640 800/225-2470 800/225-5163	1970	Scudder, Stevens & Clark, Inc.	$293.6 Mil	$1,000/ 0	n	Fund
SECURAL Mutual Funds, Inc. *Special Equity Fund* 2401 S. Memorial Dr. Appleton, WI 54915 414/739-3161 800/426-5975	1988	SECURA Advisory Services, Inc.	$1.9 Mil	$500/ 100	i, p	Local Rep
Security Omni Fund 700 Harrison St. Topeka, KS 66636 913/295-3127 800/888-2461	1986	Security Management Company	$18.8 Mil	$100/ 20	i	Local Rep
Security Ultra Fund 700 Harrison St. Topeka, KS 66636 913/295-3127 800/888-2461	1969	Security Management Company	$66.8 Mil	$100/ 20	i	Local Rep

*Key: i=initial sales charge r=redemption fee or contingent deferred sales charge(CDSC)
t=12b-1 fee and either CDSC or redemption fee p=12b-1 fee n=none of the preceding fees N/A=not available

Aggressive Growth

Fund	Year Began	Investment Adviser	9/30/89 Assets	Minimum Initial and Subsequent Investment	Fees*	Where to Buy Shares
Seligman Capital Fund, Inc. 130 Liberty St. New York, NY 10006 212/488-0200 800/221-2450 800/522-6869 NY Only	1969	J. & W. Seligman & Co. Incorporated	$132.5 Mil	$1,000/ 50	i	Local Rep
Seligman Communications and Information Fund, Inc. 130 Liberty St. New York, NY 10006 212/488-0200 800/221-2450 800/522-6869 NY Only	1983	J. & W. Seligman & Co. Incorporated	$45.4 Mil	$1,000/ 50	i	Local Rep
Seligman Mutual Benefit Portfolios, Inc. *Seligman Capital Portfolio* 130 Liberty St. New York, NY 10006 212/488-0200 800/221-2450 800/522-6869 NY Only	1988	J. & W. Seligman & Co. Incorporated	$2.4 Mil	Not Applicable	r	Insur
Sherman, Dean Fund, Inc. 6061 NW Expressway Ste. 465, IH 10(W) San Antonio, TX 78201 512/735-7700 800/247-6375	1968	Sherman, Dean Management & Research Corporation	$3.1 Mil (e)	$1,000/ 100	p	Fund
Sigma Venture Shares, Inc. 3801 Kennett Pk., C-200 Greenville Ctr. Wilmington, DE 19807 302/652-3091 800/441-9490	1970	Sigma Management, Inc.	$45.6 Mil	$0/ 0	i, p	Local Rep
Sit "New Beginning" Growth Fund, Inc. 90 S. 7th St. Ste. 4600 Minneapolis, MN 55402 612/332-3223 800/332-5580	1982	Sit Investment Management Company	$60.8 Mil	$2,000/ 100	n	Fund
Skyline Fund *Special Equities Portfolio (The)* 350 N. Clark St. Chicago, IL 60610 312/670-6035 800/458-5222	1987	Mesirow Asset Management, Inc.	$20.2 Mil	$1,000/ 100	i, p	Local Rep

*Key: i=initial sales charge   r=redemption fee or contingent deferred sales charge(CDSC)
t=12b-1 fee and either CDSC or redemption fee   p=12b-1 fee   n=none of the preceding fees   N/A=not available

54

Aggressive Growth

Fund	Year Began	Investment Adviser	9/30/89 Assets	Minimum Initial and Subsequent Investment	Fees*	Where to Buy Shares
SLH Aggressive Growth Fund 31 W. 52nd St. New York, NY 10019 212/767-3700	1983	Shearson Asset Management Division of Shearson Lehman Hutton Inc.	$96.8 Mil	$500/ 200	i	Local Rep
SLH Investment Series, Inc. *SLH Basic Value Portfolio* 31 W. 52nd St. 15th Fl. New York, NY 10019 212/767-3700 800/334-4636 800/422-0214 NY Only	1985	SLH Asset Management Division of Shearson Lehman Hutton Inc.	$346.5 Mil	$500/ 250	t	Local Rep
SLH Investment Series, Inc. *SLH Special Equities Portfolio* 31 W. 52nd St. 15th Fl. New York, NY 10019 212/767-3700 800/334-4636, 800/422-0214 NY Only	1982	SLH Asset Management Division of Shearson Lehman Hutton Inc.	$150.2 Mil	$500/ 250	t	Local Rep
SLH Small Capitalization Fund 31 W. 52nd St. 15th Fl. New York, NY 10019 212/767-3700	1987	Shearson Asset Management Division of Shearson Lehman Hutton Inc.	$27.6 Mil	$500/ 200	i	Local Rep
State Street Capital Trust *State Street Capital Fund* One Financial Ctr. 38th Fl. Boston, MA 02111 617/482-3920	1987	State Street Research & Management Company	$9.5 Mil	$250,000/ 25,000	n	Local Rep
SteinRoe Investment Trust *SteinRoe Capital Opportunities Fund* 300 W. Adams St. P.O. Box 1143 Chicago, IL 60690 800/338-2550	1969	Stein Roe & Farnham Incorporated	$272.8 Mil	$1,000/ 100	n	Fund
SteinRoe Variable Investment Trust *Aggressive Stock Fund* 600 Atlantic Ave. Boston, MA 02210 617/722-6000 800/443-2683	1989	Stein Roe & Farnham Incorporated	N/A	Not Applicable	N/A	Insur

*Key: i=initial sales charge   r=redemption fee or contingent deferred sales charge(CDSC)
t=12b-1 fee and either CDSC or redemption fee   p=12b-1 fee   n=none of the preceding fees   N/A=not available

55

Aggressive Growth

Fund	Year Began	Investment Adviser	9/30/89 Assets	Minimum Initial and Subsequent Investment	Fees*	Where to Buy Shares
Strong Discovery Fund, Inc. P.O. Box 2936 Milwaukee, WI 53201 414/359-3400 800/368-3863	1988	Strong/ Corneliuson Capital Management, Inc.	N/A	$1,000/ 200	i	Fund
Strong Opportunity Fund, Inc. P.O. Box 2936 Milwaukee, WI 53201 414/359-3400 800/368-3863	1985	Strong/ Corneliuson Capital Management, Inc.	N/A	$1,000/ 200	i	Fund
Thomson McKinnon Investment Trust *Thomson McKinnon Opportunity Fund* One State Street Plaza New York, NY 10004 212/482-5894 800/628-1237	1984	Thomson McKinnon Asset Management L.P.	$51.7 Mil	$1,000/ 100	t	Local Rep
Transamerica Special Equity Portfolios *Lowry Market Timing Fund (The)* 1000 Louisiana Ste. 6000 Houston, TX 77002-5098 713/751-2400, 800/999-3863	1983	Transamerica Fund Management Company	$22.7 Mil	$1,000/ 50	i, p	Local Rep
Transamerica Special Series, Inc. *Transamerica Special Emerging Growth Fund* 1000 Louisiana Ste. 6000 Houston, TX 77002-5098 713/751-2400, 800/999-3863	1987	Transamerica Fund Management Company	$9.1 Mil	$1,000/ 50	t	Local Rep
Transamerica Technology Fund 1000 Louisiana Ste. 6000 Houston, TX 77002-5098 713/751-2400 800/999-3863	1986	Transamerica Fund Management Company	$61.3 Mil	$100/ 10	i, p	Local Rep
T. Rowe Price New America Growth Fund 100 E. Pratt St. Baltimore, MD 21202 301/547-2000 800/638-5660	1985	T. Rowe Price Associates, Inc.	$143.2 Mil	$2,500/ 100	n	Fund

*Key: i=initial sales charge   r=redemption fee or contingent deferred sales charge(CDSC)
       t=12b-1 fee and either CDSC or redemption fee   p=12b-1 fee   n=none of the preceding fees   N/A=not available

Aggressive Growth

Fund	Year Began	Investment Adviser	9/30/89 Assets	Minimum Initial and Subsequent Investment	Fees*	Where to Buy Shares
T. Rowe Price New Horizons Fund, Inc. 100 E. Pratt St. Baltimore, MD 21202 301/547-2000 800/638-5660	1960	T. Rowe Price Associates, Inc.	$974.7 Mil	$2,500/ 100	n	Fund
T. Rowe Price Science & Technology Fund, Inc. 100 E. Pratt St. Baltimore, MD 21202 301/547-2000 800/638-5660	1987	T. Rowe Price Associates, Inc.	$20.8 Mil	$2,500/ 100	n	Fund
T. Rowe Price Small-Cap Value Fund, Inc. 100 E. Pratt St. Baltimore, MD 21202 301/547-2000 800/638-5660	1988	T. Rowe Price Associates, Inc.	$34.7 Mil	$2,500/ 100	n	Fund
Tudor Fund One New York Plaza 31st Fl. New York, NY 10004 212/908-9582 800/223-3332	1969	Tudor Management Company, Inc.	$185.6 Mil (e)	$1,000/ 50	n	Fund
Twentieth Century Investors, Inc. *Giftrust Investors* 4500 Main St. P.O. Box 419200 Kansas City, MO 64141-6200 816/531-5575 800/345-2021	1983	Investors Research Corporation	$24.1 Mil	$100/ 0	n	Fund
Twentieth Century Investors, Inc. *Heritage Investors* 4500 Main St. P.O. Box 419200 Kansas City, MO 64141-6200 816/531-5575 800/345-2021	1987	Investors Research Corporation	$109.9 Mil	$0/ 0	n	Fund
Twentieth Century Investors, Inc. *Ultra Investors* 4500 Main St. P.O. Box 419200 Kansas City, MO 64141-6200 816/531-5575 800/345-2021	1981	Investors Research Corporation	$373.7 Mil	$0/ 0	n	Fund

*Key: i=initial sales charge   r=redemption fee or contingent deferred sales charge(CDSC)
t=12b-1 fee and either CDSC or redemption fee   p=12b-1 fee   n=none of the preceding fees   N/A=not available

Aggressive Growth

Fund	Year Began	Investment Adviser	9/30/89 Assets	Minimum Initial and Subsequent Investment	Fees*	Where to Buy Shares
Twentieth Century Investors, Inc. *Vista Investors* 4500 Main St. P.O. Box 419200 Kansas City, MO 64141-6200 816/531-5575 800/345-2021	1983	Investors Research Corporation	$267.9 Mil	$0/ 0	n	Fund
United New Concepts Fund, Inc. 2400 Pershing Rd. P.O. Box 418343 Kansas City, MO 64141-9343 816/283-4000 800/821-5664	1983	Waddell & Reed, Inc.	$77.5 Mil	$500/ 25	i	Local Rep
United Services Funds *U.S. LoCap Fund* P.O. Box 29467 San Antonio, TX 78229-0467 512/696-1234 800/873-8637	1985	United Services Advisors, Inc.	$1.3 Mil	$100/ 50	r	Fund
United Vanguard Fund, Inc. 2400 Pershing Rd. P.O. Box 418343 Kansas City, MO 64141-9343 816/283-4000 800/821-5664	1969	Waddell & Reed, Inc.	$781.4 Mil	$500/ 25	i	Local Rep
USAA Mutual Fund, Inc. *Aggressive Growth Fund* USAA Bldg. San Antonio, TX 78288 512/498-8000 800/531-8000	1981	USAA Investment Management Company	$157.0 Mil	$1,000/ 50	n	Fund
Value Line Leveraged Growth Investors, Inc. 711 Third Ave. New York, NY 10017 212/687-3965 800/223-0818	1972	Value Line, Inc.	$257.7 Mil	$1,000/ 100	n	Fund
Value Line Special Situations Fund, Inc. 711 Third Ave. New York, NY 10017 212/687-3965 800/223-0818	1956	Value Line, Inc.	$132.4 Mil	$1,000/ 100	n	Fund

*Key: i=initial sales charge   r=redemption fee or contingent deferred sales charge(CDSC)
t=12b-1 fee and either CDSC or redemption fee   p=12b-1 fee   n=none of the preceding fees   N/A=not available

Aggressive Growth

Fund	Year Began	Investment Adviser	9/30/89 Assets	Minimum Initial and Subsequent Investment	Fees*	Where to Buy Shares
Vanguard Small Capitalization Fund, Inc. Vanguard Financial Ctr. P.O. Box 2600 Valley Forge, PA 19482 215/648-6000 800/662-7447 800/362-0530 PA Only	1960	Schroder Capital Management Inc.	$19.6 Mil	$3,000/ 100	n	Fund
Vanguard Specialized Portfolios *Energy Portfolio* Vanguard Financial Ctr. P.O. Box 2600 Valley Forge, PA 19482 215/648-6000 800/662-7447, 800/362-0530 PA Only	1984	Wellington Management Company	$55.2 Mil	$3,000/ 100	r	Fund
Vanguard Specialized Portfolios *Health Care Portfolio* Vanguard Financial Ctr. P.O. Box 2600 Valley Forge, PA 19482 215/648-6000 800/662-7447, 800/362-0530 PA Only	1984	Wellington Management Company	$68.7 Mil	$3,000/ 100	r	Fund
Vanguard Specialized Portfolios *Service Economy Portfolio* Vanguard Financial Ctr. P.O. Box 2600 Valley Forge, PA 19482 215/648-6000 800/662-7447, 800/362-0530 PA Only	1984	Wellington Management Company	$28.5 Mil	$3,000/ 100	r	Fund
Vanguard Specialized Portfolios *Technology Portfolio* Vanguard Financial Ctr. P.O. Box 2600 Valley Forge, PA 19482 215/648-6000 800/662-7447, 800/362-0530 PA Only	1984	Wellington Management Company	$11.1 Mil	$3,000/ 100	r	Fund
Variable Investors Series Trust *Aggressive Growth Portfolio* 1414 Main St. Springfield, MA 01144 413/732-7100	1988	Amherst Investment Management Company, Inc.	$2.6 Mil	Not Applicable	n	Insur
Wasatch Advisors Funds, Inc. *Wasatch Aggressive Equity Fund* 68 S. Main St. Ste. 400 Salt Lake City, UT 84101 801/533-0777, 800/345-7460	1987	Wasatch Advisors Inc.	$1.0 Mil (e)	$5,000/ 1,000	n	Fund

*Key: i=initial sales charge   r=redemption fee or contingent deferred sales charge(CDSC)
t=12b-1 fee and either CDSC or redemption fee   p=12b-1 fee   n=none of the preceding fees   N/A=not available

Aggressive Growth

Fund	Year Began	Investment Adviser	9/30/89 Assets	Minimum Initial and Subsequent Investment	Fees*	Where to Buy Shares
WPG Growth Fund One New York Plaza 31st Fl. New York, NY 10004 212/908-9582 800/223-3332	1986	Tudor Management Company, Inc.	$127.2 Mil (e)	$250,000/ 25,000	n	Fund
Zweig Series Trust *Emerging Growth Series* 25 Broadway New York, NY 10004 212/361-9612 800/272-2700	1985	Zweig/Glaser Advisers	$6.7 Mil (e)	$1,000/ 100	t	Local Rep

*Key: i=initial sales charge   r=redemption fee or contingent deferred sales charge(CDSC)
t=12b-1 fee and either CDSC or redemption fee   p=12b-1 fee   n=none of the preceding fees   N/A=not available

◆ ◆ ◆ ◆

Balanced Funds

Balanced

Fund	Year Began	Investment Adviser	9/30/89 Assets	Minimum Initial and Subsequent Investment	Fees*	Where to Buy Shares
ABT Investment Series, Inc. *ABT Security Income Fund* 205 Royal Palm Way Palm Beach, FL 33480 407/655-7255 800/441-6580	1983	Palm Beach Capital Management, Ltd.	$7.5 Mil	$1,000/ 50	i, p	Local Rep
Advisers Management Trust *Balanced Portfolio* 342 Madison Ave. New York, NY 10173 212/850-8300 800/877-9700	1989	Neuberger & Berman Management Incorporated	$0.1 Mil	Not Applicable	n	Insur
Aetna Investment Advisers Fund, Inc. 151 Farmington Ave. Hartford, CT 06156 203/273-4808	1989	Aetna Life Insurance and Annuity Company	N/A	Not Applicable	N/A	Insur
Alliance Balanced Shares, Inc. 1345 Avenue of the Americas New York, NY 10105 212/969-1000 800/221-5672	1932	Alliance Capital Management L.P.	$159.3 Mil	$1,000/ 50	i, p	Local Rep
American Balanced Fund, Inc. Four Embarcadero Ctr. P.O. Box 7650 San Francisco, CA 94120-7650 415/421-9360 800/421-0180	1932	Capital Research & Management Company	$271.3 Mil	$500/ 50	i, t	Local Rep
American Pension Investors Trust *Balanced Fund* 2303 Yorktown Ave. P.O. Box 2529 Lynchburg, VA 24501 804/846-1361 800/544-6060, 800/533-4115 VA Only	1988	American Pension Investors, Inc.	$3.7 Mil	$100/ 50	p	Local Rep
American Variable Insurance Series *Asset Allocation Fund (The)* 333 S. Hope St. Los Angeles, CA 90071 213/486-9200 800/421-0180 213/486-9651 Collect	1989	Capital Research & Management Company	$8.5 Mil	Not Applicable	n	Insur

*Key: i=initial sales charge   r=redemption fee or contingent deferred sales charge(CDSC)
   t=12b-1 fee and either CDSC or redemption fee   p=12b-1 fee   n=none of the preceding fees   N/A=not available

Balanced

Fund	Year Began	Investment Adviser	9/30/89 Assets	Minimum Initial and Subsequent Investment	Fees*	Where to Buy Shares
Ameritrust's Collective Investment Retirement Fund *Balanced Portfolio* 900 Euclid Ave. P.O. Box 5937 Cleveland, OH 44101-0937 216/737-4429 800/321-1355	1987	Ameritrust Company National Association	$7.3 Mil	$250/ 100	n	Local Rep
Axe-Houghton Fund B, Inc. 400 Benedict Ave. Tarrytown, NY 10591 914/631-8131 800/366-0444	1938	Axe-Houghton Management, Inc.	$170.8 Mil	$1,000/ 0	p	Fund
Calamos Convertible Income Fund 2001 Spring Rd. Ste. 750 Oak Brook, IL 60521 312/571-7115 800/323-9943	1985	Calamos Asset Management, Inc.	$20.7 Mil (e)	$5,000/ 500	n	Fund
Calvert Social Investment Fund *Managed Growth Portfolio* 1700 Pennsylvania Ave., NW Washington, DC 20006 301/951-4820 800/368-2745	1982	Calvert Asset Management Company, Inc.	$212.2 Mil	$1,000/ 250	i, p	Local Rep
CFS Investment Trust *Kalliston Convertible Total Return Fund* 2001 Spring Rd. Ste. 750 Oak Brook, IL 60521 312/571-7115 800/323-9943	1988	Calamos Asset Management, Inc.	$0.9 Mil (e)	$1,000/ 100	i, p	Local Rep
Composite Bond & Stock Fund, Inc. W. 601 Riverside, 9th Fl. Seafirst Financial Ctr. Spokane, WA 99201 509/353-3400 800/543-8072 800/572-5828	1939	Composite Research & Management Company	$72.8 Mil	$1,000/ 50	i, p	Local Rep
Delaware Group Delaware Fund One Commerce Sq. Philadelphia, PA 19103 215/988-1200 800/523-4640	1937	Delaware Management Company, Inc.	$368.8 Mil	$25/ 25	i	Local Rep

*Key: i=initial sales charge   r=redemption fee or contingent deferred sales charge(CDSC)
t=12b-1 fee and either CDSC or redemption fee   p=12b-1 fee   n=none of the preceding fees   N/A=not available

Balanced

Fund	Year Began	Investment Adviser	9/30/89 Assets	Minimum Initial and Subsequent Investment	Fees*	Where to Buy Shares
Dodge & Cox Balanced Fund One Post St. 35th Fl. San Francisco, CA 94104 415/981-1710	1931	Dodge & Cox	$48.2 Mil	$1,000/ 100	n	Fund
Dolphin FRIC Convertible Fund 10900 Wilshire Blvd. Ste. 1050 Los Angeles, CA 90024 213/208-4938	1986	Froley, Revy Investment Company, Inc.	$8.1 Mil (e)	$2,500/ 100	i	Local Rep
DR Balanced Fund 535 Madison Ave. New York, NY 10022 212/906-7658 800/356-6454	1989	Dillon, Read Capital Inc.	N/A	$100,000/ 5,000	n	Fund
Eaton Vance Investors Fund 24 Federal St. Boston, MA 02110 617/482-8260 800/225-6265	1932	Eaton Vance Management, Inc.	$214.4 Mil	$1,000/ 50	i, p	Local Rep
Federated Stock and Bond Fund, Inc. Federated Investors Twr. Pittsburgh, PA 15222-3779 412/288-1900 800/245-5000	1934	Federated Management	$88.4 Mil	$25,000/ 0	n	Local Rep
Fidelity Puritan Trust *Fidelity Balanced Fund* 82 Devonshire St. Boston, MA 02109 617/570-7000 800/544-6666	1986	Fidelity Management & Research Company	$150.8 Mil	$2,500/ 250	i	Fund
George Putnam Fund of Boston One Post Office Sq. Boston, MA 02109 617/292-1000 800/225-2465	1937	Putnam Management Company, Inc.	$428.9 Mil	$500/ 50	i	Local Rep

*Key: i=initial sales charge   r=redemption fee or contingent deferred sales charge(CDSC)
t=12b-1 fee and either CDSC or redemption fee   p=12b-1 fee   n=none of the preceding fees   N/A=not available

Balanced

Fund	Year Began	Investment Adviser	9/30/89 Assets	Minimum Initial and Subsequent Investment	Fees*	Where to Buy Shares
Greenfield Fund, Inc. 230 Park Ave. Ste. 910 New York, NY 10169 212/986-2600	1965	V.C. Management (of Conn.), Inc.	N/A	$2,000/ 1,000	r	Fund
Horace Mann Balanced Fund, Inc. P.O. Box 4657 Springfield, IL 62708-4657 217/789-2500	1983	CIGNA Investments, Inc.	N/A	Not Applicable	r	Insur
IDS Mutual, Inc. IDS Tower 10 Minneapolis, MN 55440 612/372-3131 800/328-8300	1940	IDS Financial Corporation	$1.7 Bil	$100/ 100	i, p	Local Rep
Integra Fund 600 New Hampshire Ave., NW Ste. 720 Washington, DC 20037 202/965-4150	1986	ABD Securities Corporation	N/A	$10,000/ 1,000	N/A	Local Rep
Investment Portfolios *Total Return Portfolio* 120 S. LaSalle St. Chicago, IL 60603 312/781-1121 800/621-1148	1986	Kemper Financial Services, Inc.	$544.6 Mil	$250/ 50	t	Local Rep
Loomis-Sayles Mutual Fund Back Bay Annex P.O. Box 449 Boston, MA 02116 617/578-1333 800/345-4048	1929	Loomis, Sayles & Company, Inc.	$323.4 Mil	$1,000/ 50	n	Fund
MacKay-Shields MainStay Series Fund *MainStay Total Return Fund* 51 Madison Ave. New York, NY 10010 212/576-7000 800/522-4202	1987	MacKay-Shields Financial Corporation	$22.6 Mil	$500/ 50	t	Local Rep

*Key: i=initial sales charge   r=redemption fee or contingent deferred sales charge(CDSC)
t=12b-1 fee and either CDSC or redemption fee   p=12b-1 fee   n=none of the preceding fees   N/A=not available

Balanced

Fund	Year Began	Investment Adviser	9/30/89 Assets	Minimum Initial and Subsequent Investment	Fees*	Where to Buy Shares
ManuLife Series Fund, Inc. *Balanced Assets Fund* 200 Bloor St. East N. Tower 5 Toronto, Ont., Canada M4W 1E5 416/926-6700	1984	Manufacturers Adviser Corporation	$9.3 Mil (e)	Not Applicable	n	Insur
MassMutual Integrity Funds *MassMutual Balanced Fund* 1295 State St. Springfield, MA 01111 413/788-8411 800/542-6767 800/854-9100 MA Only	1988	Massachusetts Mutual Life Insurance Company	$35.6 Mil	$500/ 25	i, p	Local Rep
Merrill Lynch Retirement Benefit Investment Program, Inc. *Full Investment Portfolio* Class A Class B P.O. Box 9011 Princeton, NJ 08543-9011 609/282-2800, 800/637-3863	1988 1985	Merrill Lynch Asset Management Inc.	$1.7 Bil	$1,000/50 $1,000/50	i t	LRep LRep
Merrill Lynch Series Fund *Balanced Portfolio* P.O. Box 9011 Princeton, NJ 08543-9011 609/282-2800 800/524-4458	1988	Fund Asset Management, Inc.	$20.9 Mil	Not Applicable	n	Insur
Merrill Lynch Variable Series Funds *American Balanced Fund* P.O. Box 9011 Princeton, NJ 08543-9011 609/282-2800 800/524-4458	1988	Merrill Lynch Asset Management Inc.	$3.2 Mil	Not Applicable	n	Insur
MIMLIC Asset Allocation Fund, Inc. 400 N. Robert St. St. Paul, MN 55101-2098 612/223-4252 800/443-3677	1984	MIMLIC Asset Management Company	$8.3 Mil	$250/ 25	i, p	Local Rep
MONY Series Fund *Diversified Portfolio* 500 Frank W. Burr Blvd. 71-13 Glenpointe Ctr. West Teaneck, NJ 07666 201/907-6669	1985	MONY Life Insurance Company of America	$12.6 Mil	Not Applicable	n	Insur

*Key: i=initial sales charge   r=redemption fee or contingent deferred sales charge(CDSC)
t=12b-1 fee and either CDSC or redemption fee   p=12b-1 fee   n=none of the preceding fees   N/A=not available

67

Balanced

Fund	Year Began	Investment Adviser	9/30/89 Assets	Minimum Initial and Subsequent Investment	Fees*	Where to Buy Shares
National Total Income Fund 600 Third Ave. New York, NY 10016 203/863-5600 800/237-1718	1940	National Securities & Research Corporation	$186.7 Mil	$250/ 25	i	Local Rep
North American Security Trust *Moderate Asset Allocation Portfolio* 695 Atlantic Ave. P.O. Box 9064 GMF Boston, MA 02205 617/439-6960, 800/344-1029	1986	NASL Financial Services, Inc.	$41.4 Mil (e)	$1,000/ 100	i, p	Local Rep
Nottingham Investment Trust *FBP Contrarian Fund* P.O. Drawer 8315 Rocky Mount, NC 27804 919/972-9922 800/525-FUND 800/525-3863	1989	Flippin, Bruce & Porter, Inc.	$1.2 Mil	$25,000/ 1,000	n	Fund
Nottingham Investment Trust *Jamestown Fund (The)* P.O. Drawer 8315 Rocky Mount, NC 27804 919/972-9922 800/525-FUND 800/525-3863	1989	Lowe, Brockenbrough, Tierney & Tattersall, Inc.	$2.5 Mil	$100,000/ 10,000	r	Fund
Ohio National Fund, Inc. *Omni Portfolio* 237 William Howard Taft Cincinnati, OH 45219 513/861-3600	1984	O.N. Investment Management Company	$31.1 Mil	Not Applicable	n	Insur
Olympic Trust *Balanced Income Fund* 800 W. 6th St. Ste. 540 Los Angeles, CA 90017-2708 213/623-7833 800/346-7301	1985	Hotchkis & Wiley	$7.9 Mil	$25,000/ 0	n	Fund
Pax World Fund, Inc. 224 State St. Portsmouth, NH 03801 603/431-8022	1971	Pax World Management Corporation	$87.7 Mil	$250/ 50	p	Fund

*Key: i=initial sales charge   r=redemption fee or contingent deferred sales charge(CDSC)
t=12b-1 fee and either CDSC or redemption fee   p=12b-1 fee   n=none of the preceding fees   N/A=not available

Balanced

Fund	Year Began	Investment Adviser	9/30/89 Assets	Minimum Initial and Subsequent Investment	Fees*	Where to Buy Shares
Phoenix Series Fund *Phoenix Balanced Fund Series* 101 Munson St. Greenfield, MA 01301 203/253-1000 800/243-1574	1981	Phoenix Investment Counsel, Inc.	$450.8 Mil	$500/ 25	i	Local Rep
Piper Jaffray Investment Trust Inc. *Balanced Fund* 222 S. 9th St. Piper Jaffray Twr. Minneapolis, MN 55402 612/342-6426 800/333-6000	1987	Piper Capital Management Incorporated	$15.9 Mil	$0/ 0	i, p	Local Rep
Plymouth Fund *Plymouth Income & Growth Portfolio* 82 Devonshire St. Boston, MA 02109 617/570-7000 800/544-6666	1987	Fidelity Management & Research Company	$45.6 Mil	$1,000/ 100	i, p	Local Rep
PNCG Asset Allocation Fund, Inc. 121 SW Morrison Ste. 1415 Portland, OR 97204 503/295-0919 800/541-9732	1989	PNCG Fund Advisers, Inc.	N/A	$1,000/ 500	i, p	Local Rep
Quest For Value Accumulation Trust *Managed Portfolio* Oppenheimer Tower World Financial Ctr. New York, NY 10281 212/667-7587 800/232-FUND	1988	Quest For Value Advisors	$15.9 Mil	Not Applicable	n	Insur
Rea-Graham Fund, Inc. *Rea-Graham Balanced Fund* 10966 Chalon Rd. Los Angeles, CA 90077 213/208-2282 800/433-1998	1982	James Buchanan Rea, Inc.	$48.5 Mil	$1,000/ 200	i	Local Rep
SafeGuard Balanced Portfolio 16 Industrial Blvd. Paoli, PA 19301 215/251-0550 800/523-7798	1988	Provident Institutional Management Corporation	$1.1 Mil	$1,000/ 100	i, p	Local Rep

*Key: i=initial sales charge   r=redemption fee or contingent deferred sales charge(CDSC)
    t=12b-1 fee and either CDSC or redemption fee   p=12b-1 fee   n=none of the preceding fees   N/A=not available

Balanced

Fund	Year Began	Investment Adviser	9/30/89 Assets	Minimum Initial and Subsequent Investment	Fees*	Where to Buy Shares
Sentinel Group Funds, Inc. *Balanced Fund Series* National Life Dr. Montpelier, VT 05604 802/229-3900 800/282-3863	1938	Sentinel Advisors, Inc.	$73.8 Mil	$250/ 25	i	Local Rep
Sigma Trust Shares One International Place 100 Oliver St. Boston, MA 02110 302/652-3091 800/441-9490	1931	Sigma Management, Inc.	$56.2 Mil	$0/ 0	i, p	Local Rep
Skyline Fund *Balanced Portfolio (The)* 350 N. Clark St. Chicago, IL 60610 312/670-6035 800/458-5222	1987	Mesirow Asset Management, Inc.	$12.7 Mil	$1,000/ 100	i, p	Local Rep
Specialty Managers Trust *Multiple Allocation Series* 1925 Century Park East Ste. 2350 Los Angeles, CA 90067 213/556-5499 800/423-4891	1989	Zweig Advisors, Inc.	N/A	Not Applicable	n	Insur
State Farm Balanced Fund, Inc. One State Farm Plaza Bloomington, IL 61710 309/766-2029	1967	State Farm Investment Management Corporation	$87.2 Mil (e)	$50/ 50	n	Fund
Strong Investment Fund, Inc. P.O. Box 2936 Milwaukee, WI 53201 414/359-3400 800/368-3863	1981	Strong/ Corneliuson Capital Management, Inc.	N/A	$250/ 200	i	Fund
Templeton Variable Products Series Fund *Templeton Asset Allocation Fund (The)* 700 Central Ave. P.O. Box 33030 St. Petersburg, FL 33733-8030 813/823-8712, 800/237-0738	1988	Templeton, Galbraith & Hansberger, Ltd.	N/A	Not Applicable	n	Insur

*Key: i=initial sales charge   r=redemption fee or contingent deferred sales charge(CDSC)
     t=12b-1 fee and either CDSC or redemption fee   p=12b-1 fee   n=none of the preceding fees   N/A=not available

70

Balanced

Fund	Year Began	Investment Adviser	9/30/89 Assets	Minimum Initial and Subsequent Investment	Fees*	Where to Buy Shares
Thompson, Unger & Plumb Fund, Inc. 4610 University Ave. P.O. Box 55320 Madison, WI 53705 608/231-1676	1987	Thompson, Unger & Plumb, Inc.	$7.8 Mil (e)	$1,000/ 250	n	Fund
Triflex Fund, Inc. Two Moody Plaza Galveston, TX 77550 409/763-2767 800/231-4639 800/392-9753 TX Only	1978	Securities Management & Research, Inc.	$20.1 Mil	$250/ 50	i	Local Rep
Twentieth Century Investors, Inc. *Balanced Investors* 4500 Main St. P.O. Box 419200 Kansas City, MO 64141-6200 816/531-5575 800/345-2021	1988	Investors Research Corporation	$28.0 Mil	$0/ 0	n	Fund
United Continental Income Fund, Inc. 2400 Pershing Rd. P.O. Box 418343 Kansas City, MO 64141-9343 816/283-4000 800/821-5664	1970	Waddell & Reed, Inc.	$319.7 Mil	$500/ 25	i	Local Rep
USAA Investment Trust *Balanced Portfolio* USAA Bldg. San Antonio, TX 78288 512/498-8000 800/531-8000	1989	USAA Investment Management Company	$23.8 Mil	$1,000/ 50	n	Fund
USAA Investment Trust *Cornerstone Fund* USAA Bldg. San Antonio, TX 78288 512/498-8000 800/531-8000	1984	USAA Investment Management Company	$522.2 Mil	$1,000/ 50	n	Fund
Vanguard Convertible Securities Fund, Inc. Vanguard Financial Ctr. P.O. Box 2600 Valley Forge, PA 19482 215/648-6000 800/662-7447 800/362-0530 PA Only	1986	Desai Capital Management, Inc.	$64.8 Mil	$3,000/ 100	n	Fund

*Key: i=initial sales charge r=redemption fee or contingent deferred sales charge(CDSC) t=12b-1 fee and either CDSC or redemption fee p=12b-1 fee n=none of the preceding fees N/A=not available

Balanced

Fund	Year Began	Investment Adviser	9/30/89 Assets	Minimum Initial and Subsequent Investment	Fees*	Where to Buy Shares
Vanguard STAR Fund Vanguard Financial Ctr. P.O. Box 2600 Valley Forge, PA 19482 215/648-6000 800/662-7447 800/362-0530 PA Only	1985	Vanguard Group, Inc.	$916.8 Mil	$500/ 100	n	Fund
Wellington Fund Vanguard Financial Ctr. P.O. Box 2600 Valley Forge, PA 19482 215/648-6000 800/662-7447 800/362-0530 PA Only	1929	Wellington Management Company	$2.0 Bil	$3,000/ 100	n	Fund

*Key: i=initial sales charge   r=redemption fee or contingent deferred sales charge(CDSC)
t=12b-1 fee and either CDSC or redemption fee   p=12b-1 fee   n=none of the preceding fees   N/A=not available

72

◆ ◆ ◆ ◆

Corporate Bond Funds

Corporate Bond

Fund	Year Began	Investment Adviser	9/30/89 Assets	Minimum Initial and Subsequent Investment	Fees*	Where to Buy Shares
AARP Income Trust *AARP General Bond Fund* AARP Investment Program 175 Federal St. Boston, MA 02110-2267 800/253-2277	1984	AARP/Scudder Financial Management Company	$128.7 Mil	$250/ 0	n	Fund
AIM Convertible Securities, Inc. 11 Greenway Plaza Ste. 1919 Houston, TX 77046 713/626-1919 800/231-0803 800/392-9681 TX Only	1978	AIM Advisors, Inc.	$13.8 Mil	$1,000/ 100	i, p	Local Rep
Alliance Bond Fund *Monthly Income Portfolio* 1345 Avenue of the Americas New York, NY 10105 212/969-1000 800/221-5672	1974	Alliance Capital Management L.P.	$57.6 Mil	$250/ 50	i, p	Local Rep
American Capital Corporate Bond Fund, Inc. 2800 Post Oak Blvd. Houston, TX 77056 713/993-0500 800/421-5666	1963	American Capital Asset Management, Inc.	$232.1 Mil	$500/ 50	i, p	Local Rep
American Capital Life Investment Trust *American Capital Corporate Bond Portfolio* 2800 Post Oak Blvd. Houston, TX 77056 713/993-0500 800/421-5666	1987	American Capital Asset Management, Inc.	$11.3 Mil	Not Applicable	n	Insur
American Pension Investors Trust *Investment Grade Securities Fund* 2303 Yorktown Ave. P.O. Box 2529 Lynchburg, VA 24501 804/846-1361, 800/544-6060, 800/533-4115 VA Only	1988	American Pension Investors, Inc.	$2.4 Mil	$100/ 50	p	Local Rep
Boston Company Fund *Government Income Fund* One Boston Place Boston, MA 02019 617/956-9740 800/225-5267 800/343-6324	1979	Boston Company Advisors, Inc.	$83.5 Mil	$1,000/ 0	p	Fund

*Key: i=initial sales charge   r=redemption fee or contingent deferred sales charge(CDSC)
      t=12b-1 fee and either CDSC or redemption fee   p=12b-1 fee   n=none of the preceding fees   N/A=not available

Corporate Bond

Fund	Year Began	Investment Adviser	9/30/89 Assets	Minimum Initial and Subsequent Investment	Fees*	Where to Buy Shares
Calvert Social Investment Fund *Bond Portfolio* 1700 Pennsylvania Ave., NW Washington, DC 20006 301/951-4820 800/368-2745	1987	Calvert Asset Management Company, Inc.	$12.7 Mil	$1,000/ 250	i, p	Local Rep
Carillon Fund, Inc. *Bond Portfolio (The)* 1876 Waycross Rd. P.O. Box 5304 Cincinnati, OH 45201 513/595-2600 800/999-1840	1984	Carillon Advisers, Inc.	$15.5 Mil	Not Applicable	n	Insur
Chubb America Fund, Inc. *Bond Portfolio* One Granite Place Concord, NH 03301 603/224-7741	1986	Chubb Investment Advisory Corporation	$2.2 Mil (e)	Not Applicable	n	Insur
CIGNA Annuity Fund *Income Fund* CIGNA Corporation Hartford, CT 06152 203/726-6000 800/562-4462	1982	CIGNA Investments, Inc.	$28.4 Mil	Not Applicable	n	Insur
Composite Deferred Series, Inc. *Income Portfolio* W. 601 Riverside, 9th Fl. Seafirst Financial Ctr. Spokane, WA 99201 509/353-3400 800/543-8072, 800/572-5828	1987	Composite Research & Management Company	$3.6 Mil	Not Applicable	r	Insur
Corporate Fund Investment Accumulation Program, Inc. P.O. Box 9011 Princeton, NJ 08543-9011 609/282-2800 800/221-3150	1977	Fund Asset Management, Inc.	N/A	$0/ 0	n	Local Rep
Dreyfus A Bonds Plus, Inc. 666 Old Country Rd. Garden City, NY 11530 718/895-1206 800/645-6561	1976	Dreyfus Corporation	$280.3 Mil	$2,500/ 100	n	Fund

*Key: i=initial sales charge   r=redemption fee or contingent deferred sales charge(CDSC)
t=12b-1 fee and either CDSC or redemption fee   p=12b-1 fee   n=none of the preceding fees   N/A=not available

Corporate Bond

Fund	Year Began	Investment Adviser	9/30/89 Assets	Minimum Initial and Subsequent Investment	Fees*	Where to Buy Shares
Federated Floating Rate Trust Federated Investors Twr. Pittsburgh, PA 15222-3779 412/288-1900 800/245-5000	1986	Federated Management	$76.5 Mil	$25,000/ 0	n	Local Rep
Fidelity Fixed-Income Trust *Fidelity Flexible Bond Portfolio* 82 Devonshire St. Boston, MA 02109 617/570-7000 800/544-6666	1971	Fidelity Management & Research Company	$384.7 Mil	$2,500/ 250	n	Fund
Fidelity Fixed-Income Trust *Fidelity Short-Term Bond Portfolio* 82 Devonshire St. Boston, MA 02109 617/570-7000 800/544-6666	1986	Fidelity Management & Research Company	$210.4 Mil	$1,000/ 250	n	Fund
Fidelity Intermediate Bond Fund 82 Devonshire St. Boston, MA 02109 617/570-7000 800/544-6666	1975	Fidelity Management & Research Company	$604.5 Mil	$1,000/ 250	n	Fund
First Boston Investment Funds, Inc. *Corporate Cash Fund* c/o Vanguard Financial Ctr. P.O. Box 1102 Valley Forge, PA 19482-1102 215/648-6069 800/541-4905	1988	First Boston Asset Management Corporation	N/A	$1.0 Mil/ 10,000	n	Fund
Franklin Managed Trust *Franklin Investment Grade Income Portfolio* 777 Mariners Island Blvd. San Mateo, CA 94404 415/570-3000 800/632-2180 800/632-2350	1987	Franklin Advisers, Inc.	$15.5 Mil	$100/ 25	i, p	Local Rep
IDS Bond Fund, Inc. IDS Tower 10 Minneapolis, MN 55440 612/372-3131 800/328-8300	1974	IDS Financial Corporation	$1.8 Bil	$100/ 100	i, p	Local Rep

*Key: i=initial sales charge   r=redemption fee or contingent deferred sales charge(CDSC)
       t=12b-1 fee and either CDSC or redemption fee   p=12b-1 fee   n=none of the preceding fees   N/A=not available

77

Corporate Bond

Fund	Year Began	Investment Adviser	9/30/89 Assets	Minimum Initial and Subsequent Investment	Fees*	Where to Buy Shares
IDS Selective Fund, Inc. IDS Tower 10 Minneapolis, MN 55440 612/372-3131 800/328-8300	1945	IDS Financial Corporation	$1.1 Bil	$100/ 100	i, p	Local Rep
IDS Strategy Fund, Inc. *Income Fund* IDS Tower 10 Minneapolis, MN 55440 612/372-3131 800/328-8300	1984	IDS Financial Corporation	$213.6 Mil	$100/ 100	t	Local Rep
Imperial Portfolios, Inc. *High Grade Corporate Bond Portfolio (The)* 9275 Sky Park Ct. P.O. Box 82997 San Diego, CA 92138 619/292-2379 800/347-5588	1988	First Imperial Advisors, Inc.	N/A	$1,000/ 100	N/A	Local Rep
Industrial Series Trust *Mackenzie Fixed Income Trust* 1200 N. Federal Hwy. #200 Boca Raton, FL 33432 407/393-8900 800/456-5111	1985	Mackenzie Financial Corporation	$20.5 Mil (e)	$250/ 50	i, p	Local Rep
Integrated Income Plus Fund, Inc. 10 Union Square East New York, NY 10003 212/353-7000 800/858-8850	1986	Integrated Resources Asset Management Corp.	$30.3 Mil	$500/ 100	t	Local Rep
Intermediate Bond Fund of America 333 S. Hope St. Los Angeles, CA 90071 213/486-9200 800/421-0180 213/486-9651 Collect	1988	Capital Research & Management Company	$104.1 Mil	$1,000/ 50	i, t	Local Rep
John Hancock Bond Trust 101 Huntington Ave. Boston, MA 02199-7603 617/375-1500 800/225-5291	1973	John Hancock Advisers, Inc.	$1.1 Bil	$1,000/ 25	i	Local Rep

*Key: i=initial sales charge   r=redemption fee or contingent deferred sales charge(CDSC)
t=12b-1 fee and either CDSC or redemption fee   p=12b-1 fee   n=none of the preceding fees   N/A=not available

Corporate Bond

Fund	Year Began	Investment Adviser	9/30/89 Assets	Minimum Initial and Subsequent Investment	Fees*	Where to Buy Shares
Keystone America Investment Grade Bond Fund 99 High St. Boston, MA 02110 617/338-3200 800/343-2898 800/225-1587	1987	Keystone Custodian Funds, Inc.	$29.0 Mil	$1,000/ 0	i, t	Local Rep
Keystone Custodian Funds, Inc. B-2 Series 99 High St. Boston, MA 02110 617/338-3200 800/343-2898 800/225-1587	1932	Keystone Custodian Funds, Inc.	$990.9 Mil	$250/ 0	t	Local Rep
Life of Virginia Series Fund, Inc. *Bond Portfolio* 6610 W. Broad St. Richmond, VA 23230 804/281-6000 800/822-6000	1985	AON Advisors, Inc.	$3.1 Mil (e)	Not Applicable	n	Insur
Massachusetts Financial Bond Fund 500 Boylston St. Boston, MA 02116 617/954-5000 800/343-2829	1974	Massachusetts Financial Services Company	$311.7 Mil	$1,000/ 25	i	Local Rep
Merrill Lynch Corporate Bond Fund, Inc. *High Quality Portfolio* *Class A* *Class B* P.O. Box 9011 Princeton, NJ 08543-9011 609/282-2800, 800/637-3863	1980 1988	Fund Asset Management, Inc.	$381.7 Mil	$1,000/100 $1,000/100	i t	LRep LRep
Merrill Lynch Corporate Bond Fund, Inc. *Intermediate Term Portfolio* P.O. Box 9011 Princeton, NJ 08543-9011 609/282-2800 800/637-3863	1980	Fund Asset Management, Inc.	$87.0 Mil	$1,000/ 100	i	Local Rep
Merrill Lynch Series Fund *Long Term Corporate Bond Portfolio* P.O. Box 9011 Princeton, NJ 08543-9011 609/282-2800 800/524-4458	1981	Fund Asset Management, Inc.	$124.3 Mil	Not Applicable	n	Insur

*Key: i=initial sales charge   r=redemption fee or contingent deferred sales charge(CDSC)
t=12b-1 fee and either CDSC or redemption fee   p=12b-1 fee   n=none of the preceding fees   N/A=not available

Corporate Bond

Fund	Year Began	Investment Adviser	9/30/89 Assets	Minimum Initial and Subsequent Investment	Fees*	Where to Buy Shares
Merrill Lynch Variable Series Funds *Prime Bond Fund* P.O. Box 9011 Princeton, NJ 08543-9011 609/282-2800 800/524-4458	1982	Merrill Lynch Asset Management Inc.	$27.3 Mil	Not Applicable	n	Insur
MFS Lifetime Investment Program *Lifetime Quality Bond Trust* 500 Boylston St. Boston, MA 02116 617/954-5000 800/343-2829	1988	Lifetime Advisers, Inc.	$9.6 Mil	$1,000/ 50	t	Local Rep
NASL Series Trust *Bond Trust* 695 Atlantic Ave. P.O. Box 9064 GMF Boston, MA 02205 617/439-6960 800/344-1029	1985	NASL Financial Services, Inc.	$26.6 Mil	Not Applicable	r	Insur
Nationwide Investing Foundation *Bond Fund* One Nationwide Plaza Box 1492 Columbus, OH 43216 614/249-7855 800/848-0920, 800/282-1440 OH Only	1980	Nationwide Financial Services, Inc.	$35.9 Mil	$250/ 25	i	Local Rep
North Carolina Cash Management Trust *Term Portfolio* 82 Devonshire St. Boston, MA 02109 617/570-7000 800/222-3232	1987	Fidelity Management & Research Company	$81.5 Mil	$0/ 0	p	Local Rep
Ohio National Fund, Inc. *Bond Portfolio* 237 William Howard Taft Cincinnati, OH 45219 513/861-3600	1982	O.N. Investment Management Company	$3.9 Mil	Not Applicable	n	Insur
Oppenheimer Variable Account Funds *Oppenheimer Bond Fund* 3410 S. Galena St. Denver, CO 80231 303/671-3200 800/525-7048	1985	Oppenheimer Management Corporation	$11.8 Mil	Not Applicable	n	Insur

*Key: i=initial sales charge   r=redemption fee or contingent deferred sales charge(CDSC)
t=12b-1 fee and either CDSC or redemption fee   p=12b-1 fee   n=none of the preceding fees   N/A=not available

Corporate Bond

Fund	Year Began	Investment Adviser	9/30/89 Assets	Minimum Initial and Subsequent Investment	Fees*	Where to Buy Shares
PaineWebber Fixed Income Portfolios *Investment Grade Bond Portfolio* 1285 Avenue of the Americas PaineWebber Bldg. New York, NY 10019 212/713-2000, 800/544-9300	1984	Mitchell Hutchins Asset Management Inc.	$253.2 Mil	$1,000/ 100	i	Local Rep
PaineWebber Series Trust *Corporate Bond Portfolio* 1285 Avenue of the Americas PaineWebber Bldg. New York, NY 10019 212/713-2000	1987	Mitchell Hutchins Asset Management Inc.	N/A	Not Applicable	N/A	Insur
Phoenix Series Fund *Phoenix High Quality Bond Fund Series* 101 Munson St. Greenfield, MA 01301 203/253-1000 800/243-1574	1983	Phoenix Investment Counsel, Inc.	$19.5 Mil	$500/ 25	i	Local Rep
Pilgrim Foreign Investors *Pilgrim High Income Fund* 10100 Santa Monica Blvd. 21st Fl. Los Angeles, CA 90067 213/551-0833 800/334-3444 800/331-1080	1987	Pilgrim Management Corporation	$10.0 Mil	$5,000/ 1,000	i, p	Local Rep
Pioneer Bond Fund 60 State St. Boston, MA 02109-1975 617/742-7825 800/225-6292	1978	Pioneering Management Corporation	$68.1 Mil	$1,000/ 100	i	Local Rep
Princor Bond Fund, Inc. 711 High St. Des Moines, IA 50309 515/247-5711 800/247-4123 800/622-5344 IA Only	1987	Principal Management, Inc.	$12.9 Mil	$1,000/ 50	i, p	Local Rep
Rochester Convertible Funds, Inc. *Growth Fund* 379 Park Ave. Rochester, NY 14607 716/442-5500	1986	Fielding Management Company, Inc.	N/A	$2,000/ 100	i, p	Local Rep

*Key: i=initial sales charge   r=redemption fee or contingent deferred sales charge(CDSC)
t=12b-1 fee and either CDSC or redemption fee   p=12b-1 fee   n=none of the preceding fees   N/A=not available

Corporate Bond

Fund	Year Began	Investment Adviser	9/30/89 Assets	Minimum Initial and Subsequent Investment	Fees*	Where to Buy Shares
Security Income Fund *Corporate Bond Series* 700 Harrison St. Topeka, KS 66636 913/295-3127 800/888-2461	1970	Security Management Company	$55.2 Mil	$100/ 20	i, p	Local Rep
SteinRoe Income Trust *SteinRoe High-Yield Bonds* 300 W. Adams St. P.O. Box 1143 Chicago, IL 60690 800/338-2550	1986	Stein Roe & Farnham Incorporated	$101.2 Mil	$1,000/ 100	n	Fund
SteinRoe Variable Investment Trust *Investment Grade Bond Fund* 600 Atlantic Ave. Boston, MA 02210 617/722-6000 800/443-2683	1989	Stein Roe & Farnham Incorporated	N/A	Not Applicable	N/A	Insur
Tower Series Funds, Inc. *Bond Series* P.O. Box 418 Tampa, FL 33601 813/229-5052	1982	Tower Investment Group, Inc.	$3.8 Mil	$500/ 100	i	Local Rep
Vanguard Fixed-Income Securities Fund, Inc. *Investment Grade Bond Portfolio* Vanguard Financial Ctr. P.O. Box 2600 Valley Forge, PA 19482 215/648-6000, 800/662-7447, 800/362-0530 PA Only	1973	Wellington Management Company	$897.5 Mil	$3,000/ 100	n	Fund
Vanguard Fixed-Income Securities Fund, Inc. *Short Term Bond Portfolio* Vanguard Financial Ctr. P.O. Box 2600 Valley Forge, PA 19482 215/648-6000 800/662-7447, 800/362-0530 PA Only	1982	Vanguard Group, Inc.	$553.0 Mil	$3,000/ 100	n	Fund
Winthrop Focus Fund *Winthrop Fixed Income Portfolio* 140 Broadway 42nd Fl. New York, NY 10005 212/504-4000 800/225-8011, 800/521-3036	1987	Wood, Struthers & Winthrop Management Corporation	$5.6 Mil (e)	$1,000/ 100	t	Local Rep

*Key: i=initial sales charge   r=redemption fee or contingent deferred sales charge(CDSC)
    t=12b-1 fee and either CDSC or redemption fee   p=12b-1 fee   n=none of the preceding fees   N/A=not available

Corporate Bond

Fund	Year Began	Investment Adviser	9/30/89 Assets	Minimum Initial and Subsequent Investment	Fees*	Where to Buy Shares
Wright Managed Bond Trust *Wright Total Return Bond Fund* 24 Federal St. 5th Fl. Boston, MA 02110 617/482-8260 800/225-6265	1983	Wright Investors Service	$66.2 Mil	$1,000/ 0	p	Local Rep

*Key: i=initial sales charge   r=redemption fee or contingent deferred sales charge(CDSC)
     t=12b-1 fee and either CDSC or redemption fee   p=12b-1 fee   n=none of the preceding fees   N/A=not available

◆ ◆ ◆ ◆

Flexible Portfolio Funds

Flexible Portfolio

Fund	Year Began	Investment Adviser	9/30/89 Assets	Minimum Initial and Subsequent Investment	Fees*	Where to Buy Shares
ADTEK Fund, Inc. 4920 W. Vliet St. Milwaukee, WI 53208 414/257-1842	1984	Heath, Schneider, Mueller & Toll Company, Inc.	$13.0 Mil	$250/ 50	n	Fund
American Capital Life Investment Trust *American Capital Multiple Strategy Portfolio* 2800 Post Oak Blvd. Houston, TX 77056 713/993-0500 800/421-5666	1987	American Capital Asset Management, Inc.	$37.3 Mil	Not Applicable	n	Insur
Anchor Pathway Fund *Asset Allocation Series (The)* 2201 E. Camelback Phoenix, AZ 85016 602/955-0300 800/528-9679	1989	Capital Research & Management Company	N/A	Not Applicable	n	Insur
Bankers National Series Trust *BNL Multiple Strategies Portfolio* 44 U.S. Hwy. 46 Pine Brook, NJ 07058 201/808-9596 800/888-4918	1987	Conseco Capital Management, Inc.	$2.5 Mil	Not Applicable	n	Insur
Blanchard Strategic Growth Fund 41 Madison Ave. 24th Fl. New York, NY 10010 212/779-7979 800/922-7771	1986	Sheffield Management Company	$251.9 Mil	$3,000/ 200	p	Fund
Carillon Investment Trust *Carillon Capital Fund* 1876 Waycross Rd. P.O. Box 5304 Cincinnati, OH 45201 513/595-2600 800/999-1840	1988	Carillon Advisers, Inc.	$21.6 Mil	$500/ 50	i	Local Rep
Christos Trust *Christos Fund* 975 Oak St. Ste. 625 Eugene, OR 97401 503/686-2744 800/999-3303	1988	Thomas D. Kienlen Corp.	$6.5 Mil	$5,000/ 100	i, p	Local Rep

*Key: i=initial sales charge   r=redemption fee or contingent deferred sales charge(CDSC)
t=12b-1 fee and either CDSC or redemption fee   p=12b-1 fee   n=none of the preceding fees   N/A=not available

Flexible Portfolio

Fund	Year Began	Investment Adviser	9/30/89 Assets	Minimum Initial and Subsequent Investment	Fees*	Where to Buy Shares
Collective Investment Trust for Seafirst Retirement Accounts *Asset Allocation Fund (The)* 701 Fifth Ave. P.O. Box 84248 Seattle, WA 98124 206/358-6119, 800/323-9919	1988	Seattle-First National Bank	$4.2 Mil (e)	$500/ 0	n	Fund
Colonial/Hancock Liberty Trust *Colonial/Hancock Liberty Asset Allocation Fund* One Financial Ctr. Boston, MA 02111 617/426-3750 800/225-2365, 800/426-3750	1987	Colonial Management Associates, Inc.	$3.7 Mil	Not Applicable	n	Insur
Dean Witter Managed Assets Trust Two World Trade Ctr. New York, NY 10048 212/392-2550 800/869-3863	1988	Dean Witter Reynolds Inc. - InterCapital Division	$288.6 Mil	$1,000/ 100	t	Local Rep
Dean Witter Strategist Fund Two World Trade Ctr. New York, NY 10048 212/392-2550 800/869-3863	1988	Dean Witter Reynolds Inc. - InterCapital Division	$64.3 Mil	$1,000/ 100	i, p	Local Rep
Dean Witter Variable Investment Series *Managed Assets Portfolio* Two World Trade Ctr. New York, NY 10048 212/392-2550 800/869-3863	1987	Dean Witter Reynolds Inc. - InterCapital Division	$83.7 Mil	Not Applicable	n	Insur
EBI Series Trust *EBI Flex Fund* 1315 Peachtree St., NE Ste. 500 Atlanta, GA 30309 404/892-0666 800/554-1156	1988	INVESCO Capital Management, Inc.	N/A	$100,000/ 5,000	r	Local Rep
FBL Series Fund, Inc. *Managed Portfolio* 5400 University Ave. W. Des Moines, IA 50265 515/225-5400 800/247-4170 800/422-3175 IA Only	1987	FBL Investment Advisory Services, Inc.	$3.4 Mil	$250/ 0	t	Local Rep

*Key: i=initial sales charge   r=redemption fee or contingent deferred sales charge(CDSC)
t=12b-1 fee and either CDSC or redemption fee   p=12b-1 fee   n=none of the preceding fees   N/A=not available

Flexible Portfolio

Fund	Year Began	Investment Adviser	9/30/89 Assets	Minimum Initial and Subsequent Investment	Fees*	Where to Buy Shares
Fidelity Charles Street Trust *Fidelity Asset Manager* 82 Devonshire St. Boston, MA 02109 617/570-7000 800/544-6666	1988	Fidelity Management & Research Company	N/A	$2,500/ 250	N/A	Fund
Huntington Investment Trust *Huntington CPI+ Fund* 251 S. Lake Ave. Ste. 600 Pasadena, CA 91101 213/681-3700 800/826-0188	1989	Huntington Advisers, Inc.	$5.9 Mil	$10,000/ 1,000	i, p	Local Rep
IDS Managed Retirement Fund, Inc. IDS Tower 10 Minneapolis, MN 55440 612/372-3131 800/328-8300	1985	IDS Financial Corporation	$720.9 Mil	$50/ 50	i, p	Local Rep
INVESCO Institutional Series Trust *INVESCO Institutional Flex Fund* 1315 Peachtree St., NE Ste. 500 Atlanta, GA 30309 404/892-0666, 800/554-1156	1987	INVESCO Capital Management, Inc.	N/A	$1.0 Mil/ 5,000	n	Local Rep
Janus Flexible Income Fund P.O. Box 44339 Denver, CO 80201-4339 303/333-3863 800/525-3713	1987	Janus Capital Corporation	$16.7 Mil	$1,000/ 50	n	Fund
John Hancock Asset Allocation Trust 101 Huntington Ave. Boston, MA 02199-7603 617/375-1500 800/225-5291	1988	John Hancock Advisers, Inc.	$15.1 Mil	$1,000/ 25	i	Local Rep
Maxus Fund 3550 Lander Rd. 2nd Fl. Pepper Pike, OH 44124 216/292-3434	1985	Investment Strategies Inc.	$12.1 Mil	$1,000/ 100	p	Local Rep

*Key: i=initial sales charge   r=redemption fee or contingent deferred sales charge(CDSC)
     t=12b-1 fee and either CDSC or redemption fee   p=12b-1 fee   n=none of the preceding fees   N/A=not available

Flexible Portfolio

Fund	Year Began	Investment Adviser	9/30/89 Assets	Minimum Initial and Subsequent Investment	Fees*	Where to Buy Shares
Merrill Lynch Global Allocation Fund, Inc. *Class A* *Class B* P.O. Box 9011 Princeton, NJ 08543-9011 609/282-2800 800/637-3863	1989 1989	Merrill Lynch Asset Management Inc.	$161.8 Mil	$1,000/50 $1,000/50	i t	LRep LRep
MetLife-State Street Income Trust *MetLife-State Street Managed Assets* One Financial Ctr. 30th Fl. Boston, MA 02111 617/348-2000, 800/882-0052	1988	MetLife-State Street Investment Services, Inc.	$40.0 Mil	$250/ 25	i, p	Local Rep
Morison Asset Allocation Fund, Inc. 1221 Nicollet Mall Ste. 700 Minneapolis, MN 55403 612/332-1588 800/325-9244	1986	Morison Asset Management, Inc.	$16.3 Mil	$500/ 50	i	Local Rep
Mutual of America Investment Corporation *Composite Fund (The)* 666 Fifth Ave. New York, NY 10103 212/399-1600 800/223-0898	1986	Mutual of America Life Insurance Company	N/A	Not Applicable	n	Insur
Oppenheimer Asset Allocation Fund Two World Trade Ctr. New York, NY 10048-0669 212/323-0200 800/525-7048	1987	Oppenheimer Management Corporation	$76.2 Mil	$1,000/ 25	i, p	Local Rep
Oppenheimer Variable Account Funds *Oppenheimer Multiple Strategies Fund* 3410 S. Galena St. Denver, CO 80231 303/671-3200 800/525-7048	1987	Oppenheimer Management Corporation	$112.5 Mil	Not Applicable	n	Insur
Overland Express Funds, Inc. *Asset Allocation Fund (The)* 114 E. Capitol Ave. Little Rock, AR 72201 501/374-4361 800/458-6589	1988	Wells Fargo Bank, N.A.	$20.8 Mil	$1,000/ 100	i	Local Rep

*Key: i=initial sales charge   r=redemption fee or contingent deferred sales charge(CDSC)
t=12b-1 fee and either CDSC or redemption fee   p=12b-1 fee   n=none of the preceding fees   N/A=not available

Flexible Portfolio

Fund	Year Began	Investment Adviser	9/30/89 Assets	Minimum Initial and Subsequent Investment	Fees*	Where to Buy Shares
PaineWebber Master Series, Inc. *PaineWebber Master Asset Allocation Fund* 1285 Avenue of the Americas PaineWebber Bldg. New York, NY 10019 212/713-2000, 800/647-1568	1986	Mitchell Hutchins Asset Management Inc.	$619.2 Mil	$1,000/ 100	t	Local Rep
PaineWebber Series Trust *Asset Allocation Portfolio* 1285 Avenue of the Americas PaineWebber Bldg. New York, NY 10019 212/713-2000	1987	Mitchell Hutchins Asset Management Inc.	N/A	Not Applicable	N/A	Insur
Phoenix Total Return Fund 101 Munson St. Greenfield, MA 01301 203/253-1000 800/243-1574	1982	Phoenix Investment Counsel, Inc.	$33.8 Mil	$500/ 50	i, p	Local Rep
Primary Trend Fund, Inc. First Financial Centre 700 N. Water St. Milwaukee, WI 53202 414/271-7870 800/443-6544	1986	Arnold Investment Counsel, Inc.	$45.1 Mil (e)	$5,000/ 100	n	Fund
Princor Managed Fund, Inc. 711 High St. Des Moines, IA 50309 515/247-5711 800/247-4123 800/622-5344 IA Only	1987	Principal Management, Inc.	$20.4 Mil	$300/ 50	i, p	Local Rep
Prudential-Bache FlexiFund *Aggressively Managed Portfolio (The)* One Seaport Plaza New York, NY 10292 212/214-1215 800/225-1852	1987	Prudential Mutual Fund Management	$69.7 Mil	$1,000/ 100	t	Local Rep
Prudential-Bache FlexiFund *Conservatively Managed Portfolio (The)* One Seaport Plaza New York, NY 10292 212/214-1215 800/225-1852	1987	Prudential Mutual Fund Management	$131.4 Mil	$1,000/ 100	t	Local Rep

*Key: i=initial sales charge   r=redemption fee or contingent deferred sales charge(CDSC)
t=12b-1 fee and either CDSC or redemption fee   p=12b-1 fee   n=none of the preceding fees   N/A=not available

Flexible Portfolio

Fund	Year Began	Investment Adviser	9/30/89 Assets	Minimum Initial and Subsequent Investment	Fees*	Where to Buy Shares
Putnam Capital Manager Trust *PCM Multi-Strategy Fund* One Post Office Sq. Boston, MA 02109 617/292-1000 800/225-2465	1988	Putnam Management Company, Inc.	$37.7 Mil	Not Applicable	r	Insur
Quest For Value Family of Funds *Asset Allocation Portfolio* Oppenheimer Tower World Financial Ctr. New York, NY 10281 212/667-7587 800/232-FUND	1988	Quest For Value Advisors	$3.6 Mil	$1,000/ 250	i, p	Local Rep
Quest For Value Family of Funds *Small Capitalization Portfolio* Oppenheimer Tower World Financial Ctr. New York, NY 10281 212/667-7587, 800/232-FUND	1988	Quest For Value Advisors	$2.2 Mil	$1,000/ 250	i, p	Local Rep
Rightime Fund, Inc. *Rightime Fund (The)* The Forst Pavilion Ste. 1000 Wyncote, PA 19095-1596 215/572-7288 800/242-1421 800/222-3317 PA only	1985	Rightime Econometrics	N/A	$2,000/ 100	p	Local Rep
Rightime Fund, Inc. *Rightime Growth Fund (The)* The Forst Pavilion Ste. 1000 Wyncote, PA 19095-1596 215/572-7288 800/242-1421 800/222-3317 PA only	1988	Rightime Econometrics	N/A	$2,000/ 100	i, p	Local Rep
Schield Portfolios Series *Timed Asset Allocation Fund* 390 Union Blvd. Ste. 410 Denver, CO 80228 303/985-9999 800/826-8154 800/233-4971 CO Only	1988	Schield Management Company	$8.5 Mil	$1,000/ 100	i, p	Local Rep
SLH Multiple Opportunities Portfolio L.P. 31 W. 52nd St. New York, NY 10019 212/767-3700	1987	Shearson Lehman Investment Strategy Advisors Inc.	$272.6 Mil	$100,000/ 10,000	t	Local Rep

*Key: i=initial sales charge   r=redemption fee or contingent deferred sales charge(CDSC)
t=12b-1 fee and either CDSC or redemption fee   p=12b-1 fee   n=none of the preceding fees   N/A=not available

Flexible Portfolio

Fund	Year Began	Investment Adviser	9/30/89 Assets	Minimum Initial and Subsequent Investment	Fees*	Where to Buy Shares
SLH Special Equity Portfolios *SLH Strategic Investors Portfolio* 31 W. 52nd St. New York, NY 10019 212/767-3700	1987	Boston Company Advisors, Inc.	$202.6 Mil	$500/ 200	t	Local Rep
SMITH HAYES Trust, Inc. *Asset Allocation Portfolio* NBC Ctr. Ste. 780 Lincoln, NE 68508 402/476-3000 800/422-7791 NE Only	1988	SMITH HAYES Portfolio Management, Inc.	N/A	$25,000/ 1,000	N/A	Local Rep
Sower Series Fund, Inc. *Discretionary Portfolio* 5900 "O" St. Lincoln, NE 68510 402/467-1122	1987	Ameritas Investment Advisors, Inc.	N/A	Not Applicable	n	Insur
Specialty Managers Trust *Fully Managed Series* 1925 Century Park E. Ste. 2350 Los Angeles, CA 90067 213/556-5499 800/423-4891	1989	Weiss, Peck & Greer Advisers, Inc.	N/A	Not Applicable	n	Insur
SteinRoe Variable Investment Trust *Aggressive Managed Assets Fund* 600 Atlantic Ave. Boston, MA 02210 617/722-6000 800/443-2683	1989	Stein Roe & Farnham Incorporated	N/A	Not Applicable	N/A	Insur
Strong Total Return Fund, Inc. P.O. Box 2936 Milwaukee, WI 53201 414/359-3400 800/368-3863	1981	Strong/ Corneliuson Capital Management, Inc.	N/A	$250/ 200	i	Fund
Value Line Strategic Asset Management Trust 711 Third Ave. New York, NY 10017 212/687-3965 800/223-0818	1987	Value Line, Inc.	$59.2 Mil	Not Applicable	n	Insur

*Key: i=initial sales charge   r=redemption fee or contingent deferred sales charge(CDSC)
t=12b-1 fee and either CDSC or redemption fee   p=12b-1 fee   n=none of the preceding fees   N/A=not available

Flexible Portfolio

Fund	Year Began	Investment Adviser	9/30/89 Assets	Minimum Initial and Subsequent Investment	Fees*	Where to Buy Shares
Vanguard Asset Allocation Fund Vanguard Financial Ctr. P.O. Box 2600 Valley Forge, PA 19482 215/648-6000 800/662-7447 800/362-0530 PA Only	1988	Mellon Capital Management	$107.1 Mil	$3,000/ 100	n	Fund
Variable Investors Series Trust *Multiple Strategies Portfolio* 1414 Main St. Springfield, MA 01144 413/732-7100	1987	Amherst Investment Management Company, Inc.	$11.3 Mil	Not Applicable	n	Insur
Weston Portfolios, Inc. *New Century Capital Portfolio* 45 William St. Wellesley, MA 02181 617/239-0445	1989	Weston Financial Group, Inc.	$42.7 Mil	$5,000/ 100	p	Fund
Weston Portfolios, Inc. *New Century I Portfolio* 45 William St. Wellesley, MA 02181 617/239-0445	1989	Weston Financial Group, Inc.	$17.5 Mil	$5,000/ 100	p	Fund

*Key: i=initial sales charge   r=redemption fee or contingent deferred sales charge(CDSC)
t=12b-1 fee and either CDSC or redemption fee   p=12b-1 fee   n=none of the preceding fees   N/A=not available

◆ ◆ ◆ ◆

GNMA (Ginnie Mae) Funds

Ginnie Mae

Fund	Year Began	Investment Adviser	9/30/89 Assets	Minimum Initial and Subsequent Investment	Fees*	Where to Buy Shares
Alliance Mortgage Securities Income Fund, Inc. 1345 Avenue of the Americas New York, NY 10105 212/969-1000 800/221-5672	1983	Alliance Capital Management L.P.	$584.4 Mil	$250/ 50	i, p	Local Rep
American Capital Federal Mortgage Trust 2800 Post Oak Blvd. Houston, TX 77056 713/993-0500 800/421-5666	1986	American Capital Asset Management, Inc.	$38.8 Mil	$500/ 50	i, p	Local Rep
Bankers National Series Trust *BNL Mortgaged-Backed Securities Portfolio* 44 U.S. Hwy. 46 Pine Brook, NJ 07058 201/808-9596 800/888-4918	1987	Conseco Capital Management, Inc.	$8.0 Mil	Not Applicable	n	Insur
Benham Government Income Trust *Benham GNMA Income Fund* 755 Page Mill Rd. Palo Alto, CA 94304 415/858-2400 800/227-8380 800/982-6150 CA Only	1985	Benham Management Corporation	$263.9 Mil (e)	$1,000/ 100	n	Fund
Boston Company Fund *GNMA Fund* One Boston Place Boston, MA 02019 617/956-9740 800/225-5267 800/343-6324	1986	Boston Company Advisors, Inc.	$13.0 Mil (e)	$1,000/ 0	p	Fund
Chubb Investment Funds, Inc. *Chubb Government Securities Fund* One Granite Place Concord, NH 03301 603/224-7741	1987	Chubb Asset Managers, Inc.	N/A	$1,000/ 100	i, p	Local Rep
Composite U.S. Government Securities, Inc. W. 601 Riverside, 9th Fl. Seafirst Financial Ctr. Spokane, WA 99201 509/353-3400 800/543-8072 800/572-5828	1982	Composite Research & Management Company	$78.7 Mil	$1,000/ 50	i, p	Local Rep

*Key: i=initial sales charge   r=redemption fee or contingent deferred sales charge(CDSC)
t=12b-1 fee and either CDSC or redemption fee   p=12b-1 fee   n=none of the preceding fees   N/A=not available

Ginnie Mae

Fund	Year Began	Investment Adviser	9/30/89 Assets	Minimum Initial and Subsequent Investment	Fees*	Where to Buy Shares
Delaware Group Government Fund *Government Income Series* *Original Class* One Commerce Sq. Philadelphia, PA 19103 215/988-1200, 800/523-4640	1985	Delaware Management Company, Inc.	$137.7 Mil	$1,000/25	i, p	Local Rep
Dreyfus Foreign Investors GNMA Fund, L.P. 666 Old Country Rd. Garden City, NY 11530 718/895-1650 800/346-3621	1987	Dreyfus Corporation	$1.3 Mil	$1,000/ 100	i, p	Fund
Dreyfus GNMA Fund, Inc. 666 Old Country Rd. Garden City, NY 11530 718/895-1206 800/645-6561	1985	Dreyfus Corporation	$1.6 Bil	$2,500/ 100	p	Fund
FBL Series Fund, Inc. *Ginnie Mae Portfolio* 5400 University Ave. W. Des Moines, IA 50265 515/225-5400 800/247-4170 800/422-3175 IA Only	1987	FBL Investment Advisory Services, Inc.	$2.0 Mil	$250/ 0	t	Local Rep
Federated GNMA Trust Federated Investors Twr. Pittsburgh, PA 15222-3779 412/288-1900 800/245-5000	1982	Federated Management	$1.4 Bil	$25,000/ 0	n	Local Rep
Federated Variable Rate Mortgage Securities Trust Federated Investors Twr. Pittsburgh, PA 15222-3779 412/288-1900 800/245-5000	1987	Federated Management	$14.2 Mil	$25,000/ 0	n	Local Rep
Fidelity Income Fund *Fidelity Ginnie Mae Portfolio* 82 Devonshire St. Boston, MA 02109 617/570-7000 800/544-6666	1985	Fidelity Management & Research Company	$627.7 Mil	$1,000/ 250	n	Fund

*Key: i=initial sales charge   r=redemption fee or contingent deferred sales charge(CDSC)
t=12b-1 fee and either CDSC or redemption fee   p=12b-1 fee   n=none of the preceding fees   N/A=not available

98

Ginnie Mae

Fund	Year Began	Investment Adviser	9/30/89 Assets	Minimum Initial and Subsequent Investment	Fees*	Where to Buy Shares
Fidelity Income Fund *Fidelity Mortgage Securities Portfolio* 82 Devonshire St. Boston, MA 02109 617/570-7000 800/544-6666	1984	Fidelity Management & Research Company	$401.6 Mil	$1,000/ 250	n	Fund
First Trust America Fund L.P. 500 W. Madison Ste. 3000 Chicago, IL 60606 312/559-3000 800/621-4770	1987	Clayton Brown Advisors, Inc.	$8.9 Mil (e)	$25,000/ 0	i, p	Local Rep
Franklin Custodian Funds, Inc. *U.S. Government Securities Series* 777 Mariners Island Blvd. San Mateo, CA 94404 415/570-3000 800/632-2180, 800/632-2350	1970	Franklin Advisers, Inc.	$11.3 Bil	$100/ 25	i	Local Rep
Franklin Investors Securities Trust *Franklin Adjustable Rate Mortgage Fund* 777 Mariners Island Blvd. San Mateo, CA 94404 415/570-3000 800/632-2180, 800/632-2350	1987	Franklin Advisers, Inc.	$45.6 Mil	$100/ 25	i, p	Local Rep
Franklin Partners Funds *Franklin Tax-Advantaged U.S. Government Securities Fund* 777 Mariners Island Blvd. San Mateo, CA 94404 415/570-3000 800/632-2180 800/632-2350	1987	Franklin Advisers, Inc.	$60.0 Mil	$2,500/ 100	i	Local Rep
Franklin Pennsylvania Investors Fund *U.S. Government Securities Portfolio* 777 Mariners Island Blvd. San Mateo, CA 94404 415/570-3000 800/632-2180, 800/632-2350	1986	Franklin Advisers, Inc.	$2.2 Mil	$100/ 25	i	Local Rep
Hartford GNMA/Mortgage Security Fund, Inc. 200 Hopmeadow St. P.O. Box 2999 Hartford, CT 06104-2999 203/843-8245 800/227-1371	1985	Hartford Investment Management Company, Inc.	$82.9 Mil	Not Applicable	n	Insur

*Key: i=initial sales charge   r=redemption fee or contingent deferred sales charge(CDSC)
   t=12b-1 fee and either CDSC or redemption fee   p=12b-1 fee   n=none of the preceding fees   N/A=not available

99

Ginnie Mae

Fund	Year Began	Investment Adviser	9/30/89 Assets	Minimum Initial and Subsequent Investment	Fees*	Where to Buy Shares
Home Investors Government Guaranteed Income Fund, Inc. 10 Union Square East New York, NY 10003 212/353-7000 800/858-8850	1983	Integrated Resources Asset Management Corp.	$152.8 Mil	$500/ 100	t	Local Rep
Institutional Fiduciary Trust *GNMA Portfolio* 777 Mariners Island Blvd. San Mateo, CA 94404 415/570-3000 800/632-2180 800/632-2350	1985	Franklin Trust Company	N/A	$25,000/ 0	n	Local Rep
Investors Preference Fund for Income, Inc. 50 Main St. White Plains, NY 10606 914/397-2168 800/541-0830	1987	Dollar Dry Dock Investment Management Corporation	$26.3 Mil (e)	$1,000/ 100	i	Local Rep
John Hancock U.S. Government Guaranteed Mortgages Trust 101 Huntington Ave. Boston, MA 02199-7603 617/375-1500 800/225-5291	1985	John Hancock Advisers, Inc.	$347.2 Mil	$1,000/ 25	i	Local Rep
Lexington GNMA Income Fund, Inc. Park 80 W., Plaza Two P.O. Box 1515 Saddle Brook, NJ 07662 201/845-7300 800/526-0056	1973	Lexington Management Corporation	$93.5 Mil	$1,000/ 50	n	Fund
Management of Managers Group of Funds *Intermediate Mortgage Securities Fund* 200 Connecticut Ave. 8th Fl. Norwalk, CT 06854 203/855-2200	1986	Evaluation Associates Investment Management Co.	$96.9 Mil	$0/ 0	n	Local Rep
Merrill Lynch Retirement/Income Fund, Inc. P.O. Box 9011 Princeton, NJ 08543-9011 609/282-2800 800/637-3863	1986	Merrill Lynch Asset Management Inc.	$1.7 Bil	$1,000/ 50	t	Local Rep

*Key: i=initial sales charge   r=redemption fee or contingent deferred sales charge(CDSC)
t=12b-1 fee and either CDSC or redemption fee   p=12b-1 fee   n=none of the preceding fees   N/A=not available

Ginnie Mae

Fund	Year Began	Investment Adviser	9/30/89 Assets	Minimum Initial and Subsequent Investment	Fees*	Where to Buy Shares
MIMLIC Mortgage Securities Income Fund, Inc. 400 N. Robert St. St. Paul, MN 55101-2098 612/223-4252 800/443-3677	1984	MIMLIC Asset Management Company	$14.6 Mil	$250/ 25	i	Local Rep
Oppenheimer GNMA Fund Two World Trade Ctr. New York, NY 10048-0669 212/323-0200 800/525-7048	1986	Oppenheimer Management Corporation	$55.5 Mil	$1,000/ 25	i, p	Local Rep
Pacific Horizon Funds, Inc. *GNMA Extra Fund* 156 W. 56th St. Ste. 1902 New York, NY 10019 212/492-1600 800/367-6075	1987	Security Pacific National Bank	$3.1 Mil	$1,000/ 100	i, p	Local Rep
Pacific Investment Management Institutional Trust *Mortgage Plus Portfolio* 840 Newport Ctr. Dr. Ste. 300 Newport Beach, CA 92660 714/640-3031, 800/443-6915	1987	Pacific Investment Management Company	N/A	$200,000/ 10,000	n	Fund
PaineWebber Fixed Income Portfolios *GNMA Portfolio* 1285 Avenue of the Americas PaineWebber Bldg. New York, NY 10019 212/713-2000 800/544-9300	1984	Mitchell Hutchins Asset Management Inc.	$973.5 Mil	$1,000/ 100	i	Local Rep
Pilgrim Foreign Investors *Pilgrim Government Securities Fund* 10100 Santa Monica Blvd. 21st Fl. Los Angeles, CA 90067 213/551-0833 800/334-3444, 800/331-1080	1987	Pilgrim Management Corporation	$10.6 Mil	$5,000/ 1,000	i, p	Local Rep
Pilgrim GNMA Fund 10100 Santa Monica Blvd. 21st Fl. Los Angeles, CA 90067 213/551-0833 800/334-3444 800/331-1080	1984	Pilgrim Management Corporation	$138.3 Mil	$1,000/ 100	i, p	Local Rep

*Key: i=initial sales charge   r=redemption fee or contingent deferred sales charge(CDSC)
t=12b-1 fee and either CDSC or redemption fee   p=12b-1 fee   n=none of the preceding fees   N/A=not available

Ginnie Mae

Fund	Year Began	Investment Adviser	9/30/89 Assets	Minimum Initial and Subsequent Investment	Fees*	Where to Buy Shares
Piper Jaffray Investment Trust Inc. *Government Income Fund* 222 S. 9th St. Piper Jaffray Twr. Minneapolis, MN 55402 612/342-6426 800/333-6000	1987	Piper Capital Management Incorporated	$85.4 Mil	$0/ 0	i, p	Local Rep
Premier GNMA Fund 666 Old Country Rd. Garden City, NY 11530 718/895-1650 800/346-3621	1987	Dreyfus Corporation	$24.9 Mil	$1,000/ 100	i, p	Local Rep
Premier Income Fund 666 Old Country Rd. Garden City, NY 11530 718/895-1650 800/346-3621	1987	Dreyfus Corporation	$3.0 Mil	$1,000/ 100	i, p	Local Rep
Princor Government Securities Income Fund, Inc. 711 High St. Des Moines, IA 50309 515/247-5711 800/247-4123 800/622-5344 IA Only	1985	Principal Management, Inc.	$54.5 Mil	$1,000/ 50	i, p	Local Rep
Prudential-Bache GNMA Fund One Seaport Plaza New York, NY 10292 212/214-1215 800/225-1852	1982	Prudential Mutual Fund Management	$217.4 Mil	$1,000/ 100	t	Local Rep
Putnam GNMA Plus Trust One Post Office Sq. Boston, MA 02109 617/292-1000 800/225-2465	1986	Putnam Management Company, Inc.	$1.0 Bil	$500/ 50	i, p	Local Rep
Putnam U.S. Government Guaranteed Securities Income Trust One Post Office Sq. Boston, MA 02109 617/292-1000 800/225-2465	1984	Putnam Management Company, Inc.	$1.4 Bil	$500/ 50	i	Local Rep

*Key: i=initial sales charge   r=redemption fee or contingent deferred sales charge(CDSC)
t=12b-1 fee and either CDSC or redemption fee   p=12b-1 fee   n=none of the preceding fees   N/A=not available

Ginnie Mae

Fund	Year Began	Investment Adviser	9/30/89 Assets	Minimum Initial and Subsequent Investment	Fees*	Where to Buy Shares
SBL Fund *Government Securities Series* 700 Harrison St. 6th Fl. Topeka, KS 66636 913/295-3127 800/888-2461	1986	Security Management Company	$28.9 Mil	Not Applicable	n	Insur
Scudder GNMA Fund 175 Federal St. Boston, MA 02110 617/439-4640 800/225-2470 800/225-5163	1985	Scudder, Stevens & Clark, Inc.	$253.3 Mil	$1,000/ 0	n	Fund
Security Income Fund *U.S. Government Series* 700 Harrison St. Topeka, KS 66636 913/295-3127 800/888-2461	1985	Security Management Company	$4.1 Mil	$100/ 20	i, p	Local Rep
SEI Cash+Plus Trust *GNMA Portfolio* 680 E. Swedesford Rd. No. 7 Wayne, PA 19087 215/254-1000 800/345-1151	1987	Wellington Management Company	$7.4 Mil	$0/ 0	p	Local Rep
Seligman High Income Fund Series *Secured Mortgage Income Series* 130 Liberty St. New York, NY 10006 212/488-0200 800/221-2450, 800/522-6869 NY Only	1985	J. & W. Seligman & Co. Incorporated	$38.4 Mil	$1,000/ 50	i, p	Local Rep
SLH Managed Governments Inc. 31 W. 52nd St. New York, NY 10019 212/767-3700	1984	Bernstein-Macaulay Division of Shearson Lehman Hutton Inc.	$584.4 Mil	$500/ 200	i	Local Rep
SLH Special Income Portfolios *SLH Mortgage Securities Portfolio* 31 W. 52nd St. New York, NY 10019 212/767-3700	1986	Bernstein-Macaulay Division of Shearson Lehman Hutton Inc.	$790.3 Mil (e)	$500/ 200	t	Local Rep

*Key: i=initial sales charge   r=redemption fee or contingent deferred sales charge(CDSC)
t=12b-1 fee and either CDSC or redemption fee   p=12b-1 fee   n=none of the preceding fees   N/A=not available

Ginnie Mae

Fund	Year Began	Investment Adviser	9/30/89 Assets	Minimum Initial and Subsequent Investment	Fees*	Where to Buy Shares
Smith Barney Funds, Inc. *Monthly Payment Government Portfolio* 1345 Avenue of the Americas New York, NY 10105 212/698-5349 800/544-7835	1986	Smith, Barney Advisers, Inc.	$16.5 Mil (e)	$10,000/ 50	i	Local Rep
Smith Barney Funds, Inc. *U.S. Government Securities Portfolio* 1345 Avenue of the Americas New York, NY 10105 212/698-5349 800/544-7835	1984	Smith, Barney Advisers, Inc.	$325.6 Mil (e)	$3,000/ 50	i	Local Rep
Smith Barney Variable Account Funds, Inc. *U.S. Government/High Quality Securities Portfolio* 1345 Avenue of the Americas New York, NY 10105 212/698-5349 800/544-7835	1989	Smith, Barney Advisers, Inc.	N/A	Not Applicable	N/A	Insur
SteinRoe Variable Investment Trust *Mortgage Securities Income Fund* 600 Atlantic Ave. Boston, MA 02210 617/722-6000 800/443-2683	1989	Stein Roe & Farnham Incorporated	N/A	Not Applicable	N/A	Insur
T. Rowe Price GNMA Fund 100 E. Pratt St. Baltimore, MD 21202 301/547-2000 800/638-5660	1985	T. Rowe Price Associates, Inc.	$364.5 Mil	$2,500/ 100	n	Fund
United Services Funds *U.S. GNMA Fund* P.O. Box 29467 San Antonio, TX 78229-0467 512/696-1234 800/873-8637	1986	United Services Advisors, Inc.	$5.9 Mil	$100/ 50	n	Fund
Vanguard Fixed-Income Securities Fund, Inc. *GNMA Portfolio* Vanguard Financial Ctr. P.O. Box 2600 Valley Forge, PA 19482 215/648-6000 800/662-7447, 800/362-0530 PA Only	1980	Wellington Management Company	$2.0 Bil	$3,000/ 100	n	Fund

*Key: i=initial sales charge   r=redemption fee or contingent deferred sales charge(CDSC)
t=12b-1 fee and either CDSC or redemption fee   p=12b-1 fee   n=none of the preceding fees   N/A=not available

◆ ◆ ◆ ◆

Global Bond Funds

Global Bond

Fund	Year Began	Investment Adviser	9/30/89 Assets	Minimum Initial and Subsequent Investment	Fees*	Where to Buy Shares
AMA Income Fund, Inc. *Global Income Portfolio* 5 Sentry Pkwy. W, Ste. 120 P.O. Box 1111 Blue Bell, PA 19422 215/825-0400 800/AMA-FUND	1987	AMA Advisers, Inc.	$16.1 Mil	$1,000/ 0	p	Fund
AMA Income Fund, Inc. *Global Short Term Portfolio* 5 Sentry Pkwy. W, Ste. 120 P.O. Box 1111 Blue Bell, PA 19422 215/825-0400 800/AMA-FUND	1987	AMA Advisers, Inc.	$17.5 Mil	$1,000/ 0	p	Fund
Capital World Bond Fund, Inc. 333 S. Hope St. Los Angeles, CA 90071 213/486-9200 800/421-0180 213/486-9651 Collect	1987	Capital Research & Management Company	$35.4 Mil	$0/ 0	i, t	Local Rep
Dreyfus Strategic World Revenues, L.P. 666 Old Country Rd. Garden City, NY 11530 718/895-1347 800/648-9048	1987	Dreyfus Corporation	$14.9 Mil	$2,500/ 500	i, p	Local Rep
Fenimore International Fund, Inc. *Fixed Income Series* 60 Broad St. New York, NY 10004 212/232-5000 800/272-2700	1987	Drexel Burnham Lambert International Management Corporation	$12.6 Mil (e)	$1,000/ 100	t	Local Rep
Fidelity Investment Trust *Fidelity Global Bond Fund* 82 Devonshire St. Boston, MA 02109 617/570-7000 800/544-6666	1986	Fidelity Management & Research Company	$45.1 Mil	$2,500/ 250	r	Fund
Franklin Investors Securities Trust *Franklin Global Opportunity Income Fund* 777 Mariners Island Blvd. San Mateo, CA 94404 415/570-3000 800/632-2180, 800/632-2350	1988	Franklin Advisers, Inc.	$8.9 Mil	$100/ 25	i	Local Rep

*Key: i=initial sales charge   r=redemption fee or contingent deferred sales charge(CDSC)
t=12b-1 fee and either CDSC or redemption fee   p=12b-1 fee   n=none of the preceding fees   N/A=not available

Global Bond

Fund	Year Began	Investment Adviser	9/30/89 Assets	Minimum Initial and Subsequent Investment	Fees*	Where to Buy Shares
Freedom Investment Trust II *Freedom Global Income Plus Fund* One Beacon St. Boston, MA 02108 617/523-3170 800/225-6258 800/392-6037 MA Only	1987	Freedom Capital Management Corporation	$253.0 Mil	$1,000/ 100	t	Local Rep
G.T. Global Income Series, Inc. *G.T. Global Bond Fund* 50 California St. 27th Fl. San Francisco, CA 94111 415/392-6181 800/824-1580	1988	G.T. Capital Management Inc.	$33.1 Mil (e)	$500/ 100	i, p	Local Rep
G.T. Global Income Series, Inc. *G.T. Global Government Income Fund* 50 California St. 27th Fl. San Francisco, CA 94111 415/392-6181, 800/824-1580	1988	G.T. Capital Management Inc.	$95.3 Mil (e)	$500/ 100	i, p	Local Rep
IDS Global Bond Fund, Inc. IDS Tower 10 Minneapolis, MN 55440 612/372-3131 800/328-8300	1989	IDS Financial Corporation	$10.0 Mil	$2,000/ 100	i, p	Local Rep
Investment Trust of Boston *World Income Portfolio* 399 Boylston St. 9th Fl. Boston, MA 02116 800/888-4823	1989	Back Bay Advisors, Inc. UBS Phillips & Drew International	$4.1 Mil	$1,000/ 100	i, p	Local Rep
John Hancock World Trust *World Fixed Income Portfolio* 101 Huntington Ave. Boston, MA 02199-7603 617/375-1500 800/225-5291	1987	John Hancock Advisers, Inc.	$0.4 Mil	$1,000/ 25	i, p	Local Rep
Keystone America Global Income Fund *Global Income Portfolio* 99 High St. Boston, MA 02110 617/338-3200 800/343-2898 800/225-1587	1987	Keystone Custodian Funds, Inc.	$8.8 Mil	$1,000/ 0	i, p	Local Rep

*Key: i=initial sales charge   r=redemption fee or contingent deferred sales charge(CDSC)
   t=12b-1 fee and either CDSC or redemption fee   p=12b-1 fee   n=none of the preceding fees   N/A=not available

Global Bond

Fund	Year Began	Investment Adviser	9/30/89 Assets	Minimum Initial and Subsequent Investment	Fees*	Where to Buy Shares
Kleinwort Benson Investment Strategies *Kleinwort Benson Global Income Fund* 200 Park Ave., 24th Fl. New York, NY 10166 212/687-2515, 800/237-4218, 800/233-9164	1987	Kleinwort Benson International Investment Ltd.	$6.9 Mil	$1,000/ 100	p	Fund
Lord Abbett Global Fund, Inc. *Income Series* The General Motors Bldg. 767 Fifth Ave. New York, NY 10153 212/848-1800 800/223-4224	1988	Lord, Abbett & Co.	$25.7 Mil	$1,000/ 0	i, p	Local Rep
Massachusetts Financial International Trust-Bond Portfolio 500 Boylston St. Boston, MA 02116 617/954-5000 800/343-2829	1981	Massachusetts Financial Services Company	$134.9 Mil	$1,000/ 25	i	Local Rep
Meeschaert International Bond Trust 28 Hill Farm Rd. RFD #2 Box 151 St. Johnsbury, VT 05819 802/748-2400	1986	Meeschaert Investment Management Corp.	N/A	$500/ 0	t	Local Rep
Merrill Lynch Retirement Global Bond Fund *Class A* *Class B* P.O. Box 9011 Princeton, NJ 08543-9011 609/282-2800 800/637-3863	1988 1986	Merrill Lynch Asset Management Inc.	$282.0 Mil	$1,000/50 $1,000/50	i t	LRep LRep
MFS Lifetime Investment Program *Lifetime Intermediate Income Trust* 500 Boylston St. Boston, MA 02116 617/954-5000 800/343-2829	1988	Lifetime Advisers, Inc.	$65.8 Mil	$1,000/ 50	t	Local Rep
NASL Series Trust *Global Government Bond Trust* 695 Atlantic Ave. P.O. Box 9064 GMF Boston, MA 02205 617/439-6960 800/344-1029	1988	NASL Financial Services, Inc.	$3.4 Mil	Not Applicable	r	Insur

*Key: i=initial sales charge   r=redemption fee or contingent deferred sales charge(CDSC)
t=12b-1 fee and either CDSC or redemption fee   p=12b-1 fee   n=none of the preceding fees   N/A=not available

Global Bond

Fund	Year Began	Investment Adviser	9/30/89 Assets	Minimum Initial and Subsequent Investment	Fees*	Where to Buy Shares
New England Global Government Fund 399 Boylston St. Boston, MA 02116 617/267-7055 800/634-8025	1988	Back Bay Advisors, Inc. UBS Phillips & Drew International	$25.6 Mil	$1,000/ 25	i, p	Local Rep
Pacific Investment Management Institutional Trust *International Bond Portfolio* 840 Newport Ctr. Dr. Ste. 300 Newport Beach, CA 92660 714/640-3031, 800/443-6915	1988	Pacific Investment Management Company	N/A	$200,000/ 10,000	n	Fund
PaineWebber Investment Series *PaineWebber Master Global Income Fund* 1285 Avenue of the Americas PaineWebber Bldg. New York, NY 10019 212/713-2000, 800/647-1568	1987	Mitchell Hutchins Asset Management Inc.	$985.2 Mil	$1,000/ 100	t	Local Rep
PaineWebber Series Trust *Global Income Portfolio* 1285 Avenue of the Americas PaineWebber Bldg. New York, NY 10019 212/713-2000	1987	Mitchell Hutchins Asset Management Inc.	N/A	Not Applicable	N/A	Insur
Pilgrim Foreign Investors *Pilgrim International Bond Fund* 10100 Santa Monica Blvd. 21st Fl. Los Angeles, CA 90067 213/551-0833 800/334-3444, 800/331-1080	1987	Pilgrim Management Corporation	$6.2 Mil	$5,000/ 1,000	i, p	Local Rep
Putnam Global Governmental Income Trust One Post Office Sq. Boston, MA 02109 617/292-1000 800/225-2465	1987	Putnam Management Company, Inc.	$158.4 Mil	$500/ 50	i, p	Local Rep
Scudder International Bond Fund 175 Federal St. Boston, MA 02110 617/439-4640 800/225-2470 800/225-5163	1988	Scudder, Stevens & Clark, Inc.	$17.9 Mil	$1,000/ 0	n	Fund

*Key: i=initial sales charge   r=redemption fee or contingent deferred sales charge(CDSC)
t=12b-1 fee and either CDSC or redemption fee   p=12b-1 fee   n=none of the preceding fees   N/A=not available

Global Bond

Fund	Year Began	Investment Adviser	9/30/89 Assets	Minimum Initial and Subsequent Investment	Fees*	Where to Buy Shares
SLH Special Income Portfolios *SLH Global Bond Portfolio* 31 W. 52nd St. New York, NY 10019 212/767-3700	1986	SLH Global Asset Management S.A.	$90.4 Mil	$500/ 200	t	Local Rep
Templeton Income Trust *Templeton Income Fund* 700 Central Ave. P.O. Box 33030 St. Petersburg, FL 33733-8030 813/823-8712 800/237-0738	1986	Templeton Investment Counsel, Inc.	$116.2 Mil	$500/ 25	i	Local Rep
T. Rowe Price International Trust *T. Rowe Price International Bond Fund* 100 E. Pratt St. Baltimore, MD 21202 301/547-2000 800/638-5660	1986	Rowe Price-Fleming International, Inc.	$268.4 Mil	$2,500/ 100	n	Fund
Van Eck Funds *World Income Fund* 122 E. 42nd St. New York, NY 10168 212/687-5200 800/221-2220	1987	Van Eck Associates Corporation	$37.8 Mil	$1,000/ 100	i, p	Local Rep
Variable Investors Series Trust *World Bond Portfolio* 1414 Main St. Springfield, MA 01144 413/732-7100	1988	Amherst Investment Management Company, Inc.	$3.4 Mil	Not Applicable	N/A	Insur

*Key: i=initial sales charge   r=redemption fee or contingent deferred sales charge(CDSC)
t=12b-1 fee and either CDSC or redemption fee   p=12b-1 fee   n=none of the preceding fees   N/A=not available

◆ ◆ ◆ ◆

Global Equity Funds

Global Equity

Fund	Year Began	Investment Adviser	9/30/89 Assets	Minimum Initial and Subsequent Investment	Fees*	Where to Buy Shares
Alliance Global Fund *World Equities Fund* 1345 Avenue of the Americas New York, NY 10105 212/969-1000 800/221-5672	1986	Alliance Capital Management L.P.	$1.8 Mil	$250/ 50	i, p	Local Rep
AMA Growth Fund, Inc. *Global Growth Portfolio* 5 Sentry Pkwy. W, Ste. 120 P.O. Box 1111 Blue Bell, PA 19422 215/825-0400 800/AMA-FUND	1987	AMA Advisers, Inc.	$110.0 Mil	$1,000/ 0	p	Fund
Colonial Value Investing Portfolios - Equity Portfolio *Diversified Return Fund* One Financial Ctr. Boston, MA 02111 617/426-3750 800/225-2365, 800/426-3750	1988	Colonial Management Associates, Inc.	$15.6 Mil	$500/ 100	t	Local Rep
Dean Witter World Wide Investment Trust Two World Trade Ctr. New York, NY 10048 212/392-2550 800/869-3863	1983	Dean Witter Reynolds Inc. - InterCapital Division	$315.6 Mil	$1,000/ 100	t	Local Rep
Dreyfus Strategic World Investing, L.P. 666 Old Country Rd. Garden City, NY 11530 718/895-1347 800/648-9048	1987	Dreyfus Corporation	$17.5 Mil	$2,500/ 500	i, p	Fund
Equitec Siebel Fund Group *Equitec Siebel Global Fund Series* 7677 Oakport St. P.O. Box 2470 Oakland, CA 94614 415/430-9900 800/869-8900	1988	Siebel Capital Management, Inc.	$2.2 Mil (e)	$1,000/ 0	t	Local Rep
Evergreen Global Real Estate Equity Fund 2500 Westchester Ave. Purchase, NY 10577 914/694-2020 800/235-0064	1989	Evergreen Asset Management Corporation	$6.9 Mil (e)	$2,000/ 0	n	Fund

*Key: i=initial sales charge   r=redemption fee or contingent deferred sales charge(CDSC)
t=12b-1 fee and either CDSC or redemption fee   p=12b-1 fee   n=none of the preceding fees   N/A=not available

Global Equity

Fund	Year Began	Investment Adviser	9/30/89 Assets	Minimum Initial and Subsequent Investment	Fees*	Where to Buy Shares
First Investors International Securities Fund, Inc. 120 Wall St. New York, NY 10005 212/208-6000	1982	First Investors Management Company, Inc.	$106.3 Mil	$200/ 50	i, p	Local Rep
Freedom Investment Trust II *Freedom Global Fund* One Beacon St. Boston, MA 02108 617/523-3170 800/225-6258 800/392-6037 MA Only	1986	Freedom Capital Management Corporation	$37.1 Mil	$1,000/ 100	t	Local Rep
Fund Source *BIL International Growth Fund* 230 Park Ave. 12th Fl. New York, NY 10169 212/309-8400 800/845-8406	1988	BIL, Trainer Wortham Inc.	$7.8 Mil (e)	$1,000/ 100	i, p	Local Rep
G.T. Global Growth Series *G.T. Worldwide Growth Fund* 50 California St. 27th Fl. San Francisco, CA 94111 415/392-6181 800/824-1580	1987	G.T. Capital Management Inc.	$18.8 Mil (e)	$500/ 100	i, p	Local Rep
IDS Strategy Fund, Inc. *Pan Pacific Growth Fund* IDS Tower 10 Minneapolis, MN 55440 612/372-3131 800/328-8300	1987	IDS Financial Corporation	$49.8 Mil	$100/ 100	t	Local Rep
John Hancock Global Trust 101 Huntington Ave. Boston, MA 02199-7603 617/375-1500 800/225-5291	1985	John Hancock Advisers, Inc.	$114.9 Mil	$1,000/ 25	i	Local Rep
Kemper Global Income Fund 120 S. LaSalle St. Chicago, IL 60603 312/781-1121 800/621-1148	1989	Kemper Financial Services, Inc.	N/A	$1,000/ 100	N/A	Local Rep

*Key: i=initial sales charge   r=redemption fee or contingent deferred sales charge(CDSC)
t=12b-1 fee and either CDSC or redemption fee   p=12b-1 fee   n=none of the preceding fees   N/A=not available

Global Equity

Fund	Year Began	Investment Adviser	9/30/89 Assets	Minimum Initial and Subsequent Investment	Fees*	Where to Buy Shares
Keystone America Global Opportunity Fund 99 High St. Boston, MA 02110 617/338-3200 800/343-2898 800/225-1587	1988	Keystone Custodian Funds, Inc.	$1.4 Mil	$1,000/ 0	i, t	Local Rep
Lexington Global Fund, Inc. Park 80 W., Plaza Two P.O. Box 1515 Saddle Brook, NJ 07662 201/845-7300 800/526-0056	1987	Lexington Management Corporation	$46.8 Mil	$1,000/ 50	i	Local Rep
Lord Abbett Global Fund, Inc. *Equity Series* The General Motors Bldg. 767 Fifth Ave. New York, NY 10153 212/848-1800 800/223-4224	1988	Lord, Abbett & Co.	$21.5 Mil	$1,000/ 0	i, p	Local Rep
MacKay-Shields MainStay Series Fund *MainStay Global Fund* 51 Madison Ave. New York, NY 10010 212/576-7000 800/522-4202	1987	Gamma Advisers Ltd.	$19.2 Mil	$500/ 50	t	Local Rep
Merrill Lynch Global Convertible Fund, Inc. *Class A* *Class B* P.O. Box 9011 Princeton, NJ 08543-9011 609/282-2800 800/637-3863	1988 1988	Merrill Lynch Asset Management Inc.	$32.7 Mil	$1,000/50 $1,000/50	i t	LRep LRep
Merrill Lynch International Holdings, Inc. *Class A* *Class B* P.O. Box 9011 Princeton, NJ 08543-9011 609/282-2800 800/637-3863	1984 1988	Merrill Lynch Asset Management Inc.	$200.9 Mil	$1,000/50 $1,000/50	i t	LRep LRep
Merrill Lynch Series Fund *Global Strategy Portfolio* P.O. Box 9011 Princeton, NJ 08543-9011 609/282-2800 800/524-4458	1987	Fund Asset Management, Inc.	$10.6 Mil	Not Applicable	n	Insur

*Key: i=initial sales charge   r=redemption fee or contingent deferred sales charge(CDSC)
t=12b-1 fee and either CDSC or redemption fee   p=12b-1 fee   n=none of the preceding fees   N/A=not available

Global Equity

Fund	Year Began	Investment Adviser	9/30/89 Assets	Minimum Initial and Subsequent Investment	Fees*	Where to Buy Shares
MFS Lifetime Investment Program *Lifetime Global Equity Trust* 500 Boylston St. Boston, MA 02116 617/954-5000 800/343-2829	1986	Lifetime Advisers, Inc.	$47.8 Mil	$1,000/ 50	t	Local Rep
NASL Series Trust *Global Equity Trust* 695 Atlantic Ave. P.O. Box 9064 GMF Boston, MA 02205 617/439-6960 800/344-1029	1988	NASL Financial Services, Inc.	$17.1 Mil	Not Applicable	r	Insur
National Strategic Allocation Fund 600 Third Ave. New York, NY 10016 203/863-5600 800/237-1718	1987	National Securities & Research Corporation	$106.5 Mil	$1,000/ 25	i, p	Local Rep
New Perspective Fund, Inc. 333 S. Hope St. Los Angeles, CA 90071 213/486-9200 800/421-0180 213/486-9651 Collect	1973	Capital Research & Management Company	$1.2 Bil	$250/ 50	i, t	Local Rep
Oppenheimer Global Fund Two World Trade Ctr. New York, NY 10048-0669 212/323-0200 800/525-7048	1969	Oppenheimer Management Corporation	$522.5 Mil	$1,000/ 25	i	Local Rep
PaineWebber Classic Atlas Fund 1285 Avenue of the Americas PaineWebber Bldg. New York, NY 10019 212/713-2000 800/544-9300	1983	Mitchell Hutchins Asset Management Inc.	$202.5 Mil	$1,000/ 100	i, p	Local Rep
PaineWebber Classic World Fund, Inc. 1285 Avenue of the Americas PaineWebber Bldg. New York, NY 10019 212/713-2000 800/544-9300	1989	Mitchell Hutchins Asset Management Inc.	N/A	$1,000/ 100	N/A	Local Rep

*Key: i=initial sales charge   r=redemption fee or contingent deferred sales charge(CDSC)
t=12b-1 fee and either CDSC or redemption fee   p=12b-1 fee   n=none of the preceding fees   N/A=not available

Global Equity

Fund	Year Began	Investment Adviser	9/30/89 Assets	Minimum Initial and Subsequent Investment	Fees*	Where to Buy Shares
PaineWebber Series Trust *Global Growth Portfolio* 1285 Avenue of the Americas PaineWebber Bldg. New York, NY 10019 212/713-2000	1987	Mitchell Hutchins Asset Management Inc.	N/A	Not Applicable	N/A	Insur
Plymouth Investment Series *Plymouth Global Natural Resources Portfolio* 82 Devonshire St. Boston, MA 02109 617/570-7000 800/544-6666	1987	Fidelity Management & Research Company	$2.1 Mil	$1,000/ 100	i, p	Local Rep
Princor World Fund, Inc. 711 High St. Des Moines, IA 50309 515/247-5711 800/247-4123 800/622-5344 IA Only	1983	Principal Management, Inc.	$14.9 Mil	$300/ 50	i, p	Local Rep
Prudential-Bache Global Fund, Inc. One Seaport Plaza New York, NY 10292 212/214-1215 800/225-1852	1984	Prudential Mutual Fund Management	$409.1 Mil	$1,000/ 100	t	Local Rep
Prudential-Bache Global Genesis Fund, Inc. One Seaport Plaza New York, NY 10292 212/214-1215 800/225-1852	1988	Prudential Mutual Fund Management	$20.8 Mil	$1,000/ 100	t	Local Rep
Prudential-Bache Global Natural Resources Fund, Inc. One Seaport Plaza New York, NY 10292 212/214-1215 800/225-1852	1987	Prudential Mutual Fund Management	$52.6 Mil	$1,000/ 100	t	Local Rep
Putnam International Equities Fund One Post Office Sq. Boston, MA 02109 617/292-1000 800/225-2465	1967	Putnam Management Company, Inc.	$507.6 Mil	$500/ 50	i	Local Rep

*Key: i=initial sales charge   r=redemption fee or contingent deferred sales charge(CDSC)
t=12b-1 fee and either CDSC or redemption fee   p=12b-1 fee   n=none of the preceding fees   N/A=not available

Global Equity

Fund	Year Began	Investment Adviser	9/30/89 Assets	Minimum Initial and Subsequent Investment	Fees*	Where to Buy Shares
Sci/Tech Holdings, Inc. *Class A* *Class B* P.O. Box 9011 Princeton, NJ 08543-9011 609/282-2800 800/637-3863	1983 1988	Merrill Lynch Asset Management Inc.	$160.2 Mil	$1,000/50 $1,000/50	i t	LRep LRep
Scudder Global Fund 175 Federal St. Boston, MA 02110 617/439-4640 800/225-2470 800/225-5163	1986	Scudder, Stevens & Clark, Inc.	$124.7 Mil	$1,000/ 0	n	Fund
SLH Global Opportunities Fund 31 W. 52nd St. New York, NY 10019 212/767-3700	1984	SLH Global Asset Management S.A.	$93.3 Mil	$500/ 200	i	Local Rep
SLH Investment Series, Inc. *SLH Global Equity Portfolio* 31 W. 52nd St. 15th Fl. New York, NY 10019 212/767-3700 800/334-4636 800/422-0214 NY Only	1987	SLH Asset Management Division of Shearson Lehman Hutton Inc.	$9.7 Mil	$500/ 250	t	Local Rep
SoGen International Fund, Inc. 50 Rockefeller Plaza New York, NY 10020 212/832-0022 800/334-2143	1970	Sogen Securities Corp.	$150.7 Mil	$1,000/ 100	i, p	Local Rep
Templeton Funds, Inc. *World Fund* 700 Central Ave. P.O. Box 33030 St. Petersburg, FL 33733-8030 813/823-8712 800/237-0738	1978	Templeton, Galbraith & Hansberger, Ltd.	$4.8 Bil	$500/ 25	i	Local Rep

*Key: i=initial sales charge   r=redemption fee or contingent deferred sales charge(CDSC)
      t=12b-1 fee and either CDSC or redemption fee   p=12b-1 fee   n=none of the preceding fees   N/A=not available

Global Equity

Fund	Year Began	Investment Adviser	9/30/89 Assets	Minimum Initial and Subsequent Investment	Fees*	Where to Buy Shares
Templeton Global Funds, Inc. *Templeton Global Fund* 700 Central Ave. P.O. Box 33030 St. Petersburg, FL 33733-8030 813/823-8712 800/237-0738	1981	Templeton, Galbraith & Hansberger, Ltd.	$938.2 Mil	$0/ 0	i	Local Rep
Templeton Growth Fund, Inc. 700 Central Ave. P.O. Box 33030 St. Petersburg, FL 33733-8030 813/823-8712 800/237-0738	1987	Templeton Investment Counsel Limited	$2.4 Bil	$500/ 25	i	Local Rep
Thomson McKinnon Investment Trust *Thomson McKinnon Global Fund* One State Street Plaza New York, NY 10004 212/482-5894 800/628-1237	1986	Thomson McKinnon Asset Management L.P.	$56.1 Mil	$1,000/ 100	t	Local Rep
Transamerica Special Series, Inc. *Transamerica Special Global Growth Fund* 1000 Louisiana Ste. 6000 Houston, TX 77002-5098 713/751-2400, 800/999-3863	1986	Transamerica Fund Management Company	$8.0 Mil (e)	$1,000/ 50	t	Local Rep
Tyndall-Newport Fund, Inc. *Tyndall-Newport Global Growth Fund* 1500 Forest Ave., Ste. 223 P.O. Box 8687 Richmond, VA 23226 804/285-8211 800/527-9500	1987	Tyndall-Newport Fund Management, Inc.	$2.4 Mil (e)	$1,000/ 100	i	Local Rep
United International Growth Fund, Inc. 2400 Pershing Rd. P.O. Box 418343 Kansas City, MO 64141-9343 816/283-4000 800/821-5664	1970	Waddell & Reed, Inc.	$280.4 Mil	$500/ 25	i	Local Rep
Van Eck Funds *World Trends Fund* 122 E. 42nd St. New York, NY 10168 212/687-5200 800/221-2220	1985	Van Eck Associates Corporation	$63.8 Mil	$1,000/ 100	i, p	Local Rep

*Key: i=initial sales charge   r=redemption fee or contingent deferred sales charge(CDSC)
t=12b-1 fee and either CDSC or redemption fee   p=12b-1 fee   n=none of the preceding fees   N/A=not available

121

Global Equity

Fund	Year Began	Investment Adviser	9/30/89 Assets	Minimum Initial and Subsequent Investment	Fees*	Where to Buy Shares
Variable Investors Series Trust *World Equity Portfolio* 1414 Main St. Springfield, MA 01144 413/732-7100	1988	Amherst Investment Management Company, Inc.	$2.0 Mil	Not Applicable	N/A	Insur
Yamaichi Funds, Inc. *Yamaichi Global Fund* Two World Trade Ctr. Ste. 9828 New York, NY 10048 212/466-6800	1988	Yamaichi Capital Management, Inc.	N/A	$2,500/ 500	i, p	Local Rep

*Key: i=initial sales charge   r=redemption fee or contingent deferred sales charge(CDSC)
t=12b-1 fee and either CDSC or redemption fee   p=12b-1 fee   n=none of the preceding fees   N/A=not available

122

◆ ◆ ◆ ◆

Growth Funds

Growth

Fund	Year Began	Investment Adviser	9/30/89 Assets	Minimum Initial and Subsequent Investment	Fees*	Where to Buy Shares
AAL Mutual Funds *AAL Capital Growth Fund (The)* 222 W. College Ave. Appleton, WI 54919 414/734-5721 800/553-6319	1987	AAL Advisors Inc.	$71.9 Mil	$500/ 50	i, p	Local Rep
AARP Growth Trust *AARP Capital Growth Fund* AARP Investment Program 175 Federal St. Boston, MA 02110-2267 800/253-2277	1984	AARP/Scudder Financial Management Company	$179.7 Mil	$250/ 0	n	Fund
Acorn Fund, Inc. Two N. LaSalle St. Ste. 500 Chicago, IL 60602-3790 312/621-0630 800/9ACORN-9	1970	Harris Associates, L.P.	$854.7 Mil	$4,000/ 1,000	n	Fund
Advantage Growth Fund 60 State St. Boston, MA 02109 617/742-5900 800/243-8115	1986	Boston Security Counsellors	$30.7 Mil	$500/ 250	t	Local Rep
Advantage Special Fund 60 State St. Boston, MA 02109 617/742-5900 800/243-8115	1986	Boston Security Counsellors	$4.3 Mil	$500/ 250	t	Local Rep
Advisers Management Trust *Growth Portfolio* 342 Madison Ave. New York, NY 10173 212/850-8300 800/877-9700	1984	Neuberger & Berman Management Incorporated	$85.5 Mil	Not Applicable	n	Insur
Aetna Variable Fund 151 Farmington Ave. Hartford, CT 06156 203/273-4808	1970	Aetna Life Insurance and Annuity Company	$2.5 Bil (e)	Not Applicable	n	Insur

*Key: i=initial sales charge   r=redemption fee or contingent deferred sales charge(CDSC)
t=12b-1 fee and either CDSC or redemption fee   p=12b-1 fee   n=none of the preceding fees   N/A=not available

Growth

Fund	Year Began	Investment Adviser	9/30/89 Assets	Minimum Initial and Subsequent Investment	Fees*	Where to Buy Shares
AIM Equity Funds, Inc. *AIM Weingarten Fund* 11 Greenway Plaza Ste. 1919 Houston, TX 77046 713/626-1919 800/231-0803 800/392-9681 TX Only	1967	AIM Advisors, Inc.	$406.1 Mil	$1,000/ 100	i, p	Local Rep
AIM Summit Investors Fund, Inc. 11 Greenway Plaza Ste. 1919 Houston, TX 77046 713/626-1919 800/231-0803 800/392-9681 TX Only	1982	AIM Advisors, Inc.	$247.3 Mil	$0/ 0	i	Local Rep
Alger American Fund *Alger American Growth Portfolio* 75 Maiden Lane New York, NY 10038 212/806-8800 800/223-3810	1988	Fred Alger Management, Inc.	$0.1 Mil	Not Applicable	n	Insur
Alger Fund *Alger Growth Portfolio* 75 Maiden Lane New York, NY 10038 212/806-8800 800/223-3810	1986	Fred Alger Management, Inc.	$6.0 Mil	$1,000/ 100	t	Fund
Alliance Counterpoint Fund 1345 Avenue of the Americas New York, NY 10105 212/969-1000 800/221-5672	1985	Alliance Capital Management L.P.	$60.5 Mil	$1,000/ 250	i, p	Local Rep
Alliance Fund, Inc. 1345 Avenue of the Americas New York, NY 10105 212/969-1000 800/221-5672	1938	Alliance Capital Management L.P.	$880.6 Mil	$250/ 50	i, p	Local Rep
Alliance Technology Fund, Inc. 1345 Avenue of the Americas New York, NY 10105 212/969-1000 800/221-5672	1982	Alliance Capital Management L.P.	$156.3 Mil	$250/ 50	i, p	Local Rep

*Key: i=initial sales charge   r=redemption fee or contingent deferred sales charge(CDSC)
t=12b-1 fee and either CDSC or redemption fee   p=12b-1 fee   n=none of the preceding fees   N/A=not available

126

Growth

Fund	Year Began	Investment Adviser	9/30/89 Assets	Minimum Initial and Subsequent Investment	Fees*	Where to Buy Shares
Altura Fund *Growth Fund* 1900 E. Dublin-Granville Rd. Columbus, OH 43229 614/899-4600 800/338-4385	1986	United Bank of Denver National Association	N/A	$2,500/ 50	N/A	Fund
AMA Growth Fund, Inc. *Classic Growth Portfolio* 5 Sentry Pkwy. W, Ste. 120 P.O. Box 1111 Blue Bell, PA 19422 215/825-0400 800/AMA-FUND	1967	AMA Advisers, Inc.	$35.8 Mil	$1,000/ 0	p	Fund
AMCAP Fund, Inc. 333 S. Hope St. Los Angeles, CA 90071 213/486-9200 800/421-0180 213/486-9651 Collect	1967	Capital Research & Management Company	$2.1 Bil	$1,000/ 50	i, t	Local Rep
American Capital Comstock Fund, Inc. 2800 Post Oak Blvd. Houston, TX 77056 713/993-0500 800/421-5666	1967	American Capital Asset Management, Inc.	$959.4 Mil	$500/ 50	i	Local Rep
American Capital Enterprise Fund, Inc. 2800 Post Oak Blvd. Houston, TX 77056 713/993-0500 800/421-5666	1953	American Capital Asset Management, Inc.	$604.5 Mil	$500/ 50	i, p	Local Rep
American Capital Exchange Fund, Inc. 2800 Post Oak Blvd. Houston, TX 77056 713/993-0500 800/421-5666	1976	American Capital Asset Management, Inc.	$45.0 Mil	Not Applicable	n	Not Offering Shares
American Capital Growth Fund, Inc. 2800 Post Oak Blvd. Houston, TX 77056 713/993-0500 800/421-5666	1964	American Capital Asset Management, Inc.	$13.4 Mil	$25/ 25	n	Local Rep

*Key: i=initial sales charge   r=redemption fee or contingent deferred sales charge(CDSC)
t=12b-1 fee and either CDSC or redemption fee   p=12b-1 fee   n=none of the preceding fees   N/A=not available

Growth

Fund	Year Began	Investment Adviser	9/30/89 Assets	Minimum Initial and Subsequent Investment	Fees*	Where to Buy Shares
American Capital Pace Fund, Inc. 2800 Post Oak Blvd. Houston, TX 77056 713/993-0500 800/421-5666	1968	American Capital Asset Management, Inc.	$2.5 Bil	$500/ 50	i, p	Local Rep
American Eagle Fund, Inc. ***American Eagle Growth Series*** 100 Light St. Baltimore, MD 21202 301/547-3894 800/622-3363	1987	Axe-Houghton Management, Inc.	$8.0 Mil	Not Applicable	r	Insur
American General Series Portfolio Company ***Social Awareness Fund*** 2929 Allen Pkwy. P.O. Box 3206 Houston, TX 77253 713/526-5251	1989	Variable Annuity Life Insurance Company	N/A	Not Applicable	N/A	Insur
American General Series Portfolio Company ***Stock Index Fund*** 2929 Allen Pkwy. P.O. Box 3206 Houston, TX 77253 713/526-5251	1987	Variable Annuity Life Insurance Company	$27.4 Mil	Not Applicable	n	Insur
American General Series Portfolio Company ***Timed Opportunity Fund*** 2929 Allen Pkwy. P.O. Box 3206 Houston, TX 77253 713/526-5251	1983	Variable Annuity Life Insurance Company	$106.0 Mil	Not Applicable	r	Insur
American Growth Fund, Inc. 410 17th St. Ste. 800 Denver, CO 80202 303/623-6137 800/525-2406	1958	Investment Research Corporation	$59.9 Mil (e)	$500/ 25	i	Local Rep
American Investors Option Fund, Inc. 777 W. Putnam Ave. P.O. Box 2500 Greenwich, CT 06836 203/531-5000 800/243-5353	1986	D.H. Blair Advisors, Inc.	$0.4 Mil (e)	$400/ 20	i	Fund

*Key: i=initial sales charge   r=redemption fee or contingent deferred sales charge(CDSC)
t=12b-1 fee and either CDSC or redemption fee   p=12b-1 fee   n=none of the preceding fees   N/A=not available

Growth

Fund	Year Began	Investment Adviser	9/30/89 Assets	Minimum Initial and Subsequent Investment	Fees*	Where to Buy Shares
American National Growth Fund, Inc. Two Moody Plaza Galveston, TX 77550 409/763-2767 800/231-4639 800/392-9753 TX Only	1953	Securities Management & Research, Inc.	$109.1 Mil	$20/ 20	i	Local Rep
American Pension Investors Trust *Growth Fund* 2303 Yorktown Ave. P.O. Box 2529 Lynchburg, VA 24501 804/846-1361 800/544-6060, 800/533-4115 VA Only	1985	American Pension Investors, Inc.	$35.7 Mil	$100/ 50	p	Local Rep
American Variable Insurance Series *Growth Fund (The)* 333 S. Hope St. Los Angeles, CA 90071 213/486-9200 800/421-0180 213/486-9651 Collect	1984	Capital Research & Management Company	$127.9 Mil	Not Applicable	n	Insur
AMEV Advantage Portfolios, Inc. *Capital Appreciation Portfolio* P.O. Box 64284 St. Paul, MN 55164 612/738-4000 800/872-2638	1988	AMEV Advisers, Inc.	$13.4 Mil	$500/ 50	i, p	Local Rep
AMEV Growth Fund, Inc. P.O. Box 64284 St. Paul, MN 55164 612/738-4000 800/872-2638	1963	AMEV Advisers, Inc.	$239.2 Mil	$500/ 50	i	Local Rep
AMEV Special Fund, Inc. P.O. Box 64284 St. Paul, MN 55164 612/738-4000 800/872-2638	1966	AMEV Advisers, Inc.	$27.8 Mil	$500/ 50	n	Fund
Amway Mutual Fund, Inc. 7575 E. Fulton Rd. Ada, MI 49355 616/676-6288 800/346-2670	1970	Amway Management Company	$39.4 Mil	$500/ 50	i	Local Rep

*Key: i=initial sales charge   r=redemption fee or contingent deferred sales charge(CDSC)
t=12b-1 fee and either CDSC or redemption fee   p=12b-1 fee   n=none of the preceding fees   N/A=not available

Growth

Fund	Year Began	Investment Adviser	9/30/89 Assets	Minimum Initial and Subsequent Investment	Fees*	Where to Buy Shares
Anchor Pathway Fund *Growth Series (The)* 2201 E. Camelback Phoenix, AZ 85016 602/955-0300 800/528-9679	1987	Capital Research & Management Company	N/A	Not Applicable	n	Insur
Armstrong Associates, Inc. 1445 Ross LB212 Dallas, TX 75202 214/720-9101	1967	Portfolios, Inc.	$9.8 Mil (e)	$250/ 0	n	Local Rep
Associated Planners Investment Trust *Associated Planners Stock Fund* 1925 Century Park East 19th Fl. Los Angeles, CA 90067 213/553-6740	1984	Associated Planners Management Company	$15.9 Mil (e)	$500/ 50	i	Local Rep
Axe-Houghton Stock Fund, Inc. 400 Benedict Ave. Tarrytown, NY 10591 914/631-8131 800/366-0444	1932	Axe-Houghton Management, Inc.	$71.1 Mil	$1,000/ 0	p	Fund
Baird Capital Development Fund, Inc. 777 E. Wisconsin Ave. Milwaukee, WI 53202 414/765-3500 800/792-2473	1984	Robert W. Baird & Company, Inc.	N/A	$1,000/ 100	i, p	Local Rep
Baker Fund *Equity Series* 1601 NW Expressway 20th Fl. Oklahoma City, OK 73118 405/842-1400 800/654-3248	1986	James Baker & Company	$14.9 Mil (e)	$1,000/ 100	p	Local Rep
Bankers National Series Trust *BNL Common Stock Portfolio* 44 U.S. Hwy. 46 Pine Brook, NJ 07058 201/808-9596 800/888-4918	1983	Conseco Capital Management, Inc.	$12.0 Mil	Not Applicable	n	Insur

*Key: i=initial sales charge   r=redemption fee or contingent deferred sales charge(CDSC)
t=12b-1 fee and either CDSC or redemption fee   p=12b-1 fee   n=none of the preceding fees   N/A=not available

130

Growth

Fund	Year Began	Investment Adviser	9/30/89 Assets	Minimum Initial and Subsequent Investment	Fees*	Where to Buy Shares
Boston Company Fund *Capital Appreciation Fund* One Boston Place Boston, MA 02019 617/956-9740 800/225-5267 800/343-6324	1947	Boston Company Advisors, Inc.	$639.4 Mil	$1,000/ 0	p	Fund
Boston Company Fund *Special Growth Fund* One Boston Place Boston, MA 02019 617/956-9740 800/225-5267 800/343-6324	1982	Boston Company Advisors, Inc.	$49.0 Mil	$1,000/ 0	p	Fund
Boston Company Index and Blue Chip Trust *Equity Index Fund* One Boston Place Boston, MA 02108 617/451-2010 800/225-5267	1988	Boston Company Advisors, Inc.	$0.4 Mil	$1,000/ 0	p	Fund
Boston Company Index and Blue Chip Trust *Small Capitalization Equity Index Fund* One Boston Place Boston, MA 02108 617/451-2010 800/225-5267	1988	Boston Company Advisors, Inc.	$1.5 Mil	$1,000/ 0	p	Fund
Bull & Bear Capital Growth Fund, Inc. 11 Hanover Sq. New York, NY 10005 212/785-0900 800/847-4200	1959	Bull & Bear Equity Advisers, Inc.	$64.1 Mil (e)	$1,000/ 100	p	Fund
Calvert-Ariel Growth Fund 1700 Pennsylvania Ave., NW Washington, DC 20006 301/951-4820 800/368-2745	1986	Ariel Capital Management, Inc.	$141.6 Mil	$2,000/ 250	i, p	Local Rep
Calvert Fund *Equity Portfolio* 1700 Pennsylvania Ave., NW Washington, DC 20006 301/951-4820 800/368-2745	1982	Calvert Asset Management Company, Inc.	$8.3 Mil	$2,000/ 250	p	Fund

Growth

Fund	Year Began	Investment Adviser	9/30/89 Assets	Minimum Initial and Subsequent Investment	Fees*	Where to Buy Shares
Calvert Fund *Washington Area Growth Fund* 1700 Pennsylvania Ave., NW Washington, DC 20006 301/951-4820 800/368-2745	1985	Calvert Asset Management Company, Inc.	$21.5 Mil	$2,000/ 250	t	Local Rep
Calvert Social Investment Fund *Equity Portfolio* 1700 Pennsylvania Ave., NW Washington, DC 20006 301/951-4820 800/368-2745	1987	Calvert Asset Management Company, Inc.	$8.0 Mil	$1,000/ 250	i, p	Local Rep
Capital Supervisors Helios Fund, Inc. 20 N. Clark St. Ste. 700 Chicago, IL 60602 312/236-8271	1983	Capital Supervisors, Inc.	$38.0 Mil	$2,500/ 500	n	Local Rep
Capstone Equity Series, Inc. *Capstone EquityGuard Stock Fund* 1100 Milan St., Ste. 3500 P.O. Box 3167 Houston, TX 77253-3167 713/750-8000, 800/262-6631	1988	Skye Investment Advisors, Inc.	$3.9 Mil	$200/ 0	i	Local Rep
Cardinal Fund, Inc. 155 E. Broad St. Columbus, OH 43215 614/464-5511 800/848-7734 800/262-9446 OH only	1966	Ohio Company	$175.1 Mil (e)	$250/ 50	i	Local Rep
Carnegie-Cappiello Trust *Growth Series* 1100 The Halle Bldg. 1228 Euclid Ave. Cleveland, OH 44115-1831 216/781-4440 800/321-2322	1984	Carnegie Capital Management Company	$74.4 Mil	$1,000/ 250	i, p	Local Rep
Cashman Farrell Value Fund, Inc. 1100 Milan St., Ste. 3500 P.O. Box 3167 Houston, TX 77253-3167 713/750-8000 800/262-6631	1986	Cashman Farrell & Associates	$11.3 Mil	$200/ 0	i	Local Rep

*Key: i=initial sales charge   r=redemption fee or contingent deferred sales charge(CDSC)
t=12b-1 fee and either CDSC or redemption fee   p=12b-1 fee   n=none of the preceding fees   N/A=not available

Growth

Fund	Year Began	Investment Adviser	9/30/89 Assets	Minimum Initial and Subsequent Investment	Fees*	Where to Buy Shares
Chubb America Fund, Inc. *World Growth Stock Portfolio* One Granite Place Concord, NH 03301 603/224-7741	1985	Chubb Investment Advisory Corporation	$11.2 Mil (e)	Not Applicable	n	Insur
Chubb Investment Funds, Inc. *Chubb Growth Fund* One Granite Place Concord, NH 03301 603/224-7741	1987	Chubb Asset Managers, Inc.	N/A	$1,000/ 100	i, p	Local Rep
CIGNA Annuity Fund *Equity Fund* CIGNA Corporation Hartford, CT 06152 203/726-6000 800/562-4462	1982	CIGNA Investments, Inc.	$54.7 Mil	Not Applicable	n	Insur
CIGNA Growth Fund One Financial Plaza Springfield, MA 01103 413/784-0100 800/56CIGNA	1968	CIGNA Investments, Inc.	$193.8 Mil	$500/ 50	i, p	Local Rep
CIGNA Variable Products Group *Companion Fund* One Financial Plaza Springfield, MA 01103 413/784-0100 800/56CIGNA	1968	CIGNA Investments, Inc.	$71.7 Mil	Not Applicable	n	Insur
Clipper Fund, Inc. 9601 Wilshire Blvd. Ste. 828 Beverly Hills, CA 90210 213/278-5033	1984	Pacific Financial Research	$103.6 Mil (e)	$25,000/ 1,000	r	Fund
Collective Investment Trust for Citibank IRAs *Equity Portfolio* 153 E. 53rd St. 4th Fl. New York, NY 10043 212/559-4677 800/CITI-IRA	1983	Citibank N.A.	$154.9 Mil	$250/ 0	n	Fund

*Key: i=initial sales charge   r=redemption fee or contingent deferred sales charge(CDSC)
t=12b-1 fee and either CDSC or redemption fee   p=12b-1 fee   n=none of the preceding fees   N/A=not available

Growth

Fund	Year Began	Investment Adviser	9/30/89 Assets	Minimum Initial and Subsequent Investment	Fees*	Where to Buy Shares
Collective Investment Trust for Seafirst Retirement Accounts *Blue Chip Fund (The)* 701 Fifth Ave. P.O. Box 84248 Seattle, WA 98124 206/358-6119, 800/323-9919	1988	Seattle-First National Bank	$5.1 Mil (e)	$500/ 0	n	Fund
Colonial Growth Shares Trust One Financial Ctr. Boston, MA 02111 617/426-3750 800/225-2365 800/426-3750	1959	Colonial Management Associates, Inc.	$120.7 Mil	$250/ 25	i	Local Rep
Columbia Growth Fund, Inc. 1301 SW 5th Ave. P.O. Box 1350 Portland, OR 97207 503/222-3600 800/547-1707	1967	Columbia Funds Management Company	$263.9 Mil	$1,000/ 100	n	Fund
Common Sense Trust *Common Sense Growth Fund* 2800 Post Oak Blvd. Houston, TX 77056 713/993-0500 800/421-5666	1987	Common Sense Investment Advisers	$773.9 Mil	$250/ 25	i	Local Rep
Compass Capital Group *Growth Fund* 1900 E. Dublin-Granville Rd. Columbus, OH 43229 614/899-4600 800/338-4385	1988	Midlantic National Bank	N/A	$2,500/ 100	N/A	Fund
Composite Deferred Series, Inc. *Growth Portfolio* W. 601 Riverside, 9th Fl. Seafirst Financial Ctr. Spokane, WA 99201 509/353-3400 800/543-8072, 800/572-5828	1987	Composite Research & Management Company	$1.8 Mil	Not Applicable	r	Insur
Connecticut Mutual Financial Services Series Fund I, Inc. *Growth Portfolio* 140 Garden St. Hartford, CT 06154 203/727-6500 800/243-0018	1982	G.R. Phelps & Company, Inc.	$53.5 Mil	Not Applicable	r	Insur

*Key: i=initial sales charge   r=redemption fee or contingent deferred sales charge(CDSC)
t=12b-1 fee and either CDSC or redemption fee   p=12b-1 fee   n=none of the preceding fees   N/A=not available

Growth

Fund	Year Began	Investment Adviser	9/30/89 Assets	Minimum Initial and Subsequent Investment	Fees*	Where to Buy Shares
Connecticut Mutual Investment Accounts, Inc. *Connecticut Mutual Growth Account* 140 Garden St. Hartford, CT 06154 203/727-6500 800/243-0018	1985	G.R. Phelps & Company, Inc.	$36.7 Mil	$1,000/ 50	i	Local Rep
Counsellors Capital Appreciation Fund 466 Lexington Ave. New York, NY 10017-3147 212/878-0600 800/888-6878	1987	Warburg, Pincus Counsellors, Inc.	$61.1 Mil	$25,000/ 5,000	n	Fund
Country Capital Growth Fund, Inc. 1701 Towanda Ave. Bloomington, IL 61701 309/557-2444 800/322-3838 IL Only	1966	Country Capital Management Company	$78.9 Mil	$1,000/ 25	i	Local Rep
Cumberland Growth Fund, Inc. 614 Landis Ave. P.O. Box 663 Vineland, NJ 08360 609/692-6690 800/257-7013 800/232-6692 NJ Only	1960	Cumberland Advisors, Pty.	$2.4 Mil	$1,000/ 0	n	Fund
Dean Witter American Value Fund Two World Trade Ctr. New York, NY 10048 212/392-2550 800/869-3863	1980	Dean Witter Reynolds Inc. - InterCapital Division	$100.2 Mil	$1,000/ 100	t	Local Rep
Dean Witter Natural Resource Development Securities Inc. Two World Trade Ctr. New York, NY 10048 212/392-2550 800/869-3863	1981	Dean Witter Reynolds Inc. - InterCapital Division	$141.7 Mil	$1,000/ 100	t	Local Rep
Dean Witter Variable Investment Series *Equity Portfolio* Two World Trade Ctr. New York, NY 10048 212/392-2550 800/869-3863	1984	Dean Witter Reynolds Inc. - InterCapital Division	$50.5 Mil	Not Applicable	n	Insur

*Key: i=initial sales charge   r=redemption fee or contingent deferred sales charge(CDSC)
    t=12b-1 fee and either CDSC or redemption fee   p=12b-1 fee   n=none of the preceding fees   N/A=not available

Growth

Fund	Year Began	Investment Adviser	9/30/89 Assets	Minimum Initial and Subsequent Investment	Fees*	Where to Buy Shares
Delaware Group DelCap Fund *Concept I Series* One Commerce Sq. Philadelphia, PA 19103 215/988-1200 800/523-4640	1986	Delaware Management Company, Inc.	$138.6 Mil	$1,000/ 25	i, p	Local Rep
Dividend/Growth Fund, Inc. *Growth Series* 107 N. Adams St. Rockville, MD 20850 301/251-1002 800/638-2042	1983	American Investment Managers, Inc.	$0.06 Mil (e)	$1,000/ 100	n	Local Rep
Dreman Mutual Group, Inc. *Dreman Contrarian Portfolio (The)* 10 Exchange Place Jersey City, NJ 07302 201/332-8228 800/533-1608	1988	Dreman Value Management, Inc.	$9.2 Mil	$5,000/ 1,000	p	Local Rep
Dreyfus Growth Opportunity Fund, Inc. 666 Old Country Rd. Garden City, NY 11530 718/895-1206 800/645-6561	1972	Dreyfus Corporation	$557.9 Mil	$2,500/ 100	n	Fund
Dreyfus New Leaders Fund, Inc. 666 Old Country Rd. Garden City, NY 11530 718/895-1206 800/645-6561	1985	Dreyfus Corporation	$198.2 Mil	$2,500/ 100	p	Fund
Dreyfus Third Century Fund, Inc. 666 Old Country Rd. Garden City, NY 11530 718/895-1206 800/645-6561	1972	Dreyfus Corporation	$175.0 Mil	$2,500/ 100	n	Fund
Eaton Vance Growth Fund 24 Federal St. Boston, MA 02110 617/482-8260 800/225-6265	1954	Eaton Vance Management, Inc.	$92.1 Mil	$1,000/ 50	i, p	Local Rep

*Key: i=initial sales charge   r=redemption fee or contingent deferred sales charge(CDSC)
t=12b-1 fee and either CDSC or redemption fee   p=12b-1 fee   n=none of the preceding fees   N/A=not available

Growth

Fund	Year Began	Investment Adviser	9/30/89 Assets	Minimum Initial and Subsequent Investment	Fees*	Where to Buy Shares
Eaton Vance Natural Resources Trust 24 Federal St. Boston, MA 02110 617/482-8260 800/225-6265	1987	Eaton Vance Management, Inc.	$3.0 Mil	$1,000/ 50	t	Local Rep
Eaton Vance Special Equities Fund 24 Federal St. Boston, MA 02110 617/482-8260 800/225-6265	1968	Eaton Vance Management, Inc.	$55.3 Mil	$1,000/ 50	i, p	Local Rep
Enterprise Equity Portfolios *Enterprise Growth Portfolio* 1200 Ashwood Pkwy. Ste. 290 Atlanta, GA 30338 404/396-8118 800/432-4320	1968	Enterprise Capital Management, Inc.	$45.0 Mil (e)	$500/ 25	t	Local Rep
Equitable Funds *Equitable Growth Fund (The)* 1755 Broadway 3rd Fl. New York, NY 10019 212/641-8100	1987	Equitable Capital Management Corporation	N/A	$1,000/ 100	t	Local Rep
Excel Value Fund, Inc. 16955 Via Del Campo Ste. 200 San Diego, CA 92127 619/485-9400 800/333-9235	1982	Excel Advisors, Inc.	$3.6 Mil (e)	$2,000/ 250	i, p	Local Rep
Fasciano Fund, Inc. 190 S. LaSalle St. Ste. 2800 Chicago, IL 60603 312/444-6050	1988	Fasciano Company, Inc.	N/A	$2,000/ 100	n	Fund
FBL Series Fund, Inc. *Blue Chip Portfolio* 5400 University Ave. W. Des Moines, IA 50265 515/225-5400 800/247-4170 800/422-3175 IA Only	1987	FBL Investment Advisory Services, Inc.	$2.2 Mil	$250/ 0	t	Local Rep

*Key: i=initial sales charge   r=redemption fee or contingent deferred sales charge(CDSC)
t=12b-1 fee and either CDSC or redemption fee   p=12b-1 fee   n=none of the preceding fees   N/A=not available

Growth

Fund	Year Began	Investment Adviser	9/30/89 Assets	Minimum Initial and Subsequent Investment	Fees*	Where to Buy Shares
FFB Funds Trust *FFB Equity Fund* 230 Park Ave. 12th Fl. New York, NY 10169 212/309-8400 800/845-8406	1986	First Fidelity Bank, N.A.	$1.8 Mil (e)	$1,000/ 100	p	Local Rep
Fidelity Capital Trust *Fidelity Value Fund* 82 Devonshire St. Boston, MA 02109 617/570-7000 800/544-6666	1978	Fidelity Management & Research Company	$152.2 Mil	$1,000/ 250	n	Fund
Fidelity Contrafund 82 Devonshire St. Boston, MA 02109 617/570-7000 800/544-6666 617/523-1919 MA Only	1961	Fidelity Management & Research Company	$308.6 Mil	$1,000/ 250	n	Fund
Fidelity Destiny Portfolios *Destiny I* 82 Devonshire St. Boston, MA 02109 617/570-7000 800/544-6666	1970	Fidelity Management & Research Company	$1.8 Bil	$50/ 25	i	Local Rep
Fidelity Destiny Portfolios *Destiny II* 82 Devonshire St. Boston, MA 02109 617/570-7000 800/544-6666	1985	Fidelity Management & Research Company	$169.0 Mil	$50/ 25	i	Local Rep
Fidelity Securities Fund *Fidelity Blue Chip Growth Fund* 82 Devonshire St. Boston, MA 02109 617/570-7000 800/544-6666	1987	Fidelity Management & Research Company	$58.5 Mil	$2,500/ 250	i	Fund
Fidelity Select Portfolios *Environmental Services Portfolio* 82 Devonshire St. Boston, MA 02109 617/570-7000 800/544-6666	1989	Fidelity Management & Research Company	N/A	$1,000/ 250	N/A	Fund

*Key: i=initial sales charge   r=redemption fee or contingent deferred sales charge(CDSC)
t=12b-1 fee and either CDSC or redemption fee   p=12b-1 fee   n=none of the preceding fees   N/A=not available

Growth

Fund	Year Began	Investment Adviser	9/30/89 Assets	Minimum Initial and Subsequent Investment	Fees*	Where to Buy Shares
Fidelity Trend Fund 82 Devonshire St. Boston, MA 02109 617/570-7000 800/544-6666 617/523-1919 MA Only	1957	Fidelity Management & Research Company	$926.5 Mil	$1,000/ 250	n	Fund
Financial Horizons Investment Trust *Growth Fund* One Nationwide Plaza P.O. Box 182008 Columbus, OH 43218 800/533-5622	1988	Nationwide Financial Services, Inc.	$0.6 Mil	$1,000/ 100	t	Local Rep
Financial Independence Trust *Growth Fund* 700 Dixie Terminal Bldg. Cincinnati, OH 45202 513/629-2000 800/543-8721 800/582-7396 OH Only	1983	Financial Independence Trust Advisers, Inc.	$10.1 Mil	$1,000/ 0	i, p	Local Rep
First Eagle Fund of America, Inc. 45 Broadway New York, NY 10006 212/943-9200 800/451-3623	1987	Arnhold and S. Bleich-roeder, Inc.	$87.1 Mil	$25,000/ 1,000	r	Fund
First Investors Life Series Fund *Growth Series* 120 Wall St. New York, NY 10005 212/208-6000	1986	First Investors Management Company, Inc.	$0.3 Mil	Not Applicable	n	Insur
First Investors Value Fund, Inc. 120 Wall St. New York, NY 10005 212/208-6000	1983	First Investors Management Company, Inc.	$5.8 Mil	$200/ 50	i	Local Rep
Flex-Funds *Growth Fund (The)* 6000 Memorial Dr. P.O. Box 7177 Dublin, OH 43017 614/766-7000 800/325-FLEX	1985	R. Meeder & Associates, Inc.	$34.3 Mil	$2,500/ 100	p	Fund

*Key: i=initial sales charge   r=redemption fee or contingent deferred sales charge(CDSC)
       t=12b-1 fee and either CDSC or redemption fee   p=12b-1 fee   n=none of the preceding fees   N/A=not available

Growth

Fund	Year Began	Investment Adviser	9/30/89 Assets	Minimum Initial and Subsequent Investment	Fees*	Where to Buy Shares
Flex-Funds *Muirfield Fund (The)* 6000 Memorial Dr. P.O. Box 7177 Dublin, OH 43017 614/766-7000 800/325-FLEX	1988	R. Meeder & Associates, Inc.	$28.4 Mil	$2,500/ 100	p	Local Rep
FPA Capital Fund, Inc. 10301 W. Pico Blvd. Los Angeles, CA 90064 213/277-4900 800/421-4374	1968	First Pacific Advisors, Inc.	$82.1 Mil	$100/ 25	i	Local Rep
Franklin Custodian Funds, Inc. *Growth Series* 777 Mariners Island Blvd. San Mateo, CA 94404 415/570-3000 800/632-2180 800/632-2350	1948	Franklin Advisers, Inc.	$134.5 Mil	$100/ 25	i	Local Rep
Franklin Equity Fund 777 Mariners Island Blvd. San Mateo, CA 94404 415/570-3000 800/632-2180 800/632-2350	1933	Franklin Advisers, Inc.	$425.8 Mil	$100/ 25	i	Local Rep
Franklin Managed Trust *Franklin Rising Dividends Portfolio* 777 Mariners Island Blvd. San Mateo, CA 94404 415/570-3000 800/632-2180 800/632-2350	1987	Franklin Advisers, Inc.	$40.8 Mil	$100/ 25	i, p	Local Rep
Franklin Pennsylvania Investors Fund *Equity Portfolio* 777 Mariners Island Blvd. San Mateo, CA 94404 415/570-3000 800/632-2180 800/632-2350	1986	Franklin Advisers, Inc.	$0.5 Mil	$100/ 25	i	Local Rep
Frank Russell Investment Company *Equity II* 909 A St. Tacoma, WA 98402 206/627-7001 800/972-0700	1981	Frank Russell Investment Management Company	$70.4 Mil	$0/ 0	n	Local Rep

*Key: i=initial sales charge   r=redemption fee or contingent deferred sales charge(CDSC)
t=12b-1 fee and either CDSC or redemption fee   p=12b-1 fee   n=none of the preceding fees   N/A=not available

Growth

Fund	Year Began	Investment Adviser	9/30/89 Assets	Minimum Initial and Subsequent Investment	Fees*	Where to Buy Shares
Frank Russell Investment Company *Special Growth* 909 A St. Tacoma, WA 98402 206/627-7001 800/972-0700	1985	Frank Russell Investment Management Company	$61.8 Mil	$0/ 0	n	Local Rep
Freedom Investment Trust *Freedom Equity Value Fund* One Beacon St. Boston, MA 02108 617/523-3170 800/225-6258 800/392-6037 MA Only	1987	Freedom Capital Management Corporation	$25.2 Mil	$1,000/ 100	t	Local Rep
Freedom Investment Trust *Freedom Regional Bank Fund* One Beacon St. Boston, MA 02108 617/523-3170 800/225-6258 800/392-6037 MA Only	1985	Freedom Capital Management Corporation	$81.0 Mil	$1,000/ 100	t	Local Rep
Freedom Investment Trust III *Freedom Environmental Fund* One Beacon St. Boston, MA 02108 617/523-3170 800/225-6258 800/392-6037 MA Only	1989	Freedom Capital Management Corporation	N/A	$1,000/ 100	N/A	Local Rep
Gabelli Asset Fund Grand Central Station P.O. Box 1634 New York, NY 10163 212/490-3670 800/422-3554	1986	Gabelli Funds, Inc.	$291.6 Mil (e)	$25,000/ 0	p	Fund
Gabelli Growth Fund Grand Central Station P.O. Box 1634 New York, NY 10163 212/490-3670 800/422-3554	1987	Gabelli Funds, Inc.	$51.6 Mil (e)	$1,000/ 0	t	Fund
Gateway Trust *Gateway Growth Plus Fund* P.O. Box 458167 Cincinnati, OH 45245 513/248-2700 800/354-6339	1986	Gateway Investment Advisers, Inc.	$7.7 Mil (e)	$500/ 100	n	Fund

*Key: i=initial sales charge   r=redemption fee or contingent deferred sales charge(CDSC) t=12b-1 fee and either CDSC or redemption fee   p=12b-1 fee   n=none of the preceding fees   N/A=not available

Growth

Fund	Year Began	Investment Adviser	9/30/89 Assets	Minimum Initial and Subsequent Investment	Fees*	Where to Buy Shares
General Securities Incorporated 701 4th Ave. South 10th Fl. Minneapolis, MN 55415-1655 612/332-1212 800/331-4923	1951	Craig-Hallum, Inc.	$18.5 Mil (e)	$100/ 10	r	Fund
GIT Equity Trust *GIT Equity Select Growth Portfolio* 1655 Fort Myer Dr. Arlington, VA 22209 703/528-6500 800/336-3063	1983	Bankers Finance Investment Management Corp.	$3.2 Mil	$1,000/ 0	n	Fund
Gradison Growth Trust *Established Growth Fund* 580 Walnut St. Cincinnati, OH 45202-3198 513/579-5700 800/869-5999	1983	Gradison & Company, Inc.	$126.1 Mil	$1,000/ 50	p	Local Rep
Greenspring Fund, Incorporated The Quadrangle, Ste. 322 Village of Cross Keys Baltimore, MD 21210 301/435-9000	1983	Key Equity Management Corporation	$28.6 Mil (e)	$1,000/ 250	n	Fund
Growth Fund of America, Inc. Four Embarcadero Ctr. P.O. Box 7650 San Francisco, CA 94120-7650 415/421-9360 800/421-0180	1959	Capital Research & Management Company	$1.7 Bil	$1,000/ 50	i, t	Local Rep
Growth Fund of Washington, Inc. (The) 1101 Vermont Ave., NW Washington, DC 20005 202/842-5665 800/972-9274	1985	GEICO Investment Services Company	$61.9 Mil	$1,000/ 500	i, p	Local Rep
Growth Industry Shares, Inc. 135 S. LaSalle St. Chicago, IL 60603 312/236-1600 800/635-2886	1946	William Blair & Company	$63.9 Mil (e)	$1,000/ 250	n	Fund

*Key: i=initial sales charge   r=redemption fee or contingent deferred sales charge(CDSC)
t=12b-1 fee and either CDSC or redemption fee   p=12b-1 fee   n=none of the preceding fees   N/A=not available

Growth

Fund	Year Began	Investment Adviser	9/30/89 Assets	Minimum Initial and Subsequent Investment	Fees*	Where to Buy Shares
G.T. Global Growth Series *G.T. America Growth Fund* 50 California St. 27th Fl. San Francisco, CA 94111 415/392-6181 800/824-1580	1987	G.T. Capital Management Inc.	$3.4 Mil (e)	$500/ 100	i, p	Local Rep
G.T. Global Health Care Fund 50 California St. 27th Fl. San Francisco, CA 94111 415/392-6181 800/824-1580	1989	G.T. Capital Management Inc.	N/A	$500/ 100	N/A	Local Rep
Guardian Park Ave. Fund 201 Park Ave. S. New York, NY 10003 212/598-8259 800/221-3253	1972	Guardian Investor Services Corporation	$229.6 Mil	$1,000/ 100	i	Local Rep
Harbor Fund *Harbor Growth Fund* One SeaGate Toledo, OH 43666 419/247-2477 800/422-1050	1986	Harbor Capital Advisors, Inc.	$146.6 Mil	$2,000/ 500	n	Fund
Hartwell Growth Fund, Inc. c/o Furman Selz 230 Park Ave. New York, NY 10169 212/309-8400 800/624-FUND	1966	Hartwell Management Company, Inc.	$19.5 Mil	$2,000/ 100	i	Local Rep
Harvest Funds, Inc. *Growth Portfolio* 4000 Park Rd. Charlotte, NC 28209 704/523-9407 800/366-2277	1987	Bass Capital Management	$17.9 Mil (e)	$1,000/ 50	i, p	Local Rep
Heartland Group *Heartland Value Fund* 790 N. Milwaukee St. Milwaukee, WI 53202 414/347-7276 800/432-7856	1984	Heartland Advisors, Inc.	$34.9 Mil	$1,000/ 100	i, p	Local Rep

*Key: i=initial sales charge   r=redemption fee or contingent deferred sales charge(CDSC)
t=12b-1 fee and either CDSC or redemption fee   p=12b-1 fee   n=none of the preceding fees   N/A=not available

143

Growth

Fund	Year Began	Investment Adviser	9/30/89 Assets	Minimum Initial and Subsequent Investment	Fees*	Where to Buy Shares
Helmsman Fund *Growth Equity Portfolio* 1900 E. Dublin-Granville Rd. Columbus, OH 43229 614/899-4600 800/338-4385	1989	Bank One, Indianapolis, N.A. Bank One, Milwaukee, N.A.	N/A	$2,500/ 0	N/A	Fund
Heritage Capital Appreciation Trust 880 Carillon Pkwy. St. Petersburg, FL 33716 813/573-3800	1985	Heritage Asset Management, Inc.	$63.1 Mil	$1,000/ 100	i, p	Local Rep
Highmark Group *Special Growth Fund* 1900 E. Dublin-Granville Rd. Columbus, OH 43229 614/899-4600 800/338-4385	1987	Merus Capital Management	N/A	$1,000/ 100	N/A	Fund
Home Life Equity Fund, Inc. One Centennial Plaza Piscataway, NJ 08854 212/428-2000	1971	Home Life Insurance Company	$42.6 Mil	Not Applicable	n	Insur
Horace Mann Growth Fund, Inc. P.O. Box 4657 Springfield, IL 62708-4657 217/789-2500	1957	CIGNA Investments, Inc.	$102.2 Mil	Not Applicable	r	Insur
HVA Stock Fund, Inc. 200 Hopmeadow St. P.O. Box 2999 Hartford, CT 06104-2999 203/843-8245 800/227-1371	1976	Hartford Investment Management Company, Inc. Wellington Management Company	$252.1 Mil	Not Applicable	n	Insur
IAI Regional Fund, Inc. 1100 Dain Twr. P.O. Box 357 Minneapolis, MN 55440 612/371-7780	1980	Investment Advisers, Inc.	$119.5 Mil	$5,000/ 1,000	n	Local Rep

*Key: i=initial sales charge   r=redemption fee or contingent deferred sales charge(CDSC)
       t=12b-1 fee and either CDSC or redemption fee   p=12b-1 fee   n=none of the preceding fees   N/A=not available

Growth

Fund	Year Began	Investment Adviser	9/30/89 Assets	Minimum Initial and Subsequent Investment	Fees*	Where to Buy Shares
IDEX Fund 201 Highland Ave. Largo, FL 34640 813/585-6565 800/237-3055 800/782-7152 FL Only	1985	IDEX Management, Inc.	$91.3 Mil	$25/ 25	i	Local Rep
IDEX Fund 3 201 Highland Ave. Largo, FL 34640 813/585-6565 800/237-3055 800/782-7152 FL Only	1987	IDEX Management, Inc.	$99.1 Mil	$50/ 50	i	Local Rep
IDEX II 201 Highland Ave. Largo, FL 34640 813/585-6565 800/237-3055 800/782-7152 FL Only	1986	IDEX Management, Inc.	$89.7 Mil	$50/ 50	i	Local Rep
IDS Growth Fund, Inc. IDS Tower 10 Minneapolis, MN 55440 612/372-3131 800/328-8300	1972	IDS Financial Corporation	$719.3 Mil	$100/ 100	i, p	Local Rep
IDS Life Capital Resource Fund, Inc. IDS Tower 10 Minneapolis, MN 55440 612/372-3131 800/328-8300	1981	IDS Financial Corporation	$658.0 Mil	Not Applicable	r	Insur
IDS New Dimensions Fund, Inc. IDS Tower 10 Minneapolis, MN 55440 612/372-3131 800/328-8300	1968	IDS Financial Corporation	$761.4 Mil	$100/ 100	i, p	Local Rep
Imperial Portfolios, Inc. ***S&P 100 Portfolio (The)*** 9275 Sky Park Ct. P.O. Box 82997 San Diego, CA 92138 619/292-2379 800/347-5588	1988	First Imperial Advisors, Inc.	N/A	$1,000/ 100	N/A	Local Rep

*Key: i=initial sales charge   r=redemption fee or contingent deferred sales charge(CDSC)
t=12b-1 fee and either CDSC or redemption fee   p=12b-1 fee   n=none of the preceding fees   N/A=not available

Growth

Fund	Year Began	Investment Adviser	9/30/89 Assets	Minimum Initial and Subsequent Investment	Fees*	Where to Buy Shares
Industrial Series Trust *Mackenzie American Fund* 1200 N. Federal Hwy. #200 Boca Raton, FL 33432 407/393-8900 800/456-5111	1985	Mackenzie Financial Corporation	$44.0 Mil (e)	$250/ 50	i	Local Rep
Integrated Capital Appreciation Fund, Inc. 10 Union Square East New York, NY 10003 212/353-7000 800/858-8850	1985	Integrated Resources Asset Management Corp.	$202.3 Mil	$500/ 100	t	Local Rep
Integrated Equity Portfolios *Growth Portfolio* 10 Union Square East New York, NY 10003 212/353-7000 800/858-8850	1987	Integrated Resources Asset Management Corp.	$49.9 Mil	$1,000/ 100	i, p	Local Rep
Integrated Multi-Asset Portfolios, Inc. *Vantage Asset Allocation Fund* 10 Union Square East New York, NY 10003 212/353-7000 800/858-8850	1989	Integrated Resources Asset Management Corp.	$2.2 Mil	$1,000/ 100	i	Local Rep
Integrated Resources Series Trust *Growth Portfolio* One Bridge Plaza Fort Lee, NJ 07024 201/461-0606 800/821-5100	1984	Integrated Resources Asset Management Corp.	$177.7 Mil	Not Applicable	n	Insur
Investment Portfolios *Equity Portfolio* 120 S. LaSalle St. Chicago, IL 60603 312/781-1121 800/621-1148	1984	Kemper Financial Services, Inc.	$307.3 Mil	$250/ 50	t	Local Rep
ISI Growth Fund, Inc. 3801 Kennett Pk., C-200 Greenville Ctr. Wilmington, DE 19807 302/652-3091 800/441-9490	1968	Sigma Management, Inc.	$10.3 Mil	$0/ 0	i	Local Rep

*Key: i=initial sales charge   r=redemption fee or contingent deferred sales charge(CDSC)
t=12b-1 fee and either CDSC or redemption fee   p=12b-1 fee   n=none of the preceding fees   N/A=not available

146

Growth

Fund	Year Began	Investment Adviser	9/30/89 Assets	Minimum Initial and Subsequent Investment	Fees*	Where to Buy Shares
Ivy Fund *Ivy Growth Fund* 40 Industrial Park Rd. Hingham, MA 02043 617/749-1416 800/235-3322	1962	Ivy Management, Inc.	$203.6 Mil	$1,000/ 0	n	Fund
Ivy Fund *Ivy Institutional Investors Fund* 40 Industrial Park Rd. Hingham, MA 02043 617/749-1416 800/235-3322	1984	Ivy Management, Inc.	$26.6 Mil	$1,000/ 0	n	Fund
Janus Fund P.O. Box 44339 Denver, CO 80201-4339 303/333-3863 800/525-3713	1969	Janus Capital Corporation	$695.5 Mil	$1,000/ 50	n	Fund
Janus Twenty Fund P.O. Box 44339 Denver, CO 80201-4339 303/333-3863 800/525-3713	1985	Janus Capital Corporation	$68.7 Mil	$1,000/ 50	n	Fund
John Hancock Growth Trust 101 Huntington Ave. Boston, MA 02199-7603 617/375-1500 800/225-5291	1968	John Hancock Advisers, Inc.	$122.1 Mil	$500/ 25	i	Local Rep
Kemper Growth Fund 120 S. LaSalle St. Chicago, IL 60603 312/781-1121 800/621-1148	1966	Kemper Financial Services, Inc.	$336.1 Mil	$1,000/ 100	i	Local Rep
Kemper Technology Fund 120 S. LaSalle St. Chicago, IL 60603 312/781-1121 800/621-1148	1948	Kemper Financial Services, Inc.	$544.3 Mil	$1,000/ 100	i	Local Rep

*Key: i=initial sales charge   r=redemption fee or contingent deferred sales charge(CDSC)
t=12b-1 fee and either CDSC or redemption fee   p=12b-1 fee   n=none of the preceding fees   N/A=not available

147

Growth

Fund	Year Began	Investment Adviser	9/30/89 Assets	Minimum Initial and Subsequent Investment	Fees*	Where to Buy Shares
Keystone Custodian Funds, Inc. K-2 Series 99 High St. Boston, MA 02110 617/338-3200 800/343-2898 800/225-1587	1932	Keystone Custodian Funds, Inc.	$373.0 Mil	$250/ 0	t	Local Rep
Keystone Custodian Funds, Inc. S-3 Series 99 High St. Boston, MA 02110 617/338-3200 800/343-2898 800/225-1587	1932	Keystone Custodian Funds, Inc.	$275.9 Mil	$250/ 0	t	Local Rep
Kidder, Peabody MarketGuard Appreciation Fund 20 Exchange Place New York, NY 10005 212/510-5552	1987	Webster Management Corporation	$26.1 Mil	$1,500/ 500	i	Local Rep
LBVIP Series Fund, Inc. *Growth Series* 625 Fourth Ave. South Minneapolis, MN 55415 612/339-8091 800/328-4552 800/752-4208 MN Only	1988	Lutheran Brotherhood Research Corp.	$13.0 Mil	Not Applicable	n	Insur
Legg Mason Value Trust, Inc. 111 S. Calvert St. P.O. Box 1476 Baltimore, MD 21203-1476 30l/539-3400 800/822-5544 800/492-7777 MD Only	1982	Legg Mason Fund Adviser, Inc.	$856.3 Mil	$1,000/ 500	p	Local Rep
Lehman Opportunity Fund, Inc. 55 Water St. 34th Fl. New York, NY 10041 212/668-8578 800/221-5350	1979	Lehman Management Company, Inc.	$120.5 Mil	$1,000/ 100	n	Fund
Lexington Technical Strategy Fund, Inc. Park 80 W., Plaza Two P.O. Box 1515 Saddle Brook, NJ 07662 201/845-7300 800/526-0056	1987	Lexington Management Corporation	$9.0 Mil	$1,000/ 50	i	Local Rep

*Key: i=initial sales charge   r=redemption fee or contingent deferred sales charge(CDSC)
t=12b-1 fee and either CDSC or redemption fee   p=12b-1 fee   n=none of the preceding fees   N/A=not available

148

Growth

Fund	Year Began	Investment Adviser	9/30/89 Assets	Minimum Initial and Subsequent Investment	Fees*	Where to Buy Shares
Life of Virginia Series Fund, Inc. *Common Stock Portfolio* 6610 W. Broad St. Richmond, VA 23230 804/281-6000 800/822-6000	1985	AON Advisors, Inc.	$2.8 Mil (e)	Not Applicable	n	Insur
Loomis-Sayles Capital Development Fund Back Bay Annex P.O. Box 449 Boston, MA 02116 617/578-1333 800/345-4048	1960	Loomis, Sayles & Company, Inc.	$215.5 Mil	$1,000/ 50	n	Fund
Lord Abbett Value Appreciation Fund, Inc. The General Motors Bldg. 767 Fifth Ave. New York, NY 10153 212/848-1800 800/223-4224	1983	Lord, Abbett & Co.	$205.6 Mil	$1,000/ 0	i	Local Rep
L. Roy Papp Stock Fund, Inc. 4400 N. 32nd St. Ste. 280 Phoenix, AZ 85018 602/956-0980	1989	L. Roy Papp & Associates	N/A	$10,000/ 2,000	N/A	Fund
MacKay-Shields MainStay Series Fund *MainStay Value Fund* 51 Madison Ave. New York, NY 10010 212/576-7000 800/522-4202	1986	MacKay-Shields Financial Corporation	$26.9 Mil	$500/ 50	t	Local Rep
Main Street Funds, Inc. *Asset Allocation Fund* 3410 S. Galena St. Denver, CO 80231 303/671-3200 800/548-1225	1988	Oppenheimer Management Corporation	$0.8 Mil	$1,000/ 25	i, p	Local Rep
Management of Managers Group of Funds *Capital Appreciation Fund* 200 Connecticut Ave. 8th Fl. Norwalk, CT 06854 203/855-2200	1984	Evaluation Associates Investment Management Co.	$60.7 Mil	$0/ 0	n	Local Rep

*Key: i=initial sales charge   r=redemption fee or contingent deferred sales charge(CDSC)
t=12b-1 fee and either CDSC or redemption fee   p=12b-1 fee   n=none of the preceding fees   N/A=not available

149

Growth

Fund	Year Began	Investment Adviser	9/30/89 Assets	Minimum Initial and Subsequent Investment	Fees*	Where to Buy Shares
Management of Managers Group of Funds *Core Equity Fund* 200 Connecticut Ave. 8th Fl. Norwalk, CT 06854 203/855-2200	1987	Evaluation Associates Investment Management Co.	$38.1 Mil	$0/ 0	n	Local Rep
Mariner Funds Trust *Mariner Equity Fund* 600 W. Hillsboro Blvd. Ste. 300 Deerfield Beach, FL 33441 305/421-8878 800/634-2536	1986	Marinvest Inc.	$4.5 Mil	$1,000/ 250	p	Local Rep
Massachusetts Capital Development Fund 500 Boylston St. Boston, MA 02116 617/954-5000 800/343-2829	1970	Massachusetts Financial Services Company	$852.2 Mil	$1,000/ 25	i	Local Rep
Massachusetts Investors Growth Stock Fund 500 Boylston St. Boston, MA 02116 617/954-5000 800/343-2829	1932	Massachusetts Financial Services Company	$928.1 Mil	$1,000/ 25	i	Local Rep
MassMutual Integrity Funds *MassMutual Capital Appreciation Fund* 1295 State St. Springfield, MA 01111 413/788-8411 800/542-6767 800/854-9100 MA Only	1988	Massachusetts Mutual Life Insurance Company	$15.0 Mil	$500/ 25	i, p	Local Rep
MBL Growth Fund, Inc. 520 Broad St. Newark, NJ 07101 201/481-8000 800/333-4726	1982	Markston Investment Management	$55.4 Mil	Not Applicable	n	Insur
Meeschaert Capital Accumulation Trust 28 Hill Farm Rd. RFD #2 Box 151 St. Johnsbury, VT 05819 802/748-2400	1960	Meeschaert Investment Management Corp.	$37.6 Mil (e)	$1,000/ 100	p	Local Rep

*Key: i=initial sales charge   r=redemption fee or contingent deferred sales charge(CDSC)
t=12b-1 fee and either CDSC or redemption fee   p=12b-1 fee   n=none of the preceding fees   N/A=not available

Growth

Fund	Year Began	Investment Adviser	9/30/89 Assets	Minimum Initial and Subsequent Investment	Fees*	Where to Buy Shares
Meridian Fund, Inc. 60 E. Sir Francis Drake Blvd. Ste. 306 Larkspur, CA 94939 415/461-6237 800/446-6662 800/445-5553 CA Only	1984	Aster Capital Management, Inc.	$9.9 Mil	$2,000/ 500	n	Fund
Merrill Lynch Fund For Tomorrow, Inc. *Class A* *Class B* P.O. Box 9011 Princeton, NJ 08543-9011 609/282-2800 800/637-3863	 1988 1984	Merrill Lynch Asset Management Inc.	$613.6 Mil	 $500/50 $500/50	 i t	 LRep LRep
Merrill Lynch Natural Resources Trust *Class A* *Class B* P.O. Box 9011 Princeton, NJ 08543-9011 609/282-2800 800/637-3863	 1988 1985	Merrill Lynch Asset Management Inc.	$474.6 Mil	 $500/50 $500/50	 i t	 LRep LRep
Merrill Lynch Series Fund ***Growth Stock Portfolio*** P.O. Box 9011 Princeton, NJ 08543-9011 609/282-2800 800/524-4458	1981	Fund Asset Management, Inc.	$81.1 Mil	Not Applicable	n	Insur
Merrill Lynch Series Fund ***Natural Resources Portfolio*** P.O. Box 9011 Princeton, NJ 08543-9011 609/282-2800 800/524-4458	1987	Fund Asset Management, Inc.	$10.4 Mil	Not Applicable	n	Insur
Merrill Lynch Special Value Fund, Inc. *Class A* *Class B* P.O. Box 9011 Princeton, NJ 08543-9011 609/282-2800 800/637-3863	 1978 1988	Fund Asset Management, Inc.	$77.6 Mil	 $250/50 $250/50	 i t	 LRep LRep
Merrill Lynch Variable Series Funds ***Equity Growth Fund*** P.O. Box 9011 Princeton, NJ 08543-9011 609/282-2800 800/524-4458	1982	Merrill Lynch Asset Management Inc.	$7.2 Mil	Not Applicable	n	Insur

*Key: i=initial sales charge   r=redemption fee or contingent deferred sales charge(CDSC)
      t=12b-1 fee and either CDSC or redemption fee   p=12b-1 fee   n=none of the preceding fees   N/A=not available

Growth

Fund	Year Began	Investment Adviser	9/30/89 Assets	Minimum Initial and Subsequent Investment	Fees*	Where to Buy Shares
Merrill Lynch Variable Series Funds *Natural Resources Focus Fund* P.O. Box 9011 Princeton, NJ 08543-9011 609/282-2800 800/524-4458	1988	Merrill Lynch Asset Management Inc.	$2.5 Mil	Not Applicable	n	Insur
Merriman Investment Trust *Merriman Timed Asset Allocation Fund* 1200 Westlake Ave. North No. 507 Seattle, WA 98109 206/285-8877 800/423-4893	1989	Merriman Investment Management Company	$9.1 Mil	$1,000/ 100	n	Fund
Merriman Investment Trust *Merriman Timed Blue Chip Fund* 1200 Westlake Ave. North No. 507 Seattle, WA 98109 206/285-8877 800/423-4893	1988	Merriman Investment Management Company	$8.7 Mil	$1,000/ 100	n	Fund
Merriman Investment Trust *Merriman Timed Capital Appreciation Fund* 1200 Westlake Ave. North No. 507 Seattle, WA 98109 206/285-8877 800/423-4893	1989	Merriman Investment Management Company	$8.7 Mil	$1,000/ 100	n	Fund
MFS Lifetime Investment Program *Lifetime Capital Growth Trust* 500 Boylston St. Boston, MA 02116 617/954-5000 800/343-2829	1986	Lifetime Advisers, Inc.	$200.0 Mil	$1,000/ 50	t	Local Rep
MFS Lifetime Investment Program *Lifetime Managed Sectors Trust* 500 Boylston St. Boston, MA 02116 617/954-5000 800/343-2829	1986	Lifetime Advisers, Inc.	$183.2 Mil	$1,000/ 50	t	Local Rep
MFS Managed Sectors Trust 500 Boylston St. Boston, MA 02116 617/954-5000 800/343-2829	1986	Massachusetts Financial Services Company	$137.6 Mil	$1,000/ 25	i, p	Local Rep

*Key: i=initial sales charge   r=redemption fee or contingent deferred sales charge(CDSC)
        t=12b-1 fee and either CDSC or redemption fee   p=12b-1 fee   n=none of the preceding fees   N/A=not available

Growth

Fund	Year Began	Investment Adviser	9/30/89 Assets	Minimum Initial and Subsequent Investment	Fees*	Where to Buy Shares
MidAmerica Mutual Fund, Inc. 433 Edgewood Rd., NE Cedar Rapids, IA 52499 319/398-8511 800/553-4287 800/342-4490 IA Only	1959	MidAmerica Management Corporation	$37.1 Mil	$10/ 10	i	Local Rep
MIM Mutual Funds, Inc. *Stock, Convertible & Option Growth Fund* 4500 Rockside Rd. Ste. 440 Independence, OH 44131-6809 216/642-3000 800/233-1240	1986	Mathematical Investing Systems, Inc.	$7.4 Mil	$250/ 50	p	Fund
Monetta Fund, Inc. 1776-B S. Naperville Rd. Ste. 101 Wheaton, IL 60187-8133 312/462-9800	1986	Monetta Financial Services, Inc.	$3.7 Mil	$500/ 100	n	Fund
Monitrend Mutual Fund *S&P 100 Index Series* 272 Closter Dock Rd. Ste. 1 Closter, NJ 07624 201/767-5400 800/251-1970	1987	Monitrend Investment Management, Inc.	$0.5 Mil (e)	$1,000/ 50	i, p	Local Rep
Monitrend Mutual Fund *Value Series* 272 Closter Dock Rd. Ste. 1 Closter, NJ 07624 201/767-5400 800/251-1970	1984	Monitrend Investment Management, Inc.	$12.4 Mil (e)	$1,000/ 50	i, p	Local Rep
MONY Series Fund *Equity Growth Portfolio* 500 Frank W. Burr Blvd. 71-13 Glenpointe Ctr. West Teaneck, NJ 07666 201/907-6669	1985	MONY Life Insurance Company of America	$5.5 Mil	Not Applicable	n	Insur
MONY Variable Account-A 500 Frank W. Burr Blvd. 71-13 Glenpointe Ctr. West Teaneck, NJ 07666 201/907-6669	1969	MONY Advisers, Inc.	$98.9 Mil (e)	Not Applicable	n	Insur

*Key: i=initial sales charge   r=redemption fee or contingent deferred sales charge(CDSC)
t=12b-1 fee and either CDSC or redemption fee   p=12b-1 fee   n=none of the preceding fees   N/A=not available

Growth

Fund	Year Began	Investment Adviser	9/30/89 Assets	Minimum Initial and Subsequent Investment	Fees*	Where to Buy Shares
Morgan Keegan Southern Capital Fund 50 Front St. 21st. Fl. Memphis, TN 38103 901/524-4100 800/238-7127	1986	Southern Capital Advisors, Inc.	$8.1 Mil	$1,000/ 500	i, p	Local Rep
Mutual Benefit Fund 520 Broad St. Newark, NJ 07101 201/481-8000 800/333-4726	1970	Markston Investment Management	$33.6 Mil	$250/ 50	i	Local Rep
Mutual of Omaha Growth Fund, Inc. 10235 Regency Circle Omaha, NE 68114 402/397-8555 800/228-9596	1968	Mutual of Omaha Fund Management Company	$49.6 Mil	$250/ 50	i	Local Rep
NASL Series Trust *Equity Trust* 695 Atlantic Ave. P.O. Box 9064 GMF Boston, MA 02205 617/439-6960 800/344-1029	1985	NASL Financial Services, Inc.	$29.9 Mil	Not Applicable	r	Insur
National Aviation & Technology Corporation 50 Broad St. New York, NY 10004 212/482-8100 800/654-0001	1928	American Fund Advisors, Inc.	$107.5 Mil	$1,000/ 100	i	Local Rep
National Telecommunications & Technology Fund, Inc. 50 Broad St. New York, NY 10004 212/482-8100 800/654-0001	1983	American Fund Advisors, Inc.	$43.3 Mil	$1,000/ 100	i	Local Rep
National Value Fund, Inc. 50 Broad St. New York, NY 10004 212/482-8100 800/654-0001	1986	American Fund Advisors, Inc.	$2.5 Mil	$1,000/ 100	i	Local Rep

*Key: i=initial sales charge   r=redemption fee or contingent deferred sales charge(CDSC)
t=12b-1 fee and either CDSC or redemption fee   p=12b-1 fee   n=none of the preceding fees   N/A=not available

154

Growth

Fund	Year Began	Investment Adviser	9/30/89 Assets	Minimum Initial and Subsequent Investment	Fees*	Where to Buy Shares
Nationwide Investing Foundation *Growth Fund* One Nationwide Plaza Box 1492 Columbus, OH 43216 614/249-7855 800/848-0920, 800/282-1440 OH Only	1961	Nationwide Financial Services, Inc.	$269.2 Mil	$250/ 25	i	Local Rep
Neuberger & Berman Genesis Fund, Inc. 342 Madison Ave. New York, NY 10173 212/850-8300 800/877-9700	1988	Neuberger & Berman Management Incorporated	$20.8 Mil	$1,000/ 100	r	Fund
Neuberger & Berman Manhattan Fund, Inc. 342 Madison Ave. New York, NY 10173 212/850-8300 800/877-9700	1966	Neuberger & Berman Management Incorporated	$432.9 Mil	$1,000/ 100	n	Fund
Neuberger & Berman Partners Fund, Inc. 342 Madison Ave. New York, NY 10173 212/850-8300 800/877-9700	1968	Neuberger & Berman Management Incorporated	$787.2 Mil	$1,000/ 100	n	Fund
Neuberger & Berman Selected Sectors Plus Energy, Inc. 342 Madison Ave. New York, NY 10173 212/850-8300 800/877-9700	1955	Neuberger & Berman Management Incorporated	$441.3 Mil	$1,000/ 100	n	Fund
New Alternatives Fund, Inc. 295 Northern Blvd. Great Neck, NY 11021 516/466-0808	1982	Accrued Equities Inc.	$10.4 Mil	$2,650/ 500	i	Fund
New Economy Fund 333 S. Hope St. Los Angeles, CA 90071 213/486-9200 800/421-0180 213/486-9651 Collect	1983	Capital Research & Management Company	$902.8 Mil	$1,000/ 50	i, t	Local Rep

*Key: i=initial sales charge   r=redemption fee or contingent deferred sales charge(CDSC)
t=12b-1 fee and either CDSC or redemption fee   p=12b-1 fee   n=none of the preceding fees   N/A=not available

Growth

Fund	Year Began	Investment Adviser	9/30/89 Assets	Minimum Initial and Subsequent Investment	Fees*	Where to Buy Shares
New England Growth Fund 399 Boylston St. Boston, MA 02116 617/267-6600 800/343-7104	1968	Loomis, Sayles & Company, Inc.	$579.8 Mil	$1,000/ 25	i, p	Local Rep
New England Zenith Fund ***Stock Index Series*** 501 Boylston St. Boston, MA 02116 617/267-7055 800/634-8025	1987	Back Bay Advisors, Inc.	$15.0 Mil	Not Applicable	n	Insur
Newton Growth Fund, Inc. 330 E. Kilbourn Ave. Ste. 1150 Milwaukee, WI 53202 414/271-0440 800/247-7039 800/242-7229 WI Only	1960	Marshall & Ilsley Investment Management Corporation	$35.2 Mil	$1,000/ 50	n	Fund
North American Security Trust ***Aggressive Asset Allocation Portfolio*** 695 Atlantic Ave. P.O. Box 9064 GMF Boston, MA 02205 617/439-6960, 800/344-1029	1988	NASL Financial Services, Inc.	N/A	$1,000/ 100	i, p	Local Rep
North American Security Trust ***Growth Portfolio*** 695 Atlantic Ave. P.O. Box 9064 GMF Boston, MA 02205 617/439-6960 800/344-1029	1986	NASL Financial Services, Inc.	$32.7 Mil (e)	$1,000/ 100	i, p	Local Rep
Ohio National Fund, Inc. ***Equity Portfolio*** 237 William Howard Taft Cincinnati, OH 45219 513/861-3600	1969	O.N. Investment Management Company	$40.9 Mil	Not Applicable	n	Insur
Omni Investment Fund 53 W. Jackson Blvd. Ste. 818 Chicago, IL 60604 312/922-0431 800/223-9790	1985	Perkins, Wolf, McDonnell & Company	$13.1 Mil	$3,000/ 1,000	n	Fund

*Key: i=initial sales charge   r=redemption fee or contingent deferred sales charge(CDSC)
t=12b-1 fee and either CDSC or redemption fee   p=12b-1 fee   n=none of the preceding fees   N/A=not available

Growth

Fund	Year Began	Investment Adviser	9/30/89 Assets	Minimum Initial and Subsequent Investment	Fees*	Where to Buy Shares
One Hundred Fund, Inc. 899 Logan St. Ste. 211 Denver, CO 80203 303/837-1020 800/333-1001	1966	Berger Associates	$14.0 Mil	$250/ 50	p	Fund
Oppenheimer Blue Chip Fund 3410 S. Galena St. Denver, CO 80231 303/671-3200 800/525-7048	1986	Oppenheimer Management Corporation	$18.2 Mil	$1,000/ 25	i, p	Local Rep
Oppenheimer Fund Two World Trade Ctr. New York, NY 10048-0669 212/323-0200 800/525-7048	1958	Oppenheimer Management Corporation	$217.7 Mil	$1,000/ 25	i	Local Rep
Oppenheimer Ninety-Ten Fund Two World Trade Ctr. New York, NY 10048-0669 212/323-0200 800/525-7048	1985	Oppenheimer Management Corporation	$16.4 Mil	$10,000/ 1,000	i	Local Rep
Oppenheimer Special Fund Two World Trade Ctr. New York, NY 10048-0669 212/323-0200 800/525-7048	1973	Oppenheimer Management Corporation	$570.2 Mil	$1,000/ 25	i	Local Rep
Oppenheimer Variable Account Funds *Oppenheimer Growth Fund* 3410 S. Galena St. Denver, CO 80231 303/671-3200 800/525-7048	1985	Oppenheimer Management Corporation	$18.8 Mil	Not Applicable	n	Insur
Orange County Growth Fund 3151 Airway Ave. Ste. H-1 Costa Mesa, CA 92626 714/957-1217	1988	Newport Securities Corporation	N/A	$2,000/ 100	N/A	Local Rep

*Key: i=initial sales charge   r=redemption fee or contingent deferred sales charge(CDSC)
t=12b-1 fee and either CDSC or redemption fee   p=12b-1 fee   n=none of the preceding fees   N/A=not available

Growth

Fund	Year Began	Investment Adviser	9/30/89 Assets	Minimum Initial and Subsequent Investment	Fees*	Where to Buy Shares
Over-The-Counter Securities Fund 275 Commerce Dr., Ste. 228 P.O. Box 1537 Ft. Washington, PA 19034-1537 215/643-2510 800/523-2578	1956	Review Management Corp.	$326.9 Mil (e)	$500/ 50	i, p	Local Rep
Pacific Investment Management Institutional Trust *Growth Stock Portfolio* 840 Newport Ctr. Dr. Ste. 300 Newport Beach, CA 92660 714/640-3031, 800/443-6915	1987	Pacific Investment Management Company	$2.9 Mil (e)	$200,000/ 10,000	n	Fund
PaineWebber Classic Growth Fund 1285 Avenue of the Americas PaineWebber Bldg. New York, NY 10019 212/713-2000 800/544-9300	1985	Mitchell Hutchins Asset Management Inc.	$62.3 Mil	$1,000/ 100	i, p	Local Rep
PaineWebber Master Series, Inc. *PaineWebber Master Growth Fund* 1285 Avenue of the Americas PaineWebber Bldg. New York, NY 10019 212/713-2000, 800/647-1568	1986	Mitchell Hutchins Asset Management Inc.	$88.7 Mil	$1,000/ 100	t	Local Rep
PaineWebber Series Trust *Growth Portfolio* 1285 Avenue of the Americas PaineWebber Bldg. New York, NY 10019 212/713-2000	1987	Mitchell Hutchins Asset Management Inc.	N/A	Not Applicable	N/A	Insur
Paribas Trust for Institutions *Quantus Equity Managed Portfolio* 787 Seventh Ave. 30th Fl., Equitable Bldg. New York, NY 10019 212/841-3200	1986	Intech/Paribas Asset Management	$7.0 Mil (e)	$5,000/ 2,000	t	Local Rep
Paribas Trust for Institutions *Quantus II* 787 Seventh Ave. 30th Fl., Equitable Bldg. New York, NY 10019 212/841-3200	1986	Intech/Paribas Asset Management	$59.9 Mil (e)	$5.0 Mil/ 10,000	n	Local Rep

*Key: i=initial sales charge   r=redemption fee or contingent deferred sales charge(CDSC)
t=12b-1 fee and either CDSC or redemption fee   p=12b-1 fee   n=none of the preceding fees   N/A=not available

Growth

Fund	Year Began	Investment Adviser	9/30/89 Assets	Minimum Initial and Subsequent Investment	Fees*	Where to Buy Shares
Parnassus Fund 244 California St. San Francisco, CA 94111 415/362-3505 800/999-3505	1985	Parnassus Financial Management	$22.7 Mil	$2,000/ 500	i	Fund
Pasadena Investment Trust *Pasadena Fundamental Value Fund (The)* 600 N. Rosemead Blvd. Pasadena, CA 91107-2101 818/351-4276 800/882-2855	1987	Roger Engemann Management Co., Inc.	$2.6 Mil (e)	$1,000/ 100	n	Fund
Pennsylvania Mutual Fund, Inc. 1414 Avenue of the Americas New York, NY 10019 212/355-7311 800/221-4268	1962	Quest Advisory Corp.	N/A	$2,000/ 50	r	Fund
Phoenix Multi-Portfolio Fund *Phoenix Capital Appreciation* 101 Munson St. Greenfield, MA 01301 203/253-1000 800/243-1574	1989	Phoenix Investment Counsel, Inc.	N/A	$500/ 25	N/A	Local Rep
Phoenix Series Fund *Phoenix Growth Fund Series* 101 Munson St. Greenfield, MA 01301 203/253-1000 800/243-1574	1958	Phoenix Investment Counsel, Inc.	$690.2 Mil	$500/ 25	i	Local Rep
Pilgrim MagnaCap Fund, Inc. 10100 Santa Monica Blvd. 21st Fl. Los Angeles, CA 90067 213/551-0833 800/334-3444 800/331-1080	1970	Pilgrim Management Corporation	$219.6 Mil	$1,000/ 100	i, p	Local Rep
Piper Jaffray Investment Trust Inc. *Sector Performance Fund* 222 S. 9th St. Piper Jaffray Twr. Minneapolis, MN 55402 612/342-6426 800/333-6000	1987	Piper Capital Management Incorporated	$12.5 Mil	$0/ 0	i, p	Local Rep

*Key: i=initial sales charge   r=redemption fee or contingent deferred sales charge(CDSC)
t=12b-1 fee and either CDSC or redemption fee   p=12b-1 fee   n=none of the preceding fees   N/A=not available

Growth

Fund	Year Began	Investment Adviser	9/30/89 Assets	Minimum Initial and Subsequent Investment	Fees*	Where to Buy Shares
Piper Jaffray Investment Trust Inc. *Value Fund* 222 S. 9th St. Piper Jaffray Twr. Minneapolis, MN 55402 612/342-6426 800/333-6000	1987	Piper Capital Management Incorporated	$37.0 Mil	$0/ 0	i, p	Local Rep
Plymouth Fund *Plymouth Growth Opportunities Portfolio* 82 Devonshire St. Boston, MA 02109 617/570-7000 800/544-6666	1987	Fidelity Management & Research Company	$31.4 Mil	$1,000/ 100	i, p	Local Rep
PNCG Equity Fund, Inc. 121 SW Morrison Ste. 1415 Portland, OR 97204 503/295-0919 800/541-9732	1989	PNCG Fund Advisers, Inc.	N/A	$1,000/ 500	i, p	Local Rep
Portfolios for Diversified Investment *Diversified Equity Appreciation Fund* 3411 Silverside Rd. Webster Bldg., Ste. 204 Wilmington, DE 19810 212/640-6155, 800/221-8120, 800/441-7450	1984	Provident Institutional Management Corporation	$6.7 Mil (e)	$1,000/ 0	n	Local Rep
PRIMECAP Fund Vanguard Financial Ctr. P.O. Box 2600 Valley Forge, PA 19482 215/648-6000 800/662-7447 800/362-0530 PA Only	1984	PRIMECAP Management Company	$275.7 Mil	$25,000/ 1,000	n	Fund
Princor Growth Fund, Inc. 711 High St. Des Moines, IA 50309 515/247-5711 800/247-4123 800/622-5344 IA Only	1969	Principal Management, Inc.	$34.2 Mil	$300/ 50	i, p	Local Rep
Professional Portfolios Trust *Timed Equity Fund* 429 N. Pennsylvania St. Indianapolis, IN 46204-1897 317/634-3300 800/862-7283	1988	Unified Management Corporation	$0.4 Mil	$200/ 25	p	Local Rep

*Key: i=initial sales charge   r=redemption fee or contingent deferred sales charge(CDSC)
    t=12b-1 fee and either CDSC or redemption fee   p=12b-1 fee   n=none of the preceding fees   N/A=not available

Growth

Fund	Year Began	Investment Adviser	9/30/89 Assets	Minimum Initial and Subsequent Investment	Fees*	Where to Buy Shares
Prudential-Bache Equity Fund One Seaport Plaza New York, NY 10292 212/214-1215 800/225-1852	1982	Prudential Mutual Fund Management	$601.1 Mil	$1,000/ 100	t	Local Rep
Prudential-Bache Option Growth Fund, Inc. One Seaport Plaza New York, NY 10292 212/214-1215 800/225-1852	1983	Prudential Mutual Fund Management	$66.9 Mil	$1,000/ 100	t	Local Rep
Prudential-Bache Research Fund, Inc. One Seaport Plaza New York, NY 10292 212/214-1215 800/225-1852	1983	Prudential-Bache Investment Management	$380.7 Mil	$1,000/ 100	t	Local Rep
Prudent Speculator Fund *Prudent Speculator Large Cap Fund (The)* 4023 W. 6th St. Los Angeles, CA 90020 800/444-4778	1989	Prudent Speculator Group	N/A	$5,000/ 500	N/A	Fund
Putnam Investors Fund One Post Office Sq. Boston, MA 02109 617/292-1000 800/225-2465	1925	Putnam Management Company, Inc.	$710.5 Mil	$500/ 50	i	Local Rep
Quest For Value Accumulation Trust *Equity Portfolio* Oppenheimer Tower World Financial Ctr. New York, NY 10281 212/667-7587 800/232-FUND	1988	Quest For Value Advisors	$4.1 Mil	Not Applicable	n	Insur
Quest For Value Accumulation Trust *Small Cap Portfolio* Oppenheimer Tower World Financial Ctr. New York, NY 10281 212/667-7587 800/232-FUND	1988	Quest For Value Advisors	$1.9 Mil	Not Applicable	n	Insur

*Key: i=initial sales charge   r=redemption fee or contingent deferred sales charge(CDSC)
       t=12b-1 fee and either CDSC or redemption fee   p=12b-1 fee   n=none of the preceding fees   N/A=not available

Growth

Fund	Year Began	Investment Adviser	9/30/89 Assets	Minimum Initial and Subsequent Investment	Fees*	Where to Buy Shares
Quest For Value Family of Funds *Quest For Value Fund, Inc.* Oppenheimer Tower World Financial Ctr. New York, NY 10281 212/667-7587 800/232-FUND	1980	Quest For Value Advisors	$79.4 Mil	$1,000/ 250	i, p	Local Rep
Retirement Investment Trust *Equity Growth Fund* 16 HCB 98 P.O. Box 2558 Houston, TX 77252-8098 713/546-7775	1988	None	N/A	$500/ 100	n	Fund
Rightime Fund, Inc. *Rightime Blue Chip Fund (The)* The Forst Pavilion Ste. 1000 Wyncote, PA 19095-1596 215/572-7288 800/242-1421, 800/222-3317 PA only	1987	Rightime Econometrics	N/A	$2,000/ 100	N/A	Local Rep
RNC Regency Fund, Inc. 11601 Wilshire Blvd. 24th Fl. Los Angeles, CA 90025 213/477-6543 800/225-9655	1985	RNC Capital Management Co.	$14.4 Mil (e)	$1,000/ 100	i, p	Local Rep
Rochester Growth Fund, Inc. 379 Park Ave. Rochester, NY 14607 716/442-5500	1983	Fielding Management Company, Inc.	$1.8 Mil (e)	$2,000/ 100	i, p	Local Rep
Rockwood Growth Fund, Inc. 545 Shoup Ave., #243 P.O. Box 50313 Idaho Falls, ID 83405 208/522-5593	1986	Aspen Securities & Advisory, Inc.	$1.5 Mil (e)	$1,000/ 0	n	Fund
Rodney Square Multi-Manager Fund *Growth Portfolio (The)* Rodney Square North Wilmington, DE 19890 302/651-1923 800/225-5084	1987	Rodney Square Management Corporation	N/A	$1,000/ 0	i, p	Local Rep

*Key: i=initial sales charge   r=redemption fee or contingent deferred sales charge(CDSC)
t=12b-1 fee and either CDSC or redemption fee   p=12b-1 fee   n=none of the preceding fees   N/A=not available

Growth

Fund	Year Began	Investment Adviser	9/30/89 Assets	Minimum Initial and Subsequent Investment	Fees*	Where to Buy Shares
Rodney Square Multi-Manager Fund *Value Portfolio (The)* Rodney Square North Wilmington, DE 19890 302/651-1923 800/225-5084	1987	Rodney Square Management Corporation	N/A	$1,000/ 0	i, p	Local Rep
SAFECO Growth Fund, Inc. SAFECO Plaza Seattle, WA 98185 206/545-5530 800/426-6730	1967	SAFECO Asset Management Company	$81.5 Mil	$1,000/ 100	n	Fund
Salem Funds *Salem Growth Portfolio (The)* 99 High St. Boston, MA 02110 617/338-3200 800/641-2580 800/343-3424	1985	First Union National Bank of N. Carolina	$93.0 Mil	$1,000/ 0	p	Fund
SBL Fund *Growth Series* 700 Harrison St. 6th Fl. Topeka, KS 66636 913/295-3127 800/888-2461	1977	Security Management Company	$152.5 Mil	Not Applicable	n	Insur
SBSF Funds *SBSF Growth Fund* 45 Rockefeller Plaza 33rd Fl. New York, NY 10111 212/903-1200 800/422-7273	1983	Spears, Benzak, Salomon & Farrell	$87.7 Mil (e)	$0/ 0	n	Fund
Schield Portfolios Series *Value Portfolio* 390 Union Blvd. Ste. 410 Denver, CO 80228 303/985-9999 800/826-8154 800/233-4971 CO Only	1986	Schield Management Company	$2.8 Mil	$1,000/ 100	i, p	Local Rep
Schroder Capital Funds, Inc. *Schroder U.S. Equity Fund* 787 Seventh Ave. 29th Fl. New York, NY 10019 212/422-6550	1969	Schroder Capital Management International Inc.	N/A	$500/ 100	N/A	Fund

*Key: i=initial sales charge   r=redemption fee or contingent deferred sales charge(CDSC)
t=12b-1 fee and either CDSC or redemption fee   p=12b-1 fee   n=none of the preceding fees   N/A=not available

Growth

Fund	Year Began	Investment Adviser	9/30/89 Assets	Minimum Initial and Subsequent Investment	Fees*	Where to Buy Shares
Scudder Capital Growth Fund, Inc. 175 Federal St. Boston, MA 02110 617/439-4640 800/225-2470 800/225-5163	1956	Scudder, Stevens & Clark, Inc.	$1.0 Bil	$1,000/ 0	n	Fund
Scudder Fund, Inc. *Lazard Equity Fund* One Rockefeller Plaza New York, NY 10020 212/957-5403 800/854-8525	1987	Lazard Freres & Co.	$16.9 Mil	$2,500/ 100	n	Fund
Security Action Fund 700 Harrison St. Topeka, KS 66636 913/295-3127 800/888-2461	1982	Security Management Company	$218.1 Mil	$50/ 50	i	Local Rep
Security Equity Fund 700 Harrison St. 6th Fl. Topeka, KS 66636 913/295-3127 800/888-2461	1962	Security Management Company	$283.7 Mil	$100/ 20	i	Local Rep
SEI Institutional Managed Trust *Capital Appreciation Portfolio* 680 E. Swedesford Rd. No. 7 Wayne, PA 19087 215/254-1000, 800/345-1151	1988	Sun Bank Investment Management Group	$47.3 Mil	$0/ 0	p	Local Rep
Select Capital Growth Fund, Inc. 20 Washington Ave. South Minneapolis, MN 55401 612/372-5605	1971	Washington Square Capital, Inc.	$12.4 Mil	Not Applicable	n	Insur
Selected Special Shares, Inc. 1331 Euclid Ave. Cleveland, OH 44115 312/641-7862 800/553-5533	1969	Selected Financial Services, Inc.	$49.5 Mil	$1,000/ 100	p	Local Rep

*Key: i=initial sales charge   r=redemption fee or contingent deferred sales charge(CDSC)
    t=12b-1 fee and either CDSC or redemption fee   p=12b-1 fee   n=none of the preceding fees   N/A=not available

Growth

Fund	Year Began	Investment Adviser	9/30/89 Assets	Minimum Initial and Subsequent Investment	Fees*	Where to Buy Shares
Select Managed Fund, Inc. 20 Washington Ave. South Minneapolis, MN 55401 612/372-5605	1986	Washington Square Capital, Inc.	$21.1 Mil	Not Applicable	n	Insur
Seligman Frontier Fund, Inc. 130 Liberty St. New York, NY 10006 212/488-0200 800/221-2450 800/522-6869 NY Only	1984	J. & W. Seligman & Co. Incorporated	$23.0 Mil	$1,000/ 50	n	Local Rep
Seligman Growth Fund, Inc. 130 Liberty St. New York, NY 10006 212/488-0200 800/221-2450 800/522-6869 NY Only	1937	J. & W. Seligman & Co. Incorporated	$597.0 Mil	$1,000/ 50	i	Local Rep
Sentinel Group Funds, Inc. *Growth Fund Series* National Life Dr. Montpelier, VT 05604 802/229-3900 800/282-3863	1969	Sentinel Advisors, Inc.	$51.8 Mil	$250/ 50	i	Local Rep
Sentry Fund, Inc. 1800 N. Point Dr. Stevens Point, WI 54481 715/346-6000 800/533-7827	1970	Sentry Investment Management Inc.	$49.1 Mil (e)	$200/ 20	i	Local Rep
Shearson Lehman Series Fund *SLH IDS Appreciation Portfolio* 31 W. 52nd St. New York, NY 10019 212/767-3700	1986	Shearson Asset Management Division of Shearson Lehman Hutton Inc.	$8.2 Mil	Not Applicable	n	Insur
Sigma Capital Shares, Inc. 3801 Kennett Pk., C-200 Greenville Ctr. Wilmington, DE 19807 302/652-3091 800/441-9490	1967	Sigma Management, Inc.	$93.7 Mil	$0/ 0	i, p	Local Rep

*Key: i=initial sales charge   r=redemption fee or contingent deferred sales charge(CDSC)
t=12b-1 fee and either CDSC or redemption fee   p=12b-1 fee   n=none of the preceding fees   N/A=not available

Growth

Fund	Year Began	Investment Adviser	9/30/89 Assets	Minimum Initial and Subsequent Investment	Fees*	Where to Buy Shares
Sigma Special Fund, Inc. 3801 Kennett Pk., C-200 Greenville Ctr. Wilmington, DE 19807 302/652-3091 800/441-9490	1969	Sigma Management, Inc.	$22.9 Mil	$0/ 0	i, p	Local Rep
Sigma Value Shares, Inc. 3801 Kennett Pk., C-200 Greenville Ctr. Wilmington, DE 19807 302/652-3091 800/441-9490	1976	Newbold's Asset Management	$11.3 Mil	$0/ 0	i, p	Local Rep
SLH Appreciation Fund, Inc. 31 W. 52nd St. New York, NY 10019 212/767-3700	1969	Shearson Asset Management Division of Shearson Lehman Hutton Inc.	$910.5 Mil	$500/ 200	i	Local Rep
SLH Fundamental Value Fund 31 W. 52nd St. New York, NY 10019 212/767-3700	1981	Shearson Asset Management Division of Shearson Lehman Hutton Inc.	$89.2 Mil	$500/ 200	i	Local Rep
SLH Investment Series, Inc. ***SLH Growth Portfolio*** 31 W. 52nd St. 15th Fl. New York, NY 10019 212/767-3700 800/334-4636 800/422-0214 NY Only	1982	SLH Asset Management Division of Shearson Lehman Hutton Inc.	$941.0 Mil	$500/ 250	t	Local Rep
SLH Principal Return Fund ***Zeros and Appreciation Series 1996*** 31 W. 52nd St. New York, NY 10019 212/767-3700	1988	Shearson Asset Management Division of Shearson Lehman Hutton Inc.	$166.9 Mil	$1,000/ 1,000	i	Local Rep
SLH Special Equity Portfolios ***SLH Growth and Opportunity Portfolio*** 31 W. 52nd St. New York, NY 10019 212/767-3700	1986	Lehman Management Company, Inc.	$215.8 Mil	$500/ 200	t	Local Rep

*Key: i=initial sales charge   r=redemption fee or contingent deferred sales charge(CDSC)
t=12b-1 fee and either CDSC or redemption fee   p=12b-1 fee   n=none of the preceding fees   N/A=not available

Growth

Fund	Year Began	Investment Adviser	9/30/89 Assets	Minimum Initial and Subsequent Investment	Fees*	Where to Buy Shares
SLH Special Equity Portfolios *SLH Sector Analysis Portfolio* 31 W. 52nd St. New York, NY 10019 212/767-3700	1987	Boston Company Advisors, Inc.	$315.4 Mil	$500/ 200	t	Local Rep
SLH Telecommunications Trust *SLH Telecommunications Growth Fund* One Boston Place Boston, MA 02019 617/956-9740 800/225-5267, 800/343-6324	1983	Boston Company Advisors, Inc.	$40.5 Mil	Not Applicable	r	Not Offering Shares
Smith Barney Equity Funds, Inc. 1345 Avenue of the Americas New York, NY 10105 212/698-5349 800/544-7835	1968	Smith, Barney Advisers, Inc.	$83.7 Mil	$3,000/ 50	i, p	Local Rep
SMITH HAYES Trust, Inc. *Covered Option Writing Portfolio* NBC Ctr. Ste. 780 Lincoln, NE 68508 402/476-3000 800/422-7791 NE Only	1988	SMITH HAYES Portfolio Management, Inc.	N/A	$25,000/ 1,000	N/A	Local Rep
SMITH HAYES Trust, Inc. *Defensive Growth Portfolio* NBC Ctr. Ste. 780 Lincoln, NE 68508 402/476-3000 800/422-7791 NE Only	1988	SMITH HAYES Portfolio Management, Inc.	N/A	$25,000/ 1,000	N/A	Local Rep
SMITH HAYES Trust, Inc. *Value Portfolio* NBC Ctr. Ste. 780 Lincoln, NE 68508 402/476-3000 800/422-7791 NE Only	1988	SMITH HAYES Portfolio Management, Inc.	N/A	$25,000/ 1,000	N/A	Local Rep
Southeastern Asset Management Funds Trust *Southeastern Asset Management Small-Cap Fund* 860 Ridgelake Blvd. Ste. 301 Memphis, TN 38119 901/761-2474, 800/445-9469	1989	Southeastern Asset Management, Inc.	$41.5 Mil	$50,000/ 1,000	n	Fund

*Key: i=initial sales charge   r=redemption fee or contingent deferred sales charge(CDSC)
t=12b-1 fee and either CDSC or redemption fee   p=12b-1 fee   n=none of the preceding fees   N/A=not available

Growth

Fund	Year Began	Investment Adviser	9/30/89 Assets	Minimum Initial and Subsequent Investment	Fees*	Where to Buy Shares
Southeastern Asset Management Funds Trust *Southeastern Asset Management Value Trust* 860 Ridgelake Blvd. Ste. 301 Memphis, TN 38119 901/761-2474, 800/445-9469	1987	Southeastern Asset Management, Inc.	$140.4 Mil	$50,000/ 1,000	n	Fund
Southeastern Growth Fund, Inc. 707 E. Main St. Richmond, VA 23219 804/649-2311 800/321-0038	1985	Wheat Investment Advisors	$115.4 Mil	$1,000/ 500	t	Local Rep
Sower Series Fund, Inc. *Growth Portfolio* 5900 "O" St. Lincoln, NE 68510 402/467-1122	1987	Ameritas Investment Advisors, Inc.	N/A	Not Applicable	n	Insur
Specialty Managers Trust *All-Growth Series* 1925 Century Park East Ste. 2350 Los Angeles, CA 90067 213/556-5499 800/423-4891	1989	J.M. Hartwell Management Company	N/A	Not Applicable	n	Insur
Spencer Trust *Spencer Growth Fund* 908 Town & Country Blvd. Ste. 602 Houston, TX 77024 713/621-7688 800/458-1446	1988	Spencer Capital Management Company, Inc.	N/A	$250/ 50	i, p	Local Rep
State Farm Growth Fund, Inc. One State Farm Plaza Bloomington, IL 61710 309/766-2029	1967	State Farm Investment Management Corporation	$378.3 Mil (e)	$50/ 50	n	Fund
State Street Fund for Foundations and Endowments *Equity Growth Portfolio* One Financial Ctr. 38th Fl. Boston, MA 02111 617/482-3920	1986	State Street Research & Management Company	$5.6 Mil	$100,000/ 0	n	Local Rep

*Key: i=initial sales charge   r=redemption fee or contingent deferred sales charge(CDSC)
t=12b-1 fee and either CDSC or redemption fee   p=12b-1 fee   n=none of the preceding fees   N/A=not available

Growth

Fund	Year Began	Investment Adviser	9/30/89 Assets	Minimum Initial and Subsequent Investment	Fees*	Where to Buy Shares
SteinRoe Investment Trust *SteinRoe Special Fund* 300 W. Adams St. P.O. Box 1143 Chicago, IL 60690 800/338-2550	1968	Stein Roe & Farnham Incorporated	$322.1 Mil	$1,000/ 100	n	Fund
SteinRoe Investment Trust *SteinRoe Stock Fund* 300 W. Adams St. P.O. Box 1143 Chicago, IL 60690 800/338-2550	1958	Stein Roe & Farnham Incorporated	$206.5 Mil	$1,000/ 100	n	Fund
SteinRoe Variable Investment Trust *Managed Growth Stock Fund* 600 Atlantic Ave. Boston, MA 02210 617/722-6000 800/443-2683	1989	Stein Roe & Farnham Incorporated	N/A	Not Applicable	N/A	Insur
Surveyor Fund, Inc. 1345 Avenue of the Americas New York, NY 10105 212/969-1000 800/221-5672	1966	Alliance Capital Management L.P.	$113.6 Mil	$250/ 50	i, p	Local Rep
TCI Portfolios, Inc. *TCI Growth* 4500 Main St. P.O. Box 419385 Kansas City, MO 64141-9385 816/932-4731	1987	Investors Research Corporation	$32.6 Mil	Not Applicable	n	Insur
Templeton Real Estate Trust 700 Central Ave. P.O. Box 33030 St. Petersburg, FL 33733-8030 813/823-8712 800/237-0738	1989	Templeton, Galbraith & Hansberger, Ltd.	$1.5 Mil	$1,000/ 25	i	Local Rep
Templeton Variable Annuity Fund 700 Central Ave. P.O. Box 33030 St. Petersburg, FL 33733-8030 813/823-8712 800/237-0738	1988	Templeton, Galbraith & Hansberger, Ltd.	N/A	Not Applicable	n	Insur

*Key: i=initial sales charge   r=redemption fee or contingent deferred sales charge(CDSC)
t=12b-1 fee and either CDSC or redemption fee   p=12b-1 fee   n=none of the preceding fees   N/A=not available

169

Growth

Fund	Year Began	Investment Adviser	9/30/89 Assets	Minimum Initial and Subsequent Investment	Fees*	Where to Buy Shares
Templeton Variable Products Series Fund *Templeton Stock Fund* 700 Central Ave. P.O. Box 33030 St. Petersburg, FL 33733-8030 813/823-8712 800/237-0738	1988	Templeton, Galbraith & Hansberger, Ltd.	N/A	Not Applicable	n	Insur
Thomson McKinnon Investment Trust *Thomson McKinnon Growth Fund* One State Street Plaza New York, NY 10004 212/482-5894 800/628-1237	1984	Thomson McKinnon Asset Management L.P.	$373.5 Mil	$1,000/ 100	t	Local Rep
Transamerica Special Series, Inc. *Transamerica Special Blue Chip Fund* 1000 Louisiana Ste. 6000 Houston, TX 77002-5098 713/751-2400, 800/999-3863	1987	Transamerica Fund Management Company	$6.5 Mil	$1,000/ 50	t	Local Rep
Transamerica Special Series, Inc. *Transamerica Special Natural Resources Fund* 1000 Louisiana Ste. 6000 Houston, TX 77002-5098 713/751-2400, 800/999-3863	1987	Transamerica Fund Management Company	$3.7 Mil	$1,000/ 50	t	Local Rep
Transamerica Sunbelt Growth Fund, Inc. 1000 Louisiana Ste. 6000 Houston, TX 77002-5098 713/751-2400 800/999-3863	1982	Transamerica Fund Management Company	$35.0 Mil	$100/ 10	i, p	Local Rep
T. Rowe Price Capital Appreciation Fund 100 E. Pratt St. Baltimore, MD 21202 301/547-2000 800/638-5660	1986	T. Rowe Price Associates, Inc.	$134.2 Mil	$2,500/ 100	n	Fund
T. Rowe Price Growth Stock Fund, Inc. 100 E. Pratt St. Baltimore, MD 21202 301/547-2000 800/638-5660	1950	T. Rowe Price Associates, Inc.	$1.5 Bil	$2,500/ 100	n	Fund

*Key: i=initial sales charge   r=redemption fee or contingent deferred sales charge(CDSC)
t=12b-1 fee and either CDSC or redemption fee   p=12b-1 fee   n=none of the preceding fees   N/A=not available

170

Growth

Fund	Year Began	Investment Adviser	9/30/89 Assets	Minimum Initial and Subsequent Investment	Fees*	Where to Buy Shares
T. Rowe Price New Era Fund, Inc. 100 E. Pratt St. Baltimore, MD 21202 301/547-2000 800/638-5660	1969	T. Rowe Price Associates, Inc.	$804.8 Mil	$2,500/ 100	n	Fund
Twentieth Century Investors, Inc. *Growth Investors* 4500 Main St. P.O. Box 419200 Kansas City, MO 64141-6200 816/531-5575 800/345-2021	1958	Investors Research Corporation	$1.7 Bil	$0/ 0	n	Fund
Twentieth Century Investors, Inc. *Select Investors* 4500 Main St. P.O. Box 419200 Kansas City, MO 64141-6200 816/531-5575 800/345-2021	1958	Investors Research Corporation	$2.8 Bil	$0/ 0	n	Fund
Unified Growth Fund, Inc. 429 N. Pennsylvania St. Indianapolis, IN 46204-1897 317/634-3300 800/862-7283	1970	Unified Management Corporation	$17.4 Mil	$200/ 25	n	Fund
United Funds, Inc. *United Accumulative Fund* 2400 Pershing Rd. P.O. Box 418343 Kansas City, MO 64141-9343 816/283-4000 800/821-5664	1940	Waddell & Reed, Inc.	$888.3 Mil	$500/ 25	i	Local Rep
United Funds, Inc. *United Science and Energy Fund* 2400 Pershing Rd. P.O. Box 418343 Kansas City, MO 64141-9343 816/283-4000 800/821-5664	1950	Waddell & Reed, Inc.	$250.9 Mil	$500/ 25	i	Local Rep
United Services Funds *U.S. Growth Fund* P.O. Box 29467 San Antonio, TX 78229-0467 512/696-1234 800/873-8637	1983	United Services Advisors, Inc.	$5.8 Mil	$100/ 50	n	Fund

*Key: i=initial sales charge   r=redemption fee or contingent deferred sales charge(CDSC)
t=12b-1 fee and either CDSC or redemption fee   p=12b-1 fee   n=none of the preceding fees   N/A=not available

171

Growth

Fund	Year Began	Investment Adviser	9/30/89 Assets	Minimum Initial and Subsequent Investment	Fees*	Where to Buy Shares
United Services Funds *U.S. Real Estate Fund* P.O. Box 29467 San Antonio, TX 78229-0467 512/696-1234 800/873-8637	1987	United Services Advisors, Inc.	$6.3 Mil	$100/ 50	n	Fund
USAA Mutual Fund, Inc. *Growth Fund* USAA Bldg. San Antonio, TX 78288 512/498-8000 800/531-8000	1971	USAA Investment Management Company	$229.3 Mil	$1,000/ 50	n	Fund
Value Line Centurion Fund, Inc. 711 Third Ave. New York, NY 10017 212/687-3965 800/223-0818	1983	Value Line, Inc.	$163.0 Mil	Not Applicable	n	Insur
Value Line Fund, Inc. 711 Third Ave. New York, NY 10017 212/687-3965 800/223-0818	1950	Value Line, Inc.	$207.8 Mil	$1,000/ 100	n	Fund
Vance Sanders Special Fund, Inc. 24 Federal St. Boston, MA 02110 617/482-8260 800/225-6265	1968	Eaton Vance Management, Inc.	$59.6 Mil	$1,000/ 50	i	Local Rep
Vanguard Index Trust *Extended Market Portfolio* Vanguard Financial Ctr. P.O. Box 2600 Valley Forge, PA 19482 215/648-6000 800/662-7447 800/362-0530 PA Only	1987	Vanguard Group, Inc.	$129.7 Mil	$3,000/ 100	n	Fund
Vanguard World Fund *U.S. Growth Portfolio* Vanguard Financial Ctr. P.O. Box 2600 Valley Forge, PA 19482 215/648-6000 800/662-7447 800/362-0530 PA Only	1959	Lincoln Capital Management Company	$189.4 Mil	$3,000/ 100	n	Fund

*Key: i=initial sales charge   r=redemption fee or contingent deferred sales charge(CDSC)
t=12b-1 fee and either CDSC or redemption fee   p=12b-1 fee   n=none of the preceding fees   N/A=not available

Growth

Fund	Year Began	Investment Adviser	9/30/89 Assets	Minimum Initial and Subsequent Investment	Fees*	Where to Buy Shares
Variable Insurance Products Fund *Growth Portfolio* 82 Devonfield St. Boston, MA 02109 617/570-7000 800/544-6666	1986	Fidelity Management & Research Company	$58.5 Mil	Not Applicable	n	Insur
Variable Investors Series Trust *Common Stock Portfolio* 1414 Main St. Springfield, MA 01144 413/732-7100	1977	Amherst Investment Management Company, Inc.	$29.9 Mil	Not Applicable	n	Insur
Variable Investors Series Trust *Natural Resources Portfolio* 1414 Main St. Springfield, MA 01144 413/732-7100	1988	Amherst Investment Management Company, Inc.	$1.3 Mil	Not Applicable	n	Insur
Variable Stock Fund, Inc. One Monarch Place 12th Fl. Springfield, MA 01144 413/784-6857	1957	Amherst Investment Management Company, Inc.	$9.9 Mil	$50/ 25	n	Fund
Volumetric Fund, Inc. 87 Violet Dr. Pearl River, NY 10965 914/623-7637 800/541-3863	1987	Volumetric Advisers, Inc.	$4.9 Mil	$500/ 300	n	Fund
Voyageur GRANIT Growth Stock Fund, Inc. 100 S. Fifth St. Ste. 2200 Minneapolis, MN 55402 612/341-6728 800/553-2143 800/247-2143 MN Only	1985	Voyageur Fund Managers	$11.4 Mil	$1,000/ 100	i, p	Local Rep
Wade Fund, Inc. 5100 Poplar Ave. Ste. 2224 Memphis, TN 38137 901/682-4613	1949	Maury Wade & Company	$0.5 Mil	$500/ 0	n	Fund

*Key: i=initial sales charge   r=redemption fee or contingent deferred sales charge(CDSC)
t=12b-1 fee and either CDSC or redemption fee   p=12b-1 fee   n=none of the preceding fees   N/A=not available

173

Growth

Fund	Year Began	Investment Adviser	9/30/89 Assets	Minimum Initial and Subsequent Investment	Fees*	Where to Buy Shares
Wasatch Advisors Funds, Inc. *Wasatch Growth Fund* 68 S. Main St. Ste. 400 Salt Lake City, UT 84101 801/533-0777 800/345-7460	1987	Wasatch Advisors Inc.	$3.2 Mil (e)	$5,000/ 1,000	n	Fund
Wealth Monitors Fund 1001 E. 101st Terr. Ste. 220 Kansas City, MO 64131 816/941-7990	1986	Wealth Monitors, Inc.	$2.4 Mil	$1,000/ 100	p	Fund
Weitz Value Fund, Inc. 9290 W. Dodge Rd. The Mark, Ste. 405 Omaha, NE 68114-3323 402/391-1980	1986	Wallace R. Weitz & Company	$23.0 Mil	$25,000/ 5,000	n	Fund
Winthrop Focus Fund *Winthrop Growth Portfolio* 140 Broadway 42nd Fl. New York, NY 10005 212/504-4000 800/225-8011 800/521-3036	1987	Wood, Struthers & Winthrop Management Corporation	$55.7 Mil (e)	$1,000/ 100	t	Local Rep
W.L. Morgan Growth Fund Vanguard Financial Ctr. P.O. Box 2600 Valley Forge, PA 19482 215/648-6000 800/662-7447 800/362-0530 PA Only	1968	Wellington Management Company	$739.6 Mil	$3,000/ 100	n	Fund
Zweig Series Trust *Blue Chip Series* 25 Broadway New York, NY 10004 212/361-9612 800/272-2700	1985	Zweig/Glaser Advisers	$20.5 Mil (e)	$1,000/ 100	t	Local Rep
Zweig Series Trust *Priority Selection List Series* 25 Broadway New York, NY 10004 212/361-9612 800/272-2700	1987	Zweig/Glaser Advisers	$13.1 Mil (e)	$1,000/ 100	t	Local Rep

*Key: i=initial sales charge   r=redemption fee or contingent deferred sales charge(CDSC)
      t=12b-1 fee and either CDSC or redemption fee   p=12b-1 fee   n=none of the preceding fees   N/A=not available

◆　◆　◆　◆

Growth and Income Funds

Growth and Income

Fund	Year Began	Investment Adviser	9/30/89 Assets	Minimum Initial and Subsequent Investment	Fees*	Where to Buy Shares
AARP Growth Trust *AARP Growth and Income Fund* AARP Investment Program 175 Federal St. Boston, MA 02110-2267 800/253-2277	1984	AARP/Scudder Financial Management Company	$236.3 Mil	$250/ 0	n	Fund
ABT Growth and Income Trust 205 Royal Palm Way Palm Beach, FL 33480 407/655-7255 800/441-6580	1967	Palm Beach Capital Management, Ltd.	$107.2 Mil	$1,000/ 50	i, p	Local Rep
Adam Investors, Inc. 80 E. Sir Francis Drake Blvd. Larkspur, CA 94939 415/461-3850	1984	Siebel Capital Management, Inc.	$4.8 Mil (e)	$25,000/ 5,000	n	Fund
Aetna Guaranteed Equity Trust 151 Farmington Ave. Hartford, CT 06156 203/273-4808	1987	Aetna Life Insurance and Annuity Company	$312.3 Mil (e)	Not Applicable	n	Insur
Aetna Series Trust *Aetna High Quality Stock Fund* Federated Investors Twr. 26th Fl. Pittsburgh, PA 15222-3779 412/288-1900 800/245-4770	1988	Federated Advisers	$3.8 Mil	$500/ 100	n	Fund
Affiliated Fund, Inc. The General Motors Bldg. 767 Fifth Ave. New York, NY 10153 212/848-1800 800/223-4224	1934	Lord, Abbett & Co.	$3.7 Bil	$250/ 0	i	Local Rep
AIM Equity Funds, Inc. *AIM Charter Fund* 11 Greenway Plaza Ste. 1919 Houston, TX 77046 713/626-1919 800/231-0803 800/392-9681 TX Only	1968	AIM Advisors, Inc.	$72.3 Mil	$1,000/ 100	i, p	Local Rep

*Key: i=initial sales charge   r=redemption fee or contingent deferred sales charge(CDSC)
      t=12b-1 fee and either CDSC or redemption fee   p=12b-1 fee   n=none of the preceding fees   N/A=not available

Growth and Income

Fund	Year Began	Investment Adviser	9/30/89 Assets	Minimum Initial and Subsequent Investment	Fees*	Where to Buy Shares
Alliance Convertible Fund 1345 Avenue of the Americas New York, NY 10105 212/969-1000 800/221-5672	1986	Alliance Capital Management L.P.	$77.0 Mil	$250/ 50	i, p	Local Rep
Alliance Dividend Shares, Inc. 1345 Avenue of the Americas New York, NY 10105 212/969-1000 800/221-5672	1932	Alliance Capital Management L.P.	$388.3 Mil	$1,000/ 50	i, p	Local Rep
AMA Growth Fund, Inc. *Growth plus Income Portfolio* 5 Sentry Pkwy. W, Ste. 120 P.O. Box 1111 Blue Bell, PA 19422 215/825-0400 800/AMA-FUND	1987	AMA Advisers, Inc.	$10.8 Mil	$1,000/ 0	p	Fund
American Capital Harbor Fund, Inc. 2800 Post Oak Blvd. Houston, TX 77056 713/993-0500 800/421-5666	1956	American Capital Asset Management, Inc.	$384.5 Mil	$500/ 50	i, p	Local Rep
American Capital Life Investment Trust *American Capital Common Stock Portfolio* 2800 Post Oak Blvd. Houston, TX 77056 713/993-0500 800/421-5666	1986	American Capital Asset Management, Inc.	$31.3 Mil	Not Applicable	n	Insur
American Eagle Fund, Inc. *American Eagle Balanced Series* 100 Light St. Baltimore, MD 21202 301/547-3894 800/622-3363	1987	Axe-Houghton Management, Inc.	$2.9 Mil	Not Applicable	r	Insur
American General Series Portfolio Company *Capital Conservation Fund* 2929 Allen Pkwy. P.O. Box 3206 Houston, TX 77253 713/526-5251	1985	Variable Annuity Life Insurance Company	$15.9 Mil	Not Applicable	r	Insur

*Key: i=initial sales charge   r=redemption fee or contingent deferred sales charge(CDSC)
     t=12b-1 fee and either CDSC or redemption fee   p=12b-1 fee   n=none of the preceding fees   N/A=not available

Growth and Income

Fund	Year Began	Investment Adviser	9/30/89 Assets	Minimum Initial and Subsequent Investment	Fees*	Where to Buy Shares
American General Series Portfolio Company *Quality Growth Fund* 2929 Allen Pkwy. P.O. Box 3206 Houston, TX 77253 713/526-5251	1987	Variable Annuity Life Insurance Company	$432.9 Mil	Not Applicable	n	Insur
American Leaders Fund, Inc. Federated Investors Twr. Liberty Ctr. Pittsburgh, PA 15222-3779 412/288-1900 800/245-0242	1969	Federated Advisers	$156.3 Mil	$500/ 100	i	Local Rep
American Mutual Fund, Inc. 333 S. Hope St. Los Angeles, CA 90071 213/486-9200 800/421-0180 213/486-9651 Collect	1949	Capital Research & Management Company	$3.2 Bil	$250/ 50	i, t	Local Rep
American Variable Insurance Series *Growth-Income Fund (The)* 333 S. Hope St. Los Angeles, CA 90071 213/486-9200 800/421-0180 213/486-9651 Collect	1984	Capital Research & Management Company	$245.9 Mil	Not Applicable	n	Insur
AMEV Advantage Portfolios, Inc. *Asset Allocation Portfolio* P.O. Box 64284 St. Paul, MN 55164 612/738-4000 800/872-2638	1988	AMEV Advisers, Inc.	$8.5 Mil	$500/ 50	i, p	Local Rep
AMEV Capital Fund, Inc. P.O. Box 64284 St. Paul, MN 55164 612/738-4000 800/872-2638	1949	AMEV Advisers, Inc.	$142.1 Mil	$500/ 50	i	Local Rep
Analytic Optioned Equity Fund, Inc. 2222 Martin St. Ste. 230 Irvine, CA 92715 714/833-0294	1978	Analytic Investment Management, Inc.	$112.5 Mil	$5,000/ 500	n	Fund

Growth and Income

Fund	Year Began	Investment Adviser	9/30/89 Assets	Minimum Initial and Subsequent Investment	Fees*	Where to Buy Shares
Anchor Pathway Fund *Growth-Income Series (The)* 2201 E. Camelback Phoenix, AZ 85016 602/955-0300 800/528-9679	1987	Capital Research & Management Company	N/A	Not Applicable	n	Insur
Avondale Investment Trust *Avondale Total Return Fund* 1105 Holliday Wichita Falls, TX 76301 817/761-3777	1988	Herbert R. Smith, Incorporated	$1.3 Mil	$1,000/ 250	i	Local Rep
Baird Blue Chip Fund, Inc. 777 E. Wisconsin Ave. Milwaukee, WI 53202 414/765-3500 800/792-2473	1987	Robert W. Baird & Company, Inc.	N/A	$1,000/ 100	i, p	Local Rep
Bankers National Series Trust *BNL Convertible Portfolio* 44 U.S. Hwy. 46 Pine Brook, NJ 07058 201/808-9596 800/888-4918	1987	Conseco Capital Management, Inc.	$3.5 Mil	Not Applicable	n	Insur
Bartlett Capital Trust *Basic Value Fund* 36 E. Fourth St. Cincinnati, OH 45202 513/621-4612 800/543-0863	1983	Bartlett & Company	$115.8 Mil	$5,000/ 100	n	Local Rep
BB&K Fund Group *BB&K Diversa Fund* 2755 Campus Dr. San Mateo, CA 94403 415/571-5800 800/882-8383	1986	Bailard, Biehl & Kaiser, Inc.	$101.2 Mil (e)	$25,000/ 2,000	n	Fund
Big E Pathfinder Family of Mutual Funds *Big E Pathfinder Total Return Fund (The)* 320 Empire Tower Buffalo, NY 14202 716/855-7891	1988	Empire of America Advisory Services, Inc.	$2.8 Mil (e)	$500/ 100	i, p	Local Rep

*Key: i=initial sales charge   r=redemption fee or contingent deferred sales charge(CDSC)
t=12b-1 fee and either CDSC or redemption fee   p=12b-1 fee   n=none of the preceding fees   N/A=not available

Growth and Income

Fund	Year Began	Investment Adviser	9/30/89 Assets	Minimum Initial and Subsequent Investment	Fees*	Where to Buy Shares
Boston Company Index and Blue Chip Trust *Blue Chip Fund* One Boston Place Boston, MA 02108 617/451-2010 800/225-5267	1988	Boston Company Advisors, Inc.	$0.3 Mil	$0/ 500	p	Fund
Bridges Investment Fund, Inc. 8401 W. Dodge Rd. 256 Durham Plaza Omaha, NE 68114 402/397-4700	1963	Bridges Investment Counsel, Inc.	$10.8 Mil	$700/ 150	r	Fund
Bull & Bear Equity-Income Fund, Inc. 11 Hanover Sq. New York, NY 10005 212/785-0900 800/847-4200	1961	Bull & Bear Equity Advisers, Inc.	$11.6 Mil (e)	$1,000/ 100	p	Fund
Burnham Fund, Inc. (The) 25 Broadway New York, NY 10004 212/361-9612 800/272-2700	1961	Burnham Asset Management Corp.	$161.1 Mil	$1,000/ 100	i	Local Rep
Capital Income Builder, Inc. 333 S. Hope St. Los Angeles, CA 90071 213/486-9200 800/421-0180 213/486-9651 Collect	1987	Capital Research & Management Company	$192.5 Mil	$0/ 0	i, t	Local Rep
Carillon Fund, Inc. *Equity Portfolio (The)* 1876 Waycross Rd. P.O. Box 5304 Cincinnati, OH 45201 513/595-2600 800/999-1840	1984	Carillon Advisers, Inc.	$52.6 Mil	Not Applicable	n	Insur
Carnegie-Cappiello Trust *Total Return Series* 1100 The Halle Bldg. 1228 Euclid Ave. Cleveland, OH 44115-1831 216/781-4440 800/321-2322	1985	Carnegie Capital Management Company	$77.4 Mil	$1,000/ 250	i, p	Local Rep

*Key: i=initial sales charge r=redemption fee or contingent deferred sales charge(CDSC)
t=12b-1 fee and either CDSC or redemption fee p=12b-1 fee n=none of the preceding fees N/A=not available

Growth and Income

Fund	Year Began	Investment Adviser	9/30/89 Assets	Minimum Initial and Subsequent Investment	Fees*	Where to Buy Shares
Century Shares Trust One Liberty Sq. Boston, MA 02109 617/482-3060 800/321-1928	1928	None	$127.3 Mil (e)	$500/ 25	n	Fund
Chubb America Fund, Inc. *Domestic Growth Portfolio* One Granite Place Concord, NH 03301 603/224-7741	1986	Chubb Investment Advisory Corporation	$9.8 Mil (e)	Not Applicable	n	Insur
Chubb Investment Funds, Inc. *Chubb Total Return Fund* One Granite Place Concord, NH 03301 603/224-7741	1987	Chubb Asset Managers, Inc.	N/A	$1,000/ 100	i, p	Local Rep
CIGNA Annuity Fund *Growth and Income Fund* CIGNA Corporation Hartford, CT 06152 203/726-6000 800/562-4462	1987	CIGNA Investments, Inc.	$5.2 Mil	Not Applicable	n	Insur
CIGNA Value Fund One Financial Plaza Springfield, MA 01103 413/784-0100 800/56CIGNA	1983	CIGNA Investments, Inc.	$72.8 Mil	$500/ 50	i, p	Local Rep
Collective Investment Trust for Citibank IRAs *Balanced Portfolio* 153 E. 53rd St. 4th Fl. New York, NY 10043 212/559-4677 800/CITI-IRA	1983	Citibank N.A.	$173.6 Mil	$250/ 0	n	Fund
Colonial Equity Index Portfolios *Colonial Small Stock Index Trust* One Financial Ctr. Boston, MA 02111 617/426-3750 800/225-2365, 800/426-3750	1986	Colonial Management Associates, Inc.	$46.1 Mil	$250/ 25	i, p	Local Rep

*Key: i=initial sales charge   r=redemption fee or contingent deferred sales charge(CDSC)
       t=12b-1 fee and either CDSC or redemption fee   p=12b-1 fee   n=none of the preceding fees   N/A=not available

Growth and Income

Fund	Year Began	Investment Adviser	9/30/89 Assets	Minimum Initial and Subsequent Investment	Fees*	Where to Buy Shares
Colonial Equity Index Portfolios *Colonial United States Equity Index Trust* One Financial Ctr. Boston, MA 02111 617/426-3750 800/225-2365, 800/426-3750	1986	Colonial Management Associates, Inc.	$34.9 Mil	$250/ 25	i, p	Local Rep
Colonial Fund One Financial Ctr. Boston, MA 02111 617/426-3750 800/225-2365 800/426-3750	1959	Colonial Management Associates, Inc.	$326.2 Mil	$250/ 25	i	Local Rep
Colonial/Hancock Liberty Trust *Colonial/Hancock Liberty Growth and Income Fund* One Financial Ctr. Boston, MA 02111 617/426-3750 800/225-2365, 800/426-3750	1987	Colonial Management Associates, Inc.	$5.9 Mil	Not Applicable	n	Insur
Colonial/Hancock Liberty Trust *Colonial/Hancock Liberty Inflation Hedge Fund* One Financial Ctr. Boston, MA 02111 617/426-3750 800/225-2365, 800/426-3750	1987	Colonial Management Associates, Inc.	$0.3 Mil	Not Applicable	n	Insur
Colonial Value Investing Portfolios - Equity Portfolio *Inflation Hedge Fund* One Financial Ctr. Boston, MA 02111 617/426-3750 800/225-2365, 800/426-3750	1988	Colonial Management Associates, Inc.	$4.4 Mil	$500/ 100	t	Local Rep
Common Sense Trust *Common Sense Growth and Income Fund* 2800 Post Oak Blvd. Houston, TX 77056 713/993-0500 800/421-5666	1987	Common Sense Investment Advisers	$272.5 Mil	$250/ 25	i	Local Rep
Composite Growth Fund, Inc. W. 601 Riverside, 9th Fl. Seafirst Financial Ctr. Spokane, WA 99201 509/353-3400 800/543-8072 800/572-5828	1949	Composite Research & Management Company	$75.1 Mil	$1,000/ 50	i, p	Local Rep

*Key: i=initial sales charge   r=redemption fee or contingent deferred sales charge(CDSC)
t=12b-1 fee and either CDSC or redemption fee   p=12b-1 fee   n=none of the preceding fees   N/A=not available

Growth and Income

Fund	Year Began	Investment Adviser	9/30/89 Assets	Minimum Initial and Subsequent Investment	Fees*	Where to Buy Shares
Composite Northwest 50 Index Fund, Inc. W. 601 Riverside, 9th Fl. Seafirst Financial Ctr. Spokane, WA 99201 509/353-3400 800/543-8072 800/572-5828	1986	Composite Research & Management Company	$17.1 Mil	$1,000/ 50	i, p	Local Rep
Concord Income Trust *Convertible Portfolio* Park 80 W., Plaza Two Saddle Brook, NJ 07662 201/845-7300 800/526-0056	1988	Moore & Schley Advisory Corporation	$6.9 Mil (e)	$1,000/ 100	i	Local Rep
Connecticut Mutual Financial Services Series Fund I, Inc. *Total Return Portfolio* 140 Garden St. Hartford, CT 06154 203/727-6500 800/243-0018	1982	G.R. Phelps & Company, Inc.	$216.3 Mil	Not Applicable	r	Insur
Connecticut Mutual Investment Accounts, Inc. *Connecticut Mutual Total Return Account* 140 Garden St. Hartford, CT 06154 203/727-6500 800/243-0018	1985	G.R. Phelps & Company, Inc.	$64.2 Mil	$1,000/ 50	i	Local Rep
Convertible Securities and Income, Inc. Federated Investors Twr. Liberty Ctr. Pittsburgh, PA 15222-3779 412/288-1900 800/245-0242	1987	Federated Advisers	$33.7 Mil	$500/ 100	i, p	Local Rep
Dean Witter Convertible Securities Trust Two World Trade Ctr. New York, NY 10048 212/392-2550 800/869-3863	1985	Dean Witter Reynolds Inc. - InterCapital Division	$822.3 Mil	$1,000/ 100	t	Local Rep
Dean Witter Dividend Growth Securities Inc. Two World Trade Ctr. New York, NY 10048 212/392-2550 800/869-3863	1981	Dean Witter Reynolds Inc. - InterCapital Division	$2.5 Bil	$1,000/ 100	t	Local Rep

*Key: i=initial sales charge   r=redemption fee or contingent deferred sales charge(CDSC)
t=12b-1 fee and either CDSC or redemption fee   p=12b-1 fee   n=none of the preceding fees   N/A=not available

Growth and Income

Fund	Year Began	Investment Adviser	9/30/89 Assets	Minimum Initial and Subsequent Investment	Fees*	Where to Buy Shares
Dean Witter Utilities Fund Two World Trade Ctr. New York, NY 10048 212/392-2550 800/869-3863	1988	Dean Witter Reynolds Inc. - InterCapital Division	$921.5 Mil	$1,000/ 100	t	Local Rep
Dean Witter Value-Added Market Series *Equity Portfolio* Two World Trade Ctr. New York, NY 10048 212/392-2550 800/869-3863	1987	Dean Witter Reynolds Inc. - InterCapital Division	$118.6 Mil	$1,000/ 100	t	Local Rep
Dividend/Growth Fund, Inc. *Dividend Series* 107 N. Adams St. Rockville, MD 20850 301/251-1002 800/638-2042	1967	American Investment Managers, Inc.	$2.8 Mil (e)	$1,000/ 100	n	Local Rep
Dodge & Cox Stock Fund One Post St. 35th Fl. San Francisco, CA 94104 415/981-1710	1965	Dodge & Cox	$112.9 Mil	$1,000/ 100	n	Fund
Dreman Mutual Group, Inc. *Dreman High Return Portfolio (The)* 10 Exchange Place Jersey City, NJ 07302 201/332-8228 800/533-1608	1988	Dreman Value Management, Inc.	$4.0 Mil	$5,000/ 1,000	p	Local Rep
DR Equity Fund 535 Madison Ave. New York, NY 10022 212/906-7658 800/356-6454	1986	Dillon, Read Capital Inc.	$62.4 Mil	$100,000/ 5,000	n	Fund
Dreyfus Capital Value Fund, Inc. 666 Old Country Rd. Garden City, NY 11530 718/895-1206 800/645-6561	1985	Dreyfus Corporation	$607.2 Mil	$2,500/ 100	i, p	Local Rep

*Key: i=initial sales charge   r=redemption fee or contingent deferred sales charge(CDSC)
    t=12b-1 fee and either CDSC or redemption fee   p=12b-1 fee   n=none of the preceding fees   N/A=not available

185

Growth and Income

Fund	Year Began	Investment Adviser	9/30/89 Assets	Minimum Initial and Subsequent Investment	Fees*	Where to Buy Shares
Dreyfus Fund Incorporated 666 Old Country Rd. Garden City, NY 11530 718/895-1206 800/645-6561	1947	Dreyfus Corporation	$2.6 Bil	$2,500/ 100	n	Fund
Dreyfus Index Fund, Inc. 666 Old Country Rd. Garden City, NY 11530 718/895-1206 800/645-6561	1987	Wells Fargo Investment Advisors	$18.4 Mil (e)	$1.0 Mil/ 100,000	n	Fund
Dreyfus Life and Annuity Index Fund, Inc. 666 Old Country Rd. Garden City, NY 11530 718/895-1206 800/645-6561	1989	Wells Fargo Investment Advisors	N/A	Not Applicable	N/A	Insur
Eaton Vance Equity-Income Trust 24 Federal St. Boston, MA 02110 617/482-8260 800/225-6265	1987	Eaton Vance Management, Inc.	$6.3 Mil	$1,000/ 50	t	Local Rep
Eaton Vance Stock Fund 24 Federal St. Boston, MA 02110 617/482-8260 800/225-6265	1931	Eaton Vance Management, Inc.	$90.0 Mil	$1,000/ 50	i	Local Rep
Eaton Vance Total Return Trust 24 Federal St. Boston, MA 02110 617/482-8260 800/225-6265	1981	Eaton Vance Management, Inc.	$492.3 Mil	$1,000/ 50	i, p	Local Rep
EBI Funds, Inc. **EBI Equity Fund** 1315 Peachtree St., NE Ste. 500 Atlanta, GA 30309 404/892-0666 800/554-1156	1984	INVESCO Capital Management, Inc.	N/A	$100,000/ 5,000	t	Local Rep

*Key: i=initial sales charge   r=redemption fee or contingent deferred sales charge(CDSC)
t=12b-1 fee and either CDSC or redemption fee   p=12b-1 fee   n=none of the preceding fees   N/A=not available

Growth and Income

Fund	Year Began	Investment Adviser	9/30/89 Assets	Minimum Initial and Subsequent Investment	Fees*	Where to Buy Shares
Eclipse Financial Asset Trust *Eclipse Balanced Fund* 144 E. 30th St. New York, NY 10016 212/696-4130 800/872-2710	1989	Towneley Capital Management, Inc.	N/A	$3,000/ 0	n	Fund
Eclipse Financial Asset Trust *Eclipse Equity Fund* 144 E. 30th St. New York, NY 10016 212/696-4130 800/872-2710	1987	Towneley Capital Management, Inc.	$192.1 Mil (e)	$3,000/ 0	n	Fund
Elite Group *Elite Growth & Income Fund (The)* 1206 IBM Bldg. Seattle, WA 98101 206/624-5863 800/654-5261 800/423-1068 WA Only	1987	R.S. McCormick & Company, Inc.	$3.8 Mil	$1,000/ 50	n	Fund
Endowments, Inc. Four Embarcadero Ctr. P.O. Box 7650 San Francisco, CA 94120-7650 415/421-9360 800/421-0180	1969	Capital Research & Management Company	$43.6 Mil	$50,000/ 0	n	Fund
Equitable Funds *Equitable Balanced Fund (The)* 1755 Broadway 3rd Fl. New York, NY 10019 212/641-8100	1987	Equitable Capital Management Corporation	N/A	$1,000/ 100	t	Local Rep
Equitec Siebel Fund Group *Equitec Siebel Total Return Fund Series* 7677 Oakport St. P.O. Box 2470 Oakland, CA 94614 415/430-9900 800/869-8900	1985	Siebel Capital Management, Inc.	$130.3 Mil (e)	$1,000/ 0	t	Local Rep
Evergreen American Retirement Trust 2500 Westchester Ave. Purchase, NY 10577 914/694-2020 800/235-0064	1988	Evergreen Asset Management Corporation	N/A	$2,000/ 0	n	Fund

*Key: i=initial sales charge   r=redemption fee or contingent deferred sales charge(CDSC)
          t=12b-1 fee and either CDSC or redemption fee   p=12b-1 fee   n=none of the preceding fees   N/A=not available

187

Growth and Income

Fund	Year Began	Investment Adviser	9/30/89 Assets	Minimum Initial and Subsequent Investment	Fees*	Where to Buy Shares
Evergreen Total Return Fund 2500 Westchester Ave. Purchase, NY 10577 914/694-2020 800/235-0064	1978	Evergreen Asset Management Corporation	$1.4 Bil (e)	$2,000/ 0	n	Fund
Exchange Fund of Boston, Inc. 24 Federal St. Boston, MA 02110 617/482-8260 800/225-6265	1963	Eaton Vance Management, Inc.	$63.4 Mil	Not Applicable	n	Not Offering Shares
FBL Series Fund, Inc. *Growth Common Stock Portfolio* 5400 University Ave. W. Des Moines, IA 50265 515/225-5400 800/247-4170 800/422-3175 IA Only	1971	FBL Investment Advisory Services, Inc.	$38.1 Mil	$250/ 0	r	Local Rep
Federated Exchange Fund, Ltd. Federated Investors Twr. Pittsburgh, PA 15222-3779 412/288-1948 800/245-2423	1976	Federated Advisers	$104.5 Mil	Not Applicable	n	Not Offering Shares
Federated Stock Trust Federated Investors Twr. Pittsburgh, PA 15222-3779 412/288-1900 800/245-5000	1982	Federated Management	$607.1 Mil	$25,000/ 0	n	Local Rep
Fenimore Asset Management Trust *FAM Value Fund* Box 399 Cobleskill, NY 12043 518/234-7543	1986	Fenimore Asset Management, Inc.	$3.9 Mil (e)	$2,000/ 100	r	Fund
Fidelity Devonshire Trust *Fidelity Real Estate Investment Portfolio* 82 Devonshire St. Boston, MA 02109 617/570-7000 800/544-6666	1986	Fidelity Management & Research Company	$58.1 Mil	$2,500/ 250	i	Fund

*Key: i=initial sales charge   r=redemption fee or contingent deferred sales charge(CDSC)
t=12b-1 fee and either CDSC or redemption fee   p=12b-1 fee   n=none of the preceding fees   N/A=not available

Growth and Income

Fund	Year Began	Investment Adviser	9/30/89 Assets	Minimum Initial and Subsequent Investment	Fees*	Where to Buy Shares
Fidelity Financial Trust *Fidelity Convertible Securities Fund* 82 Devonshire St. Boston, MA 02109 617/570-7000 800/544-6666	1987	Fidelity Management & Research Company	$57.6 Mil	$2,500/ 250	n	Fund
Fidelity Fund, Inc. 82 Devonshire St. Boston, MA 02109 617/570-7000 800/544-6666	1930	Fidelity Management & Research Company	$1.1 Bil	$1,000/ 250	n	Fund
Fidelity Institutional Trust *Fidelity U.S. Equity Index Portfolio* 82 Devonshire St. Boston, MA 02109 617/570-7000 800/843-3001	1988	Fidelity Management & Research Company	$278.9 Mil	$100,000/ 0	n	Local Rep
Fidelity Securities Fund *Fidelity Growth & Income Portfolio* 82 Devonshire St. Boston, MA 02109 617/570-7000 800/544-6666	1986	Fidelity Management & Research Company	$1.4 Bil	$2,500/ 250	i	Fund
Fiduciary Exchange Fund, Inc. 24 Federal St. 5th Fl. Boston, MA 02110 617/482-8260 800/225-6265	1966	Eaton Vance Management, Inc.	$53.0 Mil	Not Applicable	n	Not Offering Shares
Fortress High Quality Stock Fund Federated Investors Twr. Pittsburgh, PA 15222-3779 412/288-1900 800/245-5000	1985	Federated Advisers	$22.2 Mil	$1,500/ 100	i, t	Local Rep
FPA Paramount Fund, Inc. 10301 W. Pico Blvd. Los Angeles, CA 90064 213/277-4900 800/421-4374	1958	First Pacific Advisers, Inc.	$217.2 Mil	$1,500/ 100	i	Local Rep

*Key: i=initial sales charge   r=redemption fee or contingent deferred sales charge(CDSC)
t=12b-1 fee and either CDSC or redemption fee   p=12b-1 fee   n=none of the preceding fees   N/A=not available

189

Growth and Income

Fund	Year Began	Investment Adviser	9/30/89 Assets	Minimum Initial and Subsequent Investment	Fees*	Where to Buy Shares
FPA Perennial Fund, Inc. 10301 W. Pico Blvd. Los Angeles, CA 90064 213/277-4900 800/421-4374	1984	First Pacific Advisors, Inc.	$56.7 Mil	$1,500/ 100	i	Local Rep
Franklin Custodian Funds, Inc. *Utilities Series* 777 Mariners Island Blvd. San Mateo, CA 94404 415/570-3000 800/632-2180 800/632-2350	1948	Franklin Advisers, Inc.	$652.1 Mil	$100/ 25	i	Local Rep
Franklin Investors Securities Trust *Franklin Convertible Securities Fund* 777 Mariners Island Blvd. San Mateo, CA 94404 415/570-3000 800/632-2180, 800/632-2350	1987	Franklin Advisers, Inc.	$16.7 Mil	$100/ 25	i	Local Rep
Frank Russell Investment Company *Diversified Equity* 909 A St. Tacoma, WA 98402 206/627-7001 800/972-0700	1985	Frank Russell Investment Management Company	$247.4 Mil	$0/ 0	n	Local Rep
Frank Russell Investment Company *Equity I* 909 A St. Tacoma, WA 98402 206/627-7001 800/972-0700	1981	Frank Russell Investment Management Company	$304.1 Mil	$0/ 0	n	Local Rep
Frank Russell Investment Company *Equity Q Fund* 909 A St. Tacoma, WA 98402 206/627-7001 800/972-0700	1987	Frank Russell Investment Management Company	N/A	$0/ 0	N/A	Local Rep
Frank Russell Investment Company *Quantitative Equity Fund* 909 A St. Tacoma, WA 98402 206/627-7001 800/972-0700	1987	Frank Russell Investment Management Company	$125.3 Mil	$0/ 0	n	Local Rep

*Key: i=initial sales charge r=redemption fee or contingent deferred sales charge(CDSC)
t=12b-1 fee and either CDSC or redemption fee p=12b-1 fee n=none of the preceding fees N/A=not available

Growth and Income

Fund	Year Began	Investment Adviser	9/30/89 Assets	Minimum Initial and Subsequent Investment	Fees*	Where to Buy Shares
Frank Russell Investment Company *Real Estate Securities Fund* 909 A St. Tacoma, WA 98402 206/627-7001 800/972-0700	1989	Frank Russell Investment Management Company	N/A	$0/ 0	N/A	Local Rep
Fundamental Investors, Inc. 333 S. Hope St. Los Angeles, CA 90071 213/486-9200 800/421-0180 213/486-9651 Collect	1932	Capital Research & Management Company	$780.4 Mil	$250/ 50	i, t	Local Rep
Fund of America, Inc. 2800 Post Oak Blvd. Houston, TX 77056 713/993-0500 800/421-5666	1946	American Capital Asset Management, Inc.	$189.1 Mil	$500/ 50	i, p	Local Rep
Gabelli Convertible Securities Fund Grand Central Station P.O. Box 1634 New York, NY 10163 212/490-3670 800/422-3554	1989	Gabelli Funds, Inc.	N/A	$25,000/ 0	N/A	Fund
Gamma Partners, Inc. 80 E. Sir Francis Drake Blvd. Larkspur, CA 94939 415/461-3850	1984	Siebel Capital Management, Inc.	$2.9 Mil (e)	$25,000/ 1,000	n	Fund
Gardner Managed Assets Trust 105 Hazel Path P.O. Box 1256 Hendersonville, TN 37077-1256 615/824-8027 800/247-4783 TN Only	1987	Harvey L. Gardner & Associates, Inc.	$5.5 Mil	$250/ 25	p	Local Rep
GW Sierra Trust Funds *GW Growth and Income Fund* 888 S. Figueroa St. 11th Fl. Los Angeles, CA 90017-0970 213/488-2200 800/331-3426 800/221-9876 CA ONLY	1989	Great Western Financial Advisors Corp.	N/A	$1,000/ 100	t	Local Rep

*Key: i=initial sales charge   r=redemption fee or contingent deferred sales charge(CDSC)
t=12b-1 fee and either CDSC or redemption fee   p=12b-1 fee   n=none of the preceding fees   N/A=not available

Growth and Income

Fund	Year Began	Investment Adviser	9/30/89 Assets	Minimum Initial and Subsequent Investment	Fees*	Where to Buy Shares
Harbor Fund *Harbor U.S. Equities Fund* One SeaGate Toledo, OH 43666 419/247-2477 800/422-1050	1987	Harbor Capital Advisors, Inc.	$62.9 Mil	$2,000/ 500	n	Fund
Hartford Index Fund, Inc. 200 Hopmeadow St. P.O. Box 2999 Hartford, CT 06104-2999 203/843-8245 800/227-1371	1987	Hartford Investment Management Company, Inc.	$16.8 Mil	Not Applicable	n	Insur
Heritage Convertible Income-Growth Trust 880 Carillon Pkwy. St. Petersburg, FL 33716 813/573-3800	1986	Heritage Asset Management, Inc.	$24.4 Mil	$1,000/ 100	i, p	Local Rep
Home Group Trust *Home Growth and Income Fund* 59 Maiden Lane 21st Fl. New York, NY 10038 212/530-6016 800/729-3863	1988	Home Capital Services, Inc.	$19.6 Mil	$1,000/ 100	i, p	Local Rep
HVA Advisers Fund, Inc. 200 Hopmeadow St. P.O. Box 2999 Hartford, CT 06104-2999 203/843-8245 800/227-1371	1983	Hartford Investment Management Company, Inc. Wellington Management Company	$339.9 Mil (e)	Not Applicable	n	Insur
IAI Stock Fund, Inc. 1100 Dain Twr. P.O. Box 357 Minneapolis, MN 55440 612/371-7780	1971	Investment Advisers, Inc.	$72.7 Mil	$5,000/ 1,000	n	Local Rep
IDS Equity Plus Fund, Inc. IDS Tower 10 Minneapolis, MN 55440 612/372-3131 800/328-8300	1957	IDS Financial Corporation	$399.3 Mil	$100/ 100	i, p	Local Rep

*Key: i=initial sales charge   r=redemption fee or contingent deferred sales charge(CDSC)
     t=12b-1 fee and either CDSC or redemption fee   p=12b-1 fee   n=none of the preceding fees   N/A=not available

Growth and Income

Fund	Year Began	Investment Adviser	9/30/89 Assets	Minimum Initial and Subsequent Investment	Fees*	Where to Buy Shares
IDS Life Managed Fund, Inc. IDS Tower 10 Minneapolis, MN 55440 612/372-3131 800/328-8300	1986	IDS Financial Corporation	$461.2 Mil	Not Applicable	r	Insur
IDS Stock Fund, Inc. IDS Tower 10 Minneapolis, MN 55440 612/372-3131 800/328-8300	1945	IDS Financial Corporation	$1.4 Bil	$100/100	i, p	Local Rep
IDS Strategy Fund, Inc. *Equity Fund* IDS Tower 10 Minneapolis, MN 55440 612/372-3131 800/328-8300	1984	IDS Financial Corporation	$294.1 Mil	$100/100	t	Local Rep
Industrial Series Trust *Mackenzie North American Total Return Fund* 1200 N. Federal Hwy. #200 Boca Raton, FL 33432 407/393-8900 800/456-5111	1985	Mackenzie Investment Management Inc.	$160.9 Mil (e)	$250/50	i	Local Rep
Institutional Fiduciary Trust *Equity Portfolio* 777 Mariners Island Blvd. San Mateo, CA 94404 415/570-3000 800/632-2180 800/632-2350	1985	Franklin Trust Company	N/A	$25,000/0	n	Local Rep
Integrated Multi-Asset Portfolios, Inc. *Total Return Portfolio* 10 Union Square East New York, NY 10003 212/353-7000 800/858-8850	1987	Integrated Resources Asset Management Corp.	$37.2 Mil	$1,000/100	i, p	Local Rep
Integrated Resources Series Trust *Aggressive Multi-Asset Portfolio* One Bridge Plaza Fort Lee, NJ 07024 201/461-0606 800/821-5100	1987	Integrated Resources Asset Management Corp.	$114.6 Mil	Not Applicable	r	Insur

*Key: i=initial sales charge   r=redemption fee or contingent deferred sales charge(CDSC)
t=12b-1 fee and either CDSC or redemption fee   p=12b-1 fee   n=none of the preceding fees   N/A=not available

Growth and Income

Fund	Year Began	Investment Adviser	9/30/89 Assets	Minimum Initial and Subsequent Investment	Fees*	Where to Buy Shares
Integrated Resources Series Trust *Multi-Asset Portfolio* One Bridge Plaza Fort Lee, NJ 07024 201/461-0606 800/821-5100	1987	Integrated Resources Asset Management Corp.	$172.3 Mil	Not Applicable	r	Insur
Integrated Resources Series Trust *Natural Resources Portfolio* One Bridge Plaza Fort Lee, NJ 07024 201/461-0606 800/821-5100	1988	Integrated Resources Asset Management Corp.	$15.0 Mil	Not Applicable	r	Insur
INVESCO Institutional Series Trust *INVESCO Institutional Equity Fund* 1315 Peachtree St., NE Ste. 500 Atlanta, GA 30309 404/892-0666, 800/554-1156	1986	INVESCO Capital Management, Inc.	N/A	$1.0 Mil/ 5,000	n	Local Rep
Investment Company of America 333 S. Hope St. Los Angeles, CA 90071 213/486-9200 800/421-0180 213/486-9651 Collect	1933	Capital Research & Management Company	$5.4 Bil	$250/ 50	i, t	Local Rep
Investment Trust of Boston *Growth Opportunities Portfolio* 399 Boylston St. 9th Fl. Boston, MA 02116 800/888-4823	1931	Back Bay Advisors, Inc.	$63.9 Mil	$1,000/ 100	i, p	Local Rep
ISI Trust Fund 3801 Kennett Pk., C-200 Greenville Ctr. Wilmington, DE 19807 302/652-3091 800/441-9490	1938	Sigma Management, Inc.	$110.4 Mil	$0/ 0	i	Local Rep
Kemper Blue Chip Fund 120 S. LaSalle St. Chicago, IL 60603 312/781-1121 800/621-1148	1987	Kemper Financial Services, Inc.	$25.9 Mil	$1,000/ 100	i, p	Local Rep

*Key: i=initial sales charge   r=redemption fee or contingent deferred sales charge(CDSC)
   t=12b-1 fee and either CDSC or redemption fee   p=12b-1 fee   n=none of the preceding fees   N/A=not available

Growth and Income

Fund	Year Began	Investment Adviser	9/30/89 Assets	Minimum Initial and Subsequent Investment	Fees*	Where to Buy Shares
Kemper Total Return Fund 120 S. LaSalle St. Chicago, IL 60603 312/781-1121 800/621-1148	1964	Kemper Financial Services, Inc.	$971.1 Mil	$1,000/ 100	i	Local Rep
Keystone Custodian Funds, Inc. S-1 Series 99 High St. Boston, MA 02110 617/338-3200 800/343-2898 800/225-1587	1932	Keystone Custodian Funds, Inc.	$183.3 Mil	$250/ 0	t	Local Rep
Legg Mason Total Return Trust, Inc. 111 S. Calvert St. P.O. Box 1476 Baltimore, MD 21203-1476 30l/539-3400 800/822-5544 800/492-7777 MD Only	1985	Legg Mason Fund Adviser, Inc.	$32.4 Mil	$1,000/ 500	p	Local Rep
Lehman Investors Fund, Inc. 55 Water St. 34th Fl. New York, NY 10041 212/668-8578 800/221-5350	1958	Lehman Management Company, Inc.	$407.3 Mil	$500/ 50	i	Local Rep
Lepercq-Istel Trust *Lepercq-Istel Fund* 345 Park Ave. 23rd Fl. New York, NY 10154 212/702-0100 800/338-1579	1953	Lepercq, de Neuflize & Company, Incorporated	$21.7 Mil (e)	$500/ 0	p	Fund
Lexington Corporate Leaders Trust Fund Park 80 W., Plaza Two P.O. Box 1515 Saddle Brook, NJ 07662 201/845-7300 800/526-0056	1935	None	N/A	$1,000/ 50	i	Local Rep
Lexington Research Fund, Inc. Park 80 W., Plaza Two P.O. Box 1515 Saddle Brook, NJ 07662 201/845-7300 800/526-0056	1959	Lexington Management Corporation	$132.7 Mil	$1,000/ 50	n	Fund

*Key: i=initial sales charge   r=redemption fee or contingent deferred sales charge(CDSC)
t=12b-1 fee and either CDSC or redemption fee   p=12b-1 fee   n=none of the preceding fees   N/A=not available

Growth and Income

Fund	Year Began	Investment Adviser	9/30/89 Assets	Minimum Initial and Subsequent Investment	Fees*	Where to Buy Shares
Life of Virginia Series Fund, Inc. *Total Return Portfolio* 6610 W. Broad St. Richmond, VA 23230 804/281-6000 800/822-6000	1985	AON Advisors, Inc.	$2.8 Mil (e)	Not Applicable	n	Insur
LMH Fund, Ltd. 253 Post Rd. West P.O. Box 830 Westport, CT 06881 203/222-1624 800/422-2564 800/522-2564 CT Only	1983	Heine Management Group, Inc.	$37.8 Mil (e)	$2,500/ 1,000	n	Local Rep
Lord Abbett Fundamental Value Fund, Inc. The General Motors Bldg. 767 Fifth Ave. New York, NY 10153 212/848-1800 800/223-4224	1986	Lord, Abbett & Co.	$20.2 Mil	$1,000/ 0	i, p	Local Rep
Lutheran Brotherhood Fund, Inc. 625 Fourth Ave. South Minneapolis, MN 55415 612/339-8091 800/328-4552 800/752-4208 MN Only	1970	Lutheran Brotherhood Research Corp.	$305.2 Mil	$500/ 50	i	Local Rep
MacKay-Shields MainStay Series Fund *MainStay Convertible Fund* 51 Madison Ave. New York, NY 10010 212/576-7000 800/522-4202	1986	MacKay-Shields Financial Corporation	$24.0 Mil	$500/ 50	t	Local Rep
Mackenzie Funds Inc. *Growth and Income Fund* 1200 N. Federal Hwy. #200 Boca Raton, FL 33432 407/393-8900 800/456-5111	1988	Mackenzie Investment Management Inc.	N/A	$250/ 50	i, p	Local Rep
Managed Assets Trust 99 High St. Boston, MA 02110 617/338-3200 800/343-2898 800/225-1587	1983	Keystone Custodian Funds, Inc.	$79.0 Mil	Not Applicable	n	Insur

*Key: i=initial sales charge   r=redemption fee or contingent deferred sales charge(CDSC)
t=12b-1 fee and either CDSC or redemption fee   p=12b-1 fee   n=none of the preceding fees   N/A=not available

Growth and Income

Fund	Year Began	Investment Adviser	9/30/89 Assets	Minimum Initial and Subsequent Investment	Fees*	Where to Buy Shares
Management of Managers Group of Funds *Income Equity Fund* 200 Connecticut Ave. 8th Fl. Norwalk, CT 06854 203/855-2200	1984	Evaluation Associates Investment Management Co.	$125.1 Mil	$0/ 0	n	Local Rep
ManuLife Series Fund, Inc. *Common Stock Fund* 200 Bloor St. East N. Tower 5 Toronto, Ont., Canada M4W 1E5 416/926-6700	1987	Manufacturers Adviser Corporation	N/A	Not Applicable	N/A	Insur
ManuLife Series Fund, Inc. *Real Estate Securities Fund* 200 Bloor St. East N. Tower 5 Toronto, Ont., Canada M4W 1E5 416/926-6700	1987	Manufacturers Adviser Corporation	N/A	Not Applicable	N/A	Insur
Massachusetts Financial Development Fund 500 Boylston St. Boston, MA 02116 617/954-5000 800/343-2829	1971	Massachusetts Financial Services Company	$232.7 Mil	$1,000/ 25	i	Local Rep
Massachusetts Investors Trust 500 Boylston St. Boston, MA 02116 617/954-5000 800/343-2829	1924	Massachusetts Financial Services Company	$1.4 Bil	$1,000/ 25	i	Local Rep
MassMutual Integrity Funds *MassMutual Value Stock Fund* 1295 State St. Springfield, MA 01111 413/788-8411 800/542-6767 800/854-9100 MA Only	1988	Massachusetts Mutual Life Insurance Company	$36.5 Mil	$500/ 25	i, p	Local Rep
Maxus Equity Fund 3550 Lander Rd. 2nd Fl. Pepper Pike, OH 44124 216/292-3434	1989	Investment Strategies Inc.	N/A	$1,000/ 100	N/A	Local Rep

*Key: i=initial sales charge   r=redemption fee or contingent deferred sales charge(CDSC)
t=12b-1 fee and either CDSC or redemption fee   p=12b-1 fee   n=none of the preceding fees   N/A=not available

Growth and Income

Fund	Year Began	Investment Adviser	9/30/89 Assets	Minimum Initial and Subsequent Investment	Fees*	Where to Buy Shares
Merrill Lynch Basic Value Fund, Inc.		Fund Asset Management, Inc.	$2.2 Bil			
Class A	1977			$250/50	i	LRep
Class B	1988			$250/50	t	LRep
P.O. Box 9011 Princeton, NJ 08543-9011 609/282-2800 800/637-3863						
Merrill Lynch Capital Fund, Inc.		Merrill Lynch Asset Management Inc.	$988.8 Mil			
Class A	1973			$250/50	i	LRep
Class B	1988			$250/50	t	LRep
P.O. Box 9011 Princeton, NJ 08543-9011 609/282-2800 800/637-3863						
Merrill Lynch Equi-Bond I Fund, Inc.	1978	Fund Asset Management, Inc.	$12.6 Mil	$1,000/ 500	i, r	Local Rep
P.O. Box 9011 Princeton, NJ 08543-9011 609/282-2800 800/637-3863						
Merrill Lynch Retirement Equity Fund		Merrill Lynch Asset Management Inc.	$498.1 Mil			
Class A	1988			$1,000/50	t	LRep
Class B	1987			$1,000/50	t	LRep
P.O. Box 9011 Princeton, NJ 08543-9011 609/282-2800 800/637-3863						
Merrill Lynch Series Fund *Capital Stock Portfolio*	1981	Fund Asset Management, Inc.	$129.7 Mil	Not Applicable	n	Insur
P.O. Box 9011 Princeton, NJ 08543-9011 609/282-2800 800/221-3150						
Merrill Lynch Series Fund *Multiple Strategy Portfolio*	1985	Fund Asset Management, Inc.	$1.2 Bil	Not Applicable	n	Insur
P.O. Box 9011 Princeton, NJ 08543-9011 609/282-2800 800/524-4458						
Merrill Lynch Strategic Dividend Fund		Merrill Lynch Asset Management Inc.	$346.3 Mil			
Class A	1988			$1,000/50	i	LRep
Class B	1987			$1,000/50	t	LRep
P.O. Box 9011 Princeton, NJ 08543-9011 609/282-2800 800/637-3863						

*Key: i=initial sales charge   r=redemption fee or contingent deferred sales charge(CDSC)
t=12b-1 fee and either CDSC or redemption fee   p=12b-1 fee   n=none of the preceding fees   N/A=not available

Growth and Income

Fund	Year Began	Investment Adviser	9/30/89 Assets	Minimum Initial and Subsequent Investment	Fees*	Where to Buy Shares
Merrill Lynch Variable Series Funds *Flex Strategy Fund* P.O. Box 9011 Princeton, NJ 08543-9011 609/282-2800 800/524-4458	1986	Merrill Lynch Asset Management Inc.	$47.2 Mil	Not Applicable	n	Insur
Merrill Lynch Variable Series Funds *Quality Equity Fund* P.O. Box 9011 Princeton, NJ 08543-9011 609/282-2800 800/524-4458	1982	Merrill Lynch Asset Management Inc.	$28.1 Mil	Not Applicable	n	Insur
MetLife-State Street Equity Trust *MetLife-State Street Equity Investment Fund* One Financial Ctr. 30th Fl. Boston, MA 02111 617/348-2000, 800/882-0052	1986	MetLife-State Street Investment Services, Inc.	$25.6 Mil	$250/ 25	i, p	Local Rep
Mills Value Fund, Inc. 1108 E. Main St., 14th Fl. P.O. Box 1796 Richmond, VA 23214 804/649-2400	1988	Mills Value Adviser, Inc.	$11.2 Mil	$2,000/ 1,000	i, p	Local Rep
MIMLIC Investors Fund I, Inc. 400 N. Robert St. St. Paul, MN 55101-2098 612/223-4252 800/443-3677	1984	MIMLIC Asset Management Company	$11.8 Mil	$250/ 25	i	Local Rep
Mutual of America Investment Corporation *Stock Fund (The)* 666 Fifth Ave. New York, NY 10103 212/399-1600 800/223-0898	1986	Mutual of America Life Insurance Company	N/A	Not Applicable	n	Insur
Mutual Series Fund, Inc. *Mutual Beacon Fund* 51 J.F. Kennedy Pkwy. Short Hills, NJ 07078 201/912-2100 800/448-3863	1961	Heine Securities Corp.	$416.0 Mil	$50,000/ 1,000	n	Fund

*Key: i=initial sales charge   r=redemption fee or contingent deferred sales charge(CDSC)
t=12b-1 fee and either CDSC or redemption fee   p=12b-1 fee   n=none of the preceding fees   N/A=not available

Growth and Income

Fund	Year Began	Investment Adviser	9/30/89 Assets	Minimum Initial and Subsequent Investment	Fees*	Where to Buy Shares
Mutual Series Fund, Inc. *Mutual Qualified Fund* 51 J.F. Kennedy Pkwy. Short Hills, NJ 07078 201/912-2100 800/448-3863	1980	Heine Securities Corp.	$1.6 Bil	$1,000/ 50	n	Fund
Mutual Series Fund, Inc. *Mutual Shares Fund* 51 J.F. Kennedy Pkwy. Short Hills, NJ 07078 201/912-2100 800/448-3863	1949	Heine Securities Corp.	$3.6 Bil	$5,000/ 100	n	Fund
National Real Estate Trust *National Real Estate Stock Fund* 600 Third Ave. New York, NY 10016 203/863-5600 800/237-1718	1985	National Securities & Research Corporation	$24.4 Mil	$500/ 25	i, p	Local Rep
National Stock Fund 600 Third Ave. New York, NY 10016 203/863-5600 800/237-1718	1944	National Securities & Research Corporation	$246.7 Mil	$250/ 25	i	Local Rep
National Total Return Fund 600 Third Ave. New York, NY 10016 203/863-5600 800/237-1718	1945	National Securities & Research Corporation	$278.6 Mil	$250/ 25	i	Local Rep
Nationwide Investing Foundation *Nationwide Fund* One Nationwide Plaza Box 1492 Columbus, OH 43216 614/249-7855 800/848-0920, 800/282-1440 OH Only	1933	Nationwide Financial Services, Inc.	$478.3 Mil	$250/ 25	i	Local Rep
Nationwide Separate Account Trust *Common Stock Fund* One Nationwide Plaza Box 1492 Columbus, OH 43216 614/249-7855 800/848-0920, 800/282-1440 OH Only	1982	Nationwide Financial Services, Inc.	$188.5 Mil	Not Applicable	n	Insur

*Key: i=initial sales charge   r=redemption fee or contingent deferred sales charge(CDSC)
t=12b-1 fee and either CDSC or redemption fee   p=12b-1 fee   n=none of the preceding fees   N/A=not available

Growth and Income

Fund	Year Began	Investment Adviser	9/30/89 Assets	Minimum Initial and Subsequent Investment	Fees*	Where to Buy Shares
Neuberger & Berman Guardian Fund, Inc. 342 Madison Ave. New York, NY 10173 212/850-8300 800/877-9700	1950	Neuberger & Berman Management Incorporated	$611.0 Mil	$1,000/ 100	n	Fund
New England Equity Income Fund 399 Boylston St. Boston, MA 02116 617/267-6600 800/343-7104	1968	Loomis, Sayles & Company, Inc.	$62.6 Mil	$1,000/ 25	i, p	Local Rep
New England Retirement Equity Fund 399 Boylston St. Boston, MA 02116 617/267-6600 800/343-7104	1970	Loomis, Sayles & Company, Inc.	$152.1 Mil	$1,000/ 25	i, p	Local Rep
New England Zenith Fund *Managed Series* 501 Boylston St. Boston, MA 02116 617/267-7055 800/634-8025	1987	Back Bay Advisors, Inc.	$18.2 Mil	Not Applicable	n	Insur
Noddings Convertible Strategies Fund Two MidAmerica Plaza Ste. 920 Oakbrook Terrace, IL 60181 312/954-1322 800/544-7785	1985	Noddings Investment Group, Inc.	$6.0 Mil	$1,000/ 100	n	Fund
Olympus Equity Plus Fund 230 Park Ave. New York, NY 10169 212/309-8400 800/626-FUND	1986	Furman Selz Mager Dietz & Birney Incorporated	$8.8 Mil (e)	$1,000/ 100	i, p	Local Rep
One Hundred and One Fund, Inc. 899 Logan St. Ste. 211 Denver, CO 80203 303/837-1020 800/333-1001	1966	Berger Associates	$1.8 Mil	$250/ 50	p	Fund

*Key: i=initial sales charge   r=redemption fee or contingent deferred sales charge(CDSC)
t=12b-1 fee and either CDSC or redemption fee   p=12b-1 fee   n=none of the preceding fees   N/A=not available

Growth and Income

Fund	Year Began	Investment Adviser	9/30/89 Assets	Minimum Initial and Subsequent Investment	Fees*	Where to Buy Shares
Oppenheimer Total Return Fund, Inc. 3410 S. Galena St. Denver, CO 80231 303/671-3200 800/525-7048	1948	Oppenheimer Management Corporation	$382.2 Mil	$1,000/ 25	i, p	Local Rep
Pacific Horizon Funds, Inc. *Convertible Securities Fund* 156 W. 56th St. Ste. 1902 New York, NY 10019 212/492-1600 800/367-6075	1987	Security Pacific National Bank	$0.7 Mil	$1,000/ 100	i, p	Local Rep
Pacific Investment Management Institutional Trust *Market Mirror Stock Portfolio* 840 Newport Ctr. Dr. Ste. 300 Newport Beach, CA 92660 714/640-3031, 800/443-6915	1987	Pacific Investment Management Company	$2.8 Mil (e)	$200,000/ 10,000	n	Fund
PaineWebber Classic Growth and Income Fund 1285 Avenue of the Americas PaineWebber Bldg. New York, NY 10019 212/713-2000 800/544-9300	1983	Mitchell Hutchins Asset Management Inc.	$56.2 Mil	$1,000/ 100	i, p	Local Rep
PaineWebber Investment Series *PaineWebber Master Energy-Utility Fund* 1285 Avenue of the Americas PaineWebber Bldg. New York, NY 10019 212/713-2000, 800/647-1568	1987	Mitchell Hutchins Asset Management Inc.	$20.0 Mil	$1,000/ 100	t	Local Rep
PaineWebber Series Trust *Growth & Income Portfolio* 1285 Avenue of the Americas PaineWebber Bldg. New York, NY 10019 212/713-2000	1987	Mitchell Hutchins Asset Management Inc.	N/A	Not Applicable	N/A	Insur
Parkstone Group of Funds *Small Capitalization Value Fund* 1900 E. Dublin-Granville Rd. Columbus, OH 43229 614/899-4600 800/338-4385	1987	Securities Counsel, Inc.	N/A	$1,000/ 0	N/A	Fund

*Key: i=initial sales charge   r=redemption fee or contingent deferred sales charge(CDSC)
t=12b-1 fee and either CDSC or redemption fee   p=12b-1 fee   n=none of the preceding fees   N/A=not available

Growth and Income

Fund	Year Began	Investment Adviser	9/30/89 Assets	Minimum Initial and Subsequent Investment	Fees*	Where to Buy Shares
Pasadena Investment Trust *Pasadena Growth & Income Fund (The)* 600 N. Rosemead Blvd. Pasadena, CA 91107-2101 818/351-4276 800/882-2855	1989	Roger Engemann Management Co., Inc.	N/A	$1,000/ 1,000	N/A	Fund
Phillips Capital Investments, Inc. P.O. Box 796787 Dallas, TX 75379 214/380-2448	1989	Phillips Capital Management, Inc.	$2.3 Mil	$5,000/ 2,000	r	Fund
Phoenix Series Fund *Phoenix Convertible Fund Series* 101 Munson St. Greenfield, MA 01301 203/253-1000 800/243-1574	1980	Phoenix Investment Counsel, Inc.	$157.1 Mil	$500/ 25	i	Local Rep
Pine Street Fund, Inc. 140 Broadway 42nd Fl. New York, NY 10005 212/504-4000 800/225-8011 800/521-3036	1949	Wood, Struthers & Winthrop Management Corporation	$55.7 Mil (e)	$1,000/ 100	n	Fund
Pioneer Fund 60 State St. Boston, MA 02109-1975 617/742-7825 800/225-6292	1928	Pioneering Management Corporation	$1.6 Bil	$50/ 50	i	Local Rep
Pioneer II 60 State St. Boston, MA 02109-1975 617/742-7825 800/225-6292	1969	Pioneering Management Corporation	$4.4 Bil	$50/ 50	i	Local Rep
Pioneer Three 60 State St. Boston, MA 02109-1975 617/742-7825 800/225-6292	1982	Pioneering Management Corporation	$719.7 Mil	$1,000/ 100	i	Local Rep

*Key: i=initial sales charge   r=redemption fee or contingent deferred sales charge(CDSC)
t=12b-1 fee and either CDSC or redemption fee   p=12b-1 fee   n=none of the preceding fees   N/A=not available

Growth and Income

Fund	Year Began	Investment Adviser	9/30/89 Assets	Minimum Initial and Subsequent Investment	Fees*	Where to Buy Shares
PNCG Growth Fund, Inc. 121 SW Morrison Ste. 1415 Portland, OR 97204 503/295-0919 800/541-9732	1987	PNCG Fund Advisers, Inc.	$3.2 Mil (e)	$1,000/ 500	i, p	Local Rep
PRA Securities Trust *PRA Real Estate Securities Fund* 44 Montgomery St. 37th Fl. San Francisco, CA 94104 415/296-8700	1989	PRA Securities Advisors, L.P.	N/A	$100,000/ 0	n	Local Rep
Principal Preservation Portfolios, Inc. *S&P 100 Plus Portfolio* 215 N. Main St. West Bend, WI 53095 414/334-5521 800/826-4600	1986	B.C. Ziegler and Company	$20.4 Mil	$1,000/ 250	i	Local Rep
Princor Capital Accumulation Fund, Inc. 711 High St. Des Moines, IA 50309 515/247-5711 800/247-4123 800/622-5344 IA Only	1969	Principal Management, Inc.	$126.5 Mil	$300/ 50	i, p	Local Rep
Professional Portfolios Trust *Total Return Fund* 429 N. Pennsylvania St. Indianapolis, IN 46204-1897 317/634-3300 800/862-7283	1988	Unified Management Corporation	$0.3 Mil	$200/ 25	p	Local Rep
Prudential-Bache Corporate Dividend Fund, Inc. One Seaport Plaza New York, NY 10292 212/214-1215 800/225-1852	1983	Prudential Mutual Fund Management	$4.0 Mil	$25,000/ 1,000	p	Local Rep
Public Employees Retirement Trust 618 S. 19th St. Arlington, VA 22202 703/521-0785 804/782-7347	1987	Public Service Investment Management Corporation	N/A	$250/ 100	n	Fund

*Key: i=initial sales charge   r=redemption fee or contingent deferred sales charge(CDSC)
t=12b-1 fee and either CDSC or redemption fee   p=12b-1 fee   n=none of the preceding fees   N/A=not available

Growth and Income

Fund	Year Began	Investment Adviser	9/30/89 Assets	Minimum Initial and Subsequent Investment	Fees*	Where to Buy Shares
Putnam Capital Manager Trust *PCM Growth and Income Fund* One Post Office Sq. Boston, MA 02109 617/292-1000 800/225-2465	1988	Putnam Management Company, Inc.	$80.0 Mil	Not Applicable	r	Insur
Putnam Convertible Income - Growth Trust One Post Office Sq. Boston, MA 02109 617/292-1000 800/225-2465	1972	Putnam Management Company, Inc.	$867.9 Mil	$500/ 50	i	Local Rep
Putnam Energy-Resources Trust One Post Office Sq. Boston, MA 02109 617/292-1000 800/225-2465	1980	Putnam Management Company, Inc.	$113.5 Mil	$500/ 50	i	Local Rep
Putnam Fund for Growth and Income One Post Office Sq. Boston, MA 02109 617/292-1000 800/225-2465	1957	Putnam Management Company, Inc.	$1.9 Bil	$500/ 50	i	Local Rep
Retirement Investment Trust *Balanced Fund* 16 HCB 98 P.O. Box 2558 Houston, TX 77252-8098 713/546-7775	1988	None	N/A	$500/ 100	n	Fund
RNC Convertible Securities Fund, Inc. 11601 Wilshire Blvd. 24th Fl. Los Angeles, CA 90025 213/477-6543 800/225-9655	1986	RNC Capital Management Co.	$25.0 Mil (e)	$1,000/ 100	i, p	Local Rep
RNC Westwind Fund 11601 Wilshire Blvd. 24th Fl. Los Angeles, CA 90025 213/477-6543 800/225-9655	1986	RNC Capital Management Co.	$7.4 Mil (e)	$1,000/ 100	i, p	Local Rep

*Key: i=initial sales charge   r=redemption fee or contingent deferred sales charge(CDSC)
t=12b-1 fee and either CDSC or redemption fee   p=12b-1 fee   n=none of the preceding fees   N/A=not available

Growth and Income

Fund	Year Began	Investment Adviser	9/30/89 Assets	Minimum Initial and Subsequent Investment	Fees*	Where to Buy Shares
Rochester Tax Managed Fund 379 Park Ave. Rochester, NY 14607 716/442-5500	1968	Fielding Management Company, Inc.	$15.2 Mil (e)	$2,000/ 100	i, p	Local Rep
Rodney Square Multi-Manager Fund *Total Return Portfolio (The)* Rodney Square North Wilmington, DE 19890 302/651-1923 800/225-5084	1987	Rodney Square Management Corporation	$19.4 Mil (e)	$1,000/ 0	i, p	Local Rep
SAFECO Equity Fund, Inc. SAFECO Plaza Seattle, WA 98185 206/545-5530 800/426-6730	1932	SAFECO Asset Management Company	$53.9 Mil	$1,000/ 100	n	Fund
SBL Fund *Income & Growth Series* 700 Harrison St. 6th Fl. Topeka, KS 66636 913/295-3127 800/888-2461	1977	Security Management Company	$151.5 Mil	Not Applicable	n	Insur
SBSF Funds *SBSF Convertible Securities Fund* 45 Rockefeller Plaza 33rd Fl. New York, NY 10111 212/903-1200 800/422-7273	1988	Spears, Benzak, Salomon & Farrell	$12.0 Mil	$0/ 0	n	Fund
Scudder Equity Income Fund 175 Federal St. Boston, MA 02110 617/439-4640 800/225-2470 800/225-5163	1987	Scudder, Stevens & Clark, Inc.	$18.7 Mil	$1,000/ 0	n	Fund
Scudder Growth & Income Fund 175 Federal St. Boston, MA 02110 617/439-4640 800/225-2470 800/225-5163	1929	Scudder, Stevens & Clark, Inc.	$499.6 Mil	$1,000/ 0	n	Fund

*Key: i=initial sales charge   r=redemption fee or contingent deferred sales charge(CDSC)
t=12b-1 fee and either CDSC or redemption fee   p=12b-1 fee   n=none of the preceding fees   N/A=not available

Growth and Income

Fund	Year Began	Investment Adviser	9/30/89 Assets	Minimum Initial and Subsequent Investment	Fees*	Where to Buy Shares
Second Fiduciary Exchange Fund, Inc. 24 Federal St. Boston, MA 02110 617/482-8260 800/225-6265	1967	Eaton Vance Management, Inc.	$69.2 Mil (e)	Not Applicable	n	Not Offering Shares
SECURAL Mutual Funds, Inc. *Stock Fund* 2401 S. Memorial Dr. Appleton, WI 54915 414/739-3161 800/426-5975	1988	SECURA Advisory Services, Inc.	$0.3 Mil	$500/ 100	i, p	Local Rep
Security Investment Fund 700 Harrison St. Topeka, KS 66636 913/295-3127 800/888-2461	1944	Security Management Company	$85.0 Mil	$100/ 20	i	Local Rep
SEI Index Funds *S&P 500 Index Portfolio* 680 E. Swedesford Rd. No. 7 Wayne, PA 19087 215/254-1000 800/345-1151	1985	Manufacturers National Bank of Detroit	$160.3 Mil	$0/ 0	p	Local Rep
SEI Institutional Managed Trust *Value Portfolio* 680 E. Swedesford Rd. No. 7 Wayne, PA 19087 215/254-1000 800/345-1151	1987	Dreman Value Management Inc.	$111.8 Mil	$0/ 0	p	Local Rep
Selected American Shares, Inc. 1331 Euclid Ave. Cleveland, OH 44115 312/641-7862 800/553-5533	1933	Selected Financial Services, Inc.	$392.4 Mil	$1,000/ 100	p	Local Rep
Seligman Common Stock Fund, Inc. 130 Liberty St. New York, NY 10006 212/488-0200 800/221-2450 800/522-6869 NY Only	1930	J. & W. Seligman & Co. Incorporated	$516.6 Mil	$1,000/ 50	i	Local Rep

*Key: i=initial sales charge   r=redemption fee or contingent deferred sales charge(CDSC)
t=12b-1 fee and either CDSC or redemption fee   p=12b-1 fee   n=none of the preceding fees   N/A=not available

Growth and Income

Fund	Year Began	Investment Adviser	9/30/89 Assets	Minimum Initial and Subsequent Investment	Fees*	Where to Buy Shares
Seligman Mutual Benefit Portfolios, Inc. *Seligman Common Stock Portfolio* 130 Liberty St. New York, NY 10006 212/488-0200 800/221-2450, 800/522-6869 NY Only	1988	J. & W. Seligman & Co. Incorporated	$7.1 Mil	Not Applicable	r	Insur
Sentinel Group Funds, Inc. *Common Stock Fund Series* National Life Dr. Montpelier, VT 05604 802/229-3900 800/282-3863	1934	Sentinel Advisors, Inc.	$596.7 Mil	$250/ 25	i	Local Rep
Shearson Lehman Series Fund *SLH IDS Total Return Portfolio* 31 W. 52nd St. New York, NY 10019 212/767-3700	1986	Boston Company Advisors, Inc.	$5.9 Mil	Not Applicable	n	Insur
Siebel Capital Partners, Inc. 80 E. Sir Francis Drake Blvd. Larkspur, CA 94939 415/461-3850	1983	Siebel Capital Management, Inc.	$24.4 Mil (e)	$250,000/ 5,000	n	Fund
Sigma Investment Shares, Inc. 3801 Kennett Pk., C-200 Greenville Ctr. Wilmington, DE 19807 302/652-3091 800/441-9490	1950	Sigma Management, Inc.	$111.0 Mil	$0/ 0	i, p	Local Rep
SLH Master Series, Inc. *SLH Convertible Securities Fund* 31 W. 52nd St. 15th Fl. New York, NY 10019 212/767-3700 800/334-4636, 800/422-0214 NY Only	1987	SLH Asset Management Division of Shearson Lehman Hutton Inc.	$6.9 Mil	$500/ 250	i	Local Rep
SLH Special Income Portfolios *SLH Convertible Portfolio* 31 W. 52nd St. New York, NY 10019 212/767-3700	1986	Bernstein-Macaulay Division of Shearson Lehman Hutton Inc.	$145.5 Mil	$500/ 200	t	Local Rep

*Key: i=initial sales charge   r=redemption fee or contingent deferred sales charge(CDSC)
t=12b-1 fee and either CDSC or redemption fee   p=12b-1 fee   n=none of the preceding fees   N/A=not available

Growth and Income

Fund	Year Began	Investment Adviser	9/30/89 Assets	Minimum Initial and Subsequent Investment	Fees*	Where to Buy Shares
SLH Telecommunications Trust *SLH Telecommunications Income Fund* One Boston Place Boston, MA 02019 617/956-9740 800/225-5267, 800/343-6324	1983	Boston Company Advisors, Inc.	$103.3 Mil	Not Applicable	r	Not Offering Shares
SMA Investment Trust *Growth Fund* 440 Lincoln St. Worcester, MA 01605 508/852-1000	1985	State Mutual Life Assurance Company of America	$75.0 Mil	Not Applicable	n	Insur
SMA Investment Trust *Income Appreciation Fund* 440 Lincoln St. Worcester, MA 01605 508/852-1000	1985	State Mutual Life Assurance Company of America	$11.6 Mil	Not Applicable	n	Insur
Smith Barney Funds, Inc. *Income and Growth Portfolio* 1345 Avenue of the Americas New York, NY 10105 212/698-5349 800/544-7835	1966	Smith, Barney Advisers, Inc.	$588.6 Mil	$3,000/ 50	i	Local Rep
Smith Barney Variable Account Funds, Inc. *Income and Growth Portfolio* 1345 Avenue of the Americas New York, NY 10105 212/698-5349 800/544-7835	1989	Smith, Barney Advisers, Inc.	N/A	Not Applicable	N/A	Insur
SMITH HAYES Trust, Inc. *Balanced Portfolio* NBC Ctr. Ste. 780 Lincoln, NE 68508 402/476-3000 800/422-7791 NE Only	1988	SMITH HAYES Portfolio Management, Inc.	N/A	$25,000/ 1,000	N/A	Local Rep
Sovereign Investors, Inc. 985 Old Eagle School Rd. Ste. 515A Wayne, PA 19087 215/254-0703	1936	Sovereign Advisers, Inc.	$63.7 Mil	$30/ 30	i, p	Local Rep

*Key: i=initial sales charge   r=redemption fee or contingent deferred sales charge(CDSC)
t=12b-1 fee and either CDSC or redemption fee   p=12b-1 fee   n=none of the preceding fees   N/A=not available

Growth and Income

Fund	Year Began	Investment Adviser	9/30/89 Assets	Minimum Initial and Subsequent Investment	Fees*	Where to Buy Shares
Specialty Managers Trust *Real Estate Series* 1925 Century Park East Ste. 2350 Los Angeles, CA 90067 213/556-5499 800/423-4891	1989	Cohen & Steers Capital Management, Inc.	N/A	Not Applicable	n	Insur
State Street Exchange Trust *State Street Exchange Fund* One Financial Ctr. 38th Fl. Boston, MA 02111 617/482-3920	1976	State Street Research & Management Company	$139.0 Mil (e)	Not Applicable	n	Not Offering Shares
State Street Growth Trust *State Street Growth Fund* One Financial Ctr. 38th Fl. Boston, MA 02111 617/482-3920	1960	State Street Research & Management Company	$283.3 Mil (e)	Not Applicable	r	Not Offering Shares
State Street Investment Trust One Financial Ctr. 38th Fl. Boston, MA 02111 617/482-3920	1924	State Street Research & Management Company	$597.4 Mil	Not Applicable	r	Not Offering Shares
SteinRoe Investment Trust *SteinRoe Growth & Income Fund* 300 W. Adams St. P.O. Box 1143 Chicago, IL 60690 800/338-2550	1987	Stein Roe & Farnham Incorporated	$15.9 Mil	$1,000/ 100	n	Fund
SteinRoe Investment Trust *SteinRoe Prime Equities* 300 W. Adams St. P.O. Box 1143 Chicago, IL 60690 800/338-2550	1987	Stein Roe & Farnham Incorporated	$32.6 Mil	$1,000/ 100	n	Fund
SteinRoe Variable Investment Trust *Managed Assets Fund* 600 Atlantic Ave. Boston, MA 02210 617/722-6000 800/443-2683	1989	Stein Roe & Farnham Incorporated	N/A	Not Applicable	N/A	Insur

*Key: i=initial sales charge   r=redemption fee or contingent deferred sales charge(CDSC)
t=12b-1 fee and either CDSC or redemption fee   p=12b-1 fee   n=none of the preceding fees   N/A=not available

Growth and Income

Fund	Year Began	Investment Adviser	9/30/89 Assets	Minimum Initial and Subsequent Investment	Fees*	Where to Buy Shares
Stratton Growth Fund, Inc. 610 W. Germantown Pike Ste. 361 Plymouth Meeting, PA 19462 215/941-0255 800/634-5726	1972	Stratton Management Company	$24.0 Mil	$1,000/ 100	n	Fund
Thomson McKinnon Investment Trust *Thomson McKinnon Convertible Securities Fund* One State Street Plaza New York, NY 10004 212/482-5894 800/628-1237	1988	Thomson McKinnon Asset Management L.P.	$45.2 Mil	$1,000/ 100	t	Local Rep
Transamerica Investment Trust *Transamerica Growth and Income Fund* 1000 Louisiana Ste. 6000 Houston, TX 77002-5098 713/751-2400, 800/999-3863	1949	Transamerica Fund Management Company	$68.9 Mil	$100/ 10	i, p	Local Rep
Transamerica Special Series, Inc. *Transamerica Special Convertible Securities Fund* 1000 Louisiana Ste. 6000 Houston, TX 77002-5098 713/751-2400, 800/999-3863	1986	Transamerica Fund Management Company	$10.5 Mil	$1,000/ 50	t	Local Rep
T. Rowe Price Growth & Income Fund, Inc. 100 E. Pratt St. Baltimore, MD 21202 301/547-2000 800/638-5660	1982	T. Rowe Price Associates, Inc.	$569.7 Mil	$2,500/ 100	n	Fund
Trustees' Commingled Fund *U.S. Equity Portfolio* Vanguard Financial Ctr. P.O. Box 2600 Valley Forge, PA 19482 215/648-6000 800/662-7447 800/362-0530 PA Only	1980	Batterymarch Financial Management	$137.2 Mil	$10,000/ 1,000	n	Fund
Unified Mutual Shares, Inc. 429 N. Pennsylvania St. Indianapolis, IN 46204-1897 317/634-3300 800/862-7283	1963	Unified Management Corporation	$17.8 Mil	$200/ 25	n	Fund

*Key: i=initial sales charge   r=redemption fee or contingent deferred sales charge(CDSC)
t=12b-1 fee and either CDSC or redemption fee   p=12b-1 fee   n=none of the preceding fees   N/A=not available

Growth and Income

Fund	Year Began	Investment Adviser	9/30/89 Assets	Minimum Initial and Subsequent Investment	Fees*	Where to Buy Shares
United Retirement Shares, Inc. 2400 Pershing Rd. P.O. Box 418343 Kansas City, MO 64141-9343 816/283-4000 800/821-5664	1972	Waddell & Reed, Inc.	$134.3 Mil	$500/ 25	i	Local Rep
United Services Funds *U.S. Good & Bad Times Fund* P.O. Box 29467 San Antonio, TX 78229-0467 512/696-1234 800/873-8637	1981	United Services Advisors, Inc.	$13.6 Mil	$100/ 50	n	Fund
U.S. Boston Investment Company *Boston Growth and Income* 6 New England Executive Pk. Burlington, MA 01803 617/272-6420	1985	U.S. Boston Investment Management Corporation	$35.5 Mil	$5,000/ 0	t	Local Rep
U.S. Trend Fund, Inc. 1100 Milan St., Ste. 3500 P.O. Box 3167 Houston, TX 77253-3167 713/750-8000 800/262-6631	1952	Capstone Asset Management Company	$89.6 Mil	$200/ 0	i	Local Rep
Value Line Convertible Fund, Inc. 711 Third Ave. New York, NY 10017 212/687-3965 800/223-0818	1985	Value Line, Inc.	$59.4 Mil	$1,000/ 250	n	Fund
Vance Sanders Exchange Fund 24 Federal St. Boston, MA 02110 617/482-8260 800/225-6265	1976	Eaton Vance Management, Inc.	$173.2 Mil	Not Applicable	n	Not Offering Shares
Vanguard Index Trust *500 Portfolio* Vanguard Financial Ctr. P.O. Box 2600 Valley Forge, PA 19482 215/648-6000 800/662-7447 800/362-0530 PA Only	1976	Vanguard Group, Inc.	$1.7 Bil	$3,000/ 100	n	Fund

*Key: i=initial sales charge   r=redemption fee or contingent deferred sales charge(CDSC)
t=12b-1 fee and either CDSC or redemption fee   p=12b-1 fee   n=none of the preceding fees   N/A=not available

Growth and Income

Fund	Year Began	Investment Adviser	9/30/89 Assets	Minimum Initial and Subsequent Investment	Fees*	Where to Buy Shares
Vanguard Quantitative Portfolios, Inc. Vanguard Financial Ctr. P.O. Box 2600 Valley Forge, PA 19482 215/648-6000 800/662-7447 800/362-0530 PA Only	1986	Franklin Portfolio Associates, Inc.	$170.4 Mil	$3,000/ 100	n	Fund
Van Kampen Merritt Growth and Income Fund 1001 Warrenville Rd. Lisle, IL 60532 312/719-6000 800/225-2222	1986	Van Kampen Merritt Investment Advisory Corp.	$37.8 Mil	$1,500/ 100	i, p	Local Rep
Variable Investors Series Trust *Real Estate Investment Portfolio* 1414 Main St. Springfield, MA 01144 413/732-7100	1987	Amherst Investment Management Company, Inc.	$3.4 Mil	Not Applicable	n	Insur
Washington Mutual Investors Fund, Inc. 1101 Vermont Ave., NW Washington, DC 20005 202/842-5665	1952	Capital Research & Management Company	$4.1 Bil	$250/ 50	i, t	Local Rep
Wayne Hummer Growth Fund Trust 175 W. Jackson Blvd. Chicago, IL 60604 312/431-1700 800/621-4477 800/972-5566 IL Only	1983	Wayne Hummer Management Company	$24.0 Mil	$1,000/ 500	n	Local Rep
Westwood Fund 666 Old Country Rd. Garden City, NY 11530 212/688-2323 800/323-7023 800/323-1243	1986	Westwood Management Corporation	$58.8 Mil	$25,000/ 5,000	i	Local Rep
Windsor Fund Vanguard Financial Ctr. P.O. Box 2600 Valley Forge, PA 19482 215/648-6000 800/662-7447 800/362-0530 PA Only	1958	Wellington Management Company	$8.7 Bil	$10,000/ 100	n	Fund

*Key: i=initial sales charge   r=redemption fee or contingent deferred sales charge(CDSC)
t=12b-1 fee and either CDSC or redemption fee   p=12b-1 fee   n=none of the preceding fees   N/A=not available

Growth and Income

Fund	Year Began	Investment Adviser	9/30/89 Assets	Minimum Initial and Subsequent Investment	Fees*	Where to Buy Shares
Windsor II Vanguard Financial Ctr. P.O. Box 2600 Valley Forge, PA 19482 215/648-6000 800/662-7447 800/362-0530 PA Only	1985	Barrow, Hanley, Mewhinney & Strauss, Inc. INVESCO Capital Management	$2.2 Bil	$1,500/ 100	n	Fund
WPG Fund One New York Plaza 31st Fl. New York, NY 10004 212/908-9582 800/223-3332	1979	Weiss, Peck & Greer Advisers, Inc.	$37.2 Mil (e)	$1,000/ 50	n	Fund
Wright Managed Equity Trust ***Wright Junior Blue Chip Equities Fund*** 24 Federal St. Boston, MA 02110 617/482-8260 800/225-6265	1985	Wright Investors Service	$105.2 Mil	$1,000/ 0	p	Local Rep
Wright Managed Equity Trust ***Wright Quality Core Equities Fund*** 24 Federal St. Boston, MA 02110 617/482-8260 800/225-6265	1985	Wright Investors Service	$54.3 Mil	$1,000/ 0	p	Local Rep
Wright Managed Equity Trust ***Wright Selected Blue Chip Equities Fund*** 24 Federal St. Boston, MA 02110 617/482-8260 800/225-6265	1983	Wright Investors Service	$123.6 Mil	$1,000/ 0	p	Local Rep
Zweig Series Trust ***Convertible Securities Series*** 25 Broadway New York, NY 10004 212/361-9612 800/272-2700	1986	Zweig/Glaser Advisers	$9.7 Mil (e)	$1,000/ 100	t	Local Rep

*Key: i=initial sales charge   r=redemption fee or contingent deferred sales charge(CDSC)
t=12b-1 fee and either CDSC or redemption fee   p=12b-1 fee   n=none of the preceding fees   N/A=not available

High-yield Bond Funds

High-yield Bond

Fund	Year Began	Investment Adviser	9/30/89 Assets	Minimum Initial and Subsequent Investment	Fees*	Where to Buy Shares
Advantage High Yield Bond Fund 60 State St. Boston, MA 02109 617/742-5900 800/243-8115	1988	Boston Security Counsellors	$10.1 Mil	$500/ 250	t	Local Rep
Aetna Series Trust *Aetna High Income Securities Fund* Federated Investors Twr. 26th Fl. Pittsburgh, PA 15222-3779 412/288-1900 800/245-4770	1988	Federated Advisers	$4.9 Mil	$500/ 100	n	Fund
AGE High Income Fund, Inc. 777 Mariners Island Blvd. San Mateo, CA 94404 415/570-3000 800/632-2180 800/632-2350	1969	Franklin Advisers, Inc.	$2.2 Bil	$100/ 25	i	Local Rep
AIM High Yield Securities, Inc. 11 Greenway Plaza Ste. 1919 Houston, TX 77046 713/626-1919 800/231-0803 800/392-9681 TX Only	1977	AIM Advisors, Inc.	$66.6 Mil	$1,000/ 100	i, p	Local Rep
Alliance Bond Fund *High-Yield Portfolio* 1345 Avenue of the Americas New York, NY 10105 212/969-1000 800/221-5672	1985	Alliance Capital Management L.P.	$223.7 Mil	$250/ 50	i, p	Local Rep
American Capital High Yield Investments, Inc. 2800 Post Oak Blvd. Houston, TX 77056 713/993-0500 800/421-5666	1978	American Capital Asset Management, Inc.	$505.9 Mil	$500/ 50	i, p	Local Rep
American General High Yield Accumulation Fund, Inc. 2800 Post Oak Blvd. Houston, TX 77056 713/993-0500 800/421-5666	1982	American Capital Asset Management, Inc.	$38.2 Mil	Not Applicable	n	Insur

*Key: i=initial sales charge   r=redemption fee or contingent deferred sales charge(CDSC)
t=12b-1 fee and either CDSC or redemption fee   p=12b-1 fee   n=none of the preceding fees   N/A=not available

217

High-yield Bond

Fund	Year Began	Investment Adviser	9/30/89 Assets	Minimum Initial and Subsequent Investment	Fees*	Where to Buy Shares
American High-Income Trust 333 S. Hope St. Los Angeles, CA 90071 213/486-9200 800/421-0180 213/486-9651 Collect	1988	Capital Research & Management Company	$125.3 Mil	$1,000/ 50	i, t	Local Rep
American Investors Income Fund, Inc. 777 W. Putnam Ave. P.O. Box 2500 Greenwich, CT 06836 203/531-5000 800/243-5353	1975	D.H. Blair Advisors, Inc.	$15.5 Mil (e)	$1,000/ 100	i	Local Rep
American Variable Insurance Series *High-Yield Bond Fund (The)* 333 S. Hope St. Los Angeles, CA 90071 213/486-9200 800/421-0180 213/486-9651 Collect	1984	Capital Research & Management Company	$46.1 Mil	Not Applicable	n	Insur
AMEV Advantage Portfolios, Inc. *High Yield Portfolio* P.O. Box 64284 St. Paul, MN 55164 612/738-4000 800/872-2638	1988	AMEV Advisers, Inc.	$23.0 Mil	$500/ 50	i, p	Local Rep
Anchor Pathway Fund *High-Yield Bond Series (The)* 2201 E. Camelback Phoenix, AZ 85016 602/955-0300 800/528-9679	1987	Capital Research & Management Company	N/A	Not Applicable	n	Insur
Bankers National Series Trust *BNL High Yield Portfolio* 44 U.S. Hwy. 46 Pine Brook, NJ 07058 201/808-9596 800/888-4918	1987	Conseco Capital Management, Inc.	$2.5 Mil	Not Applicable	n	Insur
Bull & Bear Incorporated *Bull & Bear High Yield Fund* 11 Hanover Sq. New York, NY 10005 212/785-0900 800/847-4200	1983	Bull & Bear Fixed Income Advisers, Inc.	$82.4 Mil (e)	$1,000/ 100	p	Fund

*Key: i=initial sales charge   r=redemption fee or contingent deferred sales charge(CDSC)
t=12b-1 fee and either CDSC or redemption fee   p=12b-1 fee   n=none of the preceding fees   N/A=not available

High-yield Bond

Fund	Year Began	Investment Adviser	9/30/89 Assets	Minimum Initial and Subsequent Investment	Fees*	Where to Buy Shares
Champion High Yield Fund-USA 3410 S. Galena St. Denver, CO 80231 303/671-3200 800/327-3069	1988	Champion Asset Management Corporation	$20.6 Mil	$1,000/ 25	i, p	Local Rep
CIGNA High Yield Fund One Financial Plaza Springfield, MA 01103 413/784-0100 800/56CIGNA	1978	CIGNA Investments, Inc.	$289.0 Mil	$500/ 50	i, p	Local Rep
Colonial/Hancock Liberty Trust *Colonial/Hancock Liberty Aggressive Income Fund* One Financial Ctr. Boston, MA 02111 617/426-3750 800/225-2365, 800/426-3750	1987	Colonial Management Associates, Inc.	$1.3 Mil	Not Applicable	n	Insur
Colonial High Yield Securities Trust One Financial Ctr. Boston, MA 02111 617/426-3750 800/225-2365 800/426-3750	1971	Colonial Management Associates, Inc.	$418.3 Mil	$250/ 25	i, p	Local Rep
Colonial Value Investing Portfolios - Income Portfolio *High Income Fund* One Financial Ctr. Boston, MA 02111 617/426-3750 800/225-2365, 800/426-3750	1987	Colonial Management Associates, Inc.	$66.2 Mil	$500/ 100	t	Local Rep
Constitution Funds, Inc. *High Yield Fund* Two World Trade Ctr. New York, NY 10048-0669 212/323-0200 800/525-7048	1988	Oppenheimer Management Corporation	$4.3 Mil	$1,000/ 250	i, p	Local Rep
Dean Witter High Yield Securities Inc. Two World Trade Ctr. New York, NY 10048 212/392-2550 800/869-3863	1979	Dean Witter Reynolds Inc. - InterCapital Division	$1.6 Bil	$1,000/ 100	i	Local Rep

*Key: i=initial sales charge   r=redemption fee or contingent deferred sales charge(CDSC)
t=12b-1 fee and either CDSC or redemption fee   p=12b-1 fee   n=none of the preceding fees   N/A=not available

High-yield Bond

Fund	Year Began	Investment Adviser	9/30/89 Assets	Minimum Initial and Subsequent Investment	Fees*	Where to Buy Shares
Dean Witter Variable Investment Series *High Yield Portfolio* Two World Trade Ctr. New York, NY 10048 212/392-2550 800/869-3863	1984	Dean Witter Reynolds Inc. - InterCapital Division	$139.5 Mil	Not Applicable	n	Insur
Delaware Group Delchester High-Yield Bond Fund *Delchester I* One Commerce Sq. Philadelphia, PA 19103 215/988-1200 800/523-4640	1970	Delaware Management Company, Inc.	$668.5 Mil	$25/ 25	i	Local Rep
Delaware Group Delchester High-Yield Bond Fund *Delchester II* One Commerce Sq. Philadelphia, PA 19103 215/988-1200 800/523-4640	1987	Delaware Management Company, Inc.	$87.4 Mil	$25/ 25	i, p	Local Rep
Eaton Vance Corporate High Income Dollar Fund, L.P. 24 Federal St. Boston, MA 02110 617/482-8260 800/225-6265	1987	Eaton Vance Management, Inc.	$20.9 Mil	$5,000/ 50	i, p	Local Rep
Eaton Vance High Income Trust 24 Federal St. Boston, MA 02110 617/482-8260 800/225-6265	1986	Eaton Vance Management, Inc.	$281.9 Mil	$1,000/ 50	t	Local Rep
Enterprise Income Portfolios *Enterprise High-Yield Bond Portfolio* 1200 Ashwood Pkwy. Ste. 290 Atlanta, GA 30338 404/396-8118, 800/432-4320	1987	Enterprise Capital Management, Inc.	$26.4 Mil (e)	$500/ 25	t	Local Rep
Equitec Siebel Fund Group *Equitec Siebel High Yield Bond Fund Series* 7677 Oakport St. P.O. Box 2470 Oakland, CA 94614 415/430-9900 800/869-8900	1986	Siebel Capital Management, Inc.	$29.1 Mil (e)	$1,000/ 0	t	Local Rep

*Key: i=initial sales charge   r=redemption fee or contingent deferred sales charge(CDSC)
t=12b-1 fee and either CDSC or redemption fee   p=12b-1 fee   n=none of the preceding fees   N/A=not available

High-yield Bond

Fund	Year Began	Investment Adviser	9/30/89 Assets	Minimum Initial and Subsequent Investment	Fees*	Where to Buy Shares
Executive Investors Trust *Executive Investors High Yield Fund* 120 Wall St. New York, NY 10005 212/208-6000	1987	Executive Investors Management Company, Inc.	$21.4 Mil	$1,000/ 50	i, p	Local Rep
FBL Series Fund, Inc. *High Yield Bond Portfolio* 5400 University Ave. W. Des Moines, IA 50265 515/225-5400 800/247-4170 800/422-3175 IA Only	1987	FBL Investment Advisory Services, Inc.	$3.1 Mil	$250/ 0	t	Local Rep
Federated High Income Securities, Inc. Federated Investors Twr. Liberty Ctr. Pittsburgh, PA 15222-3779 412/288-1900 800/245-0242	1977	Federated Advisers	$369.9 Mil	$500/ 100	i	Local Rep
Federated High Yield Trust Federated Investors Twr. Pittsburgh, PA 15222-3779 412/288-1900 800/245-5000	1984	Federated Management	$192.8 Mil	$25,000/ 0	n	Local Rep
Fidelity Summer Street Trust *Fidelity High Income Fund* 82 Devonshire St. Boston, MA 02109 617/570-7000 800/544-6666	1977	Fidelity Management & Research Company	$1.6 Bil	$2,500/ 250	n	Fund
First Investors Bond Appreciation Fund, Inc. 120 Wall St. New York, NY 10005 212/208-6000	1978	First Investors Management Company, Inc.	$97.9 Mil	$1,000/ 100	i, p	Local Rep
First Investors Fund For Income, Inc. 120 Wall St. New York, NY 10005 212/208-6000	1971	First Investors Management Company, Inc.	$1.5 Bil	$200/ 50	i, p	Local Rep

*Key: i=initial sales charge   r=redemption fee or contingent deferred sales charge(CDSC)
t=12b-1 fee and either CDSC or redemption fee   p=12b-1 fee   n=none of the preceding fees   N/A=not available

High-yield Bond

Fund	Year Began	Investment Adviser	9/30/89 Assets	Minimum Initial and Subsequent Investment	Fees*	Where to Buy Shares
First Investors High Yield Fund, Inc. 120 Wall St. New York, NY 10005 212/208-6000	1986	First Investors Management Company, Inc.	$740.8 Mil	$1,000/ 50	i, p	Local Rep
First Investors Life Series Fund *Bond Appreciation Series* 120 Wall St. New York, NY 10005 212/208-6000	1986	First Investors Management Company, Inc.	$0.7 Mil	Not Applicable	n	Insur
First Investors Special Bond Fund, Inc. 120 Wall St. New York, NY 10005 212/208-6000	1979	First Investors Management Company, Inc.	$89.3 Mil	Not Applicable	n	Insur
Franklin Partners Funds *Franklin Tax-Advantaged High Yield Securities Fund* 777 Mariners Island Blvd. San Mateo, CA 94404 415/570-3000 800/632-2180 800/632-2350	1987	Franklin Advisers, Inc.	$36.0 Mil	$2,500/ 100	i	Local Rep
Franklin Pennsylvania Investors Fund *High Income Portfolio* 777 Mariners Island Blvd. San Mateo, CA 94404 415/570-3000 800/632-2180 800/632-2350	1986	Franklin Advisers, Inc.	$1.0 Mil	$100/ 25	i	Local Rep
GIT Income Trust *GIT Income Trust Maximum Income Portfolio* 1655 Fort Myer Dr. Arlington, VA 22209 703/528-6500 800/336-3063	1983	Bankers Finance Investment Management Corp.	$8.9 Mil	$1,000/ 0	n	Fund
Highmark Group *Bond Fund* 1900 E. Dublin-Granville Rd. Columbus, OH 43229 614/899-4600 800/338-4385	1987	Merus Capital Management	N/A	$1,000/ 100	N/A	Fund

*Key: i=initial sales charge   r=redemption fee or contingent deferred sales charge(CDSC)
t=12b-1 fee and either CDSC or redemption fee   p=12b-1 fee   n=none of the preceding fees   N/A=not available

High-yield Bond

Fund	Year Began	Investment Adviser	9/30/89 Assets	Minimum Initial and Subsequent Investment	Fees*	Where to Buy Shares
High Yield Bond Trust 99 High St. Boston, MA 02110 617/338-3200 800/343-2898 800/225-1587	1982	Keystone Custodian Funds, Inc.	$11.6 Mil	Not Applicable	n	Insur
Home Group Trust *Home High Yield Bond Fund* 59 Maiden Lane 21st Fl. New York, NY 10038 212/530-6016 800/729-3863	1988	Home Capital Services, Inc.	$26.0 Mil	$1,000/ 100	i, p	Local Rep
IDS Extra Income Fund, Inc. IDS Tower 10 Minneapolis, MN 55440 612/372-3131 800/328-8300	1983	IDS Financial Corporation	$1.3 Bil	$100/ 100	i, p	Local Rep
Imperial Portfolios, Inc. *High Yield Portfolio (The)* 9275 Sky Park Ct. P.O. Box 82997 San Diego, CA 92138 619/292-2379 800/347-5588	1988	First Imperial Advisors, Inc.	N/A	$1,000/ 100	N/A	Local Rep
Integrated Income Portfolios *High Yield Portfolio* 10 Union Square East New York, NY 10003 212/353-7000 800/858-8850	1986	Integrated Resources Asset Management Corp.	$27.5 Mil	$1,000/ 100	i, p	Local Rep
Integrated Resources Series Trust *High Yield Portfolio* One Bridge Plaza Fort Lee, NJ 07024 201/461-0606 800/821-5100	1986	Integrated Resources Asset Management Corp.	$41.5 Mil	Not Applicable	n	Insur
Investment Portfolios *High Yield Portfolio* 120 S. LaSalle St. Chicago, IL 60603 312/781-1121 800/621-1148	1984	Kemper Financial Services, Inc.	$779.3 Mil	$250/ 50	t	Local Rep

*Key: i=initial sales charge   r=redemption fee or contingent deferred sales charge(CDSC)
t=12b-1 fee and either CDSC or redemption fee   p=12b-1 fee   n=none of the preceding fees   N/A=not available

High-yield Bond

Fund	Year Began	Investment Adviser	9/30/89 Assets	Minimum Initial and Subsequent Investment	Fees*	Where to Buy Shares
Investment Trust of Boston *High Income Portfolio* 399 Boylston St. 9th Fl. Boston, MA 02116 800/888-4823	1984	Back Bay Advisors, Inc.	$10.2 Mil	$1,000/ 100	i, p	Local Rep
John Hancock High Income Trust *Fixed Income Portfolio* 101 Huntington Ave. Boston, MA 02199-7603 617/375-1500 800/225-5291	1986	John Hancock Advisers, Inc.	$102.4 Mil	$1,000/ 25	i, p	Local Rep
Kemper High Yield Fund, Inc. 120 S. LaSalle St. Chicago, IL 60603 312/781-1121 800/621-1148	1978	Kemper Financial Services, Inc.	$1.6 Bil	$1,000/ 100	i	Local Rep
Keystone America High Yield Bond Fund 99 High St. Boston, MA 02110 617/338-3200 800/343-2898 800/225-1587	1987	Keystone Custodian Funds, Inc.	$128.1 Mil	$1,000/ 0	i, t	Local Rep
Keystone Custodian Funds, Inc. B-4 Series 99 High St. Boston, MA 02110 617/338-3200 800/343-2898 800/225-1587	1932	Keystone Custodian Funds, Inc.	$1.0 Bil	$250/ 0	t	Local Rep
LBVIP Series Fund, Inc. *High Yield Series* 625 Fourth Ave. South Minneapolis, MN 55415 612/339-8091 800/328-4552 800/752-4208 MN Only	1988	Lutheran Brotherhood Research Corp.	$16.4 Mil	Not Applicable	n	Insur
Lord Abbett Bond-Debenture Fund, Inc. The General Motors Bldg. 767 Fifth Ave. New York, NY 10153 212/848-1800 800/223-4224	1971	Lord, Abbett & Co.	$692.8 Mil	$1,000/ 0	i	Local Rep

*Key: i=initial sales charge   r=redemption fee or contingent deferred sales charge(CDSC)
t=12b-1 fee and either CDSC or redemption fee   p=12b-1 fee   n=none of the preceding fees   N/A=not available

High-yield Bond

Fund	Year Began	Investment Adviser	9/30/89 Assets	Minimum Initial and Subsequent Investment	Fees*	Where to Buy Shares
Lutheran Brotherhood High Yield Fund, Inc. 625 Fourth Ave. South Minneapolis, MN 55415 612/339-8091 800/328-4552 800/752-4208 MN Only	1987	Lutheran Brotherhood Research Corp.	$155.7 Mil	$500/ 50	i	Local Rep
MacKay-Shields MainStay Series Fund *MainStay High Yield Corporate Bond Fund* 51 Madison Ave. New York, NY 10010 212/576-7000 800/522-4202	1986	MacKay-Shields Financial Corporation	$179.8 Mil	$500/ 50	t	Local Rep
Massachusetts Financial High Income Trust - I 500 Boylston St. Boston, MA 02116 617/954-5000 800/343-2829	1978	Massachusetts Financial Services Company	$737.7 Mil	$1,000/ 25	i	Local Rep
Massachusetts Financial High Income Trust - II 500 Boylston St. Boston, MA 02116 617/954-5000 800/343-2829	1987	Massachusetts Financial Services Company	$42.1 Mil	$1,000/ 25	i	Local Rep
Merrill Lynch Corporate Bond Fund, Inc. *High Income Portfolio* *Class A* *Class B* P.O. Box 9011 Princeton, NJ 08543-9011 609/282-2800, 800/637-3863	1978 1988	Fund Asset Management, Inc.	$762.6 Mil	$1,000/100 $1,000/100	i t	LRep LRep
Merrill Lynch Series Fund *High Yield Portfolio* P.O. Box 9011 Princeton, NJ 08543-9011 609/282-2800 800/524-4458	1986	Fund Asset Management, Inc.	$68.5 Mil	Not Applicable	n	Insur
Merrill Lynch Variable Series Funds *High Current Income Fund* P.O. Box 9011 Princeton, NJ 08543-9011 609/282-2800 800/524-4458	1982	Merrill Lynch Asset Management Inc.	$14.8 Mil	Not Applicable	n	Insur

*Key: i=initial sales charge   r=redemption fee or contingent deferred sales charge(CDSC)
t=12b-1 fee and either CDSC or redemption fee   p=12b-1 fee   n=none of the preceding fees   N/A=not available

High-yield Bond

Fund	Year Began	Investment Adviser	9/30/89 Assets	Minimum Initial and Subsequent Investment	Fees*	Where to Buy Shares
MetLife-State Street Income Trust *MetLife-State Street High Income Fund* One Financial Ctr. 30th Fl. Boston, MA 02111 617/348-2000, 800/882-0052	1986	MetLife-State Street Investment Services, Inc.	$130.8 Mil	$250/ 25	i, p	Local Rep
MFS Government Premium Account 500 Boylston St. Boston, MA 02116 617/954-5000 800/343-2829	1988	Massachusetts Financial Services Company	$262.5 Mil	$5,000/ 250	i, p	Local Rep
MFS Lifetime Investment Program *Lifetime High Income Trust* 500 Boylston St. Boston, MA 02116 617/954-5000 800/343-2829	1986	Lifetime Advisers, Inc.	$138.8 Mil	$1,000/ 50	t	Local Rep
MidAmerica High Yield Fund, Inc. 433 Edgewood Rd., NE Cedar Rapids, IA 52499 319/398-8511 800/553-4287 800/342-4490 IA Only	1985	MidAmerica Management Corporation	$21.6 Mil	$1,000/ 50	i	Local Rep
National Bond Fund 600 Third Ave. New York, NY 10016 203/863-5600 800/237-1718	1940	National Securities & Research Corporation	$547.9 Mil	$250/ 25	i	Local Rep
Oppenheimer High Yield Fund 3410 S. Galena St. Denver, CO 80231 303/671-3200 800/525-7048	1978	Oppenheimer Management Corporation	$833.2 Mil	$1,000/ 25	i	Local Rep
Oppenheimer Variable Account Funds *Oppenheimer High Income Fund* 3410 S. Galena St. Denver, CO 80231 303/671-3200 800/525-7048	1986	Oppenheimer Management Corporation	$26.7 Mil	Not Applicable	n	Insur

*Key: i=initial sales charge   r=redemption fee or contingent deferred sales charge(CDSC)
t=12b-1 fee and either CDSC or redemption fee   p=12b-1 fee   n=none of the preceding fees   N/A=not available

High-yield Bond

Fund	Year Began	Investment Adviser	9/30/89 Assets	Minimum Initial and Subsequent Investment	Fees*	Where to Buy Shares
Pacific Horizon Funds, Inc. *High Yield Bond Portfolio* 156 W. 56th St. Ste. 1902 New York, NY 10019 212/492-1600 800/367-6075	1984	Security Pacific National Bank	$20.4 Mil	$1,000/ 100	i, p	Local Rep
PaineWebber Fixed Income Portfolios *High Yield Bond Portfolio* 1285 Avenue of the Americas PaineWebber Bldg. New York, NY 10019 212/713-2000 800/544-9300	1984	Mitchell Hutchins Asset Management Inc.	$349.4 Mil	$1,000/ 100	i	Local Rep
PaineWebber Series Trust *High Yield Bond Portfolio* 1285 Avenue of the Americas PaineWebber Bldg. New York, NY 10019 212/713-2000	1987	Mitchell Hutchins Asset Management Inc.	N/A	Not Applicable	N/A	Insur
Phoenix Series Fund *Phoenix High Yield Fund Series* 101 Munson St. Greenfield, MA 01301 203/253-1000 800/243-1574	1980	Phoenix Investment Counsel, Inc.	$142.3 Mil	$500/ 25	i	Local Rep
Pilgrim High Yield Trust 10100 Santa Monica Blvd. 21st Fl. Los Angeles, CA 90067 213/551-0833 800/334-3444 800/331-1080	1939	Pilgrim Management Corporation	$34.5 Mil	$1,000/ 100	i, p	Local Rep
Plymouth Fund *Plymouth High Yield Portfolio* 82 Devonshire St. Boston, MA 02109 617/570-7000 800/544-6666	1987	Fidelity Management & Research Company	$14.1 Mil	$1,000/ 250	i, p	Local Rep
Princor High Yield Fund, Inc. 711 High St. Des Moines, IA 50309 515/247-5711 800/247-4123 800/622-5344 IA Only	1987	Principal Management, Inc.	$12.8 Mil	$1,000/ 50	i, p	Local Rep

*Key: i=initial sales charge   r=redemption fee or contingent deferred sales charge(CDSC)
t=12b-1 fee and either CDSC or redemption fee   p=12b-1 fee   n=none of the preceding fees   N/A=not available

227

High-yield Bond

Fund	Year Began	Investment Adviser	9/30/89 Assets	Minimum Initial and Subsequent Investment	Fees*	Where to Buy Shares
Professional Portfolios Trust *High Yield Fund* 429 N. Pennsylvania St. Indianapolis, IN 46204-1897 317/634-3300 800/862-7283	1988	Unified Management Corporation	$0.6 Mil	$200/ 25	p	Local Rep
Prudential-Bache High Yield Fund, Inc. One Seaport Plaza New York, NY 10292 212/214-1215 800/225-1852	1979	Prudential Mutual Fund Management	$2.8 Bil	$1,000/ 100	t	Local Rep
Putnam Capital Manager Trust *PCM High Yield Fund* One Post Office Sq. Boston, MA 02109 617/292-1000 800/225-2465	1988	Putnam Management Company, Inc.	$30.5 Mil	Not Applicable	r	Insur
Putnam High Yield Trust One Post Office Sq. Boston, MA 02109 617/292-1000 800/225-2465	1978	Putnam Management Company, Inc.	$2.3 Bil	$500/ 50	i	Local Rep
Putnam High Yield Trust II One Post Office Sq. Boston, MA 02109 617/292-1000 800/225-2465	1986	Putnam Management Company, Inc.	$387.9 Mil	$500/ 50	i, p	Local Rep
Rochester Convertible Funds, Inc. *Income Fund* 379 Park Ave. Rochester, NY 14607 716/442-5500	1986	Fielding Management Company, Inc.	N/A	$2,000/ 100	i, p	Local Rep
Royce Fund *Income Series* 1414 Avenue of the Americas New York, NY 10019 212/355-7311 800/221-4268	1986	Quest Advisory Corp.	N/A	$2,000/ 50	t	Local Rep

*Key: i=initial sales charge   r=redemption fee or contingent deferred sales charge(CDSC)
t=12b-1 fee and either CDSC or redemption fee   p=12b-1 fee   n=none of the preceding fees   N/A=not available

High-yield Bond

Fund	Year Began	Investment Adviser	9/30/89 Assets	Minimum Initial and Subsequent Investment	Fees*	Where to Buy Shares
SAFECO High-Yield Bond Fund, Inc. SAFECO Plaza Seattle, WA 98185 206/545-5530 800/426-6730	1988	SAFECO Asset Management Company	$9.1 Mil	$1,000/ 100	n	Fund
SBL Fund *High Yield Series* 700 Harrison St. 6th Fl. Topeka, KS 66636 913/295-3127 800/888-2461	1984	Security Management Company	$11.0 Mil	Not Applicable	n	Insur
Schield Portfolios Series *High Yield Bond Portfolio* 390 Union Blvd. Ste. 410 Denver, CO 80228 303/985-9999 800/826-8154 800/233-4971 CO Only	1987	Schield Management Company	$7.6 Mil	$1,000/ 100	i, p	Local Rep
Security Income Fund *High Yield Series* 700 Harrison St. Topeka, KS 66636 913/295-3127 800/888-2461	1986	Security Management Company	$10.0 Mil	$100/ 20	i, p	Local Rep
Select High Yield Fund, Inc. 20 Washington Ave. South Minneapolis, MN 55401 612/372-5605	1983	Washington Square Capital, Inc.	$9.1 Mil	Not Applicable	n	Insur
Seligman High Income Fund Series *High-Yield Bond Series* 130 Liberty St. New York, NY 10006 212/488-0200 800/221-2450 800/522-6869 NY Only	1985	J. & W. Seligman & Co. Incorporated	$52.1 Mil	$1,000/ 50	i, p	Local Rep
Shearson Lehman Series Fund *SLH IDS High Income Portfolio* 31 W. 52nd St. New York, NY 10019 212/767-3700	1986	Bernstein-Macaulay Division of Shearson Lehman Hutton Inc.	$4.7 Mil	Not Applicable	n	Insur

*Key: i=initial sales charge   r=redemption fee or contingent deferred sales charge(CDSC)
t=12b-1 fee and either CDSC or redemption fee   p=12b-1 fee   n=none of the preceding fees   N/A=not available

High-yield Bond

Fund	Year Began	Investment Adviser	9/30/89 Assets	Minimum Initial and Subsequent Investment	Fees*	Where to Buy Shares
Skyline Fund *Monthly Income Portfolio (The)* 350 N. Clark St. Chicago, IL 60610 312/670-6035 800/458-5222	1988	Mesirow Asset Management, Inc.	$9.4 Mil	$1,000/ 100	i, p	Local Rep
SLH High Yield Fund Inc. 31 W. 52nd St. New York, NY 10019 212/767-3700	1980	Bernstein-Macaulay Division of Shearson Lehman Hutton Inc.	$439.0 Mil	$500/ 200	i	Local Rep
SLH Special Income Portfolios *SLH High Income Bond Portfolio* 31 W. 52nd St. New York, NY 10019 212/767-3700	1986	Bernstein-Macaulay Division of Shearson Lehman Hutton Inc.	$537.6 Mil	$500/ 200	t	Local Rep
SteinRoe Variable Investment Trust *High Yield Bond Fund* 600 Atlantic Ave. Boston, MA 02210 617/722-6000 800/443-2683	1989	Stein Roe & Farnham Incorporated	N/A	Not Applicable	N/A	Insur
Transamerica Special Series, Inc. *Transamerica Special High Yield Bond Fund* 1000 Louisiana Ste. 6000 Houston, TX 77002-5098 713/751-2400, 800/999-3863	1987	Transamerica Fund Management Company	$34.8 Mil	$1,000/ 50	t	Local Rep
T. Rowe Price High Yield Fund, Inc. 100 E. Pratt St. Baltimore, MD 21202 301/547-2000 800/638-5660	1984	T. Rowe Price Associates, Inc.	$1.1 Bil	$2,500/ 100	n	Fund
United High Income Fund, Inc. 2400 Pershing Rd. P.O. Box 418343 Kansas City, MO 64141-9343 816/283-4000 800/821-5664	1979	Waddell & Reed, Inc.	$1.2 Bil	$500/ 25	i	Local Rep

*Key: i=initial sales charge   r=redemption fee or contingent deferred sales charge(CDSC)
       t=12b-1 fee and either CDSC or redemption fee   p=12b-1 fee   n=none of the preceding fees   N/A=not available

High-yield Bond

Fund	Year Began	Investment Adviser	9/30/89 Assets	Minimum Initial and Subsequent Investment	Fees*	Where to Buy Shares
United High Income Fund II, Inc. 2400 Pershing Rd. P.O. Box 418343 Kansas City, MO 64141-9343 816/283-4000 800/821-5664	1986	Waddell & Reed, Inc.	$313.1 Mil	$500/ 25	i	Local Rep
Value Line Aggressive Income Trust 711 Third Ave. New York, NY 10017 212/687-3965 800/223-0818	1986	Value Line, Inc.	$36.3 Mil	$1,000/ 250	n	Fund
Vanguard Fixed-Income Securities Fund, Inc. *High Yield Bond Portfolio* Vanguard Financial Ctr. P.O. Box 2600 Valley Forge, PA 19482 215/648-6000 800/662-7447, 800/362-0530 PA Only	1978	Wellington Management Company	$1.1 Bil	$3,000/ 100	n	Fund
Van Kampen Merritt High Yield Fund 1001 Warrenville Rd. Lisle, IL 60532 312/719-6000 800/225-2222	1986	Van Kampen Merritt Investment Advisory Corp.	$319.8 Mil	$1,500/ 100	i, p	Local Rep
Variable Insurance Products Fund *High Income Portfolio* 82 Devonshire St. Boston, MA 02109 617/570-7000 800/544-6666	1985	Fidelity Management & Research Company	$34.7 Mil	Not Applicable	n	Insur
Variable Investors Series Trust *High Income Bond Portfolio* 1414 Main St. Springfield, MA 01144 413/732-7100	1987	Amherst Investment Management Company, Inc.	$4.3 Mil	Not Applicable	n	Insur
Venture Income (+) Plus, Inc. 124 E. Marcy St. P.O. Box 1688 Santa Fe, NM 87504-1688 505/983-4335 800/545-2098	1980	Venture Advisers, L.P.	$43.3 Mil	$1,000/ 25	i, p	Local Rep

*Key: i=initial sales charge   r=redemption fee or contingent deferred sales charge(CDSC)
t=12b-1 fee and either CDSC or redemption fee   p=12b-1 fee   n=none of the preceding fees   N/A=not available

◆ ◆ ◆ ◆

Income-bond Funds

Income-bond

Fund	Year Began	Investment Adviser	9/30/89 Assets	Minimum Initial and Subsequent Investment	Fees*	Where to Buy Shares
Advisers Management Trust *Limited Maturity Bond Portfolio* 342 Madison Ave. New York, NY 10173 212/850-8300 800/877-9700	1984	Neuberger & Berman Management Incorporated	$28.7 Mil	Not Applicable	n	Insur
Aetna Income Shares 151 Farmington Ave. Hartford, CT 06156 203/273-4808	1973	Aetna Life Insurance and Annuity Company	$285.9 Mil (e)	Not Applicable	n	Insur
Alliance Bond Fund *High-Grade Portfolio* 1345 Avenue of the Americas New York, NY 10105 212/969-1000 800/221-5672	1973	Alliance Capital Management L.P.	$2.2 Mil	$250/ 50	i, p	Local Rep
Alliance Short-Term Multi-Market Trust P.O. Box 1520 Secaucus, NJ 07096 201/319-4000 800/221-5672	1989	Alliance Capital Management L.P.	$173.2 Mil	$250/ 50	i, p	Local Rep
Alpine Mutual Fund Trust *Catholic Income Trust (The)* 650 S. Cherry St. Ste. 700 Denver, CO 80222 303/321-2211 800/826-6677	1989	Alpine Capital Management Corporation	N/A	$250/ 250	N/A	Local Rep
AMA Income Fund, Inc. *U.S. Government Income Plus Portfolio* 5 Sentry Pkwy. W, Ste. 120 P.O. Box 1111 Blue Bell, PA 19422 215/825-0400 800/AMA-FUND	1974	AMA Advisers, Inc.	$39.7 Mil	$1,000/ 0	p	Fund
Axe-Houghton Income Fund, Inc. 400 Benedict Ave. Tarrytown, NY 10591 914/631-8131 800/366-0444	1934	Axe-Houghton Management, Inc.	$63.1 Mil	$1,000/ 0	p	Fund

*Key: i=initial sales charge   r=redemption fee or contingent deferred sales charge(CDSC)
t=12b-1 fee and either CDSC or redemption fee   p=12b-1 fee   n=none of the preceding fees   N/A=not available

Income-bond

Fund	Year Began	Investment Adviser	9/30/89 Assets	Minimum Initial and Subsequent Investment	Fees*	Where to Buy Shares
Bartlett Capital Trust *Fixed Income Fund* 36 E. Fourth St. Cincinnati, OH 45202 513/621-4612 800/543-0863	1986	Bartlett & Company	$165.2 Mil	$5,000/ 100	n	Local Rep
Bond Fund of America, Inc. 333 S. Hope St. Los Angeles, CA 90071 213/486-9200 800/421-0180 213/486-9651 Collect	1974	Capital Research & Management Company	$1.4 Bil	$1,000/ 50	i, t	Local Rep
Bond Portfolio for Endowments, Inc. Four Embarcadero Ctr. P.O. Box 7650 San Francisco, CA 94120-7650 415/421-9360 800/421-0180	1972	Capital Research & Management Company	$39.2 Mil	$50,000/ 0	n	Fund
Boston Company Index and Blue Chip Trust *Bond Index Fund* One Boston Place Boston, MA 02108 617/451-2010 800/225-5267	1988	Boston Company Advisors, Inc.	$9.7 Mil (e)	$1,000/ 0	p	Fund
Calvert Fund *Income Portfolio* 1700 Pennsylvania Ave., NW Washington, DC 20006 301/951-4820 800/368-2745	1982	Calvert Asset Management Company, Inc.	$22.9 Mil	$2,000/ 250	i, p	Local Rep
CIGNA Income Fund One Financial Plaza Springfield, MA 01103 413/784-0100 800/56CIGNA	1968	CIGNA Investments, Inc.	$222.1 Mil	$500/ 50	i, p	Local Rep
Collective Investment Trust for Seafirst Retirement Accounts *Bond Fund (The)* 701 Fifth Ave. P.O. Box 84248 Seattle, WA 98124 206/358-6119, 800/323-9919	1988	Seattle-First National Bank	$2.0 Mil (e)	$500/ 0	n	Fund

*Key: i=initial sales charge   r=redemption fee or contingent deferred sales charge(CDSC)
     t=12b-1 fee and either CDSC or redemption fee   p=12b-1 fee   n=none of the preceding fees   N/A=not available

Income-bond

Fund	Year Began	Investment Adviser	9/30/89 Assets	Minimum Initial and Subsequent Investment	Fees*	Where to Buy Shares
Columbia Fixed Income Securities Fund, Inc. 1301 SW 5th Ave. P.O. Box 1350 Portland, OR 97207 503/222-3600 800/547-1707	1983	Columbia Funds Management Company	$105.8 Mil	$1,000/ 100	n	Fund
Conestoga Family of Funds *Fixed Income Fund* 1900 E. Dublin-Granville Rd. Columbus, OH 43229 614/899-4600 800/338-4385	1989	Meridian Investment Company	N/A	$0/ 0	N/A	Fund
Conestoga Family of Funds *Limited Maturity Fund* 1900 E. Dublin-Granville Rd. Columbus, OH 43229 614/899-4600 800/338-4385	1989	Meridian Investment Company	N/A	$0/ 0	N/A	Fund
Connecticut Mutual Financial Services Series Fund I, Inc. *Income Portfolio* 140 Garden St. Hartford, CT 06154 203/727-6500 800/243-0018	1982	G.R. Phelps & Company, Inc.	$40.8 Mil	Not Applicable	r	Insur
Counsellors Fixed Income Fund 466 Lexington Ave. New York, NY 10017-3147 212/878-0600 800/888-6878	1987	Warburg, Pincus Counsellors, Inc.	$85.0 Mil	$25,000/ 5,000	n	Fund
Dean Witter Intermediate Income Securities Two World Trade Ctr. New York, NY 10048 212/392-2550 800/869-3863	1989	Dean Witter Reynolds Inc. - InterCapital Division	$84.2 Mil	$1,000/ 100	t	Local Rep
Dean Witter Variable Investment Series *Quality Income Plus Portfolio* Two World Trade Ctr. New York, NY 10048 212/392-2550 800/869-3863	1987	Dean Witter Reynolds Inc. - InterCapital Division	$42.5 Mil	Not Applicable	n	Insur

*Key: i=initial sales charge   r=redemption fee or contingent deferred sales charge(CDSC)
t=12b-1 fee and either CDSC or redemption fee   p=12b-1 fee   n=none of the preceding fees   N/A=not available

237

Income-bond

Fund	Year Began	Investment Adviser	9/30/89 Assets	Minimum Initial and Subsequent Investment	Fees*	Where to Buy Shares
Dean Witter World Wide Income Trust Two World Trade Ctr. New York, NY 10048 212/392-2550 800/869-3863	1989	Dean Witter Reynolds Inc. - InterCapital Division	$383.4 Mil	$1,000/ 100	i, t	Local Rep
Dodge & Cox Income Fund One Post St. 35th Fl. San Francisco, CA 94104 415/981-1710	1989	Dodge & Cox	$29.4 Mil	$1,000/ 100	n	Fund
Dreman Mutual Group, Inc. ***Dreman Bond Portfolio (The)*** 10 Exchange Place Jersey City, NJ 07302 201/332-8228 800/533-1608	1988	Dreman Value Management, Inc.	$4.5 Mil	$5,000/ 1,000	p	Local Rep
EBI Funds, Inc. ***EBI Income Fund*** 1315 Peachtree St., NE Ste. 500 Atlanta, GA 30309 404/892-0666 800/554-1156	1984	INVESCO Capital Management, Inc.	N/A	$100,000/ 5,000	t	Local Rep
Elite Group ***Elite Income Fund (The)*** 1206 IBM Bldg. Seattle, WA 98101 206/624-5863 800/654-5261 800/423-1068 WA Only	1987	R.S. McCormick & Company, Inc.	$2.6 Mil	$1,000/ 50	n	Fund
FBL Series Fund, Inc. ***High Quality Bond Portfolio*** 5400 University Ave. W. Des Moines, IA 50265 515/225-5400 800/247-4170 800/422-3175 IA Only	1987	FBL Investment Advisory Services, Inc.	$3.3 Mil	$250/ 0	t	Local Rep
Federated Bond Fund Federated Investors Twr. Pittsburgh, PA 15222-3779 412/288-1900 800/245-5000	1985	Federated Management	$36.1 Mil	$25,000/ 0	n	Local Rep

*Key: i=initial sales charge   r=redemption fee or contingent deferred sales charge(CDSC)
t=12b-1 fee and either CDSC or redemption fee   p=12b-1 fee   n=none of the preceding fees   N/A=not available

Income-bond

Fund	Year Began	Investment Adviser	9/30/89 Assets	Minimum Initial and Subsequent Investment	Fees*	Where to Buy Shares
Flex-Funds *Bond Fund (The)* 6000 Memorial Dr. P.O. Box 7177 Dublin, OH 43017 614/766-7000 800/325-FLEX	1985	R. Meeder & Associates, Inc.	$4.8 Mil	$2,500/ 100	p	Fund
FPA New Income, Inc. 10301 W. Pico Blvd. Los Angeles, CA 90064 213/277-4900 800/421-4374	1969	First Pacific Advisors, Inc.	$20.9 Mil	$100/ 25	i	Local Rep
Frank Russell Investment Company *Diversified Bond* 909 A St. Tacoma, WA 98402 206/627-7001 800/972-0700	1985	Frank Russell Investment Management Company	$223.4 Mil	$0/ 0	n	Local Rep
Frank Russell Investment Company *Fixed Income I* 909 A St. Tacoma, WA 98402 206/627-7001 800/972-0700	1981	Frank Russell Investment Management Company	$282.5 Mil	$0/ 0	n	Local Rep
Frank Russell Investment Company *Fixed Income II* 909 A St. Tacoma, WA 98402 206/627-7001 800/972-0700	1981	Frank Russell Investment Management Company	$86.0 Mil	$0/ 0	n	Local Rep
Frank Russell Investment Company *Volatility Constrained Bond* 909 A St. Tacoma, WA 98402 206/627-7001 800/972-0700	1985	Frank Russell Investment Management Company	$206.9 Mil	$0/ 0	n	Local Rep
GIT Income Trust *GIT Income Trust A-Rated Income Portfolio* 1655 Fort Myer Dr. Arlington, VA 22209 703/528-6500 800/336-3063	1983	Bankers Finance Investment Management Corp.	$6.4 Mil	$1,000/ 0	n	Fund

*Key: i=initial sales charge   r=redemption fee or contingent deferred sales charge(CDSC)
t=12b-1 fee and either CDSC or redemption fee   p=12b-1 fee   n=none of the preceding fees   N/A=not available

239

Income-bond

Fund	Year Began	Investment Adviser	9/30/89 Assets	Minimum Initial and Subsequent Investment	Fees*	Where to Buy Shares
Harbor Fund *Harbor Bond Fund* One SeaGate Toledo, OH 43666 419/247-2477 800/422-1050	1987	Harbor Capital Advisors, Inc.	$20.0 Mil	$2,000/ 500	n	Fund
Hartford Bond/Debt Securities Fund, Inc. 200 Hopmeadow St. P.O. Box 2999 Hartford, CT 06104-2999 203/843-8245 800/227-1371	1976	Hartford Investment Management Company, Inc.	$58.3 Mil	Not Applicable	n	Insur
Harvest Funds, Inc. *Income Portfolio* 4000 Park Rd. Charlotte, NC 28209 704/523-9407 800/366-2277	1988	Bass Capital Management	$5.8 Mil (e)	$1,000/ 50	i, p	Local Rep
Home Life Bond Fund, Inc. One Centennial Plaza Piscataway, NJ 08854 212/428-2000	1983	Home Life Insurance Company	$8.8 Mil	Not Applicable	n	Insur
Horace Mann Income Fund, Inc. P.O. Box 4657 Springfield, IL 62708-4657 217/789-2500	1983	CIGNA Investments, Inc.	N/A	Not Applicable	r	Insur
IAI Bond Fund, Inc. 1100 Dain Twr. P.O. Box 357 Minneapolis, MN 55440 612/371-7780	1977	Investment Advisers, Inc.	$61.7 Mil	$5,000/ 1,000	n	Local Rep
IDEX Total Income Trust 201 Highland Ave. Largo, FL 34640 813/585-6565 800/237-3055 800/782-7152 FL Only	1987	IDEX Management, Inc.	$27.9 Mil	$500/ 50	i	Local Rep

*Key: i=initial sales charge   r=redemption fee or contingent deferred sales charge(CDSC)
t=12b-1 fee and either CDSC or redemption fee   p=12b-1 fee   n=none of the preceding fees   N/A=not available

Income-bond

Fund	Year Began	Investment Adviser	9/30/89 Assets	Minimum Initial and Subsequent Investment	Fees*	Where to Buy Shares
IDS Life Special Income Fund, Inc. IDS Tower 10 Minneapolis, MN 55440 612/372-3131 800/328-8300	1981	IDS Financial Corporation	$573.6 Mil	Not Applicable	r	Insur
IDS Strategy Fund, Inc. *Short-Term Income Fund* IDS Tower 10 Minneapolis, MN 55440 612/372-3131 800/328-8300	1984	IDS Financial Corporation	$108.5 Mil	$100/ 100	t	Local Rep
Income Portfolios *Limited Term Series* 82 Devonshire St. Boston, MA 02109 617/570-7000 800/343-9184 617/570-4750 MA Only	1984	Fidelity Management & Research Company	$416.5 Mil	$1.0 Mil/ 0	n	Local Rep
INVESCO Institutional Series Trust *INVESCO Institutional Income Fund* 1315 Peachtree St., NE Ste. 500 Atlanta, GA 30309 404/892-0666, 800/554-1156	1986	INVESCO Capital Management, Inc.	N/A	$1.0 Mil/ 5,000	n	Local Rep
Investment Trust of Boston *Premium Income Portfolio* 399 Boylston St. 9th Fl. Boston, MA 02116 800/888-4823	1989	Back Bay Advisors, Inc.	$4.9 Mil	$1,000/ 0	i, p	Local Rep
Investors Income Fund, Inc. 1100 Milan St., Ste. 3500 P.O. Box 3167 Houston, TX 77253-3167 713/750-8000 800/262-6631	1968	Capstone Asset Management Company	$20.2 Mil	$200/ 0	i	Local Rep
Kemper Income & Capital Preservation Fund, Inc. 120 S. LaSalle St. Chicago, IL 60603 312/781-1121 800/621-1148	1974	Kemper Financial Services, Inc.	$395.3 Mil	$1,000/ 100	i	Local Rep

*Key: i=initial sales charge   r=redemption fee or contingent deferred sales charge(CDSC)
t=12b-1 fee and either CDSC or redemption fee   p=12b-1 fee   n=none of the preceding fees   N/A=not available

Income-bond

Fund	Year Began	Investment Adviser	9/30/89 Assets	Minimum Initial and Subsequent Investment	Fees*	Where to Buy Shares
Keystone Custodian Funds, Inc. B-1 Series 99 High St. Boston, MA 02110 617/338-3200 800/343-2898 800/225-1587	1932	Keystone Custodian Funds, Inc.	$447.8 Mil	$250/ 0	t	Local Rep
Legg Mason Income Trust *Legg Mason Investment Grade Income Portfolio* 111 S. Calvert St. P.O. Box 1476 Baltimore, MD 21203-1476 30l/539-3400 800/822-5544, 800/492-7777 MD Only	1987	Western Asset Management Company	$10.4 Mil (e)	$1,000/ 500	p	Local Rep
Lutheran Brotherhood Income Fund, Inc. 625 Fourth Ave. South Minneapolis, MN 55415 612/339-8091 800/328-4552 800/752-4208 MN Only	1972	Lutheran Brotherhood Research Corp.	$726.3 Mil	$500/ 50	i	Local Rep
Management of Managers Group of Funds *Fixed Income Securities Fund* 200 Connecticut Ave. 8th Fl. Norwalk, CT 06854 203/855-2200	1984	Evaluation Associates Investment Management Co.	$43.8 Mil	$0/ 0	n	Local Rep
Management of Managers Group of Funds *Short and Intermediate Fixed Income Securities Fund* 200 Connecticut Ave. 8th Fl. Norwalk, CT 06854 203/855-2200	1984	Evaluation Associates Investment Management Co.	$165.2 Mil	$0/ 0	n	Local Rep
Management of Managers Group of Funds *Short Term Fixed Income Securities Fund* 200 Connecticut Ave. 8th Fl. Norwalk, CT 06854 203/855-2200	1987	Evaluation Associates Investment Management Co.	$11.3 Mil	$0/ 0	n	Local Rep
MassMutual Integrity Funds *MassMutual Investment Grade Bond Fund* 1295 State St. Springfield, MA 01111 413/788-8411 800/542-6767 800/854-9100 MA Only	1988	Massachusetts Mutual Life Insurance Company	$98.2 Mil	$500/ 25	i, p	Local Rep

*Key: i=initial sales charge   r=redemption fee or contingent deferred sales charge(CDSC)
t=12b-1 fee and either CDSC or redemption fee   p=12b-1 fee   n=none of the preceding fees   N/A=not available

Income-bond

Fund	Year Began	Investment Adviser	9/30/89 Assets	Minimum Initial and Subsequent Investment	Fees*	Where to Buy Shares
MIM Mutual Funds, Inc. *Bond Income Fund* 4500 Rockside Rd. Ste. 440 Independence, OH 44131-6809 216/642-3000 800/233-1240	1986	Mathematical Investing Systems, Inc.	$9.5 Mil	$250/ 50	p	Fund
MONY Series Fund *Intermediate Term Bond Portfolio* 500 Frank W. Burr Blvd. 71-13 Glenpointe Ctr. West Teaneck, NJ 07666 201/907-6669	1985	MONY Life Insurance Company of America	$20.7 Mil	Not Applicable	n	Insur
MONY Series Fund *Long Term Bond Portfolio* 500 Frank W. Burr Blvd. 71-13 Glenpointe Ctr. West Teaneck, NJ 07666 201/907-6669	1985	MONY Life Insurance Company of America	$20.5 Mil	Not Applicable	n	Insur
Mutual of America Investment Corporation *Bond Fund (The)* 666 Fifth Ave. New York, NY 10103 212/399-1600 800/223-0898	1986	Mutual of America Life Insurance Company	N/A	Not Applicable	n	Insur
Neuberger & Berman Limited Maturity Bond Fund 342 Madison Ave. New York, NY 10173 212/850-8300 800/877-9700	1986	Neuberger & Berman Management Incorporated	$107.9 Mil	$10,000/ 200	n	Fund
Neuberger & Berman Money Market Plus 342 Madison Ave. New York, NY 10173 212/850-8300 800/877-9700	1986	Neuberger & Berman Management Incorporated	$100.0 Mil	$2,000/ 200	n	Fund
New England Bond Income Fund 399 Boylston St. Boston, MA 02116 617/267-6600 800/343-7104	1973	Back Bay Advisors, Inc.	$73.4 Mil	$1,000/ 25	i, p	Local Rep

*Key: i=initial sales charge   r=redemption fee or contingent deferred sales charge(CDSC)
t=12b-1 fee and either CDSC or redemption fee   p=12b-1 fee   n=none of the preceding fees   N/A=not available

Income-bond

Fund	Year Began	Investment Adviser	9/30/89 Assets	Minimum Initial and Subsequent Investment	Fees*	Where to Buy Shares
New England Zenith Fund *Bond Income Series* 501 Boylston St. Boston, MA 02116 617/267-7055 800/634-8025	1983	Back Bay Advisors, Inc.	$22.2 Mil	Not Applicable	n	Insur
Newton Income Fund, Inc. *Newton Income Fund* 330 E. Kilbourn Ave. Ste. 1150 Milwaukee, WI 53202 414/271-0440 800/247-7039 800/242-7229 WI Only	1970	Marshall & Ilsley Investment Management Corporation	$17.7 Mil	$1,000/ 50	n	Fund
Pacific Investment Management Institutional Trust *Long Duration Portfolio* 840 Newport Ctr. Dr. Ste. 300 Newport Beach, CA 92660 714/640-3031, 800/443-6915	1987	Pacific Investment Management Company	N/A	$200,000/ 10,000	n	Fund
Pacific Investment Management Institutional Trust *Low Duration Portfolio* 840 Newport Ctr. Dr. Ste. 300 Newport Beach, CA 92660 714/640-3031, 800/443-6915	1987	Pacific Investment Management Company	$163.8 Mil (e)	$200,000/ 10,000	n	Fund
Pacific Investment Management Institutional Trust *Short-Term Portfolio* 840 Newport Ctr. Dr. Ste. 300 Newport Beach, CA 92660 714/640-3031, 800/443-6915	1987	Pacific Investment Management Company	$17.1 Mil (e)	$200,000/ 10,000	n	Fund
Pacific Investment Management Institutional Trust *Total Return Portfolio* 840 Newport Ctr. Dr. Ste. 300 Newport Beach, CA 92660 714/640-3031, 800/443-6915	1987	Pacific Investment Management Company	$304.7 Mil (e)	$200,000/ 10,000	n	Fund
PaineWebber Master Series, Inc. *PaineWebber Master Income Fund* 1285 Avenue of the Americas PaineWebber Bldg. New York, NY 10019 212/713-2000, 800/647-1568	1986	Mitchell Hutchins Asset Management Inc.	$211.1 Mil	$1,000/ 100	t	Local Rep

*Key: i=initial sales charge   r=redemption fee or contingent deferred sales charge(CDSC)
t=12b-1 fee and either CDSC or redemption fee   p=12b-1 fee   n=none of the preceding fees   N/A=not available

Income-bond

Fund	Year Began	Investment Adviser	9/30/89 Assets	Minimum Initial and Subsequent Investment	Fees*	Where to Buy Shares
Parkstone Group of Funds *Bond Fund* 1900 E. Dublin-Granville Rd. Columbus, OH 43229 614/899-4600 800/338-4385	1987	Securities Counsel, Inc.	N/A	$1,000/ 0	N/A	Fund
Parkstone Group of Funds *Limited Maturity Bond Fund* 1900 E. Dublin-Granville Rd. Columbus, OH 43229 614/899-4600 800/338-4385	1987	Securities Counsel, Inc.	N/A	$1,000/ 0	N/A	Fund
Plymouth Fund *Plymouth Short-Term Bond Portfolio* 82 Devonshire St. Boston, MA 02109 617/570-7000 800/544-6666	1987	Fidelity Management & Research Company	$12.8 Mil	$1,000/ 100	i, p	Local Rep
PNCG Income Fund, Inc. 121 SW Morrison Ste. 1415 Portland, OR 97204 503/295-0919 800/541-9732	1989	PNCG Fund Advisers, Inc.	N/A	$1,000/ 500	i, p	Local Rep
Portfolios for Diversified Investment *Diversified Fixed Income Fund* 3411 Silverside Rd. Webster Bldg., Ste. 204 Wilmington, DE 19810 212/640-6155, 800/221-8120, 800/441-7450	1986	Provident Institutional Management Corporation	$13.4 Mil (e)	$1,000/ 0	n	Local Rep
Prudential-Bache Structured Maturity Fund One Seaport Plaza New York, NY 10292 212/214-1215 800/225-1852	1989	Prudential Mutual Fund Management	$78.3 Mil	$1,000/ 100	N/A	Local Rep
Putnam Capital Manager Trust *PCM U.S. Government and High Grade Bond Fund* One Post Office Sq. Boston, MA 02109 617/292-1000 800/225-2465	1988	Putnam Management Company, Inc.	$50.1 Mil	Not Applicable	r	Insur

*Key: i=initial sales charge   r=redemption fee or contingent deferred sales charge(CDSC)
t=12b-1 fee and either CDSC or redemption fee   p=12b-1 fee   n=none of the preceding fees   N/A=not available

245

Income-bond

Fund	Year Began	Investment Adviser	9/30/89 Assets	Minimum Initial and Subsequent Investment	Fees*	Where to Buy Shares
Putnam Tax-Free High Income Fund One Post Office Sq. Boston, MA 02109 617/292-1000 800/225-2465	1989	Putnam Management Company, Inc.	$132.9 Mil	$500/ 50	N/A	Local Rep
Quest For Value Accumulation Trust *Bond Portfolio* Oppenheimer Tower World Financial Ctr. New York, NY 10281 212/667-7587 800/232-FUND	1988	Quest For Value Advisors	$2.2 Mil	Not Applicable	n	Insur
RNC Income Fund, Inc. 11601 Wilshire Blvd. 24th Fl. Los Angeles, CA 90025 213/477-6543 800/225-9655	1986	RNC Capital Management Co.	$10.6 Mil (e)	$1,000/ 100	i, p	Local Rep
SAFECO Intermediate-Term Bond Fund, Inc. SAFECO Plaza Seattle, WA 98185 206/545-5530 800/426-6730	1988	SAFECO Asset Management Company	$6.2 Mil	$1,000/ 100	n	Fund
Scudder Funds Trust *Short Term Bond* 175 Federal St. Boston, MA 02110 617/439-4640 800/225-2470 800/225-5163	1984	Scudder, Stevens & Clark, Inc.	$37.3 Mil	$1,000/ 0	n	Fund
SEI Index Funds *Bond Index Portfolio* 680 E. Swedesford Rd. No. 7 Wayne, PA 19087 215/254-1000 800/345-1151	1986	Manufacturers National Bank of Detroit	$11.6 Mil	$0/ 0	p	Local Rep
SEI Institutional Managed Trust *Bond Portfolio* 680 E. Swedesford Rd. No. 7 Wayne, PA 19087 215/254-1000 800/345-1151	1987	Boatmen's Trust Company	$27.6 Mil	$0/ 0	p	Local Rep

*Key: i=initial sales charge   r=redemption fee or contingent deferred sales charge(CDSC)
t=12b-1 fee and either CDSC or redemption fee   p=12b-1 fee   n=none of the preceding fees   N/A=not available

246

Income-bond

Fund	Year Began	Investment Adviser	9/30/89 Assets	Minimum Initial and Subsequent Investment	Fees*	Where to Buy Shares
SEI Institutional Managed Trust *Limited Volatility Bond Portfolio* 680 E. Swedesford Rd. No. 7 Wayne, PA 19087 215/254-1000, 800/345-1151	1987	Bank One, Indianapolis, N.A.	$42.7 Mil	$0/ 0	p	Local Rep
Seligman Mutual Benefit Portfolios, Inc. *Seligman Fixed Income Securities Portfolio* 130 Liberty St. New York, NY 10006 212/488-0200 800/221-2450, 800/522-6869 NY Only	1988	J. & W. Seligman & Co. Incorporated	$3.3 Mil	Not Applicable	r	Insur
Sentinel Group Funds, Inc. *Bond Fund Series* National Life Dr. Montpelier, VT 05604 802/229-3900 800/282-3863	1969	Sentinel Advisors, Inc.	$29.3 Mil	$250/ 25	i	Local Rep
Sigma Income Shares, Inc. 3801 Kennett Pk., C-200 Greenville Ctr. Wilmington, DE 19807 302/652-3091 800/441-9490	1974	Sigma Management, Inc.	$36.7 Mil	$0/ 0	i, p	Local Rep
Sit "New Beginning" Investment Reserve Fund, Inc. 90 S. 7th St. Ste. 4600 Minneapolis, MN 55402 612/332-3223 800/332-5580	1985	Sit Investment Management Company	$4.3 Mil	$2,000/ 100	n	Fund
SLH Investment Series, Inc. *SLH Investment Grade Bond Portfolio* 31 W. 52nd St. 15th Fl. New York, NY 10019 212/767-3700 800/334-4636, 800/422-0214 NY Only	1982	SLH Asset Management Division of Shearson Lehman Hutton Inc.	$472.1 Mil	$500/ 250	t	Local Rep
Smith Barney Funds, Inc. *Income Return Account Portfolio* 1345 Avenue of the Americas New York, NY 10105 212/698-5349 800/544-7835	1985	Smith, Barney Advisers, Inc.	$25.1 Mil	$10,000/ 50	i	Local Rep

*Key: i=initial sales charge   r=redemption fee or contingent deferred sales charge(CDSC)
t=12b-1 fee and either CDSC or redemption fee   p=12b-1 fee   n=none of the preceding fees   N/A=not available

247

Income-bond

Fund	Year Began	Investment Adviser	9/30/89 Assets	Minimum Initial and Subsequent Investment	Fees*	Where to Buy Shares
Smith Barney Variable Account Funds, Inc. *Reserve Account Portfolio* 1345 Avenue of the Americas New York, NY 10105 212/698-5349 800/544-7835	1989	Smith, Barney Advisers, Inc.	N/A	Not Applicable	N/A	Insur
Sower Series Fund, Inc. *Bond Portfolio* 5900 "O" St. Lincoln, NE 68510 402/467-1122	1987	Ameritas Investment Advisors, Inc.	N/A	Not Applicable	n	Insur
Specialty Managers Trust *Limited Maturity Bond Series* 1925 Century Park East Ste. 2350 Los Angeles, CA 90067 213/556-5499 800/423-4891	1989	Neuberger & Berman Management, Inc.	N/A	Not Applicable	n	Insur
SteinRoe Income Trust *SteinRoe Managed Bonds* 300 W. Adams St. P.O. Box 1143 Chicago, IL 60690 800/338-2550	1978	Stein Roe & Farnham Incorporated	$164.1 Mil	$1,000/ 100	n	Fund
Strong Advantage Fund P.O. Box 2936 Milwaukee, WI 53201 414/359-3400 800/368-3863	1988	Strong/ Corneliuson Capital Management, Inc.	N/A	$1,000/ 200	n	Fund
Strong Short-Term Bond Fund Inc. P.O. Box 2936 Milwaukee, WI 53201 414/359-3400 800/368-3863	1987	Strong/ Corneliuson Capital Management, Inc.	N/A	$1,000/ 200	n	Fund
Templeton Variable Products Series Fund *Templeton Bond Fund (The)* 700 Central Ave. P.O. Box 33030 St. Petersburg, FL 33733-8030 813/823-8712 800/237-0738	1988	Templeton, Galbraith & Hansberger, Ltd.	N/A	Not Applicable	n	Insur

*Key: i=initial sales charge   r=redemption fee or contingent deferred sales charge(CDSC)
t=12b-1 fee and either CDSC or redemption fee   p=12b-1 fee   n=none of the preceding fees   N/A=not available

Income-bond

Fund	Year Began	Investment Adviser	9/30/89 Assets	Minimum Initial and Subsequent Investment	Fees*	Where to Buy Shares
Thomson McKinnon Investment Trust *Thomson McKinnon Income Fund* One State Street Plaza New York, NY 10004 212/482-5894 800/628-1237	1984	Thomson McKinnon Asset Management L.P.	$579.3 Mil	$1,000/ 100	t	Local Rep
Transamerica Bond Fund *Transamerica Investment Quality Bond Fund* 1000 Louisiana Ste. 6000 Houston, TX 77002-5098 713/751-2400 800/999-3863	1980	Transamerica Fund Management Company	$97.9 Mil	$100/ 10	i, p	Local Rep
Transamerica Bond Fund *Transamerica Premium Limited Term Account* 1000 Louisiana Ste. 6000 Houston, TX 77002-5098 713/751-2400 800/999-3863	1986	Transamerica Fund Management Company	$3.6 Mil	$10,000/ 500	i	Local Rep
T. Rowe Price New Income Fund, Inc. 100 E. Pratt St. Baltimore, MD 21202 301/547-2000 800/638-5660	1973	T. Rowe Price Associates, Inc.	$991.2 Mil	$2,500/ 100	n	Fund
T. Rowe Price Short-Term Bond Fund, Inc. 100 E. Pratt St. Baltimore, MD 21202 301/547-2000 800/638-5660	1984	T. Rowe Price Associates, Inc.	$215.0 Mil	$2,500/ 100	n	Fund
Twentieth Century Investors, Inc. *Long-Term Bond* 4500 Main St. P.O. Box 419200 Kansas City, MO 64141-6200 816/531-5575 800/345-2021	1987	Investors Research Corporation	$58.0 Mil	$0/ 0	n	Fund
United Funds, Inc. *United Bond Fund* 2400 Pershing Rd. P.O. Box 418343 Kansas City, MO 64141-9343 816/283-4000 800/821-5664	1964	Waddell & Reed, Inc.	$383.8 Mil	$500/ 25	i	Local Rep

*Key: i=initial sales charge   r=redemption fee or contingent deferred sales charge(CDSC)
t=12b-1 fee and either CDSC or redemption fee   p=12b-1 fee   n=none of the preceding fees   N/A=not available

249

Income-bond

Fund	Year Began	Investment Adviser	9/30/89 Assets	Minimum Initial and Subsequent Investment	Fees*	Where to Buy Shares
Vanguard Bond Market Fund, Inc. Vanguard Financial Ctr. P.O. Box 2600 Valley Forge, PA 19482 215/648-6000 800/662-7447 800/362-0530 PA Only	1986	Vanguard Group, Inc.	$117.2 Mil	$3,000/ 100	n	Fund
Variable Insurance Products Fund II *Short-Term Portfolio* 82 Devonshire St. Boston, MA 02109 617/570-7000 800/544-6666	1989	Fidelity Management & Research Company	N/A	Not Applicable	N/A	Insur
Variable Investors Series Trust *U.S. Government Bond Portfolio* 1414 Main St. Springfield, MA 01144 413/732-7100	1987	Amherst Investment Management Company, Inc.	$10.3 Mil	Not Applicable	n	Insur
Wright Managed Bond Trust *Wright Current Income Fund* 24 Federal St. 5th Fl. Boston, MA 02110 617/482-8260 800/225-6265	1987	Wright Investors Service	$12.4 Mil	$1,000/ 0	p	Local Rep
Wright Managed Bond Trust *Wright Near Term Bond Fund* 24 Federal St. 5th Fl. Boston, MA 02110 617/482-8260 800/225-6265	1983	Wright Investors Service	$223.7 Mil (e)	$1,000/ 0	p	Local Rep
Zweig Series Trust *Bond-Debenture Series* 25 Broadway New York, NY 10004 212/361-9612 800/272-2700	1985	Zweig/Glaser Advisers	$16.0 Mil (e)	$1,000/ 100	t	Local Rep

*Key: i=initial sales charge   r=redemption fee or contingent deferred sales charge(CDSC)
t=12b-1 fee and either CDSC or redemption fee   p=12b-1 fee   n=none of the preceding fees   N/A=not available

♦ ♦ ♦ ♦

Income-equity Funds

Income-equity

Fund	Year Began	Investment Adviser	9/30/89 Assets	Minimum Initial and Subsequent Investment	Fees*	Where to Buy Shares
ABT Utility Income Fund, Inc. 205 Royal Palm Way Palm Beach, FL 33480 407/655-7255 800/441-6580	1978	Palm Beach Capital Management, Ltd.	$124.6 Mil	$1,000/ 50	i, p	Local Rep
Alger American Fund *Alger American Income and Growth Portfolio* 75 Maiden Lane New York, NY 10038 212/806-8800 800/223-3810	1988	Fred Alger Management, Inc.	$0.02 Mil	Not Applicable	n	Insur
Alger Fund *Alger Income and Growth Portfolio* 75 Maiden Lane New York, NY 10038 212/806-8800 800/223-3810	1986	Fred Alger Management, Inc.	$2.7 Mil	$1,000/ 100	t	Fund
Amana Mutual Funds Trust *Income Series* 520 Herald Bldg. 1155 N. State St. Bellingham, WA 98225 206/734-9900	1986	Saturna Capital Corporation	$4.4 Mil	$100/ 25	p	Fund
American Asset Management Corporation *American Asset Dividend Fund* 107 S. Main St. Ste. 100 Salt Lake City, UT 84111 801/328-3333	1987	American Asset Management Corporation	N/A	$10/ 10	N/A	Fund
American Asset Management Corporation *American Asset Yield Fund* 107 S. Main St. Ste. 100 Salt Lake City, UT 84111 801/328-3333	1986	American Asset Management Corporation	N/A	$10/ 10	N/A	Local Rep
American Eagle Fund, Inc. *American Eagle Income Series* 100 Light St. Baltimore, MD 21202 301/547-3894 800/622-3363	1987	Axe-Houghton Management, Inc.	$1.2 Mil	Not Applicable	r	Insur

*Key: i=initial sales charge   r=redemption fee or contingent deferred sales charge(CDSC)
t=12b-1 fee and either CDSC or redemption fee   p=12b-1 fee   n=none of the preceding fees   N/A=not available

Income-equity

Fund	Year Began	Investment Adviser	9/30/89 Assets	Minimum Initial and Subsequent Investment	Fees*	Where to Buy Shares
American National Income Fund, Inc. Two Moody Plaza Galveston, TX 77550 409/763-2767 800/231-4639 800/392-9753 TX Only	1970	Securities Management & Research, Inc.	$66.4 Mil	$100/ 20	i	Local Rep
CFS Investment Trust *Kalliston Preferred Plus Fund* 2001 Spring Rd. Ste. 750 Oak Brook, IL 60521 312/571-7115 800/323-9943	1988	Calamos Asset Management, Inc.	$0.6 Mil (e)	$5,000/ 1,000	i, p	Local Rep
CIGNA Utilities Fund One Financial Plaza Springfield, MA 01103 413/784-0100 800/56CIGNA	1988	CIGNA Investments, Inc.	$46.1 Mil	$500/ 50	i, p	Local Rep
Compass Capital Group *Equity Income Fund* 1900 E. Dublin-Granville Rd. Columbus, OH 43229 614/899-4600 800/338-4385	1988	Midlantic National Bank	N/A	$2,500/ 100	N/A	Fund
Conestoga Family of Funds *Equity Fund* 1900 E. Dublin-Granville Rd. Columbus, OH 43229 614/899-4600 800/338-4385	1989	Meridian Investment Company	N/A	$0/ 0	N/A	Fund
Constitution Funds, Inc. *Equity Income Fund* Two World Trade Ctr. New York, NY 10048-0669 212/323-0200 800/525-7048	1988	Oppenheimer Management Corporation	$6.2 Mil	$1,000/ 250	i, p	Local Rep
Delaware Group Decatur Fund *Decatur I Series* One Commerce Sq. Philadelphia, PA 19103 215/988-1200 800/523-4640	1957	Delaware Management Company, Inc.	$1.9 Bil	$25/ 25	i	Local Rep

*Key: i=initial sales charge   r=redemption fee or contingent deferred sales charge(CDSC)
      t=12b-1 fee and either CDSC or redemption fee   p=12b-1 fee   n=none of the preceding fees   N/A=not available

Income-equity

Fund	Year Began	Investment Adviser	9/30/89 Assets	Minimum Initial and Subsequent Investment	Fees*	Where to Buy Shares
Delaware Group Decatur Fund *Decatur II Series* One Commerce Sq. Philadelphia, PA 19103 215/988-1200 800/523-4640	1986	Delaware Management Company, Inc.	$311.4 Mil	$25/ 25	i, p	Local Rep
Enterprise Equity Portfolios *Enterprise Growth and Income Portfolio* 1200 Ashwood Pkwy. Ste. 290 Atlanta, GA 30338 404/396-8118, 800/432-4320	1987	Enterprise Capital Management, Inc.	$21.1 Mil (e)	$500/ 25	t	Local Rep
Equitec Siebel Fund Group II *Equity Income Fund Series* 7677 Oakport St. P.O. Box 2470 Oakland, CA 94614 415/430-9900 800/869-8900	1987	Siebel Capital Management, Inc.	$1.2 Mil (e)	$1,000/ 0	i, p	Local Rep
Equity Portfolio: Income 82 Devonshire St. Boston, MA 02109 617/570-7000 800/843-3001 617/570-5511 MA Only	1983	Fidelity Management & Research Company	$494.7 Mil	$500,000/ 0	n	Local Rep
Federated Utility Trust Federated Investors Twr. Pittsburgh, PA 15222-3779 412/288-1900 800/245-5000	1987	Federated Management	$16.8 Mil	$25,000/ 0	n	Local Rep
Fidelity Devonshire Trust *Fidelity Equity-Income Fund* 82 Devonshire St. Boston, MA 02109 617/570-7000 800/544-6666	1965	Fidelity Management & Research Company	$5.2 Bil	$1,000/ 250	i	Fund
Fidelity Devonshire Trust *Fidelity Utilities Income Fund* 82 Devonshire St. Boston, MA 02109 617/570-7000 800/544-6666	1987	Fidelity Management & Research Company	$142.4 Mil	$2,500/ 250	i	Fund

*Key: i=initial sales charge   r=redemption fee or contingent deferred sales charge(CDSC)
t=12b-1 fee and either CDSC or redemption fee   p=12b-1 fee   n=none of the preceding fees   N/A=not available

Income-equity

Fund	Year Began	Investment Adviser	9/30/89 Assets	Minimum Initial and Subsequent Investment	Fees*	Where to Buy Shares
Fidelity Puritan Trust *Fidelity Puritan Fund* 82 Devonshire St. Boston, MA 02109 617/570-7000 800/544-6666	1947	Fidelity Management & Research Company	$4.9 Bil	$1,000/ 250	i	Fund
Financial Independence Trust *Utility Income Fund* 700 Dixie Terminal Bldg. Cincinnati, OH 45202 513/629-2000 800/543-8721 800/582-7396 OH Only	1989	Financial Independence Trust Advisers, Inc.	$1.4 Mil	$1,000/ 0	i, p	Local Rep
First Investors Fund *First Investors Blue Chip Fund* 120 Wall St. New York, NY 10005 212/208-6000	1989	First Investors Management Company, Inc.	$20.3 Mil	$1,000/ 100	i, p	Local Rep
Flex-Funds *Income and Growth Fund (The)* 6000 Memorial Dr. P.O. Box 7177 Dublin, OH 43017 614/766-7000 800/325-FLEX	1985	R. Meeder & Associates, Inc.	$2.1 Mil	$2,500/ 100	p	Fund
Franklin Investors Securities Trust *Franklin Special Equity Income Fund* 777 Mariners Island Blvd. San Mateo, CA 94404 415/570-3000 800/632-2180, 800/632-2350	1988	Franklin Advisers, Inc.	$6.4 Mil	$100/ 25	i	Local Rep
Frank Russell Investment Company *Equity Income* 909 A St. Tacoma, WA 98402 206/627-7001 800/972-0700	1985	Frank Russell Investment Management Company	$101.8 Mil	$0/ 0	n	Local Rep
Frank Russell Investment Company *Equity III* 909 A St. Tacoma, WA 98402 206/627-7001 800/972-0700	1981	Frank Russell Investment Management Company	$137.3 Mil	$0/ 0	n	Local Rep

*Key: i=initial sales charge r=redemption fee or contingent deferred sales charge(CDSC)
t=12b-1 fee and either CDSC or redemption fee p=12b-1 fee n=none of the preceding fees N/A=not available

Income-equity

Fund	Year Began	Investment Adviser	9/30/89 Assets	Minimum Initial and Subsequent Investment	Fees*	Where to Buy Shares
Harbor Fund *Harbor Value Fund* One SeaGate Toledo, OH 43666 419/247-2477 800/422-1050	1987	Harbor Capital Advisors, Inc.	$23.2 Mil	$2,000/ 500	n	Fund
Helmsman Fund *Disciplined Equity Portfolio* 1900 E. Dublin-Granville Rd. Columbus, OH 43229 614/899-4600 800/338-4385	1989	Bank One, Indianapolis, N.A. Bank One, Milwaukee, N.A.	N/A	$2,500/ 0	N/A	Fund
Helmsman Fund *Income Equity Portfolio* 1900 E. Dublin-Granville Rd. Columbus, OH 43229 614/899-4600 800/338-4385	1989	Bank One, Indianapolis, N.A. Bank One, Milwaukee, N.A.	N/A	$2,500/ 0	N/A	Fund
Highmark Group *Income Equity Fund* 1900 E. Dublin-Granville Rd. Columbus, OH 43229 614/899-4600 800/338-4385	1987	Merus Capital Management	N/A	$1,000/ 100	N/A	Fund
IDS Utilities Income Fund, Inc. IDS Tower 10 Minneapolis, MN 55440 612/372-3131 800/328-8300	1988	IDS Financial Corporation	$102.9 Mil	$100/ 100	i, p	Local Rep
Keystone America Equity Income Fund 99 High St. Boston, MA 02110 617/338-3200 800/343-2898 800/225-1587	1987	Keystone Custodian Funds, Inc.	$23.7 Mil	$1,000/ 0	i, t	Local Rep
Keystone America Fund of Growth Stock 99 High St. Boston, MA 02110 617/338-3200 800/343-2898 800/225-1587	1987	Keystone Custodian Funds, Inc.	$5.9 Mil	$1,000/ 0	i, t	Local Rep

*Key: i=initial sales charge   r=redemption fee or contingent deferred sales charge(CDSC)
t=12b-1 fee and either CDSC or redemption fee   p=12b-1 fee   n=none of the preceding fees   N/A=not available

Income-equity

Fund	Year Began	Investment Adviser	9/30/89 Assets	Minimum Initial and Subsequent Investment	Fees*	Where to Buy Shares
Keystone Custodian Funds, Inc. K-1 Series 99 High St. Boston, MA 02110 617/338-3200 800/343-2898 800/225-1587	1932	Keystone Custodian Funds, Inc.	$748.4 Mil	$250/ 0	t	Local Rep
Kidder, Peabody Equity Income Fund, Inc. 20 Exchange Place New York, NY 10005 212/510-5552	1985	Webster Management Corporation	$59.3 Mil	$1,500/ 500	t	Local Rep
Main Street Funds, Inc. *Income & Growth Fund* 3410 S. Galena St. Denver, CO 80231 303/671-3200 800/548-1225	1988	Oppenheimer Management Corporation	$4.2 Mil	$1,000/ 25	i, p	Local Rep
MassMutual Integrity Funds *MassMutual Corporate Cash Fund* 1295 State St. Springfield, MA 01111 413/788-8411 800/542-6767 800/854-9100 MA Only	1988	Massachusetts Mutual Life Insurance Company	$11.3 Mil	$25,000/ 2,500	i, p	Local Rep
Merrill Lynch Corporate Dividend Fund, Inc. P.O. Box 9011 Princeton, NJ 08543-9011 609/282-2800 800/637-3863	1984	Merrill Lynch Asset Management Inc.	$90.1 Mil	$10,000/ 5,000	i	Local Rep
MetLife-State Street Equity Trust *MetLife-State Street Equity Income Fund* One Financial Ctr. 30th Fl. Boston, MA 02111 617/348-2000, 800/882-0052	1986	MetLife-State Street Investment Services, Inc.	$42.6 Mil	$250/ 25	i, p	Local Rep
MFS Lifetime Investment Program *Lifetime Dividends Plus Trust* 500 Boylston St. Boston, MA 02116 617/954-5000 800/343-2829	1986	Lifetime Advisers, Inc.	$181.3 Mil (e)	$1,000/ 50	t	Local Rep

*Key: i=initial sales charge r=redemption fee or contingent deferred sales charge(CDSC)
t=12b-1 fee and either CDSC or redemption fee p=12b-1 fee n=none of the preceding fees N/A=not available

Income-equity

Fund	Year Began	Investment Adviser	9/30/89 Assets	Minimum Initial and Subsequent Investment	Fees*	Where to Buy Shares
MIM Mutual Funds, Inc. *Stock, Convertible & Option Income Fund* 4500 Rockside Rd. Ste. 440 Independence, OH 44131-6809 216/642-3000 800/233-1240	1986	Mathematical Investing Systems, Inc.	$13.4 Mil	$250/ 50	p	Fund
MONY Series Fund *Equity Income Portfolio* 500 Frank W. Burr Blvd. 71-13 Glenpointe Ctr. West Teaneck, NJ 07666 201/907-6669	1985	MONY Life Insurance Company of America	$6.4 Mil	Not Applicable	n	Insur
National Real Estate Trust *National Real Estate Income Fund* 600 Third Ave. New York, NY 10016 203/863-5600 800/237-1718	1987	National Securities & Research Corporation	$15.8 Mil	$500/ 25	i, p	Local Rep
North American Security Trust *Conservative Asset Allocation Portfolio* 695 Atlantic Ave. P.O. Box 9064 GMF Boston, MA 02205 617/439-6960, 800/344-1029	1986	NASL Financial Services, Inc.	$8.6 Mil (e)	$1,000/ 100	i, p	Local Rep
Olympic Trust *Equity Income Fund* 800 W. 6th St. Ste. 540 Los Angeles, CA 90017-2708 213/623-7833 800/346-7301	1987	Hotchkis & Wiley	$54.7 Mil	$25,000/ 0	n	Fund
Oppenheimer Equity Income Fund 3410 S. Galena St. Denver, CO 80231 303/671-3200 800/525-7048	1970	Oppenheimer Management Corporation	$1.2 Bil	$1,000/ 25	i	Local Rep
Parkstone Group of Funds *Equity Fund* 1900 E. Dublin-Granville Rd. Columbus, OH 43229 614/899-4600 800/338-4385	1989	Securities Counsel, Inc.	N/A	$1,000/ 0	N/A	Fund

*Key: i=initial sales charge   r=redemption fee or contingent deferred sales charge(CDSC)
t=12b-1 fee and either CDSC or redemption fee   p=12b-1 fee   n=none of the preceding fees   N/A=not available

259

Income-equity

Fund	Year Began	Investment Adviser	9/30/89 Assets	Minimum Initial and Subsequent Investment	Fees*	Where to Buy Shares
Parkstone Group of Funds *High Income Equity Fund* 1900 E. Dublin-Granville Rd. Columbus, OH 43229 614/899-4600 800/338-4385	1987	Securities Counsel, Inc.	N/A	$1,000/ 0	N/A	Fund
Patriot Group Investment Trust *Patriot Corporate Cash Fund* 211 Congress St. Boston, MA 02110 617/426-3310 800/843-0090	1986	Patriot Advisers, Inc.	$27.7 Mil (e)	$50,000/ 10,000	i, p	Local Rep
Principal Preservation Portfolios, Inc. *Dividend Achievers Portfolio* 215 N. Main St. West Bend, WI 53095 414/334-5521 800/826-4600	1987	B.C. Ziegler and Company	$12.9 Mil	$1,000/ 250	i	Local Rep
Progressive Income Equity Fund, Inc. Federated Investors Twr. Pittsburgh, PA 15222-3779 412/288-1900 800/245-5051	1987	Passport Research, Ltd.	$45.0 Mil	$500/ 100	i	Local Rep
Prudential-Bache Equity Income Fund One Seaport Plaza New York, NY 10292 212/214-1215 800/225-1852	1987	Prudential Mutual Fund Management	$131.8 Mil	$1,000/ 100	t	Local Rep
Prudential-Bache Utility Fund, Inc. One Seaport Plaza New York, NY 10292 212/214-1215 800/225-1852	1981	Prudential Mutual Fund Management	$2.2 Bil	$1,000/ 100	t	Local Rep
Retirement Investment Trust *Equity Income Fund* 16 HCB 98 P.O. Box 2558 Houston, TX 77252-8098 713/546-7775	1988	None	N/A	$500/ 100	n	Fund

---

*Key: i=initial sales charge   r=redemption fee or contingent deferred sales charge(CDSC)
t=12b-1 fee and either CDSC or redemption fee   p=12b-1 fee   n=none of the preceding fees   N/A=not available

Income-equity

Fund	Year Began	Investment Adviser	9/30/89 Assets	Minimum Initial and Subsequent Investment	Fees*	Where to Buy Shares
Royce Fund *Total Return Series* 1414 Avenue of the Americas New York, NY 10019 212/355-7311 800/221-4268	1986	Quest Advisory Corp.	N/A	$2,000/ 50	t	Local Rep
SAFECO Income Fund, Inc. SAFECO Plaza Seattle, WA 98185 206/545-5530 800/426-6730	1969	SAFECO Asset Management Company	$232.8 Mil	$1,000/ 100	n	Fund
SafeGuard Equity Growth and Income Portfolio 16 Industrial Blvd. Paoli, PA 19301 215/251-0550 800/523-7798	1988	Provident Institutional Management Corporation	$1.1 Mil	$1,000/ 0	i, p	Local Rep
SEI Institutional Managed Trust *Equity Income Portfolio* 680 E. Swedesford Rd. No. 7 Wayne, PA 19087 215/254-1000 800/345-1151	1988	Merus Capital Management, Inc.	$30.9 Mil	$0/ 0	p	Local Rep
Sit "New Beginning" Income & Growth Fund, Inc. 90 S. 7th St. Ste. 4600 Minneapolis, MN 55402 612/332-3223 800/332-5580	1982	Sit Investment Management Company	$15.4 Mil	$2,000/ 100	n	Fund
SMITH HAYES Trust, Inc. *Convertible Portfolio* NBC Ctr. Ste. 780 Lincoln, NE 68508 402/476-3000 800/422-7791 NE Only	1988	SMITH HAYES Portfolio Management, Inc.	N/A	$25,000/ 1,000	N/A	Local Rep
Specialty Managers Trust *Natural Resources Series* 1925 Century Park East Ste. 2350 Los Angeles, CA 90067 213/556-5499 800/423-4891	1989	Van Eck Associates Corporation	N/A	Not Applicable	n	Insur

*Key: i=initial sales charge   r=redemption fee or contingent deferred sales charge(CDSC)
t=12b-1 fee and either CDSC or redemption fee   p=12b-1 fee   n=none of the preceding fees   N/A=not available

Income-equity

Fund	Year Began	Investment Adviser	9/30/89 Assets	Minimum Initial and Subsequent Investment	Fees*	Where to Buy Shares
State Street Fund for Foundations and Endowments *Equity Income Portfolio* One Financial Ctr. 38th Fl. Boston, MA 02111 617/482-3920	1986	State Street Research & Management Company	N/A	$100,000/ 0	N/A	Local Rep
SteinRoe Investment Trust *SteinRoe Total Return Fund* 300 W. Adams St. P.O. Box 1143 Chicago, IL 60690 800/338-2550	1949	Stein Roe & Farnham Incorporated	$144.9 Mil	$1,000/ 100	n	Fund
Stratton Monthly Dividend Shares, Inc. 610 W. Germantown Pike Ste. 361 Plymouth Meeting, PA 19462 215/941-0255 800/634-5726	1971	Stratton Management Company	$35.0 Mil	$2,000/ 100	n	Fund
Tower Series Funds, Inc. *Equity Income Series* P.O. Box 418 Tampa, FL 33601 813/229-5052	1983	Tower Investment Group, Inc.	$0.8 Mil (e)	$500/ 100	i	Local Rep
T. Rowe Price Equity Income Fund 100 E. Pratt St. Baltimore, MD 21202 301/547-2000 800/638-5660	1985	T. Rowe Price Associates, Inc.	$939.6 Mil	$2,500/ 100	n	Fund
United Funds, Inc. *United Income Fund* 2400 Pershing Rd. P.O. Box 418343 Kansas City, MO 64141-9343 816/283-4000 800/821-5664	1940	Waddell & Reed, Inc.	$1.6 Bil	$500/ 25	i	Local Rep
United Services Funds *U.S. Income Fund* P.O. Box 29467 San Antonio, TX 78229-0467 512/696-1234 800/873-8637	1983	United Services Advisors, Inc.	$10.0 Mil	$100/ 50	n	Fund

*Key: i=initial sales charge   r=redemption fee or contingent deferred sales charge(CDSC)
t=12b-1 fee and either CDSC or redemption fee   p=12b-1 fee   n=none of the preceding fees   N/A=not available

Income-equity

Fund	Year Began	Investment Adviser	9/30/89 Assets	Minimum Initial and Subsequent Investment	Fees*	Where to Buy Shares
USAA Mutual Fund, Inc. *Income Stock Fund* USAA Bldg. San Antonio, TX 78288 512/498-8000 800/531-8000	1987	USAA Investment Management Company	$55.2 Mil	$1,000/ 50	n	Fund
Vanguard Adjustable Rate Preferred Stock Fund Vanguard Financial Ctr. P.O. Box 2600 Valley Forge, PA 19482 215/648-6000 800/662-7447 800/362-0530 PA Only	1983	Wellington Management Company	$39.2 Mil	$25,000/ 1,000	n	Fund
Vanguard Equity Income Fund, Inc. Vanguard Financial Ctr. P.O. Box 2600 Valley Forge, PA 19482 215/648-6000 800/662-7447 800/362-0530 PA Only	1988	Newell Associates	$266.6 Mil	$3,000/ 100	n	Fund
Vanguard High Yield Stock Fund Vanguard Financial Ctr. P.O. Box 2600 Valley Forge, PA 19482 215/648-6000 800/662-7447 800/362-0530 PA Only	1975	Wellington Management Company	$169.8 Mil	$3,000/ 100	n	Fund
Vanguard Preferred Stock Fund Vanguard Financial Ctr. P.O. Box 2600 Valley Forge, PA 19482 215/648-6000 800/662-7447 800/362-0530 PA Only	1975	Wellington Management Company	$64.6 Mil	$3,000/ 100	n	Fund
Variable Insurance Products Fund *Equity-Income Portfolio* 82 Devonshire St. Boston, MA 02109 617/570-7000 800/544-6666	1986	Fidelity Management & Research Company	$128.5 Mil	Not Applicable	n	Insur
Weiss Peck & Greer Funds Trust *WPG Dividend Income Fund* One New York Plaza 31st Fl. New York, NY 10004 212/908-9582 800/223-3332	1988	Weiss, Peck & Greer Advisers, Inc.	$8.8 Mil (e)	$1,000/ 50	p	Fund

*Key: i=initial sales charge   r=redemption fee or contingent deferred sales charge(CDSC)
t=12b-1 fee and either CDSC or redemption fee   p=12b-1 fee   n=none of the preceding fees   N/A=not available

◆ ◆ ◆ ◆

Income-mixed Funds

Income-mixed

Fund	Year Began	Investment Adviser	9/30/89 Assets	Minimum Initial and Subsequent Investment	Fees*	Where to Buy Shares
AAL Mutual Funds *AAL Income Fund (The)* 222 W. College Ave. Appleton, WI 54919 414/734-5721 800/553-6319	1987	AAL Advisors Inc.	$71.5 Mil	$500/ 50	i, p	Local Rep
Advantage Income Fund 60 State St. Boston, MA 02109 617/742-5900 800/243-8115	1986	Boston Security Counsellors	$57.1 Mil	$500/ 250	t	Local Rep
Alger American Fund *Alger American Fixed Income Portfolio* 75 Maiden Lane New York, NY 10038 212/806-8800 800/223-3810	1989	Fred Alger Management, Inc.	$0.1 Mil	Not Applicable	n	Insur
Altura Fund *Income Fund* 1900 E. Dublin-Granville Rd. Columbus, OH 43229 614/899-4600 800/338-4385	1986	United Bank of Denver National Association	N/A	$2,500/ 50	N/A	Fund
Altura Fund *Tax-Free Income Fund* 1900 E. Dublin-Granville Rd. Columbus, OH 43229 614/899-4600 800/338-4385	1986	United Bank of Denver National Association	N/A	$2,500/ 50	N/A	Fund
Bartlett Management Trust *Bartlett Enhanced Cash Reserves* 36 E. Fourth St. Cincinnati, OH 45202 513/621-4612 800/543-0863	1988	Bartlett & Company	$99.4 Mil	$5,000/ 100	n	Local Rep
Collective Investment Trust for Citibank IRAs *Income Portfolio* 153 E. 53rd St. 4th Fl. New York, NY 10043 212/559-4677 800/CITI-IRA	1983	Citibank N.A.	$54.5 Mil	$250/ 0	n	Fund

*Key: i=initial sales charge   r=redemption fee or contingent deferred sales charge(CDSC)
t=12b-1 fee and either CDSC or redemption fee   p=12b-1 fee   n=none of the preceding fees   N/A=not available

Income-mixed

Fund	Year Began	Investment Adviser	9/30/89 Assets	Minimum Initial and Subsequent Investment	Fees*	Where to Buy Shares
Colonial Corporate Cash Trust I One Financial Ctr. Boston, MA 02111 617/426-3750 800/225-2365 800/426-3750	1981	Colonial Management Associates, Inc.	$148.7 Mil	$25,000/ 5,000	i, p	Local Rep
Colonial Corporate Cash Trust II One Financial Ctr. Boston, MA 02111 617/426-3750 800/225-2365 800/426-3750	1983	Colonial Management Associates, Inc.	$96.8 Mil	$25,000/ 5,000	i, p	Local Rep
Colonial Income Trust One Financial Ctr. Boston, MA 02111 617/426-3750 800/225-2365 800/426-3750	1969	Colonial Management Associates, Inc.	$163.4 Mil	$250/ 25	i, p	Local Rep
Compass Capital Group *Fixed Income Fund* 1900 E. Dublin-Granville Rd. Columbus, OH 43229 614/899-4600 800/338-4385	1988	Midlantic National Bank	N/A	$2,500/ 100	N/A	Fund
Compass Capital Group *Short/Intermediate Fund* 1900 E. Dublin-Granville Rd. Columbus, OH 43229 614/899-4600 800/338-4385	1988	Midlantic National Bank	N/A	$2,500/ 100	N/A	Fund
Composite Income Fund, Inc. W. 601 Riverside, 9th Fl. Seafirst Financial Ctr. Spokane, WA 99201 509/353-3400 800/543-8072 800/572-5828	1976	Composite Research & Management Company	$126.1 Mil	$1,000/ 50	i, p	Local Rep
Connecticut Mutual Investment Accounts, Inc. *Connecticut Mutual Income Account* 140 Garden St. Hartford, CT 06154 203/727-6500 800/243-0018	1985	G.R. Phelps & Company, Inc.	$18.5 Mil	$1,000/ 50	i	Local Rep

*Key: i=initial sales charge   r=redemption fee or contingent deferred sales charge(CDSC)
t=12b-1 fee and either CDSC or redemption fee   p=12b-1 fee   n=none of the preceding fees   N/A=not available

Income-mixed

Fund	Year Began	Investment Adviser	9/30/89 Assets	Minimum Initial and Subsequent Investment	Fees*	Where to Buy Shares
Country Capital Income Fund, Inc. 1701 Towanda Ave. Bloomington, IL 61701 309/557-2444 800/322-3838 IL Only	1978	Country Capital Management Company	$5.8 Mil	$1,000/ 25	i	Local Rep
Dean Witter Tax-Advantaged Corporate Trust Two World Trade Ctr. New York, NY 10048 212/392-2550 800/869-3863	1984	Dean Witter Reynolds Inc. - InterCapital Division	$64.3 Mil	$10,000/ 100	p	Local Rep
Dreyfus Convertible Securities Fund, Inc. 666 Old Country Rd. Garden City, NY 11530 718/895-1206 800/645-6561	1971	Dreyfus Corporation	$267.4 Mil	$2,500/ 100	n	Fund
Dreyfus Strategic Income 666 Old Country Rd. Garden City, NY 11530 718/895-1347 800/648-9048	1986	Dreyfus Corporation	$41.4 Mil	$2,500/ 500	i, p	Fund
Eaton Vance Income Fund of Boston 24 Federal St. Boston, MA 02110 617/482-8260 800/225-6265	1971	Eaton Vance Management, Inc.	$85.6 Mil	$1,000/ 50	i, p	Local Rep
Eaton Vance Prime Rate Reserves 24 Federal St. Boston, MA 02110 617/482-8260 800/225-6265	1989	Eaton Vance Management, Inc.	$1.6 Bil	$5,000/ 50	r	Local Rep
Federated Corporate Cash Trust Federated Investors Twr. Pittsburgh, PA 15222-3779 412/288-1900 800/245-5000	1984	Federated Management	$25.1 Mil	$25,000/ 0	n	Local Rep

*Key: i=initial sales charge   r=redemption fee or contingent deferred sales charge(CDSC)
t=12b-1 fee and either CDSC or redemption fee   p=12b-1 fee   n=none of the preceding fees   N/A=not available

Income-mixed

Fund	Year Began	Investment Adviser	9/30/89 Assets	Minimum Initial and Subsequent Investment	Fees*	Where to Buy Shares
Fidelity Corporate Trust *Fidelity Adjustable Rate Preferred Portfolio* 82 Devonshire St. Boston, MA 02109 617/570-7000 800/343-9184	1984	Fidelity Management & Research Company	$61.1 Mil	$50,000/ 0	n	Local Rep
Fidelity Qualified Dividend Fund 82 Devonshire St. Boston, MA 02109 617/570-7000 800/343-9184 617/570-5600 MA Only	1981	Fidelity Management & Research Company	$58.5 Mil	$50,000/ 0	n	Local Rep
First Investors Life Series Fund *High Yield Series* 120 Wall St. New York, NY 10005 212/208-6000	1986	First Investors Management Company, Inc.	$13.5 Mil	Not Applicable	n	Insur
First Investors Qualified Dividend Fund, Inc. 120 Wall St. New York, NY 10005 212/208-6000	1983	First Investors Management Company, Inc.	$9.0 Mil	$5,000/ 500	p	Local Rep
First Prairie Diversified Asset Fund 666 Old Country Rd. 4th Fl. Garden City, NY 11530 516/296-3300 800/821-1185	1986	First National Bank of Chicago	$7.1 Mil	$1,000/ 100	i, p	Local Rep
Flag Investors Telephone Income Fund 135 E. Baltimore St. P.O. Box 515 Baltimore, MD 21203 301/727-1700 800/767-3524	1983	Flag Investors Management Corp.	$131.5 Mil (e)	$2,000/ 1,000	i, p	Local Rep
Flagship Basic Value Fund One First National Plaza Ste. 910 Dayton, OH 45402 513/461-0332 800/227-4648 800/354-7447 OH Only	1983	Flagship Financial Inc.	$32.0 Mil	$25,000/ 10,000	p	Local Rep

*Key: i=initial sales charge   r=redemption fee or contingent deferred sales charge(CDSC)
t=12b-1 fee and either CDSC or redemption fee   p=12b-1 fee   n=none of the preceding fees   N/A=not available

Income-mixed

Fund	Year Began	Investment Adviser	9/30/89 Assets	Minimum Initial and Subsequent Investment	Fees*	Where to Buy Shares
Franklin Custodian Funds, Inc. *Income Series* 777 Mariners Island Blvd. San Mateo, CA 94404 415/570-3000 800/632-2180 800/632-2350	1948	Franklin Advisers, Inc.	$1.2 Bil	$100/ 25	i	Local Rep
Franklin Managed Trust *Franklin Corporate Cash Portfolio* 777 Mariners Island Blvd. San Mateo, CA 94404 415/570-3000 800/632-2180 800/632-2350	1987	Franklin Advisers, Inc.	$24.8 Mil	$25,000/ 5,000	i, p	Local Rep
GEICO Qualified Dividend Fund GEICO Plaza Washington, DC 20076 301/986-2200 800/832-6232	1984	GEICO Investment Services Company	$19.8 Mil (e)	$10,000/ 1,000	p	Fund
GIT Equity Trust *GIT Equity Income Portfolio* 1655 Fort Myer Dr. Arlington, VA 22209 703/528-6500 800/336-3063	1983	Bankers Finance Investment Management Corp.	$2.0 Mil	$1,000/ 0	n	Fund
Helmsman Fund *Income Portfolio* 1900 E. Dublin-Granville Rd. Columbus, OH 43229 614/899-4600 800/338-4385	1989	Bank One, Indianapolis, N.A. Bank One, Milwaukee, N.A.	N/A	$2,500/ 0	N/A	Fund
IAI Reserve Fund, Inc. 1100 Dain Twr. P.O. Box 357 Minneapolis, MN 55440 612/371-7780	1986	Investment Advisers, Inc.	$92.7 Mil	$5,000/ 1,000	n	Local Rep
Income Fund of America, Inc. 333 S. Hope St. Los Angeles, CA 90071 213/486-9200 800/421-0180 213/486-9651 Collect	1970	Capital Research & Management Company	$1.4 Bil	$1,000/ 50	i, t	Local Rep

*Key: i=initial sales charge   r=redemption fee or contingent deferred sales charge(CDSC)
t=12b-1 fee and either CDSC or redemption fee   p=12b-1 fee   n=none of the preceding fees   N/A=not available

Income-mixed

Fund	Year Began	Investment Adviser	9/30/89 Assets	Minimum Initial and Subsequent Investment	Fees*	Where to Buy Shares
Income Portfolios *Short-Intermediate Fixed-Income Series* 82 Devonshire St. Boston, MA 02109 617/570-7000 800/544-6666	1987	Fidelity Management & Research Company	$2.1 Mil	$0/ 0	n	Local Rep
Integrated Income Portfolios *Convertible Securities Portfolio* 10 Union Square East New York, NY 10003 212/353-7000 800/858-8850	1987	Integrated Resources Asset Management Corp.	$21.9 Mil	$1,000/ 100	i, p	Local Rep
Integrated Resources Series Trust *Convertible Securities Portfolio* One Bridge Plaza Fort Lee, NJ 07024 201/461-0606 800/821-5100	1987	Integrated Resources Asset Management Corp.	$21.4 Mil	Not Applicable	r	Insur
Integrated Resources Series Trust *Fixed Income Portfolio* One Bridge Plaza Fort Lee, NJ 07024 201/461-0606 800/821-5100	1984	Integrated Resources Asset Management Corp.	$41.5 Mil	Not Applicable	n	Insur
Investment Portfolios *Diversified Income Portfolio* 120 S. LaSalle St. Chicago, IL 60603 312/781-1121 800/621-1148	1984	Kemper Financial Services, Inc.	$363.4 Mil	$250/ 50	t	Local Rep
Kemper Diversified Income Fund 120 S. LaSalle St. Chicago, IL 60603 312/781-1121 800/621-1148	1977	Kemper Financial Services, Inc.	$310.7 Mil	$1,000/ 100	i	Local Rep
LBVIP Series Fund, Inc. *Income Series* 625 Fourth Ave. South Minneapolis, MN 55415 612/339-8091 800/328-4552 800/752-4208 MN Only	1988	Lutheran Brotherhood Research Corp.	$13.9 Mil	Not Applicable	n	Insur

*Key: i=initial sales charge   r=redemption fee or contingent deferred sales charge(CDSC)
t=12b-1 fee and either CDSC or redemption fee   p=12b-1 fee   n=none of the preceding fees   N/A=not available

Income-mixed

Fund	Year Began	Investment Adviser	9/30/89 Assets	Minimum Initial and Subsequent Investment	Fees*	Where to Buy Shares
ManuLife Series Fund, Inc. *Capital Growth Bond Fund* 200 Bloor St. East N. Tower 5 Toronto, Ont., Canada M4W 1E5 416/926-6700	1984	Manufacturers Adviser Corporation	$21.5 Mil (e)	Not Applicable	n	Insur
Massachusetts Financial Total Return Trust 500 Boylston St. Boston, MA 02116 617/954-5000 800/343-2829	1970	Massachusetts Financial Services Company	$610.4 Mil	$1,000/ 25	i	Local Rep
MIMLIC Fixed Income Securities Fund, Inc. 400 N. Robert St. St. Paul, MN 55101-2098 612/223-4252 800/443-3677	1987	MIMLIC Asset Management Company	$4.0 Mil	$250/ 25	i	Local Rep
Mutual of Omaha Income Fund, Inc. 10235 Regency Circle Omaha, NE 68114 402/397-8555 800/228-9596	1968	Mutual of Omaha Fund Management Company	$165.1 Mil	$250/ 50	i	Local Rep
OLDE Custodian Fund *OLDE Intermediate C.U. Investment Series* 751 Griswold Detroit, MI 48226 313/961-6666	1988	OLDE Asset Management, Inc.	$0.9 Mil	$1,000/ 500	i	Local Rep
Oppenheimer Strategic Income Fund 3410 S. Galena St. Denver, CO 80231 303/671-3200 800/525-7048	1989	Oppenheimer Management Corporation	N/A	$1,000/ 25	N/A	Local Rep
Pilgrim Corporate Investors Fund, Inc. 10100 Santa Monica Blvd. 21st Fl. Los Angeles, CA 90067 213/551-0833 800/334-3444 800/331-1080	1983	Pilgrim Management Corporation	$115.1 Mil	$5,000/ 1,000	i, p	Local Rep

*Key: i=initial sales charge   r=redemption fee or contingent deferred sales charge(CDSC)
t=12b-1 fee and either CDSC or redemption fee   p=12b-1 fee   n=none of the preceding fees   N/A=not available

Income-mixed

Fund	Year Began	Investment Adviser	9/30/89 Assets	Minimum Initial and Subsequent Investment	Fees*	Where to Buy Shares
Pilgrim Preferred Fund 10100 Santa Monica Blvd. 21st Fl. Los Angeles, CA 90067 213/551-0833 800/334-3444 800/331-1080	1986	Pilgrim Management Corporation	$92.8 Mil	$5,000/ 1,000	i, p	Local Rep
Provident Fund for Income, Inc. 2800 Post Oak Blvd. Houston, TX 77056 713/993-0500 800/421-5666	1957	American Capital Asset Management, Inc.	$105.3 Mil	$500/ 50	i	Local Rep
Prudential-Bache IncomeVertible Plus Fund, Inc. One Seaport Plaza New York, NY 10292 212/214-1215 800/225-1852	1985	Prudential Mutual Fund Management	$551.2 Mil	$1,000/ 100	t	Local Rep
Putnam Corporate Cash Trust - Adjustable Rate Preferred Portfolio One Post Office Sq. Boston, MA 02109 617/292-1000 800/225-2465	1984	Putnam Management Company, Inc.	$150.7 Mil	$25,000/ 5,000	i	Local Rep
Putnam Corporate Cash Trust - Diversified Strategies Portfolio One Post Office Sq. Boston, MA 02109 617/292-1000 800/225-2465	1984	Putnam Management Company, Inc.	$138.8 Mil	$25,000/ 5,000	i	Local Rep
Putnam Diversified Income Trust One Post Office Sq. Boston, MA 02109 617/292-1000 800/225-2465	1988	Putnam Management Company, Inc.	$106.8 Mil	$500/ 50	i	Local Rep
Putnam Income Fund One Post Office Sq. Boston, MA 02109 617/292-1000 800/225-2465	1954	Putnam Management Company, Inc.	$396.2 Mil	$500/ 50	i	Local Rep

*Key: i=initial sales charge   r=redemption fee or contingent deferred sales charge(CDSC)
     t=12b-1 fee and either CDSC or redemption fee   p=12b-1 fee   n=none of the preceding fees   N/A=not available

Income-mixed

Fund	Year Began	Investment Adviser	9/30/89 Assets	Minimum Initial and Subsequent Investment	Fees*	Where to Buy Shares
Quest For Value Family of Funds *Fixed Income Portfolio* Oppenheimer Tower World Financial Ctr. New York, NY 10281 212/667-7587 800/232-FUND	1988	Quest For Value Advisors	$0.4 Mil	$1,000/ 250	i, p	Local Rep
Retirement Investment Trust *Income Fund* 16 HCB 98 P.O. Box 2558 Houston, TX 77252-8098 713/546-7775	1988	None	N/A	$500/ 100	n	Fund
SafeGuard Fixed Income Portfolio 16 Industrial Blvd. Paoli, PA 19301 215/251-0550 800/523-7798	1988	Provident Institutional Management Corporation	$1.1 Mil	$1,000/ 100	i, p	Local Rep
Salem Funds *Salem Fixed Income Portfolio (The)* 99 High St. Boston, MA 02110 617/338-3200 800/641-2580 800/343-3424	1989	First Union National Bank of N. Carolina	$8.8 Mil	$1,000/ 0	p	Fund
Scudder Income Fund 175 Federal St. Boston, MA 02110 617/439-4640 800/225-2470 800/225-5163	1928	Scudder, Stevens & Clark, Inc.	$263.4 Mil	$1,000/ 0	n	Fund
SECURAL Mutual Funds, Inc. *Fixed Income Fund* 2401 S. Memorial Dr. Appleton, WI 54915 414/739-3161 800/426-5975	1988	SECURA Advisory Services, Inc.	$0.5 Mil	$500/ 100	i, p	Local Rep
Seligman Income Fund, Inc. 130 Liberty St. New York, NY 10006 212/488-0200 800/221-2450 800/522-6869 NY Only	1947	J. & W. Seligman & Co. Incorporated	$159.9 Mil	$1,000/ 50	i	Local Rep

*Key: i=initial sales charge   r=redemption fee or contingent deferred sales charge(CDSC)
t=12b-1 fee and either CDSC or redemption fee   p=12b-1 fee   n=none of the preceding fees   N/A=not available

Income-mixed

Fund	Year Began	Investment Adviser	9/30/89 Assets	Minimum Initial and Subsequent Investment	Fees*	Where to Buy Shares
Seligman Mutual Benefit Portfolios, Inc. *Seligman Income Portfolio* 130 Liberty St. New York, NY 10006 212/488-0200 800/221-2450 800/522-6869 NY Only	1988	J. & W. Seligman & Co. Incorporated	$2.8 Mil	Not Applicable	r	Insur
SLH Special Income Portfolios *SLH Utility Portfolio* 31 W. 52nd St. New York, NY 10019 212/767-3700	1988	Bernstein-Macaulay Division of Shearson Lehman Hutton Inc.	$532.8 Mil	$500/ 200	t	Local Rep
State Street Fund for Foundations and Endowments *Fixed Income Portfolio* One Financial Ctr. 38th Fl. Boston, MA 02111 617/482-3920	1986	State Street Research & Management Company	$5.0 Mil	$100,000/ 0	n	Local Rep
Strong Income Fund, Inc. P.O. Box 2936 Milwaukee, WI 53201 414/359-3400 800/368-3863	1985	Strong/ Corneliuson Capital Management, Inc.	N/A	$1,000/ 200	n	Fund
Treasurer's Fund, Inc. *Auction Rate Preferred Portfolio* 8 Sound Shore Dr. Greenwich, CT 06830 203/629-2090 800/877-3863	1988	Gabelli-O'Connor Fixed Income Mutual Funds Management Company	N/A	$100,000/ 0	n	Local Rep
Treasurer's Fund, Inc. *Limited Term Portfolio* 8 Sound Shore Dr. Greenwich, CT 06830 203/629-2090 800/877-3863	1988	Gabelli-O'Connor Fixed Income Mutual Funds Management Company	N/A	$100,000/ 0	n	Local Rep
Unified Income Fund, Inc. 429 N. Pennsylvania St. Indianapolis, IN 46204-1897 317/634-3300 800/862-7283	1977	Unified Management Corporation	$7.3 Mil	$500/ 25	n	Fund

*Key: i=initial sales charge   r=redemption fee or contingent deferred sales charge(CDSC)
t=12b-1 fee and either CDSC or redemption fee   p=12b-1 fee   n=none of the preceding fees   N/A=not available

Income-mixed

Fund	Year Began	Investment Adviser	9/30/89 Assets	Minimum Initial and Subsequent Investment	Fees*	Where to Buy Shares
USAA Mutual Fund, Inc. *Income Fund* USAA Bldg. San Antonio, TX 78288 512/498-8000 800/531-8000	1974	USAA Investment Management Company	$332.2 Mil	$1,000/ 50	n	Fund
Value Line Income Fund, Inc. 711 Third Ave. New York, NY 10017 212/687-3965 800/223-0818	1952	Value Line, Inc.	$145.5 Mil	$1,000/ 100	n	Fund
Variable Investors Series Trust *Equity Income Portfolio* 1414 Main St. Springfield, MA 01144 413/732-7100	1988	Amherst Investment Management Company, Inc.	$1.4 Mil	Not Applicable	n	Insur
Wasatch Advisors Funds, Inc. *Wasatch Income Fund* 68 S. Main St. Ste. 400 Salt Lake City, UT 84101 801/533-0777 800/345-7460	1987	Wasatch Advisors Inc.	$1.1 Mil (e)	$5,000/ 1,000	n	Fund
Weitz Series Fund, Inc. *Fixed Income Series* 9290 W. Dodge Rd. The Mark, Ste. 405 Omaha, NE 68114-3323 402/391-1980	1988	Wallace R. Weitz & Company	$1.4 Mil	$10,000/ 5,000	n	Fund
Wellesley Income Fund Vanguard Financial Ctr. P.O. Box 2600 Valley Forge, PA 19482 215/648-6000 800/662-7447 800/362-0530 PA Only	1970	Wellington Management Company	$722.8 Mil	$3,000/ 100	n	Fund

*Key: i=initial sales charge   r=redemption fee or contingent deferred sales charge(CDSC)
t=12b-1 fee and either CDSC or redemption fee   p=12b-1 fee   n=none of the preceding fees   N/A=not available

♦ ♦ ♦ ♦

International Funds

International

Fund	Year Began	Investment Adviser	9/30/89 Assets	Minimum Initial and Subsequent Investment	Fees*	Where to Buy Shares
Alliance Global Fund *Canadian Fund* 1345 Avenue of the Americas New York, NY 10105 212/969-1000 800/221-5672	1952	Alliance Capital Management L.P.	$34.2 Mil	$250/ 50	i, p	Local Rep
Alliance International Fund 1345 Avenue of the Americas New York, NY 10105 212/969-1000 800/221-5672	1981	Alliance Capital Management L.P.	$197.7 Mil	$250/ 50	i, p	Local Rep
American General Series Portfolio Company *International Equities Fund* 2929 Allen Pkwy. P.O. Box 3206 Houston, TX 77253 713/526-5251	1989	Variable Annuity Life Insurance Company	N/A	Not Applicable	N/A	Insur
Bartlett Capital Trust *Bartlett Value International Fund* 36 E. Fourth St. Cincinnati, OH 45202 513/621-4612 800/543-0863	1989	Bartlett & Company	N/A	$5,000/ 100	N/A	Local Rep
Bull & Bear Overseas Fund Ltd. 11 Hanover Sq. New York, NY 10005 212/785-0900 800/847-4200	1987	Bull & Bear International Advisers, Inc.	$0.8 Mil (e)	$1,000/ 100	p	Fund
Capstone International Series Trust *European Plus Fund* 1100 Milan St., Ste. 3500 P.O. Box 3167 Houston, TX 77253-3167 713/750-8000 800/262-6631	1987	CCF International Finance Corporation	$9.8 Mil	$10,000/ 0	i	Local Rep
Capstone International Series Trust *Nikko Japan Tilt Fund* 350 Park Ave. New York, NY 10022 212/319-2730	1989	Nikko Capital Management, Inc.	N/A	$50,000/ 0	N/A	Local Rep

*Key: i=initial sales charge   r=redemption fee or contingent deferred sales charge(CDSC)
t=12b-1 fee and either CDSC or redemption fee   p=12b-1 fee   n=none of the preceding fees   N/A=not available

International

Fund	Year Began	Investment Adviser	9/30/89 Assets	Minimum Initial and Subsequent Investment	Fees*	Where to Buy Shares
Colonial Equity Index Portfolios *Colonial International Equity Index Trust* One Financial Ctr. Boston, MA 02111 617/426-3750 800/225-2365, 800/426-3750	1986	Colonial Management Associates, Inc.	$12.6 Mil	$250/ 25	i, p	Local Rep
Counsellors International Equity Fund, Inc. 466 Lexington Ave. New York, NY 10017-3147 212/878-0600 800/888-6878	1989	Warburg, Pincus Counsellors, Inc.	$13.0 Mil	$25,000/ 5,000	N/A	Fund
EBI Series Trust *International Fund* 1315 Peachtree St., NE Ste. 500 Atlanta, GA 30309 404/892-0666 800/554-1156	1988	INVESCO Capital Management, Inc.	N/A	$100,000/ 5,000	r	Local Rep
Enterprise Equity Portfolios *Enterprise International Growth Portfolio* 1200 Ashwood Pkwy. Ste. 290 Atlanta, GA 30338 404/396-8118, 800/432-4320	1987	Enterprise Capital Management, Inc.	$5.6 Mil (e)	$500/ 25	t	Local Rep
EuroPacific Growth Fund 333 S. Hope St. Los Angeles, CA 90071 213/486-9200 800/421-0180 213/486-9651 Collect	1984	Capital Research & Management Company	$323.6 Mil	$250/ 50	i, t	Local Rep
European Emerging Companies Fund 275 Commerce Dr., Ste. 228 P.O. Box 1537 Ft. Washington, PA 19034-1537 215/643-2510 800/523-2578	1988	Review Management Corp.	N/A	$500/ 50	i, p	Local Rep
Fenimore International Fund, Inc. *Equity Series* 60 Broad St. New York, NY 10004 212/232-5000 800/272-2700	1986	Drexel Burnham Lambert International Management Corporation	$51.2 Mil (e)	$1,000/ 100	t	Local Rep

*Key: i=initial sales charge   r=redemption fee or contingent deferred sales charge(CDSC)
t=12b-1 fee and either CDSC or redemption fee   p=12b-1 fee   n=none of the preceding fees   N/A=not available

282

International

Fund	Year Began	Investment Adviser	9/30/89 Assets	Minimum Initial and Subsequent Investment	Fees*	Where to Buy Shares
Fidelity Investment Trust *Fidelity Canada Fund* 82 Devonshire St. Boston, MA 02109 617/570-7000 800/544-6666	1987	Fidelity Management & Research Company	$25.5 Mil	$2,500/ 250	i, r	Fund
Fidelity Investment Trust *Fidelity Europe Fund* 82 Devonshire St. Boston, MA 02109 617/570-7000 800/544-6666	1986	Fidelity Management & Research Company	$108.2 Mil	$2,500/ 250	i, r	Fund
Fidelity Investment Trust *Fidelity International Growth & Income Fund* 82 Devonshire St. Boston, MA 02109 617/570-7000 800/544-6666	1986	Fidelity Management & Research Company	$27.9 Mil	$2,500/ 250	i, r	Fund
Fidelity Investment Trust *Fidelity Overseas Fund* 82 Devonshire St. Boston, MA 02109 617/570-7000 800/544-6666	1984	Fidelity Management & Research Company	$953.9 Mil	$2,500/ 250	i	Fund
Fidelity Investment Trust *Fidelity Pacific Basin Fund* 82 Devonshire St. Boston, MA 02109 617/570-7000 800/544-6666	1986	Fidelity Management & Research Company	$121.2 Mil	$2,500/ 250	i, r	Fund
Flag Investors International Trust 135 E. Baltimore St. P.O. Box 515 Baltimore, MD 21203 301/727-1700 800/767-3524	1986	Bessemer Trust Co., N.A.	$31.7 Mil (e)	$2,000/ 1,000	i, p	Local Rep
Frank Russell Investment Company *International* 909 A St. Tacoma, WA 98402 206/627-7001 800/972-0700	1983	Frank Russell Investment Management Company	$180.6 Mil	$0/ 0	n	Local Rep

*Key: i=initial sales charge   r=redemption fee or contingent deferred sales charge(CDSC)
      t=12b-1 fee and either CDSC or redemption fee   p=12b-1 fee   n=none of the preceding fees   N/A=not available

International

Fund	Year Began	Investment Adviser	9/30/89 Assets	Minimum Initial and Subsequent Investment	Fees*	Where to Buy Shares
Frank Russell Investment Company *International Securities* 909 A St. Tacoma, WA 98402 206/627-7001 800/972-0700	1985	Frank Russell Investment Management Company	$114.9 Mil	$0/ 0	n	Local Rep
FT International Trust Federated Investors Twr. Pittsburgh, PA 15222-3779 412/288-1900 800/245-5000	1984	Fir Tree Advisers, Inc.	$62.2 Mil	$25,000/ 0	n	Local Rep
Funds of Australia, Inc. *Income Fund of Australia* 560 Hudson St. Hackensack, NJ 07601 201/641-8630 800/683-0596	1989	Lawrence Field, Inc.	N/A	$100/ 100	N/A	Local Rep
G.T. Global Growth Series *G.T. Europe Growth Fund* 50 California St. 27th Fl. San Francisco, CA 94111 415/392-6181 800/824-1580	1985	G.T. Capital Management Inc.	$25.8 Mil (e)	$500/ 100	i, p	Local Rep
G.T. Global Growth Series *G.T. International Growth Fund* 50 California St. 27th Fl. San Francisco, CA 94111 415/392-6181 800/824-1580	1985	G.T. Capital Management Inc.	$57.0 Mil (e)	$500/ 100	i, p	Local Rep
G.T. Global Growth Series *G.T. Japan Growth Fund* 50 California St. 27th Fl. San Francisco, CA 94111 415/392-6181 800/824-1580	1985	G.T. Capital Management Inc.	$24.4 Mil (e)	$500/ 100	i, p	Local Rep
G.T. Global Growth Series *G.T. Pacific Growth Fund* 50 California St. 27th Fl. San Francisco, CA 94111 415/392-6181 800/824-1580	1977	G.T. Capital Management Inc.	$88.8 Mil (e)	$500/ 100	i, p	Local Rep

*Key: i=initial sales charge   r=redemption fee or contingent deferred sales charge(CDSC)
t=12b-1 fee and either CDSC or redemption fee   p=12b-1 fee   n=none of the preceding fees   N/A=not available

International

Fund	Year Began	Investment Adviser	9/30/89 Assets	Minimum Initial and Subsequent Investment	Fees*	Where to Buy Shares
Harbor Fund *Harbor International Fund* One SeaGate Toledo, OH 43666 419/247-2477 800/422-1050	1987	Harbor Capital Advisors, Inc.	$29.5 Mil	$2,000/ 500	n	Fund
Hard Currency Fund 251 S. Lake Ave. Ste. 600 Pasadena, CA 91101 213/681-3700 800/826-0188	1989	Bankers Trust Investment Management Limited	N/A	$2,500/ 1,000	N/A	Local Rep
High Income Currency Fund 251 S. Lake Ave. Ste. 600 Pasadena, CA 91101 213/681-3700 800/826-0188	1989	Bankers Trust Investment Management Limited	N/A	$2,500/ 1,000	N/A	Local Rep
IAI International Fund, Inc. 1100 Dain Twr. P.O. Box 357 Minneapolis, MN 55440 612/371-7780	1987	Investment Advisers, Inc.	$23.9 Mil	$5,000/ 1,000	n	Local Rep
IDS International Fund, Inc. IDS Tower 10 Minneapolis, MN 55440 612/372-3131 800/328-8300	1984	IDS Financial Corporation	$208.8 Mil	$100/ 100	i, p	Local Rep
Institutional International Funds, Inc. *Foreign Equity Fund* 100 E. Pratt St. Baltimore, MD 21202 301/547-2000 800/638-5660	1989	Rowe Price-Fleming International, Inc.	N/A	$100,000/ 25,000	n	Fund
Integrated Resources Series Trust *Foreign Securities Portfolio* One Bridge Plaza Fort Lee, NJ 07024 201/461-0606 800/821-5100	1987	Integrated Resources Asset Management Corp.	$34.7 Mil	Not Applicable	n	Insur

*Key: i=initial sales charge   r=redemption fee or contingent deferred sales charge(CDSC)
    t=12b-1 fee and either CDSC or redemption fee   p=12b-1 fee   n=none of the preceding fees   N/A=not available

International

Fund	Year Began	Investment Adviser	9/30/89 Assets	Minimum Initial and Subsequent Investment	Fees*	Where to Buy Shares
International Fund for Institutions 3411 Silverside Rd. Webster Bldg., Ste. 204 Wilmington, DE 19810 302/478-6945 800/221-8120 800/640-6155 NY Only	1984	Boston Company Advisors, Inc.	$14.8 Mil	$5,000/ 0	n	Local Rep
INVESCO Institutional Series Trust *INVESCO Institutional International Fund* 1315 Peachtree St., NE Ste. 500 Atlanta, GA 30309 404/892-0666, 800/554-1156	1987	INVESCO Capital Management, Inc.	N/A	$1.0 Mil/ 5,000	n	Local Rep
Ivy Fund *Ivy International Fund* 40 Industrial Park Rd. Hingham, MA 02043 617/749-1416 800/235-3322	1986	Ivy Management, Inc.	$52.2 Mil	$1,000/ 0	n	Fund
Japan Fund 345 Park Ave. New York, NY 10154 617/439-4640 800/225-2470 800/225-5163	1963	Asia Management Company	$419.1 Mil	$1,000/ 0	n	Fund
John Hancock World Trust *Pacific Basin Equities Portfolio* 101 Huntington Ave. Boston, MA 02199-7603 617/375-1500 800/225-5291	1987	John Hancock Advisers, Inc.	$5.3 Mil	$1,000/ 25	i, p	Local Rep
Kemper International Fund 120 S. LaSalle St. Chicago, IL 60603 312/781-1121 800/621-1148	1981	Kemper International Management, Inc.	$188.4 Mil	$1,000/ 100	i	Local Rep
Keystone International Fund, Inc. 99 High St. Boston, MA 02110 617/338-3200 800/343-2898 800/225-1587	1954	Keystone Custodian Funds, Inc.	$121.8 Mil	$250/ 0	t	Local Rep

*Key: i=initial sales charge   r=redemption fee or contingent deferred sales charge(CDSC)
t=12b-1 fee and either CDSC or redemption fee   p=12b-1 fee   n=none of the preceding fees   N/A=not available

International

Fund	Year Began	Investment Adviser	9/30/89 Assets	Minimum Initial and Subsequent Investment	Fees*	Where to Buy Shares
Kleinwort Benson Investment Strategies *Kleinwort Benson International Equity Fund* 200 Park Ave., 24th Fl. New York, NY 10166 212/687-2515, 800/237-4218, 800/233-9164	1980	Kleinwort Benson International Investment Ltd.	$69.6 Mil	$1,000/ 100	p	Fund
Mackenzie Funds Inc. *Canada Fund* 1200 N. Federal Hwy. #200 Boca Raton, FL 33432 407/393-8900 800/456-5111	1987	Mackenzie Financial Corporation	$10.4 Mil (e)	$250/ 50	i, p	Local Rep
Management of Managers Group of Funds *International Equity Fund* 200 Connecticut Ave. 8th Fl. Norwalk, CT 06854 203/855-2200	1986	Evaluation Associates Investment Management Co.	$7.9 Mil	$0/ 0	n	Local Rep
Merrill Lynch Developing Capital Markets Fund, Inc. P.O. Box 9011 Princeton, NJ 08543-9011 609/282-2800 800/637-3863	1989	Fund Asset Management, Inc.	N/A	$5,000/ 1,000	r	Local Rep
Merrill Lynch EuroFund *Class A* *Class B* P.O. Box 9011 Princeton, NJ 08543-9011 609/282-2800 800/637-3863	1988 1987	Merrill Lynch Asset Management Inc.	$230.4 Mil	$500/50 $500/50	t t	LRep LRep
Merrill Lynch Pacific Fund, Inc. *Class A* *Class B* P.O. Box 9011 Princeton, NJ 08543-9011 609/282-2800 800/637-3863	1976 1988	Merrill Lynch Asset Management Inc.	$323.4 Mil	$250/50 $250/50	i t	LRep LRep
Nomura Pacific Basin Fund, Inc. 180 Maiden Lane New York, NY 10038 212/208-9300 800/833-0018	1985	Nomura Capital Management, Inc.	$73.8 Mil	$10,000/ 5,000	n	Local Rep

*Key: i=initial sales charge   r=redemption fee or contingent deferred sales charge(CDSC)
t=12b-1 fee and either CDSC or redemption fee   p=12b-1 fee   n=none of the preceding fees   N/A=not available

International

Fund	Year Began	Investment Adviser	9/30/89 Assets	Minimum Initial and Subsequent Investment	Fees*	Where to Buy Shares
Professional Portfolios Trust *International Fund* 429 N. Pennsylvania St. Indianapolis, IN 46204-1897 317/634-3300 800/862-7283	1988	Unified Management Corporation	$0.2 Mil	$200/ 25	p	Local Rep
Rodney Square International Securities Fund, Inc. *Rodney Square International Equity Fund (The)* Rodney Square North Wilmington, DE 19890 302/651-1923 800/225-5084	1987	Wilmington Trust Company	N/A	$1,000/ 0	i, p	Local Rep
Scudder International Fund, Inc. 175 Federal St. Boston, MA 02110 617/439-4640 800/225-2470 800/225-5163	1953	Scudder, Stevens & Clark, Inc.	$678.9 Mil	$1,000/ 0	n	Fund
Sigma World Fund, Inc. 3801 Kennett Pk., C-200 Greenville Ctr. Wilmington, DE 19807 302/652-3091 800/441-9490	1985	Sigma Management, Inc.	$7.5 Mil	$0/ 0	i, p	Local Rep
SLH Investment Series, Inc. *SLH European Portfolio* 31 W. 52nd St. 15th Fl. New York, NY 10019 212/767-3700 800/334-4636 800/422-0214 NY Only	1987	SLH Asset Management Division of Shearson Lehman Hutton Inc.	$4.5 Mil	$500/ 250	t	Local Rep
SLH Investment Series, Inc. *SLH Pacific Portfolio* 31 W. 52nd St. 15th Fl. New York, NY 10019 212/767-3700 800/334-4636 800/422-0214 NY Only	1987	SLH Asset Management Division of Shearson Lehman Hutton Inc.	$4.7 Mil	$500/ 250	t	Local Rep
SLH Special Equity Portfolios *SLH International Equity Portfolio* 31 W. 52nd St. New York, NY 10019 212/767-3700	1986	SLH Global Asset Management S.A.	$70.6 Mil	$500/ 200	t	Local Rep

*Key: i=initial sales charge   r=redemption fee or contingent deferred sales charge(CDSC)
t=12b-1 fee and either CDSC or redemption fee   p=12b-1 fee   n=none of the preceding fees   N/A=not available

International

Fund	Year Began	Investment Adviser	9/30/89 Assets	Minimum Initial and Subsequent Investment	Fees*	Where to Buy Shares
SteinRoe Investment Trust *SteinRoe International Growth Fund* 300 W. Adams St. P.O. Box 1143 Chicago, IL 60690 800/338-2550	1987	Stein Roe & Farnham Incorporated	$17.3 Mil	$1,000/ 100	n	Fund
SteinRoe Variable Investment Trust *International Stock Fund* 600 Atlantic Ave. Boston, MA 02210 617/722-6000 800/443-2683	1989	Stein Roe & Farnham Incorporated	N/A	Not Applicable	N/A	Insur
Templeton Funds, Inc. *Foreign Fund* 700 Central Ave. P.O. Box 33030 St. Petersburg, FL 33733-8030 813/823-8712 800/237-0738	1982	Templeton, Galbraith & Hansberger, Ltd.	$460.1 Mil	$500/ 25	i	Local Rep
T. Rowe Price International Equity Fund, Inc. 100 E. Pratt St. Baltimore, MD 21202 301/547-2000 800/638-5660	1989	Rowe Price-Fleming International, Inc.	N/A	Not Applicable	n	Insur
T. Rowe Price International Trust *T. Rowe Price International Discovery Fund* 100 E. Pratt St. Baltimore, MD 21202 301/547-2000 800/638-5660	1989	Rowe Price-Fleming International, Inc.	$37.8 Mil	$2,500/ 100	n	Fund
T. Rowe Price International Trust *T. Rowe Price International Stock Fund* 100 E. Pratt St. Baltimore, MD 21202 301/547-2000 800/638-5660	1980	Rowe Price-Fleming International, Inc.	$857.6 Mil	$2,500/ 100	n	Fund
Trustees' Commingled Fund *International Equity Portfolio* Vanguard Financial Ctr. P.O. Box 2600 Valley Forge, PA 19482 215/648-6000 800/662-7447, 800/362-0530 PA Only	1983	Batterymarch Financial Management	$597.4 Mil	$10,000/ 1,000	n	Fund

*Key: i=initial sales charge   r=redemption fee or contingent deferred sales charge(CDSC)
t=12b-1 fee and either CDSC or redemption fee   p=12b-1 fee   n=none of the preceding fees   N/A=not available

International

Fund	Year Began	Investment Adviser	9/30/89 Assets	Minimum Initial and Subsequent Investment	Fees*	Where to Buy Shares
Tyndall-Newport Fund, Inc. *Tyndall-Newport Far East Fund* 1500 Forest Ave., Ste. 223 P.O. Box 8687 Richmond, VA 23226 804/285-8211 800/527-9500	1985	Tyndall-Newport Fund Management, Inc.	$2.5 Mil (e)	$1,000/ 100	i	Local Rep
Tyndall-Newport Fund, Inc. *Tyndall-Newport Tiger Fund* 1500 Forest Ave., Ste. 223 P.O. Box 8687 Richmond, VA 23226 804/285-8211 800/527-9500	1989	Tyndall-Newport Fund Management, Inc.	N/A	$1,000/ 100	N/A	Local Rep
USAA Investment Trust *International Fund* USAA Bldg. San Antonio, TX 78288 512/498-8000 800/531-8000	1988	USAA Investment Management Company	$12.9 Mil	$1,000/ 50	n	Fund
U.S. Boston Investment Company *Boston Foreign Growth and Income* 6 New England Executive Pk. Burlington, MA 01803 617/272-6420	1987	U.S. Boston Investment Management Corporation	$24.1 Mil	$5,000/ 0	t	Local Rep
Vanguard World Fund *International Growth Portfolio* Vanguard Financial Ctr. P.O. Box 2600 Valley Forge, PA 19482 215/648-6000 800/662-7447, 800/362-0530 PA Only	1981	Schroder Capital Management Inc.	$584.3 Mil	$3,000/ 100	n	Fund
Variable Insurance Products Fund *Overseas Portfolio* 82 Devonshire St. Boston, MA 02109 617/570-7000 800/544-6666	1986	Fidelity Management & Research Company	$18.0 Mil	Not Applicable	n	Insur
Weiss, Peck & Greer International Fund One New York Plaza 31st Fl. New York, NY 10004 212/908-9582 800/223-3332	1989	Weiss, Peck & Greer Advisers, Inc.	N/A	$1,000/ 50	N/A	Fund

*Key: i=initial sales charge   r=redemption fee or contingent deferred sales charge(CDSC)
t=12b-1 fee and either CDSC or redemption fee   p=12b-1 fee   n=none of the preceding fees   N/A=not available

◆ ◆ ◆ ◆

Long-term Municipal Bond Funds

Long-term Municipal Bond

Fund	Year Began	Investment Adviser	9/30/89 Assets	Minimum Initial and Subsequent Investment	Fees*	Where to Buy Shares
AAL Mutual Funds *AAL Municipal Bond Fund (The)* 222 W. College Ave. Appleton, WI 54919 414/734-5721 800/553-6319	1987	AAL Advisors Inc.	$71.9 Mil	$1,000/ 50	i, p	Local Rep
AARP Insured Tax Free Income Trust *AARP Insured Tax Free General Bond Fund* AARP Investment Program 175 Federal St. Boston, MA 02110-2267 800/253-2277	1984	AARP/Scudder Financial Management Company	$524.7 Mil	$250/ 0	n	Fund
Advantage Trust *Advantage Tax-Free Bond Fund* 600 Atlantic Ave. Boston, MA 02210 617/722-6000 800/443-2683	1987	Liberty Asset Management Company	$4.9 Mil (e)	$500/ 50	i, p	Local Rep
Aetna Series Trust *Aetna Municipal Bond Fund* Federated Investors Twr. 26th Fl. Pittsburgh, PA 15222-3779 412/288-1900 800/245-4770	1988	Federated Advisers	$5.4 Mil	$500/ 100	n	Fund
Alliance Tax-Free Income Fund *High Bracket Tax-Free Portfolio* 1345 Avenue of the Americas New York, NY 10105 212/969-1000 800/221-5672	1987	Alliance Capital Management L.P.	$105.5 Mil	$250/ 50	i, p	Local Rep
Alliance Tax-Free Income Fund *High Income Tax-Free Portfolio* 1345 Avenue of the Americas New York, NY 10105 212/969-1000 800/221-5672	1987	Alliance Capital Management L.P.	$121.9 Mil	$250/ 50	i, p	Local Rep
Alpine Mutual Fund Trust *National Municipal Asset Trust* 650 S. Cherry St. Ste. 700 Denver, CO 80222 303/321-2211 800/826-6677	1987	Alpine Capital Management Corporation	$3.1 Mil (e)	$1,000/ 250	i	Local Rep

*Key: i=initial sales charge   r=redemption fee or contingent deferred sales charge(CDSC)
t=12b-1 fee and either CDSC or redemption fee   p=12b-1 fee   n=none of the preceding fees   N/A=not available

Long-term Municipal Bond

Fund	Year Began	Investment Adviser	9/30/89 Assets	Minimum Initial and Subsequent Investment	Fees*	Where to Buy Shares
American Capital Municipal Bond Fund, Inc. 2800 Post Oak Blvd. Houston, TX 77056 713/993-0500 800/421-5666	1976	American Capital Asset Management, Inc.	$231.0 Mil	$500/ 50	i, p	Local Rep
American Capital Tax-Exempt Trust *High Yield Municipal Portfolio* 2800 Post Oak Blvd. Houston, TX 77056 713/993-0500 800/421-5666	1986	American Capital Asset Management, Inc.	$230.4 Mil	$500/ 50	i, p	Local Rep
American Capital Tax-Exempt Trust *Insured Municipal Portfolio* 2800 Post Oak Blvd. Houston, TX 77056 713/993-0500 800/421-5666	1986	American Capital Asset Management, Inc.	$36.4 Mil	$500/ 50	i, p	Local Rep
AMEV Tax-Free Fund, Inc. *National Portfolio* P.O. Box 64284 St. Paul, MN 55164 612/738-4000 800/872-2638	1986	AMEV Advisers, Inc.	$35.6 Mil	$500/ 50	i	Local Rep
Benham National Tax-Free Trust *Intermediate-Term Portfolio* 755 Page Mill Rd. Palo Alto, CA 94304 415/858-2400 800/227-8380 800/982-6150 CA Only	1984	Benham Management Corporation	$23.0 Mil	$1,000/ 100	n	Fund
Benham National Tax-Free Trust *Long-Term Portfolio* 755 Page Mill Rd. Palo Alto, CA 94304 415/858-2400 800/227-8380 800/982-6150 CA Only	1984	Benham Management Corporation	$35.1 Mil	$1,000/ 100	n	Fund
Big E Pathfinder Family of Mutual Funds *Big E Pathfinder Tax-Free Income Fund (The)* 320 Empire Tower Buffalo, NY 14202 716/855-7891	1988	Empire of America Advisory Services, Inc.	$4.8 Mil (e)	$500/ 100	i, p	Local Rep

*Key: i=initial sales charge   r=redemption fee or contingent deferred sales charge(CDSC)
t=12b-1 fee and either CDSC or redemption fee   p=12b-1 fee   n=none of the preceding fees   N/A=not available

Long-term Municipal Bond

Fund	Year Began	Investment Adviser	9/30/89 Assets	Minimum Initial and Subsequent Investment	Fees*	Where to Buy Shares
Boston Company Tax-Free Municipal Funds *Tax-Free Bond Fund* One Boston Place Boston, MA 02019 617/956-9740 800/225-5267 800/343-6324	1985	Boston Company Advisors, Inc.	$13.2 Mil	$1,000/ 0	p	Local Rep
Bull & Bear Municipal Securities, Inc. *Bull & Bear Tax-Free Income Fund* 11 Hanover Sq. New York, NY 10005 212/785-0900 800/847-4200	1984	Bull & Bear Fixed Income Advisers, Inc.	$20.0 Mil (e)	$1,000/ 100	p	Fund
Calvert Tax-Free Reserves *Long-Term Portfolio* 1700 Pennsylvania Ave., NW Washington, DC 20006 301/951-4820 800/368-2745	1983	Calvert Asset Management Company, Inc.	$44.1 Mil	$2,000/ 250	i, p	Local Rep
Carnegie Tax Exempt Income Trust *National High-Yield Fund* 1100 The Halle Bldg. 1228 Euclid Ave. Cleveland, OH 44115-1831 216/781-4440 800/321-2322	1986	Carnegie Capital Management Company	$34.2 Mil	$1,000/ 250	i, p	Local Rep
Chubb Investment Funds, Inc. *Chubb Tax-Exempt Fund* One Granite Place Concord, NH 03301 603/224-7741	1987	Chubb Asset Managers, Inc.	N/A	$1,000/ 100	i, p	Local Rep
CIGNA Municipal Bond Fund One Financial Plaza Springfield, MA 01103 413/784-0100 800/56CIGNA	1976	CIGNA Investments, Inc.	$253.6 Mil	$500/ 50	i, p	Local Rep
Colonial Tax-Exempt Trust *Colonial Tax-Exempt High Yield Fund* One Financial Ctr. Boston, MA 02111 617/426-3750 800/225-2365 800/426-3750	1978	Colonial Management Associates, Inc.	$1.5 Bil	$250/ 25	i, p	Local Rep

*Key: i=initial sales charge   r=redemption fee or contingent deferred sales charge(CDSC)
t=12b-1 fee and either CDSC or redemption fee   p=12b-1 fee   n=none of the preceding fees   N/A=not available

Long-term Municipal Bond

Fund	Year Began	Investment Adviser	9/30/89 Assets	Minimum Initial and Subsequent Investment	Fees*	Where to Buy Shares
Colonial Tax-Exempt Trust *Colonial Tax-Exempt Insured Fund* One Financial Ctr. Boston, MA 02111 617/426-3750 800/225-2365 800/426-3750	1985	Colonial Management Associates, Inc.	$118.5 Mil	$250/ 25	i, p	Local Rep
Colonial Value Investing Portfolios - Income Portfolio *High Yield Municipal Bond Fund* One Financial Ctr. Boston, MA 02111 617/426-3750, 800/225-2365, 800/426-3750	1987	Colonial Management Associates, Inc.	$31.8 Mil	$500/ 100	t	Local Rep
Common Sense Trust *Common Sense Municipal Bond Fund* 2800 Post Oak Blvd. Houston, TX 77056 713/993-0500 800/421-5666	1988	Common Sense Investment Advisers	$22.9 Mil	$250/ 25	i	Local Rep
Compass Capital Group *Municipal Bond Fund* 1900 E. Dublin-Granville Rd. Columbus, OH 43229 614/899-4600 800/338-4385	1989	Midlantic National Bank	N/A	$2,500/ 100	N/A	Fund
Composite Tax-Exempt Bond Fund, Inc. W. 601 Riverside, 9th Fl. Seafirst Financial Ctr. Spokane, WA 99201 509/353-3400 800/543-8072 800/572-5828	1977	Composite Research & Management Company	$102.4 Mil	$1,000/ 50	i, p	Local Rep
Constitution Funds, Inc. *Tax-Exempt Income Fund* Two World Trade Ctr. New York, NY 10048-0669 212/323-0200 800/525-7048	1988	Oppenheimer Management Corporation	$2.0 Mil	$1,000/ 250	i, p	Local Rep
Country Capital Tax-Exempt Bond Fund, Inc. 1701 Towanda Ave. Bloomington, IL 61701 309/557-2444 800/322-3838 IL Only	1978	Country Capital Management Company	$14.3 Mil	$1,000/ 25	i	Local Rep

*Key: i=initial sales charge   r=redemption fee or contingent deferred sales charge(CDSC)
t=12b-1 fee and either CDSC or redemption fee   p=12b-1 fee   n=none of the preceding fees   N/A=not available

Long-term Municipal Bond

Fund	Year Began	Investment Adviser	9/30/89 Assets	Minimum Initial and Subsequent Investment	Fees*	Where to Buy Shares
Dean Witter Tax-Exempt Securities Trust Two World Trade Ctr. New York, NY 10048 212/392-2550 800/869-3863	1980	Dean Witter Reynolds Inc. - InterCapital Division	$994.5 Mil	$1,000/ 100	i	Local Rep
Delaware Group Tax-Free Fund *USA Insured Series* One Commerce Sq. Philadelphia, PA 19103 215/988-1200 800/523-4640	1985	Delaware Management Company, Inc.	$54.0 Mil	$1,000/ 25	i	Local Rep
Delaware Group Tax-Free Fund *USA Series* One Commerce Sq. Philadelphia, PA 19103 215/988-1200 800/523-4640	1984	Delaware Management Company, Inc.	$525.8 Mil	$1,000/ 25	i	Local Rep
Dreyfus Insured Tax Exempt Bond Fund, Inc. 666 Old Country Rd. Garden City, NY 11530 718/895-1206 800/645-6561	1985	Dreyfus Corporation	$187.2 Mil	$2,500/ 100	p	Fund
Dreyfus Intermediate Tax Exempt Bond Fund, Inc. 666 Old Country Rd. Garden City, NY 11530 718/895-1206 800/645-6561	1983	Dreyfus Corporation	$1.1 Bil	$2,500/ 100	n	Fund
Dreyfus Short-Intermediate Tax Exempt Bond Fund 666 Old Country Rd. Garden City, NY 11530 718/895-1206 800/645-6561	1987	Dreyfus Corporation	$61.5 Mil	$2,500/ 100	p	Fund
Dreyfus Tax Exempt Bond Fund, Inc. 666 Old Country Rd. Garden City, NY 11530 718/895-1206 800/645-6561	1976	Dreyfus Corporation	$3.5 Bil	$2,500/ 100	n	Fund

*Key: i=initial sales charge   r=redemption fee or contingent deferred sales charge(CDSC)
t=12b-1 fee and either CDSC or redemption fee   p=12b-1 fee   n=none of the preceding fees   N/A=not available

Long-term Municipal Bond

Fund	Year Began	Investment Adviser	9/30/89 Assets	Minimum Initial and Subsequent Investment	Fees*	Where to Buy Shares
Eaton Vance High Yield Municipals Trust 24 Federal St. Boston, MA 02110 617/482-8260 800/225-6265	1985	Eaton Vance Management, Inc.	$988.0 Mil	$1,000/ 50	t	Local Rep
Eaton Vance Municipal Bond Fund L.P. 24 Federal St. Boston, MA 02110 617/482-8260 800/225-6265	1978	Eaton Vance Management, Inc.	$73.5 Mil	$1,000/ 50	i	Local Rep
Equitable Funds *Equitable Tax Exempt Fund (The)* 1755 Broadway 3rd Fl. New York, NY 10019 212/641-8100	1987	Equitable Capital Management Corporation	N/A	$1,000/ 100	t	Local Rep
Equitec Siebel Fund Group II *National Tax-Free Income Fund* 7677 Oakport St. P.O. Box 2470 Oakland, CA 94614 415/430-9900, 800/869-8900	1989	Siebel Capital Management, Inc.	N/A	$1,000/ 0	i	Local Rep
Federated Intermediate Municipal Trust Federated Investors Twr. Pittsburgh, PA 15222-3779 412/288-1900 800/245-5000	1985	Federated Management	$84.1 Mil	$25,000/ 0	n	Local Rep
Federated Short-Intermediate Municipal Trust Federated Investors Twr. Pittsburgh, PA 15222-3779 412/288-1900 800/245-5000	1981	Federated Management	$164.8 Mil	$25,000/ 0	n	Local Rep
Federated Tax-Free Income Fund, Inc. Federated Investors Twr. Liberty Ctr. Pittsburgh, PA 15222-3779 412/288-1900 800/245-0242	1976	Federated Advisers	$458.9 Mil	$500/ 100	i	Local Rep

*Key: i=initial sales charge   r=redemption fee or contingent deferred sales charge(CDSC)
t=12b-1 fee and either CDSC or redemption fee   p=12b-1 fee   n=none of the preceding fees   N/A=not available

Long-term Municipal Bond

Fund	Year Began	Investment Adviser	9/30/89 Assets	Minimum Initial and Subsequent Investment	Fees*	Where to Buy Shares
Fidelity Court Street Trust *Fidelity High Yield Municipals* 82 Devonshire St. Boston, MA 02109 617/570-7000 800/544-6666	1977	Fidelity Management & Research Company	$1.6 Bil	$2,500/ 250	n	Fund
Fidelity Limited Term Municipals 82 Devonshire St. Boston, MA 02109 617/570-7000 800/544-6666	1977	Fidelity Management & Research Company	$427.7 Mil	$2,500/ 250	n	Fund
Fidelity Municipal Trust *Fidelity Aggressive Tax-Free Portfolio* 82 Devonshire St. Boston, MA 02109 617/570-7000 800/544-6666	1985	Fidelity Management & Research Company	$539.4 Mil	$2,500/ 250	r	Fund
Fidelity Municipal Trust *Fidelity Insured Tax-Free Portfolio* 82 Devonshire St. Boston, MA 02109 617/570-7000 800/544-6666	1985	Fidelity Management & Research Company	$164.4 Mil	$2,500/ 250	n	Fund
Fidelity Municipal Trust *Fidelity Municipal Bond Portfolio* 82 Devonshire St. Boston, MA 02109 617/570-7000 800/544-6666	1976	Fidelity Management & Research Company	$994.2 Mil	$2,500/ 250	n	Fund
Fidelity Municipal Trust *Fidelity Short-Term Tax-Free Portfolio* 82 Devonshire St. Boston, MA 02109 617/570-7000 800/544-6666	1986	Fidelity Management & Research Company	$61.3 Mil	$2,500/ 250	n	Fund
Financial Horizons Investment Trust *Municipal Bond Fund* One Nationwide Plaza P.O. Box 182008 Columbus, OH 43218 800/533-5622	1988	Nationwide Financial Services, Inc.	$1.1 Mil	$1,000/ 100	t	Local Rep

*Key: i=initial sales charge   r=redemption fee or contingent deferred sales charge(CDSC)
t=12b-1 fee and either CDSC or redemption fee   p=12b-1 fee   n=none of the preceding fees   N/A=not available

Long-term Municipal Bond

Fund	Year Began	Investment Adviser	9/30/89 Assets	Minimum Initial and Subsequent Investment	Fees*	Where to Buy Shares
First Investors Insured Tax Exempt Fund, Inc. 120 Wall St. New York, NY 10005 212/208-6000	1977	First Investors Management Company, Inc.	$1.0 Bil	$2,000/ 500	i, p	Local Rep
First Prairie Tax Exempt Bond Fund, Inc. *Insured Series* 666 Old Country Rd. 4th Fl. Garden City, NY 11530 516/296-3300 800/821-1185	1989	First National Bank of Chicago	$1.0 Mil	$1,000/ 100	i, p	Local Rep
First Prairie Tax Exempt Bond Fund, Inc. *Intermediate Series* 666 Old Country Rd. 4th Fl. Garden City, NY 11530 516/296-3300 800/821-1185	1988	First National Bank of Chicago	$3.8 Mil	$1,000/ 100	i, p	Local Rep
First Trust Tax-Free Bond Fund *Income Series* 500 W. Madison Ste. 3000 Chicago, IL 60606 312/559-3000 800/621-4770	1986	Clayton Brown Advisors, Inc.	$19.0 Mil (e)	$25,000/ 0	i, p	Local Rep
First Trust Tax-Free Bond Fund *Insured Series* 500 W. Madison Ste. 3000 Chicago, IL 60606 312/559-3000 800/621-4770	1986	Clayton Brown Advisors, Inc.	$12.9 Mil (e)	$25,000/ 0	i, p	Local Rep
Flagship Tax Exempt Funds *All-American Tax Exempt Fund* One First National Plaza Ste. 910 Dayton, OH 45402 513/461-0332 800/227-4648 800/354-7447 OH Only	1988	Flagship Financial Inc.	$37.9 Mil	$3,000/ 50	i, p	Local Rep
Flagship Tax Exempt Funds *Insured Tax Exempt Fund* One First National Plaza Ste. 910 Dayton, OH 45402 513/461-0332 800/227-4648 800/354-7447 OH Only	1988	Flagship Financial Inc.	$1.1 Mil	$3,000/ 50	i, p	Local Rep

*Key: i=initial sales charge   r=redemption fee or contingent deferred sales charge(CDSC)
t=12b-1 fee and either CDSC or redemption fee   p=12b-1 fee   n=none of the preceding fees   N/A=not available

Long-term Municipal Bond

Fund	Year Began	Investment Adviser	9/30/89 Assets	Minimum Initial and Subsequent Investment	Fees*	Where to Buy Shares
Flagship Tax Exempt Funds *Limited Term Tax Exempt Fund* One First National Plaza Ste. 910 Dayton, OH 45402 513/461-0332 800/227-4648 800/354-7447 OH Only	1987	Flagship Financial Inc.	$13.7 Mil	$3,000/ 50	i, p	Local Rep
Fortress High Yield Municipal Fund, Inc. Federated Investors Twr. Pittsburgh, PA 15222-3779 412/288-1900 800/245-5051	1987	Federated Advisers	$63.2 Mil	$1,500/ 100	i, t	Local Rep
Franklin Federal Tax-Free Income Fund 777 Mariners Island Blvd. San Mateo, CA 94404 415/570-3000 800/632-2180 800/632-2350	1983	Franklin Advisers, Inc.	$3.8 Bil	$100/ 25	i	Local Rep
Franklin Tax-Free Trust *Franklin High Yield Tax-Free Income Fund* 777 Mariners Island Blvd. San Mateo, CA 94404 415/570-3000 800/632-2180 800/632-2350	1986	Franklin Advisers, Inc.	$1.4 Bil	$100/ 25	i	Local Rep
Franklin Tax-Free Trust *Franklin Insured Tax-Free Income Fund* 777 Mariners Island Blvd. San Mateo, CA 94404 415/570-3000 800/632-2180 800/632-2350	1985	Franklin Advisers, Inc.	$656.4 Mil	$100/ 25	i	Local Rep
Freedom Investment Trust *Freedom Managed Tax Exempt Fund* One Beacon St. Boston, MA 02108 617/523-3170 800/225-6258 800/392-6037 MA Only	1987	Freedom Capital Management Corporation	$103.0 Mil	$1,000/ 100	t	Local Rep
General Tax Exempt Bond Fund, Inc. 666 Old Country Rd. Garden City, NY 11530 718/895-1396 800/242-8671	1984	Dreyfus Corporation	$39.3 Mil	$2,500/ 100	p	Fund

*Key: i=initial sales charge   r=redemption fee or contingent deferred sales charge(CDSC)
t=12b-1 fee and either CDSC or redemption fee   p=12b-1 fee   n=none of the preceding fees   N/A=not available

Long-term Municipal Bond

Fund	Year Began	Investment Adviser	9/30/89 Assets	Minimum Initial and Subsequent Investment	Fees*	Where to Buy Shares
GIT Tax-Free Trust *High Yield Portfolio* 1655 Fort Myer Dr. Arlington, VA 22209 703/528-6500 800/336-3063	1982	Bankers Finance Investment Management Corp.	$40.8 Mil	$1,000/ 0	p	Fund
GW Sierra Trust Funds *GW California Municipal Income Fund* 888 S. Figueroa St. 11th Fl. Los Angeles, CA 90017-0970 213/488-2200 800/331-3426, 800/221-9876 CA ONLY	1989	Great Western Financial Advisors Corp.	N/A	$1,000/ 100	t	Local Rep
Home Group Trust *Home National Tax-Free Fund* 59 Maiden Lane 21st Fl. New York, NY 10038 212/530-6016 800/729-3863	1987	Home Capital Services, Inc.	$4.1 Mil	$1,000/ 100	i	Local Rep
Horizon Funds *Horizon Intermediate Tax-Exempt Fund* 156 W. 56th St. Ste. 1902 New York, NY 10019 212/492-1600 800/367-6075	1987	Security Pacific National Bank	$0.02 Mil (e)	$5,000/ 0	n	Local Rep
IDS High Yield Tax-Exempt Fund, Inc. IDS Tower 10 Minneapolis, MN 55440 612/372-3131 800/328-8300	1979	IDS Financial Corporation	$4.4 Bil	$100/ 100	i, p	Local Rep
IDS Special Tax-Exempt Series Trust *IDS Insured Tax-Exempt Fund* IDS Tower 10 Minneapolis, MN 55440 612/372-3131 800/328-8300	1986	IDS Financial Corporation	$93.5 Mil	$2,000/ 100	i, p	Local Rep
IDS Tax-Exempt Bond Fund, Inc. IDS Tower 10 Minneapolis, MN 55440 612/372-3131 800/328-8300	1976	IDS Financial Corporation	$955.8 Mil	$100/ 100	i, p	Local Rep

*Key: i=initial sales charge   r=redemption fee or contingent deferred sales charge(CDSC)
   t=12b-1 fee and either CDSC or redemption fee   p=12b-1 fee   n=none of the preceding fees   N/A=not available

Long-term Municipal Bond

Fund	Year Began	Investment Adviser	9/30/89 Assets	Minimum Initial and Subsequent Investment	Fees*	Where to Buy Shares
Industrial Series Trust *Mackenzie National Municipal Fund* 1200 N. Federal Hwy. #200 Boca Raton, FL 33432 407/393-8900 800/456-5111	1988	Mackenzie Investment Management Inc.	$6.3 Mil (e)	$250/ 50	i, p	Local Rep
Institutional Fiduciary Trust *Federal Tax-Exempt Portfolio* 777 Mariners Island Blvd. San Mateo, CA 94404 415/570-3000 800/632-2180 800/632-2350	1985	Franklin Trust Company	N/A	$25,000/ 0	n	Local Rep
Integrated Tax Free Portfolios *STRIPES Portfolio* 10 Union Square East New York, NY 10003 212/353-7000 800/858-8850	1985	Integrated Resources Asset Management Corp.	$100.4 Mil	$1,000/ 100	i, p	Local Rep
John Hancock Tax-Exempt Income Trust 101 Huntington Ave. Boston, MA 02199-7603 617/375-1500 800/225-5291	1976	John Hancock Advisers, Inc.	$374.6 Mil	$1,000/ 25	i, p	Local Rep
Kemper Municipal Bond Fund, Inc. 120 S. LaSalle St. Chicago, IL 60603 312/781-1121 800/621-1148	1976	Kemper Financial Services, Inc.	$1.8 Bil	$1,000/ 100	i	Local Rep
Keystone America Tax Free Income Fund 99 High St. Boston, MA 02110 617/338-3200 800/343-2898 800/225-1587	1987	Keystone Custodian Funds, Inc.	$160.3 Mil	$1,000/ 0	i, t	Local Rep
Keystone Tax Exempt Trust 99 High St. Boston, MA 02110 617/338-3200 800/343-2898 800/225-1587	1985	Keystone Custodian Funds, Inc.	$576.2 Mil	$10,000/ 0	t	Local Rep

*Key: i=initial sales charge   r=redemption fee or contingent deferred sales charge(CDSC)
     t=12b-1 fee and either CDSC or redemption fee   p=12b-1 fee   n=none of the preceding fees   N/A=not available

Long-term Municipal Bond

Fund	Year Began	Investment Adviser	9/30/89 Assets	Minimum Initial and Subsequent Investment	Fees*	Where to Buy Shares
Keystone Tax Free Fund 99 High St. Boston, MA 02110 617/338-3200 800/343-2898 800/225-1587	1978	Keystone Custodian Funds, Inc.	$893.7 Mil	$10,000/ 0	t	Local Rep
Kidder, Peabody Tax Free Income Fund *National Series* 20 Exchange Place New York, NY 10005 212/510-5552	1985	Webster Management Corporation	$28.1 Mil	$0/ 0	i	Local Rep
Lexington Tax Exempt Bond Trust Park 80 W., Plaza Two P.O. Box 1515 Saddle Brook, NJ 07662 201/845-7300 800/526-0056	1986	Lexington Management Corporation	$12.4 Mil	$1,000/ 50	n	Fund
Limited Term Municipal Fund, Inc. *Limited Term Municipal Fund* *National Portfolio* 119 E. Marcy St. Ste. 202 Santa Fe, NM 87501 505/984-0200, 800/847-0200	1984	Thornburg Management Company, Inc.	$189.3 Mil (e)	$2,500/ 100	i, p	Local Rep
Lord Abbett Tax-Free Income Fund, Inc. *National Series* The General Motors Bldg. 767 Fifth Ave. New York, NY 10153 212/848-1800 800/223-4224	1984	Lord, Abbett & Co.	$304.5 Mil	$1,000/ 0	i	Local Rep
Lutheran Brotherhood Municipal Bond Fund, Inc. 625 Fourth Ave. South Minneapolis, MN 55415 612/339-8091 800/328-4552 800/752-4208 MN Only	1976	Lutheran Brotherhood Research Corp.	$338.0 Mil	$500/ 50	i	Local Rep
MacKay-Shields MainStay Series Fund *MainStay Tax Free Bond Fund* 51 Madison Ave. New York, NY 10010 212/576-7000 800/522-4202	1986	MacKay-Shields Financial Corporation	$113.2 Mil	$500/ 50	t	Local Rep

*Key: i=initial sales charge   r=redemption fee or contingent deferred sales charge(CDSC)
    t=12b-1 fee and either CDSC or redemption fee   p=12b-1 fee   n=none of the preceding fees   N/A=not available

Long-term Municipal Bond

Fund	Year Began	Investment Adviser	9/30/89 Assets	Minimum Initial and Subsequent Investment	Fees*	Where to Buy Shares
Main Street Funds, Inc. *Tax-Free Income Fund* 3410 S. Galena St. Denver, CO 80231 303/671-3200 800/548-1225	1989	Oppenheimer Management Corporation	$0.8 Mil	$1,000/ 25	i, p	Local Rep
Management of Managers Group of Funds *Municipal Bond Fund* 200 Connecticut Ave. 8th Fl. Norwalk, CT 06854 203/855-2200	1984	Evaluation Associates Investment Management Co.	$21.7 Mil	$0/ 0	n	Local Rep
MassMutual Integrity Funds *MassMutual Tax-Exempt Bond Fund* 1295 State St. Springfield, MA 01111 413/788-8411 800/542-6767 800/854-9100 MA Only	1988	Massachusetts Mutual Life Insurance Company	$25.0 Mil	$500/ 25	i, p	Local Rep
Merrill Lynch Municipal Bond Fund, Inc. *High Yield Portfolio* *Class A* *Class B* P.O. Box 9011 Princeton, NJ 08543-9011 609/282-2800, 800/637-3863	1979 1988	Fund Asset Management, Inc.	$1.5 Bil	$1,000/100 $1,000/100	i t	LRep LRep
Merrill Lynch Municipal Bond Fund, Inc. *Insured Portfolio* *Class A* *Class B* P.O. Box 9011 Princeton, NJ 08543-9011 609/282-2800, 800/637-3863	1977 1988	Fund Asset Management, Inc.	$2.2 Bil	$1,000/100 $1,000/100	i t	LRep LRep
Merrill Lynch Municipal Bond Fund, Inc. *Limited Maturity Portfolio* P.O. Box 9011 Princeton, NJ 08543-9011 609/282-2800 800/637-3863	1979	Fund Asset Management, Inc.	$370.3 Mil	$1,000/ 100	i	Local Rep
Merrill Lynch Municipal Series Trust *Merrill Lynch Municipal Income Fund* *Class A* *Class B* P.O. Box 9011 Princeton, NJ 08543-9011 609/282-2800, 800/637-3863	1988 1986	Merrill Lynch Asset Management Inc.	$134.4 Mil	$1,000/50 $1,000/50	i t	LRep LRep

*Key: i=initial sales charge   r=redemption fee or contingent deferred sales charge(CDSC)
t=12b-1 fee and either CDSC or redemption fee   p=12b-1 fee   n=none of the preceding fees   N/A=not available

Long-term Municipal Bond

Fund	Year Began	Investment Adviser	9/30/89 Assets	Minimum Initial and Subsequent Investment	Fees*	Where to Buy Shares
MetLife-State Street Tax-Exempt Trust *MetLife-State Street Tax-Exempt Fund* One Financial Ctr. 30th Fl. Boston, MA 02111 617/348-2000, 800/882-0052	1986	MetLife-State Street Investment Services, Inc.	$60.0 Mil	$250/ 25	i, p	Local Rep
MFS Lifetime Investment Program *Lifetime Managed Municipal Bond Trust* 500 Boylston St. Boston, MA 02116 617/954-5000 800/343-2829	1986	Lifetime Advisers, Inc.	$324.0 Mil	$1,000/ 50	t	Local Rep
MFS Managed High Yield Municipal Bond Trust 500 Boylston St. Boston, MA 02116 617/954-5000 800/343-2829	1984	Massachusetts Financial Services Company	$479.2 Mil	$1,000/ 25	i	Local Rep
MFS Managed Municipal Bond Trust 500 Boylston St. Boston, MA 02116 617/954-5000 800/343-2829	1976	Massachusetts Financial Services Company	$1.2 Bil	$1,000/ 25	i	Local Rep
MidAmerica Tax-Exempt Bond Fund, Inc. 433 Edgewood Rd., NE Cedar Rapids, IA 52499 319/398-8511 800/553-4287 800/342-4490 IA Only	1985	MidAmerica Management Corporation	$14.8 Mil	$2,000/ 50	i	Local Rep
Midwest Group Tax Free Trust *Limited Term Portfolio* 700 Dixie Terminal Bldg. Cincinnati, OH 45202 513/629-2000 800/543-8721 800/582-7396 OH Only	1981	Midwest Advisory Services Inc.	$18.0 Mil	$1,000/ 0	i	Local Rep
Muni Bond Funds *Limited Term Portfolio* 1345 Avenue of the Americas New York, NY 10105 212/698-5349 800/544-7835	1988	Mutual Management Corp.	$14.7 Mil	$10,000/ 50	i	Local Rep

Long-term Municipal Bond

Fund	Year Began	Investment Adviser	9/30/89 Assets	Minimum Initial and Subsequent Investment	Fees*	Where to Buy Shares
Muni Bond Funds *National Portfolio* 1345 Avenue of the Americas New York, NY 10105 212/698-5349 800/544-7835	1986	Mutual Management Corp.	$130.3 Mil	$10,000/ 50	i	Local Rep
Municipal Fund for Temporary Investment *InterMuni Fund* 3411 Silverside Rd. Webster Bldg., Ste. 204 Wilmington, DE 19810 302/478-6945 800/221-8120, 800/640-6155 NY Only	1982	Provident Institutional Management Corporation	$40.6 Mil (e)	$5,000/ 0	n	Local Rep
Municipal Fund for Temporary Investment *LongMuni Fund* 3411 Silverside Rd. Webster Bldg., Ste. 204 Wilmington, DE 19810 302/478-6945 800/221-8120, 800/640-6155 NY Only	1987	Provident Institutional Management Corporation	$5.1 Mil	$5,000/ 0	p	Local Rep
Municipal Fund Investment Accumulation Program, Inc. P.O. Box 9011 Princeton, NJ 08543-9011 609/282-2800 800/221-3150	1977	Fund Asset Management, Inc.	N/A	$0/ 0	n	Local Rep
Mutual of Omaha Tax-Free Income Fund, Inc. 10235 Regency Circle Omaha, NE 68114 402/397-8555 800/228-9596	1976	Mutual of Omaha Fund Management Company	$346.4 Mil	$1,000/ 50	i	Local Rep
National Securities Tax Exempt Bonds, Inc. 600 Third Ave. New York, NY 10016 203/863-5600 800/237-1718	1976	National Securities & Research Corporation	$94.5 Mil	$1,000/ 25	i	Local Rep
Nationwide Tax-Free Fund One Nationwide Plaza Box 1492 Columbus, OH 43216 614/249-7855 800/848-0920 800/282-1440 OH Only	1986	Nationwide Financial Services, Inc.	$69.9 Mil	$1,000/ 100	t	Local Rep

*Key: i=initial sales charge   r=redemption fee or contingent deferred sales charge(CDSC)
t=12b-1 fee and either CDSC or redemption fee   p=12b-1 fee   n=none of the preceding fees   N/A=not available

Long-term Municipal Bond

Fund	Year Began	Investment Adviser	9/30/89 Assets	Minimum Initial and Subsequent Investment	Fees*	Where to Buy Shares
Neuberger & Berman Municipal Securities Trust 342 Madison Ave. New York, NY 10173 212/850-8300 800/877-9700	1987	Neuberger & Berman Management Incorporated	$10.0 Mil	$5,000/ 200	n	Fund
New England Tax Exempt Income Fund 399 Boylston St. Boston, MA 02116 617/267-6600 800/343-7104	1977	Back Bay Advisors, Inc.	$137.2 Mil	$1,000/ 25	i, p	Local Rep
Nuveen Insured Tax-Free Bond Fund, Inc. *National Portfolio* 333 W. Wacker Dr. Chicago, IL 60606 312/917-7844 800/621-7210	1987	Nuveen Advisory Corp.	$91.9 Mil	$1,000/ 100	i	Local Rep
Nuveen Municipal Bond Fund, Inc. 333 W. Wacker Dr. Chicago, IL 60606 312/917-7844 800/621-7210	1976	Nuveen Advisory Corp.	$1.1 Bil	$1,000/ 100	i	Local Rep
Olympus Tax-Exempt Money Market Fund *Olympus Tax-Exempt High Yield Series* 230 Park Ave. New York, NY 10169 212/309-8400 800/626-FUND	1989	Furman Selz Mager Dietz & Birney Incorporated	$19.9 Mil (e)	$1,000/ 100	i, t	Local Rep
Oppenheimer Tax-Free Bond Fund Two World Trade Ctr. New York, NY 10048-0669 212/323-0200 800/525-7048	1976	Oppenheimer Management Corporation	$212.3 Mil	$1,000/ 25	i, p	Local Rep
PaineWebber Managed Municipal Trust *PaineWebber Tax-Exempt Income Fund* 1285 Avenue of the Americas PaineWebber Bldg. New York, NY 10019 212/713-2000, 800/544-9300	1984	Mitchell Hutchins Asset Management Inc.	$307.9 Mil	$1,000/ 100	i	Local Rep

*Key: i=initial sales charge   r=redemption fee or contingent deferred sales charge(CDSC)
     t=12b-1 fee and either CDSC or redemption fee   p=12b-1 fee   n=none of the preceding fees   N/A=not available

Long-term Municipal Bond

Fund	Year Began	Investment Adviser	9/30/89 Assets	Minimum Initial and Subsequent Investment	Fees*	Where to Buy Shares
PaineWebber Municipal Series *PaineWebber Classic High Yield Municipal Fund* 1285 Avenue of the Americas PaineWebber Bldg. New York, NY 10019 212/713-2000, 800/544-9300	1987	Mitchell Hutchins Asset Management Inc.	$57.0 Mil	$1,000/ 100	i, p	Local Rep
Parkstone Group of Funds *Municipal Bond Fund* 1900 E. Dublin-Granville Rd. Columbus, OH 43229 614/899-4600 800/338-4385	1987	Securities Counsel, Inc.	N/A	$1,000/ 0	N/A	Fund
Phoenix Multi-Portfolio Fund *Phoenix Tax-Exempt Bond Portfolio* 101 Munson St. Greenfield, MA 01301 203/253-1000 800/243-1574	1988	Phoenix Investment Counsel, Inc.	$16.3 Mil	$500/ 25	i, p	Local Rep
Pioneer Municipal Bond Fund 60 State St. Boston, MA 02109-1975 617/742-7825 800/225-6292	1986	Pioneering Management Corporation	$27.7 Mil	$1,000/ 100	i	Local Rep
Piper Jaffray Investment Trust Inc. *National Tax-Exempt Fund* 222 S. 9th St. Piper Jaffray Twr. Minneapolis, MN 55402 612/342-6426 800/333-6000	1988	Piper Capital Management Incorporated	$35.8 Mil	$0/ 0	i, p	Local Rep
Plymouth Investment Series *Plymouth High Income Municipal Portfolio* 82 Devonshire St. Boston, MA 02109 617/570-7000 800/544-6666	1987	Fidelity Management & Research Company	$5.7 Mil	$1,000/ 250	i, p	Local Rep
Premier Tax Exempt Bond Fund 666 Old Country Rd. Garden City, NY 11530 718/895-1650 800/346-3621	1986	Dreyfus Corporation	$49.4 Mil	$1,000/ 100	i, p	Fund

*Key: i=initial sales charge   r=redemption fee or contingent deferred sales charge(CDSC)
t=12b-1 fee and either CDSC or redemption fee   p=12b-1 fee   n=none of the preceding fees   N/A=not available

Long-term Municipal Bond

Fund	Year Began	Investment Adviser	9/30/89 Assets	Minimum Initial and Subsequent Investment	Fees*	Where to Buy Shares
Principal Preservation Portfolios, Inc. *Insured Tax-Exempt Portfolio* 215 N. Main St. West Bend, WI 53095 414/334-5521 800/826-4600	1986	B.C. Ziegler and Company	$17.6 Mil	$1,000/ 250	i	Local Rep
Principal Preservation Portfolios, Inc. *Tax-Exempt Portfolio* 215 N. Main St. West Bend, WI 53095 414/334-5521 800/826-4600	1984	B.C. Ziegler and Company	$74.7 Mil	$1,000/ 250	i	Local Rep
Princor Tax-Exempt Bond Fund, Inc. 711 High St. Des Moines, IA 50309 515/247-5711 800/247-4123 800/622-5344 IA Only	1986	Principal Management, Inc.	$35.1 Mil	$1,000/ 50	i, p	Local Rep
Prudential-Bache Municipal Bond Fund *High Yield Series (The)* One Seaport Plaza New York, NY 10292 212/214-1215 800/225-1852	1987	Prudential Mutual Fund Management	$531.2 Mil	$1,000/ 100	t	Local Rep
Prudential-Bache Municipal Bond Fund *Insured Series (The)* One Seaport Plaza New York, NY 10292 212/214-1215 800/225-1852	1987	Prudential Mutual Fund Management	$428.7 Mil	$1,000/ 100	t	Local Rep
Prudential-Bache Municipal Bond Fund *Modified Term Series (The)* One Seaport Plaza New York, NY 10292 212/214-1215 800/225-1852	1987	Prudential Mutual Fund Management	$45.2 Mil	$1,000/ 100	t	Local Rep
Prudential-Bache National Municipals Fund, Inc. One Seaport Plaza New York, NY 10292 212/214-1215 800/225-1852	1980	Prudential Mutual Fund Management	$978.3 Mil	$1,000/ 100	t	Local Rep

*Key: i=initial sales charge   r=redemption fee or contingent deferred sales charge(CDSC)
t=12b-1 fee and either CDSC or redemption fee   p=12b-1 fee   n=none of the preceding fees   N/A=not available

Long-term Municipal Bond

Fund	Year Began	Investment Adviser	9/30/89 Assets	Minimum Initial and Subsequent Investment	Fees*	Where to Buy Shares
Putnam Tax Exempt Income Fund One Post Office Sq. Boston, MA 02109 617/292-1000 800/225-2465	1976	Putnam Management Company, Inc.	$1.2 Bil	$500/ 50	i	Local Rep
Putnam Tax-Free Income Trust *High Yield Fund* One Post Office Sq. Boston, MA 02109 617/292-1000 800/225-2465	1985	Putnam Management Company, Inc.	$632.1 Mil	$500/ 50	t	Local Rep
Putnam Tax-Free Income Trust *Insured Fund* One Post Office Sq. Boston, MA 02109 617/292-1000 800/225-2465	1985	Putnam Management Company, Inc.	$278.9 Mil	$500/ 50	t	Local Rep
Rochester Fund Municipals, Inc. 379 Park Ave. Rochester, NY 14607 716/442-5500	1986	Fielding Management Company, Inc.	N/A	$2,000/ 100	i, p	Local Rep
SAFECO Municipal Bond Fund, Inc. SAFECO Plaza Seattle, WA 98185 206/545-5530 800/426-6730	1981	SAFECO Asset Management Company	$267.4 Mil	$1,000/ 100	n	Fund
SafeGuard Tax-Free Bond Portfolio 16 Industrial Blvd. Paoli, PA 19301 215/251-0550 800/523-7798	1988	Provident Institutional Management Corporation	$1.1 Mil	$1,000/ 100	i, p	Local Rep
Salem Funds *Salem Tax Free Portfolio (The)* 99 High St. Boston, MA 02110 617/338-3200 800/641-2580 800/343-3424	1989	First Union National Bank of N. Carolina	N/A	$1,000/ 0	n	Fund

*Key: i=initial sales charge   r=redemption fee or contingent deferred sales charge(CDSC)
t=12b-1 fee and either CDSC or redemption fee   p=12b-1 fee   n=none of the preceding fees   N/A=not available

311

Long-term Municipal Bond

Fund	Year Began	Investment Adviser	9/30/89 Assets	Minimum Initial and Subsequent Investment	Fees*	Where to Buy Shares
Scudder High Yield Tax Free Fund 175 Federal St. Boston, MA 02110 617/439-4640 800/225-2470 800/225-5163	1987	Scudder, Stevens & Clark, Inc.	$106.8 Mil	$1,000/ 0	n	Fund
Scudder Managed Municipal Bonds 175 Federal St. Boston, MA 02110 617/439-4640 800/225-2470 800/225-5163	1976	Scudder, Stevens & Clark, Inc.	$659.5 Mil	$1,000/ 0	n	Fund
Scudder Tax-Free Target Fund *Tax Free 90* 175 Federal St. Boston, MA 02110 617/439-4640 800/225-2470 800/225-5163	1983	Scudder, Stevens & Clark, Inc.	$58.9 Mil	$1,000/ 0	n	Fund
Scudder Tax-Free Target Fund *Tax Free 93* 175 Federal St. Boston, MA 02110 617/439-4640 800/225-2470 800/225-5163	1983	Scudder, Stevens & Clark, Inc.	$79.6 Mil	$1,000/ 0	n	Fund
Scudder Tax-Free Target Fund *Tax Free 96* 175 Federal St. Boston, MA 02110 617/439-4640 800/225-2470 800/225-5163	1985	Scudder, Stevens & Clark, Inc.	$33.9 Mil	$1,000/ 0	n	Fund
Sears Tax-Exempt Reinvestment Fund Two World Trade Ctr. New York, NY 10048 212/392-2550 800/869-3863	1983	Dean Witter Reynolds Inc. - InterCapital Division	$49.7 Mil	$0/ 0	n	Local Rep
SECURAL Mutual Funds, Inc. *Municipal Bond Fund* 2401 S. Memorial Dr. Appleton, WI 54915 414/739-3161 800/426-5975	1988	SECURA Advisory Services, Inc.	$0.5 Mil	$500/ 100	i, p	Local Rep

*Key: i=initial sales charge   r=redemption fee or contingent deferred sales charge(CDSC)
t=12b-1 fee and either CDSC or redemption fee   p=12b-1 fee   n=none of the preceding fees   N/A=not available

Long-term Municipal Bond

Fund	Year Began	Investment Adviser	9/30/89 Assets	Minimum Initial and Subsequent Investment	Fees*	Where to Buy Shares
Security Tax-Exempt Fund 700 Harrison St. Topeka, KS 66636 913/295-3127 800/888-2461	1984	Security Management Company	$20.0 Mil	$100/ 20	i	Local Rep
Seligman Tax-Exempt Fund Series, Inc. *National Tax-Exempt Series* 130 Liberty St. New York, NY 10006 212/488-0200 800/221-2450 800/522-6869 NY Only	1983	J. & W. Seligman & Co. Incorporated	$140.4 Mil	$1,000/ 50	i	Local Rep
Sigma Tax-Free Bond Fund, Inc. 3801 Kennett Pk., C-200 Greenville Ctr. Wilmington, DE 19807 302/652-3091 800/441-9490	1979	Sigma Management, Inc.	$24.7 Mil	$0/ 0	i, p	Local Rep
Sit "New Beginning" Tax-Free Income Fund, Inc. 90 S. 7th St. Ste. 4600 Minneapolis, MN 55402 612/332-3223 800/332-5580	1988	Sit Investment Management Company	$15.7 Mil	$2,000/ 100	n	Fund
SLH Managed Municipals Inc. 31 W. 52nd St. New York, NY 10019 212/767-3700	1981	Bernstein-Macaulay Division of Shearson Lehman Hutton Inc.	$1.5 Bil	$500/ 200	i	Local Rep
SLH Special Income Portfolios *SLH Tax Exempt Income Portfolio* 31 W. 52nd St. New York, NY 10019 212/767-3700	1985	Bernstein-Macaulay Division of Shearson Lehman Hutton Inc.	$551.9 Mil	$500/ 200	t	Local Rep
State Farm Municipal Bond Fund, Inc. One State Farm Plaza Bloomington, IL 61710 309/766-2029	1977	State Farm Investment Management Corporation	$106.7 Mil (e)	$1,000/ 500	n	Fund

*Key: i=initial sales charge   r=redemption fee or contingent deferred sales charge(CDSC)
t=12b-1 fee and either CDSC or redemption fee   p=12b-1 fee   n=none of the preceding fees   N/A=not available

313

Long-term Municipal Bond

Fund	Year Began	Investment Adviser	9/30/89 Assets	Minimum Initial and Subsequent Investment	Fees*	Where to Buy Shares
SteinRoe Tax-Exempt Income Trust *SteinRoe High-Yield Municipals* 300 W. Adams St. P.O. Box 1143 Chicago, IL 60690 800/338-2550	1984	Stein Roe & Farnham Incorporated	$278.3 Mil	$1,000/ 100	n	Fund
SteinRoe Tax-Exempt Income Trust *SteinRoe Intermediate Municipals* 300 W. Adams St. P.O. Box 1143 Chicago, IL 60690 800/338-2550	1985	Stein Roe & Farnham Incorporated	$95.1 Mil	$1,000/ 100	n	Fund
SteinRoe Tax-Exempt Income Trust *SteinRoe Managed Municipals* 300 W. Adams St. P.O. Box 1143 Chicago, IL 60690 800/338-2550	1977	Stein Roe & Farnham Incorporated	$515.3 Mil	$1,000/ 100	n	Fund
Strong Tax-Free Funds *Strong Tax-Free Income Fund, Inc.* P.O. Box 2936 Milwaukee, WI 53201 414/359-3400 800/368-3863	1986	Strong/ Corneliuson Capital Management, Inc.	N/A	$2,500/ 200	n	Fund
Tax-Exempt Bond Fund of America, Inc. 333 S. Hope St. Los Angeles, CA 90071 213/486-9200 800/421-0180 213/486-9651 Collect	1979	Capital Research & Management Company	$456.6 Mil	$1,000/ 50	i, t	Local Rep
Tax-Exempt Portfolios *Limited Term Series* 82 Devonshire St. Boston, MA 02109 617/570-7000 800/343-9184 617/570-4750 MA Only	1985	Fidelity Management & Research Company	$122.7 Mil	$100,000/ 0	n	Fund
Tax-Free Investments Trust *Intermediate Portfolio* AIM Tax-Free Inter. Shares Institutional Inter. Shares 11 Greenway Plaza Ste. 1919 Houston, TX 77046 713/626-1919, 800/231-0803, 800/392-9681 TX Only	1987 1987	AIM Advisors, Inc.	$4.9 Mil	$1,000/100 $1.0 mil/0	i, p n	LRep LRep

*Key: i=initial sales charge   r=redemption fee or contingent deferred sales charge(CDSC)
t=12b-1 fee and either CDSC or redemption fee   p=12b-1 fee   n=none of the preceding fees   N/A=not available

Long-term Municipal Bond

Fund	Year Began	Investment Adviser	9/30/89 Assets	Minimum Initial and Subsequent Investment	Fees*	Where to Buy Shares
Templeton Tax Free Trust *Templeton Insured Tax Free Fund* 700 Central Ave. P.O. Box 33030 St. Petersburg, FL 33733-8030 813/823-8712 800/237-0738	1989	Templeton, Galbraith & Hansberger, Ltd.	$0.4 Mil	$1,000/ 25	i	Local Rep
Thomson McKinnon Investment Trust *Thomson McKinnon Tax-Exempt Fund* One State Street Plaza New York, NY 10004 212/482-5894 800/628-1237	1985	Thomson McKinnon Asset Management L.P.	$60.6 Mil	$1,000/ 100	t	Local Rep
Transamerica Special Series, Inc. *Transamerica Special High Yield Tax Free Fund* 1000 Louisiana Ste. 6000 Houston, TX 77002-5098 713/751-2400, 800/999-3863	1986	Transamerica Fund Management Company	$28.4 Mil	$1,000/ 50	t	Local Rep
Transamerica Tax Free Fund, Inc. *Transamerica Tax Free Income Fund* 1000 Louisiana Ste. 6000 Houston, TX 77002-5098 713/751-2400, 800/999-3863	1983	Transamerica Fund Management Company	$21.9 Mil	$100/ 10	i, p	Local Rep
Treasurer's Fund, Inc. *Tax Exempt Limited Term Portfolio* 8 Sound Shore Dr. Greenwich, CT 06830 203/629-2090 800/877-3863	1988	Gabelli-O'Connor Fixed Income Mutual Funds Management Company	N/A	$100,000/ 0	n	Local Rep
T. Rowe Price Tax-Free High Yield Fund, Inc. 100 E. Pratt St. Baltimore, MD 21202 301/547-2000 800/638-5660	1985	T. Rowe Price Associates, Inc.	$393.9 Mil	$2,500/ 100	n	Fund
T. Rowe Price Tax-Free Income Fund, Inc. 100 E. Pratt St. Baltimore, MD 21202 301/547-2000 800/638-5660	1976	T. Rowe Price Associates, Inc.	$1.1 Bil	$2,500/ 100	n	Fund

*Key: i=initial sales charge   r=redemption fee or contingent deferred sales charge(CDSC)
t=12b-1 fee and either CDSC or redemption fee   p=12b-1 fee   n=none of the preceding fees   N/A=not available

Long-term Municipal Bond

Fund	Year Began	Investment Adviser	9/30/89 Assets	Minimum Initial and Subsequent Investment	Fees*	Where to Buy Shares
T. Rowe Price Tax-Free Short - Intermediate Fund, Inc. 100 E. Pratt St. Baltimore, MD 21202 301/547-2000 800/638-5660	1983	T. Rowe Price Associates, Inc.	$210.2 Mil	$2,500/ 100	n	Fund
Twentieth Century Investors, Inc. *Tax-Exempt Intermediate Term* 4500 Main St. P.O. Box 419200 Kansas City, MO 64141-6200 816/531-5575 800/345-2021	1987	Investors Research Corporation	$20.2 Mil	$0/ 0	n	Fund
Twentieth Century Investors, Inc. *Tax-Exempt Long Term* 4500 Main St. P.O. Box 419200 Kansas City, MO 64141-6200 816/531-5575 800/345-2021	1987	Investors Research Corporation	$20.0 Mil	$0/ 0	n	Fund
Unified Municipal Fund, Inc. *General Series* 429 N. Pennsylvania St. Indianapolis, IN 46204-1897 317/634-3300 800/862-7283	1985	Unified Management Corporation	$5.1 Mil	$1,000/ 25	n	Fund
United Municipal Bond Fund, Inc. 2400 Pershing Rd. P.O. Box 418343 Kansas City, MO 64141-9343 816/283-4000 800/821-5664	1976	Waddell & Reed, Inc.	$594.3 Mil	$500/ 25	i	Local Rep
United Municipal High Income Fund, Inc. 2400 Pershing Rd. P.O. Box 418343 Kansas City, MO 64141-9343 816/283-4000 800/821-5664	1986	Waddell & Reed, Inc.	$168.7 Mil	$500/ 25	i	Local Rep
United Services Funds *U.S. Tax Free Fund* P.O. Box 29467 San Antonio, TX 78229-0467 512/696-1234 800/873-8637	1984	United Services Advisors, Inc.	$9.2 Mil	$100/ 50	n	Fund

*Key: i=initial sales charge   r=redemption fee or contingent deferred sales charge(CDSC)
t=12b-1 fee and either CDSC or redemption fee   p=12b-1 fee   n=none of the preceding fees   N/A=not available

Long-term Municipal Bond

Fund	Year Began	Investment Adviser	9/30/89 Assets	Minimum Initial and Subsequent Investment	Fees*	Where to Buy Shares
USAA Tax Exempt Fund, Inc. *High Yield Fund* USAA Bldg. San Antonio, TX 78288 512/498-8000 800/531-8000	1982	USAA Investment Management Company	$1.1 Bil	$3,000/ 50	n	Fund
USAA Tax Exempt Fund, Inc. *Intermediate-Term Fund* USAA Bldg. San Antonio, TX 78288 512/498-8000 800/531-8000	1982	USAA Investment Management Company	$431.5 Mil	$3,000/ 50	n	Fund
Value Line Tax Exempt Fund, Inc. *High Yield Portfolio* 711 Third Ave. New York, NY 10017 212/687-3965 800/223-0818	1984	Value Line, Inc.	$267.9 Mil	$1,000/ 250	n	Fund
Vanguard Municipal Bond Fund *High-Yield Portfolio* Vanguard Financial Ctr. P.O. Box 2600 Valley Forge, PA 19482 215/648-6000 800/662-7447, 800/362-0530 PA Only	1978	Vanguard Group, Inc.	$866.8 Mil	$3,000/ 100	n	Fund
Vanguard Municipal Bond Fund *Insured Long-Term Municipal Bond Portfolio* Vanguard Financial Ctr. P.O. Box 2600 Valley Forge, PA 19482 215/648-6000, 800/662-7447, 800/362-0530 PA Only	1984	Vanguard Group, Inc.	$938.4 Mil	$3,000/ 100	n	Fund
Vanguard Municipal Bond Fund *Intermediate-Term Portfolio* Vanguard Financial Ctr. P.O. Box 2600 Valley Forge, PA 19482 215/648-6000 800/662-7447, 800/362-0530 PA Only	1977	Vanguard Group, Inc.	$1.0 Bil	$3,000/ 100	n	Fund
Vanguard Municipal Bond Fund *Limited-Term Portfolio* Vanguard Financial Ctr. P.O. Box 2600 Valley Forge, PA 19482 215/648-6000 800/662-7447, 800/362-0530 PA Only	1987	Vanguard Group, Inc.	$168.1 Mil	$3,000/ 100	n	Fund

*Key: i=initial sales charge   r=redemption fee or contingent deferred sales charge(CDSC)
t=12b-1 fee and either CDSC or redemption fee   p=12b-1 fee   n=none of the preceding fees   N/A=not available

Long-term Municipal Bond

Fund	Year Began	Investment Adviser	9/30/89 Assets	Minimum Initial and Subsequent Investment	Fees*	Where to Buy Shares
Vanguard Municipal Bond Fund *Long-Term Portfolio* Vanguard Financial Ctr. P.O. Box 2600 Valley Forge, PA 19482 215/648-6000 800/662-7447, 800/362-0530 PA Only	1977	Vanguard Group, Inc.	$626.9 Mil	$3,000/ 100	n	Fund
Van Kampen Merritt Insured Tax Free Income Fund 1001 Warrenville Rd. Lisle, IL 60532 312/719-6000 800/225-2222	1984	Van Kampen Merritt Investment Advisory Corp.	$603.6 Mil	$1,500/ 100	i, p	Local Rep
Van Kampen Merritt Tax Free High Income Fund 1001 Warrenville Rd. Lisle, IL 60532 312/719-6000 800/225-2222	1985	Van Kampen Merritt Investment Advisory Corp.	$616.3 Mil	$1,500/ 100	i, p	Local Rep
Venture Muni (+) Plus 124 E. Marcy St. P.O. Box 1688 Santa Fe, NM 87504-1688 505/983-4335 800/545-2098	1984	Venture Advisers, L.P.	$71.3 Mil	$1,000/ 25	t	Local Rep
Voyageur GRANIT Insured Tax Exempt Fund, Inc. 100 S. Fifth St. Ste. 2200 Minneapolis, MN 55402 612/341-6728 800/553-2143 800/247-2143 MN Only	1985	Voyageur Fund Managers	$4.2 Mil	$1,000/ 100	i, p	Local Rep
Wright Managed Bond Trust *Wright Insured Tax Free Bond Fund* 24 Federal St. 5th Fl. Boston, MA 02110 617/482-8260 800/225-6265	1983	Wright Investors Service	$7.2 Mil	$1,000/ 0	p	Local Rep
Zweig Tax-Free Fund Inc. *Limited Term Portfolio* 25 Broadway New York, NY 10004 212/361-9612 800/272-2700	1985	Zweig/Glaser Advisers	$46.0 Mil (e)	$1,000/ 100	i	Local Rep

*Key: i=initial sales charge   r=redemption fee or contingent deferred sales charge(CDSC)
t=12b-1 fee and either CDSC or redemption fee   p=12b-1 fee   n=none of the preceding fees   N/A=not available

Long-term Municipal Bond

Fund	Year Began	Investment Adviser	9/30/89 Assets	Minimum Initial and Subsequent Investment	Fees*	Where to Buy Shares
Zweig Tax-Free Fund Inc. *Long Term Portfolio* 25 Broadway New York, NY 10004 212/361-9612 800/272-2700	1986	Zweig/Glaser Advisers	$17.4 Mil (e)	$1,000/ 100	i, p	Local Rep

*Key: i=initial sales charge   r=redemption fee or contingent deferred sales charge(CDSC)
t=12b-1 fee and either CDSC or redemption fee   p=12b-1 fee   n=none of the preceding fees   N/A=not available

319

◆ ◆ ◆ ◆

Money Market Funds

Money Market

Fund	Year Began	Investment Adviser	9/30/89 Assets	Minimum Initial and Subsequent Investment	Fees*	Where to Buy Shares
AAL Mutual Funds *AAL Money Market Fund (The)* 222 W. College Ave. Appleton, WI 54919 414/734-5721 800/553-6319	1988	AAL Advisors Inc.	$193.0 Mil	$500/ 50	p	Local Rep
AARP Cash Investment Funds *AARP Money Fund* AARP Investment Program 175 Federal St. Boston, MA 02110-2267 800/253-2277	1985	AARP/Scudder Financial Management Company	$323.2 Mil	$250/ 0	n	Fund
ABT Money Market Series, Inc. *ABT Prime Portfolio* 205 Royal Palm Way Palm Beach, FL 33480 407/655-7255 800/441-6580	1989	Palm Beach Capital Management, Ltd.	$4.2 Mil	$1,000/ 100	n	Local Rep
Active Assets Government Securities Trust Two World Trade Ctr. New York, NY 10048 212/392-2550 800/869-3863	1981	Dean Witter Reynolds Inc. - InterCapital Division	$268.8 Mil	$0/ 0	p	Local Rep
Active Assets Money Trust Two World Trade Ctr. New York, NY 10048 212/392-2550 800/869-3863	1981	Dean Witter Reynolds Inc. - InterCapital Division	$3.3 Bil	$0/ 0	p	Local Rep
Advisers Management Trust *Liquid Asset Portfolio* 342 Madison Ave. New York, NY 10173 212/850-8300 800/877-9700	1984	Neuberger & Berman Management Incorporated	$11.3 Mil	Not Applicable	n	Insur
Aetna Variable Encore Fund, Inc. 151 Farmington Ave. Hartford, CT 06156 203/273-4808	1974	Aetna Life Insurance and Annuity Company	$407.8 Mil	Not Applicable	n	Insur

*Key: i=initial sales charge   r=redemption fee or contingent deferred sales charge(CDSC)
t=12b-1 fee and either CDSC or redemption fee   p=12b-1 fee   n=none of the preceding fees   N/A=not available

Money Market

Fund	Year Began	Investment Adviser	9/30/89 Assets	Minimum Initial and Subsequent Investment	Fees*	Where to Buy Shares
Alex. Brown Cash Reserve Fund *Prime Series* Flag Investors Shares Class *Original Class* P.O. Box 515 Baltimore, MD 21203 301/727-1700, 800/767-3524	1989 1981	Flag Investors Management Corp.	$1.2 Bil	$1,500/100 $1,500/100	p p	LRep LRep
Alex. Brown Cash Reserve Fund *Treasury Series* P.O. Box 515 Baltimore, MD 21203 301/727-1700 800/767-3524	1982	Flag Investors Management Corp.	$269.8 Mil	$1,500/ 100	p	Local Rep
Alger American Fund *Alger American Money Market Portfolio* 75 Maiden Lane New York, NY 10038 212/806-8800 800/223-3810	1988	Fred Alger Management, Inc.	$0.1 Mil	Not Applicable	N/A	Insur
Alger Fund *Alger Money Market Portfolio* 75 Maiden Lane New York, NY 10038 212/806-8800 800/223-3810	1986	Fred Alger Management, Inc.	$62.2 Mil	$1,000/ 100	n	Fund
Alliance Capital Reserves 1345 Avenue of the Americas New York, NY 10105 212/969-1000 800/221-5672	1978	Alliance Capital Management L.P.	$1.8 Bil	$1,000/ 100	n	Local Rep
Alliance Government Reserves 1345 Avenue of the Americas New York, NY 10105 212/969-1000 800/221-5672	1979	Alliance Capital Management L.P.	$455.5 Mil	$1,000/ 100	n	Local Rep
Alliance Money Reserve 1345 Avenue of the Americas New York, NY 10105 212/969-1000 800/221-5672	1989	Alliance Capital Management L.P.	$785.9 Mil	$1,000/ 100	p	Local Rep

*Key: i=initial sales charge   r=redemption fee or contingent deferred sales charge(CDSC)
t=12b-1 fee and either CDSC or redemption fee   p=12b-1 fee   n=none of the preceding fees   N/A=not available

324

Money Market

Fund	Year Began	Investment Adviser	9/30/89 Assets	Minimum Initial and Subsequent Investment	Fees*	Where to Buy Shares
Altura Fund *Prime Obligations Fund* 1900 E. Dublin-Granville Rd. Columbus, OH 43229 614/899-4600 800/338-4385	1986	United Bank of Denver National Association	N/A	$1,000/ 50	N/A	Fund
AMA Money Fund, Inc. *Prime Portfolio* 5 Sentry Pkwy. W, Ste. 120 P.O. Box 1111 Blue Bell, PA 19422 215/825-0400 800/AMA-FUND	1985	AMA Advisers, Inc.	$117.9 Mil	$2,000/ 100	p	Fund
AMA Money Fund, Inc. *Treasury Portfolio* 5 Sentry Pkwy. W, Ste. 120 P.O. Box 1111 Blue Bell, PA 19422 215/825-0400 800/AMA-FUND	1982	AMA Advisers, Inc.	$18.9 Mil	$2,000/ 100	p	Fund
American Capital Government Money Market Trust 2800 Post Oak Blvd. Houston, TX 77056 713/993-0500 800/421-5666	1987	American Capital Asset Management, Inc.	$19.6 Mil	$500/ 50	p	Local Rep
American Capital Life Investment Trust *American Capital Money Market Portfolio* 2800 Post Oak Blvd. Houston, TX 77056 713/993-0500 800/421-5666	1986	American Capital Asset Management, Inc.	$26.8 Mil	Not Applicable	n	Insur
American Capital Reserve Fund, Inc. 2800 Post Oak Blvd. Houston, TX 77056 713/993-0500 800/421-5666	1974	American Capital Asset Management, Inc.	$475.9 Mil	$1,000/ 100	p	Local Rep
American General Money Market Accumulation Fund, Inc. 2800 Post Oak Blvd. Houston, TX 77056 713/993-0500 800/421-5666	1982	American Capital Asset Management, Inc.	$47.0 Mil	Not Applicable	n	Insur

*Key: i=initial sales charge   r=redemption fee or contingent deferred sales charge(CDSC)
      t=12b-1 fee and either CDSC or redemption fee   p=12b-1 fee   n=none of the preceding fees   N/A=not available

Money Market

Fund	Year Began	Investment Adviser	9/30/89 Assets	Minimum Initial and Subsequent Investment	Fees*	Where to Buy Shares
American General Series Portfolio Company *Money Market Fund* 2929 Allen Pkwy. P.O. Box 3206 Houston, TX 77253 713/526-5251	1985	Variable Annuity Life Insurance Company	$20.6 Mil	Not Applicable	r	Insur
American Investors Money Fund, Inc. 777 W. Putnam Ave. P.O. Box 2500 Greenwich, CT 06836 203/531-5000 800/243-5353	1982	D.H. Blair Advisors, Inc.	$5.2 Mil (e)	$1,000/ 100	n	Fund
American National Money Market Fund, Inc. Two Moody Plaza Galveston, TX 77550 409/763-2767 800/231-4639 800/392-9753 TX Only	1981	Securities Management & Research, Inc.	$22.1 Mil	$2,000/ 100	n	Local Rep
American Variable Insurance Series *Cash Management Fund (The)* 333 S. Hope St. Los Angeles, CA 90071 213/486-9200 800/421-0180 213/486-9651 Collect	1984	Capital Research & Management Company	$46.9 Mil	Not Applicable	n	Insur
AMEV Money Fund, Inc. P.O. Box 64284 St. Paul, MN 55164 612/738-4000 800/872-2638	1979	AMEV Advisers, Inc.	$97.4 Mil	$500/ 100	p	Local Rep
Anchor Pathway Fund *Cash Management Series (The)* 2201 E. Camelback Phoenix, AZ 85016 602/955-0300 800/528-9679	1987	Capital Research & Management Company	N/A	Not Applicable	n	Insur
Arch Fund, Inc. *Discretionary Portfolio* 3512 Silverside Rd. The Commons, No. 6 Wilmington, DE 19810 302/478-6945 800/441-7379	1982	Provident Institutional Management Corporation	N/A	$1,000/ 100	p	Local Rep

*Key: i=initial sales charge   r=redemption fee or contingent deferred sales charge(CDSC)
t=12b-1 fee and either CDSC or redemption fee   p=12b-1 fee   n=none of the preceding fees   N/A=not available

Money Market

Fund	Year Began	Investment Adviser	9/30/89 Assets	Minimum Initial and Subsequent Investment	Fees*	Where to Buy Shares
Arch Fund, Inc. *Non-Discretionary Portfolio* 3512 Silverside Rd. The Commons, No. 6 Wilmington, DE 19810 302/478-6945 800/441-7379	1983	Provident Institutional Management Corporation	N/A	$1,000/ 100	p	Local Rep
Associated Capital Institutional Trust *Money Market 1* 580 California St. San Francisco, CA 94104 415/393-0300 800/544-6295	1988	Associated Capital Investors, Inc.	$45.7 Mil	$250,000/ 25,000	n	Local Rep
Automated Cash Management Trust Federated Investors Twr. Pittsburgh, PA 15222-3779 412/288-1900 800/245-5000	1982	Federated Management	$1.2 Bil	$25,000/ 0	n	Local Rep
Automated Government Money Trust Federated Investors Twr. Pittsburgh, PA 15222-3779 412/288-1900 800/245-5000	1982	Federated Management	$3.1 Bil	$25,000/ 0	n	Local Rep
Axe-Houghton Money Market Fund, Inc. 400 Benedict Ave. Tarrytown, NY 10591 914/631-8131 800/366-0444	1981	Axe-Houghton Management, Inc.	$123.7 Mil	$1,000/ 100	p	Fund
Bankers National Series Trust *BNL Money Market Portfolio* 44 U.S. Hwy. 46 Pine Brook, NJ 07058 201/808-9596 800/888-4918	1983	Conseco Capital Management, Inc.	$6.0 Mil	Not Applicable	n	Insur
Bedford Government Money Market Portfolio 16 Industrial Blvd. Paoli, PA 19301 215/251-0550 800/523-7798	1988	Provident Institutional Management Corporation	$72.4 Mil	$1,000/ 100	p	Local Rep

*Key: i=initial sales charge   r=redemption fee or contingent deferred sales charge(CDSC)
t=12b-1 fee and either CDSC or redemption fee   p=12b-1 fee   n=none of the preceding fees   N/A=not available

Money Market

Fund	Year Began	Investment Adviser	9/30/89 Assets	Minimum Initial and Subsequent Investment	Fees*	Where to Buy Shares
Bedford Money Market Portfolio 16 Industrial Blvd. Paoli, PA 19301 215/251-0550 800/523-7798	1988	Provident Institutional Management Corporation	$187.3 Mil	$1,000/ 100	p	Local Rep
Bison Money Market Fund *Discretionary Portfolio - Class B* 3512 Silverside Rd. The Commons, No. 6 Wilmington, DE 19810 302/478-6945 800/441-7379	1983	Provident Institutional Management Corporation	$272.8 Mil	$2,000/ 0	n	Local Rep
Bison Money Market Fund *Non-Discretionary Portfolio - Class A* 3512 Silverside Rd. The Commons, No. 6 Wilmington, DE 19810 302/478-6945 800/441-7379	1982	Provident Institutional Management Corporation	$180.0 Mil	$2,000/ 0	n	Local Rep
Blanchard Government Money Market Fund 41 Madison Ave. 24th Fl. New York, NY 10010 212/779-7979 800/922-7771	1989	Sheffield Management Company	$46.8 Mil	$3,000/ 200	n	Fund
Boston Company Fund *Cash Management Fund* One Boston Place Boston, MA 02019 617/956-9740 800/225-5267 800/343-6324	1979	Boston Company Advisors, Inc.	$361.2 Mil	$1,000/ 0	p	Fund
Boston Company Fund *Government Money Fund* One Boston Place Boston, MA 02019 617/956-9740 800/225-5267 800/343-6324	1982	Boston Company Advisors, Inc.	$40.0 Mil	$1,000/ 0	p	Fund
Bull & Bear Incorporated *Bull & Bear Dollar Reserves* 11 Hanover Sq. New York, NY 10005 212/785-0900 800/847-4200	1980	Bull & Bear Fixed Income Advisers, Inc.	$96.9 Mil (e)	$1,000/ 100	p	Fund

*Key: i=initial sales charge   r=redemption fee or contingent deferred sales charge(CDSC)
t=12b-1 fee and either CDSC or redemption fee   p=12b-1 fee   n=none of the preceding fees   N/A=not available

Money Market

Fund	Year Began	Investment Adviser	9/30/89 Assets	Minimum Initial and Subsequent Investment	Fees*	Where to Buy Shares
California Investment Trust II *United States Treasury Trust (The)* 44 Montgomery St. Ste. 2200 San Francisco, CA 94104 415/398-2727, 800/225-8778	1989	CCM Partners	$4.0 Mil	$10,000/ 250	n	Fund
Calvert Social Investment Fund *Money Market Portfolio* 1700 Pennsylvania Ave., NW Washington, DC 20006 301/951-4820 800/368-2745	1982	Calvert Asset Management Company, Inc.	$139.9 Mil	$1,000/ 250	p	Fund
Capital Cash Management Trust 200 Park Ave. Ste. 4515 New York, NY 10017 212/697-6666	1974	STCM Management Company, Inc.	$2.4 Mil	$1,000/ 0	n	Local Rep
Capital Preservation Fund 755 Page Mill Rd. Palo Alto, CA 94304 415/858-2400 800/227-8380 800/982-6150 CA Only	1971	Benham Management Corporation	$2.7 Bil	$1,000/ 100	n	Fund
Capital Preservation Fund II 755 Page Mill Rd. Palo Alto, CA 94304 415/858-2400 800/227-8380 800/982-6150 CA Only	1980	Benham Management Corporation	$707.1 Mil	$1,000/ 100	n	Fund
Cardinal Government Securities Trust 155 E. Broad St. Columbus, OH 43215 614/464-5511 800/848-7734 800/262-9446 OH only	1980	Cardinal Management Corporation	$533.2 Mil	$1,000/ 100	n	Fund
Carillon Cash Reserves, Inc. 1876 Waycross Rd. P.O. Box 5304 Cincinnati, OH 45201 513/595-2600 800/999-1840	1982	Carillon Advisers, Inc.	$111.4 Mil	$1,000/ 100	n	Fund

*Key: i=initial sales charge   r=redemption fee or contingent deferred sales charge(CDSC)
t=12b-1 fee and either CDSC or redemption fee   p=12b-1 fee   n=none of the preceding fees   N/A=not available

329

Money Market

Fund	Year Began	Investment Adviser	9/30/89 Assets	Minimum Initial and Subsequent Investment	Fees*	Where to Buy Shares
Carillon Fund, Inc. *Money Market Portfolio (The)* 1876 Waycross Rd. P.O. Box 5304 Cincinnati, OH 45201 513/595-2600 800/999-1840	1984	Carillon Advisers, Inc.	$11.1 Mil	Not Applicable	n	Insur
Carnegie Government Securities Trust *Money Market Series* 1100 The Halle Bldg. 1228 Euclid Ave. Cleveland, OH 44115-1831 216/781-4440 800/321-2322	1980	Carnegie Capital Management Company	$91.8 Mil	$1,000/ 250	n	Local Rep
Cascades Trust *Cascades Cash Fund* 200 Park Ave. Ste. 4515 New York, NY 10017 212/697-6666	1989	Qualivest Capital Management, Inc.	N/A	$1,000/ 0	N/A	Fund
Cash Accumulation Trust *National Government Fund* One State Street Plaza New York, NY 10004 212/482-5894 800/628-1237	1984	Thomson McKinnon Asset Management L.P.	$64.8 Mil	$500/ 100	p	Local Rep
Cash Accumulation Trust *National Money Market Fund* One State Street Plaza New York, NY 10004 212/482-5894 800/628-1237	1984	Thomson McKinnon Asset Management L.P.	$2.4 Bil	$500/ 100	p	Local Rep
Cash Assets Trust *Cash Assets Trust* 200 Park Ave. Ste. 4515 New York, NY 10017 212/697-6666 800/228-4227	1985	Hawaiian Trust Company, Limited	$351.3 Mil	$1,000/ 0	n	Fund
Cash Assets Trust *U.S. Treasuries Cash Assets Trust* 200 Park Ave. Ste. 4515 New York, NY 10017 212/697-6666 800/228-4227	1988	Hawaiian Trust Company, Limited	$27.7 Mil	$1,000/ 0	n	Fund

*Key: i=initial sales charge   r=redemption fee or contingent deferred sales charge(CDSC)
t=12b-1 fee and either CDSC or redemption fee   p=12b-1 fee   n=none of the preceding fees   N/A=not available

Money Market

Fund	Year Began	Investment Adviser	9/30/89 Assets	Minimum Initial and Subsequent Investment	Fees*	Where to Buy Shares
Cash Equivalent Fund, Inc. *Government Securities Portfolio* 120 S. LaSalle St. Chicago, IL 60603 312/781-1121 800/621-1148	1981	Kemper Financial Services, Inc.	$3.1 Bil	$1,000/ 100	p	Local Rep
Cash Equivalent Fund, Inc. *Money Market Portfolio* 120 S. LaSalle St. Chicago, IL 60603 312/781-1121 800/621-1148	1979	Kemper Financial Services, Inc.	$7.1 Bil	$1,000/ 100	p	Local Rep
Cash Income Trust 99 High St. Boston, MA 02110 617/338-3200 800/343-2898 800/225-1587	1981	Keystone Custodian Funds, Inc.	$0.8 Mil	Not Applicable	n	Insur
Cash Management Trust of America 333 S. Hope St. Los Angeles, CA 90071 213/486-9200 800/421-0180 213/486-9651 Collect	1976	Capital Research & Management Company	$1.4 Bil	$5,000/ 50	p	Local Rep
Cash Preservation Money Market Portfolio 16 Industrial Blvd. Paoli, PA 19301 215/251-0550 800/523-7798	1988	Provident Institutional Management Corporation	$2.8 Mil	$1,000/ 100	p	Local Rep
Cash Trust Series *Government Cash Series* Federated Investors Twr. Pittsburgh, PA 15222-3779 412/288-1900 800/245-5051	1989	Federated Advisers	$38.6 Mil	$1,000/ 500	N/A	Local Rep
Cash Trust Series *Prime Cash Series* Federated Investors Twr. Pittsburgh, PA 15222-3779 412/288-1900 800/245-5051	1989	Federated Advisers	$17.7 Mil	$1,000/ 500	N/A	Local Rep

*Key: i=initial sales charge   r=redemption fee or contingent deferred sales charge(CDSC)
t=12b-1 fee and either CDSC or redemption fee   p=12b-1 fee   n=none of the preceding fees   N/A=not available

Money Market

Fund	Year Began	Investment Adviser	9/30/89 Assets	Minimum Initial and Subsequent Investment	Fees*	Where to Buy Shares
CBA Money Fund P.O. Box 9011 Princeton, NJ 08543-9011 201/560-5507 800/262-4636 800/262-3276	1983	Fund Asset Management, Inc.	$716.8 Mil	$0/ 0	p	Local Rep
Centennial Government Trust 3410 S. Galena St. Denver, CO 80231 303/671-3200 800/525-7048	1982	Centennial Capital Corporation	$197.7 Mil	$500/ 25	p	Local Rep
Centennial Money Market Trust 3410 S. Galena St. Denver, CO 80231 303/671-3200 800/525-7048	1982	Centennial Capital Corporation	$387.2 Mil	$500/ 25	p	Local Rep
Chapman Funds, Inc. *Chapman Institutional Cash Management Fund (The)* Two Hopkins Plaza 10th Fl. Baltimore, MD 21201 301/625-9656	1989	Chapman Capital Management, Inc.	N/A	$1.0 Mil/ 0	N/A	Fund
Chestnut Street Cash Fund, Inc. *Portfolio A* 3411 Silverside Rd. Webster Bldg., Ste. 204 Wilmington, DE 19810 302/478-6945 800/441-7379	1985	Bernstein-Macaulay Division of Shearson Lehman Hutton Inc.	$104.7 Mil	$1,500/ 0	n	Local Rep
Chestnut Street Cash Fund, Inc. *Portfolio B* 3411 Silverside Rd. Webster Bldg., Ste. 204 Wilmington, DE 19810 302/478-6945 800/441-7379	1985	Provident Institutional Management Corporation	$301.7 Mil	$1,500/ 0	n	Local Rep
Chubb America Fund, Inc. *Money Market Portfolio* One Granite Place Concord, NH 03301 603/224-7741	1985	Chubb Investment Advisory Corporation	$2.3 Mil (e)	Not Applicable	n	Insur

*Key: i=initial sales charge   r=redemption fee or contingent deferred sales charge(CDSC)
t=12b-1 fee and either CDSC or redemption fee   p=12b-1 fee   n=none of the preceding fees   N/A=not available

Money Market

Fund	Year Began	Investment Adviser	9/30/89 Assets	Minimum Initial and Subsequent Investment	Fees*	Where to Buy Shares
Chubb Investment Funds, Inc. *Chubb Money Market Fund* One Granite Place Concord, NH 03301 603/224-7741	1987	Chubb Asset Managers, Inc.	N/A	$1,000/ 100	i, p	Local Rep
Churchill Cash Reserves Trust 200 Park Ave. Ste. 4515 New York, NY 10017 212/697-6666	1985	Citizens Fidelity Bank & Trust Company	$288.4 Mil	$1,000/ 0	n	Local Rep
CIGNA Annuity Fund *Money Market Fund* CIGNA Corporation Hartford, CT 06152 203/726-6000 800/562-4462	1981	CIGNA Investments, Inc.	$46.0 Mil	Not Applicable	n	Insur
CIGNA Cash Funds *CIGNA Cash Fund* One Financial Plaza Springfield, MA 01103 413/784-0100 800/56CIGNA	1982	CIGNA Investments, Inc.	$112.0 Mil	$1,000/ 100	p	Local Rep
CIGNA Money Market Fund One Financial Plaza Springfield, MA 01103 413/784-0100 800/56CIGNA	1974	CIGNA Investments, Inc.	$160.7 Mil	$500/ 50	i, p	Local Rep
CMA Government Securities Fund P.O. Box 9011 Princeton, NJ 08543-9011 201/560-5507 800/262-4636 800/262-3276	1982	Fund Asset Management, Inc.	$2.9 Bil	$0/ 0	p	Local Rep
CMA Money Fund P.O. Box 9011 Princeton, NJ 08543-9011 201/560-5507 800/262-4636 800/262-3276	1977	Fund Asset Management, Inc.	$26.8 Bil	$0/ 0	p	Local Rep

*Key: i=initial sales charge   r=redemption fee or contingent deferred sales charge(CDSC)
t=12b-1 fee and either CDSC or redemption fee   p=12b-1 fee   n=none of the preceding fees   N/A=not available

333

Money Market

Fund	Year Began	Investment Adviser	9/30/89 Assets	Minimum Initial and Subsequent Investment	Fees*	Where to Buy Shares
Collective Investment Trust for Citibank IRAs *Short Term Portfolio* 153 E. 53rd St. 4th Fl. New York, NY 10043 212/559-4677 800/CITI-IRA	1983	Citibank N.A.	$9.1 Mil	$250/ 0	n	Fund
Collective Investment Trust for Seafirst Retirement Accounts *Money Market Fund (The)* 701 Fifth Ave. P.O. Box 84248 Seattle, WA 98124 206/358-6119, 800/323-9919	1988	Seattle-First National Bank	$23.6 Mil (e)	$500/ 0	n	Fund
Colonial Government Money Market Trust One Financial Ctr. Boston, MA 02111 617/426-3750 800/225-2365 800/426-3750	1980	Colonial Management Associates, Inc.	$86.6 Mil	$250/ 25	n	Local Rep
Colonial/Hancock Liberty Trust *Colonial/Hancock Liberty Money Market Fund* One Financial Ctr. Boston, MA 02111 617/426-3750 800/225-2365, 800/426-3750	1987	Colonial Management Associates, Inc.	$4.0 Mil	Not Applicable	n	Insur
Colonial Value Investing Portfolios - Income Portfolio *Money Market Fund* One Financial Ctr. Boston, MA 02111 617/426-3750 800/225-2365, 800/426-3750	1987	Colonial Management Associates, Inc.	$18.4 Mil	$500/ 100	t	Local Rep
Columbia Daily Income Company 1301 SW 5th Ave. P.O. Box 1350 Portland, OR 97207 503/222-3600 800/547-1707	1974	Columbia Funds Management Company	$680.9 Mil	$1,000/ 100	n	Fund
Command Government Fund One Seaport Plaza New York, NY 10292 212/214-1215 800/872-7787	1982	Prudential Mutual Fund Management	$203.2 Mil	$10,000/ 0	p	Local Rep

*Key: i=initial sales charge   r=redemption fee or contingent deferred sales charge(CDSC)
t=12b-1 fee and either CDSC or redemption fee   p=12b-1 fee   n=none of the preceding fees   N/A=not available

334

Money Market

Fund	Year Began	Investment Adviser	9/30/89 Assets	Minimum Initial and Subsequent Investment	Fees*	Where to Buy Shares
Command Money Fund One Seaport Plaza New York, NY 10292 212/214-1215 800/872-7787	1982	Prudential Mutual Fund Management	$2.6 Bil	$10,000/0	p	Local Rep
Common Sense Trust *Common Sense Money Market Fund* 2800 Post Oak Blvd. Houston, TX 77056 713/993-0500 800/421-5666	1987	Common Sense Investment Advisers	$61.3 Mil	$250/25	n	Local Rep
Compass Capital Group *Cash Reserve Fund* 1900 E. Dublin-Granville Rd. Columbus, OH 43229 614/899-4600 800/338-4385	1989	Midlantic National Bank	N/A	$5,000/100	N/A	Fund
Compass Capital Group *U.S. Treasury Fund* 1900 E. Dublin-Granville Rd. Columbus, OH 43229 614/899-4600 800/338-4385	1989	Midlantic National Bank	N/A	$5,000/100	N/A	Fund
Composite Cash Management Company *Money Market Portfolio* W. 601 Riverside, 9th Fl. Seafirst Financial Ctr. Spokane, WA 99201 509/353-3400 800/543-8072, 800/572-5828	1979	Composite Research & Management Company	$248.2 Mil	$1,000/50	p	Fund
Composite Deferred Series, Inc. *Money Market Portfolio* W. 601 Riverside, 9th Fl. Seafirst Financial Ctr. Spokane, WA 99201 509/353-3400 800/543-8072, 800/572-5828	1987	Composite Research & Management Company	$0.4 Mil	Not Applicable	r	Insur
Conestoga Family of Funds *Cash Management Fund* 1900 E. Dublin-Granville Rd. Columbus, OH 43229 614/899-4600 800/338-4385	1989	Meridian Investment Company	N/A	$1,000/0	N/A	Fund

*Key: i=initial sales charge   r=redemption fee or contingent deferred sales charge(CDSC)
t=12b-1 fee and either CDSC or redemption fee   p=12b-1 fee   n=none of the preceding fees   N/A=not available

Money Market

Fund	Year Began	Investment Adviser	9/30/89 Assets	Minimum Initial and Subsequent Investment	Fees*	Where to Buy Shares
Conestoga Family of Funds *U.S. Treasury Securities Fund* 1900 E. Dublin-Granville Rd. Columbus, OH 43229 614/899-4600 800/338-4385	1989	Meridian Investment Company	N/A	$1,000/ 0	N/A	Fund
Connecticut Mutual Financial Services Series Fund I, Inc. *Money Market Portfolio* 140 Garden St. Hartford, CT 06154 203/727-6500 800/243-0018	1982	G.R. Phelps & Company, Inc.	$59.9 Mil	Not Applicable	r	Insur
Connecticut Mutual Investment Accounts, Inc. *Connecticut Mutual Liquid Account* 140 Garden St. Hartford, CT 06154 203/727-6500 800/243-0018	1982	G.R. Phelps & Company, Inc.	$88.2 Mil	$1,000/ 50	p	Local Rep
Consolidated Asset Management Fund P.O. Box 9006 Valley Forge, PA 19485-9006 215/971-9500 800/423-2345	1981	Declaration Investment Advisors	$45.6 Mil	$0/ 0	p	Fund
Cortland Trust *General Money Market Fund* AIM Class Original Class 3 University Plaza Hackensack, NJ 07601 201/342-6066, 800/433-1918	1987 1985	Cortland Financial Group, Inc.	$924.2 Mil	$1,000/0 $100/25	p p	LRep LRep
Cortland Trust *U.S. Government Fund* 3 University Plaza Hackensack, NJ 07601 201/342-6066 800/433-1918	1985	Cortland Financial Group, Inc.	$87.4 Mil	$100/ 25	p	Local Rep
Counsellors Cash Reserve Fund, Inc. 466 Lexington Ave. New York, NY 10017-3147 212/878-0600 800/888-6878	1985	Warburg, Pincus Counsellors, Inc.	$267.6 Mil	$1,000/ 500	n	Fund

*Key: i=initial sales charge   r=redemption fee or contingent deferred sales charge(CDSC)
t=12b-1 fee and either CDSC or redemption fee   p=12b-1 fee   n=none of the preceding fees   N/A=not available

336

Money Market

Fund	Year Began	Investment Adviser	9/30/89 Assets	Minimum Initial and Subsequent Investment	Fees*	Where to Buy Shares
Country Capital Money Market Fund, Inc. 1701 Towanda Ave. Bloomington, IL 61701 309/557-2444 800/322-3838 IL Only	1981	Country Capital Management Company	$19.1 Mil	$1,000/ 25	n	Local Rep
Daily Cash Accumulation Fund, Inc. 3410 S. Galena St. Denver, CO 80231 303/671-3200 800/525-7048	1978	Centennial Capital Corporation	$4.7 Bil	$500/ 25	p	Local Rep
Daily Money Fund *Money Market Portfolio* 82 Devonshire St. Boston, MA 02109 617/570-7000 800/343-9184 617/570-4750 MA Only	1983	Fidelity Management & Research Company	$1.0 Bil	$1,000/ 250	n	Local Rep
Daily Money Fund *U.S. Treasury Portfolio* 82 Devonshire St. Boston, MA 02109 617/570-7000 800/343-9184 617/570-4750 MA Only	1983	Fidelity Management & Research Company	$998.2 Mil	$1,000/ 250	n	Local Rep
Daiwa Money Fund Inc. One World Financial Ctr. 200 Liberty St. New York, NY 10281 212/945-0100	1981	Daiwa International Capital Management Corp.	$15.2 Mil	$2,500/ 100	n	Fund
Dean Witter/Sears Liquid Asset Fund Inc. Two World Trade Ctr. New York, NY 10048 212/392-2550 800/869-3863	1975	Dean Witter Reynolds Inc. - InterCapital Division	$11.0 Bil	$5,000/ 100	p	Local Rep
Dean Witter/Sears U.S. Government Money Market Trust Two World Trade Ctr. New York, NY 10048 212/392-2550 800/869-3863	1982	Dean Witter Reynolds Inc. - InterCapital Division	$802.2 Mil	$1,000/ 50	p	Local Rep

*Key: i=initial sales charge   r=redemption fee or contingent deferred sales charge(CDSC)
t=12b-1 fee and either CDSC or redemption fee   p=12b-1 fee   n=none of the preceding fees   N/A=not available

Money Market

Fund	Year Began	Investment Adviser	9/30/89 Assets	Minimum Initial and Subsequent Investment	Fees*	Where to Buy Shares
Dean Witter Variable Investment Series *Money Market Portfolio* Two World Trade Ctr. New York, NY 10048 212/392-2550 800/869-3863	1984	Dean Witter Reynolds Inc. - InterCapital Division	$70.1 Mil	Not Applicable	n	Insur
Delaware Group Cash Reserve *Original Class* One Commerce Sq. Philadelphia, PA 19103 215/988-1200 800/523-4640	1978	Delaware Management Company, Inc.	$1.1 Bil	$1,000/25	n	Fund
Delaware Group Treasury Reserves *Cashiers Series* *Original Class* One Commerce Sq. Philadelphia, PA 19103 215/988-1200, 800/523-4640	1982	Delaware Management Company, Inc.	$31.3 Mil	$1,000/25	n	Fund
Dreman Mutual Group, Inc. *Dreman Cash Portfolio (The)* 10 Exchange Place Jersey City, NJ 07302 201/332-8228 800/533-1608	1989	Dreman Value Management, Inc.	N/A	$5,000/ 1,000	N/A	Local Rep
Dreyfus Cash Management 666 Old Country Rd. Garden City, NY 11530 718/895-1650 800/346-3621	1985	Dreyfus Corporation	$3.2 Bil	$10.0 Mil/ 0	n	Local Rep
Dreyfus Cash Management Plus, Inc. 666 Old Country Rd. Garden City, NY 11530 718/895-1650 800/346-3621	1987	Dreyfus Corporation	$728.8 Mil	$10.0 Mil/ 0	n	Fund
Dreyfus Dollar International Fund, Inc. 666 Old Country Rd. Garden City, NY 11530 718/895-1397 800/358-5566	1983	Dreyfus Corporation	$30.1 Mil	$5,000/ 500	p	Fund

*Key: i=initial sales charge   r=redemption fee or contingent deferred sales charge(CDSC)
t=12b-1 fee and either CDSC or redemption fee   p=12b-1 fee   n=none of the preceding fees   N/A=not available

Money Market

Fund	Year Began	Investment Adviser	9/30/89 Assets	Minimum Initial and Subsequent Investment	Fees*	Where to Buy Shares
Dreyfus Government Cash Management 666 Old Country Rd. Garden City, NY 11530 718/895-1650 800/346-3621	1985	Dreyfus Corporation	$1.4 Bil	$10.0 Mil/ 0	n	Local Rep
Dreyfus Institutional Money Market Fund *Government Securities Series* 666 Old Country Rd. Garden City, NY 11530 718/895-1650 800/346-3621	1982	Dreyfus Corporation	$269.6 Mil	$50,000/ 100	n	Local Rep
Dreyfus Institutional Money Market Fund *Money Market Series* 666 Old Country Rd. Garden City, NY 11530 718/895-1650 800/346-3621	1982	Dreyfus Corporation	$727.2 Mil	$50,000/ 100	n	Local Rep
Dreyfus Liquid Assets, Inc. 666 Old Country Rd. Garden City, NY 11530 718/895-1206 800/645-6561	1974	Dreyfus Corporation	$7.7 Bil	$2,500/ 100	n	Fund
Dreyfus Money Market Instruments, Inc. *Government Securities Series* 666 Old Country Rd. Garden City, NY 11530 718/895-1206 800/645-6561	1979	Dreyfus Corporation	$679.5 Mil	$2,500/ 100	n	Fund
Dreyfus Money Market Instruments, Inc. *Money Market Series* 666 Old Country Rd. Garden City, NY 11530 718/895-1396 800/242-8671	1975	Dreyfus Corporation	$374.0 Mil	$50,000/ 100	n	Local Rep
Dreyfus Treasury Cash Management 666 Old Country Rd. Garden City, NY 11530 718/895-1650 800/346-3621	1986	Dreyfus Corporation	$813.7 Mil	$10.0 Mil/ 0	n	Local Rep

*Key: i=initial sales charge   r=redemption fee or contingent deferred sales charge(CDSC)
t=12b-1 fee and either CDSC or redemption fee   p=12b-1 fee   n=none of the preceding fees   N/A=not available

Money Market

Fund	Year Began	Investment Adviser	9/30/89 Assets	Minimum Initial and Subsequent Investment	Fees*	Where to Buy Shares
Dreyfus Treasury Prime Cash Management 666 Old Country Rd. Garden City, NY 11530 718/895-1650 800/346-3621	1988	Dreyfus Corporation	$229.2 Mil	$10.0 Mil/ 0	n	Local Rep
Dreyfus U.S. Guaranteed Money Market Account, L.P. 666 Old Country Rd. Garden City, NY 11530 718/895-1347 800/648-9048	1987	Dreyfus Corporation	$124.0 Mil	$2,500/ 100	n	Fund
Dreyfus Worldwide Dollar Money Market Fund, Inc. 666 Old Country Rd. Garden City, NY 11530 718/895-1206 800/645-6561	1989	Dreyfus Corporation	$3.1 Bil	$2,500/ 100	N/A	Local Rep
Eaton Vance Cash Management Fund 24 Federal St. Boston, MA 02110 617/482-8260 800/225-6265	1974	Eaton Vance Management, Inc.	$223.1 Mil	$1,000/ 50	n	Local Rep
Eaton Vance Liquid Assets Trust 24 Federal St. Boston, MA 02110 617/482-8260 800/225-6265	1987	Eaton Vance Management, Inc.	$11.3 Mil	$1,000/ 50	t	Local Rep
EBI Funds, Inc. *EBI Cash Management Fund* 1315 Peachtree St., NE Ste. 500 Atlanta, GA 30309 404/892-0666 800/554-1156	1984	INVESCO Capital Management, Inc.	N/A	$10,000/ 1,000	n	Local Rep
Edward D. Jones & Co. Daily Passport Cash Trust Federated Investors Twr. Pittsburgh, PA 15222-3779 412/288-1900 314/851-2000	1980	Passport Research, Ltd.	$1.9 Bil	$1,000/ 1,000	n	Local Rep

*Key: i=initial sales charge   r=redemption fee or contingent deferred sales charge(CDSC)
t=12b-1 fee and either CDSC or redemption fee   p=12b-1 fee   n=none of the preceding fees   N/A=not available

Money Market

Fund	Year Began	Investment Adviser	9/30/89 Assets	Minimum Initial and Subsequent Investment	Fees*	Where to Buy Shares
Equitec Siebel Fund Group *Equitec Siebel Cash Equivalent Fund Series* 7677 Oakport St. P.O. Box 2470 Oakland, CA 94614 415/430-9900 800/869-8900	1986	Siebel Capital Management, Inc.	$31.5 Mil (e)	$1,000/ 0	t	Local Rep
Equitec Siebel Fund Group II *Money Market Fund Series* 7677 Oakport St. P.O. Box 2470 Oakland, CA 94614 415/430-9900 800/869-8900	1989	Siebel Capital Management, Inc.	N/A	$1,000/ 0	n	Local Rep
Evergreen Money Market Trust 2500 Westchester Ave. Purchase, NY 10577 914/694-2020 800/235-0064	1987	Evergreen Asset Management Corporation	$368.5 Mil (e)	$2,000/ 0	n	Fund
FBL Money Market Fund, Inc. 5400 University Ave. W. Des Moines, IA 50265 515/225-5400 800/247-4170 800/422-3175 IA Only	1981	FBL Investment Advisory Services, Inc.	$57.6 Mil	$500/ 0	n	Local Rep
FBL Series Fund, Inc. *Money Market Portfolio* 5400 University Ave. W. Des Moines, IA 50265 515/225-5400 800/247-4170 800/422-3175 IA Only	1987	FBL Investment Advisory Services, Inc.	$3.0 Mil	$250/ 0	t	Local Rep
Federated Master Trust Federated Investors Twr. Pittsburgh, PA 15222-3779 412/288-1900 800/245-5000	1978	Federated Research	$2.3 Bil	$25,000/ 0	n	Local Rep
Federated Short-Term U.S. Government Trust Federated Investors Twr. Pittsburgh, PA 15222-3779 412/288-1900 800/245-5000	1987	Federated Research	$972.6 Mil	$25,000/ 0	n	Local Rep

*Key: i=initial sales charge   r=redemption fee or contingent deferred sales charge(CDSC) t=12b-1 fee and either CDSC or redemption fee   p=12b-1 fee   n=none of the preceding fees   N/A=not available

341

Money Market

Fund	Year Began	Investment Adviser	9/30/89 Assets	Minimum Initial and Subsequent Investment	Fees*	Where to Buy Shares
FFB Funds Trust *FFB Cash Management Fund* 230 Park Ave. 12th Fl. New York, NY 10169 212/309-8400 800/845-8406	1986	First Fidelity Bank, N.A.	$450.2 Mil	$1,000/ 100	p	Local Rep
FFB Funds Trust *FFB U.S. Government Fund* 230 Park Ave. 12th Fl. New York, NY 10169 212/309-8400 800/845-8406	1986	First Fidelity Bank, N.A.	$275.6 Mil	$1,000/ 100	p	Local Rep
FFB Funds Trust *FFB U.S. Treasury Fund* 230 Park Ave. 12th Fl. New York, NY 10169 212/309-8400 800/845-8406	1986	First Fidelity Bank, N.A.	$122.3 Mil	$1,000/ 100	p	Local Rep
Fidelity Cash Reserves 82 Devonshire St. Boston, MA 02109 617/570-7000 800/544-6666	1979	Fidelity Management & Research Company	$10.7 Bil	$1,000/ 250	n	Fund
Fidelity Charles Street Trust *Fidelity U.S. Government Reserves* 82 Devonshire St. Boston, MA 02109 617/570-7000 800/544-6666	1981	Fidelity Management & Research Company	$1.5 Bil	$1,000/ 250	n	Fund
Fidelity Daily Income Trust 82 Devonshire St. Boston, MA 02109 617/570-7000 800/544-6666	1974	Fidelity Management & Research Company	$2.8 Bil	$5,000/ 500	n	Fund
Fidelity Institutional Cash Portfolios *Domestic Money Market Portfolio* 82 Devonshire St. Boston, MA 02109 617/570-7000 800/544-6666	1988	Fidelity Management & Research Company	N/A	$50.0 Mil/ 0	N/A	Local Rep

*Key: i=initial sales charge   r=redemption fee or contingent deferred sales charge(CDSC)
t=12b-1 fee and either CDSC or redemption fee   p=12b-1 fee   n=none of the preceding fees   N/A=not available

342

Money Market

Fund	Year Began	Investment Adviser	9/30/89 Assets	Minimum Initial and Subsequent Investment	Fees*	Where to Buy Shares
Fidelity Institutional Cash Portfolios *Money Market Portfolio* 82 Devonshire St. Boston, MA 02109 617/570-7000 800/544-6666	1985	Fidelity Management & Research Company	$3.3 Bil	$50.0 Mil/ 0	n	Local Rep
Fidelity Institutional Cash Portfolios *U.S. Government Portfolio* 82 Devonshire St. Boston, MA 02109 617/570-7000 800/544-6666	1985	Fidelity Management & Research Company	$2.3 Bil	$50.0 Mil/ 0	n	Local Rep
Fidelity Institutional Cash Portfolios *U.S. Treasury Portfolio* 82 Devonshire St. Boston, MA 02109 617/570-7000 800/544-6666	1985	Fidelity Management & Research Company	$1.2 Bil	$50.0 Mil/ 0	n	Local Rep
Fidelity Institutional Cash Portfolios *U.S. Treasury Portfolio II* 82 Devonshire St. Boston, MA 02109 617/570-7000 800/544-6666	1985	Fidelity Management & Research Company	$924.0 Mil	$50.0 Mil/ 0	n	Local Rep
Fidelity Money Market Trust *Domestic Money Market Portfolio* 82 Devonshire St. Boston, MA 02109 617/570-7000 800/343-9184	1979	Fidelity Management & Research Company	$1.2 Bil	$100,000/ 0	n	Local Rep
Fidelity Money Market Trust *Retirement Government Money Market Portfolio* 82 Devonshire St. Boston, MA 02109 617/570-7000 800/343-9184	1988	Fidelity Management & Research Company	N/A	$100,000/ 0	N/A	Local Rep
Fidelity Money Market Trust *Retirement Money Market Portfolio* 82 Devonshire St. Boston, MA 02109 617/570-7000 800/343-9184	1988	Fidelity Management & Research Company	N/A	$100,000/ 0	N/A	Local Rep

*Key: i=initial sales charge   r=redemption fee or contingent deferred sales charge(CDSC)
t=12b-1 fee and either CDSC or redemption fee   p=12b-1 fee   n=none of the preceding fees   N/A=not available

Money Market

Fund	Year Began	Investment Adviser	9/30/89 Assets	Minimum Initial and Subsequent Investment	Fees*	Where to Buy Shares
Fidelity Money Market Trust *U.S. Government Portfolio* 82 Devonshire St. Boston, MA 02109 617/570-7000 800/343-9184	1979	Fidelity Management & Research Company	$511.8 Mil	$100,000/ 0	n	Local Rep
Fidelity Money Market Trust *U.S. Treasury Portfolio* 82 Devonshire St. Boston, MA 02109 617/570-7000 800/343-9184	1981	Fidelity Management & Research Company	$314.4 Mil	$100,000/ 0	n	Local Rep
Fidelity Select Portfolios *Money Market Portfolio* 82 Devonshire St. Boston, MA 02109 617/570-7000 800/544-6666	1985	Fidelity Management & Research Company	$664.0 Mil	$1,000/ 250	i, r	Fund
Fidelity Summer Street Trust *Spartan Money Market Fund* 82 Devonshire St. Boston, MA 02109 617/570-7000 800/544-6666	1989	Fidelity Management & Research Company	$4.3 Bil	$20,000/ 1,000	n	Fund
Fidelity U.S. Treasury Money Market Fund, L.P. 82 Devonshire St. Boston, MA 02109 617/570-7000 800/544-6666	1988	Fidelity Management & Research Company	$107.9 Mil	$2,500/ 250	n	Fund
Financial Horizons Investment Trust *Cash Reserve Fund* One Nationwide Plaza P.O. Box 182008 Columbus, OH 43218 800/533-5622	1988	Nationwide Financial Services, Inc.	$2.1 Mil	$1,000/ 100	t	Local Rep
Financial Reserves Fund 82 Devonshire St. Boston, MA 02109 617/570-7000 800/343-5409	1983	Fidelity Management & Research Company	$462.5 Mil	$0/ 0	n	Local Rep

*Key: i=initial sales charge   r=redemption fee or contingent deferred sales charge(CDSC)
     t=12b-1 fee and either CDSC or redemption fee   p=12b-1 fee   n=none of the preceding fees   N/A=not available

Money Market

Fund	Year Began	Investment Adviser	9/30/89 Assets	Minimum Initial and Subsequent Investment	Fees*	Where to Buy Shares
First Investors Cash Management Fund, Inc. 120 Wall St. New York, NY 10005 212/208-6000	1978	First Investors Management Company, Inc.	$299.9 Mil	$1,000/ 100	n	Local Rep
First Investors Life Series Fund *Cash Management Series* 120 Wall St. New York, NY 10005 212/208-6000	1986	First Investors Management Company, Inc.	$2.0 Mil	Not Applicable	n	Insur
First Prairie Money Market Fund *Government Series* 666 Old Country Rd. 4th Fl. Garden City, NY 11530 516/296-3300 800/821-1185	1987	First National Bank of Chicago	$249.8 Mil	$1,000/ 100	p	Local Rep
First Prairie Money Market Fund *Money Market Series* 666 Old Country Rd. 4th Fl. Garden City, NY 11530 516/296-3300 800/821-1185	1986	First National Bank of Chicago	$305.7 Mil	$1,000/ 100	p	Local Rep
First Variable Rate Fund for Government Income 1700 Pennsylvania Ave., NW Washington, DC 20006 301/951-4820 800/368-2745	1976	Calvert Asset Management Company, Inc.	$363.2 Mil	$2,000/ 250	n	Fund
Flex-Funds *Money Market Fund (The)* 6000 Memorial Dr. P.O. Box 7177 Dublin, OH 43017 614/766-7000 800/325-FLEX	1985	R. Meeder & Associates, Inc.	$216.1 Mil	$2,500/ 100	p	Fund
Fort Washington Money Market Fund Federated Investors Twr. Pittsburgh, PA 15222-3779 412/288-1900 800/245-3391	1982	Comerica Investment Advisers, Inc. Federated Management	$75.8 Mil	$5,000/ 100	n	Local Rep

*Key: i=initial sales charge   r=redemption fee or contingent deferred sales charge(CDSC)
t=12b-1 fee and either CDSC or redemption fee   p=12b-1 fee   n=none of the preceding fees   N/A=not available

Money Market

Fund	Year Began	Investment Adviser	9/30/89 Assets	Minimum Initial and Subsequent Investment	Fees*	Where to Buy Shares
Franklin Federal Money Fund 777 Mariners Island Blvd. San Mateo, CA 94404 415/570-3000 800/632-2180 800/632-2350	1980	Franklin Advisers, Inc.	$139.4 Mil	$500/ 25	n	Fund
Franklin Money Fund 777 Mariners Island Blvd. San Mateo, CA 94404 415/570-3000 800/632-2180 800/632-2350	1976	Franklin Advisers, Inc.	$1.5 Bil	$500/ 25	n	Fund
Frank Russell Investment Company *Money Market* 909 A St. Tacoma, WA 98402 206/627-7001 800/972-0700	1981	Frank Russell Investment Management Company	$13.9 Mil	$0/ 0	n	Local Rep
Frank Russell Investment Company *U.S. Government Money Market* 909 A St. Tacoma, WA 98402 206/627-7001 800/972-0700	1985	Frank Russell Investment Management Company	$85.5 Mil	$0/ 0	n	Local Rep
Freedom Fund *Government Money Market Portfolio* 82 Devonshire St. Boston, MA 02109 617/570-7000 800/343-5409	1987	Key Trust Company	$34.3 Mil (e)	$1,000/ 0	n	Local Rep
Freedom Fund *Money Market Portfolio* 82 Devonshire St. Boston, MA 02109 617/570-7000 800/343-5409	1982	Key Trust Company	$216.5 Mil (e)	$1,000/ 0	n	Local Rep
Freedom Investment Trust *Freedom Money Market Fund* One Beacon St. Boston, MA 02108 617/523-3170 800/225-6258 800/392-6037 MA Only	1987	Freedom Capital Management Corporation	$5.9 Mil	$1,000/ 100	n	Local Rep

*Key: i=initial sales charge   r=redemption fee or contingent deferred sales charge(CDSC)
t=12b-1 fee and either CDSC or redemption fee   p=12b-1 fee   n=none of the preceding fees   N/A=not available

Money Market

Fund	Year Began	Investment Adviser	9/30/89 Assets	Minimum Initial and Subsequent Investment	Fees*	Where to Buy Shares
Freedom Mutual Fund *Freedom Cash Management Fund* One Beacon St. Boston, MA 02108 617/523-3170 800/225-6258 800/392-6037 MA Only	1981	Freedom Capital Management Corporation	$1.1 Bil	$1,000/ 100	n	Local Rep
Freedom Mutual Fund *Freedom Government Securities Fund* One Beacon St. Boston, MA 02108 617/523-3170 800/225-6258 800/392-6037 MA Only	1982	Freedom Capital Management Corporation	$179.5 Mil	$1,000/ 100	n	Local Rep
Fund Source *Government Trust* 230 Park Ave. 12th Fl. New York, NY 10169 212/309-8400 800/845-8406	1988	San Diego Financial Capital Management, Inc.	$162.7 Mil	$1,000/ 100	n	Local Rep
Fund Source *Money Trust* 230 Park Ave. 12th Fl. New York, NY 10169 212/309-8400 800/845-8406	1985	Republic National Bank of New York	$117.9 Mil	$1,000/ 0	n	Local Rep
Fund Source *Washington Money Trust* 230 Park Ave. 12th Fl. New York, NY 10169 212/309-8400 800/845-8406	1987	National Bank of Washington	$150.8 Mil	$1,000/ 100	p	Local Rep
Galaxy Fund *Government Fund* 3512 Silverside Rd. The Commons, No. 6 Wilmington, DE 19810 302/478-6945 800/441-7379	1986	Norstar Investment Advisory Services, Inc.	$332.5 Mil	$0/ 0	p	Local Rep
Galaxy Fund *Money Market Fund* 3512 Silverside Rd. The Commons, No. 6 Wilmington, DE 19810 302/478-6945 800/441-7379	1986	Norstar Investment Advisory Services, Inc.	$400.1 Mil	$0/ 0	p	Local Rep

*Key: i=initial sales charge   r=redemption fee or contingent deferred sales charge(CDSC)
t=12b-1 fee and either CDSC or redemption fee   p=12b-1 fee   n=none of the preceding fees   N/A=not available

Money Market

Fund	Year Began	Investment Adviser	9/30/89 Assets	Minimum Initial and Subsequent Investment	Fees*	Where to Buy Shares
General Government Securities Money Market Fund, Inc. 666 Old Country Rd. Garden City, NY 11530 718/895-1396 800/242-8671	1983	Dreyfus Corporation	$303.1 Mil	$2,500/ 100	p	Fund
General Money Market Fund, Inc. 666 Old Country Rd. Garden City, NY 11530 718/895-1396 800/242-8671	1982	Dreyfus Corporation	$817.5 Mil	$2,500/ 100	p	Fund
Government Investors Trust 1655 Fort Myer Dr. Arlington, VA 22209 703/528-6500 800/336-3063	1979	Bankers Finance Investment Management Corp.	$169.7 Mil	$1,000/ 0	n	Fund
Government Securities Cash Fund GEICO Plaza Washington, DC 20076 301/986-2200 800/832-6232	1982	GEICO Investment Services Company	$15.2 Mil	$1,000/ 100	n	Fund
Gradison Cash Reserves Trust 580 Walnut St. Cincinnati, OH 45202-3198 513/579-5700 800/869-5999	1976	Gradison & Company, Inc.	$613.4 Mil	$1,000/ 50	p	Local Rep
Gradison U.S. Government Trust 580 Walnut St. Cincinnati, OH 45202-3198 513/579-5700 800/869-5999	1982	Gradison & Company, Inc.	$31.5 Mil	$1,000/ 50	p	Local Rep
G.T. Money Market Series *G.T. Money Market Fund* 50 California St. 27th Fl. San Francisco, CA 94111 415/392-6181 800/824-1580	1985	G.T. Capital Management Inc.	$13.3 Mil (e)	$500/ 100	n	Local Rep

*Key: i=initial sales charge   r=redemption fee or contingent deferred sales charge(CDSC)
t=12b-1 fee and either CDSC or redemption fee   p=12b-1 fee   n=none of the preceding fees   N/A=not available

Money Market

Fund	Year Began	Investment Adviser	9/30/89 Assets	Minimum Initial and Subsequent Investment	Fees*	Where to Buy Shares
Guardian Cash Management Trust 201 Park Ave. South New York, NY 10003 212/598-8259 800/221-3253	1982	Guardian Investor Services Corporation	$30.8 Mil	$1,000/ 100	n	Fund
GW Sierra Trust Funds *GW U.S. Government Money Market Fund* 888 S. Figueroa St. 11th Fl. Los Angeles, CA 90017-0970 213/488-2200 800/331-3426, 800/221-9876 CA ONLY	1989	Great Western Financial Advisors Corp.	N/A	$1,000/ 100	p	Local Rep
Harbor Fund *Harbor Money Market Fund* One SeaGate Toledo, OH 43666 419/247-2477 800/422-1050	1987	Harbor Capital Advisors, Inc.	$43.4 Mil	$2,000/ 500	n	Fund
Hartford Money Market Fund, Inc. 200 Hopmeadow St. P.O. Box 2999 Hartford, CT 06104-2999 203/843-8255 800/343-1250 800/243-3337 MA Only	1982	Hartford Investment Management Company, Inc.	$19.7 Mil	$500/ 100	n	Fund
Hartford U.S. Government Money Market Fund, Inc. 200 Hopmeadow St. P.O. Box 2999 Hartford, CT 06104-2999 203/843-8245 800/227-1371	1983	Hartford Investment Management Company, Inc.	$7.5 Mil	Not Applicable	n	Insur
Heartland Group *Heartland Money Market Fund* 790 N. Milwaukee St. Milwaukee, WI 53202 414/347-7276 800/432-7856	1988	Heartland Advisors, Inc.	N/A	$1,000/ 100	p	Local Rep
Helmsman Fund *Prime Obligations Portfolio* 1900 E. Dublin-Granville Rd. Columbus, OH 43229 614/899-4600 800/338-4385	1989	Bank One, Indianapolis, N.A. Bank One, Milwaukee, N.A.	N/A	$1,000/ 0	N/A	Fund

*Key: i=initial sales charge   r=redemption fee or contingent deferred sales charge(CDSC)
        t=12b-1 fee and either CDSC or redemption fee   p=12b-1 fee   n=none of the preceding fees   N/A=not available

Money Market

Fund	Year Began	Investment Adviser	9/30/89 Assets	Minimum Initial and Subsequent Investment	Fees*	Where to Buy Shares
Heritage Cash Trust 880 Carillon Pkwy. St. Petersburg, FL 33716 813/573-3800	1985	Heritage Asset Management, Inc.	$510.2 Mil	$2,500/ 100	p	Local Rep
Highmark Group *Diversified Obligations Fund* 1900 E. Dublin-Granville Rd. Columbus, OH 43229 614/899-4600 800/338-4385	1987	Merus Capital Management	N/A	$1,000/ 100	N/A	Fund
Highmark Group *U.S. Government Obligations Fund* 1900 E. Dublin-Granville Rd. Columbus, OH 43229 614/899-4600 800/338-4385	1987	Merus Capital Management	N/A	$1,000/ 100	N/A	Fund
Highmark Group *U.S. Treasury Obligations Fund* 1900 E. Dublin-Granville Rd. Columbus, OH 43229 614/899-4600 800/338-4385	1987	Merus Capital Management	N/A	$1,000/ 100	N/A	Fund
High Yield Cash Trust Federated Investors Twr. Pittsburgh, PA 15222-3779 412/288-1900 800/245-5000	1982	Federated Research	$106.7 Mil	$25,000/ 0	n	Local Rep
Hilliard-Lyons Government Fund Inc. Hilliard-Lyons Ctr. P.O. Box 32760 Louisville, KY 40232-2760 502/588-8400 800/444-1854	1980	J.J.B. Hilliard, W.L. Lyons, Inc.	$115.7 Mil	$3,000/ 500	n	Local Rep
Home Group Trust *Home Cash Reserves* 59 Maiden Lane 21st Fl. New York, NY 10038 212/530-6016 800/729-3863	1988	Home Capital Services, Inc.	$619.9 Mil	$1,000/ 100	p	Local Rep

*Key: i=initial sales charge   r=redemption fee or contingent deferred sales charge(CDSC)
t=12b-1 fee and either CDSC or redemption fee   p=12b-1 fee   n=none of the preceding fees   N/A=not available

Money Market

Fund	Year Began	Investment Adviser	9/30/89 Assets	Minimum Initial and Subsequent Investment	Fees*	Where to Buy Shares
Home Group Trust *Home Government Reserves* 59 Maiden Lane 21st Fl. New York, NY 10038 212/530-6016 800/729-3863	1988	Home Capital Services, Inc.	$64.3 Mil	$1,000/ 100	p	Local Rep
Home Life Liquid Fund, Inc. One Centennial Plaza Piscataway, NJ 08854 212/428-2000	1983	Home Life Insurance Company	$13.0 Mil	Not Applicable	n	Insur
Horace Mann Short-Term Investment Fund, Inc. P.O. Box 4657 Springfield, IL 62708-4657 217/789-2500	1983	CIGNA Investments, Inc.	N/A	Not Applicable	r	Insur
Horizon Funds *Horizon Prime Fund* 156 W. 56th St. Ste. 1902 New York, NY 10019 212/492-1600 800/367-6075	1987	Security Pacific National Bank	$625.9 Mil	$500,000/ 0	n	Local Rep
Horizon Funds *Horizon Treasury Fund* 156 W. 56th St. Ste. 1902 New York, NY 10019 212/492-1600 800/367-6075	1987	Security Pacific National Bank	$326.6 Mil	$500,000/ 0	n	Local Rep
HVA Money Market Fund, Inc. 200 Hopmeadow St. P.O. Box 2999 Hartford, CT 06104-2999 203/843-8245 800/227-1371	1976	Hartford Investment Management Company, Inc.	$130.4 Mil	Not Applicable	n	Insur
IDS Cash Management Fund, Inc. IDS Tower 10 Minneapolis, MN 55440 612/372-3131 800/328-8300	1975	IDS Financial Corporation	$1.5 Bil	$2,000/ 100	p	Local Rep

*Key: i=initial sales charge   r=redemption fee or contingent deferred sales charge(CDSC)
t=12b-1 fee and either CDSC or redemption fee   p=12b-1 fee   n=none of the preceding fees   N/A=not available

Money Market

Fund	Year Began	Investment Adviser	9/30/89 Assets	Minimum Initial and Subsequent Investment	Fees*	Where to Buy Shares
IDS Life Moneyshare Fund, Inc. IDS Tower 10 Minneapolis, MN 55440 612/372-3131 800/328-8300	1981	IDS Financial Corporation	$171.7 Mil	Not Applicable	r	Insur
IDS Planned Investment Account IDS Tower 10 Minneapolis, MN 55440 612/372-3131 800/328-8300	1989	IDS Financial Corporation	$8.3 Mil	$2,000/ 100	p	Local Rep
Income Portfolios *State and Local Asset Management: Government Bond Portfolio* 82 Devonshire St. Boston, MA 02109 617/570-7000 800/544-6666	1988	Fidelity Management & Research Company	N/A	$0/ 0	N/A	Fund
Income Portfolios *State and Local Asset Management: Government Money Market Portfolio* 82 Devonshire St. Boston, MA 02109 617/570-7000 800/544-6666	1987	Fidelity Management & Research Company	$691.9 Mil	$0/ 0	n	Fund
Income Portfolios *State and Local Asset Management: The California Portfolio* 82 Devonshire St. Boston, MA 02109 617/570-7000 800/544-6666	1987	Fidelity Management & Research Company	$115.5 Mil	$0/ 0	n	Fund
Industrial Series Trust *Mackenzie Cash Management Fund* 1200 N. Federal Hwy. #200 Boca Raton, FL 33432 407/393-8900 800/456-5111	1985	Mackenzie Investment Management Inc.	$6.8 Mil (e)	$250/ 50	p	Local Rep
Institutional Fiduciary Trust *Franklin Government Investors Money Market Portfolio* 777 Mariners Island Blvd. San Mateo, CA 94404 415/570-3000, 800/632-2180, 800/632-2350	1988	Franklin Advisers, Inc.	$69.4 Mil	$1,000/ 0	n	Local Rep

*Key: i=initial sales charge   r=redemption fee or contingent deferred sales charge(CDSC)
     t=12b-1 fee and either CDSC or redemption fee   p=12b-1 fee   n=none of the preceding fees   N/A=not available

Money Market

Fund	Year Began	Investment Adviser	9/30/89 Assets	Minimum Initial and Subsequent Investment	Fees*	Where to Buy Shares
Institutional Fiduciary Trust *Franklin U.S. Government Securities Money Market Portfolio* 777 Mariners Island Blvd. San Mateo, CA 94404 415/570-3000, 800/632-2180, 800/632-2350	1988	Franklin Advisers, Inc.	$98.0 Mil	$1,000/0	n	Local Rep
Institutional Fiduciary Trust *Money Market Portfolio* 777 Mariners Island Blvd. San Mateo, CA 94404 415/570-3000 800/632-2180 800/632-2350	1985	Franklin Advisers, Inc.	$128.6 Mil	$50,000/0	p	Local Rep
Integrated Cash Fund, Inc. 10 Union Square East New York, NY 10003 212/353-7000 800/858-8850	1987	Integrated Resources Asset Management Corp.	$63.1 Mil	$1,000/100	p	Local Rep
Integrated Money Market Securities, Inc. 10 Union Square East New York, NY 10003 212/353-7000 800/858-8850	1984	Integrated Resources Asset Management Corp.	$447.7 Mil	$1,000/100	p	Local Rep
Integrated Resources Series Trust *Money Market Portfolio* One Bridge Plaza Fort Lee, NJ 07024 201/461-0606 800/821-5100	1984	Integrated Resources Asset Management Corp.	$220.2 Mil	Not Applicable	n	Insur
International Cash Portfolios *Global Cash Portfolio* 251 S. Lake Ave. Ste. 600 Pasadena, CA 91101 213/681-3700 800/826-0188	1986	Bankers Trust Investment Management Limited	$87.0 Mil	$2,500/1,000	i, p	Local Rep
International Cash Portfolios *U.S. CASH Portfolio* 251 S. Lake Ave. Ste. 600 Pasadena, CA 91101 213/681-3700 800/826-0188	1986	Bankers Trust Investment Management Limited	$15.4 Mil	$2,500/1,000	n	Local Rep

*Key: i=initial sales charge   r=redemption fee or contingent deferred sales charge(CDSC)
t=12b-1 fee and either CDSC or redemption fee   p=12b-1 fee   n=none of the preceding fees   N/A=not available

Money Market

Fund	Year Began	Investment Adviser	9/30/89 Assets	Minimum Initial and Subsequent Investment	Fees*	Where to Buy Shares
INVESCO Treasurers Series Trust *Money Reserve Fund* 1315 Peachtree St., NE Ste. 500 Atlanta, GA 30309 404/892-0666 800/554-1156	1988	INVESCO Capital Management, Inc.	N/A	$1.0 Mil/ 5,000	N/A	Local Rep
Investment Portfolios *Money Market Portfolio* 120 S. LaSalle St. Chicago, IL 60603 312/781-1121 800/621-1148	1984	Kemper Financial Services, Inc.	$307.7 Mil	$250/ 50	t	Local Rep
Investment Trust of Boston *Liquid Reserves Portfolio* 399 Boylston St. 9th Fl. Boston, MA 02116 800/888-4823	1989	Back Bay Advisors, Inc.	$3.4 Mil	$1,000/ 100	n	Local Rep
Investors Cash Reserve Fund, Inc. 1100 Milan St., Ste. 3500 P.O. Box 3167 Houston, TX 77253-3167 713/750-8000 800/262-6631	1980	Capstone Asset Management Company	$20.9 Mil	$1,000/ 0	n	Local Rep
Ivy Fund *Ivy Money Market Fund* 40 Industrial Park Rd. Hingham, MA 02043 617/749-1416 800/235-3322	1987	Ivy Management, Inc.	$17.5 Mil	$1,000/ 0	p	Fund
John Hancock Cash Management Trust 101 Huntington Ave. Boston, MA 02199-7603 617/375-1500 800/225-5291	1979	John Hancock Advisers, Inc.	$274.1 Mil	$1,000/ 25	p	Local Rep
Kemper Money Market Fund *Government Securities Portfolio* 120 S. LaSalle St. Ste. 1120 Chicago, IL 60603 312/781-1121 800/621-1048	1981	Kemper Financial Services, Inc.	$558.3 Mil	$1,000/ 100	n	Fund

*Key: i=initial sales charge   r=redemption fee or contingent deferred sales charge(CDSC)
t=12b-1 fee and either CDSC or redemption fee   p=12b-1 fee   n=none of the preceding fees   N/A=not available

354

Money Market

Fund	Year Began	Investment Adviser	9/30/89 Assets	Minimum Initial and Subsequent Investment	Fees*	Where to Buy Shares
Kemper Money Market Fund *Money Market Portfolio* 120 S. LaSalle St. Ste. 1120 Chicago, IL 60603 312/781-1121 800/621-1048	1974	Kemper Financial Services, Inc.	$7.0 Bil	$1,000/ 100	n	Fund
Keystone America Money Market Fund 99 High St. Boston, MA 02110 617/338-3200 800/343-2898 800/225-1587	1987	Keystone Custodian Funds, Inc.	$12.9 Mil	$1,000/ 0	p	Local Rep
Keystone Liquid Trust 99 High St. Boston, MA 02110 617/338-3200 800/343-2898 800/225-1587	1975	Keystone Custodian Funds, Inc.	$498.6 Mil	$1,000/ 100	p	Local Rep
Kidder, Peabody Exchange Money Market Fund 20 Exchange Place New York, NY 10005 212/510-5552	1986	Webster Management Corporation	$13.9 Mil	$1,500/ 500	t	Local Rep
Kidder, Peabody Government Money Fund, Inc. 20 Exchange Place New York, NY 10005 212/510-5552	1983	Webster Management Corporation	$372.5 Mil	$1,500/ 500	n	Local Rep
Kidder, Peabody Premium Account Fund 20 Exchange Place New York, NY 10005 212/510-5552	1982	Webster Management Corporation	$1.1 Bil	$25,000/ 0	n	Local Rep
LBVIP Series Fund, Inc. *Money Market Series* 625 Fourth Ave. South Minneapolis, MN 55415 612/339-8091 800/328-4552 800/752-4208 MN Only	1988	Lutheran Brotherhood Research Corp.	$8.8 Mil	Not Applicable	n	Insur

*Key: i=initial sales charge   r=redemption fee or contingent deferred sales charge(CDSC)
t=12b-1 fee and either CDSC or redemption fee   p=12b-1 fee   n=none of the preceding fees   N/A=not available

Money Market

Fund	Year Began	Investment Adviser	9/30/89 Assets	Minimum Initial and Subsequent Investment	Fees*	Where to Buy Shares
Legg Mason Cash Reserve Trust 111 S. Calvert St. P.O. Box 1476 Baltimore, MD 21203-1476 30l/539-3400 800/822-5544 800/492-7777 MD Only	1979	Western Asset Management Company	$751.7 Mil	$1,000/ 500	n	Local Rep
Legg Mason Income Trust *Legg Mason U.S. Government Money Market Portfolio* 111 S. Calvert St. P.O. Box 1476 Baltimore, MD 21203-1476 30l/539-3400 800/822-5544, 800/492-7777 MD Only	1989	Western Asset Management Company	$87.2 Mil	$1,000/ 500	n	Local Rep
Lexington Government Securities Money Market Fund, Inc. Park 80 West, Plaza Two P.O. Box 1515 Saddle Brook, NJ 07662 201/845-7300 800/526-0056	1981	Lexington Management Corporation	$18.2 Mil	$1,000/ 50	n	Fund
Lexington Money Market Trust Park 80 West, Plaza Two P.O. Box 1515 Saddle Brook, NJ 07662 201/845-7300 800/526-0056	1976	Lexington Management Corporation	$190.7 Mil	$1,000/ 50	n	Fund
Liberty U.S. Government Money Market Trust Federated Investors Twr. Liberty Ctr. Pittsburgh, PA 15222-3779 412/288-1900 800/245-0242	1980	Federated Advisers	$1.4 Bil	$500/ 100	n	Fund
Life of Virginia Series Fund, Inc. *Money Market Portfolio* 6610 W. Broad St. Richmond, VA 23230 804/281-6000 800/822-6000	1985	AON Advisors, Inc.	$3.2 Mil (e)	Not Applicable	n	Insur
Liquid Capital Income Trust 1100 The Halle Bldg. 1228 Euclid Ave. Cleveland, OH 44115-1831 216/781-4440 800/321-2322	1974	Carnegie Capital Management Company	$1.2 Bil	$1,000/ 250	n	Local Rep

*Key: i=initial sales charge   r=redemption fee or contingent deferred sales charge(CDSC)
t=12b-1 fee and either CDSC or redemption fee   p=12b-1 fee   n=none of the preceding fees   N/A=not available

Money Market

Fund	Year Began	Investment Adviser	9/30/89 Assets	Minimum Initial and Subsequent Investment	Fees*	Where to Buy Shares
Liquid Cash Trust Federated Investors Twr. Pittsburgh, PA 15222-3779 412/288-1900 800/245-5000	1980	Federated Research Corp.	$582.7 Mil	$25,000/ 0	n	Local Rep
Liquid Green Trust 429 N. Pennsylvania St. Indianapolis, IN 46204-1897 317/634-3300 800/862-7283	1980	Unified Management Corporation	$444.9 Mil	$1,000/ 0	n	Fund
Lord Abbett Cash Reserve Fund, Inc. The General Motors Bldg. 767 Fifth Ave. New York, NY 10153 212/848-1800 800/223-4224	1979	Lord, Abbett & Co.	$210.3 Mil	$1,000/ 0	n	Fund
Lutheran Brotherhood Money Market Fund 625 Fourth Ave. South Minneapolis, MN 55415 612/339-8091 800/328-4552 800/752-4208 MN Only	1979	Lutheran Brotherhood Research Corp.	$393.8 Mil	$1,500/ 50	n	Local Rep
MacKay-Shields MainStay Series Fund *MainStay Money Market Fund* 51 Madison Ave. New York, NY 10010 212/576-7000 800/522-4202	1986	MacKay-Shields Financial Corporation	$179.3 Mil	$1,000/ 50	n	Local Rep
Management of Managers Group of Funds *Money Market Fund* 200 Connecticut Ave. 8th Fl. Norwalk, CT 06854 203/855-2200	1984	Evaluation Associates Investment Management Co.	N/A	$0/ 0	n	Local Rep
ManuLife Series Fund, Inc. *Money Market Fund* 200 Bloor St. East N. Tower 5 Toronto, Ont., Canada M4W 1E5 416/926-6700	1984	Manufacturers Adviser Corporation	$5.9 Mil (e)	Not Applicable	n	Insur

*Key: i=initial sales charge   r=redemption fee or contingent deferred sales charge(CDSC)
t=12b-1 fee and either CDSC or redemption fee   p=12b-1 fee   n=none of the preceding fees   N/A=not available

Money Market

Fund	Year Began	Investment Adviser	9/30/89 Assets	Minimum Initial and Subsequent Investment	Fees*	Where to Buy Shares
MAP-Government Fund, Inc. 520 Broad St. Newark, NJ 07102 401/751-8600 800/333-4726	1982	Mutual Benefit Financial Service Company	$36.8 Mil	$1,000/ 50	n	Local Rep
Mariner Funds Trust *Mariner Cash Management Fund* 600 W. Hillsboro Blvd. Ste. 300 Deerfield Beach, FL 33441 305/421-8878 800/634-2536	1982	Marinvest Inc.	$917.3 Mil	$1,000/ 250	p	Local Rep
Mariner Funds Trust *Mariner Government Fund* 600 W. Hillsboro Blvd. Ste. 300 Deerfield Beach, FL 33441 305/421-8878 800/634-2536	1982	Marinvest Inc.	$222.1 Mil	$1,000/ 250	p	Local Rep
Mariner Funds Trust *Mariner U.S. Treasury Fund* 600 W. Hillsboro Blvd. Ste. 300 Deerfield Beach, FL 33441 305/421-8878 800/634-2536	1983	Marinvest Inc.	$91.3 Mil	$1,000/ 250	p	Local Rep
Marketmaster Money Market Trust 3512 Silverside Rd. The Commons, No. 6 Wilmington, DE 19810 302/478-6945 800/441-7379	1987	Sovran Bank, N.A.	$346.6 Mil	$1,000/ 0	n	Local Rep
Marketmaster Trust *Government Fund* 3512 Silverside Rd. The Commons, No. 6 Wilmington, DE 19810 302/478-6945 800/441-7379	1985	Sovran Bank, N.A.	$279.0 Mil	$1,000/ 0	p	Local Rep
Marketmaster Trust *Money Market Fund* 3512 Silverside Rd. The Commons, No. 6 Wilmington, DE 19810 302/478-6945 800/441-7379	1985	Sovran Bank, N.A.	$451.3 Mil	$1,000/ 0	p	Local Rep

*Key: i=initial sales charge   r=redemption fee or contingent deferred sales charge(CDSC)
t=12b-1 fee and either CDSC or redemption fee   p=12b-1 fee   n=none of the preceding fees   N/A=not available

Money Market

Fund	Year Began	Investment Adviser	9/30/89 Assets	Minimum Initial and Subsequent Investment	Fees*	Where to Buy Shares
Market Street Fund, Inc. *Money Market Portfolio (PM Variable Money Market Sep. Acct. II)* 1600 Market St. P.O. Box 7378 Philadelphia, PA 19101 215/636-5000	1984	Providentmutual Investment Management Company	N/A	Not Applicable	N/A	Insur
Massachusetts Cash Management Trust *Government Series* 500 Boylston St. Boston, MA 02116 617/954-5000 800/343-2829	1982	Massachusetts Financial Services Company	$49.0 Mil	$1,000/ 25	n	Local Rep
Massachusetts Cash Management Trust *Prime Series* 500 Boylston St. Boston, MA 02116 617/954-5000 800/343-2829	1975	Massachusetts Financial Services Company	$673.0 Mil	$1,000/ 25	n	Local Rep
MassMutual Integrity Funds *MassMutual Money Market Fund* 1295 State St. Springfield, MA 01111 413/788-8411 800/542-6767 800/854-9100 MA Only	1983	Massachusetts Mutual Life Insurance Company	$64.5 Mil	$100/ 25	N/A	Local Rep
Master Reserves Trust *Money Market Portfolio No. I* 99 High St. Boston, MA 02110 617/338-3200 800/343-2898 800/225-1587	1976	Keystone Custodian Funds, Inc.	$251.2 Mil	$250,000/ 0	n	Local Rep
Master Reserves Trust *Money Market Portfolio No. III* 99 High St. Boston, MA 02110 617/338-3200 800/343-2898 800/225-1587	1981	Keystone Custodian Funds, Inc.	$187.6 Mil	$75.0 Mil/ 0	n	Local Rep
Master Reserves Trust *Money Market Portfolio No. VI* 99 High St. Boston, MA 02110 617/338-3200 800/343-2898 800/225-1587	1981	Keystone Custodian Funds, Inc.	$30.2 Mil	$75.0 Mil/ 0	n	Local Rep

*Key: i=initial sales charge   r=redemption fee or contingent deferred sales charge(CDSC)
t=12b-1 fee and either CDSC or redemption fee   p=12b-1 fee   n=none of the preceding fees   N/A=not available

Money Market

Fund	Year Began	Investment Adviser	9/30/89 Assets	Minimum Initial and Subsequent Investment	Fees*	Where to Buy Shares
Master Reserves Trust *Money Market Portfolio No. XVII* 99 High St. Boston, MA 02110 617/338-3200 800/343-2898 800/225-1587	1984	Keystone Custodian Funds, Inc.	$454.4 Mil	$75.0 Mil/ 0	n	Local Rep
Master Reserves Trust *Money Market Portfolio No. XX* 99 High St. Boston, MA 02110 617/338-3200 800/343-2898 800/225-1587	1982	Keystone Custodian Funds, Inc.	N/A	$75.0 Mil/ 0	n	Local Rep
Master Reserves Trust *U.S. Government Portfolio No. I* 99 High St. Boston, MA 02110 617/338-3200 800/343-2898 800/225-1587	1980	Keystone Custodian Funds, Inc.	$146.3 Mil	$75.0 Mil/ 0	n	Local Rep
Master Reserves Trust *U.S. Government Portfolio No. III* 99 High St. Boston, MA 02110 617/338-3200 800/343-2898 800/225-1587	1981	Keystone Custodian Funds, Inc.	$298.0 Mil	$75.0 Mil/ 0	n	Local Rep
Master Reserves Trust *U.S. Government Portfolio No. VI* 99 High St. Boston, MA 02110 617/338-3200 800/343-2898 800/225-1587	1981	Keystone Custodian Funds, Inc.	$19.0 Mil	$75.0 Mil/ 0	n	Local Rep
Master Reserves Trust *U.S. Government Portfolio No. X* 99 High St. Boston, MA 02110 617/338-3200 800/343-2898 800/225-1587	1982	Keystone Custodian Funds, Inc.	N/A	$75.0 Mil/ 0	n	Local Rep
McDonald Money Market Fund, Inc. 666 Old Country Rd. Garden City, NY 11530 800/553-2240	1981	McDonald & Company Securities, Inc.	$279.7 Mil	$500/ 0	p	Local Rep

*Key: i=initial sales charge   r=redemption fee or contingent deferred sales charge(CDSC)
t=12b-1 fee and either CDSC or redemption fee   p=12b-1 fee   n=none of the preceding fees   N/A=not available

Money Market

Fund	Year Began	Investment Adviser	9/30/89 Assets	Minimum Initial and Subsequent Investment	Fees*	Where to Buy Shares
McDonald U.S. Government Money Market Fund, Inc. 666 Old Country Rd. Garden City, NY 11530 800/553-2240	1989	McDonald & Company Securities, Inc.	N/A	$0/ 0	N/A	Local Rep
Merrill Lynch Government Fund, Inc. One Financial Ctr. 15th Fl. Boston, MA 02111 617/357-1460 800/225-1576	1977	Fund Asset Management, Inc.	$1.5 Bil	$5,000/ 1,000	n	Local Rep
Merrill Lynch Institutional Fund, Inc. One Financial Ctr. 15th Fl. Boston, MA 02111 617/357-1460 800/225-1576	1974	Fund Asset Management, Inc.	$1.9 Bil	$25,000/ 1,000	n	Local Rep
Merrill Lynch Ready Assets Trust P.O. Box 9011 Princeton, NJ 08543-9011 609/282-2800 800/221-7210	1975	Merrill Lynch Asset Management Inc.	$10.7 Bil	$5,000/ 1,000	p	Local Rep
Merrill Lynch Retirement Reserves Money Fund P.O. Box 9011 Princeton, NJ 08543-9011 609/282-2800 800/221-7210	1982	Merrill Lynch Asset Management Inc.	$4.6 Bil	$0/ 0	n	Local Rep
Merrill Lynch Series Fund *Money Reserve Portfolio* P.O. Box 9011 Princeton, NJ 08543-9011 609/282-2800 800/524-4458	1981	Fund Asset Management, Inc.	$829.9 Mil	Not Applicable	n	Insur
Merrill Lynch U.S.A. Government Reserves P.O. Box 9011 Princeton, NJ 08543-9011 609/282-2800 800/221-7210	1982	Merrill Lynch Asset Management Inc.	$308.4 Mil	$5,000/ 1,000	p	Local Rep

*Key: i=initial sales charge   r=redemption fee or contingent deferred sales charge(CDSC)
t=12b-1 fee and either CDSC or redemption fee   p=12b-1 fee   n=none of the preceding fees   N/A=not available

Money Market

Fund	Year Began	Investment Adviser	9/30/89 Assets	Minimum Initial and Subsequent Investment	Fees*	Where to Buy Shares
Merrill Lynch Variable Series Funds *Reserve Assets Fund* P.O. Box 9011 Princeton, NJ 08543-9011 609/282-2800 800/524-4458	1981	Merrill Lynch Asset Management Inc.	$28.8 Mil	Not Applicable	n	Insur
MetLife-State Street Money Market Trust *MetLife-State Street Money Market Fund* One Financial Ctr. 30th Fl. Boston, MA 02111 617/348-2000, 800/882-0052	1986	MetLife-State Street Investment Services, Inc.	$80.3 Mil	$250/ 25	n	Local Rep
MFS Lifetime Investment Program *Lifetime Money Market Trust* 500 Boylston St. Boston, MA 02116 617/954-5000 800/343-2829	1986	Lifetime Advisers, Inc.	$149.0 Mil	$1,000/ 50	t	Local Rep
Midwest Income Trust *Institutional Government Fund* 700 Dixie Terminal Bldg. Cincinnati, OH 45202 513/629-2000 800/543-8721 800/582-7396 OH Only	1988	Midwest Advisory Services Inc.	$121.8 Mil	$100,000/ 5,000	n	Local Rep
Midwest Income Trust *Short Term Government Fund* 700 Dixie Terminal Bldg. Cincinnati, OH 45202 513/629-2000 800/543-8721 800/582-7396 OH Only	1974	Midwest Advisory Services Inc.	$105.0 Mil	$1,000/ 0	n	Local Rep
MIMLIC Cash Fund, Inc. 400 N. Robert St. St. Paul, MN 55101-2098 612/223-4252 800/443-3677	1987	MIMLIC Asset Management Company	$24.7 Mil	$0/ 0	n	Local Rep
MIMLIC Money Market Fund, Inc. 400 N. Robert St. St. Paul, MN 55101-2098 612/223-4252 800/443-3677	1984	MIMLIC Asset Management Company	$22.8 Mil	$250/ 25	n	Local Rep

*Key: i=initial sales charge   r=redemption fee or contingent deferred sales charge(CDSC)
       t=12b-1 fee and either CDSC or redemption fee   p=12b-1 fee   n=none of the preceding fees   N/A=not available

Money Market

Fund	Year Began	Investment Adviser	9/30/89 Assets	Minimum Initial and Subsequent Investment	Fees*	Where to Buy Shares
MIM Mutual Funds, Inc. *Money Market Fund* 4500 Rockside Rd. Ste. 440 Independence, OH 44131-6809 216/642-3000 800/233-1240	1986	Mathematical Investing Systems, Inc.	N/A	$250/ 50	N/A	Fund
Money Management Plus *Government Portfolio* 1700 Pennsylvania Ave., NW Washington, DC 20006 301/951-4820 800/368-2745	1982	Calvert Asset Management Company, Inc.	$25.9 Mil	$2,000/ 250	n	Fund
Money Management Plus *Prime Portfolio* 1700 Pennsylvania Ave., NW Washington, DC 20006 301/951-4820 800/368-2745	1982	Calvert Asset Management Company, Inc.	$155.3 Mil	$2,000/ 250	n	Fund
Money Market Management Federated Investors Twr. Pittsburgh, PA 15222-3779 412/288-1948 800/245-0242	1974	Federated Advisers	$209.7 Mil	$500/ 100	n	Fund
Money Market Trust Federated Investors Twr. Pittsburgh, PA 15222-3779 412/288-1900 800/245-5000	1979	Federated Research	$1.6 Bil	$25,000/ 0	n	Local Rep
MONY Series Fund *Money Market Portfolio* 500 Frank W. Burr Blvd. 71-13 Glenpointe Ctr. West Teaneck, NJ 07666 201/907-6669	1985	MONY Life Insurance Company of America	$8.7 Mil	Not Applicable	n	Insur
MONY Variable Account-B 500 Frank W. Burr Blvd. 71-13 Glenpointe Ctr. West Teaneck, NJ 07666 201/907-6669	1983	Mutual Life Insurance Company of New York	$3.5 Mil	Not Applicable	n	Insur

*Key: i=initial sales charge   r=redemption fee or contingent deferred sales charge(CDSC)
t=12b-1 fee and either CDSC or redemption fee   p=12b-1 fee   n=none of the preceding fees   N/A=not available

Money Market

Fund	Year Began	Investment Adviser	9/30/89 Assets	Minimum Initial and Subsequent Investment	Fees*	Where to Buy Shares
Mutual of America Investment Corporation *Money Market Fund (The)* 666 Fifth Ave. New York, NY 10103 212/399-1600 800/223-0898	1986	Mutual of America Life Insurance Company	N/A	Not Applicable	n	Insur
Mutual of Omaha Cash Reserve Fund, Inc. 10235 Regency Circle Omaha, NE 68114 402/397-8555 800/228-9596	· 1980	Mutual of Omaha Fund Management Company	$52.4 Mil	$0/ 0	p	Local Rep
Mutual of Omaha Money Market Account, Inc. 10235 Regency Circle Omaha, NE 68114 402/397-8555 800/228-9596	1979	Mutual of Omaha Fund Management Company	$191.7 Mil	$1,000/ 50	n	Local Rep
NASL Series Trust *Money Market Trust* 695 Atlantic Ave. P.O. Box 9064 GMF Boston, MA 02205 617/439-6960 800/344-1029	1985	NASL Financial Services, Inc.	$18.9 Mil (e)	Not Applicable	r	Insur
National Cash Reserves, Inc. 600 Third Ave. New York, NY 10016 203/863-5600 800/237-1718	1982	National Securities & Research Corporation	$47.6 Mil	$1,000/ 25	p	Local Rep
National Liquid Reserves, Inc. *NLR Cash Portfolio* 1345 Avenue of the Americas New York, NY 10105 212/698-5349 800/544-7835	1974	Mutual Management Corp.	$1.9 Bil	$1,500/ 100	n	Local Rep
National Liquid Reserves, Inc. *NLR Government Portfolio* 1345 Avenue of the Americas New York, NY 10105 212/698-5349 800/544-7835	1984	Mutual Management Corp.	$131.9 Mil	$1,500/ 100	n	Local Rep

*Key: i=initial sales charge   r=redemption fee or contingent deferred sales charge(CDSC)
t=12b-1 fee and either CDSC or redemption fee   p=12b-1 fee   n=none of the preceding fees   N/A=not available

Money Market

Fund	Year Began	Investment Adviser	9/30/89 Assets	Minimum Initial and Subsequent Investment	Fees*	Where to Buy Shares
National Liquid Reserves, Inc. *NLR Retirement Portfolio* 1345 Avenue of the Americas New York, NY 10105 212/698-5349 800/544-7835	1986	Mutual Management Corp.	$760.6 Mil	$200/ 1	n	Local Rep
Nationwide Investing Foundation *Money Market Fund* One Nationwide Plaza Box 1492 Columbus, OH 43216 614/249-7855 800/848-0920, 800/282-1440 OH Only	1980	Nationwide Financial Services, Inc.	$520.6 Mil	$1,000/ 100	n	Local Rep
Nationwide Separate Account Trust *Money Market Fund* One Nationwide Plaza Box 1492 Columbus, OH 43216 614/249-7855 800/848-0920, 800/282-1440 OH Only	1981	Nationwide Financial Services, Inc.	$203.3 Mil	Not Applicable	n	Insur
Neuberger & Berman Cash Reserves 342 Madison Ave. New York, NY 10173 212/850-8300 800/877-9700	1988	Neuberger & Berman Management Incorporated	$227.5 Mil	$2,000/ 200	n	Fund
Neuberger & Berman Government Money Fund, Inc. 342 Madison Ave. New York, NY 10173 212/850-8300 800/877-9700	1983	Neuberger & Berman Management Incorporated	$180.0 Mil	$2,000/ 200	n	Fund
New England Cash Management Trust *Money Market Series* 399 Boylston St. Boston, MA 02116 617/267-6600 800/343-7104	1978	Back Bay Advisors, Inc.	$1.0 Bil	$1,000/ 0	n	Local Rep
New England Cash Management Trust *U.S. Government Series* 399 Boylston St. Boston, MA 02116 617/267-6600 800/343-7104	1982	Back Bay Advisors, Inc.	$57.3 Mil	$1,000/ 0	n	Local Rep

*Key: i=initial sales charge   r=redemption fee or contingent deferred sales charge(CDSC)
t=12b-1 fee and either CDSC or redemption fee   p=12b-1 fee   n=none of the preceding fees   N/A=not available

Money Market

Fund	Year Began	Investment Adviser	9/30/89 Assets	Minimum Initial and Subsequent Investment	Fees*	Where to Buy Shares
New England Zenith Fund *Money Market Series* 501 Boylston St. Boston, MA 02116 617/267-7055 800/634-8025	1983	Back Bay Advisors, Inc.	$37.3 Mil	Not Applicable	n	Insur
Newton Income Fund, Inc. *Newton Money Fund* 330 E. Kilbourn Ave. Ste. 1150 Milwaukee, WI 53202 414/271-0440 800/247-7039 800/242-7229 WI Only	1981	Marshall & Ilsley Investment Management Corporation	$147.3 Mil	$1,000/ 250	n	Fund
North American Security Trust *Money Market Portfolio* 695 Atlantic Ave. P.O. Box 9064 GMF Boston, MA 02205 617/439-6960 800/344-1029	1986	NASL Financial Services, Inc.	$7.0 Mil (e)	$1,000/ 100	p	Local Rep
North Carolina Cash Management Trust *Cash Portfolio* 82 Devonshire St. Boston, MA 02109 617/570-7000 800/222-3232	1983	Fidelity Management & Research Company	$1.1 Bil	$0/ 0	n	Local Rep
Ohio National Fund, Inc. *Money Market Portfolio* 237 William Howard Taft Cincinnati, OH 45219 513/861-3600	1980	O.N. Investment Management Company	$24.1 Mil	Not Applicable	n	Insur
OLDE Custodian Fund *OLDE Money Market Series* 751 Griswold Detroit, MI 48226 313/961-6666	1989	OLDE Asset Management, Inc.	N/A	$1,000/ 1,000	N/A	Local Rep
Olympus Money Market Fund 230 Park Ave. New York, NY 10169 212/309-8400 800/626-FUND	1986	Furman Selz Mager Dietz & Birney Incorporated	$4.2 Mil (e)	$1,000/ 100	i, p	Local Rep

*Key: i=initial sales charge   r=redemption fee or contingent deferred sales charge(CDSC)
t=12b-1 fee and either CDSC or redemption fee   p=12b-1 fee   n=none of the preceding fees   N/A=not available

Money Market

Fund	Year Began	Investment Adviser	9/30/89 Assets	Minimum Initial and Subsequent Investment	Fees*	Where to Buy Shares
Oppenheimer Cash Reserves 3410 S. Galena St. Denver, CO 80231 303/671-3200 800/525-7048	1989	Oppenheimer Management Corporation	$9.0 Mil	$1,000/ 25	p	Local Rep
Oppenheimer Money Market Fund, Inc. 3410 S. Galena St. Denver, CO 80231 303/671-3200 800/525-7048	1974	Oppenheimer Management Corporation	$913.3 Mil	$1,000/ 25	n	Local Rep
Oppenheimer Variable Account Funds *Oppenheimer Money Fund* 3410 S. Galena St. Denver, CO 80231 303/671-3200 800/525-7048	1985	Oppenheimer Management Corporation	$64.7 Mil	Not Applicable	n	Insur
Pacific American Fund, Inc. *Money Market Portfolio* 707 Wilshire Blvd. Mail Sort W10-6 Los Angeles, CA 90017 213/614-2132	1981	First Interstate Investment Services, Inc.	$697.7 Mil	$0/ 0	p	Fund
Pacific American Fund, Inc. *Short Term Government Portfolio* 707 Wilshire Blvd. Mail Sort W10-6 Los Angeles, CA 90017 213/614-2132	1982	First Interstate Investment Services, Inc.	$158.0 Mil	$0/ 0	n	Local Rep
Pacific Horizon Funds, Inc. *Government Money Market Portfolio* 156 W. 56th St. Ste. 1902 New York, NY 10019 212/492-1600 800/367-6075	1984	Security Pacific National Bank	$1.2 Bil	$1,000/ 100	p	Fund
Pacific Horizon Funds, Inc. *Money Market Portfolio* 156 W. 56th St. Ste. 1902 New York, NY 10019 212/492-1600 800/367-6075	1984	Security Pacific National Bank	$876.3 Mil	$1,000/ 100	p	Fund

*Key: i=initial sales charge   r=redemption fee or contingent deferred sales charge(CDSC)
t=12b-1 fee and either CDSC or redemption fee   p=12b-1 fee   n=none of the preceding fees   N/A=not available

Money Market

Fund	Year Began	Investment Adviser	9/30/89 Assets	Minimum Initial and Subsequent Investment	Fees*	Where to Buy Shares
PaineWebber Cashfund, Inc. 1285 Avenue of the Americas PaineWebber Bldg. New York, NY 10019 212/713-2000	1978	PaineWebber Incorporated	$4.9 Bil	$5,000/ 500	n	Local Rep
PaineWebber Master Series, Inc. *PaineWebber Master Money Fund* 1285 Avenue of the Americas PaineWebber Bldg. New York, NY 10019 212/713-2000, 800/647-1568	1986	Mitchell Hutchins Asset Management Inc.	$55.9 Mil	$1,000/ 100	t	Local Rep
PaineWebber RMA Money Fund, Inc. *Money Market Portfolio* 1285 Avenue of the Americas PaineWebber Bldg. New York, NY 10019 800/RMA-1000	1982	PaineWebber Incorporated	$3.2 Bil	$15,000/ 0	n	Local Rep
PaineWebber RMA Money Fund, Inc. *PaineWebber Retirement Money Fund* 1285 Avenue of the Americas PaineWebber Bldg. New York, NY 10019 800/RMA-1000	1988	PaineWebber Incorporated	$1.5 Bil	$25/ 0	p	Local Rep
PaineWebber RMA Money Fund, Inc. *U.S. Government Portfolio* 1285 Avenue of the Americas PaineWebber Bldg. New York, NY 10019 800/RMA-1000	1982	PaineWebber Incorporated	$363.7 Mil	$15,000/ 0	n	Local Rep
PaineWebber Series Trust *Money Market Portfolio* 1285 Avenue of the Americas PaineWebber Bldg. New York, NY 10019 212/713-2000	1987	Mitchell Hutchins Asset Management Inc.	N/A	Not Applicable	N/A	Insur
Parkstone Group of Funds *Prime Obligations Fund* 1900 E. Dublin-Granville Rd. Columbus, OH 43229 614/899-4600 800/338-4385	1987	Securities Counsel, Inc.	N/A	$1,000/ 0	N/A	Fund

*Key: i=initial sales charge   r=redemption fee or contingent deferred sales charge(CDSC)
t=12b-1 fee and either CDSC or redemption fee   p=12b-1 fee   n=none of the preceding fees   N/A=not available

368

Money Market

Fund	Year Began	Investment Adviser	9/30/89 Assets	Minimum Initial and Subsequent Investment	Fees*	Where to Buy Shares
Parkstone Group of Funds *U.S. Government Fund* 1900 E. Dublin-Granville Rd. Columbus, OH 43229 614/899-4600 800/338-4385	1989	Securities Counsel, Inc.	N/A	$1,000/ 0	N/A	Fund
Parkway Cash Fund, Inc. 985 Old Eagle School Rd. Wayne, PA 19087 215/688-8164 800/992-2207	1979	Parkway Management Corporation	$114.3 Mil	$1,000/ 0	n	Local Rep
Phoenix Series Fund *Phoenix Money Market Fund Series* 101 Munson St. Greenfield, MA 01301 203/253-1000 800/243-1574	1980	Phoenix Investment Counsel, Inc.	$146.0 Mil	$500/ 25	n	Local Rep
Pilgrim Money Market Fund 10100 Santa Monica Blvd. 21st Fl. Los Angeles, CA 90067 213/551-0833 800/334-3444 800/331-1080	1982	Pilgrim Management Corporation	$22.1 Mil	$1,000/ 100	p	Local Rep
Pinnacle Government Fund, Inc. 183 E. Main St. Ste. 1035 Rochester, NY 14604 716/262-4080 800/456-7780	1980	Chase Lincoln First Bank, N.A.	$84.7 Mil	$1,000/ 100	n	Local Rep
Pioneer Cash Reserves Fund 60 State St. Boston, MA 02109-1975 617/742-7825 800/225-6292	1987	Pioneering Management Corporation	$77.1 Mil	$2,000/ 100	n	Fund
Pioneer U.S. Government Money Fund 60 State St. Boston, MA 02109-1975 617/742-7825 800/225-6292	1988	Pioneering Management Corporation	$19.5 Mil	$2,000/ 100	n	Fund

*Key: i=initial sales charge   r=redemption fee or contingent deferred sales charge(CDSC)
     t=12b-1 fee and either CDSC or redemption fee   p=12b-1 fee   n=none of the preceding fees   N/A=not available

Money Market

Fund	Year Began	Investment Adviser	9/30/89 Assets	Minimum Initial and Subsequent Investment	Fees*	Where to Buy Shares
Piper Jaffray Investment Trust Inc. *Money Market Fund* 222 S. 9th St. Piper Jaffray Twr. Minneapolis, MN 55402 612/342-6426 800/333-6000	1987	Piper Capital Management Incorporated	$1.0 Bil	$0/ 0	p	Local Rep
Piper Jaffray Investment Trust Inc. *U.S. Government Money Market Fund* 222 S. 9th St. Piper Jaffray Twr. Minneapolis, MN 55402 612/342-6426, 800/333-6000	1988	Piper Capital Management Incorporated	$45.7 Mil	$0/ 0	p	Local Rep
PNCG Money Market Fund, Inc. 121 SW Morrison Ste. 1415 Portland, OR 97204 503/295-0919 800/541-9732	1989	PNCG Fund Advisers, Inc.	N/A	$1,000/ 500	p	Local Rep
Prime Cash Fund 200 Park Ave. Ste. 4515 New York, NY 10017 212/697-6666	1983	Security Pacific National Bank	$322.7 Mil	$1,000/ 0	n	Local Rep
Princor Cash Management Fund, Inc. 711 High St. Des Moines, IA 50309 515/247-5711 800/247-4123 800/622-5344 IA Only	1983	Principal Management, Inc.	$125.4 Mil	$1,000/ 100	n	Local Rep
Prudential-Bache Government Securities Trust *Money Market Series* One Seaport Plaza New York, NY 10292 212/214-1215 800/225-1852	1981	Prudential Mutual Fund Management	$629.6 Mil	$1,000/ 100	p	Local Rep
Prudential-Bache MoneyMart Assets Inc. One Seaport Plaza New York, NY 10292 212/214-1215 800/225-1852	1976	Prudential Mutual Fund Management	$7.9 Bil	$1,000/ 100	p	Local Rep

*Key: i=initial sales charge   r=redemption fee or contingent deferred sales charge(CDSC)
t=12b-1 fee and either CDSC or redemption fee   p=12b-1 fee   n=none of the preceding fees   N/A=not available

Money Market

Fund	Year Began	Investment Adviser	9/30/89 Assets	Minimum Initial and Subsequent Investment	Fees*	Where to Buy Shares
Prudential Institutional Liquidity Portfolio, Inc. *Institutional Government Series* One Seaport Plaza New York, NY 10292 212/214-1215 800/225-1852	1987	Prudential Mutual Fund Management	$58.2 Mil	$100,000/ 10,000	p	Local Rep
Prudential Institutional Liquidity Portfolio, Inc. *Institutional Money Market Series* One Seaport Plaza New York, NY 10292 212/214-1215 800/225-1852	1987	Prudential Mutual Fund Management	$506.4 Mil	$100,000/ 10,000	p	Local Rep
Putnam Capital Manager Trust *PCM Money Market Fund* One Post Office Sq. Boston, MA 02109 617/292-1000 800/225-2465	1988	Putnam Management Company, Inc.	$24.3 Mil	Not Applicable	r	Insur
Putnam Daily Dividend Trust One Post Office Sq. Boston, MA 02109 617/292-1000 800/225-2465	1976	Putnam Management Company, Inc.	$780.4 Mil	$1,000/ 100	n	Local Rep
Quest For Value Accumulation Trust *Money Market Portfolio* Oppenheimer Tower World Financial Ctr. New York, NY 10281 212/667-7587 800/232-FUND	1988	Quest For Value Advisors	$2.5 Mil	Not Applicable	n	Insur
Quest For Value Cash Management Trust Oppenheimer Tower World Financial Ctr. New York, NY 10281 212/667-7587 800/232-FUND	1987	Quest For Value Advisors	$620.4 Mil	$500/ 25	p	Local Rep
Retirement Investment Trust *Money Market Fund* 16 HCB 98 P.O. Box 2558 Houston, TX 77252-8098 713/546-7775	1988	None	N/A	$500/ 100	n	Fund

*Key: i=initial sales charge   r=redemption fee or contingent deferred sales charge(CDSC)
t=12b-1 fee and either CDSC or redemption fee   p=12b-1 fee   n=none of the preceding fees   N/A=not available

Money Market

Fund	Year Began	Investment Adviser	9/30/89 Assets	Minimum Initial and Subsequent Investment	Fees*	Where to Buy Shares
Retirement Planning Funds of America, Inc. *Money Market Fund* 124 E. Marcy St. P.O. Box 1688 Santa Fe, NM 87504-1688 505/983-4335 800/545-2098	1976	Venture Advisers, L.P.	$31.9 Mil	$1,000/ 25	p	Local Rep
RNC Liquid Assets Fund, Inc. 11601 Wilshire Blvd. 24th Fl. Los Angeles, CA 90025 213/477-6543 800/225-9655	1986	RNC Capital Management Co.	$107.0 Mil (e)	$1,000/ 100	p	Local Rep
Rodney Square Fund *Money Market Portfolio* Rodney Square North Wilmington, DE 19890 302/651-1923 800/225-5084	1983	Rodney Square Management Corporation	$647.8 Mil	$100/ 0	p	Local Rep
Rodney Square Fund *U.S. Government Portfolio* Rodney Square North Wilmington, DE 19890 302/651-1923 800/225-5084	1983	Rodney Square Management Corporation	$232.2 Mil	$100/ 0	p	Local Rep
SAFECO Money Market Mutual Fund, Inc. SAFECO Plaza Seattle, WA 98185 206/545-5530 800/426-6730	1982	SAFECO Asset Management Company	$209.5 Mil	$1,000/ 100	n	Fund
SafeGuard Money Market Portfolio 16 Industrial Blvd. Paoli, PA 19301 215/251-0550 800/523-7798	1988	Provident Institutional Management Corporation	$0.06 Mil	$1,000/ 100	p	Local Rep
Salem Funds *Salem Money Market Portfolio (The)* 99 High St. Boston, MA 02110 617/338-3200 800/641-2580 800/343-3424	1989	First Union National Bank of N. Carolina	$12.5 Mil	$1,000/ 0	p	Fund

*Key: i=initial sales charge   r=redemption fee or contingent deferred sales charge(CDSC)
t=12b-1 fee and either CDSC or redemption fee   p=12b-1 fee   n=none of the preceding fees   N/A=not available

Money Market

Fund	Year Began	Investment Adviser	9/30/89 Assets	Minimum Initial and Subsequent Investment	Fees*	Where to Buy Shares
Sansom Street Government Money Market Portfolio 16 Industrial Blvd. Paoli, PA 19301 215/251-0550 800/523-7798	1988	Provident Institutional Management Corporation	N/A	$1,500/ 0	p	Local Rep
Sansom Street Money Market Portfolio 16 Industrial Blvd. Paoli, PA 19301 215/251-0550 800/523-7798	1988	Provident Institutional Management Corporation	$93.6 Mil	$1,500/ 0	p	Local Rep
SBL Fund *Money Market Series* 700 Harrison St. 6th Fl. Topeka, KS 66636 913/295-3127 800/888-2461	1977	Security Management Company	$94.1 Mil	Not Applicable	n	Insur
SBSF Funds *SBSF Money Market Fund* 45 Rockefeller Plaza 33rd Fl. New York, NY 10111 212/903-1200 800/422-7273	1988	Spears, Benzak, Salomon & Farrell	$16.7 Mil	$0/ 0	n	Fund
Scudder Cash Investment Trust 175 Federal St. Boston, MA 02110 617/439-4640 800/225-2470 800/225-5163	1974	Scudder, Stevens & Clark, Inc.	$1.5 Bil	$1,000/ 0	n	Fund
Scudder Fund, Inc. *Managed Cash Fund* 345 Park Ave. New York, NY 10154 212/326-6656 800/854-8525	1985	Scudder, Stevens & Clark, Inc.	$242.4 Mil	$2,500/ 100	n	Fund
Scudder Fund, Inc. *Managed Government Fund* 345 Park Ave. New York, NY 10154 212/326-6656 800/854-8525	1985	Scudder, Stevens & Clark, Inc.	$66.8 Mil	$2,500/ 100	n	Fund

*Key: i=initial sales charge   r=redemption fee or contingent deferred sales charge(CDSC)
t=12b-1 fee and either CDSC or redemption fee   p=12b-1 fee   n=none of the preceding fees   N/A=not available

Money Market

Fund	Year Began	Investment Adviser	9/30/89 Assets	Minimum Initial and Subsequent Investment	Fees*	Where to Buy Shares
Scudder Government Money Fund 175 Federal St. Boston, MA 02110 617/439-4640 800/225-2470 800/225-5163	1981	Scudder, Stevens & Clark, Inc.	$173.2 Mil	$1,000/ 0	n	Fund
Scudder Institutional Fund, Inc. *Institutional Cash Portfolio* 345 Park Ave. New York, NY 10154 212/326-6656 800/854-8525	1986	Scudder, Stevens & Clark, Inc.	$77.3 Mil	$2.0 Mil/ 0	n	Fund
Scudder Institutional Fund, Inc. *Institutional Government Portfolio* 345 Park Ave. New York, NY 10154 212/326-6656 800/854-8525	1986	Scudder, Stevens & Clark, Inc.	$213.3 Mil	$2.0 Mil/ 0	n	Fund
Scudder Institutional Fund, Inc. *Institutional Prime Portfolio* 345 Park Ave. New York, NY 10154 212/326-6656 800/854-8525	1986	Scudder, Stevens & Clark, Inc.	$127.4 Mil	$2.0 Mil/ 0	n	Fund
Scudder Institutional Fund, Inc. *Institutional Treasury Portfolio* 345 Park Ave. New York, NY 10154 212/326-6656 800/854-8525	1986	Scudder, Stevens & Clark, Inc.	$31.3 Mil	$2.0 Mil/ 0	n	Fund
Scudder Treasurers Trust *Treasurers Money Portfolio* 175 Federal St. Boston, MA 02110 617/439-4640 800/225-2470 800/225-5163	1987	Scudder, Stevens & Clark, Inc.	$76.4 Mil	$100,000/ 0	n	Fund
Security Cash Fund 700 Harrison St. Topeka, KS 66636 913/295-3127 800/888-2461	1980	Security Management Company	$52.8 Mil	$100/ 20	n	Local Rep

*Key: i=initial sales charge   r=redemption fee or contingent deferred sales charge(CDSC)
t=12b-1 fee and either CDSC or redemption fee   p=12b-1 fee   n=none of the preceding fees   N/A=not available

374

Money Market

Fund	Year Began	Investment Adviser	9/30/89 Assets	Minimum Initial and Subsequent Investment	Fees*	Where to Buy Shares
SEI Cash+Plus Trust *Federal Securities Portfolio* 680 E. Swedesford Rd. No. 7 Wayne, PA 19087 215/254-1000 800/345-1151	1982	Wellington Management Company	$137.8 Mil	$0/ 0	p	Local Rep
SEI Cash+Plus Trust *Government Portfolio* 680 E. Swedesford Rd. No. 7 Wayne, PA 19087 215/254-1000 800/345-1151	1985	Wellington Management Company	$281.7 Mil	$100.0 Mil/ 0	p	Local Rep
SEI Cash+Plus Trust *Money Market Portfolio* 680 E. Swedesford Rd. No. 7 Wayne, PA 19087 215/254-1000 800/345-1151	1983	Wellington Management Company	$356.6 Mil	$0/ 0	p	Local Rep
SEI Cash+Plus Trust *Prime Obligation Portfolio* 680 E. Swedesford Rd. No. 7 Wayne, PA 19087 215/254-1000 800/345-1151	1987	Wellington Management Company	$350.6 Mil	$100.0 Mil/ 0	p	Local Rep
SEI Cash+Plus Trust *Treasury Portfolio* 680 E. Swedesford Rd. No. 7 Wayne, PA 19087 215/254-1000 800/345-1151	1989	Wellington Management Company	$47.8 Mil	$100.0 Mil/ 0	p	Local Rep
SEI Liquid Asset Trust *Commercial Portfolio* 680 E. Swedesford Rd. No. 7 Wayne, PA 19087 215/254-1000 800/345-1151	1982	Wellington Management Company	$188.2 Mil	$0/ 0	p	Local Rep
SEI Liquid Asset Trust *Government Portfolio* 680 E. Swedesford Rd. No. 7 Wayne, PA 19087 215/254-1000 800/345-1151	1982	Wellington Management Company	$402.4 Mil	$0/ 0	p	Local Rep

*Key: i=initial sales charge   r=redemption fee or contingent deferred sales charge(CDSC)
t=12b-1 fee and either CDSC or redemption fee   p=12b-1 fee   n=none of the preceding fees   N/A=not available

Money Market

Fund	Year Began	Investment Adviser	9/30/89 Assets	Minimum Initial and Subsequent Investment	Fees*	Where to Buy Shares
SEI Liquid Asset Trust *Prime Obligation Portfolio* 680 E. Swedesford Rd. No. 7 Wayne, PA 19087 215/254-1000 800/345-1151	1982	Wellington Management Company	$2.1 Bil	$0/ 0	p	Local Rep
SEI Liquid Asset Trust *Treasury II Portfolio* 680 E. Swedesford Rd. No. 7 Wayne, PA 19087 215/254-1000 800/345-1151	1988	Wellington Management Company	$135.4 Mil	$0/ 0	p	Local Rep
SEI Liquid Asset Trust *Treasury Portfolio* 680 E. Swedesford Rd. No. 7 Wayne, PA 19087 215/254-1000 800/345-1151	1982	Wellington Management Company	$2.3 Bil	$0/ 0	p	Local Rep
Select Cash Management Fund, Inc. 20 Washington Ave. South Minneapolis, MN 55401 612/372-5605	1981	Washington Square Capital, Inc.	$4.9 Mil	Not Applicable	n	Insur
Selected Capital Preservation Trust *Selected Daily Government Fund* 1331 Euclid Ave. Cleveland, OH 44115 312/641-7862 800/553-5533	1988	Selected Financial Services, Inc.	$96.3 Mil	$1,000/ 100	n	Local Rep
Selected Capital Preservation Trust *Selected Daily Income Fund* 1331 Euclid Ave. Cleveland, OH 44115 312/641-7862 800/553-5533	1988	Selected Financial Services, Inc.	$524.2 Mil	$1,000/ 100	n	Local Rep
Seligman Cash Management Fund, Inc. *Government Portfolio* 130 Liberty St. New York, NY 10006 212/488-0200 800/221-2450 800/522-6869 NY Only	1982	J. & W. Seligman & Co. Incorporated	$20.0 Mil	$2,000/ 100	n	Local Rep

*Key: i=initial sales charge   r=redemption fee or contingent deferred sales charge(CDSC)
t=12b-1 fee and either CDSC or redemption fee   p=12b-1 fee   n=none of the preceding fees   N/A=not available

Money Market

Fund	Year Began	Investment Adviser	9/30/89 Assets	Minimum Initial and Subsequent Investment	Fees*	Where to Buy Shares
Seligman Cash Management Fund, Inc. *Prime Portfolio* 130 Liberty St. New York, NY 10006 212/488-0200 800/221-2450 800/522-6869 NY Only	1977	J. & W. Seligman & Co. Incorporated	$328.2 Mil	$2,000/ 100	n	Local Rep
Seligman Mutual Benefit Portfolios, Inc. *Seligman Cash Management Portfolio* 130 Liberty St. New York, NY 10006 212/488-0200 800/221-2450, 800/522-6869 NY Only	1988	J. & W. Seligman & Co. Incorporated	$0.6 Mil	Not Applicable	r	Insur
Sentinel Cash Management Fund, Inc. National Life Dr. Montpelier, VT 05604 802/229-3900 800/282-3863	1981	Sentinel Advisors, Inc.	$57.1 Mil	$250/ 25	n	Local Rep
Sessions Group *PSB Government Money Market Fund* 1900 E. Dublin-Granville Rd. Columbus, OH 43229 614/899-4600 800/338-4385	1988	Perpetual Investment Advisory Service, Inc.	N/A	$1,000/ 100	N/A	Fund
Sessions Group *Riverside Capital Money Market Fund* 1900 E. Dublin-Granville Rd. Columbus, OH 43229 614/899-4600 800/338-4385	1989	National Bank of Commerce	N/A	$1,000/ 50	N/A	Fund
Sessions Group *Sun Eagle Prime Obligations Fund* 1900 E. Dublin-Granville Rd. Columbus, OH 43229 614/899-4600 800/338-4385	1989	Valley National Bank of Arizona	N/A	$1,000/ 50	N/A	Fund
Shearson Lehman Series Fund *SLH IDS Money Market Portfolio* 31 W. 52nd St. New York, NY 10019 212/767-3700	1986	Bernstein-Macaulay Division of Shearson Lehman Hutton Inc.	$1.8 Mil	Not Applicable	n	Insur

*Key: i=initial sales charge   r=redemption fee or contingent deferred sales charge(CDSC)
t=12b-1 fee and either CDSC or redemption fee   p=12b-1 fee   n=none of the preceding fees   N/A=not available

Money Market

Fund	Year Began	Investment Adviser	9/30/89 Assets	Minimum Initial and Subsequent Investment	Fees*	Where to Buy Shares
Short Term Asset Reserves 200 Park Ave. Ste. 4515 New York, NY 10017 212/697-6666	1985	Security Pacific National Bank	$28.1 Mil	$1,000/ 0	n	Local Rep
Short-Term Investments Co. *Prime Portfolio* 11 Greenway Plaza Ste. 1919 Houston, TX 77046 713/626-1919 800/231-0803 800/392-9681 TX Only	1980	AIM Advisors, Inc.	$6.5 Bil	$1.0 Mil/ 0	n	Local Rep
Short-Term Investments Co. *Treasury Portfolio* 11 Greenway Plaza Ste. 1919 Houston, TX 77046 713/626-1919 800/231-0803 800/392-9681 TX Only	1984	AIM Advisors, Inc.	$1.2 Bil	$1.0 Mil/ 0	n	Local Rep
Sigma Federal Moneyfund, Inc. 3801 Kennett Pk., C-200 Greenville Ctr. Wilmington, DE 19807 302/652-3091 800/441-9490	1980	Sigma Management, Inc.	$17.4 Mil	$500/ 100	p	Local Rep
Sigma Moneyfund, Inc. 3801 Kennett Pk., C-200 Greenville Ctr. Wilmington, DE 19807 302/652-3091 800/441-9490	1980	Sigma Management, Inc.	$28.7 Mil	$500/ 100	p	Local Rep
Silver Star Fund, Inc. *Government Portfolio* 11 Greenway Plaza Ste. 1919 Houston, TX 77046 713/626-1919 800/231-0803 800/392-9681 TX Only	1986	NCNB Texas National Bank	$160.7 Mil	$0/ 0	n	Local Rep
Silver Star Fund, Inc. *Prime Portfolio* 11 Greenway Plaza Ste. 1919 Houston, TX 77046 713/626-1919 800/231-0803 800/392-9681 TX Only	1986	NCNB Texas National Bank	$227.7 Mil	$0/ 0	n	Local Rep

*Key: i=initial sales charge   r=redemption fee or contingent deferred sales charge(CDSC)
t=12b-1 fee and either CDSC or redemption fee   p=12b-1 fee   n=none of the preceding fees   N/A=not available

Money Market

Fund	Year Began	Investment Adviser	9/30/89 Assets	Minimum Initial and Subsequent Investment	Fees*	Where to Buy Shares
SLH Daily Dividend Fund 31 W. 52nd St. New York, NY 10019 212/767-3700	1979	Bernstein-Macaulay Division of Shearson Lehman Hutton Inc.	$16.8 Bil	$2,500/ 1,000	n	Local Rep
SLH Government and Agencies Income Fund, Inc. 31 W. 52nd St. New York, NY 10019 212/767-3700	1980	Bernstein-Macaulay Division of Shearson Lehman Hutton Inc.	$3.1 Bil	$2,500/ 1,000	n	Local Rep
SLH Special Income Portfolios *SLH Money Market Portfolio* 31 W. 52nd St. New York, NY 10019 212/767-3700	1986	Bernstein-Macaulay Division of Shearson Lehman Hutton Inc.	$851.5 Mil	$500/ 200	t	Local Rep
SMA Investment Trust *Money Market Fund* 440 Lincoln St. Worcester, MA 01605 508/852-1000	1985	State Mutual Life Assurance Company of America	$12.6 Mil	Not Applicable	n	Insur
Southern Farm Bureau Cash Fund, Inc. 1401 Livingston Lane P.O. Box 691 Jackson, MS 39205 601/982-7800 800/647-8053 800/872-8514 MS Only	1981	Southern Farm Bureau Adviser, Inc.	$20.1 Mil	$500/ 100	n	Fund
Sower Series Fund, Inc. *Money Market Portfolio* 5900 "O" St. Lincoln, NE 68510 402/467-1122	1987	Ameritas Investment Advisors, Inc.	$0.3 Mil (e)	Not Applicable	n	Insur
Specialty Managers Trust *Liquid Asset Series* 1925 Century Park East Ste. 2350 Los Angeles, CA 90067 213/556-5499 800/423-4891	1989	Neuberger & Berman Management, Inc.	N/A	Not Applicable	n	Insur

*Key: i=initial sales charge   r=redemption fee or contingent deferred sales charge(CDSC)
t=12b-1 fee and either CDSC or redemption fee   p=12b-1 fee   n=none of the preceding fees   N/A=not available

379

Money Market

Fund	Year Began	Investment Adviser	9/30/89 Assets	Minimum Initial and Subsequent Investment	Fees*	Where to Buy Shares
SteinRoe Income Trust *SteinRoe Cash Reserves* 300 W. Adams St. P.O. Box 1143 Chicago, IL 60690 800/338-2550	1976	Stein Roe & Farnham Incorporated	$977.2 Mil	$1,000/ 100	n	Fund
SteinRoe Income Trust *SteinRoe Government Reserves* 300 W. Adams St. P.O. Box 1143 Chicago, IL 60690 800/338-2550	1982	Stein Roe & Farnham Incorporated	$54.6 Mil	$1,000/ 100	n	Fund
SteinRoe Variable Investment Trust *Cash Income Fund* 600 Atlantic Ave. Boston, MA 02210 617/722-6000 800/443-2683	1989	Stein Roe & Farnham Incorporated	N/A	Not Applicable	N/A	Insur
Strong Money Market Fund, Inc. P.O. Box 2936 Milwaukee, WI 53201 414/359-3400 800/368-3863	1985	Strong/ Corneliuson Capital Management, Inc.	$742.8 Mil	$1,000/ 200	n	Fund
Summit Cash Reserve Fund P.O. Box 9011 Princeton, NJ 08543-9011 609/282-2800 800/221-7210	1982	Fund Asset Management, Inc.	$757.4 Mil	$5,000/ 1,000	n	Local Rep
Templeton Income Trust *Templeton Money Fund* 700 Central Ave. P.O. Box 33030 St. Petersburg, FL 33733-8030 813/823-8712 800/237-0738	1987	Templeton Investment Counsel, Inc.	$137.4 Mil	$1,000/ 100	n	Local Rep
Templeton Variable Products Series Fund *Templeton Money Market Fund (The)* 700 Central Ave. P.O. Box 33030 St. Petersburg, FL 33733-8030 813/823-8712, 800/237-0738	1988	Templeton, Galbraith & Hansberger, Ltd.	N/A	Not Applicable	n	Insur

*Key: i=initial sales charge   r=redemption fee or contingent deferred sales charge(CDSC)
t=12b-1 fee and either CDSC or redemption fee   p=12b-1 fee   n=none of the preceding fees   N/A=not available

Money Market

Fund	Year Began	Investment Adviser	9/30/89 Assets	Minimum Initial and Subsequent Investment	Fees*	Where to Buy Shares
Temporary Investment Fund, Inc. *TempCash* 3411 Silverside Rd. Webster Bldg., Ste. 204 Wilmington, DE 19810 302/478-6945 800/221-8120, 800/821-6006	1984	Provident Institutional Management Corporation	$770.2 Mil	$5,000/ 0	p	Local Rep
Temporary Investment Fund, Inc. *TempFund* 3411 Silverside Rd. Webster Bldg., Ste. 204 Wilmington, DE 19810 302/478-6945 800/221-8120, 800/821-6006	1973	Provident Institutional Management Corporation	$5.4 Bil	$5,000/ 0	n	Local Rep
Thomson McKinnon Investment Trust *Thomson McKinnon Short-Term Fund* One State Street Plaza New York, NY 10004 212/482-5894 800/628-1237	1984	Thomson McKinnon Asset Management L.P.	$104.2 Mil	$1,000/ 100	t	Local Rep
Transamerica Cash Reserve, Inc. P.O. Box 2438 Los Angeles, CA 90051-1598 213/742-2222	1980	Transamerica Investment Services	$415.5 Mil (e)	$500/ 100	n	Fund
Transamerica Current Interest, Inc. *Transamerica Money Market Fund* 1000 Louisiana Ste. 6000 Houston, TX 77002-5098 713/751-2400, 800/999-3863	1974	Transamerica Fund Management Company	$76.3 Mil	$1,000/ 50	p	Local Rep
Transamerica Current Interest, Inc. *Transamerica Premium Cash Account* 1000 Louisiana Ste. 6000 Houston, TX 77002-5098 713/751-2400, 800/999-3863	1982	Transamerica Fund Management Company	$154.8 Mil	$10,000/ 500	n	Local Rep
Transamerica Current Interest, Inc. *Transamerica U.S. Government Cash Reserves* 1000 Louisiana Ste. 6000 Houston, TX 77002-5098 713/751-2400, 800/999-3863	1982	Transamerica Fund Management Company	$91.4 Mil	$1,000/ 50	p	Local Rep

*Key: i=initial sales charge   r=redemption fee or contingent deferred sales charge(CDSC)
t=12b-1 fee and either CDSC or redemption fee   p=12b-1 fee   n=none of the preceding fees   N/A=not available

Money Market

Fund	Year Began	Investment Adviser	9/30/89 Assets	Minimum Initial and Subsequent Investment	Fees*	Where to Buy Shares
Transamerica Special Series, Inc. *Transamerica Special Money Market Fund* 1000 Louisiana Ste. 6000 Houston, TX 77002-5098 713/751-2400, 800/999-3863	1987	Transamerica Fund Management Company	$13.5 Mil	$1,000/ 50	t	Local Rep
Treasurer's Fund, Inc. *Domestic Prime Money Market Portfolio* 8 Sound Shore Dr. Greenwich, CT 06830 203/629-2090 800/877-3863	1987	Gabelli-O'Connor Fixed Income Mutual Funds Management Company	$300.2 Mil (e)	$100,000/ 0	n	Local Rep
Treasurer's Fund, Inc. *Money Market Plus Portfolio* 8 Sound Shore Dr. Greenwich, CT 06830 203/629-2090 800/877-3863	1988	Gabelli-O'Connor Fixed Income Mutual Funds Management Company	N/A	$100,000/ 0	n	Local Rep
Trinity Liquid Assets Trust *Trinity Money Market Fund* 183 E. Main St. Ste. 1035 Rochester, NY 14604 716/262-4080 800/456-7780	1983	Chase Lincoln First Bank, N.A.	$517.7 Mil	$1,000/ 0	n	Local Rep
T. Rowe Price Prime Reserve Fund, Inc. 100 E. Pratt St. Baltimore, MD 21202 301/547-2000 800/638-5660	1976	T. Rowe Price Associates, Inc.	$4.5 Bil	$2,500/ 100	n	Fund
T. Rowe Price U.S. Treasury Money Fund, Inc. 100 E. Pratt St. Baltimore, MD 21202 301/547-2000 800/638-5660	1982	T. Rowe Price Associates, Inc.	$309.4 Mil	$2,500/ 100	n	Fund
Trust for Federal Securities *FedFund* 3411 Silverside Rd. Webster Bldg., Ste. 204 Wilmington, DE 19810 302/478-6945 800/221-8120, 800/821-6006	1975	Provident Institutional Management Corporation	$1.5 Bil	$5,000/ 0	n	Local Rep

*Key: i=initial sales charge   r=redemption fee or contingent deferred sales charge(CDSC)
t=12b-1 fee and either CDSC or redemption fee   p=12b-1 fee   n=none of the preceding fees   N/A=not available

Money Market

Fund	Year Began	Investment Adviser	9/30/89 Assets	Minimum Initial and Subsequent Investment	Fees*	Where to Buy Shares
Trust for Federal Securities *T-Fund* 3411 Silverside Rd. Webster Bldg., Ste. 204 Wilmington, DE 19810 302/478-6945 800/221-8120, 800/821-6006	1980	Provident Institutional Management Corporation	$1.4 Bil	$5,000/ 0	n	Local Rep
Trust for Government Cash Reserves Federated Investors Twr. Pittsburgh, PA 15222-3779 412/288-1900 800/245-5000	1989	Federated Research	$246.0 Mil	$25,000/ 0	n	Local Rep
Trust for Short-Term U.S. Government Securities Federated Investors Twr. Pittsburgh, PA 15222-3779 412/288-1900 800/245-5000	1975	Federated Research	$3.7 Bil	$25,000/ 0	n	Local Rep
Trust for U.S. Treasury Obligations Federated Investors Twr. Pittsburgh, PA 15222-3779 412/288-1900 800/245-5000	1979	Federated Research	$5.7 Bil	$25,000/ 0	n	Local Rep
Twentieth Century Investors, Inc. *Cash Reserve* 4500 Main St. P.O. Box 419200 Kansas City, MO 64141-6200 816/531-5575 800/345-2021	1985	Investors Research Corporation	$612.5 Mil	$0/ 0	n	Fund
United Cash Management Fund, Inc. 2400 Pershing Rd. P.O. Box 418343 Kansas City, MO 64141-9343 816/283-4000 800/821-5664	1979	Waddell & Reed, Inc.	$494.7 Mil	$1,000/ 0	n	Local Rep
United Services Funds *U.S. Treasury Securities Fund* P.O. Box 29467 San Antonio, TX 78229-0467 512/696-1234 800/873-8637	1982	United Services Advisors, Inc.	$146.0 Mil	$100/ 50	n	Fund

*Key: i=initial sales charge   r=redemption fee or contingent deferred sales charge(CDSC)
     t=12b-1 fee and either CDSC or redemption fee   p=12b-1 fee   n=none of the preceding fees   N/A=not available

Money Market

Fund	Year Began	Investment Adviser	9/30/89 Assets	Minimum Initial and Subsequent Investment	Fees*	Where to Buy Shares
USAA Mutual Fund, Inc. *Money Market Fund* USAA Bldg. San Antonio, TX 78288 512/498-8000 800/531-8000	1981	USAA Investment Management Company	$875.9 Mil	$1,000/ 50	n	Fund
Value Line Cash Fund, Inc. 711 Third Ave. New York, NY 10017 212/687-3965 800/223-0818	1979	Value Line, Inc.	$603.0 Mil	$1,000/ 100	n	Fund
Van Eck Funds *U.S. Government Money Fund* 122 E. 42nd St. New York, NY 10168 212/687-5200 800/221-2220	1986	Van Eck Associates Corporation	$47.5 Mil	$1,000/ 100	p	Local Rep
Vanguard Institutional Money Market Portfolio Vanguard Financial Ctr. P.O. Box 2600 Valley Forge, PA 19482 215/648-6000 800/662-7447 800/362-0530 PA Only	1989	Vanguard Group, Inc.	N/A	$10.0 Mil/ 0	n	Fund
Vanguard Money Market Reserves *Federal Portfolio* Vanguard Financial Ctr. P.O. Box 2600 Valley Forge, PA 19482 215/648-6000 800/662-7447, 800/362-0530 PA Only	1981	Vanguard Group, Inc.	$1.5 Bil	$3,000/ 100	n	Fund
Vanguard Money Market Reserves *Prime Portfolio* Vanguard Financial Ctr. P.O. Box 2600 Valley Forge, PA 19482 215/648-6000 800/662-7447, 800/362-0530 PA Only	1975	Vanguard Group, Inc.	$10.5 Bil	$3,000/ 100	n	Fund
Vanguard Money Market Reserves *U.S. Treasury Portfolio* Vanguard Financial Ctr. P.O. Box 2600 Valley Forge, PA 19482 215/648-6000 800/662-7447, 800/362-0530 PA Only	1983	Vanguard Group, Inc.	$365.5 Mil	$3,000/ 100	n	Fund

*Key: i=initial sales charge   r=redemption fee or contingent deferred sales charge(CDSC)
t=12b-1 fee and either CDSC or redemption fee   p=12b-1 fee   n=none of the preceding fees   N/A=not available

Money Market

Fund	Year Began	Investment Adviser	9/30/89 Assets	Minimum Initial and Subsequent Investment	Fees*	Where to Buy Shares
Van Kampen Merritt Money Market Fund 1001 Warrenville Rd. Lisle, IL 60532 312/719-6000 800/225-2222	1983	Van Kampen Merritt Investment Advisory Corp.	$46.2 Mil	$1,000/ 100	p	Local Rep
Vantage Money Market Funds *Vantage Cash Portfolio* 1345 Avenue of the Americas New York, NY 10105 212/698-5349 800/544-7835	1982	Smith Barney, Harris Upham & Co. Incorporated	$1.1 Bil	$1/ 1	n	Local Rep
Vantage Money Market Funds *Vantage Government Portfolio* 1345 Avenue of the Americas New York, NY 10105 212/698-5349 800/544-7835	1982	Smith Barney, Harris Upham & Co. Incorporated	$135.8 Mil	$1/ 1	n	Local Rep
Variable Insurance Products Fund *Money Market Portfolio* 82 Devonshire St. Boston, MA 02109 617/570-7000 800/544-6666	1982	Fidelity Management & Research Company	$134.5 Mil	Not Applicable	n	Insur
Variable Investors Series Trust *Cash Management Portfolio* 1414 Main St. Springfield, MA 01144 413/732-7100	1987	Amherst Investment Management Company, Inc.	$9.8 Mil	Not Applicable	n	Insur
Venture Trust Money Market Fund *General Purpose Portfolio (The)* 124 E. Marcy St. P.O. Box 1688 Santa Fe, NM 87504-1688 505/983-4335, 800/458-6557	1983	Venture Advisers, L.P.	$12.0 Mil	$1,000/ 25	p	Local Rep
Venture Trust Money Market Fund *Government Portfolio (The)* 124 E. Marcy St. P.O. Box 1688 Santa Fe, NM 87504-1688 505/983-4335 800/458-6557	1980	Venture Advisers, L.P.	$16.5 Mil	$1,000/ 25	p	Local Rep

*Key: i=initial sales charge   r=redemption fee or contingent deferred sales charge(CDSC)
t=12b-1 fee and either CDSC or redemption fee   p=12b-1 fee   n=none of the preceding fees   N/A=not available

Money Market

Fund	Year Began	Investment Adviser	9/30/89 Assets	Minimum Initial and Subsequent Investment	Fees*	Where to Buy Shares
Voyageur GRANIT Money Market Fund, Inc. 100 S. Fifth St. Ste. 2200 Minneapolis, MN 55402 612/341-6728 800/553-2143 800/247-2143 MN Only	1985	Voyageur Fund Managers	$46.6 Mil	$1,000/ 100	p	Local Rep
Washington Square Cash Fund 20 Washington Ave. South Minneapolis, MN 55401 612/372-5605	1983	Washington Square Capital, Inc.	$69.5 Mil	$1,000/ 50	n	Local Rep
Wayne Hummer Money Fund Trust 175 W. Jackson Blvd. Chicago, IL 60604 312/431-1700 800/621-4477 800/972-5566 IL Only	1982	Wayne Hummer Management Company	$162.8 Mil	$500/ 500	n	Local Rep
Webster Cash Reserve Fund, Inc. 20 Exchange Place New York, NY 10005 212/510-5552	1979	Webster Management Corporation	$2.0 Bil	$1,500/ 500	n	Local Rep
Weiss Peck & Greer Funds Trust *WPG Short Term Income Fund* One New York Plaza 31st Fl. New York, NY 10004 212/908-9582 800/223-3332	1988	Weiss, Peck & Greer Advisers, Inc.	$111.5 Mil	$1,000/ 50	n	Fund
William Blair Ready Reserves, Inc. 135 S. LaSalle St. Chicago, IL 60603 312/236-1600	1988	William Blair & Company	N/A	$2,500/ 1	n	Local Rep
Working Assets Money Fund 230 California St. San Francisco, CA 94111 415/989-3200 800/533-FUND	1983	Working Assets Limited Partnership	$178.9 Mil	$1,000/ 100	p	Fund

*Key: i=initial sales charge   r=redemption fee or contingent deferred sales charge(CDSC)
t=12b-1 fee and either CDSC or redemption fee   p=12b-1 fee   n=none of the preceding fees   N/A=not available

Money Market

Fund	Year Began	Investment Adviser	9/30/89 Assets	Minimum Initial and Subsequent Investment	Fees*	Where to Buy Shares
Wright Managed Money Market Trust 24 Federal St. Boston, MA 02110 617/482-8260 800/225-6265	1982	Wright Investors Service	$39.9 Mil	$1,000/ 0	p	Local Rep
Zweig Cash Fund Inc. *Government Securities Portfolio* 25 Broadway New York, NY 10004 212/361-9612 800/272-2700	1982	Zweig/Glaser Advisers	$144.7 Mil (e)	$1,000/ 100	p	Fund
Zweig Cash Fund Inc. *Money Market Portfolio* 25 Broadway New York, NY 10004 212/361-9612 800/272-2700	1981	Zweig/Glaser Advisers	$477.5 Mil	$1,000/ 100	p	Fund
Zweig Series Trust *Money Market Series* 25 Broadway New York, NY 10004 212/361-9612 800/272-2700	1985	Zweig/Glaser Advisers	$38.1 Mil	$1,000/ 100	t	Local Rep

*Key: i=initial sales charge   r=redemption fee or contingent deferred sales charge(CDSC)
t=12b-1 fee and either CDSC or redemption fee   p=12b-1 fee   n=none of the preceding fees   N/A=not available

◆ ◆ ◆ ◆

Option/Income Funds

Option/Income

Fund	Year Began	Investment Adviser	9/30/89 Assets	Minimum Initial and Subsequent Investment	Fees*	Where to Buy Shares
Colonial Strategic Income Trust *Portfolio I* One Financial Ctr. Boston, MA 02111 617/426-3750 800/225-2365 800/426-3750	1977	Colonial Management Associates, Inc.	$533.5 Mil	$250/ 25	i	Local Rep
Colonial Strategic Income Trust *Portfolio II* One Financial Ctr. Boston, MA 02111 617/426-3750 800/225-2365 800/426-3750	1984	Colonial Management Associates, Inc.	$102.2 Mil	$250/ 25	i	Local Rep
Dean Witter Option Income Trust Two World Trade Ctr. New York, NY 10048 212/392-2550 800/869-3863	1985	Dean Witter Reynolds Inc. - InterCapital Division	$230.4 Mil	$1,000/ 100	t	Local Rep
Franklin Option Fund 777 Mariners Island Blvd. San Mateo, CA 94404 415/570-3000 800/632-2180 800/632-2350	1951	Franklin Advisers, Inc.	$47.4 Mil	$100/ 25	i	Local Rep
Gateway Trust *Gateway Option Index Fund* P.O. Box 458167 Cincinnati, OH 45245 513/248-2700 800/354-6339	1977	Gateway Investment Advisers, Inc.	$27.2 Mil (e)	$500/ 100	n	Fund
Loch Ness Option Fund, Inc. 7039 Encina Lane Boca Raton, FL 33433 407/488-3589	1987	Loch Ness Investments, Inc.	$0.6 Mil (e)	$1,000/ 100	n	Fund
National Premium Income Fund 600 Third Ave. New York, NY 10016 203/863-5600 800/237-1718	1987	National Securities & Research Corporation	$12.8 Mil	$500/ 25	i, p	Local Rep

*Key: i=initial sales charge   r=redemption fee or contingent deferred sales charge(CDSC)
t=12b-1 fee and either CDSC or redemption fee   p=12b-1 fee   n=none of the preceding fees   N/A=not available

Option/Income

Fund	Year Began	Investment Adviser	9/30/89 Assets	Minimum Initial and Subsequent Investment	Fees*	Where to Buy Shares
Olympus Premium Income Fund 230 Park Ave. New York, NY 10169 212/309-8400 800/626-FUND	1986	Furman Selz Mager Dietz & Birney Incorporated	$48.3 Mil (e)	$1,000/ 100	i, p	Local Rep
Oppenheimer Premium Income Fund Two World Trade Ctr. New York, NY 10048-0669 212/323-0200 800/525-7048	1977	Oppenheimer Management Corporation	$287.6 Mil	$1,000/ 25	i	Local Rep
Putnam Option Income Trust One Post Office Sq. Boston, MA 02109 617/292-1000 800/225-2465	1977	Putnam Management Company, Inc.	$993.3 Mil	$500/ 50	i	Local Rep
Putnam Option Income Trust II One Post Office Sq. Boston, MA 02109 617/292-1000 800/225-2465	1985	Putnam Management Company, Inc.	$1.2 Bil	$500/ 50	i	Local Rep
SLH Special Income Portfolios *SLH Option/Income Portfolio* 31 W. 52nd St. New York, NY 10019 212/767-3700	1985	Boston Company Advisors, Inc.	$590.0 Mil	$500/ 200	t	Local Rep
Zweig Series Trust *Option Income Series* 25 Broadway New York, NY 10004 212/361-9612 800/272-2700	1985	Zweig/Glaser Advisers	$15.2 Mil (e)	$1,000/ 100	t	Local Rep

*Key: i=initial sales charge   r=redemption fee or contingent deferred sales charge(CDSC)
t=12b-1 fee and either CDSC or redemption fee   p=12b-1 fee   n=none of the preceding fees   N/A=not available

◆ ◆ ◆ ◆

Precious Metals/Gold Funds

Precious Metals/Gold

Fund	Year Began	Investment Adviser	9/30/89 Assets	Minimum Initial and Subsequent Investment	Fees*	Where to Buy Shares
American Pension Investors Trust *Precious Resources Fund* 2303 Yorktown Ave. P.O. Box 2529 Lynchburg, VA 24501 804/846-1361 800/544-6060, 800/533-4115 VA Only	1988	American Pension Investors, Inc.	$2.4 Mil	$100/ 50	p	Local Rep
Benham Equity Fund *Benham Gold Equities Index Fund* 755 Page Mill Rd. Palo Alto, CA 94304 415/858-2400 800/227-8380 800/982-6150 CA Only	1988	Benham Management Corporation	$22.4 Mil	$1,000/ 100	n	Fund
Blanchard Precious Metals Fund, Inc. 41 Madison Ave. 24th Fl. New York, NY 10010 212/779-7979 800/922-7771	1988	Sheffield Management Company	$27.3 Mil	$3,000/ 200	p	Fund
Bull & Bear Gold Investors, Ltd. 11 Hanover Sq. New York, NY 10005 212/785-0900 800/847-4200	1979	Bull & Bear International Advisers, Inc.	$37.5 Mil (e)	$1,000/ 100	p	Fund
Chubb America Fund, Inc. *Gold Stock Portfolio* One Granite Place Concord, NH 03301 603/224-7741	1985	Chubb Investment Advisory Corporation	$4.4 Mil (e)	Not Applicable	n	Insur
Colonial Advanced Strategies Gold Trust One Financial Ctr. Boston, MA 02111 617/426-3750 800/225-2365 800/426-3750	1985	Colonial Management Associates, Inc.	$79.6 Mil	$250/ 25	i, p	Local Rep
Enterprise Specialty Portfolios *Enterprise Precious Metals Portfolio* 1200 Ashwood Pkwy. Ste. 290 Atlanta, GA 30338 404/396-8118, 800/432-4320	1987	Enterprise Capital Management, Inc.	$4.5 Mil (e)	$500/ 25	t	Local Rep

*Key: i=initial sales charge   r=redemption fee or contingent deferred sales charge(CDSC)
t=12b-1 fee and either CDSC or redemption fee   p=12b-1 fee   n=none of the preceding fees   N/A=not available

395

Precious Metals/Gold

Fund	Year Began	Investment Adviser	9/30/89 Assets	Minimum Initial and Subsequent Investment	Fees*	Where to Buy Shares
Equitec Siebel Fund Group *Equitec Siebel Precious Metals Fund Series* 7677 Oakport St. P.O. Box 2470 Oakland, CA 94614 415/430-9900 800/869-8900	1988	Siebel Capital Management, Inc.	$2.7 Mil (e)	$1,000/ 0	t	Local Rep
Excel Midas Gold Shares, Inc. 16955 Via Del Campo Ste. 200 San Diego, CA 92127 619/485-9400 800/333-9235	1986	Excel Advisors, Inc.	$10.1 Mil (e)	$1,000/ 250	i, p	Local Rep
Fidelity Select Portfolios *American Gold Portfolio* 82 Devonshire St. Boston, MA 02109 617/570-7000 800/544-6666	1985	Fidelity Management & Research Company	$189.5 Mil	$1,000/ 250	i, r	Fund
Fidelity Select Portfolios *Precious Metals and Minerals Portfolio* 82 Devonshire St. Boston, MA 02109 617/570-7000 800/544-6666	1981	Fidelity Management & Research Company	$197.5 Mil	$1,000/ 250	i, r	Fund
Franklin Gold Fund 777 Mariners Island Blvd. San Mateo, CA 94404 415/570-3000 800/632-2180 800/632-2350	1969	Franklin Advisers, Inc.	$277.1 Mil	$100/ 25	i	Local Rep
IDS Precious Metals Fund, Inc. IDS Tower 10 Minneapolis, MN 55440 612/372-3131 800/328-8300	1985	IDS Financial Corporation	$94.7 Mil	$100/ 100	i, p	Local Rep
Institutional Fiduciary Trust *Precious Metals Portfolio* 777 Mariners Island Blvd. San Mateo, CA 94404 415/570-3000 800/632-2180 800/632-2350	1985	Franklin Trust Company	N/A	$25,000/ 0	n	Local Rep

*Key: i=initial sales charge   r=redemption fee or contingent deferred sales charge(CDSC)
t=12b-1 fee and either CDSC or redemption fee   p=12b-1 fee   n=none of the preceding fees   N/A=not available

Precious Metals/Gold

Fund	Year Began	Investment Adviser	9/30/89 Assets	Minimum Initial and Subsequent Investment	Fees*	Where to Buy Shares
International Investors Incorporated 122 E. 42nd St. New York, NY 10168 212/687-5200 800/221-2220	1955	Van Eck Management Corporation	$790.8 Mil	$1,000/ 100	i	Local Rep
Kemper Gold Fund 120 S. LaSalle St. Chicago, IL 60603 312/781-1121 800/621-1148	1988	Kemper Financial Services, Inc.	$6.8 Mil	$1,000/ 100	i, p	Local Rep
Keystone Precious Metals Holdings, Inc. 99 High St. Boston, MA 02110 617/338-3200 800/343-2898 800/225-1587	1983	Harbor Keystone Advisers, Inc.	$198.7 Mil	$250/ 0	t	Local Rep
Lexington Goldfund, Inc. Park 80 W., Plaza Two P.O. Box 1515 Saddle Brook, NJ 07662 201/845-7300 800/526-0056	1981	Lexington Management Corporation	$95.3 Mil	$1,000/ 50	n	Fund
MacKay-Shields MainStay Series Fund *MainStay Gold & Precious Metals Fund* 51 Madison Ave. New York, NY 10010 212/576-7000 800/522-4202	1987	Gamma Advisers Ltd.	$7.1 Mil	$500/ 50	t	Local Rep
Management of Managers Group of Funds *Precious Metals Fund* 200 Connecticut Ave. 8th Fl. Norwalk, CT 06854 203/855-2200	1989	Evaluation Associates Investment Management Co.	N/A	$0/ 0	n	Local Rep
MFS Lifetime Investment Program *Lifetime Gold & Precious Metals Trust* 500 Boylston St. Boston, MA 02116 617/954-5000 800/343-2829	1988	Lifetime Advisers, Inc.	$3.2 Mil	$1,000/ 50	t	Local Rep

*Key: i=initial sales charge   r=redemption fee or contingent deferred sales charge(CDSC)
t=12b-1 fee and either CDSC or redemption fee   p=12b-1 fee   n=none of the preceding fees   N/A=not available

Precious Metals/Gold

Fund	Year Began	Investment Adviser	9/30/89 Assets	Minimum Initial and Subsequent Investment	Fees*	Where to Buy Shares
Monitrend Mutual Fund *Gold Series* 272 Closter Dock Rd. Ste. 1 Closter, NJ 07624 201/767-5400 800/251-1970	1987	Monitrend Investment Management, Inc.	$1.9 Mil (e)	$1,000/ 50	i, p	Local Rep
Oppenheimer Gold & Special Minerals Fund Two World Trade Ctr. New York, NY 10048-0669 212/323-0200 800/525-7048	1983	Oppenheimer Management Corporation	$135.6 Mil	$1,000/ 25	i	Local Rep
Scudder Mutual Funds, Inc. *Scudder Gold Fund* 345 Park Ave. New York, NY 10154 617/439-4640 800/225-2470 800/225-5163	1988	Scudder, Stevens & Clark, Inc.	$11.3 Mil	$1,000/ 100	n	Fund
SLH Investment Series, Inc. *SLH Precious Metals Portfolio* 31 W. 52nd St. 15th Fl. New York, NY 10019 212/767-3700 800/334-4636, 800/422-0214 NY Only	1984	SLH Asset Management Division of Shearson Lehman Hutton Inc.	$84.8 Mil	$500/ 250	t	Local Rep
SLH Precious Metals and Minerals Fund 31 W. 52nd St. New York, NY 10019 212/767-3700	1986	SLH Global Asset Management S.A.	$35.2 Mil	$500/ 200	i	Local Rep
Thomson McKinnon Investment Trust *Thomson McKinnon Precious Metals & Natural Resources Fund* One State Street Plaza New York, NY 10004 212/482-5894, 800/628-1237	1988	Thomson McKinnon Asset Management L.P.	$6.6 Mil	$1,000/ 100	t	Local Rep
United Gold & Government Fund, Inc. 2400 Pershing Rd. P.O. Box 418343 Kansas City, MO 64141-9343 816/283-4000 800/821-5664	1985	Waddell & Reed, Inc.	$82.0 Mil	$500/ 25	i	Local Rep

*Key: i=initial sales charge   r=redemption fee or contingent deferred sales charge(CDSC)
t=12b-1 fee and either CDSC or redemption fee   p=12b-1 fee   n=none of the preceding fees   N/A=not available

Precious Metals/Gold

Fund	Year Began	Investment Adviser	9/30/89 Assets	Minimum Initial and Subsequent Investment	Fees*	Where to Buy Shares
United Services Funds *Prospector Fund* P.O. Box 29467 San Antonio, TX 78229-0467 512/696-1234 800/873-8637	1983	United Services Advisors, Inc.	$39.9 Mil	$100/ 50	r	Fund
United Services Funds *U.S. Gold Shares Fund* P.O. Box 29467 San Antonio, TX 78229-0467 512/696-1234 800/873-8637	1974	United Services Advisors, Inc.	$285.0 Mil	$100/ 50	n	Fund
United Services Funds *U.S. New Prospector Fund* P.O. Box 29467 San Antonio, TX 78229-0467 512/696-1234 800/873-8637	1985	United Services Advisors, Inc.	$92.4 Mil	$100/ 50	r	Fund
USAA Investment Trust *Gold Fund* USAA Bldg. San Antonio, TX 78288 512/498-8000 800/531-8000	1984	USAA Investment Management Company	$165.3 Mil	$1,000/ 50	n	Fund
Van Eck Funds *Gold/Resources Fund* 122 E. 42nd St. New York, NY 10168 212/687-5200 800/221-2220	1986	Van Eck Associates Corporation	$227.3 Mil	$1,000/ 100	i, p	Local Rep
Vanguard Specialized Portfolios *Gold & Precious Metals Portfolio* Vanguard Financial Ctr. P.O. Box 2600 Valley Forge, PA 19482 215/648-6000, 800/662-7447, 800/362-0530 PA Only	1984	M & G Investment Management, Ltd.	$135.8 Mil	$3,000/ 100	r	Fund

*Key: i=initial sales charge   r=redemption fee or contingent deferred sales charge(CDSC)
t=12b-1 fee and either CDSC or redemption fee   p=12b-1 fee   n=none of the preceding fees   N/A=not available

◆ ◆ ◆ ◆

Short-term Municipal Bond Funds

Short-term Municipal Bond

Fund	Year Began	Investment Adviser	9/30/89 Assets	Minimum Initial and Subsequent Investment	Fees*	Where to Buy Shares
AARP Insured Tax Free Income Trust *AARP Insured Tax Free Short Term Fund* AARP Investment Program 175 Federal St. Boston, MA 02110-2267 800/253-2277	1984	AARP/Scudder Financial Management Company	$89.6 Mil	$250/ 0	n	Fund
ABT Money Market Series, Inc. *ABT Tax-Free Portfolio* 205 Royal Palm Way Palm Beach, FL 33480 407/655-7255 800/441-6580	1989	Palm Beach Capital Management, Ltd.	$1.0 Mil	$1,000/ 100	n	Local Rep
Active Assets Tax-Free Trust Two World Trade Ctr. New York, NY 10048 212/392-2550 800/869-3863	1981	Dean Witter Reynolds Inc. - InterCapital Division	$1.1 Bil	$0/ 0	p	Local Rep
Alliance Tax-Exempt Reserves *New York Portfolio* 1345 Avenue of the Americas New York, NY 10105 212/969-1000 800/221-5672	1986	Alliance Capital Management L.P.	$56.0 Mil	$1,000/ 100	p	Local Rep
Alliance Tax-Exempt Reserves *Tax-Exempt Reserves (General)* 1345 Avenue of the Americas New York, NY 10105 212/969-1000 800/221-5672	1983	Alliance Capital Management L.P.	$798.4 Mil	$1,000/ 100	p	Local Rep
Altura Fund *Tax-Free Obligations Fund* 1900 E. Dublin-Granville Rd. Columbus, OH 43229 614/899-4600 800/338-4385	1986	United Bank of Denver National Association	N/A	$1,000/ 50	N/A	Fund
AMA Money Fund, Inc. *Tax-Free Portfolio* 5 Sentry Pkwy. W, Ste. 120 P.O. Box 1111 Blue Bell, PA 19422 215/825-0400 800/AMA-FUND	1989	AMA Advisers, Inc.	$2.8 Mil	$2,000/ 100	p	Fund

*Key: i=initial sales charge   r=redemption fee or contingent deferred sales charge(CDSC)
t=12b-1 fee and either CDSC or redemption fee   p=12b-1 fee   n=none of the preceding fees   N/A=not available

Short-term Municipal Bond

Fund	Year Began	Investment Adviser	9/30/89 Assets	Minimum Initial and Subsequent Investment	Fees*	Where to Buy Shares
American Capital Tax-Exempt Trust *Money Market Municipal Portfolio* 2800 Post Oak Blvd. Houston, TX 77056 713/993-0500 800/421-5666	1986	American Capital Asset Management, Inc.	$9.4 Mil	$500/ 50	n	Local Rep
Arch Tax-Exempt Trust *Discretionary Portfolio* 3516 Silverside Rd. The Commons, No. 6 Wilmington, DE 19810 302/478-6945 800/441-7379	1986	Mississippi Valley Advisers	$120.5 Mil	$1,000/ 0	p	Local Rep
Arch Tax-Exempt Trust *Non-Discretionary Portfolio* 3516 Silverside Rd. The Commons, No. 6 Wilmington, DE 19810 302/478-6945 800/441-7379	1986	Mississippi Valley Advisers	N/A	$1,000/ 0	p	Local Rep
Bedford Tax-Free Money Market Portfolio 16 Industrial Blvd. Paoli, PA 19301 215/251-0550 800/523-7798	1988	Provident Institutional Management Corporation	$108.1 Mil	$1,000/ 100	p	Local Rep
Benham National Tax-Free Trust *Money Market Portfolio* 755 Page Mill Rd. Palo Alto, CA 94304 415/858-2400 800/227-8380 800/982-6150 CA Only	1984	Benham Management Corporation	$94.0 Mil	$1,000/ 100	n	Fund
Bison Money Market Fund *Tax-Exempt Discretionary Portfolio* 3512 Silverside Rd. The Commons, No. 6 Wilmington, DE 19810 302/478-6945 800/441-7379	1987	Provident Institutional Management Corporation	$70.9 Mil (e)	$2,000/ 0	p	Local Rep
Bison Money Market Fund *Tax-Exempt Non-Discretionary Portfolio* 3512 Silverside Rd. The Commons, No. 6 Wilmington, DE 19810 302/478-6945 800/441-7379	1987	Provident Institutional Management Corporation	$51.8 Mil (e)	$2,000/ 0	p	Local Rep

*Key: i=initial sales charge   r=redemption fee or contingent deferred sales charge(CDSC)
t=12b-1 fee and either CDSC or redemption fee   p=12b-1 fee   n=none of the preceding fees   N/A=not available

Short-term Municipal Bond

Fund	Year Began	Investment Adviser	9/30/89 Assets	Minimum Initial and Subsequent Investment	Fees*	Where to Buy Shares
Boston Company Tax-Free Municipal Funds *Tax-Free Money Fund* One Boston Place Boston, MA 02019 617/956-9740 800/225-5267 800/343-6324	1983	Boston Company Advisors, Inc.	$22.2 Mil	$1,000/ 0	p	Local Rep
Calvert Tax-Free Reserves *Limited-Term Portfolio* 1700 Pennsylvania Ave., NW Washington, DC 20006 301/951-4820 800/368-2745	1980	Calvert Asset Management Company, Inc.	$133.5 Mil	$2,000/ 250	n	Fund
Calvert Tax-Free Reserves *Money Market Portfolio* 1700 Pennsylvania Ave., NW Washington, DC 20006 301/951-4820 800/368-2745	1980	Calvert Asset Management Company, Inc.	$848.2 Mil	$2,000/ 250	n	Fund
Cardinal Tax Exempt Money Trust 155 E. Broad St. Columbus, OH 43215 614/464-5511 800/848-7734 800/262-9446 OH only	1983	Cardinal Management Corporation	$82.1 Mil	$1,000/ 100	n	Fund
Carnegie Tax Free Income Trust 1100 The Halle Bldg. 1228 Euclid Ave. Cleveland, OH 44115-1831 216/781-4440 800/321-2322	1982	Carnegie Capital Management Company	$223.7 Mil	$1,000/ 250	n	Local Rep
Cash Accumulation Trust *National Tax-Exempt Fund* One State Street Plaza New York, NY 10004 212/482-5894 800/628-1237	1984	Thomson McKinnon Asset Management L.P.	$235.9 Mil	$500/ 100	p	Local Rep
Cash Assets Trust *Tax-Free Cash Assets Trust* 200 Park Ave. Ste. 4515 New York, NY 10017 212/697-6666 800/228-4227	1988	Hawaiian Trust Company, Limited	$57.6 Mil	$1,000/ 0	n	Fund

*Key: i=initial sales charge   r=redemption fee or contingent deferred sales charge(CDSC)
t=12b-1 fee and either CDSC or redemption fee   p=12b-1 fee   n=none of the preceding fees   N/A=not available

405

Short-term Municipal Bond

Fund	Year Began	Investment Adviser	9/30/89 Assets	Minimum Initial and Subsequent Investment	Fees*	Where to Buy Shares
Cash Equivalent Fund, Inc. *Tax-Exempt Portfolio* 120 S. LaSalle St. Chicago, IL 60603 312/781-1121 800/621-1148	1982	Kemper Financial Services, Inc.	$2.2 Bil	$1,000/ 100	p	Local Rep
Cash Preservation Tax-Free Money Market Portfolio 16 Industrial Blvd. Paoli, PA 19301 215/251-0550 800/523-7798	1988	Provident Institutional Management Corporation	N/A	$1,000/ 100	p	Local Rep
Cash Trust Series *Municipal Cash Series* Federated Investors Twr. Pittsburgh, PA 15222-3779 412/288-1900 800/245-5051	1989	Federated Advisers	$8.1 Mil	$1,000/ 500	N/A	Local Rep
Centennial Tax Exempt Trust 3410 S. Galena St. Denver, CO 80231 303/671-3200 800/525-7048	1981	Centennial Capital Corporation	$550.2 Mil	$500/ 25	p	Local Rep
Churchill Tax-Free Trust *Churchill Tax-Free Cash Fund* 200 Park Ave. Ste. 4515 New York, NY 10017 212/697-6666 800/872-5859	1988	Citizens Fidelity Bank & Trust Company	N/A	$1,000/ 0	n	Fund
CIGNA Cash Funds *CIGNA Tax-Exempt Cash Fund* One Financial Plaza Springfield, MA 01103 413/784-0100 800/56CIGNA	1982	CIGNA Investments, Inc.	$46.5 Mil	$1,000/ 100	p	Local Rep
CMA Tax-Exempt Fund P.O. Box 9011 Princeton, NJ 08543-9011 201/560-5507 800/262-4636 800/262-3276	1981	Fund Asset Management, Inc.	$7.4 Bil	$0/ 0	p	Local Rep

*Key: i=initial sales charge   r=redemption fee or contingent deferred sales charge(CDSC)
t=12b-1 fee and either CDSC or redemption fee   p=12b-1 fee   n=none of the preceding fees   N/A=not available

Short-term Municipal Bond

Fund	Year Began	Investment Adviser	9/30/89 Assets	Minimum Initial and Subsequent Investment	Fees*	Where to Buy Shares
Colonial Tax-Exempt Money Market Trust One Financial Ctr. Boston, MA 02111 617/426-3750 800/225-2365 800/426-3750	1987	Colonial Management Associates, Inc.	$47.6 Mil	$250/ 25	n	Local Rep
Command Tax-Free Fund One Seaport Plaza New York, NY 10292 212/214-1215 800/872-7787	1982	Prudential Mutual Fund Management	$666.8 Mil	$10,000/ 0	p	Local Rep
Compass Capital Group *Tax Exempt Fund* 1900 E. Dublin-Granville Rd. Columbus, OH 43229 614/899-4600 800/338-4385	1989	Midlantic National Bank	N/A	$5,000/ 100	N/A	Fund
Composite Cash Management Company *Tax-Exempt Money Market Portfolio* W. 601 Riverside, 9th Fl. Seafirst Financial Ctr. Spokane, WA 99201 509/353-3400, 800/543-8072, 800/572-5828	1988	Composite Research & Management Company	$23.3 Mil	$1,000/ 50	n	Local Rep
Conestoga Family of Funds *Tax-Free Fund* 1900 E. Dublin-Granville Rd. Columbus, OH 43229 614/899-4600 800/338-4385	1989	Meridian Investment Company	N/A	$1,000/ 0	N/A	Fund
Cortland Trust *Tax-Free Money Market Fund* 3 University Plaza Hackensack, NJ 07601 201/342-6066 800/433-1918	1985	Cortland Financial Group, Inc.	$175.0 Mil	$100/ 25	p	Local Rep
Daily Tax-Exempt Money Fund 82 Devonshire St. Boston, MA 02109 617/570-7000 800/343-9184 617/570-4750 MA Only	1983	Fidelity Management & Research Company	$218.5 Mil	$1,000/ 250	p	Local Rep

*Key: i=initial sales charge   r=redemption fee or contingent deferred sales charge(CDSC)
t=12b-1 fee and either CDSC or redemption fee   p=12b-1 fee   n=none of the preceding fees   N/A=not available

Short-term Municipal Bond

Fund	Year Began	Investment Adviser	9/30/89 Assets	Minimum Initial and Subsequent Investment	Fees*	Where to Buy Shares
Dean Witter/Sears Tax-Free Daily Income Trust Two World Trade Ctr. New York, NY 10048 212/392-2550 800/869-3863	1981	Dean Witter Reynolds Inc. - InterCapital Division	$934.6 Mil	$5,000/ 100	p	Local Rep
Delaware Group Tax-Free Money Fund *Original Class* One Commerce Sq. Philadelphia, PA 19103 215/988-1200 800/523-4640	1981	Delaware Management Company, Inc.	$58.7 Mil	$5,000/100	n	Fund
Dreyfus Tax Exempt Cash Management 666 Old Country Rd. Garden City, NY 11530 718/895-1650 800/346-3621	1985	Dreyfus Corporation	$904.6 Mil	$10.0 Mil/ 0	n	Local Rep
Dreyfus Tax Exempt Money Market Fund, Inc. 666 Old Country Rd. Garden City, NY 11530 718/895-1206 800/645-6561	1980	Dreyfus Corporation	$2.3 Bil	$2,500/ 100	n	Fund
Eaton Vance Tax Free Reserves 24 Federal St. Boston, MA 02110 617/482-8260 800/225-6265	1982	Eaton Vance Management, Inc.	$42.2 Mil	$1,000/ 50	n	Local Rep
Evergreen Tax Exempt Money Market Fund 2500 Westchester Ave. Purchase, NY 10577 914/694-2020 800/235-0064	1988	Evergreen Asset Management Corporation	$85.2 Mil (e)	$2,000/ 100	n	Fund
Federated Tax-Free Trust Federated Investors Twr. Pittsburgh, PA 15222-3779 412/288-1900 800/245-5000	1979	Federated Research	$2.1 Bil	$25,000/ 0	n	Local Rep

*Key: i=initial sales charge   r=redemption fee or contingent deferred sales charge(CDSC)
t=12b-1 fee and either CDSC or redemption fee   p=12b-1 fee   n=none of the preceding fees   N/A=not available

Short-term Municipal Bond

Fund	Year Began	Investment Adviser	9/30/89 Assets	Minimum Initial and Subsequent Investment	Fees*	Where to Buy Shares
FFB Funds Trust *FFB Tax-Free Money Market Fund* 230 Park Ave. 12th Fl. New York, NY 10169 212/309-8400 800/845-8406	1986	First Fidelity Bank, N.A.	$143.9 Mil (e)	$1,000/ 100	p	Local Rep
Fidelity Institutional Tax-Exempt Cash Portfolios 82 Devonshire St. Boston, MA 02109 617/570-7000 800/343-9184	1985	Fidelity Management & Research Company	$2.1 Bil	$50.0 Mil/ 0	n	Local Rep
Fidelity Tax-Exempt Money Market Trust 82 Devonshire St. Boston, MA 02109 617/570-7000 800/544-6666	1980	Fidelity Management & Research Company	$2.9 Bil	$5,000/ 500	n	Fund
First Investors Tax Exempt Money Market Fund, Inc. 120 Wall St. New York, NY 10005 212/208-6000	1983	First Investors Management Company, Inc.	$40.2 Mil	$1,000/ 100	p	Local Rep
First Prairie Tax Exempt Money Market Fund 666 Old Country Rd. 4th Fl. Garden City, NY 11530 516/296-3300 800/821-1185	1986	First National Bank of Chicago	$143.4 Mil	$1,000/ 100	p	Local Rep
FN Network Tax Free Money Market Fund 666 Old Country Rd. Garden City, NY 11530 800/554-4611	1988	Dreyfus Corporation	$99.3 Mil	$1,000/ 100	p	Fund
Franklin Tax-Exempt Money Fund 777 Mariners Island Blvd. San Mateo, CA 94404 415/570-3000 800/632-2180 800/632-2350	1982	Franklin Advisers, Inc.	$219.3 Mil	$500/ 25	n	Fund

*Key: i=initial sales charge   r=redemption fee or contingent deferred sales charge(CDSC)
t=12b-1 fee and either CDSC or redemption fee   p=12b-1 fee   n=none of the preceding fees   N/A=not available

409

Short-term Municipal Bond

Fund	Year Began	Investment Adviser	9/30/89 Assets	Minimum Initial and Subsequent Investment	Fees*	Where to Buy Shares
Frank Russell Investment Company *Limited Volatility Tax Free* 909 A St. Tacoma, WA 98402 206/627-7001 800/972-0700	1985	Frank Russell Investment Management Company	$31.5 Mil	$0/ 0	n	Local Rep
Frank Russell Investment Company *Tax Free Money Market Fund* 909 A St. Tacoma, WA 98402 206/627-7001 800/972-0700	1987	Frank Russell Investment Management Company	$31.8 Mil	$0/ 0	n	Local Rep
Freedom Group of Tax Exempt Funds *Freedom Tax Exempt Money Fund* One Beacon St. Boston, MA 02108 617/523-3170 800/225-6258, 800/392-6037 MA Only	1982	Freedom Capital Management Corporation	$229.7 Mil	$1,000/ 100	n	Local Rep
Galaxy Fund *Tax-Exempt Money Market Fund* 3512 Silverside Rd. The Commons, No. 6 Wilmington, DE 19810 302/478-6945 800/441-7379	1988	Norstar Investment Advisory Services, Inc.	$126.6 Mil	$0/ 0	p	Local Rep
General Tax Exempt Money Market Fund, Inc. 666 Old Country Rd. Garden City, NY 11530 718/895-1396 800/242-8671	1983	Dreyfus Corporation	$335.6 Mil	$2,500/ 100	p	Fund
GIT Tax-Free Trust *Money Market Portfolio* 1655 Fort Myer Dr. Arlington, VA 22209 703/528-6500 800/336-3063	1982	Bankers Finance Investment Management Corp.	$25.1 Mil	$1,000/ 0	p	Fund
GW Sierra Trust Funds *GW Global Income Money Market Fund* 888 S. Figueroa St. 11th Fl. Los Angeles, CA 90017-0970 213/488-2200 800/331-3426, 800/221-9876 CA ONLY	1989	Great Western Financial Advisors Corp.	N/A	$1,000/ 100	p	Local Rep

*Key: i=initial sales charge   r=redemption fee or contingent deferred sales charge(CDSC)
t=12b-1 fee and either CDSC or redemption fee   p=12b-1 fee   n=none of the preceding fees   N/A=not available

Short-term Municipal Bond

Fund	Year Began	Investment Adviser	9/30/89 Assets	Minimum Initial and Subsequent Investment	Fees*	Where to Buy Shares
Helmsman Fund *Tax-Free Obligations Portfolio* 1900 E. Dublin-Granville Rd. Columbus, OH 43229 614/899-4600 800/338-4385	1989	Bank One, Indianapolis, N.A. Bank One, Milwaukee, N.A.	N/A	$1,000/ 0	N/A	Fund
Highmark Group *Tax-Free Fund* 1900 E. Dublin-Granville Rd. Columbus, OH 43229 614/899-4600 800/338-4385	1987	Merus Capital Management	N/A	$1,000/ 100	N/A	Fund
Home Group Trust *Home Federal Tax-Free Reserves* 59 Maiden Lane 21st Fl. New York, NY 10038 212/530-6016 800/729-3863	1988	Home Capital Services, Inc.	$92.8 Mil	$1,000/ 100	p	Local Rep
Horizon Funds *Horizon Tax-Exempt Money Fund* 156 W. 56th St. Ste. 1902 New York, NY 10019 212/492-1600 800/367-6075	1987	Security Pacific National Bank	$354.4 Mil	$500,000/ 0	n	Local Rep
IDS Tax-Free Money Fund, Inc. IDS Tower 10 Minneapolis, MN 55440 612/372-3131 800/328-8300	1980	IDS Financial Corporation	$126.4 Mil	$2,000/ 100	p	Local Rep
Integrated Tax Free Portfolios *Tax Free Money Market Portfolio* 10 Union Square East New York, NY 10003 212/353-7000 800/858-8850	1987	Integrated Resources Asset Management Corp.	$24.1 Mil	$1,000/ 100	p	Local Rep
INVESCO Treasurers Series Trust *Tax-Exempt Fund* 1315 Peachtree St., NE Ste. 500 Atlanta, GA 30309 404/892-0666 800/554-1156	1988	INVESCO Capital Management, Inc.	N/A	$1.0 Mil/ 5,000	N/A	Local Rep

*Key: i=initial sales charge   r=redemption fee or contingent deferred sales charge(CDSC)
        t=12b-1 fee and either CDSC or redemption fee   p=12b-1 fee   n=none of the preceding fees   N/A=not available

Short-term Municipal Bond

Fund	Year Began	Investment Adviser	9/30/89 Assets	Minimum Initial and Subsequent Investment	Fees*	Where to Buy Shares
Kemper Money Market Fund *Tax-Exempt Portfolio* 120 S. LaSalle St. Chicago, IL 60603 312/781-1121 800/621-1148	1987	Kemper Financial Services, Inc.	$557.4 Mil	$1,000/ 100	n	Fund
Keystone America Tax Free Money Market Fund 99 High St. Boston, MA 02110 617/338-3200 800/343-2898 800/225-1587	1987	Keystone Custodian Funds, Inc.	$6.3 Mil	$1,000/ 0	p	Local Rep
Kidder, Peabody Tax Exempt Money Fund, Inc. 20 Exchange Place New York, NY 10005 212/510-5552	1983	Webster Management Corporation	$702.2 Mil	$1,500/ 500	n	Local Rep
Legg Mason Tax-Exempt Trust, Inc. 111 S. Calvert St. P.O. Box 1476 Baltimore, MD 21203-1476 301/539-3400 800/822-5544 800/492-7777 MD Only	1983	Legg Mason Fund Adviser, Inc.	$164.8 Mil	$5,000/ 500	n	Local Rep
Lexington Tax Free Money Fund, Inc. Park 80 West, Plaza Two P.O. Box 1515 Saddle Brook, NJ 07662 201/845-7300 800/526-0056	1980	Lexington Management Corporation	$75.9 Mil	$1,000/ 50	n	Fund
Liquid Green Tax-Free Trust 429 N. Pennsylvania St. Indianapolis, IN 46204-1897 317/634-3300 800/862-7283	1983	Unified Management Corporation	$76.9 Mil	$1,000/ 0	n	Fund
Management of Managers Group of Funds *Short Term Municipal Bond Fund* 200 Connecticut Ave. 8th Fl. Norwalk, CT 06854 203/855-2200	1984	Evaluation Associates Investment Management Co.	$30.7 Mil	$0/ 0	n	Local Rep

*Key: i=initial sales charge   r=redemption fee or contingent deferred sales charge(CDSC)
t=12b-1 fee and either CDSC or redemption fee   p=12b-1 fee   n=none of the preceding fees   N/A=not available

Short-term Municipal Bond

Fund	Year Began	Investment Adviser	9/30/89 Assets	Minimum Initial and Subsequent Investment	Fees*	Where to Buy Shares
Mariner Funds Trust *Mariner Tax-Free Money Market Fund* 600 W. Hillsboro Blvd. Ste. 300 Deerfield Beach, FL 33441 305/421-8878 800/634-2536	1983	Marinvest Inc.	$115.4 Mil	$1,000/ 250	p	Local Rep
Marketmaster Trust *Tax Exempt Fund* 3512 Silverside Rd. The Commons, No. 6 Wilmington, DE 19810 302/478-6945 800/441-7379	1987	Sovran Bank, N.A.	$146.8 Mil	$1,000/ 0	n	Local Rep
MassMutual Integrity Funds *MassMutual Tax-Exempt Money Market Fund* 1295 State St. Springfield, MA 01111 413/788-8411 800/542-6767 800/854-9100 MA Only	1988	Massachusetts Mutual Life Insurance Company	$15.4 Mil	$100/ 25	N/A	Local Rep
Master Reserves Tax Free Trust *Multiple User Portfolio I* 99 High St. Boston, MA 02110 617/338-3200 800/343-2898 800/225-1587	1983	Keystone Custodian Funds, Inc.	$336.6 Mil	$250,000/ 0	n	Local Rep
McDonald Tax Exempt Money Market Fund, Inc. 666 Old Country Rd. Garden City, NY 11530 800/553-2240	1985	McDonald & Company Securities, Inc.	$93.2 Mil	$500/ 0	p	Local Rep
Merrill Lynch Institutional Tax-Exempt Fund One Financial Ctr. 15th Fl. Boston, MA 02111 617/357-1460 800/225-1576	1983	Fund Asset Management, Inc.	$265.4 Mil	$5,000/ 1,000	n	Local Rep
Midwest Group Tax Free Trust *Money Market Portfolio* 700 Dixie Terminal Bldg. Cincinnati, OH 45202 513/629-2000 800/543-8721 800/582-7396 OH Only	1981	Midwest Advisory Services Inc.	$77.9 Mil	$1,000/ 0	n	Local Rep

*Key: i=initial sales charge   r=redemption fee or contingent deferred sales charge(CDSC)
      t=12b-1 fee and either CDSC or redemption fee   p=12b-1 fee   n=none of the preceding fees   N/A=not available

Short-term Municipal Bond

Fund	Year Began	Investment Adviser	9/30/89 Assets	Minimum Initial and Subsequent Investment	Fees*	Where to Buy Shares
Money Management Plus *Tax Free Portfolio* 1700 Pennsylvania Ave., NW Washington, DC 20006 301/951-4820 800/368-2745	1984	Calvert Asset Management Company, Inc.	$76.2 Mil	$2,000/ 250	p	Fund
Municipal Fund for Temporary Investment *Muni-Cash* 3411 Silverside Rd. Webster Bldg., Ste. 204 Wilmington, DE 19810 302/478-6945 800/221-8120, 800/640-6155 NY Only	1985	Provident Institutional Management Corporation	$84.2 Mil (e)	$5,000/ 0	n	Local Rep
Municipal Fund for Temporary Investment *Muni-Fund* 3411 Silverside Rd. Webster Bldg., Ste. 204 Wilmington, DE 19810 302/478-6945 800/221-8120, 800/640-6155 NY Only	1980	Provident Institutional Management Corporation	$1.2 Bil (e)	$5,000/ 0	n	Local Rep
Municipal Lease Securities Fund, Inc. 208 S. LaSalle St. No. 1816 Chicago, IL 60604 312/726-2688 800/322-6573	1986	Hutchinson Advisers	$15.8 Mil (e)	$5,000/ 0	i, p	Local Rep
Municipal Working Capital Trust 500 Boylston St. Boston, MA 02116 617/954-5000 800/343-2829	1980	Massachusetts Financial Services Company	$15.2 Mil	$1,000/ 25	n	Local Rep
Neuberger & Berman Municipal Money Fund 342 Madison Ave. New York, NY 10173 212/850-8300 800/877-9700	1984	Neuberger & Berman Management Incorporated	$175.1 Mil	$2,000/ 200	n	Fund
New England Tax Exempt Money Market Trust 399 Boylston St. Boston, MA 02116 617/267-6600 800/343-7104	1983	Back Bay Advisors, Inc.	$66.7 Mil	$1,000/ 0	n	Local Rep

Short-term Municipal Bond

Fund	Year Began	Investment Adviser	9/30/89 Assets	Minimum Initial and Subsequent Investment	Fees*	Where to Buy Shares
Nuveen Tax-Exempt Money Market Fund, Inc. 333 W. Wacker Dr. Chicago, IL 60606 312/917-7824 800/621-2431	1981	Nuveen Advisory Corp.	$1.8 Bil	$25,000/ 500	n	Local Rep
Nuveen Tax-Free Reserves, Inc. 333 W. Wacker Dr. Chicago, IL 60606 312/917-7843 800/858-4084	1982	Nuveen Advisory Corp.	$390.3 Mil	$1,000/ 100	p	Local Rep
Olympus Tax-Exempt Money Market Fund *Olympus Tax-Exempt Money Market Series* 230 Park Ave. New York, NY 10169 212/309-8400 800/626-FUND	1986	Furman Selz Mager Dietz & Birney Incorporated	$3.1 Mil (e)	$1,000/ 100	i, r	Local Rep
Oppenheimer Tax-Exempt Cash Reserves 3410 S. Galena St. Denver, CO 80231 303/671-3200 800/525-7048	1989	Oppenheimer Management Corporation	$7.4 Mil	$1,000/ 25	p	Local Rep
Pacific Horizon Tax-Exempt Money Market Portfolio, Inc. 156 W. 56th St. Ste. 1902 New York, NY 10019 212/492-1600 800/367-6075	1984	Security Pacific National Bank	$100.4 Mil	$1,000/ 100	p	Fund
PaineWebber RMA Tax-Free Fund, Inc. 1285 Avenue of the Americas PaineWebber Bldg. New York, NY 10019 800/RMA-1000	1982	PaineWebber Incorporated	$983.8 Mil	$1,000/ 100	n	Local Rep
Parkstone Group of Funds *Tax-Free Fund* 1900 E. Dublin-Granville Rd. Columbus, OH 43229 614/899-4600 800/338-4385	1989	Securities Counsel, Inc.	N/A	$1,000/ 0	N/A	Fund

*Key: i=initial sales charge   r=redemption fee or contingent deferred sales charge(CDSC)
t=12b-1 fee and either CDSC or redemption fee   p=12b-1 fee   n=none of the preceding fees   N/A=not available

415

Short-term Municipal Bond

Fund	Year Began	Investment Adviser	9/30/89 Assets	Minimum Initial and Subsequent Investment	Fees*	Where to Buy Shares
Parkway Tax-Free Reserve Fund, Inc. 985 Old Eagle School Rd. Wayne, PA 19087 215/688-8164 800/992-2207	1980	Parkway Management Corporation	$11.8 Mil (e)	$1,000/ 0	n	Local Rep
Pioneer Tax-Free Money Fund 60 State St. Boston, MA 02109-1975 617/742-7825 800/225-6292	1988	Pioneering Management Corporation	$5.1 Mil	$2,000/ 100	n	Fund
Piper Jaffray Investment Trust Inc. *Tax-Exempt Money Market Fund* 222 S. 9th St. Piper Jaffray Twr. Minneapolis, MN 55402 612/342-6426 800/333-6000	1988	Piper Capital Management Incorporated	$83.8 Mil	$0/ 0	p	Local Rep
Princor Tax-Exempt Cash Management Fund, Inc. 711 High St. Des Moines, IA 50309 515/247-5711 800/247-4123 800/622-5344 IA Only	1988	Principal Management, Inc.	$45.2 Mil	$1,000/ 100	n	Local Rep
Prudential-Bache Tax Free Money Fund, Inc. One Seaport Plaza New York, NY 10292 212/214-1215 800/225-1852	1979	Prudential Mutual Fund Management	$657.3 Mil	$1,000/ 100	p	Local Rep
Putnam Tax Exempt Money Market Fund One Post Office Sq. Boston, MA 02109 617/292-1000 800/225-2465	1987	Putnam Management Company, Inc.	$98.4 Mil (e)	$1,000/ 100	n	Local Rep
Rodney Square Tax-Exempt Fund Rodney Square North Wilmington, DE 19890 302/651-1923 800/225-5084	1986	Rodney Square Management Corporation	$258.7 Mil	$100/ 0	p	Local Rep

*Key: i=initial sales charge   r=redemption fee or contingent deferred sales charge(CDSC)
        t=12b-1 fee and either CDSC or redemption fee   p=12b-1 fee   n=none of the preceding fees   N/A=not available

Short-term Municipal Bond

Fund	Year Began	Investment Adviser	9/30/89 Assets	Minimum Initial and Subsequent Investment	Fees*	Where to Buy Shares
SAFECO Tax-Free Money Market Fund, Inc. SAFECO Plaza Seattle, WA 98185 206/545-5530 800/426-6730	1984	SAFECO Asset Management Company	$47.8 Mil	$1,000/ 100	n	Fund
SafeGuard Tax-Free Money Market Portfolio 16 Industrial Blvd. Paoli, PA 19301 215/251-0550 800/523-7798	1988	Provident Institutional Management Corporation	N/A	$1,000/ 100	p	Local Rep
Salem Funds *Salem Tax Free Money Market Portfolio (The)* 99 High St. Boston, MA 02110 617/338-3200 800/641-2580 800/343-3424	1989	First Union National Bank of N. Carolina	$31.2 Mil	$1,000/ 0	p	Fund
Sansom Street Tax-Free Money Market Portfolio 16 Industrial Blvd. Paoli, PA 19301 215/251-0550 800/523-7798	1988	Provident Institutional Management Corporation	N/A	$1,500/ 0	p	Local Rep
Scudder Fund, Inc. *Managed Tax-Free Fund* 345 Park Ave. New York, NY 10154 212/326-6656 800/854-8525	1982	Scudder, Stevens & Clark, Inc.	$100.1 Mil	$2,500/ 100	n	Fund
Scudder Institutional Fund, Inc. *Institutional Tax-Free Portfolio* 345 Park Ave. New York, NY 10154 212/326-6656 800/854-8525	1986	Scudder, Stevens & Clark, Inc.	$152.4 Mil	$2.0 Mil/ 0	n	Fund
Scudder Tax-Free Money Fund 175 Federal St. Boston, MA 02110 617/439-4640 800/225-2470 800/225-5163	1980	Scudder, Stevens & Clark, Inc.	$317.8 Mil	$1,000/ 0	n	Fund

*Key: i=initial sales charge   r=redemption fee or contingent deferred sales charge(CDSC)
t=12b-1 fee and either CDSC or redemption fee   p=12b-1 fee   n=none of the preceding fees   N/A=not available

417

Short-term Municipal Bond

Fund	Year Began	Investment Adviser	9/30/89 Assets	Minimum Initial and Subsequent Investment	Fees*	Where to Buy Shares
Scudder Treasurers Trust *Treasurers Tax Exempt Money Portfolio* 175 Federal St. Boston, MA 02110 617/439-4640 800/225-2470 800/225-5163	1987	Scudder, Stevens & Clark, Inc.	$10.8 Mil	$100,000/ 0	n	Fund
SEI Tax Exempt Trust *Institutional Tax Free Portfolio* 680 E. Swedesford Rd. No. 7 Wayne, PA 19087 215/254-1000 800/345-1151	1982	Manufacturers National Bank of Detroit	$139.1 Mil	$0/ 0	p	Local Rep
SEI Tax Exempt Trust *Tax Free Portfolio* 680 E. Swedesford Rd. No. 7 Wayne, PA 19087 215/254-1000 800/345-1151	1982	Delaware Trust Company	$474.9 Mil	$0/ 0	p	Local Rep
Selected Capital Preservation Trust *Selected Daily Tax-Exempt Fund* 1331 Euclid Ave. Cleveland, OH 44115 312/641-7862 800/553-5533	1988	Selected Financial Services, Inc.	$88.4 Mil	$1,000/ 100	n	Local Rep
Sigma Tax-Free Moneyfund, Inc. 3801 Kennett Pk., C-200 Greenville Ctr. Wilmington, DE 19807 302/652-3091 800/441-9490	1986	Sigma Management, Inc.	$2.0 Mil	$500/ 100	n	Fund
SLH Daily Tax-Free Dividend Fund 31 W. 52nd St. New York, NY 10019 212/767-3700	1982	Bernstein-Macaulay Division of Shearson Lehman Hutton Inc.	$3.0 Bil	$2,500/ 1,000	n	Local Rep
SteinRoe Tax-Exempt Income Trust *SteinRoe Tax-Exempt Money Fund* 300 W. Adams St. P.O. Box 1143 Chicago, IL 60690 800/338-2550	1983	Stein Roe & Farnham Incorporated	$250.9 Mil	$1,000/ 100	n	Fund

*Key: i=initial sales charge   r=redemption fee or contingent deferred sales charge(CDSC)
t=12b-1 fee and either CDSC or redemption fee   p=12b-1 fee   n=none of the preceding fees   N/A=not available

Short-term Municipal Bond

Fund	Year Began	Investment Adviser	9/30/89 Assets	Minimum Initial and Subsequent Investment	Fees*	Where to Buy Shares
Strong Tax-Free Funds *Strong Tax-Free Money Market Fund, Inc.* P.O. Box 2936 Milwaukee, WI 53201 414/359-3400 800/368-3863	1986	Strong/ Corneliuson Capital Management, Inc.	N/A	$2,500/ 200	n	Fund
Tax-Exempt Money Fund of America 333 S. Hope St. Los Angeles, CA 90071 213/486-9200 800/421-0180 213/486-9651 Collect	1989	Capital Research & Management Company	N/A	$2,500/ 50	N/A	Local Rep
Tax Free Instruments Trust Federated Investors Twr. Liberty Ctr. Pittsburgh, PA 15222-3779 412/288-1900 800/245-0242	1982	Federated Management	$1.3 Bil	$500/ 100	n	Local Rep
Tax-Free Investments Trust *Cash Reserve Portfolio*		AIM Advisors, Inc.	$1.4 Bil			
Flag Investors Tax-Free Cash Reserve Shares	1983			$1,500/100	p	LRep
Institutional Cash Reserve Shares 11 Greenway Plaza, Ste. 1919 Houston, TX 77046 713/626-1919, 800/231-0803, 800/392-9681 TX Only	1983			$1.0 Mil/0	n	LRep
Tax Free Money Fund, Inc. 1345 Avenue of the Americas New York, NY 10105 212/698-5349 800/544-7835	1981	Mutual Management Corp.	$1.2 Bil	$7,500/ 100	n	Local Rep
Templeton Tax Free Trust *Templeton Tax Free Money Fund* 700 Central Ave. P.O. Box 33030 St. Petersburg, FL 33733-8030 813/823-8712 800/237-0738	1988	Templeton, Galbraith & Hansberger, Ltd.	$1.1 Mil	$1,000/ 25	n	Local Rep
Transamerica Tax Free Fund, Inc. *Transamerica Tax Free Cash Reserves* 1000 Louisiana Ste. 6000 Houston, TX 77002-5098 713/751-2400, 800/999-3863	1983	Transamerica Fund Management Company	$9.7 Mil	$1,000/ 50	p	Local Rep

*Key: i=initial sales charge   r=redemption fee or contingent deferred sales charge(CDSC)
      t=12b-1 fee and either CDSC or redemption fee   p=12b-1 fee   n=none of the preceding fees   N/A=not available

419

Short-term Municipal Bond

Fund	Year Began	Investment Adviser	9/30/89 Assets	Minimum Initial and Subsequent Investment	Fees*	Where to Buy Shares
Treasurer's Fund, Inc. *Tax Exempt Money Market Portfolio* 8 Sound Shore Dr. Greenwich, CT 06830 203/629-2090 800/877-3863	1987	Gabelli-O'Connor Fixed Income Mutual Funds Management Company	$55.9 Mil (e)	$100,000/ 0	n	Local Rep
T. Rowe Price Institutional Trust *Tax-Exempt Reserve Portfolio* 100 E. Pratt St. Baltimore, MD 21202 301/547-2000 800/638-5660	1986	T. Rowe Price Associates, Inc.	$74.7 Mil	$250,000/ 0	n	Fund
T. Rowe Price Tax-Exempt Money Fund, Inc. 100 E. Pratt St. Baltimore, MD 21202 301/547-2000 800/638-5660	1981	T. Rowe Price Associates, Inc.	$1.1 Bil	$2,500/ 100	n	Fund
USAA Tax Exempt Fund, Inc. *Short-Term Fund* USAA Bldg. San Antonio, TX 78288 512/498-8000 800/531-8000	1982	USAA Investment Management Company	$250.0 Mil	$3,000/ 50	n	Fund
USAA Tax Exempt Fund, Inc. *Tax Exempt Money Market Fund* USAA Bldg. San Antonio, TX 78288 512/498-8000 800/531-8000	1984	USAA Investment Management Company	$826.0 Mil	$3,000/ 50	n	Fund
Value Line Tax Exempt Fund, Inc. *Money Market Portfolio* 711 Third Ave. New York, NY 10017 212/687-3965 800/223-0818	1984	Value Line, Inc.	$42.1 Mil	$1,000/ 250	n	Fund
Vanguard Municipal Bond Fund *Money Market Portfolio* Vanguard Financial Ctr. P.O. Box 2600 Valley Forge, PA 19482 215/648-6000 800/662-7447, 800/362-0530 PA Only	1980	Vanguard Group, Inc.	$2.1 Bil	$3,000/ 100	n	Fund

*Key: i=initial sales charge   r=redemption fee or contingent deferred sales charge(CDSC)
t=12b-1 fee and either CDSC or redemption fee   p=12b-1 fee   n=none of the preceding fees   N/A=not available

Short-term Municipal Bond

Fund	Year Began	Investment Adviser	9/30/89 Assets	Minimum Initial and Subsequent Investment	Fees*	Where to Buy Shares
Vanguard Municipal Bond Fund *Short-Term Portfolio* Vanguard Financial Ctr. P.O. Box 2600 Valley Forge, PA 19482 215/648-6000 800/662-7447, 800/362-0530 PA Only	1977	Vanguard Group, Inc.	$697.2 Mil	$3,000/ 100	n	Fund
Van Kampen Merritt Tax Free Money Fund 1001 Warrenville Rd. Lisle, IL 60532 312/719-6000 800/225-2222	1986	Van Kampen Merritt Investment Advisory Corp.	$50.8 Mil	$1,000/ 100	p	Local Rep
Venture Trust Money Market Fund *Tax-Free Portfolio (The)* 124 E. Marcy St. P.O. Box 1688 Santa Fe, NM 87504-1688 505/983-4335 800/458-6557	1983	Venture Advisers, L.P.	$12.4 Mil	$1,000/ 25	p	Local Rep
Weiss Peck & Greer Funds Trust *WPG Tax Free Money Market Fund* One New York Plaza 31st Fl. New York, NY 10004 212/908-9582, 800/223-3332	1988	Weiss, Peck & Greer Advisers, Inc.	$51.1 Mil (e)	$1,000/ 50	n	Fund
Zweig Tax-Free Fund Inc. *Money Market Portfolio* 25 Broadway New York, NY 10004 212/361-9612 800/272-2700	1983	Zweig/Glaser Advisers	$105.0 Mil (e)	$1,000/ 100	p	Fund

*Key: i=initial sales charge   r=redemption fee or contingent deferred sales charge(CDSC)
t=12b-1 fee and either CDSC or redemption fee   p=12b-1 fee   n=none of the preceding fees   N/A=not available

◆ ◆ ◆ ◆

State Municipal Bond—
Long-term Funds

State Municipal Bond—Long-term

Fund	Year Began	Investment Adviser	9/30/89 Assets	Minimum Initial and Subsequent Investment	Fees*	Where to Buy Shares
AIM Tax-Exempt Funds, Inc. *AIM California Tax-Free Intermediate Fund* 11 Greenway Plaza Ste. 1919 Houston, TX 77046 713/626-1919 800/231-0803, 800/392-9681 TX Only	1987	AIM Advisors, Inc.	$9.2 Mil	$1,000/ 100	i, p	Local Rep
Alliance Tax-Free Income Fund *California Portfolio* 1345 Avenue of the Americas New York, NY 10105 212/969-1000 800/221-5672	1987	Alliance Capital Management L.P.	$87.9 Mil	$250/ 50	i, p	Local Rep
Alliance Tax-Free Income Fund *Insured California Portfolio* 40 Rector St. New York, NY 10006 212/513-4200 800/443-4430	1985	Alliance Capital Management L.P.	$52.5 Mil	$250/ 50	i, p	Local Rep
Alliance Tax-Free Income Fund *New York Portfolio* 1345 Avenue of the Americas New York, NY 10105 212/969-1000 800/221-5672	1987	Alliance Capital Management L.P.	$68.4 Mil	$250/ 50	i, p	Local Rep
Alpine Mutual Fund Trust *California Municipal Asset Trust* 650 S. Cherry St. Ste. 700 Denver, CO 80222 303/321-2211 800/826-6677	1988	Alpine Capital Management Corporation	N/A	$1,000/ 250	i	Local Rep
American Capital California Tax-Exempt Trust 2800 Post Oak Blvd. Houston, TX 77056 713/993-0500 800/421-5666	1986	American Capital Asset Management, Inc.	$21.4 Mil	$500/ 50	i, p	Local Rep
American Capital Tax-Exempt Trust *New York Municipal Portfolio* 2800 Post Oak Blvd. Houston, TX 77056 713/993-0500 800/421-5666	1986	American Capital Asset Management, Inc.	$10.0 Mil	$500/ 50	i, p	Local Rep

*Key: i=initial sales charge   r=redemption fee or contingent deferred sales charge(CDSC)
t=12b-1 fee and either CDSC or redemption fee   p=12b-1 fee   n=none of the preceding fees   N/A=not available

State Municipal Bond—Long-term

Fund	Year Began	Investment Adviser	9/30/89 Assets	Minimum Initial and Subsequent Investment	Fees*	Where to Buy Shares
AMEV Tax-Free Fund, Inc. *Minnesota Portfolio* P.O. Box 64284 St. Paul, MN 55164 612/738-4000 800/872-2638	1986	AMEV Advisers, Inc.	$21.3 Mil	$500/ 50	i	Local Rep
Arizona Tax Free Fund, Inc. 6991 E. Camelback Rd. Ste. B302 Scottsdale, AZ 85251 602/998-5557	1983	Sea Investment Management, Inc.	$2.2 Mil (e)	$1,000/ 100	i	Local Rep
Associated Planners Investment Trust *Associated Planners California Tax-Free Fund* 1925 Century Park East 19th Fl. Los Angeles, CA 90067 213/553-6740	1987	Associated Planners Management Company	$6.3 Mil (e)	$500/ 50	i	Local Rep
Benham California Tax-Free Trust *High Yield Portfolio* 755 Page Mill Rd. Palo Alto, CA 94304 415/858-2400 800/227-8380 800/982-6150 CA Only	1987	Benham Management Corporation	$34.8 Mil	$1,000/ 100	n	Fund
Benham California Tax-Free Trust *Insured Portfolio* 755 Page Mill Rd. Palo Alto, CA 94304 415/858-2400 800/227-8380 800/982-6150 CA Only	1987	Benham Management Corporation	$43.0 Mil	$1,000/ 100	n	Fund
Benham California Tax-Free Trust *Intermediate-Term Portfolio* 755 Page Mill Rd. Palo Alto, CA 94304 415/858-2400 800/227-8380 800/982-6150 CA Only	1983	Benham Management Corporation	$168.3 Mil	$1,000/ 100	n	Fund
Benham California Tax-Free Trust *Long-Term Portfolio* 755 Page Mill Rd. Palo Alto, CA 94304 415/858-2400 800/227-8380 800/982-6150 CA Only	1983	Benham Management Corporation	$180.3 Mil	$1,000/ 100	n	Fund

*Key: i=initial sales charge   r=redemption fee or contingent deferred sales charge(CDSC)
t=12b-1 fee and either CDSC or redemption fee   p=12b-1 fee   n=none of the preceding fees   N/A=not available

426

State Municipal Bond—Long-term

Fund	Year Began	Investment Adviser	9/30/89 Assets	Minimum Initial and Subsequent Investment	Fees*	Where to Buy Shares
Big E Pathfinder Family of Mutual Funds *Big E Pathfinder New York Tax-Free Income Fund (The)* 320 Empire Tower Buffalo, NY 14202 716/855-7891	1988	Empire of America Advisory Services, Inc.	$23.1 Mil	$500/ 100	i, p	Local Rep
Boston Company Tax-Free Municipal Funds *California Tax-Free Bond Fund* One Boston Place Boston, MA 02019 617/956-9740 800/225-5267, 800/343-6324	1988	Boston Company Advisors, Inc.	$4.5 Mil	$1,000/ 0	p	Fund
Boston Company Tax-Free Municipal Funds *Massachusetts Tax-Free Bond Fund* One Boston Place Boston, MA 02019 617/956-9740 800/225-5267, 800/343-6324	1985	Boston Company Advisors, Inc.	$15.4 Mil	$1,000/ 0	p	Local Rep
Boston Company Tax-Free Municipal Funds *New York Tax-Free Bond Fund* One Boston Place Boston, MA 02019 617/956-9740 800/225-5267 800/343-6324	1988	Boston Company Advisors, Inc.	$3.0 Mil	$1,000/ 0	p	Fund
California Investment Trust I *California Tax-Free Income Fund* 44 Montgomery St. Ste. 2200 San Francisco, CA 94104 415/398-2727, 800/225-8778	1985	CCM Partners	$68.6 Mil (e)	$10,000/ 250	n	Fund
California Tax Exempt Bonds, Inc. 600 Third Ave. New York, NY 10016 203/863-5600 800/237-1718	1983	National Securities & Research Corporation	$108.3 Mil	$1,000/ 25	i	Local Rep
Carnegie Tax Exempt Income Trust *Georgia Insured Fund* 1100 The Halle Bldg. 1228 Euclid Ave. Cleveland, OH 44115-1831 216/781-4440 800/321-2322	1986	Carnegie Capital Management Company	$6.3 Mil	$1,000/ 250	i, p	Local Rep

*Key: i=initial sales charge   r=redemption fee or contingent deferred sales charge(CDSC)
t=12b-1 fee and either CDSC or redemption fee   p=12b-1 fee   n=none of the preceding fees   N/A=not available

State Municipal Bond—Long-term

Fund	Year Began	Investment Adviser	9/30/89 Assets	Minimum Initial and Subsequent Investment	Fees*	Where to Buy Shares
Carnegie Tax Exempt Income Trust *Minnesota Insured Fund* 1100 The Halle Bldg. 1228 Euclid Ave. Cleveland, OH 44115-1831 216/781-4440 800/321-2322	1986	Carnegie Capital Management Company	$11.9 Mil	$1,000/ 250	i, p	Local Rep
Carnegie Tax Exempt Income Trust *New York Insured Fund* 1100 The Halle Bldg. 1228 Euclid Ave. Cleveland, OH 44115-1831 216/781-4440 800/321-2322	1986	Carnegie Capital Management Company	$1.4 Mil (e)	$1,000/ 250	i, p	Local Rep
Carnegie Tax Exempt Income Trust *Ohio General Municipal Fund* 1100 The Halle Bldg. 1228 Euclid Ave. Cleveland, OH 44115-1831 216/781-4440 800/321-2322	1986	Carnegie Capital Management Company	$20.5 Mil	$1,000/ 250	i, p	Local Rep
Carnegie Tax Exempt Income Trust *Ohio Insured Fund* 1100 The Halle Bldg. 1228 Euclid Ave. Cleveland, OH 44115-1831 216/781-4440 800/321-2322	1986	Carnegie Capital Management Company	$16.5 Mil	$1,000/ 250	i, p	Local Rep
Churchill Tax-Free Trust *Churchill Tax-Free Fund of Kentucky* 200 Park Ave. Ste. 4515 New York, NY 10017 212/697-6666 800/872-5859	1987	Citizens Fidelity Bank & Trust Company	$28.4 Mil	$1,000/ 0	i	Local Rep
Colonial California Tax-Exempt Trust One Financial Ctr. Boston, MA 02111 617/426-3750 800/225-2365 800/426-3750	1985	Colonial Management Associates, Inc.	$152.3 Mil	$250/ 25	i, p	Local Rep
Colonial Massachusetts Tax-Exempt Trust One Financial Ctr. Boston, MA 02111 617/426-3750 800/225-2365 800/426-3750	1987	Colonial Management Associates, Inc.	$34.8 Mil	$250/ 25	i, p	Local Rep

*Key: i=initial sales charge   r=redemption fee or contingent deferred sales charge(CDSC)
t=12b-1 fee and either CDSC or redemption fee   p=12b-1 fee   n=none of the preceding fees   N/A=not available

State Municipal Bond—Long-term

Fund	Year Began	Investment Adviser	9/30/89 Assets	Minimum Initial and Subsequent Investment	Fees*	Where to Buy Shares
Colonial Michigan Tax-Exempt Trust One Financial Ctr. Boston, MA 02111 617/426-3750 800/225-2365 800/426-3750	1986	Colonial Management Associates, Inc.	$18.4 Mil	$250/ 25	i, p	Local Rep
Colonial Minnesota Tax-Exempt Trust One Financial Ctr. Boston, MA 02111 617/426-3750 800/225-2365 800/426-3750	1986	Colonial Management Associates, Inc.	$18.8 Mil	$250/ 25	i, p	Local Rep
Colonial New York Tax-Exempt Trust One Financial Ctr. Boston, MA 02111 617/426-3750 800/225-2365 800/426-3750	1985	Colonial Management Associates, Inc.	$23.9 Mil	$250/ 25	i, p	Local Rep
Colonial Ohio Tax-Exempt Trust One Financial Ctr. Boston, MA 02111 617/426-3750 800/225-2365 800/426-3750	1986	Colonial Management Associates, Inc.	$27.6 Mil	$250/ 25	i, p	Local Rep
Colorado Double Tax-Exempt Fund, Inc. 717 17th St. Ste. 2500 Denver, CO 80202 303/292-0300	1987	Colorado Funds Management Group, Inc.	$28.7 Mil (e)	$2,500/ 100	i	Local Rep
Columbia Municipal Bond Fund, Inc. 1301 SW 5th Ave. P.O. Box 1350 Portland, OR 97207 503/222-3600 800/547-1707	1984	Columbia Funds Management Company	$154.6 Mil	$1,000/ 100	n	Fund
Counsellors New York Municipal Bond Fund 466 Lexington Ave. New York, NY 10017-3147 212/878-0600 800/888-6878	1987	Warburg, Pincus Counsellors, Inc.	$19.7 Mil	$25,000/ 5,000	n	Fund

*Key: i=initial sales charge   r=redemption fee or contingent deferred sales charge(CDSC)
t=12b-1 fee and either CDSC or redemption fee   p=12b-1 fee   n=none of the preceding fees   N/A=not available

429

State Municipal Bond—Long-term

Fund	Year Began	Investment Adviser	9/30/89 Assets	Minimum Initial and Subsequent Investment	Fees*	Where to Buy Shares
Dean Witter California Tax-Free Income Fund Two World Trade Ctr. New York, NY 10048 212/392-2550 800/869-3863	1984	Dean Witter Reynolds Inc. - InterCapital Division	$541.4 Mil	$1,000/ 100	t	Local Rep
Dean Witter New York Tax-Free Income Fund Two World Trade Ctr. New York, NY 10048 212/392-2550 800/869-3863	1985	Dean Witter Reynolds Inc. - InterCapital Division	$141.6 Mil	$1,000/ 100	t	Local Rep
DMC Tax-Free Income Trust - PA One Commerce Sq. Philadelphia, PA 19103 215/988-1200 800/523-4640	1977	Delaware Management Company, Inc.	$584.7 Mil	$1,000/ 25	i	Local Rep
Double Exempt Flex Fund, Inc. 100 S. Fifth St. Ste. 2200 Minneapolis, MN 55402 612/341-6728 800/553-2143 800/247-2143 MN Only	1984	Voyageur Fund Managers	N/A	$3,000/ 100	i	Local Rep
Dreyfus California Tax Exempt Bond Fund, Inc. 666 Old Country Rd. Garden City, NY 11530 718/895-1206 800/645-6561	1983	Dreyfus Corporation	$1.4 Bil	$2,500/ 100	n	Fund
Dreyfus Massachusetts Tax Exempt Bond Fund 666 Old Country Rd. Garden City, NY 11530 718/895-1206 800/645-6561	1985	Dreyfus Corporation	$101.6 Mil	$2,500/ 100	n	Fund
Dreyfus New Jersey Tax Exempt Bond Fund, Inc. 666 Old Country Rd. Garden City, NY 11530 718/895-1206 800/645-6561	1988	Dreyfus Corporation	$235.8 Mil	$2,500/ 100	p	Fund

*Key: i=initial sales charge   r=redemption fee or contingent deferred sales charge(CDSC)
t=12b-1 fee and either CDSC or redemption fee   p=12b-1 fee   n=none of the preceding fees   N/A=not available

State Municipal Bond—Long-term

Fund	Year Began	Investment Adviser	9/30/89 Assets	Minimum Initial and Subsequent Investment	Fees*	Where to Buy Shares
Dreyfus New York Insured Tax Exempt Bond Fund 666 Old Country Rd. Garden City, NY 11530 718/895-1206 800/645-6561	1987	Dreyfus Corporation	$62.2 Mil	$2,500/ 100	p	Fund
Dreyfus New York Tax Exempt Bond Fund, Inc. 666 Old Country Rd. Garden City, NY 11530 718/895-1206 800/645-6561	1983	Dreyfus Corporation	$1.7 Bil	$2,500/ 100	n	Fund
Dreyfus New York Tax Exempt Intermediate Bond Fund 666 Old Country Rd. Garden City, NY 11530 718/895-1206 800/645-6561	1987	Dreyfus Corporation	$67.6 Mil	$2,500/ 100	p	Fund
Eaton Vance California Municipals Trust 24 Federal St. Boston, MA 02110 617/482-8260 800/225-6265	1985	Eaton Vance Management, Inc.	$260.0 Mil	$1,000/ 50	t	Local Rep
Empire Builder Tax Free Bond Fund 230 Park Ave. 13th Fl. New York, NY 10169 212/309-8400 800/845-8406	1984	Glickenhaus & Company	$58.3 Mil (e)	$1,000/ 100	i	Local Rep
Enterprise Income Portfolios *Enterprise Tax-Exempt Income Portfolio* 1200 Ashwood Pkwy. Ste. 290 Atlanta, GA 30338 404/396-8118, 800/432-4320	1987	Enterprise Capital Management, Inc.	$11.8 Mil (e)	$500/ 25	t	Local Rep
Equitec Siebel Fund Group II *California Tax-Free Income Fund Series* 7677 Oakport St. P.O. Box 2470 Oakland, CA 94614 415/430-9900, 800/869-8900	1987	Siebel Capital Management, Inc.	$7.5 Mil (e)	$1,000/ 0	i, p	Local Rep

*Key: i=initial sales charge   r=redemption fee or contingent deferred sales charge(CDSC)
t=12b-1 fee and either CDSC or redemption fee   p=12b-1 fee   n=none of the preceding fees   N/A=not available

State Municipal Bond—Long-term

Fund	Year Began	Investment Adviser	9/30/89 Assets	Minimum Initial and Subsequent Investment	Fees*	Where to Buy Shares
Fidelity California Tax Free Fund *High Yield Portfolio* 82 Devonshire St. Boston, MA 02109 617/570-7000 800/227-9639	1984	Fidelity Management & Research Company	$537.5 Mil	$2,500/ 250	n	Fund
Fidelity California Tax Free Fund *Insured Portfolio* 82 Devonshire St. Boston, MA 02109 617/570-7000 800/227-9639	1986	Fidelity Management & Research Company	$83.3 Mil	$2,500/ 250	n	Fund
Fidelity Court Street Trust *Fidelity Connecticut Tax-Free High Yield Portfolio* 82 Devonshire St. Boston, MA 02109 617/570-7000 800/544-6666	1987	Fidelity Management & Research Company	$162.9 Mil	$2,500/ 250	n	Fund
Fidelity Court Street Trust *Fidelity New Jersey Tax-Free High Yield Portfolio* 82 Devonshire St. Boston, MA 02109 617/570-7000 800/544-6666	1988	Fidelity Management & Research Company	$144.3 Mil	$2,500/ 250	n	Fund
Fidelity Massachusetts Tax-Free Fund *High Yield Portfolio* 82 Devonshire St. Boston, MA 02109 617/570-7000 800/544-6666	1983	Fidelity Management & Research Company	$641.4 Mil	$2,500/ 250	n	Fund
Fidelity Municipal Trust *Fidelity Michigan Tax-Free Portfolio* 82 Devonshire St. Boston, MA 02109 617/570-7000 800/544-6666	1985	Fidelity Management & Research Company	$210.4 Mil	$2,500/ 250	n	Fund
Fidelity Municipal Trust *Fidelity Minnesota Tax-Free Portfolio* 82 Devonshire St. Boston, MA 02109 617/570-7000 800/544-6666	1985	Fidelity Management & Research Company	$118.6 Mil	$2,500/ 250	n	Fund

*Key: i=initial sales charge   r=redemption fee or contingent deferred sales charge(CDSC)
     t=12b-1 fee and either CDSC or redemption fee   p=12b-1 fee   n=none of the preceding fees   N/A=not available

State Municipal Bond—Long-term

Fund	Year Began	Investment Adviser	9/30/89 Assets	Minimum Initial and Subsequent Investment	Fees*	Where to Buy Shares
Fidelity Municipal Trust *Fidelity Ohio Tax-Free High Yield Portfolio* 82 Devonshire St. Boston, MA 02109 617/570-7000 800/544-6666	1985	Fidelity Management & Research Company	$184.6 Mil	$2,500/ 250	n	Fund
Fidelity Municipal Trust *Fidelity Pennsylvania Tax-Free High Yield Portfolio* 82 Devonshire St. Boston, MA 02109 617/570-7000 800/544-6666	1986	Fidelity Management & Research Company	$88.0 Mil	$2,500/ 250	n	Fund
Fidelity Municipal Trust *Fidelity Texas Tax-Free Portfolio* 82 Devonshire St. Boston, MA 02109 617/570-7000 800/544-6666	1986	Fidelity Management & Research Company	$33.2 Mil	$2,500/ 250	n	Fund
Fidelity New York Tax-Free Fund *High Yield Portfolio* 82 Devonshire St. Boston, MA 02109 617/570-7000 800/544-6666	1984	Fidelity Management & Research Company	$397.3 Mil	$2,500/ 250	n	Fund
Fidelity New York Tax-Free Fund *Insured Portfolio* 82 Devonshire St. Boston, MA 02109 617/570-7000 800/544-6666	1985	Fidelity Management & Research Company	$190.4 Mil	$2,500/ 250	n	Fund
First Investors Multi-State Insured Tax Free Fund *California Series* 120 Wall St. New York, NY 10005 212/208-6000	1986	First Investors Management Company, Inc.	$4.9 Mil	$2,000/ 500	i, p	Local Rep
First Investors Multi-State Insured Tax Free Fund *Massachusetts Series* 120 Wall St. New York, NY 10005 212/208-6000	1986	First Investors Management Company, Inc.	$7.0 Mil	$2,000/ 500	i, p	Local Rep

*Key: i=initial sales charge   r=redemption fee or contingent deferred sales charge(CDSC)
t=12b-1 fee and either CDSC or redemption fee   p=12b-1 fee   n=none of the preceding fees   N/A=not available

State Municipal Bond—Long-term

Fund	Year Began	Investment Adviser	9/30/89 Assets	Minimum Initial and Subsequent Investment	Fees*	Where to Buy Shares
First Investors Multi-State Insured Tax Free Fund *Michigan Series* 120 Wall St. New York, NY 10005 212/208-6000	1986	First Investors Management Company, Inc.	$5.5 Mil	$2,000/ 500	i, p	Local Rep
First Investors Multi-State Insured Tax Free Fund *Minnesota Series* 120 Wall St. New York, NY 10005 212/208-6000	1986	First Investors Management Company, Inc.	$1.6 Mil	$2,000/ 500	i, p	Local Rep
First Investors Multi-State Insured Tax Free Fund *New Jersey Series* 120 Wall St. New York, NY 10005 212/208-6000	1988	First Investors Management Company, Inc.	$13.4 Mil	$2,000/ 500	i, p	Local Rep
First Investors Multi-State Insured Tax Free Fund *Ohio Series* 120 Wall St. New York, NY 10005 212/208-6000	1986	First Investors Management Company, Inc.	$3.3 Mil	$2,000/ 500	i, p	Local Rep
First Investors New York Insured Tax Free Fund, Inc. 120 Wall St. New York, NY 10005 212/208-6000	1984	First Investors Management Company, Inc.	$142.2 Mil	$2,000/ 500	i, p	Local Rep
First Pacific Mutual Fund, Inc. *First Hawaii Municipal Bond Fund* 1270 Queen Emma St. Ste. 607 Honolulu, HI 96813 808/599-2400	1988	Van Kampen Merritt Investment Advisory Corp.	$6.6 Mil	$1,000/ 100	t	Fund
Flagship Tax Exempt Funds *Arizona Double Tax Exempt Fund* One First National Plaza Ste. 910 Dayton, OH 45402 513/461-0332 800/227-4648, 800/354-7447 OH Only	1986	Flagship Financial Inc.	$29.7 Mil	$3,000/ 50	i, p	Local Rep

*Key: i=initial sales charge   r=redemption fee or contingent deferred sales charge(CDSC)
t=12b-1 fee and either CDSC or redemption fee   p=12b-1 fee   n=none of the preceding fees   N/A=not available

State Municipal Bond—Long-term

Fund	Year Began	Investment Adviser	9/30/89 Assets	Minimum Initial and Subsequent Investment	Fees*	Where to Buy Shares
Flagship Tax Exempt Funds *Colorado Double Tax Exempt Fund* One First National Plaza Ste. 910 Dayton, OH 45402 513/461-0332 800/227-4648, 800/354-7447 OH Only	1987	Flagship Financial Inc.	$7.1 Mil	$3,000/ 50	i, p	Local Rep
Flagship Tax Exempt Funds *Connecticut Double Tax Exempt Fund* One First National Plaza Ste. 910 Dayton, OH 45402 513/461-0332 800/227-4648, 800/354-7447 OH Only	1987	Flagship Financial Inc.	$58.5 Mil	$3,000/ 50	i, p	Local Rep
Flagship Tax Exempt Funds *Georgia Double Tax Exempt Fund* One First National Plaza Ste. 910 Dayton, OH 45402 513/461-0332 800/227-4648, 800/354-7447 OH Only	1986	Flagship Financial Inc.	$36.1 Mil	$3,000/ 50	i, p	Local Rep
Flagship Tax Exempt Funds *Kentucky Triple Tax Exempt Fund* One First National Plaza Ste. 910 Dayton, OH 45402 513/461-0332 800/227-4648, 800/354-7447 OH Only	1987	Flagship Financial Inc.	$78.7 Mil	$3,000/ 50	i, p	Local Rep
Flagship Tax Exempt Funds *Louisiana Double Tax Exempt Fund* One First National Plaza Ste. 910 Dayton, OH 45402 513/461-0332 800/227-4648, 800/354-7447 OH Only	1989	Flagship Financial Inc.	N/A	$3,000/ 50	N/A	Local Rep
Flagship Tax Exempt Funds *Michigan Triple Tax Exempt Fund* One First National Plaza Ste. 910 Dayton, OH 45402 513/461-0332 800/227-4648, 800/354-7447 OH Only	1985	Flagship Financial Inc.	$88.3 Mil	$3,000/ 50	i, p	Local Rep
Flagship Tax Exempt Funds *Missouri Double Tax Exempt Fund* One First National Plaza Ste. 910 Dayton, OH 45402 513/461-0332 800/227-4648, 800/354-7447 OH Only	1987	Flagship Financial Inc.	$14.7 Mil	$3,000/ 50	i, p	Local Rep

*Key: i=initial sales charge   r=redemption fee or contingent deferred sales charge(CDSC)
t=12b-1 fee and either CDSC or redemption fee   p=12b-1 fee   n=none of the preceding fees   N/A=not available

State Municipal Bond—Long-term

Fund	Year Began	Investment Adviser	9/30/89 Assets	Minimum Initial and Subsequent Investment	Fees*	Where to Buy Shares
Flagship Tax Exempt Funds *North Carolina Triple Tax Exempt Fund* One First National Plaza Ste. 910 Dayton, OH 45402 513/461-0332 800/227-4648, 800/354-7447 OH Only	1986	Flagship Financial Inc.	$88.8 Mil	$3,000/ 50	i, p	Local Rep
Flagship Tax Exempt Funds *Ohio Double Tax Exempt Fund* One First National Plaza Ste. 910 Dayton, OH 45402 513/461-0332 800/227-4648 800/354-7447 OH Only	1985	Flagship Financial Inc.	$204.2 Mil	$3,000/ 50	i, p	Local Rep
Flagship Tax Exempt Funds *Pennsylvania Triple Tax Exempt Fund* One First National Plaza Ste. 910 Dayton, OH 45402 513/461-0332 800/227-4648, 800/354-7447 OH Only	1986	Flagship Financial Inc.	$35.1 Mil	$3,000/ 50	i, p	Local Rep
Flagship Tax Exempt Funds *Tennessee Double Tax Exempt Fund* One First National Plaza Ste. 910 Dayton, OH 45402 513/461-0332 800/227-4648, 800/354-7447 OH Only	1987	Flagship Financial Inc.	$67.7 Mil	$3,000/ 50	i, p	Local Rep
Flagship Tax Exempt Funds *Virginia Double Tax Exempt Fund* One First National Plaza Ste. 910 Dayton, OH 45402 513/461-0332 800/227-4648, 800/354-7447 OH Only	1986	Flagship Financial Inc.	$39.6 Mil	$3,000/ 50	i, p	Local Rep
Franklin California Tax-Free Income Fund, Inc. 777 Mariners Island Blvd. San Mateo, CA 94404 415/570-3000 800/632-2180 800/632-2350	1977	Franklin Advisers, Inc.	$9.8 Bil	$100/ 25	i	Local Rep
Franklin California Tax-Free Trust *Franklin California Insured Tax-Free Income Fund, Inc.* 777 Mariners Island Blvd. San Mateo, CA 94404 415/570-3000 800/632-2180, 800/632-2350	1985	Franklin Advisers, Inc.	$258.2 Mil	$100/ 25	i	Local Rep

*Key: i=initial sales charge   r=redemption fee or contingent deferred sales charge(CDSC)
t=12b-1 fee and either CDSC or redemption fee   p=12b-1 fee   n=none of the preceding fees   N/A=not available

State Municipal Bond—Long-term

Fund	Year Began	Investment Adviser	9/30/89 Assets	Minimum Initial and Subsequent Investment	Fees*	Where to Buy Shares
Franklin New York Tax-Free Income Fund, Inc. 777 Mariners Island Blvd. San Mateo, CA 94404 415/570-3000 800/632-2180 800/632-2350	1982	Franklin Advisers, Inc.	$2.8 Bil	$100/ 25	i	Local Rep
Franklin Tax-Free Trust *Franklin Alabama Tax-Free Income Fund* 777 Mariners Island Blvd. San Mateo, CA 94404 415/570-3000 800/632-2180 800/632-2350	1987	Franklin Advisers, Inc.	$14.8 Mil	$100/ 25	i	Local Rep
Franklin Tax-Free Trust *Franklin Arizona Tax-Free Income Fund* 777 Mariners Island Blvd. San Mateo, CA 94404 415/570-3000 800/632-2180 800/632-2350	1987	Franklin Advisers, Inc.	$148.9 Mil	$100/ 25	i	Local Rep
Franklin Tax-Free Trust *Franklin Colorado Tax-Free Income Fund* 777 Mariners Island Blvd. San Mateo, CA 94404 415/570-3000 800/632-2180 800/632-2350	1987	Franklin Advisers, Inc.	$27.9 Mil	$100/ 25	i	Local Rep
Franklin Tax-Free Trust *Franklin Connecticut Tax-Free Income Fund* 777 Mariners Island Blvd. San Mateo, CA 94404 415/570-3000 800/632-2180 800/632-2350	1988	Franklin Advisers, Inc.	$13.6 Mil	$100/ 25	i	Local Rep
Franklin Tax-Free Trust *Franklin Florida Tax-Free Income Fund* 777 Mariners Island Blvd. San Mateo, CA 94404 415/570-3000 800/632-2180 800/632-2350	1987	Franklin Advisers, Inc.	$167.7 Mil	$100/ 25	i	Local Rep
Franklin Tax-Free Trust *Franklin Georgia Tax-Free Income Fund* 777 Mariners Island Blvd. San Mateo, CA 94404 415/570-3000 800/632-2180 800/632-2350	1987	Franklin Advisers, Inc.	$9.1 Mil	$100/ 25	i	Local Rep

*Key: i=initial sales charge   r=redemption fee or contingent deferred sales charge(CDSC)
t=12b-1 fee and either CDSC or redemption fee   p=12b-1 fee   n=none of the preceding fees   N/A=not available

437

State Municipal Bond—Long-term

Fund	Year Began	Investment Adviser	9/30/89 Assets	Minimum Initial and Subsequent Investment	Fees*	Where to Buy Shares
Franklin Tax-Free Trust *Franklin Indiana Tax-Free Income Fund* 777 Mariners Island Blvd. San Mateo, CA 94404 415/570-3000 800/632-2180 800/632-2350	1987	Franklin Advisers, Inc.	$8.7 Mil	$100/ 25	i	Local Rep
Franklin Tax-Free Trust *Franklin Louisiana Tax-Free Income Fund* 777 Mariners Island Blvd. San Mateo, CA 94404 415/570-3000 800/632-2180 800/632-2350	1987	Franklin Advisers, Inc.	$10.1 Mil	$100/ 25	i	Local Rep
Franklin Tax-Free Trust *Franklin Maryland Tax-Free Income Fund* 777 Mariners Island Blvd. San Mateo, CA 94404 415/570-3000 800/632-2180 800/632-2350	1988	Franklin Advisers, Inc.	$9.7 Mil	$100/ 25	i	Local Rep
Franklin Tax-Free Trust *Franklin Massachusetts Insured Tax-Free Income Fund* 777 Mariners Island Blvd. San Mateo, CA 94404 415/570-3000 800/632-2180 800/632-2350	1985	Franklin Advisers, Inc.	$118.2 Mil	$100/ 25	i	Local Rep
Franklin Tax-Free Trust *Franklin Michigan Insured Tax-Free Income Fund* 777 Mariners Island Blvd. San Mateo, CA 94404 415/570-3000 800/632-2180 800/632-2350	1985	Franklin Advisers, Inc.	$406.2 Mil	$100/ 25	i	Local Rep
Franklin Tax-Free Trust *Franklin Minnesota Insured Tax-Free Income Fund* 777 Mariners Island Blvd. San Mateo, CA 94404 415/570-3000 800/632-2180 800/632-2350	1985	Franklin Advisers, Inc.	$212.4 Mil	$100/ 25	i	Local Rep
Franklin Tax-Free Trust *Franklin Missouri Tax-Free Income Fund* 777 Mariners Island Blvd. San Mateo, CA 94404 415/570-3000 800/632-2180 800/632-2350	1987	Franklin Advisers, Inc.	$16.2 Mil	$100/ 25	i	Local Rep

*Key: i=initial sales charge   r=redemption fee or contingent deferred sales charge(CDSC)
t=12b-1 fee and either CDSC or redemption fee   p=12b-1 fee   n=none of the preceding fees   N/A=not available

State Municipal Bond—Long-term

Fund	Year Began	Investment Adviser	9/30/89 Assets	Minimum Initial and Subsequent Investment	Fees*	Where to Buy Shares
Franklin Tax-Free Trust *Franklin New Jersey Tax-Free Income Fund* 777 Mariners Island Blvd. San Mateo, CA 94404 415/570-3000 800/632-2180 800/632-2350	1988	Franklin Advisers, Inc.	$66.5 Mil	$100/ 25	i	Local Rep
Franklin Tax-Free Trust *Franklin North Carolina Tax-Free Income Fund* 777 Mariners Island Blvd. San Mateo, CA 94404 415/570-3000 800/632-2180 800/632-2350	1987	Franklin Advisers, Inc.	$18.8 Mil	$100/ 25	i	Local Rep
Franklin Tax-Free Trust *Franklin Ohio Insured Tax-Free Income Fund* 777 Mariners Island Blvd. San Mateo, CA 94404 415/570-3000 800/632-2180 800/632-2350	1985	Franklin Advisers, Inc.	$214.9 Mil	$100/ 25	i	Local Rep
Franklin Tax-Free Trust *Franklin Oregon Tax-Free Income Fund* 777 Mariners Island Blvd. San Mateo, CA 94404 415/570-3000 800/632-2180 800/632-2350	1987	Franklin Advisers, Inc.	$49.3 Mil	$100/ 25	i	Local Rep
Franklin Tax-Free Trust *Franklin Pennsylvania Tax-Free Income Fund* 777 Mariners Island Blvd. San Mateo, CA 94404 415/570-3000 800/632-2180 800/632-2350	1986	Franklin Advisers, Inc.	$132.2 Mil	$100/ 25	i	Local Rep
Franklin Tax-Free Trust *Franklin Puerto Rico Tax-Free Income Fund* 777 Mariners Island Blvd. San Mateo, CA 94404 415/570-3000 800/632-2180 800/632-2350	1985	Franklin Advisers, Inc.	$82.7 Mil	$100/ 25	i	Local Rep
Franklin Tax-Free Trust *Franklin Texas Tax-Free Income Fund* 777 Mariners Island Blvd. San Mateo, CA 94404 415/570-3000 800/632-2180 800/632-2350	1987	Franklin Advisers, Inc.	$4.1 Mil	$100/ 25	i	Local Rep

*Key: i=initial sales charge   r=redemption fee or contingent deferred sales charge(CDSC)
t=12b-1 fee and either CDSC or redemption fee   p=12b-1 fee   n=none of the preceding fees   N/A=not available

State Municipal Bond—Long-term

Fund	Year Began	Investment Adviser	9/30/89 Assets	Minimum Initial and Subsequent Investment	Fees*	Where to Buy Shares
Franklin Tax-Free Trust *Franklin Virginia Tax-Free Income Fund* 777 Mariners Island Blvd. San Mateo, CA 94404 415/570-3000 800/632-2180 800/632-2350	1987	Franklin Advisers, Inc.	$28.3 Mil	$100/ 25	i	Local Rep
General New York Tax Exempt Intermediate Bond Fund, Inc. 666 Old Country Rd. Garden City, NY 11530 718/895-1396 800/242-8671	1984	Dreyfus Corporation	$38.9 Mil	$2,500/ 100	p	Fund
GIT Tax-Free Trust *Arizona Portfolio* 1655 Fort Myer Dr. Arlington, VA 22209 703/528-6500 800/336-3063	1989	Bankers Finance Investment Management Corp.	N/A	$1,000/ 0	N/A	Fund
GIT Tax-Free Trust *Missouri Portfolio* 1655 Fort Myer Dr. Arlington, VA 22209 703/528-6500 800/336-3063	1989	Bankers Finance Investment Management Corp.	N/A	$1,000/ 0	N/A	Fund
GIT Tax-Free Trust *Virginia Portfolio* 1655 Fort Myer Dr. Arlington, VA 22209 703/528-6500 800/336-3063	1987	Bankers Finance Investment Management Corp.	$20.4 Mil	$1,000/ 0	n	Fund
Hawaiian Tax-Free Trust 200 Park Ave. Ste. 4515 New York, NY 10017 212/697-6666 800/228-4227	1985	Hawaiian Trust Company, Limited	$301.8 Mil	$1,000/ 0	i	Local Rep
IDS California Tax-Exempt Trust *IDS California Tax-Exempt Fund* IDS Tower 10 Minneapolis, MN 55440 612/372-3131 800/328-8300	1986	IDS Financial Corporation	$107.0 Mil	$100/ 100	i, p	Local Rep

*Key: i=initial sales charge   r=redemption fee or contingent deferred sales charge(CDSC)
t=12b-1 fee and either CDSC or redemption fee   p=12b-1 fee   n=none of the preceding fees   N/A=not available

State Municipal Bond—Long-term

Fund	Year Began	Investment Adviser	9/30/89 Assets	Minimum Initial and Subsequent Investment	Fees*	Where to Buy Shares
IDS Special Tax-Exempt Series Trust *IDS Massachusetts Tax-Exempt Fund* IDS Tower 10 Minneapolis, MN 55440 612/372-3131 800/328-8300	1987	IDS Financial Corporation	$14.6 Mil	$100/ 100	i, p	Local Rep
IDS Special Tax-Exempt Series Trust *IDS Michigan Tax-Exempt Fund* IDS Tower 10 Minneapolis, MN 55440 612/372-3131 800/328-8300	1987	IDS Financial Corporation	$18.7 Mil	$2,000/ 100	i, p	Local Rep
IDS Special Tax-Exempt Series Trust *IDS Minnesota Tax-Exempt Fund* IDS Tower 10 Minneapolis, MN 55440 612/372-3131 800/328-8300	1986	IDS Financial Corporation	$134.9 Mil	$2,000/ 100	i, p	Local Rep
IDS Special Tax-Exempt Series Trust *IDS New York Tax-Exempt Fund* IDS Tower 10 Minneapolis, MN 55440 612/372-3131 800/328-8300	1986	IDS Financial Corporation	$54.8 Mil	$100/ 100	i, p	Local Rep
IDS Special Tax-Exempt Series Trust *IDS Ohio Tax-Exempt Fund* IDS Tower 10 Minneapolis, MN 55440 612/372-3131 800/328-8300	1987	IDS Financial Corporation	$18.3 Mil	$2,000/ 100	i, p	Local Rep
Imperial Portfolios, Inc. *California Tax-Free Portfolio (The)* 9275 Sky Park Ct. P.O. Box 82997 San Diego, CA 92138 619/292-2379 800/347-5588	1988	First Imperial Advisors, Inc.	N/A	$2,500/ 100	N/A	Local Rep
Industrial Series Trust *Mackenzie California Municipal Fund* 1200 N. Federal Hwy. #200 Boca Raton, FL 33432 407/393-8900 800/456-5111	1988	Mackenzie Investment Management Inc.	$7.9 Mil (e)	$250/ 50	i, p	Local Rep

*Key: i=initial sales charge   r=redemption fee or contingent deferred sales charge(CDSC)
t=12b-1 fee and either CDSC or redemption fee   p=12b-1 fee   n=none of the preceding fees   N/A=not available

441

State Municipal Bond—Long-term

Fund	Year Began	Investment Adviser	9/30/89 Assets	Minimum Initial and Subsequent Investment	Fees*	Where to Buy Shares
Industrial Series Trust *Mackenzie New York Municipal Fund* 1200 N. Federal Hwy. #200 Boca Raton, FL 33432 407/393-8900 800/456-5111	1988	Mackenzie Investment Management Inc.	$6.2 Mil (e)	$250/ 50	i, p	Local Rep
Integrated Tax Free Portfolios *California Municipal Bond Portfolio* 10 Union Square East New York, NY 10003 212/353-7000 800/858-8850	1988	Integrated Resources Asset Management Corp.	$13.6 Mil (e)	$1,000/ 100	i, p	Local Rep
Investment Trust of Boston *Massachusetts Tax Free Income Portfolio* 399 Boylston St. 9th Fl. Boston, MA 02116 800/888-4823	1984	Back Bay Advisors, Inc.	$53.5 Mil	$1,000/ 100	i, p	Local Rep
John Hancock Tax-Exempt Series Trust *California Portfolio* 101 Huntington Ave. Boston, MA 02199-7603 617/375-1500 800/225-5291	1987	John Hancock Advisers, Inc.	$11.0 Mil	$1,000/ 25	i, p	Local Rep
John Hancock Tax-Exempt Series Trust *Massachusetts Portfolio* 101 Huntington Ave. Boston, MA 02199-7603 617/375-1500 800/225-5291	1987	John Hancock Advisers, Inc.	$9.4 Mil	$1,000/ 25	i, p	Local Rep
John Hancock Tax-Exempt Series Trust *New York Portfolio* 101 Huntington Ave. Boston, MA 02199-7603 617/375-1500 800/225-5291	1987	John Hancock Advisers, Inc.	$9.3 Mil	$1,000/ 25	i, p	Local Rep
Kemper California Tax-Free Income Fund, Inc. 120 S. LaSalle St. Chicago, IL 60603 312/781-1121 800/621-1148	1983	Kemper Financial Services, Inc.	$543.8 Mil	$1,000/ 100	i	Local Rep

*Key: i=initial sales charge   r=redemption fee or contingent deferred sales charge(CDSC)
t=12b-1 fee and either CDSC or redemption fee   p=12b-1 fee   n=none of the preceding fees   N/A=not available

State Municipal Bond—Long-term

Fund	Year Began	Investment Adviser	9/30/89 Assets	Minimum Initial and Subsequent Investment	Fees*	Where to Buy Shares
Kemper New York Tax-Free Income Fund 120 S. LaSalle St. Chicago, IL 60603 312/781-1121 800/621-1148	1985	Kemper Financial Services, Inc.	$79.8 Mil	$1,000/ 100	i	Local Rep
Kidder, Peabody Tax Free Income Fund *New York Series* 20 Exchange Place New York, NY 10005 212/510-5552	1985	Webster Management Corporation	$8.7 Mil	$0/ 0	i	Local Rep
Limited Term Municipal Fund, Inc. *Limited Term Municipal Fund California Portfolio* 119 E. Marcy St. Ste. 202 Santa Fe, NM 87501 505/984-0200, 800/847-0200	1987	Thornburg Management Company, Inc.	$12.5 Mil (e)	$2,500/ 100	i, p	Local Rep
Lord Abbett California Tax-Free Income Fund, Inc. The General Motors Bldg. 767 Fifth Ave. New York, NY 10153 212/848-1800 800/223-4224	1985	Lord, Abbett & Co.	$100.2 Mil	$1,000/ 0	i, p	Local Rep
Lord Abbett Tax-Free Income Fund, Inc. *New York Series* The General Motors Bldg. 767 Fifth Ave. New York, NY 10153 212/848-1800 800/223-4224	1984	Lord, Abbett & Co.	$166.8 Mil	$1,000/ 0	i	Local Rep
Lord Abbett Tax-Free Income Fund, Inc. *Texas Series* The General Motors Bldg. 767 Fifth Ave. New York, NY 10153 212/848-1800 800/223-4224	1987	Lord, Abbett & Co.	$24.5 Mil	$1,000/ 0	i	Local Rep
Mariner Funds Trust *Mariner New York Managed Bond Fund* P.O. Box 571 Marlton, NJ 08053 609/751-5220 800/634-2536	1989	Marinvest Inc.	$7.2 Mil	$1,000/ 25	N/A	Local Rep

*Key: i=initial sales charge   r=redemption fee or contingent deferred sales charge(CDSC)
t=12b-1 fee and either CDSC or redemption fee   p=12b-1 fee   n=none of the preceding fees   N/A=not available

State Municipal Bond—Long-term

Fund	Year Began	Investment Adviser	9/30/89 Assets	Minimum Initial and Subsequent Investment	Fees*	Where to Buy Shares
Merrill Lynch California Municipal Series Trust *Merrill Lynch California Municipal Bond Fund*		Fund Asset Management, Inc.	$681.5 Mil			
Class A	1988			$1,000/50	i	LRep
Class B	1985			$1,000/50	t	LRep
P.O. Box 9011 Princeton, NJ 08543-9011 609/282-2800, 800/637-3863						
Merrill Lynch Multi-State Municipal Series Trust *Merrill Lynch New York Municipal Bond Fund*		Fund Asset Management, Inc.	$639.0 Mil			
Class A	1988			$1,000/50	i	LRep
Class B	1985			$1,000/50	t	LRep
P.O. Box 9011 Princeton, NJ 08543-9011 609/282-2800, 800/637-3863						
MetLife California Tax-Free Fund One Financial Ctr. 30th Fl. Boston, MA 02111 617/348-2000 800/882-0052	1989	MetLife-State Street Investment Services, Inc.	$5.6 Mil	$250/ 50	i	Local Rep
MetLife New York Tax-Free Fund One Financial Ctr. 30th Fl. Boston, MA 02111 617/348-2000 800/882-0052	1989	MetLife-State Street Investment Services, Inc.	$6.2 Mil	$250/ 50	i	Local Rep
MFS Managed California Tax-Exempt Trust 500 Boylston St. Boston, MA 02116 617/954-5000 800/343-2829	1985	Massachusetts Financial Services Company	$66.0 Mil	$1,000/ 25	i, p	Local Rep
MFS Managed Multi-State Tax-Exempt Trust *Georgia Series* 500 Boylston St. Boston, MA 02116 617/954-5000 800/343-2829	1988	Massachusetts Financial Services Company	$9.7 Mil	$1,000/ 25	i	Local Rep
MFS Managed Multi-State Tax-Exempt Trust *Maryland Series* 500 Boylston St. Boston, MA 02116 617/954-5000 800/343-2829	1984	Massachusetts Financial Services Company	$91.4 Mil	$1,000/ 25	i, p	Local Rep

*Key: i=initial sales charge   r=redemption fee or contingent deferred sales charge(CDSC)
t=12b-1 fee and either CDSC or redemption fee   p=12b-1 fee   n=none of the preceding fees   N/A=not available

State Municipal Bond—Long-term

Fund	Year Began	Investment Adviser	9/30/89 Assets	Minimum Initial and Subsequent Investment	Fees*	Where to Buy Shares
MFS Managed Multi-State Tax-Exempt Trust *Massachusetts Series* 500 Boylston St. Boston, MA 02116 617/954-5000 800/343-2829	1985	Massachusetts Financial Services Company	$218.4 Mil	$1,000/ 25	i, p	Local Rep
MFS Managed Multi-State Tax-Exempt Trust *Michigan Series* 500 Boylston St. Boston, MA 02116 617/954-5000 800/343-2829	1988	Massachusetts Financial Services Company	$6.5 Mil	$1,000/ 25	i	Local Rep
MFS Managed Multi-State Tax-Exempt Trust *New Jersey Series* 500 Boylston St. Boston, MA 02116 617/954-5000 800/343-2829	1988	Massachusetts Financial Services Company	$7.4 Mil	$1,000/ 25	i	Local Rep
MFS Managed Multi-State Tax-Exempt Trust *New York Series* 500 Boylston St. Boston, MA 02116 617/954-5000 800/343-2829	1988	Massachusetts Financial Services Company	$14.8 Mil	$1,000/ 25	i	Local Rep
MFS Managed Multi-State Tax-Exempt Trust *North Carolina Series* 500 Boylston St. Boston, MA 02116 617/954-5000 800/343-2829	1984	Massachusetts Financial Services Company	$162.6 Mil	$1,000/ 25	i, p	Local Rep
MFS Managed Multi-State Tax-Exempt Trust *Ohio Series* 500 Boylston St. Boston, MA 02116 617/954-5000 800/343-2829	1988	Massachusetts Financial Services Company	$9.0 Mil	$1,000/ 25	i	Local Rep
MFS Managed Multi-State Tax-Exempt Trust *South Carolina Series* 500 Boylston St. Boston, MA 02116 617/954-5000 800/343-2829	1984	Massachusetts Financial Services Company	$54.0 Mil	$1,000/ 25	i, p	Local Rep

*Key: i=initial sales charge   r=redemption fee or contingent deferred sales charge(CDSC)
t=12b-1 fee and either CDSC or redemption fee   p=12b-1 fee   n=none of the preceding fees   N/A=not available

State Municipal Bond—Long-term

Fund	Year Began	Investment Adviser	9/30/89 Assets	Minimum Initial and Subsequent Investment	Fees*	Where to Buy Shares
MFS Managed Multi-State Tax-Exempt Trust *Tennessee Series* 500 Boylston St. Boston, MA 02116 617/954-5000 800/343-2829	1988	Massachusetts Financial Services Company	$48.5 Mil	$1,000/ 25	i	Local Rep
MFS Managed Multi-State Tax-Exempt Trust *Virginia Series* 500 Boylston St. Boston, MA 02116 617/954-5000 800/343-2829	1984	Massachusetts Financial Services Company	$229.1 Mil	$1,000/ 25	i, p	Local Rep
MFS Managed Multi-State Tax-Exempt Trust *West Virginia Series* 500 Boylston St. Boston, MA 02116 617/954-5000 800/343-2829	1984	Massachusetts Financial Services Company	$49.3 Mil	$1,000/ 25	i, p	Local Rep
Midwest Group Tax Free Trust *Ohio Long Term Portfolio* 700 Dixie Terminal Bldg. Cincinnati, OH 45202 513/629-2000 800/543-8721 800/582-7396 OH Only	1985	Midwest Advisory Services Inc.	$15.2 Mil	$1,000/ 0	i, p	Local Rep
Minnesota Double Exempt Capital Conservation Fund, Inc. 100 S. Fifth St. Ste. 2200 Minneapolis, MN 55402 612/341-6728 800/553-2143, 800/247-2143 MN Only	1985	Voyageur Fund Managers	N/A	$3,000/ 100	i	Local Rep
Minnesota Insured Fund, Inc. 100 S. Fifth St. Ste. 2200 Minneapolis, MN 55402 612/341-6728 800/553-2143 800/247-2143 MN Only	1987	Voyageur Fund Managers	N/A	$3,000/ 100	i	Local Rep
Muni Bond Funds *California Portfolio* 1345 Avenue of the Americas New York, NY 10105 212/698-5349 800/544-7835	1987	Mutual Management Corp.	$51.1 Mil	$10,000/ 50	i	Local Rep

*Key: i=initial sales charge   r=redemption fee or contingent deferred sales charge(CDSC)
t=12b-1 fee and either CDSC or redemption fee   p=12b-1 fee   n=none of the preceding fees   N/A=not available

446

State Municipal Bond—Long-term

Fund	Year Began	Investment Adviser	9/30/89 Assets	Minimum Initial and Subsequent Investment	Fees*	Where to Buy Shares
Muni Bond Funds *New York Portfolio* 1345 Avenue of the Americas New York, NY 10105 212/698-5349 800/544-7835	1987	Mutual Management Corp.	$16.8 Mil	$10,000/ 50	i	Local Rep
ND Tax-Free Fund, Inc. 201 S. Broadway Minot, ND 58701 701/852-5292 800/56BONDS	1988	ND Money Management, Inc.	$4.3 Mil (e)	$1,000/ 100	t	Local Rep
North Dakota Double Tax-Exempt Bond Fund, Inc. 600 17th St., S. Tower Ste. 2610 Denver, CO 80202 303/623-7500 800/242-0094	1988	Funds Management Corporation	$3.3 Mil	$5,000/ 1,000	i	Local Rep
Northwest Investors Tax-Exempt Business Trust *Idaho Extended Maturity Tax-Exempt Fund (The)* W. 717 Sprague Ave. Ste. 1115 Spokane, WA 99204 509/747-7520, 800/331-4603	1987	Clemenson Capital Management Group, Inc.	$0.7 Mil	$5,000/ 1,000	i	Local Rep
Northwest Investors Tax-Exempt Business Trust *Idaho Limited Maturity Tax-Exempt Fund (The)* W. 717 Sprague Ave. Ste. 1115 Spokane, WA 99204 509/747-7520, 800/331-4603	1987	Clemenson Capital Management Group, Inc.	$1.4 Mil	$5,000/ 1,000	i	Local Rep
Nuveen California Tax-Free Fund, Inc. *Nuveen California Insured Portfolio* 333 W. Wacker Dr. Chicago, IL 60606 312/917-7844 800/621-7210	1986	Nuveen Advisory Corp.	$37.0 Mil	$1,000/ 100	i	Local Rep
Nuveen California Tax-Free Fund, Inc. *Nuveen California Special Bond Portfolio* 333 W. Wacker Dr. Chicago, IL 60606 312/917-7844 800/621-7210	1987	Nuveen Advisory Corp.	$55.7 Mil	$1,000/ 100	i	Local Rep

*Key: i=initial sales charge   r=redemption fee or contingent deferred sales charge(CDSC)
t=12b-1 fee and either CDSC or redemption fee   p=12b-1 fee   n=none of the preceding fees   N/A=not available

State Municipal Bond—Long-term

Fund	Year Began	Investment Adviser	9/30/89 Assets	Minimum Initial and Subsequent Investment	Fees*	Where to Buy Shares
Nuveen Insured Tax-Free Bond Fund, Inc. *Massachusetts Portfolio* 333 W. Wacker Dr. Chicago, IL 60606 312/917-7844 800/621-7210	1987	Nuveen Advisory Corp.	$7.0 Mil	$1,000/ 100	i	Local Rep
Nuveen Insured Tax-Free Bond Fund, Inc. *New York Portfolio* 333 W. Wacker Dr. Chicago, IL 60606 312/917-7844 800/621-7210	1987	Nuveen Advisory Corp.	$28.9 Mil	$1,000/ 100	i	Local Rep
Nuveen Tax-Free Bond Fund, Inc. *Massachusetts Portfolio* 333 W. Wacker Dr. Chicago, IL 60606 312/917-7844 800/621-7210	1987	Nuveen Advisory Corp.	$13.9 Mil	$1,000/ 100	i	Local Rep
Nuveen Tax-Free Bond Fund, Inc. *New York Portfolio* 333 W. Wacker Dr. Chicago, IL 60606 312/917-7844 800/621-7210	1987	Nuveen Advisory Corp.	$24.8 Mil	$1,000/ 100	i	Local Rep
Nuveen Tax-Free Bond Fund, Inc. *Ohio Portfolio* 333 W. Wacker Dr. Chicago, IL 60606 312/917-7844 800/621-7210	1987	Nuveen Advisory Corp.	$34.5 Mil	$1,000/ 100	i	Local Rep
Ocean State Tax-Exempt Fund One Turks Head Place Providence, RI 02903 401/421-1411 800/331-3186	1986	Van Liew Capital, Inc.	$10.3 Mil (e)	$1,000/ 0	i, p	Local Rep
Olympus Tax-Exempt Money Market Fund *Olympus Tax-Exempt California Series* 230 Park Ave. New York, NY 10169 212/309-8400 800/626-FUND	1989	Furman Selz Mager Dietz & Birney Incorporated	$30.7 Mil (e)	$1,000/ 100	i, t	Local Rep

*Key: i=initial sales charge   r=redemption fee or contingent deferred sales charge(CDSC)
t=12b-1 fee and either CDSC or redemption fee   p=12b-1 fee   n=none of the preceding fees   N/A=not available

448

State Municipal Bond—Long-term

Fund	Year Began	Investment Adviser	9/30/89 Assets	Minimum Initial and Subsequent Investment	Fees*	Where to Buy Shares
Olympus Tax-Exempt Money Market Fund *Olympus Tax-Exempt New York Series* 230 Park Ave. New York, NY 10169 212/309-8400 800/626-FUND	1989	Furman Selz Mager Dietz & Birney Incorporated	$21.2 Mil (e)	$1,000/ 100	i, t	Local Rep
Oppenheimer California Tax Exempt Fund Two World Trade Ctr. New York, NY 10048-0669 212/323-0200 800/525-7048	1988	Oppenheimer Management Corporation	$42.6 Mil	$1,000/ 25	i, p	Local Rep
Oppenheimer New York Tax Exempt Fund Two World Trade Ctr. New York, NY 10048-0669 212/323-0200 800/525-7048	1984	Oppenheimer Management Corporation	$197.2 Mil	$1,000/ 25	i, p	Local Rep
Oppenheimer Pennsylvania Tax-Exempt Fund 3410 S. Galena St. Denver, CO 80231 303/671-3200 800/525-7048	1989	Oppenheimer Management Corporation	$0.4 Mil	$1,000/ 25	N/A	Local Rep
Oregon Municipal Bond Fund, Inc. 121 SW Morrison Ste. 1415 Portland, OR 97204 503/295-0919 800/541-9732	1984	PNCG Fund Advisers, Inc.	$20.0 Mil (e)	$1,000/ 500	i, p	Local Rep
Overland Express Funds, Inc. *California Tax-Free Bond Fund (The)* 114 E. Capitol Ave. Little Rock, AR 72201 501/374-4361 800/458-6589	1988	Wells Fargo Bank, N.A.	$54.9 Mil	$1,000/ 100	i	Local Rep
Pacific Horizon California Tax-Exempt Bond Portfolio, Inc. 156 W. 56th St. Ste. 1902 New York, NY 10019 212/492-1600 800/367-6075	1984	Security Pacific National Bank	$92.8 Mil	$1,000/ 100	i, p	Local Rep

*Key: i=initial sales charge   r=redemption fee or contingent deferred sales charge(CDSC)
t=12b-1 fee and either CDSC or redemption fee   p=12b-1 fee   n=none of the preceding fees   N/A=not available

State Municipal Bond—Long-term

Fund	Year Began	Investment Adviser	9/30/89 Assets	Minimum Initial and Subsequent Investment	Fees*	Where to Buy Shares
PaineWebber California Tax Exempt Income Fund 1285 Avenue of the Americas PaineWebber Bldg. New York, NY 10019 212/713-2000 800/544-9300	1985	Mitchell Hutchins Asset Management Inc.	$188.0 Mil	$1,000/ 100	i	Local Rep
PaineWebber Municipal Series *PaineWebber Classic New York Tax-Free Fund* 1285 Avenue of the Americas PaineWebber Bldg. New York, NY 10019 212/713-2000, 800/544-9300	1988	Mitchell Hutchins Asset Management Inc.	$16.6 Mil	$1,000/ 100	i	Local Rep
Piper Jaffray Investment Trust Inc. *Minnesota Tax-Exempt Fund* 222 S. 9th St. Piper Jaffray Twr. Minneapolis, MN 55402 612/342-6426 800/333-6000	1988	Piper Capital Management Incorporated	$50.7 Mil	$0/ 0	i, p	Local Rep
Premier California Tax Exempt Bond Fund 666 Old Country Rd. Garden City, NY 11530 718/895-1650 800/346-3621	1986	Dreyfus Corporation	$40.4 Mil	$1,000/ 100	i, p	Fund
Premier New York Tax Exempt Bond Fund 666 Old Country Rd. Garden City, NY 11530 718/895-1650 800/346-3621	1987	Dreyfus Corporation	$9.6 Mil	$1,000/ 100	i, p	Local Rep
Premier State Tax Exempt Bond Fund *Connecticut Series* 666 Old Country Rd. Garden City, NY 11530 718/895-1650 800/346-3621	1987	Dreyfus Corporation	$52.4 Mil	$1,000/ 100	i, p	Fund
Premier State Tax Exempt Bond Fund *Florida Series* 666 Old Country Rd. Garden City, NY 11530 718/895-1650 800/346-3621	1987	Dreyfus Corporation	$32.3 Mil	$1,000/ 100	i, p	Fund

*Key: i=initial sales charge   r=redemption fee or contingent deferred sales charge(CDSC)
t=12b-1 fee and either CDSC or redemption fee   p=12b-1 fee   n=none of the preceding fees   N/A=not available

450

State Municipal Bond—Long-term

Fund	Year Began	Investment Adviser	9/30/89 Assets	Minimum Initial and Subsequent Investment	Fees*	Where to Buy Shares
Premier State Tax Exempt Bond Fund *Maryland Series* 666 Old Country Rd. Garden City, NY 11530 718/895-1650 800/346-3621	1987	Dreyfus Corporation	$44.7 Mil	$1,000/ 100	i, p	Fund
Premier State Tax Exempt Bond Fund *Massachusetts Series* 666 Old Country Rd. Garden City, NY 11530 718/895-1650 800/346-3621	1987	Dreyfus Corporation	$31.0 Mil	$1,000/ 100	i, p	Fund
Premier State Tax Exempt Bond Fund *Michigan Series* 666 Old Country Rd. Garden City, NY 11530 718/895-1650 800/346-3621	1987	Dreyfus Corporation	$21.8 Mil	$1,000/ 100	i, p	Fund
Premier State Tax Exempt Bond Fund *Minnesota Series* 666 Old Country Rd. Garden City, NY 11530 718/895-1650 800/346-3621	1987	Dreyfus Corporation	$23.6 Mil	$1,000/ 100	i, p	Fund
Premier State Tax Exempt Bond Fund *Ohio Series* 666 Old Country Rd. Garden City, NY 11530 718/895-1650 800/346-3621	1987	Dreyfus Corporation	$55.2 Mil	$1,000/ 100	i, p	Fund
Premier State Tax Exempt Bond Fund *Pennsylvania Series* 666 Old Country Rd. Garden City, NY 11530 718/895-1650 800/346-3621	1987	Dreyfus Corporation	$23.5 Mil	$1,000/ 100	i, p	Fund
Premier State Tax Exempt Bond Fund *Texas Series* 666 Old Country Rd. Garden City, NY 11530 718/895-1650 800/346-3621	1987	Dreyfus Corporation	$3.9 Mil	$1,000/ 100	i, p	Fund

*Key: i=initial sales charge   r=redemption fee or contingent deferred sales charge(CDSC)
t=12b-1 fee and either CDSC or redemption fee   p=12b-1 fee   n=none of the preceding fees   N/A=not available

451

State Municipal Bond—Long-term

Fund	Year Began	Investment Adviser	9/30/89 Assets	Minimum Initial and Subsequent Investment	Fees*	Where to Buy Shares
Prudential-Bache California Municipal Fund *California Series* One Seaport Plaza New York, NY 10292 212/214-1215 800/225-1852	1984	Prudential Mutual Fund Management	$178.1 Mil	$1,000/ 100	t	Local Rep
Prudential-Bache Municipal Series Fund *Arizona Series* One Seaport Plaza New York, NY 10292 212/214-1215 800/225-1852	1984	Prudential Mutual Fund Management	$59.4 Mil	$1,000/ 100	t	Local Rep
Prudential-Bache Municipal Series Fund *Georgia Series* One Seaport Plaza New York, NY 10292 212/214-1215 800/225-1852	1984	Prudential Mutual Fund Management	$23.8 Mil	$1,000/ 100	t	Local Rep
Prudential-Bache Municipal Series Fund *Maryland Series* One Seaport Plaza New York, NY 10292 212/214-1215 800/225-1852	1985	Prudential Mutual Fund Management	$47.3 Mil	$1,000/ 100	t	Local Rep
Prudential-Bache Municipal Series Fund *Massachusetts Series* One Seaport Plaza New York, NY 10292 212/214-1215 800/225-1852	1984	Prudential Mutual Fund Management	$52.6 Mil	$1,000/ 100	t	Local Rep
Prudential-Bache Municipal Series Fund *Michigan Series* One Seaport Plaza New York, NY 10292 212/214-1215 800/225-1852	1984	Prudential Mutual Fund Management	$47.4 Mil	$1,000/ 100	t	Local Rep
Prudential-Bache Municipal Series Fund *Minnesota Series* One Seaport Plaza New York, NY 10292 212/214-1215 800/225-1852	1984	Prudential Mutual Fund Management	$22.9 Mil	$1,000/ 100	t	Local Rep

*Key: i=initial sales charge   r=redemption fee or contingent deferred sales charge(CDSC)
t=12b-1 fee and either CDSC or redemption fee   p=12b-1 fee   n=none of the preceding fees   N/A=not available

State Municipal Bond—Long-term

Fund	Year Began	Investment Adviser	9/30/89 Assets	Minimum Initial and Subsequent Investment	Fees*	Where to Buy Shares
Prudential-Bache Municipal Series Fund *New Jersey Series* One Seaport Plaza New York, NY 10292 212/214-1215 800/225-1852	1988	Prudential Mutual Fund Management	$129.4 Mil	$1,000/ 100	p	Local Rep
Prudential-Bache Municipal Series Fund *New York Series* One Seaport Plaza New York, NY 10292 212/214-1215 800/225-1852	1984	Prudential Mutual Fund Management	$339.9 Mil	$1,000/ 100	t	Local Rep
Prudential-Bache Municipal Series Fund *North Carolina Series* One Seaport Plaza New York, NY 10292 212/214-1215 800/225-1852	1985	Prudential Mutual Fund Management	$54.1 Mil	$1,000/ 100	t	Local Rep
Prudential-Bache Municipal Series Fund *Ohio Series* One Seaport Plaza New York, NY 10292 212/214-1215 800/225-1852	1984	Prudential Mutual Fund Management	$86.9 Mil	$1,000/ 100	t	Local Rep
Prudential-Bache Municipal Series Fund *Oregon Series* One Seaport Plaza New York, NY 10292 212/214-1215 800/225-1852	1984	Prudential Mutual Fund Management	$12.6 Mil	$1,000/ 100	t	Local Rep
Prudential-Bache Municipal Series Fund *Pennsylvania Series* One Seaport Plaza New York, NY 10292 212/214-1215 800/225-1852	1987	Prudential Mutual Fund Management	$121.8 Mil	$1,000/ 100	t	Local Rep
Putnam California Tax Exempt Income Fund One Post Office Sq. Boston, MA 02109 617/292-1000 800/225-2465	1983	Putnam Management Company, Inc.	$1.5 Bil	$500/ 50	i	Local Rep

*Key: i=initial sales charge   r=redemption fee or contingent deferred sales charge(CDSC)
t=12b-1 fee and either CDSC or redemption fee   p=12b-1 fee   n=none of the preceding fees   N/A=not available

453

State Municipal Bond—Long-term

Fund	Year Began	Investment Adviser	9/30/89 Assets	Minimum Initial and Subsequent Investment	Fees*	Where to Buy Shares
Putnam Massachusetts Tax Exempt Income Fund One Post Office Sq. Boston, MA 02109 617/292-1000 800/225-2465	1986	Putnam Management Company, Inc.	$70.2 Mil	$500/ 50	t	Local Rep
Putnam Michigan Tax Exempt Income Fund One Post Office Sq. Boston, MA 02109 617/292-1000 800/225-2465	1987	Putnam Management Company, Inc.	$38.6 Mil	$500/ 50	t	Local Rep
Putnam Minnesota Tax Exempt Income Fund One Post Office Sq. Boston, MA 02109 617/292-1000 800/225-2465	1986	Putnam Management Company, Inc.	$29.3 Mil	$500/ 50	t	Local Rep
Putnam New York Tax Exempt Income Fund One Post Office Sq. Boston, MA 02109 617/292-1000 800/225-2465	1983	Putnam Management Company, Inc.	$1.3 Bil	$500/ 50	i	Local Rep
Putnam Ohio Tax Exempt Income Fund One Post Office Sq. Boston, MA 02109 617/292-1000 800/225-2465	1986	Putnam Management Company, Inc.	$92.5 Mil	$500/ 50	t	Local Rep
Putnam Pennsylvania Tax Exempt Income Fund One Post Office Sq. Boston, MA 02109 617/292-1000 800/225-2465	1989	Putnam Management Company, Inc.	$8.2 Mil	$500/ 50	N/A	Local Rep
SAFECO California Tax-Free Income Fund, Inc. SAFECO Plaza Seattle, WA 98185 206/545-5530 800/426-6730	1983	SAFECO Asset Management Company	$42.6 Mil	$1,000/ 100	n	Fund

*Key: i=initial sales charge   r=redemption fee or contingent deferred sales charge(CDSC)
       t=12b-1 fee and either CDSC or redemption fee   p=12b-1 fee   n=none of the preceding fees   N/A=not available

State Municipal Bond—Long-term

Fund	Year Began	Investment Adviser	9/30/89 Assets	Minimum Initial and Subsequent Investment	Fees*	Where to Buy Shares
Scudder California Tax Free Fund 175 Federal St. Boston, MA 02110 617/439-4640 800/225-2470 800/225-5163	1983	Scudder, Stevens & Clark, Inc.	$182.1 Mil	$1,000/ 0	n	Fund
Scudder Massachusetts Tax Free Fund 175 Federal St. Boston, MA 02110 617/439-4640 800/225-2470 800/225-5163	1987	Scudder, Stevens & Clark, Inc.	$42.5 Mil	$1,000/ 0	n	Fund
Scudder New York Tax Free Fund 175 Federal St. Boston, MA 02110 617/439-4640 800/225-2470 800/225-5163	1983	Scudder, Stevens & Clark, Inc.	$130.1 Mil	$1,000/ 0	n	Fund
Scudder Ohio Tax Free Fund 175 Federal St. Boston, MA 02110 617/439-4640 800/225-2470 800/225-5163	1987	Scudder, Stevens & Clark, Inc.	$18.7 Mil	$1,000/ 0	n	Fund
Scudder Pennsylvania Tax Free Fund 175 Federal St. Boston, MA 02110 617/439-4640 800/225-2470 800/225-5163	1987	Scudder, Stevens & Clark, Inc.	$15.1 Mil	$1,000/ 0	n	Fund
Seligman California Tax-Exempt Fund Series *High-Yield Series* 130 Liberty St. New York, NY 10006 212/488-0200 800/221-2450 800/522-6869 NY Only	1984	J. & W. Seligman & Co. Incorporated	$51.1 Mil	$1,000/ 50	i	Local Rep
Seligman California Tax-Exempt Fund Series *Quality Series* 130 Liberty St. New York, NY 10006 212/488-0200 800/221-2450 800/522-6869 NY Only	1984	J. & W. Seligman & Co. Incorporated	$59.3 Mil	$1,000/ 50	i	Local Rep

*Key: i=initial sales charge   r=redemption fee or contingent deferred sales charge(CDSC)
t=12b-1 fee and either CDSC or redemption fee   p=12b-1 fee   n=none of the preceding fees   N/A=not available

State Municipal Bond—Long-term

Fund	Year Began	Investment Adviser	9/30/89 Assets	Minimum Initial and Subsequent Investment	Fees*	Where to Buy Shares
Seligman New Jersey Tax-Exempt Fund, Inc. 130 Liberty St. New York, NY 10006 212/488-0200 800/221-2450 800/522-6869 NY Only	1988	J. & W. Seligman & Co. Incorporated	$51.0 Mil	$1,000/ 50	i, p	Local Rep
Seligman Pennsylvania Tax-Exempt Fund Series *Quality Series* 130 Liberty St. New York, NY 10006 212/488-0200 800/221-2450 800/522-6869 NY Only	1986	J. & W. Seligman & Co. Incorporated	$41.9 Mil	$1,000/ 50	i, p	Local Rep
Seligman Tax-Exempt Fund Series, Inc. *Colorado Tax-Exempt Series* 130 Liberty St. New York, NY 10006 212/488-0200 800/221-2450 800/522-6869 NY Only	1986	J. & W. Seligman & Co. Incorporated	$62.5 Mil	$1,000/ 50	i	Local Rep
Seligman Tax-Exempt Fund Series, Inc. *Florida Tax-Exempt Series* 130 Liberty St. New York, NY 10006 212/488-0200 800/221-2450 800/522-6869 NY Only	1986	J. & W. Seligman & Co. Incorporated	$23.1 Mil	$1,000/ 50	i	Local Rep
Seligman Tax-Exempt Fund Series, Inc. *Georgia Tax-Exempt Series* 130 Liberty St. New York, NY 10006 212/488-0200 800/221-2450 800/522-6869 NY Only	1987	J. & W. Seligman & Co. Incorporated	$14.5 Mil	$1,000/ 50	i	Local Rep
Seligman Tax-Exempt Fund Series, Inc. *Louisiana Tax-Exempt Series* 130 Liberty St. New York, NY 10006 212/488-0200 800/221-2450 800/522-6869 NY Only	1985	J. & W. Seligman & Co. Incorporated	$43.9 Mil	$1,000/ 50	i	Local Rep
Seligman Tax-Exempt Fund Series, Inc. *Maryland Tax-Exempt Series* 130 Liberty St. New York, NY 10006 212/488-0200 800/221-2450 800/522-6869 NY Only	1985	J. & W. Seligman & Co. Incorporated	$46.6 Mil	$1,000/ 50	i	Local Rep

*Key: i=initial sales charge   r=redemption fee or contingent deferred sales charge(CDSC)
t=12b-1 fee and either CDSC or redemption fee   p=12b-1 fee   n=none of the preceding fees   N/A=not available

456

State Municipal Bond—Long-term

Fund	Year Began	Investment Adviser	9/30/89 Assets	Minimum Initial and Subsequent Investment	Fees*	Where to Buy Shares
Seligman Tax-Exempt Fund Series, Inc. *Massachusetts Tax-Exempt Series* 130 Liberty St. New York, NY 10006 212/488-0200 800/221-2450, 800/522-6869 NY Only	1983	J. & W. Seligman & Co. Incorporated	$122.5 Mil	$1,000/ 50	i	Local Rep
Seligman Tax-Exempt Fund Series, Inc. *Michigan Tax-Exempt Series* 130 Liberty St. New York, NY 10006 212/488-0200 800/221-2450 800/522-6869 NY Only	1984	J. & W. Seligman & Co. Incorporated	$111.2 Mil	$1,000/ 50	i	Local Rep
Seligman Tax-Exempt Fund Series, Inc. *Minnesota Tax-Exempt Series* 130 Liberty St. New York, NY 10006 212/488-0200 800/221-2450 800/522-6869 NY Only	1983	J. & W. Seligman & Co. Incorporated	$148.4 Mil	$1,000/ 50	i	Local Rep
Seligman Tax-Exempt Fund Series, Inc. *Missouri Tax-Exempt Series* 130 Liberty St. New York, NY 10006 212/488-0200 800/221-2450 800/522-6869 NY Only	1986	J. & W. Seligman & Co. Incorporated	$49.2 Mil	$1,000/ 50	i	Local Rep
Seligman Tax-Exempt Fund Series, Inc. *New York Tax-Exempt Series* 130 Liberty St. New York, NY 10006 212/488-0200 800/221-2450 800/522-6869 NY Only	1983	J. & W. Seligman & Co. Incorporated	$75.5 Mil	$1,000/ 50	i	Local Rep
Seligman Tax-Exempt Fund Series, Inc. *Ohio Tax-Exempt Series* 130 Liberty St. New York, NY 10006 212/488-0200 800/221-2450 800/522-6869 NY Only	1983	J. & W. Seligman & Co. Incorporated	$131.9 Mil	$1,000/ 50	i	Local Rep
Seligman Tax-Exempt Fund Series, Inc. *Oregon Tax-Exempt Series* 130 Liberty St. New York, NY 10006 212/488-0200 800/221-2450 800/522-6869 NY Only	1986	J. & W. Seligman & Co. Incorporated	$30.5 Mil	$1,000/ 50	i	Local Rep

*Key: i=initial sales charge   r=redemption fee or contingent deferred sales charge(CDSC)
t=12b-1 fee and either CDSC or redemption fee   p=12b-1 fee   n=none of the preceding fees   N/A=not available

State Municipal Bond—Long-term

Fund	Year Began	Investment Adviser	9/30/89 Assets	Minimum Initial and Subsequent Investment	Fees*	Where to Buy Shares
Seligman Tax-Exempt Fund Series, Inc. *South Carolina Tax-Exempt Series* 130 Liberty St. New York, NY 10006 212/488-0200 800/221-2450, 800/522-6869 NY Only	1987	J. & W. Seligman & Co. Incorporated	$46.5 Mil	$1,000/ 50	i	Local Rep
Sigma Pennsylvania Tax-Free Trust 3801 Kennett Pk., C-200 Greenville Ctr. Wilmington, DE 19807 302/652-3091 800/441-9490	1986	Sigma Management, Inc.	$28.3 Mil	$0/ 0	i, p	Local Rep
SLH California Municipal Fund, Inc. 31 W. 52nd St. New York, NY 10019 212/767-3700	1984	Bernstein-Macaulay Division of Shearson Lehman Hutton Inc.	$323.0 Mil	$500/ 200	i	Local Rep
SLH Massachusetts Municipals 31 W. 52nd St. New York, NY 10019 212/767-3700	1988	Bernstein-Macaulay Division of Shearson Lehman Hutton Inc.	$19.9 Mil	$500/ 200	i	Local Rep
SLH Michigan Municipals 31 W. 52nd St. New York, NY 10019 212/767-3700	1987	Bernstein-Macaulay Division of Shearson Lehman Hutton Inc.	$3.5 Mil	$500/ 200	i	Local Rep
SLH Municipal Series, Inc. *SLH Arizona Municipal Fund* One Battery Park Plaza New York, NY 10004 212/742-5000	1987	SLH Asset Management Division of Shearson Lehman Hutton Inc.	$8.1 Mil	$500/ 250	i	Local Rep
SLH New York Municipals Fund 31 W. 52nd St. New York, NY 10019 212/767-3700	1984	Bernstein-Macaulay Division of Shearson Lehman Hutton Inc.	$436.1 Mil	$500/ 200	i	Local Rep

*Key: i=initial sales charge   r=redemption fee or contingent deferred sales charge(CDSC)
t=12b-1 fee and either CDSC or redemption fee   p=12b-1 fee   n=none of the preceding fees   N/A=not available

State Municipal Bond—Long-term

Fund	Year Began	Investment Adviser	9/30/89 Assets	Minimum Initial and Subsequent Investment	Fees*	Where to Buy Shares
SLH Ohio Municipals Fund 31 W. 52nd St. New York, NY 10019 212/767-3700	1987	Bernstein-Macaulay Division of Shearson Lehman Hutton Inc.	$7.2 Mil	$500/ 0	i	Local Rep
Tax-Exempt Fund of California 333 S. Hope St. Los Angeles, CA 90071 213/486-9200 800/421-0180 213/486-9651 Collect	1986	Capital Research & Management Company	$70.1 Mil	$0/ 0	i, t	Local Rep
Tax-Exempt Fund of Maryland 1101 Vermont Ave., NW Washington, DC 20016 202/842-5665	1986	Capital Research & Management Company	$28.2 Mil	$0/ 0	i, t	Local Rep
Tax-Exempt Fund of Virginia 1101 Vermont Ave., NW Washington, DC 20016 202/842-5665	1986	Capital Research & Management Company	$29.2 Mil	$0/ 0	i, t	Local Rep
Tax-Free Fund of Colorado 200 Park Ave. Ste. 4515 New York, NY 10017 212/697-6666 800/872-2652	1987	United Bank of Denver	$44.3 Mil	$1,000/ 0	i	Local Rep
Tax-Free Trust of Arizona 200 Park Ave. Ste. 4515 New York, NY 10017 212/697-6666 800/437-1020	1986	Valley National Bank of Arizona	$103.2 Mil	$1,000/ 0	i	Local Rep
Tax-Free Trust of Oregon 200 Park Ave. Ste. 4515 New York, NY 10017 212/697-6666 800/872-6734	1986	Qualivest Capital Management, Inc.	$122.1 Mil	$1,000/ 0	i	Local Rep

*Key: i=initial sales charge   r=redemption fee or contingent deferred sales charge(CDSC)
t=12b-1 fee and either CDSC or redemption fee   p=12b-1 fee   n=none of the preceding fees   N/A=not available

State Municipal Bond—Long-term

Fund	Year Began	Investment Adviser	9/30/89 Assets	Minimum Initial and Subsequent Investment	Fees*	Where to Buy Shares
THC Fund, Inc. *Municipal Utilities Tax-Exempt Fund (Missouri)* 515 Olive St. 11th Fl. St. Louis, MO 63101 314/421-4422 800/325-7159	1988	Mutef Investment Advisors	$1.7 Mil	$1,000/ 100	i, p	Local Rep
T. Rowe Price California Tax-Free Income Trust *California Tax-Free Bond Fund* 100 E. Pratt St. Baltimore, MD 21202 301/547-2000 800/638-5660	1986	T. Rowe Price Associates, Inc.	$59.0 Mil	$2,500/ 100	n	Fund
T. Rowe Price State Tax-Free Income Trust *Maryland Tax-Free Bond Fund* 100 E. Pratt St. Baltimore, MD 21202 301/547-2000 800/638-5660	1987	T. Rowe Price Associates, Inc.	$164.5 Mil	$2,500/ 100	n	Fund
T. Rowe Price State Tax-Free Income Trust *New York Tax-Free Bond Fund* 100 E. Pratt St. Baltimore, MD 21202 301/547-2000 800/638-5660	1986	T. Rowe Price Associates, Inc.	$43.9 Mil	$2,500/ 100	n	Fund
Unified Municipal Fund, Inc. *Indiana Series* 429 N. Pennsylvania St. Indianapolis, IN 46204-1897 317/634-3300 800/862-7283	1985	Unified Management Corporation	$11.9 Mil	$1,000/ 25	n	Fund
USAA Tax Exempt Fund, Inc. *California Bond Fund* USAA Bldg. San Antonio, TX 78288 512/498-8000 800/531-8000	1989	USAA Investment Management Company	$36.8 Mil	$3,000/ 50	n	Fund
Value Line New York Tax Exempt Trust 711 Third Ave. New York, NY 10017 212/687-3965 800/223-0818	1987	Value Line, Inc.	$27.7 Mil	$1,000/ 250	n	Fund

*Key: i=initial sales charge   r=redemption fee or contingent deferred sales charge(CDSC)
t=12b-1 fee and either CDSC or redemption fee   p=12b-1 fee   n=none of the preceding fees   N/A=not available

State Municipal Bond—Long-term

Fund	Year Began	Investment Adviser	9/30/89 Assets	Minimum Initial and Subsequent Investment	Fees*	Where to Buy Shares
Vanguard California Tax-Free Fund *California Insured Long-Term Portfolio* Vanguard Financial Ctr. P.O. Box 2600 Valley Forge, PA 19482 215/648-6000, 800/662-7447, 800/362-0530 PA Only	1986	Vanguard Group, Inc.	$225.1 Mil	$3,000/ 100	n	Fund
Vanguard New Jersey Tax-Free Fund *Insured Tax-Free Portfolio* Vanguard Financial Ctr. P.O. Box 2600 Valley Forge, PA 19482 215/648-6000 800/662-7447, 800/362-0530 PA Only	1988	Vanguard Group, Inc.	$111.5 Mil	$3,000/ 100	n	Fund
Vanguard New York Insured Tax-Free Fund Vanguard Financial Ctr. P.O. Box 2600 Valley Forge, PA 19482 215/648-6000 800/662-7447 800/362-0530 PA Only	1986	Vanguard Group, Inc.	$150.5 Mil	$3,000/ 100	n	Fund
Vanguard Pennsylvania Tax-Free Fund *Insured Long-Term Portfolio* Vanguard Financial Ctr. P.O. Box 2600 Valley Forge, PA 19482 215/648-6000 800/662-7447, 800/362-0530 PA Only	1986	Vanguard Group, Inc.	$380.8 Mil	$3,000/ 100	n	Fund
Van Kampen Merritt California Insured Tax Free Fund 1001 Warrenville Rd. Lisle, IL 60532 312/719-6000 800/225-2222	1986	Van Kampen Merritt Investment Advisory Corp.	$44.6 Mil	$1,500/ 100	i, p	Local Rep
Van Kampen Merritt Pennsylvania Tax Free Income Fund 1001 Warrenville Rd. Lisle, IL 60532 312/719-6000 800/225-2222	1987	Van Kampen Merritt Investment Advisory Corp.	$40.1 Mil	$1,500/ 100	i, p	Local Rep

*Key: i=initial sales charge   r=redemption fee or contingent deferred sales charge(CDSC)
      t=12b-1 fee and either CDSC or redemption fee   p=12b-1 fee   n=none of the preceding fees   N/A=not available

461

◆ ◆ ◆ ◆

State Municipal Bond—
Short-term Funds

State Municipal Bond—Short-term

Fund	Year Began	Investment Adviser	9/30/89 Assets	Minimum Initial and Subsequent Investment	Fees*	Where to Buy Shares
Alliance Tax-Exempt Reserves *California Portfolio* 1345 Avenue of the Americas New York, NY 10105 212/969-1000 800/221-5672	1988	Alliance Capital Management L.P.	$108.1 Mil	$1,000/ 100	p	Local Rep
A.T. Ohio Tax-Free Money Fund Federated Investors Twr. Pittsburgh, PA 15222-3779 412/288-1900 800/245-3391	1985	Federated Management	$261.2 Mil	$25,000/ 0	n	Local Rep
Benham California Tax-Free Trust *Money Market Portfolio* 755 Page Mill Rd. Palo Alto, CA 94304 415/858-2400 800/227-8380 800/982-6150 CA Only	1983	Benham Management Corporation	$486.7 Mil	$1,000/ 100	n	Fund
Boston Company Tax-Free Municipal Funds *California Tax-Free Money Fund* Two World Trade Ctr. New York, NY 10048 212/321-7155	1988	Boston Company Advisors, Inc.	$14.8 Mil	$1,000/ 0	p	Fund
Boston Company Tax-Free Municipal Funds *Massachusetts Tax-Free Money Fund* One Boston Place Boston, MA 02019 617/956-9740 800/225-5267, 800/343-6324	1983	Boston Company Advisors, Inc.	$154.6 Mil	$1,000/ 0	p	Local Rep
Boston Company Tax-Free Municipal Funds *New York Tax-Free Money Fund* Two World Trade Ctr. New York, NY 10048 212/321-7155	1988	Boston Company Advisors, Inc.	$13.7 Mil	$1,000/ 0	p	Fund
California Investment Trust I *California Tax-Free Money Market Fund* 44 Montgomery St. Ste. 2200 San Francisco, CA 94104 415/398-2727, 800/225-8778	1985	CCM Partners	$78.8 Mil (e)	$10,000/ 250	n	Fund

*Key: i=initial sales charge   r=redemption fee or contingent deferred sales charge(CDSC)
t=12b-1 fee and either CDSC or redemption fee   p=12b-1 fee   n=none of the preceding fees   N/A=not available

465

State Municipal Bond—Short-term

Fund	Year Began	Investment Adviser	9/30/89 Assets	Minimum Initial and Subsequent Investment	Fees*	Where to Buy Shares
California Municipal Cash Trust Federated Investors Twr. Pittsburgh, PA 15222-3779 412/288-1900 800/245-5000	1989	Federated Management	$36.6 Mil	$25,000/ 0	n	Local Rep
Calvert Tax-Free Reserves *California Portfolio* 1700 Pennsylvania Ave., NW Washington, DC 20006 301/951-4820 800/368-2745	1989	Ariel Capital Management, Inc.	N/A	$2,000/ 250	N/A	Fund
CIGNA Cash Funds *CIGNA Tax-Exempt Cash Fund of Connecticut* One Financial Plaza Springfield, MA 01103 413/784-0100 800/56CIGNA	1989	CIGNA Investments, Inc.	$9.0 Mil	$1,000/ 50	p	Local Rep
CMA Multi-State Municipal Series Trust *CMA California Tax-Exempt Fund* P.O. Box 9011 Princeton, NJ 08543-9011 201/560-5507 800/262-4636, 800/262-3276	1988	Fund Asset Management, Inc.	$923.4 Mil	$0/ 0	p	Local Rep
CMA Multi-State Municipal Series Trust *CMA New York Tax-Exempt Fund* P.O. Box 9011 Princeton, NJ 08543-9011 201/560-5507 800/262-4636 800/262-3276	1988	Fund Asset Management, Inc.	$393.5 Mil	$0/ 0	p	Local Rep
Counsellors New York Tax Exempt Fund, Inc. 466 Lexington Ave. New York, NY 10017-3147 212/878-0600 800/888-6878	1985	Warburg, Pincus Counsellors, Inc.	$72.2 Mil	$1,000/ 500	n	Fund
Dean Witter/Sears California Tax-Free Daily Income Trust Two World Trade Ctr. New York, NY 10048 212/392-2550 800/869-3863	1988	Dean Witter Reynolds Inc. - InterCapital Division	$352.9 Mil	$5,000/ 100	p	Local Rep

*Key: i=initial sales charge   r=redemption fee or contingent deferred sales charge(CDSC)
t=12b-1 fee and either CDSC or redemption fee   p=12b-1 fee   n=none of the preceding fees   N/A=not available

466

State Municipal Bond—Short-term

Fund	Year Began	Investment Adviser	9/30/89 Assets	Minimum Initial and Subsequent Investment	Fees*	Where to Buy Shares
Dreyfus California Tax Exempt Money Market Fund 666 Old Country Rd. Garden City, NY 11530 718/895-1206 800/645-6561	1986	Dreyfus Corporation	$415.2 Mil	$2,500/ 100	n	Fund
Dreyfus New Jersey Tax Exempt Money Market Fund, Inc. 666 Old Country Rd. Garden City, NY 11530 718/895-1206 800/645-6561	1988	Dreyfus Corporation	$406.6 Mil	$2,500/ 100	n	Fund
Dreyfus New York Tax Exempt Money Market Fund 666 Old Country Rd. Garden City, NY 11530 718/895-1206 800/645-6561	1987	Dreyfus Corporation	$489.0 Mil	$2,500/ 100	n	Fund
Evergreen California Tax Exempt Money Market Fund 2500 Westchester Ave. Purchase, NY 10577 914/694-2020 800/235-0064	1988	Evergreen Asset Management Corporation	$27.4 Mil (e)	$2,000/ 100	n	Fund
Fidelity California Tax Free Fund *Money Market Portfolio* 82 Devonshire St. Boston, MA 02109 617/570-7000 800/227-9639	1984	Fidelity Management & Research Company	$775.5 Mil	$2,500/ 250	n	Fund
Fidelity Court Street Trust *Fidelity Connecticut Tax-Free Money Market Portfolio* 82 Devonshire St. Boston, MA 02109 617/570-7000 800/544-6666	1989	Fidelity Management & Research Company	N/A	$5,000/ 500	n	Fund
Fidelity Court Street Trust *Fidelity New Jersey Tax-Free Money Market Portfolio* 82 Devonshire St. Boston, MA 02109 617/570-7000 800/544-6666	1988	Fidelity Management & Research Company	$329.5 Mil	$2,500/ 250	n	Fund

*Key: i=initial sales charge   r=redemption fee or contingent deferred sales charge(CDSC)
t=12b-1 fee and either CDSC or redemption fee   p=12b-1 fee   n=none of the preceding fees   N/A=not available

467

State Municipal Bond—Short-term

Fund	Year Began	Investment Adviser	9/30/89 Assets	Minimum Initial and Subsequent Investment	Fees*	Where to Buy Shares
Fidelity Massachusetts Tax-Free Fund *Money Market Portfolio* 82 Devonshire St. Boston, MA 02109 617/570-7000 800/544-6666	1983	Fidelity Management & Research Company	$659.7 Mil	$2,500/ 250	n	Fund
Fidelity Municipal Trust *Fidelity Ohio Tax-Free Money Market Portfolio* 82 Devonshire St. Boston, MA 02109 617/570-7000 800/544-6666	1989	Fidelity Management & Research Company	N/A	$2,500/ 250	N/A	Fund
Fidelity Municipal Trust *Fidelity Pennsylvania Tax-Free Money Market Portfolio* 82 Devonshire St. Boston, MA 02109 617/570-7000 800/544-6666	1986	Fidelity Management & Research Company	$157.7 Mil	$2,500/ 250	n	Fund
Fidelity New York Tax-Free Fund *Money Market Portfolio* 82 Devonshire St. Boston, MA 02109 617/570-7000 800/544-6666 617/523-1919 MA Only	1984	Fidelity Management & Research Company	$627.5 Mil	$2,500/ 250	n	Fund
Franklin California Tax-Free Trust *Franklin California Tax-Exempt Money Fund* 777 Mariners Island Blvd. San Mateo, CA 94404 415/570-3000 800/632-2180, 800/632-2350	1985	Franklin Advisers, Inc.	$914.1 Mil	$500/ 25	n	Fund
Franklin New York Tax-Exempt Money Fund 777 Mariners Island Blvd. San Mateo, CA 94404 415/570-3000 800/632-2180 800/632-2350	1986	Franklin Advisers, Inc.	$70.7 Mil	$500/ 25	n	Fund
General California Municipal Bond Fund, Inc. 666 Old Country Rd. Garden City, NY 11530 800/242-8671	1989	Dreyfus Corporation	N/A	$2,500/ 100	N/A	Fund

*Key: i=initial sales charge   r=redemption fee or contingent deferred sales charge(CDSC)
t=12b-1 fee and either CDSC or redemption fee   p=12b-1 fee   n=none of the preceding fees   N/A=not available

468

State Municipal Bond—Short-term

Fund	Year Began	Investment Adviser	9/30/89 Assets	Minimum Initial and Subsequent Investment	Fees*	Where to Buy Shares
General California Tax Exempt Money Market Fund 666 Old Country Rd. Garden City, NY 11530 800/242-8671	1987	Dreyfus Corporation	$67.7 Mil	$2,500/ 100	n	Fund
General New York Tax Exempt Money Market Fund 666 Old Country Rd. Garden City, NY 11530 718/895-1396 800/242-8671	1986	Dreyfus Corporation	$44.9 Mil	$2,500/ 100	n	Fund
GW Sierra Trust Funds *GW California Municipal Money Market Fund* 888 S. Figueroa St. 11th Fl. Los Angeles, CA 90017-0970 213/488-2200 800/331-3426, 800/221-9876 CA Only	1989	Great Western Financial Advisors Corp.	N/A	$1,000/ 100	p	Local Rep
Highmark Group *California Tax-Free Fund* 1900 E. Dublin-Granville Rd. Columbus, OH 43229 614/899-4600 800/338-4385	1987	Merus Capital Management	N/A	$1,000/ 100	N/A	Fund
Home Group Trust *Home New York Tax-Free Reserves* 59 Maiden Lane 21st Fl. New York, NY 10038 212/530-6016 800/729-3863	1988	Home Capital Services, Inc.	$35.9 Mil	$1,000/ 100	p	Local Rep
Kidder, Peabody California Tax Exempt Money Market Fund 20 Exchange Place New York, NY 10005 212/510-5552	1987	Webster Management Corporation	$227.0 Mil	$1,500/ 500	n	Local Rep
Mariner Funds Trust *Mariner New York Tax-Free Money Market Fund* 600 W. Hillsboro Blvd. Ste. 300 Deerfield Beach, FL 33441 305/421-8878 800/634-2536	1986	Marinvest Inc.	$128.8 Mil	$1,000/ 250	p	Local Rep

*Key: i=initial sales charge   r=redemption fee or contingent deferred sales charge(CDSC)
t=12b-1 fee and either CDSC or redemption fee   p=12b-1 fee   n=none of the preceding fees   N/A=not available

469

State Municipal Bond—Short-term

Fund	Year Began	Investment Adviser	9/30/89 Assets	Minimum Initial and Subsequent Investment	Fees*	Where to Buy Shares
Massachusetts Tax-Exempt Money Market Fund 500 Boylston St. Boston, MA 02116 617/954-5000 800/343-2829	1984	Massachusetts Financial Services Company	$10.0 Mil	$1,000/ 25	p	Local Rep
Midwest Group Tax Free Trust *California Tax-Exempt Money Fund* 700 Dixie Terminal Bldg. Cincinnati, OH 45202 513/629-2000 800/543-8721, 800/582-7396 OH Only	1989	Midwest Advisory Services Inc.	$16.3 Mil	$1,000/ 0	p	Local Rep
Midwest Group Tax Free Trust *Ohio Tax Free Money Fund* 700 Dixie Terminal Bldg. Cincinnati, OH 45202 513/629-2000 800/543-8721 800/582-7396 OH Only	1987	Midwest Advisory Services Inc.	$101.2 Mil	$1,000/ 0	i, p	Local Rep
Midwest Group Tax Free Trust *Train, Smith New York Tax-Exempt Money Fund* 700 Dixie Terminal Bldg. Cincinnati, OH 45202 513/629-2000 800/543-8721, 800/582-7396 OH Only	1988	Midwest Advisory Services Inc.	$13.6 Mil	$1,000/ 0	n	Local Rep
Municipal Fund for California Investors, Inc. 3411 Silverside Rd. Webster Bldg., Ste. 204 Wilmington, DE 19810 212/323-7712 800/221-8120 800/640-6155 NY Only	1983	Provident Institutional Management Corporation	$968.3 Mil	$5,000/ 0	n	Local Rep
Municipal Fund for New York Investors, Inc. 3411 Silverside Rd. Webster Bldg., Ste. 204 Wilmington, DE 19810 212/323-7712 800/221-8120 800/640-6155 NY Only	1983	Provident Institutional Management Corporation	$355.1 Mil	$5,000/ 0	n	Local Rep
New York Municipal Cash Trust Federated Investors Twr. Pittsburgh, PA 15222-3779 412/288-1900 800/245-5000	1982	Federated Management	$213.4 Mil	$25,000/ 0	p	Local Rep

*Key: i=initial sales charge   r=redemption fee or contingent deferred sales charge(CDSC)
t=12b-1 fee and either CDSC or redemption fee   p=12b-1 fee   n=none of the preceding fees   N/A=not available

State Municipal Bond—Short-term

Fund	Year Began	Investment Adviser	9/30/89 Assets	Minimum Initial and Subsequent Investment	Fees*	Where to Buy Shares
Nuveen California Tax-Free Fund, Inc. *Money Market Portfolio*		Nuveen Advisory Corp.	N/A			
Distribution Plan	1987			$5,000/100	p	LRep
Institution Plan	1987			$5,000/100	n	LRep
Service Plan	1986			$5,000/100	p	LRep
333 W. Wacker Dr. Chicago, IL 60606 312/917-7844, 800/621-7210						
Nuveen Tax-Free Money Market Fund, Inc. *Massachusetts Portfolio*		Nuveen Advisory Corp.	N/A			
Distribution Plan	1987			$5,000/100	p	LRep
Institution Plan	1987			$5,000/100	n	LRep
Service Plan	1987			$5,000/100	p	LRep
333 W. Wacker Dr. Chicago, IL 60606 312/917-7844, 800/621-7210						
Nuveen Tax-Free Money Market Fund, Inc. *New York Portfolio*		Nuveen Advisory Corp.	N/A			
Distribution Plan	1988			$5,000/100	p	LRep
Institution Plan	1988			$5,000/100	n	LRep
Service Plan	1987			$5,000/100	p	LRep
333 W. Wacker Dr. Chicago, IL 60606 312/917-7844, 800/621-7210						
Oppenheimer New York Tax-Exempt Cash Reserves 3410 S. Galena St. Denver, CO 80231 303/671-3200 800/525-7048	1988	Oppenheimer Management Corporation	$4.9 Mil	$1,000/ 25	p	Local Rep
Overland Express Funds, Inc. *Tax-Free Money Market Fund (The)* 114 E. Capitol Ave. Little Rock, AR 72201 501/374-4361 800/458-6589	1988	Wells Fargo Bank, N.A.	$232.6 Mil	$1,000/ 100	n	Local Rep
PaineWebber RMA Money Fund, Inc. *California Tax Free Fund* 1285 Avenue of the Americas PaineWebber Bldg. New York, NY 10019 800/RMA-1000	1988	PaineWebber Incorporated	$221.1 Mil	$15,000/ 0	n	Local Rep
PaineWebber RMA Money Fund, Inc. *New York Tax Free Fund* 1285 Avenue of the Americas PaineWebber Bldg. New York, NY 10019 800/RMA-1000	1988	PaineWebber Incorporated	$71.9 Mil	$15,000/ 0	n	Local Rep

*Key: i=initial sales charge   r=redemption fee or contingent deferred sales charge(CDSC)
t=12b-1 fee and either CDSC or redemption fee   p=12b-1 fee   n=none of the preceding fees   N/A=not available

State Municipal Bond—Short-term

Fund	Year Began	Investment Adviser	9/30/89 Assets	Minimum Initial and Subsequent Investment	Fees*	Where to Buy Shares
Prudential-Bache California Municipal Fund *California Money Market Series* One Seaport Plaza New York, NY 10292 212/214-1215 800/225-1852	1989	Prudential Mutual Fund Management	$253.8 Mil	$1,000/ 100	p	Local Rep
Prudential-Bache Municipal Series Fund *New York Money Market Series* One Seaport Plaza New York, NY 10292 212/214-1215 800/225-1852	1985	Prudential Mutual Fund Management	$187.3 Mil	$1,000/ 100	p	Local Rep
Putnam California Tax Exempt Money Market Fund One Post Office Sq. Boston, MA 02109 617/292-1000 800/225-2465	1987	Putnam Management Company, Inc.	$72.4 Mil (e)	$1,000/ 100	n	Local Rep
Putnam New York Tax Exempt Money Market Fund One Post Office Sq. Boston, MA 02109 617/292-1000 800/225-2465	1987	Putnam Management Company, Inc.	$46.7 Mil (e)	$1,000/ 100	n	Local Rep
Scudder California Tax Free Money Fund 175 Federal St. Boston, MA 02110 617/439-4640 800/225-2470 800/225-5163	1987	Scudder, Stevens & Clark, Inc.	$66.5 Mil	$1,000/ 0	n	Fund
Scudder New York Tax Free Money Fund 175 Federal St. Boston, MA 02110 617/439-4640 800/225-2470 800/225-5163	1987	Scudder, Stevens & Clark, Inc.	$34.4 Mil	$1,000/ 0	n	Fund
Seligman California Tax-Exempt Fund Series *Money Market Series* 130 Liberty St. New York, NY 10006 212/488-0200 800/221-2450 800/522-6869 NY Only	1984	J. & W. Seligman & Co. Incorporated	$8.6 Mil	$1,000/ 0	p	Local Rep

*Key: i=initial sales charge   r=redemption fee or contingent deferred sales charge(CDSC)
t=12b-1 fee and either CDSC or redemption fee   p=12b-1 fee   n=none of the preceding fees   N/A=not available

State Municipal Bond—Short-term

Fund	Year Began	Investment Adviser	9/30/89 Assets	Minimum Initial and Subsequent Investment	Fees*	Where to Buy Shares
SLH California Daily Tax Free Fund 31 W. 52nd St. New York, NY 10019 212/767-3700	1985	Shearson Asset Management Division of Shearson Lehman Hutton Inc.	$666.2 Mil	$2,500/ 1,000	n	Local Rep
SLH New York Daily Tax-Free Fund 31 W. 52nd St. New York, NY 10019 212/767-3700	1985	Bernstein-Macaulay Division of Shearson Lehman Hutton Inc.	$413.2 Mil	$2,500/ 1,000	n	Local Rep
Tax-Exempt California Money Market Fund 120 S. LaSalle St. Chicago, IL 60603 312/781-1121 800/621-1148	1987	Kemper Financial Services, Inc.	$236.5 Mil	$1,000/ 100	p	Local Rep
T. Rowe Price California Tax-Free Income Trust *California Tax-Free Money Fund* 100 E. Pratt St. Baltimore, MD 21202 301/547-2000 800/638-5660	1986	T. Rowe Price Associates, Inc.	$80.6 Mil	$2,500/ 100	n	Fund
T. Rowe Price State Tax-Free Income Trust *New York Tax-Free Money Fund* 100 E. Pratt St. Baltimore, MD 21202 301/547-2000 800/638-5660	1986	T. Rowe Price Associates, Inc.	$49.3 Mil	$2,500/ 100	n	Fund
USAA Tax Exempt Fund, Inc. *California Money Market Fund* USAA Bldg. San Antonio, TX 78288 512/498-8000 800/531-8000	1989	USAA Investment Management Company	$36.3 Mil	$3,000/ 50	n	Fund
Vanguard California Tax-Free Fund *California Money Market Portfolio* Vanguard Financial Ctr. P.O. Box 2600 Valley Forge, PA 19482 215/648-6000, 800/662-7447, 800/362-0530 PA Only	1987	Vanguard Group, Inc.	$506.3 Mil	$3,000/ 100	n	Fund

*Key: i=initial sales charge   r=redemption fee or contingent deferred sales charge(CDSC)
t=12b-1 fee and either CDSC or redemption fee   p=12b-1 fee   n=none of the preceding fees   N/A=not available

State Municipal Bond—Short-term

Fund	Year Began	Investment Adviser	9/30/89 Assets	Minimum Initial and Subsequent Investment	Fees*	Where to Buy Shares
Vanguard New Jersey Tax-Free Fund *Money Market Portfolio* Vanguard Financial Ctr. P.O. Box 2600 Valley Forge, PA 19482 215/648-6000 800/662-7447, 800/362-0530 PA Only	1988	Vanguard Group, Inc.	$235.3 Mil	$3,000/ 100	n	Fund
Vanguard Pennsylvania Tax-Free Fund *Money Market Portfolio* Vanguard Financial Ctr. P.O. Box 2600 Valley Forge, PA 19482 215/648-6000 800/662-7447, 800/362-0530 PA Only	1988	Vanguard Group, Inc.	$401.4 Mil	$3,000/ 100	n	Fund

◆ ◆ ◆ ◆

U.S. Government Income Funds

U.S. Government Income

Fund	Year Began	Investment Adviser	9/30/89 Assets	Minimum Initial and Subsequent Investment	Fees*	Where to Buy Shares
AARP Income Trust **AARP GNMA and U.S. Treasury Fund** AARP Investment Program 175 Federal St. Boston, MA 02110-2267 800/253-2277	1984	AARP/Scudder Financial Management Company	$2.5 Bil	$250/ 0	n	Fund
ABT Investment Series, Inc. **ABT U.S. Government Securities Fund** 205 Royal Palm Way Palm Beach, FL 33480 407/655-7255 800/441-6580	1989	Palm Beach Capital Management, Ltd.	$4.4 Mil	$1,000/ 50	i	Local Rep
Advantage Government Securities Fund 60 State St. Boston, MA 02109 617/742-5900 800/243-8115	1986	Boston Security Counsellors	$122.3 Mil	$500/ 250	t	Local Rep
Advantage Trust **Advantage U.S. Government Securities Fund** 600 Atlantic Ave. Boston, MA 02210 617/722-6000 800/443-2683	1987	Liberty Asset Management Company	$224.6 Mil (e)	$500/ 50	i, p	Local Rep
Aetna Series Trust **Aetna U.S. Government Bond Fund** Federated Investors Twr. 26th Fl. Pittsburgh, PA 15222-3779 412/288-1900 800/245-4770	1988	Federated Advisers	$2.3 Mil	$500/ 100	n	Fund
AIM Government Funds, Inc. **AIM U.S. Government Securities Fund Series** 11 Greenway Plaza Ste. 1919 Houston, TX 77046 713/626-1919 800/231-0803, 800/392-9681 TX Only	1988	AIM Advisors, Inc.	$3.7 Mil	$1,000/ 100	i, p	Local Rep
Alliance Bond Fund **U.S. Government Portfolio** 1345 Avenue of the Americas New York, NY 10105 212/969-1000 800/221-5672	1985	Alliance Capital Management L.P.	$575.9 Mil	$250/ 50	i, p	Local Rep

*Key: i=initial sales charge   r=redemption fee or contingent deferred sales charge(CDSC)
     t=12b-1 fee and either CDSC or redemption fee   p=12b-1 fee   n=none of the preceding fees   N/A=not available

477

U.S. Government Income

Fund	Year Began	Investment Adviser	9/30/89 Assets	Minimum Initial and Subsequent Investment	Fees*	Where to Buy Shares
Altura Fund *U.S. Government Intermediate Bond Fund* 1900 E. Dublin-Granville Rd. Columbus, OH 43229 614/899-4600 800/338-4385	1986	United Bank of Denver National Association	N/A	$2,500/ 50	N/A	Fund
Altura Fund *U.S. Government Obligations Fund* 1900 E. Dublin-Granville Rd. Columbus, OH 43229 614/899-4600 800/338-4385	1986	United Bank of Denver National Association	N/A	$2,500/ 50	N/A	Fund
American Capital Government Securities, Inc. 2800 Post Oak Blvd. Houston, TX 77056 713/993-0500 800/421-5666	1984	American Capital Asset Management, Inc.	$4.7 Bil	$500/ 50	i, p	Local Rep
American Capital Life Investment Trust *American Capital Government Portfolio* 2800 Post Oak Blvd. Houston, TX 77056 713/993-0500 800/421-5666	1986	American Capital Asset Management, Inc.	$81.0 Mil	Not Applicable	n	Insur
American Funds Income Series *U.S. Government Guaranteed Securities Fund* 333 S. Hope St. Los Angeles, CA 90071 213/486-9200 800/421-0180, 213/486-9651 Collect	1985	Capital Research & Management Company	$506.5 Mil	$1,000/ 50	i, t	Local Rep
American General Series Portfolio Company *Government Securities Fund* 2929 Allen Pkwy. P.O. Box 3206 Houston, TX 77253 713/526-5251	1985	Variable Annuity Life Insurance Company	$6.5 Mil	Not Applicable	r	Insur
American Pension Investors Trust *U.S. Government Intermediate Fund* 2303 Yorktown Ave. P.O. Box 2529 Lynchburg, VA 24501 804/846-1361, 800/544-6060, 800/533-4115 VA Only	1988	American Pension Investors, Inc.	$2.8 Mil	$100/ 50	p	Local Rep

*Key: i=initial sales charge   r=redemption fee or contingent deferred sales charge(CDSC)
t=12b-1 fee and either CDSC or redemption fee   p=12b-1 fee   n=none of the preceding fees   N/A=not available

U.S. Government Income

Fund	Year Began	Investment Adviser	9/30/89 Assets	Minimum Initial and Subsequent Investment	Fees*	Where to Buy Shares
American Variable Insurance Series *U.S. Government Guaranteed/AAA-Rated Securities Fund (The)* 333 S. Hope St. Los Angeles, CA 90071 213/486-9200, 800/421-0180, 213/486-9651 Collect	1984	Capital Research & Management Company	$50.5 Mil	Not Applicable	n	Insur
Ameritrust's Collective Investment Retirement Fund *U.S. Government Securities Portfolio* 900 Euclid Ave. P.O. Box 5937 Cleveland, OH 44101-0937 216/737-4429, 800/321-1355	1987	Ameritrust Company National Association	$5.9 Mil	$250/ 100	n	Local Rep
AMEV U.S. Government Securities Fund, Inc. P.O. Box 64284 St. Paul, MN 55164 612/738-4000 800/872-2638	1973	AMEV Advisers, Inc.	$114.9 Mil	$500/ 50	i	Local Rep
Anchor Pathway Fund *U.S. Government Guaranteed/AAA-Rated Securities Series (The)* 2201 E. Camelback Phoenix, AZ 85016 602/955-0300 800/528-9679	1987	Capital Research & Management Company	N/A	Not Applicable	n	Insur
Associated Planners Investment Trust *Associated Planners Government Securities Fund* 1925 Century Park East 19th Fl. Los Angeles, CA 90067 213/553-6740	1986	Associated Planners Management Company	$5.9 Mil (e)	$500/ 50	i	Local Rep
Avondale Investment Trust *Avondale Government Securities Fund* 1105 Holliday Wichita Falls, TX 76301 817/761-3777	1987	Herbert R. Smith, Incorporated	$17.3 Mil	$5,000/ 1,000	i	Local Rep
Baker Fund *U.S. Government Series* 1601 NW Expressway 20th Fl. Oklahoma City, OK 73118 405/842-1400 800/654-3248	1986	James Baker & Company	$14.9 Mil (e)	$1,000/ 100	p	Local Rep

*Key: i=initial sales charge   r=redemption fee or contingent deferred sales charge(CDSC)
t=12b-1 fee and either CDSC or redemption fee   p=12b-1 fee   n=none of the preceding fees   N/A=not available

U.S. Government Income

Fund	Year Began	Investment Adviser	9/30/89 Assets	Minimum Initial and Subsequent Investment	Fees*	Where to Buy Shares
Bankers National Series Trust *BNL Government Securities Portfolio* 44 U.S. Hwy. 46 Pine Brook, NJ 07058 201/808-9596 800/888-4918	1983	Conseco Capital Management, Inc.	$5.9 Mil	Not Applicable	n	Insur
Benham Government Income Trust *Benham Treasury Note Fund* 755 Page Mill Rd. Palo Alto, CA 94304 415/858-2400 800/227-8380 800/982-6150 CA Only	1980	Benham Management Corporation	$84.2 Mil	$1,000/ 100	n	Fund
Benham Target Maturities Trust *Series 1990* 755 Page Mill Rd. Palo Alto, CA 94304 415/858-2400 800/227-8380 800/982-6150 CA Only	1985	Benham Management Corporation	$17.8 Mil	$1,000/ 100	n	Fund
Benham Target Maturities Trust *Series 1995* 755 Page Mill Rd. Palo Alto, CA 94304 415/858-2400 800/227-8380 800/982-6150 CA Only	1985	Benham Management Corporation	$39.2 Mil	$1,000/ 100	n	Fund
Benham Target Maturities Trust *Series 2000* 755 Page Mill Rd. Palo Alto, CA 94304 415/858-2400 800/227-8380 800/982-6150 CA Only	1985	Benham Management Corporation	$34.8 Mil	$1,000/ 100	n	Fund
Benham Target Maturities Trust *Series 2005* 755 Page Mill Rd. Palo Alto, CA 94304 415/858-2400 800/227-8380 800/982-6150 CA Only	1985	Benham Management Corporation	$25.0 Mil	$1,000/ 100	n	Fund
Benham Target Maturities Trust *Series 2010* 755 Page Mill Rd. Palo Alto, CA 94304 415/858-2400 800/227-8380 800/982-6150 CA Only	1985	Benham Management Corporation	$42.4 Mil	$1,000/ 100	n	Fund

*Key: i=initial sales charge   r=redemption fee or contingent deferred sales charge(CDSC)
t=12b-1 fee and either CDSC or redemption fee   p=12b-1 fee   n=none of the preceding fees   N/A=not available

480

U.S. Government Income

Fund	Year Began	Investment Adviser	9/30/89 Assets	Minimum Initial and Subsequent Investment	Fees*	Where to Buy Shares
Benham Target Maturities Trust *Series 2015* 755 Page Mill Rd. Palo Alto, CA 94304 415/858-2400 800/227-8380 800/982-6150 CA Only	1986	Benham Management Corporation	$197.3 Mil (e)	$1,000/ 100	n	Fund
Big E Pathfinder Family of Mutual Funds *Big E Pathfinder Government Plus Fund (The)* 320 Empire Tower Buffalo, NY 14202 716/855-7891	1988	Empire of America Advisory Services, Inc.	$60.0 Mil	$500/ 100	i, p	Local Rep
Bull & Bear Incorporated *Bull & Bear U.S. Government Guaranteed Securities Fund* 11 Hanover Sq. New York, NY 10005 212/785-0900 800/847-4200	1986	Bull & Bear Fixed Income Advisers, Inc.	$37.9 Mil (e)	$1,000/ 100	p	Fund
California Investment Trust II *U.S. Government Securities Fund* 44 Montgomery St. Ste. 2200 San Francisco, CA 94104 415/398-2727, 800/225-8778	1985	CCM Partners	$11.0 Mil (e)	$10,000/ 250	n	Fund
Calvert Fund *Limited Term Government Portfolio* 1700 Pennsylvania Ave., NW Washington, DC 20006 301/951-4820 800/368-2745	1988	Calvert Asset Management Company, Inc.	$3.6 Mil	$2,000/ 250	i, p	Local Rep
Calvert Fund *U.S. Government Portfolio* 1700 Pennsylvania Ave., NW Washington, DC 20006 301/951-4820 800/368-2745	1986	Calvert Asset Management Company, Inc.	$3.4 Mil	$2,000/ 250	i, p	Local Rep
Cardinal Government Guaranteed Fund 155 E. Broad St. Columbus, OH 43215 614/464-5511 800/848-7734 800/262-9446 OH only	1986	Cardinal Management Corporation	$118.5 Mil	$1,000/ 50	i	Local Rep

*Key: i=initial sales charge   r=redemption fee or contingent deferred sales charge(CDSC)
t=12b-1 fee and either CDSC or redemption fee   p=12b-1 fee   n=none of the preceding fees   N/A=not available

U.S. Government Income

Fund	Year Began	Investment Adviser	9/30/89 Assets	Minimum Initial and Subsequent Investment	Fees*	Where to Buy Shares
Carnegie Government Securities Trust *Carnegie High Yield Government Series* 1100 The Halle Bldg. 1228 Euclid Ave. Cleveland, OH 44115-1831 216/781-4440, 800/321-2322	1983	Carnegie Capital Management Company	$45.8 Mil	$1,000/ 250	i, p	Local Rep
Carnegie Government Securities Trust *Carnegie Intermediate Government Series* 1100 The Halle Bldg. 1228 Euclid Ave. Cleveland, OH 44115-1831 216/781-4440, 800/321-2322	1987	Carnegie Capital Management Company	$3.0 Mil	$1,000/ 250	i, p	Local Rep
Carnegie Government Securities Trust *Carnegie Long Government Series* 1100 The Halle Bldg. 1228 Euclid Ave. Cleveland, OH 44115-1831 216/781-4440, 800/321-2322	1987	Carnegie Capital Management Company	$0.7 Mil	$1,000/ 250	i, p	Local Rep
Carnegie Government Securities Trust *Carnegie Short Government Series* 1100 The Halle Bldg. 1228 Euclid Ave. Cleveland, OH 44115-1831 216/781-4440, 800/321-2322	1987	Carnegie Capital Management Company	$3.8 Mil	$1,000/ 250	i, p	Local Rep
Chapman Funds, Inc. *Chapman U.S. Treasury Money Fund (The)* Two Hopkins Plaza 10th Fl. Baltimore, MD 21201 301/625-9656	1989	Chapman Capital Management, Inc.	N/A	$1.0 Mil/ 0	N/A	Fund
CIGNA Government Securities Fund One Financial Plaza Springfield, MA 01103 413/784-0100 800/56CIGNA	1987	CIGNA Investments, Inc.	$54.3 Mil	$500/ 50	i, p	Local Rep
Colonial Government Securities Plus Trust One Financial Ctr. Boston, MA 02111 617/426-3750 800/225-2365 800/426-3750	1983	Colonial Management Associates, Inc.	$2.6 Bil	$250/ 25	i, p	Local Rep

*Key: i=initial sales charge   r=redemption fee or contingent deferred sales charge(CDSC)
t=12b-1 fee and either CDSC or redemption fee   p=12b-1 fee   n=none of the preceding fees   N/A=not available

U.S. Government Income

Fund	Year Began	Investment Adviser	9/30/89 Assets	Minimum Initial and Subsequent Investment	Fees*	Where to Buy Shares
Colonial/Hancock Liberty Trust *Colonial/Hancock Liberty Investment Grade Income Fund* One Financial Ctr. Boston, MA 02111 617/426-3750 800/225-2365, 800/426-3750	1987	Colonial Management Associates, Inc.	$6.1 Mil	Not Applicable	n	Insur
Colonial U.S. Government Trust One Financial Ctr. Boston, MA 02111 617/426-3750 800/225-2365 800/426-3750	1987	Colonial Management Associates, Inc.	$58.4 Mil	$250/ 25	i, p	Local Rep
Colonial Value Investing Portfolios - Income Portfolio *Federal Securities Fund* One Financial Ctr. Boston, MA 02111 617/426-3750 800/225-2365, 800/426-3750	1987	Colonial Management Associates, Inc.	$15.0 Mil	$500/ 100	t	Local Rep
Columbia U.S. Government Guaranteed Securities Fund, Inc. 1301 SW 5th Ave. P.O. Box 1350 Portland, OR 97207 503/222-3600 800/547-1707	1986	Columbia Funds Management Company	$12.3 Mil	$1,000/ 100	n	Fund
Common Sense Trust *Common Sense Government Fund* 2800 Post Oak Blvd. Houston, TX 77056 713/993-0500 800/421-5666	1987	Common Sense Investment Advisers	$96.0 Mil	$250/ 25	i	Local Rep
Connecticut Mutual Investment Accounts, Inc. *Connecticut Mutual Government Securities Account* 140 Garden St. Hartford, CT 06154 203/727-6500 800/243-0018	1985	G.R. Phelps & Company, Inc.	$39.4 Mil	$1,000/ 50	i	Local Rep
Constitution Funds, Inc. *U.S. Government Fund* Two World Trade Ctr. New York, NY 10048-0669 212/323-0200 800/525-7048	1988	Oppenheimer Management Corporation	$1.9 Mil	$1,000/ 250	i, p	Local Rep

*Key: i=initial sales charge   r=redemption fee or contingent deferred sales charge(CDSC)
t=12b-1 fee and either CDSC or redemption fee   p=12b-1 fee   n=none of the preceding fees   N/A=not available

483

U.S. Government Income

Fund	Year Began	Investment Adviser	9/30/89 Assets	Minimum Initial and Subsequent Investment	Fees*	Where to Buy Shares
Counsellors Intermediate Maturity Government Fund, Inc. 466 Lexington Ave. New York, NY 10017-3147 212/878-0600 800/888-6878	1988	Warburg, Pincus Counsellors, Inc.	$22.5 Mil	$25,000/ 5,000	n	Fund
Dean Witter Government Securities Plus Two World Trade Ctr. New York, NY 10048 212/392-2550 800/869-3863	1987	Dean Witter Reynolds Inc. - InterCapital Division	$1.9 Bil	$1,000/ 100	t	Local Rep
Dean Witter U.S. Government Securities Trust Two World Trade Ctr. New York, NY 10048 212/392-2550 800/869-3863	1984	Dean Witter Reynolds Inc. - InterCapital Division	$10.0 Bil	$1,000/ 100	t	Local Rep
Delaware Group Treasury Reserves *Investors Series* *Original Class* One Commerce Sq. Philadelphia, PA 19103 215/988-1200, 800/523-4640	1985	Delaware Management Company, Inc.	$110.9 Mil	$1,000/25	p	Local Rep
Dreyfus Foreign Investors U.S. Government Bond Fund, L.P. 666 Old Country Rd. Garden City, NY 11530 718/895-1650 800/346-3621	1987	Dreyfus Corporation	$0.3 Mil	$1,000/ 100	i, p	Local Rep
Dreyfus Short-Intermediate Government Fund 666 Old Country Rd. Garden City, NY 11530 718/895-1206 800/645-6561	1987	Dreyfus Corporation	$30.9 Mil	$25,000/ 100	n	Fund
Dreyfus U.S. Government Bond Fund, L.P. 666 Old Country Rd. Garden City, NY 11530 718/895-1347 800/648-9048	1987	Dreyfus Corporation	$17.9 Mil	$2,500/ 100	n	Fund

*Key: i=initial sales charge   r=redemption fee or contingent deferred sales charge(CDSC)
t=12b-1 fee and either CDSC or redemption fee   p=12b-1 fee   n=none of the preceding fees   N/A=not available

U.S. Government Income

Fund	Year Began	Investment Adviser	9/30/89 Assets	Minimum Initial and Subsequent Investment	Fees*	Where to Buy Shares
Dreyfus U.S. Government Intermediate Securities, L.P. 666 Old Country Rd. Garden City, NY 11530 718/895-1347 800/648-9048	1987	Dreyfus Corporation	$59.8 Mil	$2,500/ 100	n	Fund
Eaton Vance Government Obligations Trust 24 Federal St. Boston, MA 02110 617/482-8260 800/225-6265	1984	Eaton Vance Management, Inc.	$295.9 Mil	$1,000/ 50	i, p	Local Rep
Eaton Vance U.S. Government Income Dollar Fund, L.P. 24 Federal St. Boston, MA 02110 617/482-8260 800/225-6265	1987	Eaton Vance Management, Inc.	$4.7 Mil	$5,000/ 50	i, p	Local Rep
Enterprise Income Portfolios *Enterprise Government Securities Portfolio* 1200 Ashwood Pkwy. Ste. 290 Atlanta, GA 30338 404/396-8118, 800/432-4320	1987	Enterprise Capital Management, Inc.	$17.7 Mil (e)	$500/ 25	t	Local Rep
Equitable Funds *Equitable Government Securities Fund (The)* 1755 Broadway 3rd Fl. New York, NY 10019 212/641-8100	1987	Equitable Capital Management Corporation	N/A	$1,000/ 100	t	Local Rep
Equitec Siebel Fund Group *Equitec Siebel U.S. Government Securities Fund Series* 7677 Oakport St. P.O. Box 2470 Oakland, CA 94614 415/430-9900, 800/869-8900	1986	Siebel Capital Management, Inc.	$297.3 Mil (e)	$1,000/ 0	t	Local Rep
Equitec Siebel Fund Group II *Government Income Fund Series* 7677 Oakport St. P.O. Box 2470 Oakland, CA 94614 415/430-9900, 800/869-8900	1989	Siebel Capital Management, Inc.	N/A	$1,000/ 0	i	Local Rep

*Key: i=initial sales charge   r=redemption fee or contingent deferred sales charge(CDSC)
t=12b-1 fee and either CDSC or redemption fee   p=12b-1 fee   n=none of the preceding fees   N/A=not available

485

U.S. Government Income

Fund	Year Began	Investment Adviser	9/30/89 Assets	Minimum Initial and Subsequent Investment	Fees*	Where to Buy Shares
Federated Income Trust Federated Investors Twr. Pittsburgh, PA 15222-3779 412/288-1900 800/245-5000	1982	Federated Management	$1.0 Bil	$25,000/ 0	n	Local Rep
Federated Intermediate Government Trust Federated Investors Twr. Pittsburgh, PA 15222-3779 412/288-1900 800/245-5000	1983	Federated Management	$1.1 Bil	$25,000/ 0	n	Local Rep
Federated Short-Intermediate Government Trust Federated Investors Twr. Pittsburgh, PA 15222-3779 412/288-1900 800/245-5000	1984	Federated Management	$1.9 Bil	$25,000/ 0	n	Local Rep
Federated U.S. Government Fund Federated Investors Twr. Pittsburgh, PA 15222-3779 412/288-1900 800/245-5000	1985	Federated Management	$26.2 Mil	$25,000/ 0	n	Local Rep
Fidelity Fixed-Income Trust *Spartan Government Fund* 82 Devonshire St. Boston, MA 02109 617/570-7000 800/544-6666	1989	Fidelity Management & Research Company	N/A	$10,000/ 1,000	N/A	Fund
Fidelity Government Securities Fund 82 Devonshire St. Boston, MA 02109 617/570-7000 800/544-6666	1979	Fidelity Management & Research Company	$530.0 Mil	$1,000/ 250	n	Fund
Fidelity Income Fund *Fidelity Short-Term Government Portfolio* 82 Devonshire St. Boston, MA 02109 617/570-7000 800/544-6666	1988	Fidelity Management & Research Company	$132.5 Mil	$1,000/ 250	n	Fund

*Key: i=initial sales charge   r=redemption fee or contingent deferred sales charge(CDSC)
t=12b-1 fee and either CDSC or redemption fee   p=12b-1 fee   n=none of the preceding fees   N/A=not available

486

U.S. Government Income

Fund	Year Began	Investment Adviser	9/30/89 Assets	Minimum Initial and Subsequent Investment	Fees*	Where to Buy Shares
Fidelity U.S. Investments-Government Securities Fund, L.P. 82 Devonshire St. Boston, MA 02109 617/570-7000 800/544-6666	1988	Fidelity Management & Research Company	N/A	$2,500/ 250	N/A	Fund
Financial Horizons Investment Trust *Government Bond Fund* One Nationwide Plaza P.O. Box 182008 Columbus, OH 43218 800/533-5622	1988	Nationwide Financial Services, Inc.	$1.1 Mil	$1,000/ 100	t	Local Rep
Financial Independence Trust *U.S. Government Securities Fund* 700 Dixie Terminal Bldg. Cincinnati, OH 45202 513/629-2000 800/543-8721, 800/582-7396 OH Only	1984	Financial Independence Trust Advisers, Inc.	$29.4 Mil	$1,000/ 0	i, p	Local Rep
Financial Independence Trust *U.S. Treasury Allocation Fund* 700 Dixie Terminal Bldg. Cincinnati, OH 45202 513/629-2000 800/543-8721, 800/582-7396 OH Only	1988	Financial Independence Trust Advisers, Inc.	$75.2 Mil	$1,000/ 0	i, p	Local Rep
First Investors Government Fund, Inc. 120 Wall St. New York, NY 10005 212/208-6000	1984	First Investors Management Company, Inc.	$230.3 Mil	$1,000/ 100	i, p	Local Rep
First Investors U.S. Government Plus Fund 1st Series 120 Wall St. New York, NY 10005 212/208-6000	1985	First Investors Management Company, Inc.	$1.8 Mil	$2,400/ 100	i	Local Rep
First Investors U.S. Government Plus Fund 2nd Series 120 Wall St. New York, NY 10005 212/208-6000	1986	First Investors Management Company, Inc.	$3.6 Mil	$200/ 50	i	Local Rep

*Key: i=initial sales charge   r=redemption fee or contingent deferred sales charge(CDSC)
t=12b-1 fee and either CDSC or redemption fee   p=12b-1 fee   n=none of the preceding fees   N/A=not available

U.S. Government Income

Fund	Year Began	Investment Adviser	9/30/89 Assets	Minimum Initial and Subsequent Investment	Fees*	Where to Buy Shares
First Investors U.S. Government Plus Fund 3rd Series 120 Wall St. New York, NY 10005 212/208-6000	1986	First Investors Management Company, Inc.	$2.1 Mil	$2,400/ 100	i	Local Rep
First Trust Fund *U.S. Government Series* 500 W. Madison Ste. 3000 Chicago, IL 60606 312/559-3000 800/621-4770	1986	Clayton Brown Advisors, Inc.	$238.1 Mil (e)	$25,000/ 0	i, p	Local Rep
Fortress Total Performance U.S. Treasury Fund, Inc. Federated Investors Twr. Pittsburgh, PA 15222-3779 412/288-1900 800/245-5051	1988	Federated Advisers	$19.5 Mil	$1,500/ 100	i	Local Rep
Franklin Investors Securities Trust *Franklin Short-Intermediate U.S. Government Securities Fund* 777 Mariners Island Blvd. San Mateo, CA 94404 415/570-3000, 800/632-2180, 800/632-2350	1987	Franklin Advisers, Inc.	$28.4 Mil	$100/ 25	i	Local Rep
Freedom Investment Trust *Freedom Gold & Government Trust* One Beacon St. Boston, MA 02108 617/523-3170 800/225-6258 800/392-6037 MA Only	1984	Freedom Capital Management Corporation	$62.4 Mil	$1,000/ 100	t	Local Rep
Freedom Investment Trust *Freedom Government Plus Fund* One Beacon St. Boston, MA 02108 617/523-3170 800/225-6258 800/392-6037 MA Only	1986	Freedom Capital Management Corporation	$142.6 Mil	$1,000/ 100	t	Local Rep
Fund for U.S. Government Securities, Inc. Federated Investors Twr. Liberty Ctr. Pittsburgh, PA 15222-3779 412/288-1900 800/245-0242	1969	Federated Advisers	$1.0 Bil	$500/ 100	i	Local Rep

*Key: i=initial sales charge   r=redemption fee or contingent deferred sales charge(CDSC)
t=12b-1 fee and either CDSC or redemption fee   p=12b-1 fee   n=none of the preceding fees   N/A=not available

488

U.S. Government Income

Fund	Year Began	Investment Adviser	9/30/89 Assets	Minimum Initial and Subsequent Investment	Fees*	Where to Buy Shares
Gateway Trust *Gateway Government Bond Fund* P.O. Box 458167 Cincinnati, OH 45245 513/248-2700 800/354-6339	1988	Gateway Investment Advisers, Inc.	N/A	$500/ 100	n	Fund
GNA Investors Trust *U.S. Government Securities Fund* 3300 One Union Sq. Seattle, WA 98101 206/625-1755 800/433-0684	1987	GNA Capital Management, Inc.	$53.2 Mil	$1,500/ 100	t	Local Rep
Government Income Securities, Inc. Federated Investors Twr. Pittsburgh, PA 15222-3779 412/288-1900 800/245-5051	1986	Federated Advisers	$1.4 Bil	$1,500/ 100	i, r	Local Rep
Gradison Custodian Trust *Gradison Government Income Fund* 580 Walnut St. Cincinnati, OH 45202-3198 513/579-5700 800/869-5999	1987	Gradison & Company, Inc.	$34.8 Mil	$1,000/ 50	i, p	Local Rep
Guardian U.S. Government Trust 201 Park Ave. South New York, NY 10003 212/598-8259 800/221-3253	1989	Guardian Investor Services Corporation	N/A	$1,000/ 100	i	Local Rep
GW Sierra Trust Funds *GW U.S. Government Securities Fund* 888 S. Figueroa St. 11th Fl. Los Angeles, CA 90017-0970 213/488-2200 800/331-3426, 800/221-9876 CA ONLY	1989	Great Western Financial Advisors Corp.	N/A	$1,000/ 100	t	Local Rep
Hartford Zero Coupon Treasury Fund, Inc. 200 Hopmeadow St. P.O. Box 2999 Hartford, CT 06104-2999 203/843-8245 800/227-1371	1987	Hartford Investment Management Company, Inc.	$0.6 Mil	Not Applicable	n	Insur

*Key: i=initial sales charge   r=redemption fee or contingent deferred sales charge(CDSC)
      t=12b-1 fee and either CDSC or redemption fee   p=12b-1 fee   n=none of the preceding fees   N/A=not available

489

U.S. Government Income

Fund	Year Began	Investment Adviser	9/30/89 Assets	Minimum Initial and Subsequent Investment	Fees*	Where to Buy Shares
Heartland Group *Heartland U.S. Government Fund* 790 N. Milwaukee St. Milwaukee, WI 53202 414/347-7276 800/432-7856	1987	Heartland Advisors, Inc.	$11.4 Mil	$1,000/ 100	i, p	Local Rep
Helmsman Fund *U.S. Government Obligations Portfolio* 1900 E. Dublin-Granville Rd. Columbus, OH 43229 614/899-4600 800/338-4385	1989	Bank One, Indianapolis, N.A. Bank One, Milwaukee, N.A.	N/A	$1,000/ 0	N/A	Fund
Home Group Trust *Home Government Securities Fund* 59 Maiden Lane 21st Fl. New York, NY 10038 212/530-6016 800/729-3863	1988	Home Capital Services, Inc.	$40.9 Mil	$1,000/ 100	i, p	Local Rep
Horizon Funds *Horizon Intermediate Government Fund* 156 W. 56th St. Ste. 1902 New York, NY 10019 212/492-1600 800/367-6075	1987	Security Pacific National Bank	$0.07 Mil (e)	$5,000/ 0	n	Local Rep
IDS Federal Income Fund, Inc. IDS Tower 10 Minneapolis, MN 55440 612/372-3131 800/328-8300	1985	IDS Financial Corporation	$190.0 Mil	$100/ 100	i, p	Local Rep
Imperial Portfolios, Inc. *U.S. Government Portfolio (The)* 9275 Sky Park Ct. P.O. Box 82997 San Diego, CA 92138 619/292-2379 800/347-5588	1988	First Imperial Advisors, Inc.	N/A	$1,000/ 100	N/A	Local Rep
Income Portfolios *Short Government Series* 82 Devonshire St. Boston, MA 02109 617/570-7000 800/544-6666	1984	Fidelity Management & Research Company	$155.8 Mil	$0/ 0	n	Local Rep

*Key: i=initial sales charge   r=redemption fee or contingent deferred sales charge(CDSC)
t=12b-1 fee and either CDSC or redemption fee   p=12b-1 fee   n=none of the preceding fees   N/A=not available

490

U.S. Government Income

Fund	Year Began	Investment Adviser	9/30/89 Assets	Minimum Initial and Subsequent Investment	Fees*	Where to Buy Shares
Industrial Series Trust *Mackenzie Government Securities Trust* 1200 N. Federal Hwy. #200 Boca Raton, FL 33432 407/393-8900 800/456-5111	1985	Mackenzie Investment Management Inc.	$8.8 Mil (e)	$250/ 50	i, p	Local Rep
Integrated Income Portfolios *Government Securities Plus Portfolio* 10 Union Square East New York, NY 10003 212/353-7000 800/858-8850	1987	Integrated Resources Asset Management Corp.	$55.0 Mil	$1,000/ 100	i, p	Local Rep
Integrated Resources Series Trust *Government Securities Portfolio* One Bridge Plaza Fort Lee, NJ 07024 201/461-0606 800/821-5100	1984	Integrated Resources Asset Management Corp.	$167.4 Mil	Not Applicable	n	Insur
Integrated Resources Series Trust *Target '98 Portfolio* One Bridge Plaza Fort Lee, NJ 07024 201/461-0606 800/821-5100	1989	Integrated Resources Asset Management Corp.	$13.7 Mil	Not Applicable	n	Insur
Investment Portfolios *Government Plus Portfolio* 120 S. LaSalle St. Chicago, IL 60603 312/781-1121 800/621-1148	1984	Kemper Financial Services, Inc.	$5.9 Bil	$250/ 50	t	Local Rep
Investment Portfolios *Short-Intermediate Government Portfolio* 120 S. LaSalle St. Chicago, IL 60603 312/781-1121 800/621-1148	1989	Kemper Financial Services, Inc.	$22.0 Mil	$250/ 50	t	Local Rep
Ivy Fund *Ivy U.S. Government Income Fund* 40 Industrial Park Rd. Hingham, MA 02043 617/749-1416 800/235-3322	1987	Ivy Management, Inc.	$2.0 Mil	$1,000/ 0	p	Fund

*Key: i=initial sales charge   r=redemption fee or contingent deferred sales charge(CDSC)
t=12b-1 fee and either CDSC or redemption fee   p=12b-1 fee   n=none of the preceding fees   N/A=not available

U.S. Government Income

Fund	Year Began	Investment Adviser	9/30/89 Assets	Minimum Initial and Subsequent Investment	Fees*	Where to Buy Shares
John Hancock High Income Trust *Federal Securities Plus Portfolio* 101 Huntington Ave. Boston, MA 02199-7603 617/375-1500 800/225-5291	1987	John Hancock Advisers, Inc.	$82.0 Mil	$1,000/ 25	i, p	Local Rep
John Hancock U.S. Government Securities Trust 101 Huntington Ave. Boston, MA 02199-7603 617/375-1500 800/225-5291	1981	John Hancock Advisers, Inc.	$180.3 Mil	$500/ 25	i	Local Rep
Kemper Enhanced Government Income Fund 120 S. LaSalle St. Chicago, IL 60603 312/781-1121 800/621-1148	1987	Kemper Financial Services, Inc.	$76.7 Mil	$1,000/ 100	i, p	Local Rep
Kemper U.S. Government Securities Fund, Inc. 120 S. LaSalle St. Chicago, IL 60603 312/781-1121 800/621-1148	1977	Kemper Financial Services, Inc.	$4.4 Bil	$1,000/ 100	i	Local Rep
Keystone America Government Securities Fund 99 High St. Boston, MA 02110 617/338-3200 800/343-2898 800/225-1587	1987	Keystone Custodian Funds, Inc.	$65.2 Mil	$1,000/ 0	i, t	Local Rep
Kidder, Peabody Government Income Fund, Inc. 20 Exchange Place New York, NY 10005 212/510-5552	1985	Webster Management Corporation	$109.6 Mil	$1,500/ 500	t	Local Rep
Legg Mason Income Trust *Legg Mason U.S. Government Intermediate-Term Portfolio* 111 S. Calvert St. P.O. Box 1476 Baltimore, MD 21203-1476 301/539-3400 800/822-5544, 800/492-7777 MD Only	1987	Western Asset Management Company	$27.7 Mil (e)	$1,000/ 500	p	Local Rep

*Key: i=initial sales charge   r=redemption fee or contingent deferred sales charge(CDSC)
t=12b-1 fee and either CDSC or redemption fee   p=12b-1 fee   n=none of the preceding fees   N/A=not available

492

U.S. Government Income

Fund	Year Began	Investment Adviser	9/30/89 Assets	Minimum Initial and Subsequent Investment	Fees*	Where to Buy Shares
Lord Abbett U.S. Government Securities Fund, Inc. The General Motors Bldg. 767 Fifth Ave. New York, NY 10153 212/848-1800 800/223-4224	1932	Lord, Abbett & Co.	$1.2 Bil	$500/ 0	i, p	Local Rep
MacKay-Shields MainStay Series Fund *MainStay Government Plus Fund* 51 Madison Ave. New York, NY 10010 212/576-7000 800/522-4202	1986	MacKay-Shields Financial Corporation	$516.0 Mil	$500/ 50	t	Local Rep
Main Street Funds, Inc. *Government Securities Fund* 3410 S. Galena St. Denver, CO 80231 303/671-3200 800/548-1225	1988	Oppenheimer Management Corporation	$1.2 Mil	$1,000/ 25	i, p	Local Rep
MassMutual Integrity Funds *MassMutual U.S. Government Securities Fund* 1295 State St. Springfield, MA 01111 413/788-8411 800/542-6767 800/854-9100 MA Only	1988	Massachusetts Mutual Life Insurance Company	$28.4 Mil	$500/ 25	i, p	Local Rep
Merrill Lynch Federal Securities Trust P.O. Box 9011 Princeton, NJ 08543-9011 609/282-2800 800/637-3863	1984	Fund Asset Management, Inc.	$2.7 Bil	$1,000/ 50	i, p	Local Rep
Merrill Lynch Institutional Intermediate Fund One Financial Ctr. 15th Fl. Boston, MA 02111 617/357-1460 800/225-1576	1986	Merrill Lynch Asset Management Inc.	$212.9 Mil	$25,000/ 1,000	p	Local Rep
Merrill Lynch Series Fund *Intermediate Government Bond Portfolio* P.O. Box 9011 Princeton, NJ 08543-9011 609/282-2800 800/524-4458	1981	Fund Asset Management, Inc.	$209.9 Mil	Not Applicable	n	Insur

*Key: i=initial sales charge   r=redemption fee or contingent deferred sales charge(CDSC)
t=12b-1 fee and either CDSC or redemption fee   p=12b-1 fee   n=none of the preceding fees   N/A=not available

U.S. Government Income

Fund	Year Began	Investment Adviser	9/30/89 Assets	Minimum Initial and Subsequent Investment	Fees*	Where to Buy Shares
Merriman Investment Trust *Merriman Timed Government Fund* 1200 Westlake Ave. North No. 507 Seattle, WA 98109 206/285-8877 800/423-4893	1988	Merriman Investment Management Company	$6.6 Mil	$1,000/ 100	n	Fund
MetLife-State Street Fixed Income Trust *MetLife-State Street Government Income Fund* One Financial Ctr. 30th Fl. Boston, MA 02111 617/348-2000, 800/882-0052	1987	MetLife-State Street Investment Services, Inc.	$1.2 Bil	$10,000/ 2,000	p	Local Rep
MetLife-State Street Income Trust *MetLife-State Street Government Securities Fund* One Financial Ctr. 30th Fl. Boston, MA 02111 617/348-2000, 800/882-0052	1986	MetLife-State Street Investment Services, Inc.	$28.9 Mil	$250/ 25	i, p	Local Rep
MFS Government Guaranteed Securities Trust 500 Boylston St. Boston, MA 02116 617/954-5000 800/343-2829	1984	Massachusetts Financial Services Company	$343.6 Mil	$1,000/ 25	i, p	Local Rep
MFS Government Securities High Yield Trust 500 Boylston St. Boston, MA 02116 617/954-5000 800/343-2829	1986	Massachusetts Financial Services Company	$1.3 Bil	$1,000/ 25	i, p	Local Rep
MFS Lifetime Investment Program *Lifetime Government Income Plus Trust* 500 Boylston St. Boston, MA 02116 617/954-5000 800/343-2829	1986	Lifetime Advisers, Inc.	$3.5 Bil	$1,000/ 50	t	Local Rep
Midwest Income Trust *Intermediate Term Government Fund* 700 Dixie Terminal Bldg. Cincinnati, OH 45202 513/629-2000 800/543-8721 800/582-7396 OH Only	1981	Midwest Advisory Services Inc.	$40.4 Mil	$1,000/ 0	i	Local Rep

*Key: i=initial sales charge   r=redemption fee or contingent deferred sales charge(CDSC)
t=12b-1 fee and either CDSC or redemption fee   p=12b-1 fee   n=none of the preceding fees   N/A=not available

U.S. Government Income

Fund	Year Began	Investment Adviser	9/30/89 Assets	Minimum Initial and Subsequent Investment	Fees*	Where to Buy Shares
Monitrend Mutual Fund *Government Series* 272 Closter Dock Rd. Ste. 1 Closter, NJ 07624 201/767-5400 800/251-1970	1986	Monitrend Investment Management, Inc.	$3.0 Mil (e)	$1,000/ 50	i, p	Local Rep
Mutual of Omaha America Fund, Inc. 10235 Regency Circle Omaha, NE 68114 402/397-8555 800/228-9596	1973	Mutual of Omaha Fund Management Company	$49.8 Mil	$250/ 50	n	Local Rep
NASL Series Trust *U.S. Government Bond Trust* 695 Atlantic Ave. P.O. Box 9064 GMF Boston, MA 02205 617/439-6960 800/344-1029	1988	NASL Financial Services, Inc.	$1.0 Mil	Not Applicable	r	Insur
National Federal Securities Trust 600 Third Ave. New York, NY 10016 203/863-5600 800/237-1718	1984	National Securities & Research Corporation	$541.0 Mil	$500/ 25	i	Local Rep
Nationwide Separate Account Trust *Government Bond Fund* One Nationwide Plaza Box 1492 Columbus, OH 43216 614/249-7855 800/848-0920, 800/282-1440 OH Only	1982	Nationwide Financial Services, Inc.	$70.1 Mil	Not Applicable	n	Insur
New England Government Securities Fund 399 Boylston St. Boston, MA 02116 617/267-6600 800/343-7104	1985	Back Bay Advisors, Inc.	$178.3 Mil	$1,000/ 25	i, p	Local Rep
North American Security Trust *U.S. Government High Yield Portfolio* 695 Atlantic Ave. P.O. Box 9064 GMF Boston, MA 02205 617/439-6960, 800/344-1029	1987	NASL Financial Services, Inc.	$59.8 Mil (e)	$1,000/ 100	i, p	Local Rep

*Key: i=initial sales charge   r=redemption fee or contingent deferred sales charge(CDSC)
t=12b-1 fee and either CDSC or redemption fee   p=12b-1 fee   n=none of the preceding fees   N/A=not available

U.S. Government Income

Fund	Year Began	Investment Adviser	9/30/89 Assets	Minimum Initial and Subsequent Investment	Fees*	Where to Buy Shares
Olympus U.S. Government Plus Fund 230 Park Ave. New York, NY 10169 212/309-8400 800/626-FUND	1986	Furman Selz Mager Dietz & Birney Incorporated	$77.5 Mil (e)	$1,000/ 100	i, p	Local Rep
Oppenheimer U.S. Government Trust Two World Trade Ctr. New York, NY 10048-0669 212/323-0200 800/525-7048	1985	Oppenheimer Management Corporation	$241.9 Mil	$1,000/ 25	i, p	Local Rep
Overland Express Funds, Inc. *U.S. Government Income Fund (The)* 114 E. Capitol Ave. Little Rock, AR 72201 501/374-4361 800/458-6589	1988	Wells Fargo Bank, N.A.	$4.3 Mil	$1,000/ 100	i	Local Rep
Parkstone Group of Funds *Intermediate Government Fund* 1900 E. Dublin-Granville Rd. Columbus, OH 43229 614/899-4600 800/338-4385	1987	Securities Counsel, Inc.	N/A	$1,000/ 0	N/A	Fund
Pasadena Investment Trust *Pasadena U.S. Government Securities Fund (The)* 600 N. Rosemead Blvd. Pasadena, CA 91107-2101 818/351-4276 800/882-2855	1989	Roger Engemann Management Co., Inc.	N/A	$5,000/ 1,000	N/A	Fund
Phoenix Series Fund *Phoenix U.S. Government Securities Fund Series* 101 Munson St. Greenfield, MA 01301 203/253-1000 800/243-1574	1987	Phoenix Investment Counsel, Inc.	$10.0 Mil	$500/ 25	i	Local Rep
Pioneer U.S. Government Trust 60 State St. Boston, MA 02109-1975 617/742-7825 800/225-6292	1988	Pioneering Management Corporation	$8.8 Mil	$1,000/ 100	i, p	Local Rep

*Key: i=initial sales charge   r=redemption fee or contingent deferred sales charge(CDSC)
t=12b-1 fee and either CDSC or redemption fee   p=12b-1 fee   n=none of the preceding fees   N/A=not available

496

U.S. Government Income

Fund	Year Began	Investment Adviser	9/30/89 Assets	Minimum Initial and Subsequent Investment	Fees*	Where to Buy Shares
Piper Jaffray Investment Trust Inc. *Institutional Government Income Fund* 222 S. 9th St. Piper Jaffray Twr. Minneapolis, MN 55402 612/342-6426, 800/333-6000	1988	Piper Capital Management Incorporated	$27.5 Mil	$25,000/ 2,500	i, p	Local Rep
Plymouth Fund *Plymouth Government Securities Portfolio* 82 Devonshire St. Boston, MA 02109 617/570-7000 800/544-6666	1987	Fidelity Management & Research Company	$7.7 Mil	$1,000/ 250	i, p	Local Rep
PNCG U.S. Government Income Fund, Inc. 121 SW Morrison Ste. 1415 Portland, OR 97204 503/295-0919 800/541-9732	1989	PNCG Fund Advisers, Inc.	N/A	$1,000/ 500	i, p	Local Rep
Principal Preservation Portfolios, Inc. *Government Portfolio* 215 N. Main St. West Bend, WI 53095 414/334-5521 800/826-4600	1986	B.C. Ziegler and Company	$30.5 Mil	$1,000/ 250	i	Local Rep
Professional Portfolios Trust *Government Securities Fund* 429 N. Pennsylvania St. Indianapolis, IN 46204-1897 317/634-3300 800/862-7283	1988	Unified Management Corporation	$0.5 Mil	$200/ 25	p	Local Rep
Prudential-Bache Government Plus Fund, Inc. One Seaport Plaza New York, NY 10292 212/214-1215 800/225-1852	1985	Prudential Mutual Fund Management	$3.8 Bil	$1,000/ 100	t	Local Rep
Prudential-Bache Government Plus Fund II One Seaport Plaza New York, NY 10292 212/214-1215 800/225-1852	1986	Prudential Mutual Fund Management	$153.4 Mil	$1,000/ 100	t	Local Rep

*Key: i=initial sales charge r=redemption fee or contingent deferred sales charge(CDSC)
t=12b-1 fee and either CDSC or redemption fee p=12b-1 fee n=none of the preceding fees N/A=not available

U.S. Government Income

Fund	Year Began	Investment Adviser	9/30/89 Assets	Minimum Initial and Subsequent Investment	Fees*	Where to Buy Shares
Prudential-Bache Government Securities Trust *Intermediate Term Series* One Seaport Plaza New York, NY 10292 212/214-1215 800/225-1852	1982	Prudential Mutual Fund Management	$396.8 Mil	$1,000/ 100	p	Local Rep
Putnam Capital Preservation/Income Trust One Post Office Sq. Boston, MA 02109 617/292-1000 800/225-2465	1988	Putnam Management Company, Inc.	$52.0 Mil	$500/ 50	i, p	Local Rep
Putnam High Income Government Trust One Post Office Sq. Boston, MA 02109 617/292-1000 800/225-2465	1985	Putnam Management Company, Inc.	$7.9 Bil	$500/ 50	i, p	Local Rep
Quest For Value Family of Funds *U.S. Government High Income Portfolio* Oppenheimer Tower World Financial Ctr. New York, NY 10281 212/667-7587, 800/232-FUND	1988	Quest For Value Advisors	$72.1 Mil	$1,000/ 250	i, p	Local Rep
Retirement Planning Funds of America, Inc. *Bond Fund* 124 E. Marcy St. P.O. Box 1688 Santa Fe, NM 87504-1688 505/983-4335 800/545-2098	1976	Venture Advisers, L.P.	$63.6 Mil	$1,000/ 25	t	Local Rep
Rightime Fund, Inc. *Rightime Government Securities Fund (The)* The Forst Pavilion Ste. 1000 Wyncote, PA 19095-1596 215/572-7288 800/242-1421, 800/222-3317 PA only	1986	Rightime Econometrics	N/A	$2,000/ 100	N/A	Local Rep
RNC Short/Intermediate Government Securities Fund 11601 Wilshire Blvd. 24th Fl. Los Angeles, CA 90025 213/477-6543 800/225-9655	1988	RNC Capital Management Co.	$2.0 Mil (e)	$1,000/ 100	i, p	Local Rep

*Key: i=initial sales charge r=redemption fee or contingent deferred sales charge(CDSC)
t=12b-1 fee and either CDSC or redemption fee p=12b-1 fee n=none of the preceding fees N/A=not available

498

U.S. Government Income

Fund	Year Began	Investment Adviser	9/30/89 Assets	Minimum Initial and Subsequent Investment	Fees*	Where to Buy Shares
Rodney Square Benchmark U.S. Treasury Fund Rodney Square North Wilmington, DE 19890 302/651-1923 800/225-5084	1986	Wilmington Trust Company	N/A	$1,000/ 0	i, p	Local Rep
RXR Dynamic Government Fund, Inc. 30 Buxton Farm Rd. Ste. 116 Stamford, CT 06905 203/323-5015 800/654-5311	1987	RXR Capital Management, Inc.	$8.3 Mil (e)	$1.0 Mil/ 100,000	i, p	Local Rep
SAFECO U.S. Government Securities Fund, Inc. SAFECO Plaza Seattle, WA 98185 206/545-5530 800/426-6730	1986	SAFECO Asset Management Company	$27.1 Mil	$1,000/ 100	n	Fund
Scudder Funds Trust *U.S. Government 1990 Zero Coupon* 175 Federal St. Boston, MA 02110 617/439-4640 800/225-2470 800/225-5163	1986	Scudder, Stevens & Clark, Inc.	$3.1 Mil	$1,000/ 0	n	Fund
Scudder Funds Trust *U.S. Government 1995 Zero Coupon* 175 Federal St. Boston, MA 02110 617/439-4640 800/225-2470 800/225-5163	1986	Scudder, Stevens & Clark, Inc.	$7.5 Mil	$1,000/ 0	n	Fund
Scudder Funds Trust *U.S. Government 2000 Zero Coupon* 175 Federal St. Boston, MA 02110 617/439-4640 800/225-2470 800/225-5163	1986	Scudder, Stevens & Clark, Inc.	$24.5 Mil	$1,000/ 0	n	Fund
SECURAL Mutual Funds, Inc. *Government Bond Fund* 2401 S. Memorial Dr. Appleton, WI 54915 414/739-3161 800/426-5975	1988	SECURA Advisory Services, Inc.	$1.7 Mil	$500/ 100	i, p	Local Rep

*Key: i=initial sales charge   r=redemption fee or contingent deferred sales charge(CDSC)
t=12b-1 fee and either CDSC or redemption fee   p=12b-1 fee   n=none of the preceding fees   N/A=not available

U.S. Government Income

Fund	Year Began	Investment Adviser	9/30/89 Assets	Minimum Initial and Subsequent Investment	Fees*	Where to Buy Shares
SEI Cash+Plus Trust *Intermediate Term Government Portfolio* 680 E. Swedesford Rd. No. 7 Wayne, PA 19087 215/254-1000 800/345-1151	1987	Wellington Management Company	$113.5 Mil	$0/ 0	p	Local Rep
SEI Cash+Plus Trust *Short-Term Government Portfolio* 680 E. Swedesford Rd. No. 7 Wayne, PA 19087 215/254-1000 800/345-1151	1987	Wellington Management Company	$52.5 Mil	$0/ 0	p	Local Rep
Selected Capital Preservation Trust *Selected Government Total Return Fund* 1331 Euclid Ave. Cleveland, OH 44115 312/641-7862 800/553-5533	1987	Selected Financial Services, Inc.	$20.9 Mil	$1,000/ 100	p	Local Rep
Seligman High Income Fund Series *U.S. Government Guaranteed Securities Series* 130 Liberty St. New York, NY 10006 212/488-0200 800/221-2450, 800/522-6869 NY Only	1985	J. & W. Seligman & Co. Incorporated	$86.3 Mil	$1,000/ 50	i, p	Local Rep
Sentinel Group Funds, Inc. *Government Securities Fund* National Life Dr. Montpelier, VT 05604 802/229-3900 800/282-3863	1986	Sentinel Advisors, Inc.	$33.5 Mil	$250/ 25	i	Local Rep
Shearson Lehman Series Fund *SLH IDS Government Portfolio* 31 W. 52nd St. New York, NY 10019 212/767-3700	1986	Bernstein-Macaulay Division of Shearson Lehman Hutton Inc.	$1.6 Mil	Not Applicable	n	Insur
Short-Term Investments Co. *Limited Maturity Treasury Portfolio* AIM Shares Portfolio A Portfolio B 11 Greenway Plaza, Ste. 1919 Houston, TX 77046 713/626-1919, 800/231-0803, 800/392-9681 TX Only	1987 1987 1987	AIM Advisors, Inc.	$82.7 Mil	$1,000/100 $1.0 mil/0 $1.0 mil/0	i, p n p	LRep LRep LRep

*Key: i=initial sales charge   r=redemption fee or contingent deferred sales charge(CDSC)
   t=12b-1 fee and either CDSC or redemption fee   p=12b-1 fee   n=none of the preceding fees   N/A=not available

U.S. Government Income

Fund	Year Began	Investment Adviser	9/30/89 Assets	Minimum Initial and Subsequent Investment	Fees*	Where to Buy Shares
Sigma U.S. Government Fund, Inc. 3801 Kennett Pk., C-200 Greenville Ctr. Wilmington, DE 19807 302/652-3091 800/441-9490	1986	Sigma Management, Inc.	$13.9 Mil	$0/ 0	i, p	Local Rep
Sit "New Beginning" U.S. Government Securities Fund, Inc. 90 S. 7th St. Ste. 4600 Minneapolis, MN 55402 612/332-3223 800/332-5580	1987	Sit Investment Management Company	$10.9 Mil	$2,000/ 100	n	Fund
SLH Investment Series, Inc. *SLH Government Portfolio* 31 W. 52nd St. 15th Fl. New York, NY 10019 212/767-3700 800/334-4636 800/422-0214 NY Only	1984	SLH Asset Management Division of Shearson Lehman Hutton Inc.	$2.2 Bil (e)	$500/ 250	t	Local Rep
SLH Special Income Portfolios *SLH Intermediate Term Goverment Portfolio* 31 W. 52nd St. New York, NY 10019 212/767-3700	1985	Bernstein-Macaulay Division of Shearson Lehman Hutton Inc.	$36.9 Mil	$500/ 200	p	Local Rep
SMITH HAYES Trust, Inc. *Government/Quality Bond Portfolio* NBC Ctr. Ste. 780 Lincoln, NE 68508 402/476-3000 800/422-7791 NE Only	1988	SMITH HAYES Portfolio Management, Inc.	N/A	$25,000/ 1,000	N/A	Local Rep
State Farm Interim Fund, Inc. One State Farm Plaza Bloomington, IL 61710 309/766-2029	1977	State Farm Investment Management Corporation	$40.4 Mil (e)	$50/ 50	n	Fund
SteinRoe Income Trust *SteinRoe Governments Plus* 300 W. Adams St. P.O. Box 1143 Chicago, IL 60690 800/338-2550	1986	Stein Roe & Farnham Incorporated	$34.6 Mil	$1,000/ 100	n	Fund

*Key: i=initial sales charge   r=redemption fee or contingent deferred sales charge(CDSC)
t=12b-1 fee and either CDSC or redemption fee   p=12b-1 fee   n=none of the preceding fees   N/A=not available

U.S. Government Income

Fund	Year Began	Investment Adviser	9/30/89 Assets	Minimum Initial and Subsequent Investment	Fees*	Where to Buy Shares
SteinRoe Variable Investment Trust *Government Guaranteed Securities Fund* 600 Atlantic Ave. Boston, MA 02210 617/722-6000 800/443-2683	1989	Stein Roe & Farnham Incorporated	N/A	Not Applicable	N/A	Insur
SteinRoe Variable Investment Trust *Government Securities Zero Coupon Fund* 600 Atlantic Ave. Boston, MA 02210 617/722-6000 800/443-2683	1989	Stein Roe & Farnham Incorporated	N/A	Not Applicable	N/A	Insur
Strong Government Securities Fund, Inc. P.O. Box 2936 Milwaukee, WI 53201 414/359-3400 800/368-3863	1986	Strong/ Corneliuson Capital Management, Inc.	N/A	$1,000/ 200	n	Fund
Thomson McKinnon Investment Trust *Thomson McKinnon U.S. Government Fund* One State Street Plaza New York, NY 10004 212/482-5894 800/628-1237	1985	Thomson McKinnon Asset Management L.P.	$583.7 Mil	$1,000/ 100	t	Local Rep
Thornburg Income Trust *Limited Term U.S. Government Fund* 119 E. Marcy St. Ste. 202 Santa Fe, NM 87501 505/984-0200 800/847-0200	1987	Thornburg Management Company, Inc.	$19.8 Mil (e)	$2,500/ 100	i, p	Local Rep
Total Return U.S. Treasury Fund, Inc. *C.J. Lawrence Class* 1290 Avenue of the Americas New York, NY 10104-0101 212/468-5000 800/334-1898	1988	C.J. Lawrence, Morgan Grenfell, Inc.	N/A	$2,000/ 1,000	i, p	Local Rep
Total Return U.S. Treasury Fund, Inc. *Flag Investors Class* 135 E. Baltimore St. P.O. Box 515 Baltimore, MD 21203 301/727-1700 800/767-3524	1988	C.J. Lawrence, Morgan Grenfell, Inc.	N/A	$2,000/ 1,000	i, p	Local Rep

*Key: i=initial sales charge   r=redemption fee or contingent deferred sales charge(CDSC)
t=12b-1 fee and either CDSC or redemption fee   p=12b-1 fee   n=none of the preceding fees   N/A=not available

502

U.S. Government Income

Fund	Year Began	Investment Adviser	9/30/89 Assets	Minimum Initial and Subsequent Investment	Fees*	Where to Buy Shares
Transamerica Bond Fund *Transamerica Government Income Trust* 1000 Louisiana Ste. 6000 Houston, TX 77002-5098 713/751-2400 800/999-3863	1986	Transamerica Fund Management Company	$166.9 Mil	$250,000/ 100,000	i, p	Local Rep
Transamerica Bond Fund *Transamerica Government Securities Trust* 1000 Louisiana Ste. 6000 Houston, TX 77002-5098 713/751-2400 800/999-3863	1985	Transamerica Fund Management Company	$1.0 Bil	$1,000/ 50	i, p	Local Rep
Transamerica Special Series, Inc. *Transamerica Special Government Income Fund* 1000 Louisiana Ste. 6000 Houston, TX 77002-5098 713/751-2400, 800/999-3863	1988	Transamerica Fund Management Company	$23.0 Mil	$1,000/ 50	t	Local Rep
Treasury First, Inc. 222 Bosley Ave. Ste. C-4 Towson, MD 21204 301/494-8488 800/234-4111	1986	Vintage Advisors, Inc.	$15.1 Mil (e)	$10,000/ 0	p	Local Rep
Trust for Federal Securities *ShortFed Fund* 3411 Silverside Rd. Webster Bldg., Ste. 201 Wilmington, DE 19810 302/478-6945 800/221-8120, 800/223-8829	1987	Provident Institutional Management Corporation	$11.0 Mil (e)	$500/ 200	n	Local Rep
Twentieth Century Investors, Inc. *U.S. Governments* 4500 Main St. P.O. Box 419200 Kansas City, MO 64141-6200 816/531-5575 800/345-2021	1982	Investors Research Corporation	$436.9 Mil	$0/ 0	n	Fund
United Government Securities Fund, Inc. 2400 Pershing Rd. P.O. Box 418343 Kansas City, MO 64141-9343 816/283-4000 800/821-5664	1982	Waddell & Reed, Inc.	$104.8 Mil	$500/ 25	i	Local Rep

*Key: i=initial sales charge   r=redemption fee or contingent deferred sales charge(CDSC)
t=12b-1 fee and either CDSC or redemption fee   p=12b-1 fee   n=none of the preceding fees   N/A=not available

503

U.S. Government Income

Fund	Year Began	Investment Adviser	9/30/89 Assets	Minimum Initial and Subsequent Investment	Fees*	Where to Buy Shares
Value Line U.S. Government Securities Fund, Inc. 711 Third Ave. New York, NY 10017 212/687-3965 800/223-0818	1981	Value Line, Inc.	$244.5 Mil	$1,000/ 250	n	Fund
Value Line U.S. Government Securities Trust 711 Third Ave. New York, NY 10017 212/687-3965 800/223-0818	1987	Value Line, Inc.	$4.0 Mil	Not Applicable	n	Insur
Vanguard Fixed-Income Securities Fund, Inc. *Short Term Government Portfolio* Vanguard Financial Ctr. P.O. Box 2600 Valley Forge, PA 19482 215/648-6000, 800/662-7447, 800/362-0530 PA Only	1987	Vanguard Group, Inc.	$188.3 Mil	$3,000/ 100	n	Fund
Vanguard Fixed-Income Securities Fund, Inc. *U.S. Treasury Bond Portfolio* Vanguard Financial Ctr. P.O. Box 2600 Valley Forge, PA 19482 215/648-6000 800/662-7447, 800/362-0530 PA Only	1986	Vanguard Group, Inc.	$388.6 Mil	$3,000/ 100	n	Fund
Van Kampen Merritt U.S. Government Fund 1001 Warrenville Rd. Lisle, IL 60532 312/719-6000 800/225-2222	1984	Van Kampen Merritt Investment Advisory Corp.	$3.6 Bil	$1,500/ 100	i, p	Local Rep
Voyageur GRANIT Government Securities Fund, Inc. 100 S. Fifth St. Ste. 2200 Minneapolis, MN 55402 612/341-6728 800/553-2143 800/247-2143 MN Only	1985	Voyageur Fund Managers	$6.4 Mil	$1,000/ 100	p	Local Rep
Voyageur U.S. Government Securities Fund, Inc. 100 S. Fifth St. Ste. 2200 Minneapolis, MN 55402 612/341-6728 800/553-2143 800/247-2143 MN Only	1987	Voyageur Fund Managers	N/A	$1,000/ 100	N/A	Local Rep

*Key: i=initial sales charge   r=redemption fee or contingent deferred sales charge(CDSC)
t=12b-1 fee and either CDSC or redemption fee   p=12b-1 fee   n=none of the preceding fees   N/A=not available

U.S. Government Income

Fund	Year Began	Investment Adviser	9/30/89 Assets	Minimum Initial and Subsequent Investment	Fees*	Where to Buy Shares
Weiss Peck & Greer Funds Trust *WPG Government Securities Fund* One New York Plaza 31st Fl. New York, NY 10004 212/908-9582, 800/223-3332	1986	Weiss, Peck & Greer Advisers, Inc.	$83.5 Mil (e)	$1,000/ 50	p	Fund
Wright Managed Bond Trust *Wright Government Obligations Fund* 24 Federal St. 5th Fl. Boston, MA 02110 617/482-8260 800/225-6265	1983	Wright Investors Service	$41.5 Mil	$1,000/ 0	p	Local Rep
Zero Coupon Bond Fund *1993 Portfolio* 82 Devonshire St. Boston, MA 02109 617/570-7000 800/544-6666	1988	Fidelity Management & Research Company	$1.4 Mil	Not Applicable	n	Insur
Zero Coupon Bond Fund *1998 Portfolio* 82 Devonshire St. Boston, MA 02109 617/570-7000 800/544-6666	1988	Fidelity Management & Research Company	$1.1 Mil	Not Applicable	n	Insur
Zero Coupon Bond Fund *2003 Portfolio* 82 Devonshire St. Boston, MA 02109 617/570-7000 800/544-6666	1988	Fidelity Management & Research Company	$2.3 Mil	Not Applicable	n	Insur
Zweig Series Trust *Government Securities Series* 25 Broadway New York, NY 10004 212/361-9612 800/272-2700	1985	Zweig/Glaser Advisers	$141.0 Mil (e)	$1,000/ 100	t	Local Rep
Zweig Series Trust *Limited Term Government Series* 25 Broadway New York, NY 10004 212/361-9612 800/272-2700	1987	Zweig/Glaser Advisers	$6.7 Mil (e)	$1,000/ 100	t	Local Rep

*Key: i=initial sales charge   r=redemption fee or contingent deferred sales charge(CDSC)
t=12b-1 fee and either CDSC or redemption fee   p=12b-1 fee   n=none of the preceding fees   N/A=not available

Index

◆◆◆◆

509

514

515

518

519

521

527

Y

Z